MILITARY BRATS

LEGACIES

OF CHILDHOOD

INSIDE THE

FORTRESS

Mary Edwards Wertsch

FAWCETT COLUMBINE/NEW YORK

A Fawcett Columbine Book
Published by Ballantine Books

Copyright © 1991 by Mary Edwards Wertsch
Introduction copyright © 1991 by Pat Conroy

This edition published by arrangement with Harmony Books, a member of the Crown Publishing Group.

The publisher gratefully acknowledges permission to reprint extracts from the following: "Bless Thou the Astronauts Who Face," copyright © 1969 by Ernest K. Emurian, used by permission of the author; "The End," copyright © 1967 by Doors Music Co., written by Jim Morrison, Ray Manzarek, John Densmore, Robby Krieger, all rights reserved; *Gardens of Stone* by Nicholas Proffitt, copyright © 1983 by Nicholas Proffitt, reprinted by permission of Carroll and Graf Publishers; *The Great Santini* by Pat Conroy, copyright © 1976 by Pat Conroy, reprinted by permission of Houghton Mifflin Co.; "Incest in the Military Family" by Patricia W. Crigler in *The Military Family: Dynamics and Treatment*, edited by Kaslow and Ridenour, copyright © 1984 the Guilford Press; "The Military Family Syndrome" by Don M. LaGrone in *American Journal of Psychiatry*, copyright © 1978 by the American Psychiatric Association; "The Paternal Roots of Male Character Development" by Tess Forrest in *Psychoanalytic Review*, copyright © 1967 by the National Psychological Association for Psychoanalysis; *The Wounded Woman* by Linda Schierse Leonard, copyright © 1982 by Linda Schierse Leonard, reprinted with the permission of The Ohio University Press/Swallow Press, Athens.

Library of Congress Catalog Card Number: 91-76227

ISBN: 0-449-90706-6

Manufactured in the United States of America

First Ballantine Books Edition: June 1992

10 9 8 7 6 5 4 3 2 1

With love and gratitude
to Jim, my husband, friend, and favorite civilian;
to my mother, Dorothy,
and my brother, David,
troupers and survivors both;
and to the memory of my father,
Col. David Lincoln Edwards (1912–1985),
West Point class of '36

CONTENTS

ACKNOWLEDGMENTS

There are many to whom I wish to express my thanks for the significant roles they have played in helping me complete this book.

Mark and Lorrie Duval are the friends who took me to see the film *The Great Santini* and talked with me for hours afterward; that evening was instrumental in planting the seeds for the idea of this book. Dr. Diane Martin is a marvelously gifted Jungian analyst whose wise guidance renewed my spirit and helped me greatly in improving my relationship with my father; she has also been an invaluable source of encouragement throughout this undertaking and provided helpful comments about the material I shared with her. The Revs. Tom and Carolyn Owen-Towle, ministers at First Unitarian Church in San Diego, were warmly supportive at the critical stage when the book idea was taking root.

Pat and Lenore Conroy provided unflagging encouragement and a depth of friendship that energized this project throughout; their kindness and generosity of spirit have been light and comfort to me during dark times of struggle with some of the difficult personal material presented here. Pat's commitment to this effort, both as a military brat who believed in the idea of this book and as a writer who threw his support behind it early on, has been vital. I cannot imagine having a better ally with whom to fight the good fight.

My mother and my brother, both brave and loving people whose moral example informs this book, were consistently supportive of this project; I alone, however, take responsibility for the interpretation of our family presented here.

Tamara Dembo played a very important role as friend and adviser; the example alone of this remarkable woman has been an inspiration. Others who offered valuable support include Fran Hagstrom, Karin Junefelt, Mary Bauer, Sally and Reggie Lewis, Norris Minick, my cousin Savannah, and my cousin Alice Lane. I am also grateful to those not previously mentioned who gave of their time to read and criticize portions of the manuscript: Jim Youniss, Sandra T. Azar, Cynthia Enloe, Larry Wertsch, Bonnie and Michael Kanner-Mascolo, Sheila

Cole, Doreen Lehr, Judy Rosselli, Sarah Shaw, and Mary Kay Magistad.

Special thanks go to Margaret Garigan, my editor at Harmony and a sterling Army brat, who handled the editing with grace and wisdom and has in every way been devoted to the cause. Thanks also to Peter Guzzardi, who shepherded this book through the final stages. I am grateful to Natalie Bowen for her excellent skills as a copy editor, and to Andrea Connolly, who handled production.

I would also like to express devout thanks to the kind, responsible, and loving women who at various times cared for my children while I worked on my book: Julie Angulo, Elfrieda Van Veen, Kate Osgood, Dorie Hutchinson, Eileen Strong, Jeni Bivens, Fran Hagstrom, Natasha Selivanova, Beth and Sarah Farnham, and Ana Smolka. This is the invisible but vitally important support women provide for one another, and which for the writer-mother is in my view the late twentieth-century equivalent of Virginia Woolf's "room of one's own."

Above all there is my husband, Jim, who helped immeasurably in every way mentioned above, from initial encouragement, to guidance, to criticism of the manuscript, to doing more than his share of child care—particularly in the last three months when I needed every possible minute at the computer. He has backed me up all the way, and it is in large part because of the love, tolerance, and humor I receive from him and from our two sons that I have been able to approach this personally challenging subject from a position of emotional strength.

Finally, I owe deepest thanks to the eighty military brats who shared their stories with me. Thank you, all of you, for opening your lives and sharing your insights into our collective experience. I learned so much from you. I am the first beneficiary of your generosity; I hope I have presented your stories in a way that will allow others to benefit as I have. In the integrity and resourcefulness with which you conduct your lives and which reflect so well on our "tribe," you make me very, very proud to be a military brat.

I particularly wish to thank "Lisa," who suffered terribly in sharing her story of extreme abuse, and whose courage in doing so is a shining light to others. I pray that the public telling of her story, which she chose to do here for the first time in the interest of helping other victims of abuse, brings her the measure of peace she has long sought.

If there were such a thing as medals for military brats, all of you would deserve bronze and silver stars.

PREFACE

When I was living in Chicago in 1980, a couple of friends stopped by one night and asked me to go to a movie. The decision to drop what I was doing and go along turned out to be one of the most fateful ones I've ever made.

The movie was *The Great Santini*, made from Pat Conroy's novel about a Marine Corps pilot and his family, and the overall effect on me was like being struck by a thunderbolt. Whole scenes, whole sections of dialogue could have been lifted right from my childhood.

Not that there weren't important differences; for starters, my father had been in the Army, not the Marine Corps, and he was not a pilot. There were plenty of other differences, too. But the movie nonetheless was a revelation: It spoke to me in my own idiom, out of my own military experience—something I had yearned for without realizing it. For the first time in my life I saw that my brother and I were not, as we'd thought, rootless; we were the offspring of a lifestyle that is unique, intense, demanding, steeped in characteristic rules and values—and a lifestyle that literally millions of children have shared.

It took me several hours to calm down. What a revelation to suddenly understand that one is not alone! To all at once be given the gift of perspective on one's experience, and shown the ways to both cry and laugh about it!

In succeeding days I began to marvel that it had never occurred to me before. How was it that I had somehow grown up with the impression that other people had backgrounds, but I did not?

Then I started to piece together my assumptions about the differences between civilians and myself. They came from real places. I didn't. They knew their relatives. I didn't. They identified with a region of the country. I didn't. The implication, of course, is that all the time I was growing up, I felt my parents were in a sense more *real* than I: They came from towns in Georgia and Ohio that were rich in history, where they had friends from childhood. Their language was laced with regional idiom. They grew up knowing, really knowing, their grandparents, cousins, aunts, and uncles. They had friends from childhood who recognized in them the children they once had been, with whom they could share the sacrament of memory.

Seeing *The Great Santini* made me realize that until then I had assumed I was some kind of generic nobody, a kid from nowhere and everywhere, with an American speech so homogenized that not even the most expert linguistic detective would be able to deduce my origins. I saw that I had actually believed my life had only been "real" since I attained adulthood. And I saw how very wrong I had been.

So *The Great Santini*, as painful as it was to watch in parts—for the family depicted is a dysfunctional one, like my own, and its problems were all too familiar—was nevertheless for me a redemptive experience. Soon after, I read the novel, and in its even richer treatment of military family life I had a still more powerful feeling of connection to my origins. I realized there must be millions of us military brats caught up in the same sort of psychological diaspora, aching to get "home."

Over the next five years, I found I was full of questions about my experience as a child of the warrior society. *Santini* had given me a framework and an emotional identification, but there was much still to be explored. I knew I needed to read a book that would explain my roots inside "the Fortress," as I call the military, that would reveal the patterns of experience I share with other military brats, that would explicitly speak to the psychological legacies of the warrior life, and help me understand who I am.

That is the kind of book I needed to read, and as there were none remotely like it, that is the kind of book I have tried to write. I am a journalist, not a psychologist, but I am a journalist in search not only of ways to describe the roots I share with my subjects, but ways to understand those roots and deal with their implications. My approach is to look for patterns and try to trace them backward to their probable origin, and forward to their possible consequences. If *The Great Santini* was our first family portrait—and I have quoted liberally from it in this book because I believe it is—then what I have tried to do is part family analysis and part ethnographic description. I believe that military brats are America's most invisible minority; what I have tried to do is make us more visible—and understandable—to ourselves and to others.

It has taken me five years, during which I have had two children and, like a typical military brat, moved four times. I have done in-depth interviews with eighty military brats, all of them well into adulthood, who were raised in all four armed services. I have also done many dozens of additional interviews with military parents, teachers, physicians, psychiatrists, psychologists, social workers, historians, and scholars.

It is my contention, based on this research, that not only does the military constitute a separate and distinctly different subculture from civilian America, it exercises such a powerful shaping influence on its children that for the rest of our lives we continue to bear its stamp.

Warrior society is characterized by a rigid authoritarian structure, frequently mirrored inside its families; extreme mobility; a great deal of father absence; isolation and alienation from the civilian community; an exceedingly strict class system; a very high incidence of alcoholism, which also suggests possibly high rates of family violence; a deeply felt sense of mission; and, not least, an atmosphere of constant preparation for war, with the accompanying implication for every family that on a moment's notice the father can be sent to war, perhaps never to be seen again.

Many aspects of warrior life described in this book are not unique to the Fortress, but that does not detract from the uniqueness of Fortress life. It is the particular *combination* of characteristics, as well as its own self-perception, that sets the Fortress apart from civilian society.

Indeed, civilians will certainly see aspects of their own experience reflected in that of the military brats presented in this book. Children of police officers may be familiar with the authoritarian family structure, and the stress of knowing that the parent might be killed in the line of duty. Children of corporate executives may recognize the effects of extreme mobility. Every "PK"—preacher's kid—knows about the sense of mission that infuses the family. And the children of foreign service personnel—"dip brats," as they call themselves—know about rootlessness and the perpetual status of outsider.

There are people who carry an idealized notion of childhood in their heads, and feel cheated if their own was at variance with it—as though childhood should be free of stress and disappointment and loss. That is not the premise of this book. Nor is it the premise that these things are good in themselves. I've approached the subject of military childhood from quite another angle: that what is important is that we understand it, all of it, its joy and its pain, its humor and its cruelty, in full measure. Only if we cut through the secrecy, stoicism, and denial that are so much a part of warrior culture, only if we look at our Fortress experience unvarnished by myth, can we know who we are.

The military brats I interviewed were all very anxious to find their Fortress roots and understand the psychological legacies, positive and negative, they still carry. They understood my need to ask about very private and sometimes very dark aspects of their family experience inside the Fortress, and they were extremely candid. Because their information is so deeply personal, I have accorded them anonymity. The first names I use for the military brats are not their real names. If another person is referred to by name in a quotation, I have changed that name as well. As further protection, I have left out the names of places where interviewees reside.

They come from all parts of the country; military brats are to be found everywhere. Just over half the interviews were done in person, in several regions of the country. The rest were accomplished through a combination of phone interviews and correspondence; most often I received very lengthy taped responses to questions, after which I would follow up by letter or phone call. I received all of the names of interviewees by word of mouth, or in response to a couple of newspaper articles about my book research. There were nearly as many different sources of names as there were interviewees. I did not go to any organizations such as Adult Children of Alcoholics to find interviewees, since this would have seriously biased my research. Although this book is not presented as scientific research, I have tallied some figures in the interests of journalistic reporting. This is primarily a work of interpretive journalism; its goal is less to present a flawlessly accurate portrait of many millions of military brats—something clearly beyond the scope of what one writer can do—than to present voices that reveal aspects of our collective experience. There will be those who accuse me of giving too much space to military brats who have suffered in the course of their rearing inside the Fortress. My response is that those voices are important voices which have been stifled for too long; it is my conviction that these voices need to be heard, and indeed that we must listen to what they have to say if we are to grasp the dimensions of the Fortress experience.

There are some generalizations and assumptions in the book that I would like to clarify. Throughout, it is assumed that it is the father, not the mother, who is the member of the military, and I invariably refer to the warrior as "he." I am keenly aware of the implied sexism in this assumption, and as a feminist I do not undertake it lightly. However, when the interviewees for this book were growing up—they were born between 1932 and 1964—this was the applicable model of military family life, and indeed all of their families conformed to it. To suggest otherwise by nonsexist wording would be misleading and distracting. Today the American military is changing rapidly; there are many families in which the mother is active-duty military, and there are many single-parent families as well. These differences are bound to have important effects on the current generation of military brats, and it is my hope that someday their generation will produce a similar book to probe the new set of legacies.

For this book I interviewed as many black and Hispanic military brats as I could find, but I did not find as many as I wanted, and I suspect there are important elements of their experience I have failed to bring out. I interviewed no Asian military brats. Nor did I find any military brats who are the offspring of mixed American-Asian marriages; they present special issues which I regrettably have not covered. It is my hope that they will raise their voices and add to the military brat story, of which so little has been written.

Some readers may find that my descriptions of military routine and use of terminology reveal my Army orientation. This is not meant to be exclusionary, and was done for the sake of simplicity. As those of us reared in the military are well aware, there are major differences among the armed services, and within each service there are many distinctions, too. At some point it is necessary to generalize in order to make the commonalities clear. I believe our commonalities are far, far stronger than our differences.

Finally, a word about the term *military brat*. Of the eighty military brats interviewed for this book, only five objected to the term—two because they disliked a categorization they felt was imposed on them by the military, one because she did not like the implications of "brat," and two because they had always been told to say "Navy junior" instead. The rest all said they identified with *military brat* and used it themselves; to them it is a term of affectionate humor as well as identification. My own inquiries turned up nothing about the origin of the phrase, although I found a clue in the *Oxford Universal Dictionary* definition of *brat:* "A child (usu. implying insignificance)." I suspect that this points to a historical truth, the age-old point of view of the military-as-institution that children are a bothersome necessity, like the camp followers of whom they formed a not coincidental part. As this book makes clear, there are major ways in which that attitude still directs the military's policy toward families, to our misfortune and that of the children who are at this moment inside the Fortress.

However, that in my opinion is no reason to cast aside the term *military brat*. Why deny the truth of the way we have been regarded inside the Fortress? It is part of who we are. But only a part. As to the rest of it, the term refers to our own lived experience. And just as that experience is ours and ours alone, the term is ours too, to define as we will. That is what this book is about: a defining of who we are, in our own voices.

Some years ago the Navy launched an effort to eradicate the term *brat* and impose *Navy junior* instead. However well meaning the intention, it has not been entirely successful. Most of the Navy children interviewed for this book prefer *brat*. My inquiries with social workers at Navy bases confirmed that *Navy junior* is perceived to be a term for officer children, not enlisted ones. Perhaps sensing the elitist connotations, most of the Navy officer children interviewed for this book would not use the *junior* term to which they were supposedly entitled by their fathers' rank. In fairness to those who continue to use the term, I do not think all who use it are aware of the elitism it implies.

For my part, I've been an Army brat so long I've become very attached to the term, and I don't mind pushing my bias. I even see an advantage in being a *brat* over a *junior*. To me, *junior* implies a replica in miniature, without much autonomy or gumption, while *brat* implies not only separateness, but a certain spunkiness. And when it comes to growing up inside the Fortress and the challenge of coming to terms with the legacies of that life, I believe it is the brat qualities that see us through.

I would like to pose some challenges to the readers of this book.

To civilians: I challenge you to break down your stereotypes of military people that imprison us in simplistic cartoon figures speaking in balloons. If you listen to the voices in this book, you will find that the Fortress is a world of many-layered complexity; its warriors are not so easily dismissed as posturing martinets; its wives are not automatons; and we children might surprise you.

To military parents: I challenge you to listen to your children when they come to you with tough questions that sound uncomfortably close to recriminations. Underneath the hard surface of their questions they may well be saying, "There is so very much we weren't allowed to talk about—so much stress, so much loss, so much love. Now we are trying to figure it all out, and it would help if we could acknowledge it together, talk it through, let it go."

To military brats: I challenge you to go against the grain of all our socialization inside the Fortress, and question everything about your experience there, including all your assumptions about yourself and your family. Where there is pain to face, I ask you to call on the courage and determination that are part of our warrior legacy, and face it. In this book you will find you are not alone; there are many voices joining with yours, and because they share not only their pain but the wisdom they have gained through it, there is comfort as well. I believe you will find, as I have, that the Fortress legacy is rich in strengths, and we have much of which to be proud.

There is one question, only one, that I find not worth troubling about. I mention it because for many military brats from dysfunctional families it is one that naturally leaps to mind: Were our parents wrong to raise us in that environment? Decide as you will, but my own feeling is that the question is not only unproductive, but irrelevant. The fact is we *were* raised inside the Fortress; all further questions derive from that. Our mission is to examine what was, not what might have been, and to reconcile our Fortress roots—roots that are as rich as they are difficult— with who we are now.

INTRODUCTION

I was born and raised on federal property. America itself paid all the costs for my birth and my mother's long stay at the hospital. I was a military brat—one of America's children in the profoundest sense—and I was guaranteed free medical care and subsidized food and housing until the day I finished college and had to turn in the ID card that granted me these rights and privileges. The sound of gunfire on rifle ranges strikes an authentic chord of home in me even now. My father was a fighter pilot in the United States Marine Corps and fought for his country in three wars. I grew up invisibly in the aviator's house. We became quiet as bivalves at his approach and our lives were desperate and sad. But when the United States needed a fighter pilot, we did our best to provide one. Our contribution to the country was small, but so were we most of the time, and we gave all that we could.

Until Mary Edwards Wertsch's remarkable book *Military Brats*, no one in this country ever had the decency or took the time to thank us for our service to our country. This book is both a love letter and a troubled meditation on the way children are raised in military families. It is the first book that I know of that records the testimony of those of us who were raised in these families and analyzes our common experience. I wept while reading much of this book, I found myself roaring with laughter in other sections.

I think being a military brat is one of the strangest and most interesting ways to spend an American childhood. The military brats of America are an invisible, unorganized tribe, a federation of brothers and sisters bound by common experience, by our uniformed fathers, by the movement of families being rotated through the American mainland and to military posts in foreign lands. We are an undiscovered nation living invisibly in the body politic of this country. There are millions of us scattered throughout America, but we have no special markings or passwords to identify each other when we move into a common field of vision. We grew up strangers to ourselves. We passed through our military childhoods unremembered. We were transients, billboards to be changed, body temperatures occupying school desks for a short time.

We came and went like rented furniture, serviceable when you needed it, but unremarked upon after it was gone.

Who would have thought we were in the process of creating a brand new culture in America? Who could have known that our pain and our joy would produce such an extraordinary testament as that produced by these eighty veterans of military families who opened their hearts to Mary? Our lives may have been hard to endure, but from the clear evidence of this book, what American subdivision has produced more passionate or generous appraisers of their destinies than the voices cited here? Until now, military brats had done everything except tell their own stories. We'd never stopped to honor ourselves, out loud, for our understanding service to America. No one ever gave us our ticket to the homeland until Mary Edwards Wertsch wrote this book.

I was drafted into the Marine Corps on October 26, 1945, and I served the Corps faithfully and proudly for twenty-one years. I moved more than twenty times and I attended eleven schools in twelve years. My job was to be a stranger, to know no one's name on the first day of school, to be ignorant of all history and flow and that familial sense of relationship and proportion that makes a town safe for a child.

By necessity, I made my own private treaty with rootlessness and spent my whole life trying to fake or invent a sense of place. *Home* is a foreign word in my vocabulary and always will be. At each new base and fresh assignment, I suffered through long months of trying to catch up and learning the new steps required of those outsiders condemned to inhabit the airless margins of a child's world. None of my classmates would ever remember my name when it was time to rotate out the following summer. My family drifted in and out of that archipelago of Marine bases that begins with the Pentagon in Arlington, Virginia, and stretches down the coast to Parris Island in the South. I spent most of my childhood in North Carolina and not a single person in North Carolina knows that salient fact. I've been claimed as native son by more than a few southern states, but not by the one I spent the most time in as a child.

I've spent my life and my writing career thinking I was southern. That was only partly true and a tribute to my mother's fiery sense of belonging to the South. Because of this book, I know now that I'm something else entirely. I come from a country that has no name, the one that Mary Wertsch discovers in this book. No Carolinian, no Georgian, has ever been as close to me and what I am in my blood than those military brats who lived out their childhoods going from base to base.

My mother, the loveliest of Marine wives, always claimed to her seven children that we were in the middle of a wonderful, free-flowing life. Since it was the only life I'd ever lived, I had no choice but to believe her. She also provided me with the raw material for the protective shell I built for myself. As excuse or rationalization, it gave me comfort in the great solitude I was born into as a military brat. My mother explained that my loneliness was an act of patriotism. She knew how much the constant moving bothered me, but she convinced me that my country was somehow safer because my formidable, blue-eyed father practiced his deadly art at air stations around the South. We moved almost every year preparing for that existential moment (this is no drill, son) when my violent father would take to the air against enemies more fierce than his wife or children.

That was a darker part of my service to my country. I grew up thinking my father would one day kill me. I never remember a time when I was not afraid of my father's hands except for those bright, palmy years when Dad was waging war or serving in carrier-based squadrons overseas. I used to pray that America would go to war or for Dad to get overseas assignments that would take him to Asian cities I'd never heard of. Ironically, a time of war for the United States became both respite and separate peace for my family. When my father was off killing the enemy, his family slept securely, and not because he was making the world safe for democracy.

My mother would not let us tell anyone that Dad was knocking us around. My silence was simply another facet of my patriotism. My youth filled up with the ancient shame of a son who cannot protect his mother. It would begin with an argument and the Colonel's temper would rise (one did not argue with the Colonel or the Major or the Captain or the Lieutenant). He would backhand my mother, and her pitiful weeping would fill the room. Her seven children, quiet as Spartans, would lower their eyes and say nothing.

Later, my mother would recover and tell us that we had not seen what we had just seen. She turned us into unwitnesses of our own history. I breathed not a word of these troubling scenes to my teachers, coaches, relatives, or friends of the family. If asked, I think I'd have denied under torture that my father ever laid a hand on me. If the provost marshal had ever arrested my father for child abuse, his career in the Marine Corps would have ended at that moment. So my mother took her beatings and I took mine. My brothers and sisters, too, did their part for the Corps. We did not squeal and we earned our wings in our father's dark and high-geared squadron.

To this day, my father thinks I exaggerate the terror of my childhood. I exaggerate nothing. Mine was a forced march of blood and tears and I was always afraid in my father's house. But I did it because I had no choice and because I was a military brat conscripted at birth who had a strong and unshakeable sense of mission. I was in the middle of a long and honorable service to my country, and part of that service included letting my father practice the art of warfare against me and the rest of the family.

The military life marked me out as one of its own. I'm accustomed to order, to a chain of command, to a list of rules at poolside, a spit-shined guard at the gate, retreat at sunset, reveille at dawn, and everyone in my world must be on time. Being late was unimaginable in the world I grew up in, so I always arrive at appointments early and find it difficult to tolerate lateness in others. I always know what time it is even when I don't carry a watch.

I thought I was singular in all this, one of a kind. From Mary's book I discover that I speak in the multitongued, deep-throated voice of my tribe. By writing this book, she handed me a visa to an invisible city where I'm welcomed for the first time as a native son. Her book speaks in a language that is clear and stinging and instantly recognizable to me, yet it's a language I was not even aware I spoke. She isolates the military brats of America as a new indigenous subculture with our own customs, rites of passage, forms of communication, and folkways. When I wrote *The Great Santini* I thought I'd lived a life like no other child in this country. I had no clue that with *The Great Santini*, I had accidentally broken into the heart of both the military brat's truth and cliché. With this book, Mary astonished me and introduced me to a secret family I did not know I had.

This great family of military brats has had no voice because we've assimilated so well into the slipstreams of American life. We've never had a way of reaching out to each other, letting each other know we were around, that we endured and even prospered in our trial by father and the permanent transiency of our sturdy breed.

But Mary takes the testimony of these children of the military experience and tells us what it means. With her brilliant analysis of these far-flung anonymous voices, she lets us know that we are brothers and sisters who belong to a hidden, unpraised country. To those of us without homes or hometowns, Mary Wertsch gives, for the first time, a sense and spirit of place.

This is my paradox. Because of the military life, I'm a stranger everywhere and a stranger nowhere. I can engage anyone in a conversation, become well-liked in a matter of seconds, yet there is a distance I can never recover, a slight shiver of alienation, of not belonging, and an eye on the nearest door. The word *goodbye* will always be a killing thing to me, but so is the word *hello*. I'm pathetic in my attempts to make friends with everyone I meet, from cabdrivers to bellhops to store clerks. As a child my heart used to sink at every new move or new set of orders.

By necessity, I became an expert at spotting outsiders. All through my youth, I was grateful for unpopular children. In their unhappiness, I saw my chance for rescue and I always leapt at it. When Mary writes of military brats offering emotional blank checks to everyone in the world, she's writing the first line in my biography.

Yet I can walk away from best friends and rarely think of them again. I can close a door and not look back. There's something about my soul that's always ready to go, to break camp, to unfold the road map, to leave at night when the house inspection's done and the civilians are asleep and the open road is calling to the Marine and his family again. I left twenty towns at night singing the Marine Corps hymn and it's that hymn that sets my blood on fire each time I hear it, and takes me back to my ruined and magnificent childhood.

I brought so few gifts to the task of being a military brat. You learn who you are by testing and measuring yourself against the friends you grow up with. The military brat lacks those young, fixed critics who form opinions about your character over long, unhurried years or who pass judgment on your behavior as your personality waxes and wanes during the insoluble dilemma that is childhood. But I do know the raw artlessness of being an outsider.

Each year I began my life all over again. I grew up knowing no one well, least of all myself, and I think it damaged me. I grew up not knowing if I was smart or stupid, handsome or ugly, interesting or insipid. I was too busy reacting to the changing landscapes and climates of my life to get any clear picture of myself. I was always leaving behind what I was just about ready to become. I could never catch up to the boy I might have been if I'd grown up in one place.

In 1972, my book *The Water Is Wide* came out when I was living in Beaufort, South Carolina. It was not the most popular book in South Carolina during that season, but it was extremely popular at the Beaufort Air Station where the Marines and their wives looked to me as a living affirmation of the military way of life. I accepted an invitation to speak to the Marine Corps officers' wives' club with the deep sense that some circle was being closed. Seven years earlier my mother had been an officer in the same club and she'd produced the first racially integrated program in the club's history. Neither of us knew that my speech would mark a turning point in both our lives.

Instead of talking about my new book and my experiences teaching on Daufuskie Island, I spoke of some things I wanted to say about the Marine Corps family. I was the son of a fighter pilot, as were a lot of their kids, and I had some things to tell them. I was the first military brat who'd ever spoken to the club—I was a native son. I could hear the inheld breath of these women as I approached the taboo subject of the kind of husbands and fathers I thought Marines made. For the first time in my life I was hanging the laundry of my childhood out to dry. I told those women of the Corps that I'd met many good soldiers in my life, but precious few good fathers. I also told them of my unbounded admiration for my mother and other military wives I'd met during my career as a brat. But I told those women directly that they shouldn't let their Marines beat them or their children.

I thought I was giving a speech, but something astonishing was unleashed in that room that day. Some of the women present that day hated me, but some liked me very much. The response was electric, passionate, immediate. Some of the women approached me in tears, others in rage. But that talk to the officers' wives was the catalyst that first made me sit down and start writing the outline of *The Great Santini*.

A year later, the day after my father's retirement parade, my mother left my father after thirty-three years of marriage. Their divorce was ferocious and bitter, but it contained, miraculously, the seeds of my father's redemption. Alone and without the Corps, he realized that his children were his enemies and that all seven of us thought he hated our guts. The American soldier is not taught to love his enemy or anyone else. Love did not come easily to my father, but he started trying to learn the steps after my mother left him. It was way too late for her, but his kids were ready for it. We'd been waiting all our lives for our Dad to love us.

I had already begun the first chapters of *The Great Santini*. I wrote about a seventeen-year-old boy, a military brat who'd spent his whole life smiling and pretending that he was the happiest part of a perfect, indivisible American family. I had no experience in writing down the graffiti left along the margins of a boy's ruined heart. Because I was born a male, I had never wept for the boy who'd once withstood the slaps and blows of one of the Corps's strongest aviators. I'd never wept for my brothers or sisters or my beautiful and loyal mother, yet I'd witnessed those brutal seasons of their fear and hurt and sadness. Because I was born to be a novelist, I remembered every scene, every beating, every drop of blood shed by my sweet and innocent family for America.

As I wrote, the child of the military in me began to fall apart. I came apart at the seams. For the one thing a military brat is not allowed to do is commit an act of treason. I learned the hard way that truth is a capital offense and so did my family. I created a boy named Ben Meecham and I gave him my story. His loneliness, his unbearable solitude almost killed me as I wrote about him. Everything about the boy hurt me, but I kept writing the book because I didn't know how to stop. My marriage would fall apart and I'd spend several years trying to figure out how not to be crazy because the deep sadness of Ben Meecham and his family touched me with a pity I could not bear. His father could love him only with his fists and I found myself inconsolable as I wrote this. I would stare at pictures of myself taken in high school and could not imagine why any father would want to hit that boy's face. I wrote *The Great Santini* through tears, hating everything my father stood for and sickened by his behavior toward his family.

But in the acknowledgment of this hatred, I also found myself composing a love song to my father and to the military way of life. Once when I read *Look Homeward, Angel* in high school, I'd lamented the fact that my father didn't have an interesting, artistic profession like Thomas Wolfe's stonecutter father. But in writing *Santini*, I realized that Thomas Wolfe's father never landed jets on aircraft carriers at night, wiped out a battalion of North Korean regulars crossing the Naktong River, or flew to Cuba with his squadron with the mission to clear the Cuban skies of MIGs if the flag went up.

In writing *The Great Santini* I had to consider the fact of my father's heroism. His job was extraordinarily dangerous and I never knew it. He never once complained about the perils of his vocation. He was one of those men who make the men of other nations pause before attacking America. I learned that I would not want to be an enemy soldier or tank when Don Conroy passed overhead. My father had made orphans out of many boys and girls in Asia during those years I prayed for God to make an orphan out of me. His job was to kill people when his nation asked him to, pure and simple. And the loving of his kids was never written into his job description.

When my mother left my father she found, to her great distress, that she was leaving the protective embrace of the Corps that she'd served for more than thirty years. She was shaken and disbelieving when a divorce court granted her $500 a month in child support, but informed her she was not entitled to a dime of his retirement pay. The court affirmed that it was the Colonel who had served his country so valiantly, not she. But she'd been an exemplary wife of a Marine officer and it was a career she had carried with rare grace and distinction. Peg Conroy made the whole Marine Corps a better place to be, but her career had a value of nothing when judged in a court of law. My mother died thinking that the Marine Corps had not done right by her. She had always considered herself and her children to be part of the grand design of the military, part of the mission.

There are no ceremonies to mark the end of our career as military brats, either. We simply walk out into our destinies, into the dead center of our lives, and try to make the most of it. After my own career as a military child ended in 1967, I received not a single medal of good conduct, no silver chevrons or leaves, no letter of commendation or retirement parade. I simply walked out of one life and into another. My father cut up my ID card in front of me and told me he'd kill me if he ever caught me trying to buy liquor on base. I had the rest of my life to think about the coming of age of a military child.

Mary's book has brought it all back again—both the great parts and the hideous ones. She was brave enough to hold nothing back. I felt a great, abiding tenderness for all military brats when I read this book, and a free-flowing, unquenchable pride. Listening to the voices of these nameless men and women included here, I filled up with admiration and pity and love for all of them. We disappear and become invisible the moment we leave our fathers' homes. We lose everything except the memories of what we've done and how we did it.

Mary Edwards Wertsch tells us we did it exceptionally well.

As I was reading this book, it moved me so many times that I could feel the novelist inside me fighting to the surface for air. The novelist kept trying to change Mary's book and make it something it wasn't. I imagined that all of us could meet on some impeccably manicured field, all the military brats, in a gathering so vast that it would be like the assembling of some vivid and undauntable army. We could come together on this parade ground at dusk, million voiced and articulating our secret anthems of hurt and joy. We could praise each other in voices that understand both the magnificence and pain of our transient lives. Our greatest tragedy is that we don't know each other. Our stories could help us to see and understand what it is we all have lived through and endured.

At the end of our assembly, we could pass in review in a parade of unutterable beauty. As brats, we've watched a thousand parades on a thousand weekends. We've shined shoes and polished brass and gotten every bedroom we ever slept in ready for Saturday morning inspection. A parade would be a piece of cake for the military brats of the world.

I would put all of our fathers in the reviewing stand, and require that they come in full dress uniform and in the prime of life. I want our fathers handsome and strong and feared by all the armies of the world the day they attend our parade.

To the ancient beat of drums we could pass by those erect and silent rows of fathers. What a fearful word *father* is to so many of us, but not on this day, when the marchers keep perfect step and the command for "eyes right" roars through our disciplined ranks and we turn to face our fathers in that crowd of warriors.

In this parade, these men would understand the nature and the value of their children's sacrifice for the first time. Our fathers would stand at rigid attention. Then they would begin to salute us, one by one, and in that salute, that one sign of recognition, of acknowledgment, they would thank us for the first time. They would be thanking their own children for their fortitude and courage and generosity and long suffering, for enduring a military childhood.

But most of all the salute would be for something no military man in this country has ever acknowledged. The gathering of fighting men would be thanking their children, their fine and resourceful children, who were strangers in every town they entered, thanking them for their extraordinary service to their country, for the sacrifices they made over and over again to the United States of America, to its ideals of freedom, to its preservation, and to its everlasting honor.

Mary points out in this splendid book something that's never been pointed out before: that military brats, my lost tribe, spent their entire youth in service to this country and no one even knew we were there. This book is our acknowledgment. This book is our parade.

I wrote *The Great Santini* because in many ways the book was the only way I could take to the skies in the dark-winged jets, move through those competitive ranks of aviators and become, at last, my father's wingman.

And with this book, Mary Edwards Wertsch has taken up the guidon in her father's well-trained regiment. For this book proves that no matter how brave Col. Edwards was in battle, his daughter is every bit the warrior her father was.

—Pat Conroy

CHAPTER 1

TROUPERS

Life in the military is about fronts. Appearances. Masks. The stage persona. That's an important part of military life. Our parents were always obsessively concerned about how things looked. When we were growing up, every aspect of personal and private life was a measure of our fathers' professional competence.

—a military brat

When asked by civilians if it was really all that different to grow up in the military, we children of the Fortress sometimes draw a blank. In our gut we know it was different. Very different. But how to explain? It's possible, of course, to point out that it's all the difference between living under an authoritarian regime and living in a democracy, but that doesn't go far enough. It might supply a bird's-eye view of structure and form, but it leaves out the heart, the flavor, the drama.

And drama is the key. Growing up inside the Fortress is like being drafted into a gigantic theater company. The role of the warrior society, even in peacetime, is to exist in a state of perpetual "readiness": one continuous dress rehearsal for war. The principal actors are immaculately costumed, carefully scripted, and supplied with a vast array of props. They practice elaborate large-scale stage movements—land, air, and sea exercises simulating attacks and defenses. But even apart from such massive stagings, the minutiae of form in each costumed actor are carefully shaped to the last detail. No liberties may be taken with the way a warrior-actor stands, walks, salutes, speaks; this is not a theater of improvisation.

And then there is the supporting cast: the wives—who may lack costumes but whose lines and movements are crafted every bit as carefully—and the children, the understudies.

But the thing about the drama of the military is that it is not confined, as movies would have it, to the most spectacular scenes of families parting and reuniting, of actual combat, of military funerals. Drama is the very medium of life inside the Fortress, its color and texture, a quality that so thoroughly imbues even the most ordinary moments that it cannot be subtracted. Shopping at the commissary, riding home on a bike, sitting in a movie theater—even the most trivial actions can have a staged, rehearsed feeling to them that is largely alien to the civilian world.

Take, for example, something as inconsequential as a tape player at a base movie theater going on the blink. An Air Force son who, as a teenager, happened to be in a theater when that happened one night, described the scene: The airmen, officers, and their families were settling into their seats when, as usual, the curtains opened to reveal a gigantic American flag on the screen. On cue, everyone put down their popcorn and drinks and rose to attention, fully expecting to hear the national anthem as it played over the loudspeakers. But for some reason the tape didn't play that evening, and the silent crowd began to fidget uneasily, unsure of what to do. With the flag still on the screen, it was impossible to sit down. To stand at attention until the tape player was repaired would be absurd. But to sit down and watch the film without having performed the expected patriotic duty was unthinkable. Then an officer in the audience took charge: In a commanding voice he began reciting the Pledge of Allegiance. Every voice in the theater joined him; and at the end, like an umpire at a baseball game or a field commander ordering an attack, he shouted, "Show the film!" Only then did the audience resume their seats.

Or take another moment of everyday military life: the precise moment of 1700 hours (5:00 P.M.), any day of the week, on any American military base anywhere in the United States or abroad. At the stroke of 1700—one could set one's watch by it, if it weren't irreverent—loudspeakers all around the base sound the first bugle notes of Retreat. All movement stops. Forget rush hour, forget the beckoning of dinnertime, forget the shopping and the chores. Cars pull over. Occupants get out. Children dismount from their bikes. Pedestrians stop in their tracks. Golfers put down their clubs. In the base commissary, where the speaker system plays the same notes, shoppers halt, cash registers are silent. And everyone turns in the direction of the base's main flag. Even if they cannot see it, they all know where it is. If in uniform, they stand in stiff salute; if not, they stand straight and motionless, hand over heart. Then there is the deep BOOM-echo-echo of the cannon firing, followed by the bugle playing To the Colors. Out of vision of all but a few, the flag is being lowered for the day. In this most nationalistic of all American communities, respect must be paid.

But it bears keeping in mind that the life of the Fortress turns not merely on patriotic fervor. This is an authoritarian world. The reverential nature of the daily ritual of Retreat, one might notice, does not prevent the devout from casting indignant sidelong stares at the few cars or pedestrians that keep moving. If these violators of tradition are recognized, they will be reported. For if 1700 is the hour of patriotic witness, it is also the hour of conformity.

A mile away, perhaps less, the civilian community might as well be on another planet. No mass ritual, no patriotic devotion, no conformity, and, some would say, no sense of mission.

The Militarization of Childhood

The coaching that directs military children to assume their proper roles in the theatrical company of the Fortress begins quite early. For some it starts in the cradle. Many military brats begin life in a way that leaves little doubt about their parents' wish to imprint the warrior image.

Before they have had time even to suckle their mothers, some military children carry the freight of their parents' expectations in the form of the warrior names they are given to bear: Dwight (for Gen. Dwight D. Eisenhower), Omar (for Gen. Omar Bradley), Lewis (for Gen. Lewis "Chesty" Puller), John Paul (for Adm. John Paul Jones), Robert Lee (for Gen. Robert E. Lee). . . . The names invoke the memory of exalted generals and admirals.

And many children of warrior families are named after military bases; several of the military brats interviewed for this book carry such names. Air Force brats are particularly subject to this practice, for almost all the bases bear the names of deceased aviators, many of whom had surnames that work well as first names: Travis, George, Scott, Kelly, Luke, Hamilton, Patrick, Maxwell, Randolph, to name just a few.[1]

I also heard from reliable sources of an Army daughter named Major, after her father's rank when she was born, and of a Marine sergeant who named his baby girl Marina Cora. Lest the reader think that sergeant is unique, there is also the case of a Marine daughter interviewed for this book, the child of Mexican-American parents: Her first and last names reflect her family heritage and are thoroughly Hispanic, but her middle name is clashingly Irish. "Maureen," she explained, "was the closest he could come to naming me after the Marine Corps." She went on to say that her father nearly named her brother, his firstborn son, Gung Ho. "They would have called him G.H.," she said. "In the end he didn't do it, but he did seriously think about it."

As childhood progresses, the coaching intensifies for the part of little warrior. Indeed, a visit to any post or base exchange on a Saturday morning will likely reveal a procession of toddlers outfitted in "cammies" (camouflage fatigues), bearing toy M-16s. War toys are encouraged, from model bombers and battleships to walkie-talkies and entire arsenals of plastic weapons. G.I. Joe, popular among civilian kids as well, is standard issue to kids in many military homes, but is actually banned in some where the parents fear it will sissify their sons to play with dolls. But military brats of both sexes tell of the joys of playing with the castoff military paraphernalia their fathers brought home, from helmets and C-rations to parachutes, empty ammo cans, holsters, old fatigue jackets, spent shells, and brightly colored uniform patches.

At base chapels, children pray to a God glorified by war. In the Chapel of the Centurion at Fort Monroe, Virginia, there is even a stained glass window entitled "Power for Peace," the central element of which is a nuclear missile pointed heavenward. This is not merely a missile in a peaceful state of "readiness," but a missile moments after blastoff, still discharging curling white plumes as it begins its deadly trajectory.

In all military chapels, children hear sermons linking heavenly tribute and patriotic purpose. They often grow up singing such hymns as "The Son of God Goes Forth to War," "Fight the Good Fight with All Thy Might," "Marching with the Heroes," "Jesus, Savior, Pilot Me," and "Guard and Guide the Men Who Fly."[2] And of course there are the two bloodiest and most inspiring hymns of all, both dating from the Civil War: "The Battle Hymn of the Republic" and "Onward, Christian Soldiers."

At the government-run elementary schools on military bases, many children of warriors recall, patriotic and military songs are not just a casual part of the educational agenda. A Navy daughter recalled that at her school, "We started each day by pledging allegiance to the flag, then singing 'The Star Spangled Banner,' then 'It's a Grand Old Flag,' then 'America the Beautiful.' We had to march single file, in time, between classes." The practice is echoed within families; children of warriors grow up with such airs as "The Marines' Hymn" ("From the Halls of Montezuma . . .") or "The Air Force Hymn" ("Up we go, into the wild blue yonder . . .") as much a part of their repertoire as "Mary

Had a Little Lamb." Marines, who sing their hymn "at the drop of a field hat," in the words of *The Marine Officer's Guide*,[3] train their children to rise, as their parents do, whenever it is played or sung. Coaching like this is not confined to the Corps, of course. A daughter of a Green Beret (U.S. Army Special Forces) recalled that whenever her father and one of his buddies got together, they would play a record of Sgt. Barry Sadler's "Ballad of the Green Beret" and order their sons to stand in stiff salute.

Then there are the special days of the calendar year: Armed Forces Day, in May, is a major celebration, with air shows, parades, displays of weapons and tanks, cookouts. The Marines have an additional day that approaches the sacred: November 10, the Birthday of the Marine Corps (founded in 1775), which Marines around the world are required to celebrate. Every command has a formal ball for officers and one for enlisted, and attendance is mandatory unless duty prevents. Even solitary Marines in isolated outposts are required to celebrate the birthday of the Corps in some appropriate manner. It goes without saying that November 10 figures prominently in the lives of Marine children.[4]

For boys fourteen to seventeen years old who are particularly "gung ho"—or those whose parents wish them to be—there is also the ten-day Devil Pups summer camp at Camp Pendleton, near San Diego, run by a private corporation with the permission and extensive involvement of the Marine Corps. The purpose, according to Duncan Shaw, president of Devil Pups, Inc.,[5] is "character building, good citizenship, and physical development." While most of the 34,500 kids who have "graduated" from Devil Pups camp since 1954 have been civilians, there have been plenty of military sons as well. "It's a disciplined environment," said Shaw, "but it should not be considered anything like a boot camp." The program was founded by Marines and is still run by Marines along lines that approximate Marine Corps discipline and training, but the boys do not handle weapons, and it has been some years since their summer camp rite of passage included exposure to tear gas.

"I was in two of the Devil Pup summer camps," said the son of a Marine sergeant. "They really put you through your paces physically. You learned how to take orders and not talk back, or you'd get your butt kicked. It was nothing I hadn't experienced before."

In the day-to-day life of warrior families, conversation is typically punctuated with military expressions: Children learning a new task are "briefed" on the "SOP" (standard order of procedure). A job well done is pronounced "outstanding," a common military superlative. Children are taught to tell time in the approved military way: Bedtime, for instance, might be "twenty-one hundred" (9:00 P.M.). The children themselves are often referred to as "hands," "troops," "sailors," "Marines," "men" (regardless of gender), or even "maggots" (when the father styles himself as a particularly fearsome drill instructor), and they learn to refer to their home as their "quarters," to kitchen chores as "KP," and mopping the floor as "swabbing the decks," to making their beds as "squaring away the bunks," and to cleaning the bathrooms as "latrine detail."

Certainly by the time a military child is five years old, the values and rules of military life have been thoroughly internalized, the military identity well forged, and the child has already assumed an active stage presence as an understudy of the Fortress theater company. In my own case, the year I was five is the first year I can remember clearly thinking of myself as a child of the military. At that time we were living at Fort Myer, Virginia, and my father, an Army colonel, was working at the Pentagon.

. . . Summer, 1957. I had been learning how to read and write in preparation for first grade. One day I wandered into my sixteen-year-old brother's bedroom and, to my delight, found that I could actually read the single word emblazoned in big gold letters on the black pennant above his bed.

"Mary!" I exclaimed with joy. I had not realized I meant so much to my big brother, whom I held in fearful awe. To my consternation, my brother instantly doubled over laughing.

"Not 'Mary,' " he finally gasped. "Army!"

I was disappointed, to say the least, but the incident nevertheless left me with an enduring attachment to that shining word on the pennant. The similarity to my own name was a fact I could not overlook; to me it constituted proof of something I already felt. I was an extension of it, and it of me. No one could have convinced me otherwise.

. . . Another day that summer I set out down our front walk, clasping a little metal treasure chest in which I kept some of my favorite things. About halfway down the walk I decided to stop and look at some of them. I lifted the lid and carefully took out a decal of the U.S. flag. Suddenly a gust of wind caught the corner and, before I could catch it, the flag decal fluttered to the ground.

I cried. That decal meant a lot to me, but I knew my duty: When the U.S. flag touches the ground, it must be burned or buried immediately. Not having access to matches, I gave it a proper burial in the backyard.

. . . A second burial. My pet turtle died, presenting me with the issue of how to dispose properly of the body. I solemnly gave it a military funeral in the soft earth under the back porch, complete with improvised caisson, bugler, and, for good measure, the twenty-one-gun salute usually reserved for heads of state. At the time, we lived on the edge of Arlington National Cemetery, and our house was on the route traveled by the caisson and horses each day.

. . . About 7:15 one morning, my father set off as usual for his job at the Pentagon. I followed him out back, marveling at his rigid bearing, barrel chest, and that wondrous uniform with bright ribbons, shiny buttons, and neat silver birds on the shoulders. His uniform awed me. It was more than the buttons and birds and shiny trim on his hat. There were perfect creases down his pants. Not a spot on the smooth expanse of khaki. Not a smudge of dirt on his shiny black shoes, in which I could almost see my face. I felt unworthy in his immaculate presence.

Then, suddenly, one of the sparrows up in our oak tree scored a direct hit on his hat. I screamed with laughter as my father stomped and cursed. I was sure I'd never seen anything so funny in my whole life. The Colonel was furious, and from the sound of his curses it was hard to tell who had committed the greater outrage—the sparrow, or his five-year-old daughter.

. . . Christmas, 1957. My big present that year was a portable mono record player. I couldn't believe my good fortune. And along with the record player came my first very own record. It was wrapped in bright paper and tied with a ribbon, but I could clearly see it was a 45 rpm. Could it possibly be my current favorite, "Wake Up, Little Suzie"? Or even "You Ain't Nothin' but a Hound Dog"? I snatched the paper off.

But no. It was "The Pledge of Allegiance," sung by the U.S. Marine Corps Band. Even then, enough was enough. I've never played it, though I have it still.

. . . Dinner, en famille. It must have been 5:30 sharp. My father, still in uniform minus the jacket, was at the head of the table. Mom was holding down the other end, ready to scoot to the kitchen should anything be wanted. My brother, sixteen and sullen, was across from me. The atmosphere was grave. My brother said nothing. My mother said nothing. It must have been one of those times when no subject was safe. And Dad just sat there, ramrod straight, glowering at his food and chewing critically.

Finally, secure in my role as the little Electra of the household, I turned to my father and said, in my best casual imitation of my mother, "Pass the tomatoes, Dave." No "please," no "sir." And to top it off, I'd called him Dave.

The entire family exploded in laughter at this brazen impertinence. Even The Colonel. His face turned red. Tears ran down his cheeks. He laughed so hard his voice went up two octaves into a high-pitched, breathless "hee hee hee." My brother and mother, weak with laughter at the sacrilege, were hanging on to the table for support. It looked like the revolution had triumphed, and I was the heroine of the hour.

Five minutes later, after we had mostly recovered and the general atmosphere had calmed to reminiscent chuckles, I decided to try it again. Fatal mistake. My father roared out scorching rage. "That's enough of *that!* You will *not* call me *Dave!* And when you speak to me you will say *please* and follow it with *sir!* Is that *clear?*"

Yes, sir, it was. In the exacting theatrical world of the Fortress, such were the consequences of ad-libbing one's lines.

Scenes like these were commonplace not only in my family, but in many other families of the Fortress—although I did not fully realize this until I was almost thirty years old and saw the movie, then read the novel *The Great Santini.* Pat Conroy's evocation of a Marine Corps officer's family was so like my own I was staggered. While I watched the movie I recall I had the odd sensation of peering into an endlessly reflecting mirror: I was sitting there in the theater watching a drama of the everyday drama of the military—and meanwhile there was a parallel drama of my own past running in my head.

Nearly all the military brats interviewed for this book were familiar with *Santini* and more than familiar with its title character; if they hadn't been raised by him, they had lived next door to him. Their families were organized along the same chain of command, spoke the same scripts, were militarized in much the same way.

Take duty rosters, for instance. Quite a few of us grew up with duty rosters posted on the refrigerator. "The chores were listed for the whole week, by date and name of kid," said one Army son who later chose a career in the Marine Corps. "I remember latrine detail: We had to shine all the brass pipes, including the ones behind the commode, with Brasso, and we had to take a toothbrush to clean the dirt and mold between the tiles."

Other duties typically scheduled on rosters might include KP, polishing all the shoes in the family (with a spit shine for the warrior's), "policing the grounds," or "squaring away" the quarters. An Air Force son recalled a particular "punishment duty" that was such a frequent feature of his childhood it might as well have been one of the regular chores: sitting on the lawn and picking out the little blue bits of gravel sprayed there by the car going in and out of the driveway. Some families used a demerit system to keep track of imperfections in performance.

In many homes the week's duties were followed by formal, military-style inspections. "We did our chores on Saturday mornings," said an Army colonel's daughter, "and then we'd have to stand by our bed-room doors, lined up, and our father would come and inspect. He'd check our closets to see if the shoes were neatly lined up, and under the beds to see if we'd vacuumed and dusted there. The beds had to be made a certain way—with hospital corners—and we couldn't sit on the bedspreads, ever." Room inspections in many military households included bouncing a quarter off the bed: If it didn't bounce, the bedclothes had to be ripped off and the bed remade. An Air Force brat whose father used military lingo "in our regular operations around the house," told of inspections every Saturday. "If we didn't pass," she said, "we'd get an Article 15, which meant we were confined to quarters."

White-glove inspections, in imitation of the procedure used on special occasions in the military, represent the same idea elevated to another dimension. "My father would don a pair of white gloves, and start looking for dust," said the daughter of an Army sergeant. "He always found some on the floor behind the toilet bowl." But that father was hardly unique in the rigor of his methods. So many military brats told similar stories, one would have to think that at any given moment hundreds of military fathers must be pulling on white gloves and stern expressions and getting down on all fours to probe behind the bath-room toilet.

A civilian I know recalled a scene from childhood when he'd gone one Saturday morning to the home of a friend, the son of a retired major. In that home, he said, weekly white-glove inspections pre-vailed, but it was the mother, not the father, who performed them.[6] The civilian kid watched in consternation as the ritual proceeded. His friend's mother pulled on her glove and began running her finger across the dresser, the windowsill, every surface in the room in a concentrated, methodical search. "I clearly remember she ran her finger over the bedposts looking for dust," he said. "She didn't find any. Then she looked around and her glance fell on the top of the bedroom door. She reached up and ran her finger across the top, and it was dirty. I'll never forget the look on her face; it was almost evil. She stared at her son and slowly said, 'James. You . . . are . . . not . . . going . . . *anywhere* . . . today.' "

The notion that we children of the Fortress were raised in ways substantially different from our civilian peers is a realization that hovers on the edge of consciousness in childhood. The truth of it is undeniable, but we focus on it at our own peril. It is safer to take note of it later, when we are older and have some power over our lives.

"I knew growing up that our family didn't seem to act like civilian families," said the son of an Army colonel. "Later on, I realized that operationally there was little difference between how Dad ran one of his units and how he ran his family. The way I was made to answer the phone, for instance: 'Sir, this is Colonel [Smith's] quarters, [John] speaking, Sir.' That was standard military." Even in many homes that were far more relaxed, the way the phone was answered was pro forma military, as many interviewees attested. Asking military brats how they answered the phone as a child is like pushing a button on a tape machine: The answer is instantaneous, exact, and has the well-worn rhythm of an incantation.

It is customary in many military families for the children to say "yes, sir," "no, sir," "yes, ma'am," "no, ma'am." Of the interviewees for this book, nearly three quarters said this was law in their households. The son of an Air Force lieutenant colonel said, "It wasn't until my late twenties—and I'm thirty-eight now—that I didn't automatically say 'yes, sir,' 'no, sir' if I didn't know the person who was addressing me. Sometimes I still do; it was ground into me."

The practice appears to be slightly more common in officer families than enlisted ones, but what is interesting is that it occurs in enlisted families at all. In the military a noncommissioned officer such as a sergeant or petty officer is never addressed as "sir." An appropriate response is, for example, "Yes, Sergeant." At home, however, many of these men apparently prefer to be called sir.[7]

Theater with a Difference

It should not be surprising that military families become faithful miniatures of the larger theatrical company of the Fortress. The dramatic atmosphere is so all-consuming, and the pressure to perform so intense, that resisting it would require extraordinary determination—and anyone willing to exert that kind of strength of will is better off outside the Fortress.

But if the directors of the production make sure no detail of performance is left to chance, it is for good reason. For the backdrop to this rehearsal—invisible to the mere spectator but harrowingly real to the players—is the potential of actual war and death. The warrior-actors are preparing for roles that may, for all they know, call for their sacrifice on the battlefield. And as each day's rehearsal begins, they have no idea if it will end benignly or in death. On a military base there is no way to know if an alert called in the middle of the night is just a drill or the real thing.

A drama company, then, but one with a difference. For these actors, there is no end to the production, no moment when they can leave the role behind. A warrior must be a warrior twenty-four hours a day; the script calls for him to be ready for war at any moment. The identification of the warrior-actors with their parts is total. For them, the boundary between what is real and what is not has long since ceased to matter.

What keeps this fusion intact is the unique and insular world of the Fortress, which absorbs its players into a tight-knit culture of war. There is the kinship warriors feel for one another, reinforced at every turn. There are the stage props, from tanks and ships to rifles and C-rations. There are the thousands of rituals of the regimented life. Even the smells are important: Brasso and shoe polish, gun oil and Cosmoline, discharged weapons and heavily dyed canvas tents—all as intoxicating to these actors as the smell of greasepaint. And there are the sounds, from the boom-echo of cannon and the roar of jets to the popping of shells in the distance and the sweet bugle tones of Reveille, Assembly, Mess Call, Retreat, To the Colors, Tattoo, and Taps.

To the observer there is something intriguing about the initiated inside the Fortress, evident not just in the costumes of the warriors but in their bearing, voice, facial expression. These are men who live their parts, who carry themselves as though they had never known the comparatively chaotic, kaleidoscopic world beyond the Fortress walls. But we know otherwise. At some point each of them left someplace else, another life, and of his own volition came to the Fortress to shed his uniqueness, join himself to the warrior image.

It is a role which, these men must surely have known, would change everything in their lives: their self-image, their ties to the world outside the Fortress, their relationship to their own families of origin.

By the time we, their children, came to know them, the warrior image had long been joined. We cannot envision our fathers as other than warriors. But there was a time before our fathers came to the Fortress, a time before they learned to live the role, when they were still homegrown boys bearing the stamp of their families, their neighborhoods, their towns. It is hard for us, leafing through old family albums, to reconcile two such disparate images: the cocky, loose-limbed youth embedded in the cultural milieu of his time, and the older warrior so merged with archetype that he stands oddly outside time and place. There is a gap in understanding, a missed connection, a question that cannot be ignored because it lies at the heart of both our fathers' lives and ours.

We must know how and why they became warriors—for it is one thing to understand how the Fortress is a vastly different world from civilian society, and quite another to understand how we the children came to be part of it.

The Mask of the Warrior

It was because of this insistent need to know that I visited the Marine Corps Recruit Depot (MCRD) in San Diego late one March evening a few years ago, at the start of my research on this book. Perhaps, I reasoned, if I picked the right place and time, I could actually witness a living moment of transition, see the mold of the warrior mask as it is first applied over the uniqueness of a young man's life.

I am watching from the shadows as a bus rolls to a stop before the imposing red brick buildings of MCRD, point of entry to the Marine Corps for all recruits west of the Mississippi. The passengers, picked up minutes before at the city airport, look painfully young: perhaps seventeen or eighteen, long-haired, baby-faced, pimply. Under the glare of half a dozen spotlights, paralyzing fear can be read in their blanched faces.

A slim, ramrod-straight Marine sergeant boards the bus at once and walks down the aisle, hands clasped behind him, surveying his new crop.

"*Sit up straight, recruits!*" he suddenly barks, the astonishing loudness of his voice magnified inside the bus, and they jump. He orders them to get off the bus, single file and fast. Outside they line up for his inspection. Most of them are scruffy, disheveled, and out of shape. The contrast to the sergeant, who looks as if he was born starched and spit-shined, is almost painful to behold.

He continues to rasp out orders: *Stand up straight! Arms at your sides!* He shows them how to salute, how to scream *Yes, sir* at the top of their lungs, in unison.[8] Then he orders anyone who meant to go into the Navy instead of the Marines to stand off to one side. Sometimes, in their terror and confusion, recruits arriving at the airport board the wrong bus.

The drill instructor—DI—gives his young charges no time to reflect between orders. They're told to move quickly into a nearby building, where the open door throws a shaft of light onto the close-cropped lawn. "*Walk!* I said *walk!* Let's *go!*" Minutes later they emerge, carrying their first seabags, and hurry stiff-legged to another section of the parking lot, where they line up on the yellow footprints painted there. The DI uses no profanity, no epithets, does not lay a finger on them. Officially, these relics of the old-style Marine Corps have been banned. But he wouldn't need to use them anyway; these kids have fear written all over them. And they all desperately want to be Marines. For many this is a ticket out of joblessness or a bad home life. For others it's a quick route to manhood and self-esteem. Whatever the impetus, they consider themselves lucky to be here. There's a waiting list to get into the Corps.[9]

An observer can't help but notice that these kids all seem to know instinctively how to stand, how to respond to commands. "Partly that's because the recruiters tell them what to expect," said the Marine captain standing next to me, who is in charge of the receiving barracks. "But also it's because they arrive here expecting to live up to an image."

The image of the Corps: the few, the proud, the toughest fighters of them all—first on the beaches, first to die. In the anxious, jerky movements of these recruits—now wearing Marine fatigue jackets over their jeans, their seabags beside them—one can almost feel the electric charge, the desperate adolescent yearning to claim the role, to merge the cumulative pains of boyhood into the collective manhood of the Corps.

Of all the rites of passage, boot camp must be the most predictable— and every boy here knows it, even as he stands eyes riveted straight ahead, trembling before the future and the chill of deepening night. If he can just hack the next twelve weeks—and most particularly, the recruiter will have told him, the next fifteen days of hell—he will have left boyhood behind. He will be a Marine, incarnation of the hallowed ideal. Perhaps the thoughts of these boys are already winging ahead to graduation and a scene often played out on this base: A mother, confronted with a line of taut, disciplined, immaculate young Marines in dress blues, does not recognize her own son. Anticipating the transformation, the boys arrive already wearing awkward approximations of the mask of the warrior.

The DI, meanwhile, continues to bark his commands in rapid-fire succession, giving his charges no time to think. Hurrying the recruits is a critical part of their introduction to the Corps; the more stress they're under, the easier they are to mold.

A moment later the captain says, "It might seem like this is a lot of stress for these recruits, but compared to what goes on in training, it's very, very mild." In the days to come, commands will be thrown at recruits faster than they can obey. They will be physically driven to the point of exhaustion. Sleep will be adequate, but not enough to satisfy.

They will not be allowed off base for any reason. And in addition to the other restrictions of the ascetic life, they will not be allowed tobacco. For those with a habit, the stress goes up geometrically.

The DI, stalking the perimeter of the tightly packed square of recruits, shouts, "*And now, recruits, you will go inside for your first Marine haircut. This regulation haircut is not to humiliate or harass you. It is for hygiene purposes only, recruits.*" The first boy is peeled off from the mass and dispatched inside to stand stiffly before the chair until the barber is ready. The haircut itself takes about fifteen seconds, the wide electric razor quickly finding the contours of his skull, the hair falling to the floor in great hunks. The boy stares unblinking at a point on the ceiling, his ears full of the sound of his irrevocable decision.

The haircut is perhaps the most important thing that will happen to the recruits tonight. For despite the DI's disclaimer, this haircut is not for hygiene purposes only. It is an extremely effective way to impress on each teenager that he has entered a new life in which conformity is what counts. In the space of half an hour he has been transformed from a particular boy from a particular family in a particular town, to a member of a unit. His personal history has been erased. From now on all that counts is how well he fulfills the expectations of his sergeant.

The first mask worn in the military, then, is a blank one. Its function: to suppress the individual beneath it. Over the next weeks of grueling boot camp, the details of the mask will be filled in. By the end—if the recruit makes it to the end—he will wear the mask of the warrior: macho, aggressive, single-minded, able to respond instantly to any command, willing to lay down his life for his comrades.

It is impossible to remain indifferent or detached while watching these young boys as they apply to the portal of their manhood. The snapped orders, their fumbled compliance, the mix of emotion in their faces, the stark contrast of the lean and finely honed DI, like a ghost of their future selves come back to challenge them—all of it has a timelessness and universality about it. It is a scene as redolent of the human condition as the worn steps of a cathedral, or the votive candles that flicker their sweet dancing promise to the hopeful. And in its way, this stark monochromatic receiving barracks of the United States Marine Corps is also hallowed ground, saturated as it is in faith and dreams and the promise of blood shed for glory.

All of us wear masks, every day of our lives. We do it because it's by far the best way to function with other people. It conceals what we do not want to display, and enables us to fit what others expect. But in the military, masks are not merely a matter of convenience. They are essential.

Military readiness depends on each member of the unit reacting in a predictable manner. That's why every aspect of training reinforces conformity, why all members of the military are expected to dress alike, act alike, carry within them the same set of absolute, unquestioned beliefs, and demonstrate in all things their submission to order and authority.

A civilian therapist at the Recruit Depot put it this way: "Marines are trained to react. They're not trained to think. They're not trained to be individuals. What happens to them in recruit training is they're stripped of their individuality. And they're put together again as a *group*. They're taught the good of the group is more important than their own life or safety."

It can be no other way. In any military operation, the unit must function as smoothly and dependably as a machine.

Unit. The word itself is telling. The military is no place for an assortment of freethinkers, each with his own way of doing things, his own separate agenda. For we are talking—and this cannot be overstated—about a world vastly different from the rest of American society. We are talking about a parallel world that runs, of necessity, on a different value system.

The great paradox of the military is that its members, the self-appointed front-line guardians of our cherished American democratic values, do not live in democracy themselves. Not only is individuality not valued in the military, it is discouraged. There is no freedom of speech, save on the most innocuous level. There is no freedom of assembly for anything that is not authorized. There is not even a concept of privacy as civilians understand it, for in the military the distinction between private and public is thoroughly blurred. What a soldier does and says privately, and what his spouse and children do and say, can be held against him. And there are restrictions on such things as the expression of one's religion, which must never be allowed to distract from the overriding imperative of conformity.

To cite a recent example, in March 1986 the United States Supreme Court voted 5–4 to uphold the United States Air Force in its 1981 disciplinary action against an Orthodox Jew, Capt. Simcha Goldman, who wore his yarmulke indoors while in uniform, in violation of a uniform dress code banning all wearing of headgear indoors.[10] Justice William Rehnquist, author of the majority opinion, wrote that the free-exercise clause of the First Amendment did not apply, since the USAF did not prohibit the wearing of nonvisible religious apparel.

Dissenting opinions were among the most bitter in the Court's history. Justice William Brennan, for example, wrote, "The Court and the military services have presented patriotic Orthodox Jews with a painful dilemma—the choice between fulfilling a religious obligation and serving their country. Should the draft be reinstated, compulsion will replace choice. Although the pain the services inflict on Orthodox Jewish servicemen is clearly the result of insensitivity rather than design, it is unworthy of our military because it is unnecessary. The Court and the military have refused these servicemen their constitutional rights: we must hope that Congress will correct this wrong."[11]

What the Court majority did not—and could not—specifically say is that the constitutional guarantees available to citizens of a democracy frequently do not apply to members of an authoritarian regime such as the military. The issue in the Goldman case, from the strictly military point of view, is not that the yarmulke itself was offensive, but that its wearing implies a notion that the authoritarian military inevitably finds intolerable: that an individualistic agenda—even subservience to one's religious beliefs—holds supremacy over the military necessity of conformity at all times. The wearing of a yarmulke—or any other visible religious symbol—is in effect an advertisement that the wearer obeys a higher authority than the military—something the military reasons it cannot afford.

The Fortress, in short, is an authoritarian society. The masks worn there are authoritarian masks, each exactly like the others of its rank, each subservient to those of higher rungs. The notions of conformity, order, and obedience reign supreme.

One might ask, then, in view of the great value American society places on individuality and autonomy, what attracted these maskwearers, our fathers, to a strangely theatrical world that demands absolute self-effacement and total immersion in the dramatic part.

This is the other part of the question at the heart of military brats' lives, the one that addresses our presence in the theatrical company of the Fortress. The first part was to know *how* our fathers came to wear the mask of the warrior. Now we must know *why*.

The Reasons They Join

To say that men choose a military career out of a sense of patriotism may have a large measure of truth to it, but it is not enough of an explanation. After all, one can be quite patriotic without becoming a warrior.

There are men, of course, who become warriors because it is a family tradition; the warrior mask is conferred by one generation on the next.

There are others who joined to fight in World War II and remained because they found they had a special affinity for the life.

And there are plenty of others who came of age during the Depression, and joined the warrior society because it offered financial support, education, and benefits that could not then be matched in civilian society. Some of our best military leaders have been such men, whose best hope for making use of their considerable talents lay in the military, and who, fortunately for our country, were then in place to return the favor in World War II. The same situation applies even today to members of minority groups who continue to see more opportunity for upward mobility in the military than they have been able to find in civilian society.

On a deeper psychological level, however, there is something more to be said about the decision to merge one's identity with the mask of the warrior. It has to do with the nature of the military, which in some ways is very much like a family: It has structure, expectations, rules, penalties, and an overriding identity in which every member shares. The military in that sense is very reassuring, in its way. It offers security, identity, a sense of purpose.

It can also satisfy a need for dependence. Some men are drawn to the predictable, sheltered life of the Fortress because it offers a measure of compensation for what they did not have growing up. For such men, the theatrical company of the military represents an additional dramatic opportunity: the chance to replay the family experience, only this time with a "parent" who is dependable and approving, though strict.

Joining the military in order to put one's self in the care of a good surrogate parent is hardly the sort of thing one is likely to advertise; in fact, it is a secret so deep-seated that those who act upon on it rarely admit it, and guard their secret carefully. Ultimately, however, it is the sort of truth that is impossible to conceal totally. The children almost always know, though it has almost never been explained to them in so many words.

The daughter of a Navy commander: "My father was the son of an immigrant family which was very abusive. He enlisted in the Navy at seventeen and worked his way up to officer. The Navy gave him things he would never have had otherwise."

The daughter of an Army colonel: "My father's mother was an alcoholic, and his father, who remarried three or four times, didn't want his son. My father was sent to a military high school and joined the service right afterward."

The son of a Marine major: "My father's father was very tough on him. He ran away at age fourteen, and later joined the Marine Corps. He's the kind of man who likes to be told what to do and what is expected of him; he appreciates the clarity. But at the same time he has a very hard time with authority figures, and resists more than most people."

The son of a Navy chief petty officer: "If *my* father was an authoritarian, *his* father was a despot. My father ran away from home at age eleven and never went back. He lied about his age and enlisted in the Navy when he was fifteen or sixteen. He wanted to get as far away from home as possible."

For such men, the military life can be very satisfying. It eases anxiety by providing a solid job, a route to manhood, and separation from the family of origin, while allowing room to grow into a more secure sense of self. These men, who after all did not ask to be saddled with the problems they faced in childhood, made the best decision they could to straighten out their lives. For many, it pays off.

But for military brats, the significance doesn't end there. If the father—or mother—came to the military life seeking a surrogate parent, it means that the children are born inside the Fortress as a direct result of their parent's unresolved childhood needs. Looking at the father's reason for joining, then, is not just a means of articulating a superficial explanation for why his particular children happen to be military brats. It is a potentially ominous shadow of what is to come as they grow up. For the military offspring will almost certainly have to deal not only with the particular challenges of the Fortress life— aspects of which are the subjects of later chapters—but with the residual effects of uncommonly difficult problems in their parents' lives.

Some men wear the mask of the warrior to assume a new identity. Some wear it to protect themselves from the past. For both purposes, it works extraordinarily well. But there is a built-in danger: The mask not only protects the wearer, it transforms him. Very often the warrior becomes the authoritarian that the mask represents, no matter what he was like before.

Wearing the Mask of the Warrior into the Home

Authoritarians are made, not born, according to the psychological literature. [12] Since the Fortress is a thoroughly authoritarian society, it is to be expected that authoritarian personalities abound there—some because they were already authoritarian and sought a compatible environment, and some because the Fortress itself gradually reshaped them to fit the mold. The authoritarian mask of the warrior is not a natural fit for every would-be actor in the Fortress theater company, but evidently a great many types of people can be taught to wear it quite convincingly.

Characteristics of the authoritarian personality include very conventional behavior, submissiveness to authority, exaggerated notions of masculinity and femininity, extreme emphasis on discipline, heavy reliance on external authority for support of one's belief system, a tendency to use others as scapegoats, and rejection of all that is spontaneous or instinctual. [13]

If authoritarianism could be safely confined to the military work environment, to which it is so well suited, the problems of many military families would be vastly reduced. But this is not easy to do, given the fact that warriors are supposed to be warriors twenty-four hours a day. It may be unrealistic to expect a military man to compartmentalize his life naturally, so that when he goes home he can relate to his family as husband and father, free of the controlling behavior typical of authoritarians.

A behavioral study of 273 drill instructors at a Marine Corps recruit training facility demonstrated just how natural it is for warriors to extend their authoritarian role play into the family. [14] Dr. Peter Neidig, who headed the study, found that the stresses of this job have a direct impact on the family, as we will see.

First, it is necessary to understand that the drill instructor billet is a very prestigious position for the NCO tapped to fill it; only the very best sergeants in the service are chosen, because they must serve as role models for the raw recruits they are ordered to shape. [15] In the Marine Corps, for instance, each potential DI is subjected to a thorough investigation of his background, including personal life as well as service performance over his career. The wife, too, is interviewed. Among other things, it must be determined that the sergeant has a stable home life with no history of spouse or child abuse.

But the job of drill instructor is intensely stressful; not only is the role itself extremely demanding, the days are exceedingly long. A DI must rise by 4:30 A.M. at the latest in order to be at the barracks to wake the recruits an hour later; he typically will not leave the base until 10:00 P.M., after putting them to bed. All day long he is on stage, the star performer before an audience of as many as ninety recruits, forcing himself to hew as closely as possible to standards of absolute perfection, even changing uniforms three or four times in the course of the day to maintain his immaculate appearance. The constant pressure to be perfect in the interest of projecting an all-powerful, godlike persona to the recruits creates an extraordinarily high stress level—and a great deal of difficulty in changing roles when the DI goes home. The wives interviewed in the Neidig study frequently reported that since beginning their tours as DIs, their husbands had become "impatient, distant, demanding, and that they treat family members as they would recruits."[16] Meanwhile, the wives themselves are under tremendous stress, feeling deprived of the company of their mates and having to shoulder the burden of raising the children and managing the household by themselves.

Neidig found that the level of marital conflict became increasingly violent over the course of the two-year tour of DIs; of those with less than one year as DI, none of whom had marital violence before, 62 percent now reported either physical threats or physical abuse in the relationship with their spouse,[17] about half of which may have been heavily contributed to by the wife herself.[18] For those with more than one year as DI, the percentage reporting marital violence increased to 75 percent. At the same time, the typical DI's "level of commitment to the marriage" declined steadily. The rate of divorce among DIs was found to be "considerably higher" than among their non-DI peers— even though, as Neidig notes, "their current difficulties in relating have much more to do with the intrusion of work-related stress into the home than with a primary dissatisfaction with the marriage partner." It is apparently easier for the DI to divorce himself from his home life than to divorce himself from the warrior mask he has come to identify with so totally.

The drill field assignment is so extremely stressful, in fact, that even those marriages that hold together are sent into a downspin with potentially long-term consequences. As Neidig puts it, "The linear relationship between length of time on the drill field and increasing conflict and marital dissatisfaction can be accurately understood as an occupational hazard for this billet."[19]

To my knowledge, no one has done a comparable study on the consequences of the drill field on the children of drill instructors—but the testimony of a Marine sergeant's daughter suggested the effects can be far-reaching.

"Probably the worst experience we had growing up was when my father was a DI at MCRD," she said.

For one thing, my father dramatically changed from the kind of soft-spoken, gentle person he was before the drill field into basically the Great Santini. I think it was very difficult for my mother, having known him since he was nine years old, to see him change so dramatically over a period of two and a half years. I don't remember my father any other way than the Great Santini model, probably because I was so little when he was the other way.

When my father went to the drill field, his behavior went really out of control. From what I understand, he was considered one of the top drill instructors at MCRD, and the troops thought very highly of him for being a very tough man but a very fair one. He was tough but not brutal, not a sadist. He had tough standards for himself as well as for his troops, and as far as I know, he always lived up to those ideals. Even under the stress of war he was a person who had a certain code of conduct and lived up to it. In some ways he's one of the best examples of the soldier-guardian Plato speaks about in the *Republic*.

My father was very good at his work; he came home, though, almost always intoxicated. And my father was not a happy drunk. He was a menacing drunk. I don't remember him striking any of us, but he didn't need to. I began to be very afraid of him; we all were. The kind of menace a drill instructor needs to have was something he acquired on the drill field and was unable to let go of once he came home.

I was ten; my sister was nine, and my brothers were six and five. There would be occasions when he didn't come home, which of course caused a great deal of anguish for my mother: "Where is he? Why doesn't he call?" We knew that as it got later and later and he didn't come home, chances were that he was going to come home in bad shape. He would be irrational, and if we irritated him we would be subject to all of his raging and screaming.

There was a lot of fighting between my parents for two and a half years; at one point my mother in fact left my father. But being the good Catholic she was, she was talked out of it by her old parish priest. So we all sort of survived it.

My next-to-youngest brother took the worst of it. He was very unmacho as a child; [my father] was afraid he would turn out to be gay. In fact he isn't, and is happily married with two children. But my father was at the point where weakness could not be tolerated in your troops, and he maybe unknowingly transferred that to this six-year-old boy. It was very difficult for me to watch; I always felt like the protector of my brothers and my sister. And for that reason I became very angry with my father. It was the beginning of my distancing from him.

My father always liked to drink, but the drill field fueled his alcoholism. I think he probably drank to forget he was surrounded by sadists; a lot of the drill instructors were very cruel and in fact a little mentally unstable and actually got a lot of pleasure out of berating the recruits. I think he hated that kind of work, but he did it anyway.

The drill field was hell. It was awful. It left very lasting scars. It was full of pomp and pageantry and we attended a lot of parades—each graduating class had its parade—but it was extremely stressful for us as a family. And the fact we survived is really due in great part to my mother, who agreed in some part of her soul to be a part of this so that she could get the family through as a unit.

He never hit any of us, never hit my mother, never abused any of us sexually. But the psychological abuse we endured for almost three years became the foundation for a lot of neurosis later on. In my case I just built upon it—one more brick, one more brick, one more brick—until I got to a point in college where I went into therapy and started understanding what had happened to me. I was angry at my father for a long time, because after the drill field he didn't change his behavior very much. He drank just as much later on. . . .

I don't know what kind of scars the drill field left on my father; he seems to have recovered from it. But the scars it left on us were considerable.

Neidig developed a program for helping DIs and their wives learn to handle their stress more effectively before it propels them into violent conflict. For the DIs, it involves conscious separation from their warrior identities before entering the home at the end of the day. They are instructed to do such things as remove their hats before they get in the car, try to visualize what their wives' and kids' day has been like, change out of their uniforms as soon as they get home and before they speak to anyone.

For some wives, finding a sense of humor under stressful circumstances helps a lot. One DI wife interviewed for this book told of the time her husband came home and immediately began giving the house a white-glove inspection, running his gloved finger over the shelves and furniture. He turned to her and in a tone of unmistakable DI outrage snapped, "There's dust on this hall table!" She demurely handed him a cloth and said, "Well, then, honey, you'd better get busy!" Fortunately, her husband was able to locate his sense of humor as well.

Of the military brats interviewed for this book, more than 80 percent described their fathers as authoritarian. They insisted they were not confusing the term with the word *authoritative*, which is considered a positive value in parenting. Rather, they described fathers who were rigid in their discipline, inflexible in most matters, intolerant of dissent or even of questions, disapproving of any thought or action that seemed to depart from the conventional. Perhaps above all, these fathers tended in all things to jealously guard their position of supreme authority in the home.

One Air Force colonel's son I'll call Todd told of a father who rarely shed his authoritarian persona in the family setting. "My father would use you like a servant," he said.

> Like you were an enlisted man, for Christ's sake. He believed that rank had its privileges, and he was the commanding officer of his family.
>
> I remember once he made me come and sit next to him while he was watching television in bed. Every time he wanted the channel turned, he'd have me get up and turn it for him. Until I finally got fed up and said, "Why don't you turn the channel yourself?" And he hopped up from the bed and slapped me across the face for talking back. He really was an officer in the old pre–World War II Marine Corps sense—and that's the way he treated his family.
>
> For a long time we had to stand at attention, in military brace, whenever we talked to him. Dinner would generally be hell. We had to sit at the first quarter-inch of our chairs and eat a "square meal" like cadets. You know: when you lift your fork straight up from your plate and then move it to your mouth at a ninety-degree angle and back down like that, and you sit ramrod straight. And we could not talk at meals. That went on until my mother couldn't stand it any longer—this man was torturing her children. But she couldn't get around his rage; he had this incredible rage that was like a volcano erupting. So she moved the dinner hour for the kids to way before he got home from the office. For years, almost the only meals we ate together as a family were Sunday breakfasts, when he'd be relaxed and in a good mood. But [any other time], you'd run into his complete authoritarianism, with his kids standing at attention in military brace.

Many other military brats told similar stories: fathers who would not tolerate questions, much less disagreement, fathers who continually violated their privacy, who forbade them to engage in any activity, however trivial, that smacked of individuation.

The most commonly described domestic scene in which the father's authoritarianism was played out involved the father "helping" his child with homework. "It wasn't helping, but intimidation," said one son. "It was very, very uncomfortable. For example, spelling, which I'm not good at even today. He'd find out what the spelling words were, go over them once and expect me to write them correctly. Most of the time I was so terrified I couldn't think anyway. That would frustrate him. He didn't know how to relate to me to make me more at ease. Things would get worse and worse."

Military daughters described the trauma of their fathers helping them with their math homework. The stories were so abundant and so similar—the father ordering the daughter to understand the lesson, the daughter still not understanding, the father exploding in anger and frustration—that it seems the Fortress must have echoed at times with the sound of math books being hurled across the room. For the

authoritarian, failure is rarely seen as a matter of inability; it's seen as
disobedience.

In situations like this the child is being made a scapegoat—a very
common occurrence in authoritarian systems. It allows the authoritarian to release aggression and tension that has built up during
the work day and which, because of the nature of hierarchy, he is
powerless to direct toward his higher-ups. An underling at work or the
spouse or child at home are convenient, "safe" outlets for his pent-up
anger. Psychiatrist Don M. LaGrone, who worked with military parents and children on a large base, has written that in the military,

> since confrontation is practically prohibited and conflict is channeled
> through the chain of command, scapegoating is inevitable. The supervisor
> receives a great deal of pressure to keep his men compliant. When
> problems arise, as they always will in such a system, it is easier to single out
> someone as the cause than to examine the system. The scapegoat frequent-
> ly does a great deal to contribute to this process. This model is often carried
> home to the family. A father who feels worried about his career may focus
> on one family member as the cause of family conflict. [20]

That member might take on a permanent role as the family scapegoat,
or the role might shift among family members from day to day.

LaGrone conducted a study in which he found that an authoritarian
family structure was common to the backgrounds of most of the
problem children at a clinic serving military families. He reviewed the
records of 792 children and adolescents seen by the psychiatric staff
over a two-year period:

> The parents who came to our clinic used three methods of dealing with
> their children—authoritarian, democratic, and a mixed, inconsistent way.
> Some of the parents who felt they were democratic were actually au-
> thoritarian or inconsistent when examined. As one might expect, the
> greatest number of behavioral disorders, nearly 93 percent, came from the
> authoritarian families. The fathers in authoritarian families . . . often
> came from autocratic homes themselves and found the military comfort-
> able for that reason. Often, the only model of dealing with children they
> knew was what they learned through their own "mortification" process.
> When this process is applied to a child, especially one in the adolescent
> years, there is bound to be difficulty. [21]

There is more than one variety of authoritarianism, as the interviews
for this book demonstrated: Military families may be authoritarian to
greater or lesser degrees. In one type of military home, for instance, a
father's authoritarianism might be limited to role rigidity and an
inability to tolerate dissent; the children will be heavily bossed and
strictly controlled, but not otherwise harmed. In another type of

military home, the father might extend his authoritarian control to listening in on phone calls, hunting down personal diaries and reading them, opening private mail, grilling his children's friends and dates. In still another type, the father might combine his authoritarian control with emotional, physical, or sexual abuse.

One of the most interesting things about military families, however, is that there are warriors who thrive in the authoritarian work environment without becoming authoritarian at home. These warriors somehow have the ability to segregate their military persona from their family persona; they know how to take off the mask of the warrior when they come home to their wives and children.

Reed and Rebecca are the children of a three-star Army general who managed to keep his military personality at bay when he was at home. After an extended assignment away from home, his children said, he would usually have temporary problems readjusting to family life and try to "order everyone around"—but his strong and independent wife would take her stand and before long he would relax into his old self.

"He had a lot of respect for our mother," Reed said. "She had her own career and he encouraged her in it; she earned as much money as he did." That fact alone—that he actively encouraged his wife's civilian career—demonstrates the father's flexibility. At the time, it was highly unusual for an officer's wife to hold any kind of paying job; she was expected to devote her time to socializing with other military wives and doing volunteer work for the military.

But this family was atypical in other ways as well. The children were not forced into military-type behavior. The family almost never lived on a military post, preferring to participate in civilian life as much as possible. The children were permitted both to question their father and to disagree—and he would listen to their opinions. Despite having a very demanding job that frequently took him away from the family for extended periods, he tried to spend as much time with the children as he could, taking them fishing, hiking, camping, and attending their school events. And both Reed and Rebecca agree that in their household, males and females were equally valued. When the son chose not to make the Army his career, the father was sorely disappointed but did not reject him for that decision. To this day Reed and Rebecca enjoy a close relationship with their father based on mutual respect.[22]

Families such as this demonstrate that authoritarianism is not the only model of family life possible in the military. What we can also see in their story, however, is that the burden of overcoming the tendency toward an authoritarian family structure cannot rest solely on the warrior. Indeed, Reed and Rebecca give a great deal of credit to their mother for the strong, independent spirit that enabled her to go toe to toe with her husband when necessary. Their mother, now deceased, was not just tough-minded when it counted but had a great deal of skill in the way she handled her husband and children day to day; she was overtly appreciative of her husband, supportive of his career (as long as it didn't swallow her up), and in general was a very capable, savvy sort of person.

So much of life inside the Fortress focuses on the warrior husband that it is easy to overlook the fact that what happens in the family is not just a function of the warrior's behavior. Husband, wife, and children together form a family system—one could say a subtroupe of the larger dramatic company—in which every role affects every other. For that system to be healthy, it is important for the wife to be supportive of her husband and flexible in the way she plays her part, but assertive and self-confident in her own right. A tall order, by anyone's standards, particularly when it involves crossing swords with a warrior.

Although the majority of military brats interviewed for this book came from authoritarian families, I met several whose families seemed to fit this more relaxed model in most respects—although, for reasons such as parental alcoholism or the father's absence, these families may not have been as close as that of Reed and Rebecca. In my view there is a pressing need for thorough research to discover exactly how these more relaxed families are able to resist the cultural pressures of the Fortress to become rigid and authoritarian.

The reality of military life is that the stresses are very great—from financial problems to the frustration of living within a rigid hierarchy to constant mobility with its attendant social isolation.

On top of that, as we have seen, many men and women come to the military burdened with a host of unresolved problems from their families of origin, where they may have suffered abuse, rejection, abandonment, or the effects of parental alcoholism. The intensely theatrical world of the Fortress is likely to draw them so thoroughly into their parts that they cannot maintain a removed perspective; the roles are carried back into the family without a second thought, and the home becomes a microcosm of the larger stage.

Hall of Mirrors

One of the ways a warrior family reflects the Fortress is in its structure. In the family, no matter where the warrior falls in the rank-conscious hierarchy of the military, the father is the general, the mother is the colonel, the older siblings are noncoms, and the youngest are the miserable new recruits. Like its larger military context, the family tends to have a very clear and generally inflexible chain of command.

The virtue of this system must surely be its clarity. The person on each tier knows exactly what is expected and how far one can and cannot go. Life is accordingly streamlined and simplified. The downside is role rigidity, which can be inhibiting to personal growth and can actually contribute to family conflict when the individuals resent their powerlessness to make opinions and feelings heard. In both respects the family parallel to the military itself is exact.

The second major way warrior families resemble the military is in their rules of behavior. We have already seen how in many warrior families children are drafted from birth into the ways of the Fortress, including duty rosters, inspections, and a formal, scripted way to answer the phone. But there is more than mindless imitation in the militarization of childhood. The fact is, a family inside the Fortress isn't just a family. It is an additional means of taking the measure of a man.

The warrior, the wife, the children—everyone is watched, *all the time*, to see if they reflect well on the military. If a family is to all appearances normal and conventional, and the children are well behaved and accomplished, it means the warrior is a man who knows how to a run a tight outfit. If, however, something is amiss—the wife drinks too much, or she makes a disparaging comment about the wife of another officer, or the kids get into trouble, or are sloppy or rude—it is viewed as a direct commentary on the warrior's ability to lead and command. From this standard there is no way to escape, no place to hide.

It is like living in a hall of mirrors, where the Fortress, the warrior, and the family all reflect one another endlessly.

"A particular stress to military families is the fishbowl within which they live," reported two military physicians in a journal on family dynamics. "They reside, work, and attend school in a tightly organized and observant community that demands conformity to conservative and relatively inflexible behavioral standards. Norms and values of family members are determined, to a more than usual extent, by external agencies, with a resulting low tolerance for individual variation."[23]

The daughter of an Army colonel recalled what it was like when her family was stationed for a couple of years at a military academy; the "fishbowl" was smaller than usual, its standards even more demanding. "Everything was very political and very pretentious and my mother didn't like that," she said. "But she played the role beautifully, and so did my brothers and I. We lived in a neighborhood with three

generals and their families, and we had to know how to act. We said
our yes sirs and no sirs and answered the phone, 'Colonel [Doe's]
quarters, [Ann] speaking.' I remember my dad teaching my brothers
how to shake hands: 'Offer them your hand. Give 'em a firm grip.
Look 'em in the eye.' " Standard schooling in military families.

For the military wife—particularly the wife of an officer or senior
NCO—the role expectations are as stringent as for her husband. Every
aspect of her appearance and behavior is measured against rigid standards of propriety and conventionality. *The Army Wife*, a reference
manual much used over the years, which inspired spinoffs for the
other services, explicitly instructs the officer's wife on how to present
herself in every circumstance. The level of detail gives some notion of
the close scrutiny to which the wife is subjected. She is told how to
answer the phone (in a "low, well-modulated voice"); how to set the
table ("Place an ashtray at the top of each plate to the left of the water
glass, and in it put two or three cigarettes and a book of matches"); how
long to stay during a social call (*never* more than twenty minutes at a
commanding officer's house); how to make proper conversation ("Get
a small pronouncing dictionary . . . and read it word for word, marking
and studying any that you mispronounce"); what to wear for any
conceivable social occasion. She is warned against any hint of un-
conventionality, whether it be candles that are other than white or
ivory, or creative placement of furniture ("Don't place any piece of
furniture cater-cornered").[24]

The scrutiny of an officer's wife is not merely an accidental spinoff
of standards that hold the officer to account. For many years it was
built directly into the system in an official way. Commanding officers
had to comment on an officer's wife in the periodic evaluation report
of his service performance; on the form there was a block of space
specifically reserved for that purpose. Officially, this practice has been
discontinued—in 1987 the armed services ordered that spouses could
no longer be referred to on a service member's efficiency report—but
since the evaluations by one's superior are highly subjective in nature,
there is widespread feeling that a spouse's conduct is still taken into
consideration and may influence a service member's career.[25]

In the Army and Air Force, the evaluation forms are known as
efficiency reports; in the Navy and Marine Corps, as fitness reports.
Every active-duty member of the military, whether officer or enlisted
(above the rank of E-4), receives an evaluation annually, as well as at
the time of transfer to another job and for other special reasons. These
reports are part of the individual's permanent record, and weigh heavily when that person comes up for promotion. Receiving anything less
than a perfect rating on an efficiency or fitness report is considered a

disaster for the serviceperson, who will likely be passed over in favor of someone with a history of unblemished reports.

The following passage is from another reference manual for Army couples:

> It is particularly true in the service that a wife can make or break her husband. . . .
>
> Numerous instances are on record where an officer's efficiency has been discounted heavily, where he has failed to achieve positions of trust and distinction, and even where transfers have been made, entirely because . . . the wife was indiscreet in her speech or showed too plainly a lack of knowledge of military customs, ordinary social customs, or customs of good breeding.
>
> It should again be emphasized that the responsibility is the man's. He should instruct his wife in all things connected with the military life that she should know and should particularly warn her against criticism of the administration, as such criticism is accredited to him.[26]

The son of a Navy commander offered an example:

> There was a lot of heat on Mom to conform; that was made clear in my family, that her behavior could influence my father's career. And indeed there may have been some truth to that. Because my mom, once when my dad was at sea as executive officer on a destroyer, got ticked off at one of the junior officers' wives and chewed her out. It was nothing more serious than they'd both had too much wine and my mother said, "You're really a spoiled brat. You expect too much out of people." It just so happened that [the woman's] father-in-law was an admiral. That was it. That killed my father's career on the spot. He never advanced in the Navy from that day forward. Eight years later he retired at the same rank.

The same manual does not mince words when it comes to military kids: "The responsibility for children rests directly on the parents. . . . Children may be usually accepted as an index to the officer's general ability."[27]

All military kids grow up with an acute awareness of the military hall of mirrors. An Army daughter recalled, "My behavior reflected on my father as a sergeant. I don't know if I was ever told that directly, but I knew it. I was conscious I had to be careful. After all, he wasn't the high man on the totem pole."

An Army colonel made sure all five of his daughters knew not to slip up. "He would give us examples," one of them recalled. "He'd say, 'So and So's son was picked up shoplifting at the PX. Now they're going to transfer the whole family.' That kind of thing. The message was, 'Don't do anything to make me lose face.' Appearances were *very* important, particularly in his later career. I was led to believe that men who could not control their families, who had wild children, were really in trouble. If they couldn't control their kids, they couldn't control a platoon of men."

The son of an Air Force sergeant told a similar story. "It was in the base newspaper that an officer's son rode his bike on the airstrip, even though they had signs forbidding it. He got caught *twice*. His father was reprimanded for it. My father showed the article to us and said, 'See what happens when you mess up?' "

Most military children, to hear them talk, grow up in mortal fear of making some stupid mistake and finding out the whole family has to pay for it. Not only would it be shameful—in a society that is extraordinarily sensitive to shame—it would also provide the perfect excuse for the child to be made a scapegoat within the family. But most of the time there is not even any conscious reasoning to this effect; conforming to the expected standard of behavior is a basic term of existence that is so internalized it is not questioned. "Getting dressed up and being on your best behavior was such a huge deal it was never challenged by anyone in the family," said a Navy officer's son. "Not by me and not by my sisters. Whenever we went down to the ship, we wore nice clothes and we were clean, polished, everything. We did not misbehave, we did not act up, we did not do *any*thing we were not supposed to do—and that was true even when we were old enough to be down there by ourselves. It just *didn't happen*."

But the flip side, of course, is that some military brats who are sufficiently angry—and, one might add, self-destructive—realize that their fathers' image in the hall of mirrors is very fragile, and that this built-in vulnerability is where their power lies. It is in their power to undermine their fathers' careers by taking the stage and deliberately playing the wrong role directly into the mirror, thus shattering the image of seamless perfection that the Fortress demands.

"At one base," the daughter of an Air Force colonel recalled, "there was a fifteen-year-old girl, an admiral's daughter, who created a scandal by fucking enlisted men. I remember thinking it was a splendid way to get back at her father. Because there was an unwritten rule: 'If a man can't control his child, how can he control his men?' The emphasis was on discipline and conformity."

The son of an Air Force general recalled,

> I never caused any problems until I was older, and we were on Taiwan. We were on diplomatic passports. I was sixteen going on thirty, and we did terrible things. But my father's aide kept up with me. He'd say, "Come see me." And I'd go, and he'd tick off my sins: "I know you are driving a car, that you went to such and such a place, that you did X and X." It was amazing. Then he'd read me the riot act.

While we were in Taiwan the ambassador had several military kids sent home. That was a *terrible* thing to have happen. Once, after a boy got a girl pregnant, both were sent home. Another was sent home for an incident involving alcohol. There were also a couple of suicides: two very unhappy military sons.

Destructively rebellious behavior by military kids is a syndrome familiar to military physicians and therapists. "If a teenager in a family commits an act of delinquency or misconduct," one physician wrote in an article, "everyone knows that his father will be held responsible and the commander may become involved. Some children are well enough versed in this code that they use it—if not consciously, at least indirectly—to get a negligent father's attention to their difficulties."[28]

Adolescents who intend their rebellion to reflect badly on their families are common enough in civilian life, too, of course. The difference is that in the authoritarian warrior society the stakes are usually much higher for the parents; the warrior's entire career and social identity rides on the maintenance of a certain image, which can be dashed in seconds by a willful child. The other difference is that in the military—perhaps because the stakes are so very high—there is little distinction made between major transgressions and very minor ones. One military son told of being picked up by the Air Force Security Police for assault and battery after he and a friend hit another kid over the head with a frozen water balloon. The child was not badly hurt, but the incident was handled as though he had been. The arrested boys spent twelve hours in SP headquarters, after which their fathers came down to get them. "They were fiery mad," the son recalled. "Their commanding officer had just finished grilling them about their sons' behavior."

In another case, a teenage boy committed the unpardonable sin of teeing off on the golf course at 5:00 P.M., while Retreat was being blown, instead of standing respectfully at attention as the base's flag was lowered for the day. An officer reported him, and his father got a call from high up in the base hierarchy. The incident went down on the father's permanent record. The same thing happened to another father whose twelve-year-old son knocked over a trash can in front of the base teen club. The son was picked up by the military police, who called not the father, but the father's commanding officer.

Inside the Fortress-theater, there is really only one sin: deviating from the approved script. And it is such a grievous sin that it does not, for all practical purposes, come in degrees or shades of gray. To the authoritarian mind, all transgressions come down to the same thing—*disobedience*, which can mean nothing other than an unwillingness to comply with the system. And to authoritarians, that is intolerable in any quantity, however slight.

Warriors take the wearing of the mask very seriously. The rule, as every warrior knows, is as firm as it is simple: Either one wears the mask flawlessly, all the time, in the home or out, or one is not worthy of being called Warrior. It is immaterial whether an offense—a slip of the mask—is committed by the warrior himself or by one of his family; spouse and children are merely extensions of him, additional reflections in the hall of mirrors.

So if the families of the Fortress are militarized along with the warriors, it is not just an aberration, a gratuitous dramatic flourish in this most intense of theatrical worlds. In a sense, the militarization of the family is not even optional: The forces that require it are the very forces that define the Fortress itself. There is no escape.

Are military families substantially different from civilian families? Yes, most certainly yes. They exist in a world apart, with different norms, values, goals, rules, expectations. The members of the family wear masks and live out their assigned dramatic roles just like the warriors.

And if they thereby gain an identity and sense of mission that is strengthening, it must be said that the personal cost is also very high.

But they're troupers. Real troupers.

MASKS

The emphasis in the military is on discipline and conformity. On what you see. There is no emphasis on interiors.

—a military brat

Spend any length of time inside the Fortress and you're bound to come up against a fundamental truth: It is exceedingly difficult to get past the surface of things.

Everywhere you look, the surfaces are shined, waxed, polished to perfection. The lawns are close-cropped, the buildings freshly painted, the streets scrubbed and litter-free. It is the most supremely ordered of communities, and, it goes without saying, the most punctilious of theatrical companies. One has only to note the diligence with which the costumes, props, and sets are tended, the exaggerated attention to detail. And that is to say nothing of the flawless masks worn by all who walk within the Fortress walls. Meticulous surfaces, all.

Make no mistake. This is not the nostalgic, dreamworld orderliness of Disneyland. Nor is it the busywork of a military idled by peace.

There is a quite different reason for the zealous grooming of surfaces inside the Fortress, with a very serious dual message.

First: *This is a society prepared to wage war with the same relentless attention to detail it brings to every moment of every day.*

Second (and mind this well): *Don't even try to look beyond the surface. What you see is all you are authorized to see. The rest is off limits, classified, denied.*

It would seem to be a superficial measure of the world, this fanatical devotion of those inside the Fortress to the way things look, but in fact it is central to the purpose of the military.

The Fortress is committed to keeping things under control. And if everything is truly under control, it should be evident right there on the surface, in how things look and how people act.

Control is the heart and soul of the military, the very essence of its mission in peace or in war. A good military outfit is one that is prepared to control any situation, no matter what the variables. And of course a good military outfit should look and act at all times as if it is in tune with that mission. It's as though, in their polished appearance and rehearsed behavior, the warriors were saying, "Observe how we control ourselves, and you'll know we can control the enemy."

The notion of control does not merely describe the warrior, it defines him.

It also defines his family.

A "good" military family is one that demonstrates in all things its submission to the ways of the Fortress. It is conventional. It is predictable. It conforms in appearance and behavior to what the Fortress expects. It obeys authority. It displays to the world what ought to be displayed.

And it conceals the rest.

Whether it is in the Fortress at large or in the confines of the military home, control means suppression. It takes extraordinary and unrelenting effort to cap human emotions, keep them safely underground where they do not threaten to mar the perfect appearance of things. And that effort exacts its price—particularly within the family.

"When I was growing up," one daughter said, "I always thought we had the perfect happy family. Later, I saw it was a myth." It was not until she reached adulthood, she said, that she realized both her parents had been closet alcoholics for years, and that all three children had picked up on the family dysfunction and promptly channeled their feelings about it underground. The entire family was locked into a drama of denial. In adulthood, all three children have had problems with substance abuse—drugs, alcohol, food. "We are all massively controlling," the daughter said, "and we needed massive amounts of substances to do it." In struggling with their addictions, the children have had to discover and expose the underground emotional climate of their family. For the first time in their lives, they are violating the off-limits zone.

That bold venture into forbidden territory is the supreme challenge for the children of warriors. The Fortress insists on being taken at face value, especially by those who live within it. The children grow up knowing not to ask questions or probe for answers. But the path of noninquiry, as most learn sooner or later, is hardly the path to wisdom.

Paradoxically, if we children of the Fortress are to understand the implications of our military roots—to consciously value the positive qualities while squarely facing the negative—we must deliberately violate the cardinal rule of the society that gave us birth and trained us in its ways. Our task must be to get past the surface, search behind the masks, venture into the forbidden regions of interior life, claim for ourselves the hidden realm of feelings.

Military brats tend to know this instinctively, even in childhood. It's as though when we become old enough to awaken to reflection, our mission is there waiting, already recognized and affirmed. And very often it has already been acted upon.

There is the example of the Mansion Woods.

In the early sixties my father was stationed in France for three years. For the last two of those years we lived in La Celle St. Cloud, just outside Paris, in the housing area for American military families known as Petit Beauregard. On one side of Petit, as it was known, was a forest that was private property and separated from the housing area by an ancient, crumbling stone wall. And in the center of the forest, at the end of a wide, overgrown lane, was a once elegant chateau of wooden construction, long abandoned and on the verge of collapse.

Stately, ornate, and covered with peeling white paint, it had a regal but ghostly aspect, like a fragile white-haired grande dame returned from the grave. The Mansion—I feel sure it was capitalized in our minds—was reputed to have been a girlhood home of Josephine, Napoleon's empress. On high ground and set well back in a clearing choked with high grass, partially camouflaged by the encroaching forest, it could barely be seen from the highway below. It was alluring, mysterious, ethereal—and explicitly forbidden.

The military children of Petit Beauregard had strict orders: *Never* enter the Mansion Woods under any circumstances. My father warned that if I ever went in there I would certainly be caught and he would certainly be court-martialed—quite an exaggeration, but he clearly felt it necessary to make his point as strongly as possible.

We all knew the rule, we all knew the risks. And yet every military brat of my acquaintance considered it a personal duty—a mission, in fact—to explore the Mansion Woods and learn the secrets of the Mansion itself. This, despite the orders of our parents, despite our own awareness of the hall of mirrors, and despite the fact we knew the Mansion was guarded by an armed French caretaker and his dogs. My diaries of the time—I was eleven—tell in detail, complete with maps, of many forays into this forbidden world.

That is why I now see the Mansion Woods as a metaphor for the quest of the military brat. For those of us at Petit Beauregard, it was irresistibly compelling, precisely because it represented the exact opposite of the Fortress world we knew.

If the Fortress was a place of strict control and little freedom, the Mansion seemed an oasis of anarchy, a sanctuary of the spontaneous and instinctual.

If the Fortress was focused on surface, the Mansion represented the secret inner world we longed to know.

I confess with great regret that despite my many expeditions into the Mansion Woods, I never made it all the way inside the Mansion. I always imagined I heard the caretaker or his dogs, and would flee before I could summon the nerve to race across the clearing to the goal. Partly this was because the Mansion had been there so long, and had such an air of timelessness about it, that I assumed there would be plenty of time for me to grow in my resolve and finally attain the inner sanctum, as many older kids had done. But that summer of 1963, the Mansion was abruptly torn down.

It would be an understatement to say we missed it. The loss of the Mansion was a source of deep and abiding grief for the military brats of Petit Beauregard. Probably the American military had little or nothing to do with the destruction of the Mansion, but it was hard not to blame it anyway. To us it seemed very much in keeping with the iron rule of the Fortress: Once again the gate had clanged shut on the world of interiors.

After that I had to content myself with dreaming about the Mansion I had never entered, to making maps of the forbidden woods, to yearning for that lost secret realm. In a way, this book is my latest effort to cross that clearing and gain entrance to the house of secrets.

It is easy enough to see why the Fortress focuses entirely on surfaces, and goes to such lengths to suppress the disorder of the inner realm. Authoritarians are not self-directed; they need rules, and plenty of them, to hold them in place. They do not listen for or heed the inner voice.

But why is it that military families automatically conform to this model? Why can't a warrior family, within the safe confines of its own home, be open and expressive about its emotional life? Theoretically it is possible, but in practice it rarely happens. The reason is as simple as basic arithmetic. While it takes enormous energy to stifle inner feelings and ban their expression, it would require even greater energy to maintain a family life that is completely at odds with the warrior society around it. Forcing the family to conform to warrior notions of surface appearance is in the end far more economical. It simply makes more sense to adapt to a harsh environment than to try to function as though one lived in an entirely different one.

Still, suppressing uncomfortable emotion is a mammoth undertaking, accomplished only with unflagging effort—and the aid of three stock items borrowed from the theatrical storehouse of the military itself: the masks of secrecy, stoicism, and denial. And while it is true that civilian families, too, make use of secrecy, stoicism, and denial, it is generally not because the society around them requires it. Inside the Fortress, however, these masks are de rigueur.

The absolutely imperative quality of mask wearing is perhaps the most basic point of contrast between military and civilian society. Among civilians in America, the sacred cornerstone of values is individual rights, as articulated in the Constitution and Bill of Rights and as reflected throughout American life in the dearly held notions of free enterprise, the free press, civil rights, fair play, collective bargaining, an abundance of artistic expression, the right to sue for legal remedies, and the vigorous pursuit of pleasure. Inside the Fortress, what is sacred is not individual rights—a notion that too often runs dead against the authoritarian order—but the myth of a completely controlled, conformist society composed of individuals of unblemished character who strive at all times for perfection in their public service and in their private lives. Warriors, spouses, children—all are in service to that myth, which is the essential undergirding to the military concept of "readiness." For them, the masks of secrecy, stoicism, and denial are standard issue: the basic equipment without which the mission cannot be accomplished.

It is important to bear in mind this bedrock difference between Fortress culture and civilian society; the two sectors are so dissimilar that direct comparisons don't always work. The conditions of Fortress life are different, the pressures are different, and so the adaptations of individuals and families are also bound to be different. Since nearly everything about life inside the Fortress is extreme or exaggerated compared to its civilian counterpart, it is easy for outsiders to read pathology into family relationships that, from the military family point of view, are actually the healthiest way of relating to one another given the extreme duress of their lives.

For example, when the warrior father is overseas in the heart of a combat zone, is it pathological for his family to totally suppress their fear, to deny his vulnerability, their longing for him, their anger at his absence, their powerlessness to protect him or bring him back? Another kind of family might deal more openly with its feelings, but that does not mean the warrior family's response is pathological— particularly given the fact that in Fortress culture, denial and stoicism are expected and any other response would be looked at askance. For the family to openly display its fear and worry would even, in that context, be seen as so out of sync with Fortress values that it would reflect badly on the warrior. Military families serve the Fortress myth, but the Fortress myth also serves them: They need it to lean on. They need it to justify the stress and pain and loss that are part of their sacrifice.

To be sure, pathology does exist in military families. As we shall see, there is even reason to believe that they experience more of certain kinds of pathology, such as alcoholism. It is equally true that even in their most ordinary and benign forms, secrecy, stoicism, and denial are not without their costs to warriors and their wives and children. But the point is, seen in the fullest context of life inside the Fortress, that cost is frequently appropriate.

Military brats need to know how these masks functioned in our lives growing up, and how they continue to affect us now. We need to see those patterns in our lives, so we have the option of changing them. An understanding of the masks also makes it easier to be more forgiving of our parents once we understand the appropriateness of our early family patterns to the unique culture of the Fortress.

In other instances, where the need to deny and repress reached truly pathological proportions, as in parental alcoholism, for example, I believe that seeing how the pressures of the Fortress contributed to the problem permits a more realistic view of our parents, who were themselves vulnerable to forces beyond their control. Sometimes warrior children have a hard time bringing their parents' powerlessness into focus, because it is so at odds with the image that the parents projected for so many years. Again the Fortress myth is at work: Parents project the myth of their own perfection and invincibility; children in return project the myth onto their parents. All are reflecting the great myth of the Fortress, the unwritten and unspoken imperative of military life.

Seeing past that myth to understand our parents' vulnerability, and the role played by the Fortress, directly and indirectly, in contributing to the dysfunction, potentially opens the way to healing.

THE MASK OF SECRECY

When I was ten years old, I made my first and only visit to my father's office. At the time it was in a long, gray cinder-block building about fifteen kilometers outside Paris at Camp des Loges, then headquarters of USAREUR (U.S. Army, Europe).[1]

His office turned out to be spacious but very spare, with gray-green walls, a shiny waxed floor, and a large dark wooden desk with a few immaculately neat piles of papers at the corners. My father sat behind it in a swivel chair. Right behind him on the wall was the most magnificent map of the world I had ever seen. It was so large it took up most of the wall space, and it seemed to be made of some kind of special board that required a heavy frame. Best of all, it was covered with clusters of brightly colored pushpins. I was impressed.

"What are those for?" I inquired eagerly.

My father wheeled around in his chair, his face flushed. "None of your goddamned business!" he shouted. "That's Classified!"

Even then I thought his reaction a bit excessive, particularly since at the time he was a comptroller who handled financial affairs, not a nuclear strategist. Only much later did I realize that his snappish response, and much of his irritable behavior at the time, was perhaps because he was a frustrated line officer badly in need of a command, not to mention a war. But after that small incident I never again asked questions about his work, and still have only the vaguest idea of what he did during his thirty years in the Army. This is not unusual among military brats.

"Closed-mouthedness is part of military life," commented the daughter of an Air Force colonel. "When I was young I thought my father was a spy, because he said so little about his work. We weren't allowed to ask about it, either. I don't actually know what he did. In a footlocker once I found a lot of things stamped Classified—but in the military they stamp everything Classified."

Some fathers, to be sure, were involved in very secret work. Another daughter recalled that her father, an Air Force colonel with a doctorate in electrical engineering, worked on the first hydrogen bomb. Twice he was stationed away for six months, his whereabouts unknown to the family.

Many fathers who have seen combat, whether or not they were career military, maintain silence on their wartime experiences. As a result, few military brats can tick off the names of battles in which their fathers saw action, or repeat their fathers' war stories. "I was probably seventeen before I learned my father was a tailgunner on a fighter plane in World War II," said a Marine son.

All of this adds up to a culture in which secrecy is second nature. And the pattern is strongly repeated within the military family, in which even the most vital information is frequently parceled out on a "need to know" basis, or not revealed at all.

There is, for example, the story of a Navy family that accompanied the father on a three-year overseas tour of duty, but returned to the United States after a year because the schools were not good. The father, a lieutenant commander, made several trips home to see them over the next year, but during the last year of his tour did not come home at all. His letters, which had been coming daily, suddenly became sporadic. "We all wondered why," said his daughter,

> but we knew he did a lot of secret work. We didn't find out until later.
> My father had been involved in a terrible accident in a missile silo. He had been directing the loading of a missile into a five-story missile hatch when the crane operator swung the missile and he was knocked down the hatch. He caught himself on a ledge down below, but it ripped out every muscle, every vertebra. It was a terrible thing, it really was. He spent weeks in the hospital. But he didn't want to upset us, so he never mentioned it. He also asked the Navy not to inform us, and they didn't until he was out of the hospital. So my mother and my older sister knew about the accident at that point, but in a way they didn't know. They were thousands of miles away and couldn't see his hurt, his pain. But I knew nothing.
> All I know is that one day—I was a high school freshman—I went to answer the front door and there was a man standing there. Now my father was over six feet tall and probably weighed two hundred pounds when he left—and the man who was standing there was under six feet tall and weighed maybe a hundred and twenty. I didn't recognize him. But it was my father, and the only reason I figured that out was that he was in uniform and I thought, "Who the hell else could be here?" I had to go in the other room and cry. And he said, "It's me! Don't cry!"

Asked to speculate on why her father kept his injury a secret, denying himself the comfort of his family, the daughter said, "I think he didn't know how to accept the compassion or the love that would have been forthcoming at that point in his life. I think he would have been afraid he wouldn't know what to do with it.

"But we certainly got no word from any official, either, mind you. We just assumed that he'd been on another of his missions and we weren't privy to it."

THE MASK OF STOICISM

Closely related to secrecy in the theatrical world of the Fortress is the mask of stoicism, as can be seen in the preceding story. It is impossible to imagine life inside the Fortress without stoicism, which is in fact not just a useful mask but one of the most central virtues in the pantheon of warrior values.

For example, the Navy officer who fell down the missile silo was severely injured, but he did not request retirement with medical disability—and he must have gone to extraordinary lengths to mask his pain so as not to be forced into retirement. His daughter recounted something she overheard him tell her mother much later. When her father returned to duty he was still in great pain. The assignment was on board ship. "He was in agony," his daughter said. "I heard him say that one night he had to stand watch, and because of the prevailing attitude on board, he didn't want to pass his watch to someone else. And he literally crawled from his stateroom to the duty station. He waited until no one was looking and he crawled." To be stoic, in the eyes of warriors, is to assert one's ability to control anything, even physical pain.

The same holds true for emotional pain. Many a warrior who spends his life training to meet the enemy head-on—and even longing for the confrontation—will run the other way, wall himself off, drink himself into oblivion, do anything in his power to avoid facing the "enemy" within.

"I had a brother who died of crib death," said the daughter of a Marine fighter pilot,

and my father never came to grips with that. He acted like it never happened, though he lost thirty-five pounds right after. But he couldn't ever talk about [the death] to my mom or allow her to talk about it to him.

Later, my dad's best friend, also a pilot, died in a car accident. He was dead drunk and was trying to beat a train across the railroad tracks in a snowstorm. My father was absolutely in a state of shock. My mother, who was sad, too, but also very down-to-earth, said, "Look. He's cracked up six planes, totaled four cars, and he was a self-destructive person." But my dad had a hard time with that. It took him six months, then finally one day he broke down and cried.

Warriors believe in the mask of stoicism. They keep it close to them, wear it like a talisman empowered to ward off the evil eye. They expect stoic behavior of one another, except in the worst, most cataclysmic moments of combat.

They also expect it of their children. Military brats learn very early that their fathers—and often mothers—reward stoic behavior with approval and respect, while emotional behavior is heavily discouraged if not punished. Warrior fathers are frequently at a loss as to how to deal with behavior in their children that is other than stoic. Whether it is to protect themselves from having to face uncomfortable shows of emotion, or whether they genuinely believe stoicism is beneficial for their kids, fathers clearly go to some lengths to instill it in them.

Here is how some military brats recall their stoic childhoods:

The daughter of an Army sergeant: "We were never supposed to show hurt or pain or fear. Once I saw a horror movie, and couldn't sleep that night. I cried in my room, I was so afraid that whatever I saw in the movie was going to be in my closet or in my bed. But I couldn't tell my mother I was scared; I probably would have gotten yelled at. You had to just bite your lip, take care of it all yourself. I don't know . . . maybe if I'd known how to say, 'Hey, I'm scared,' I would have gotten some comfort. But I didn't know how to say it. If my father had heard, I'm sure he would have said, 'Leave her alone. Don't baby her.' "

The son of an Air Force sergeant: "None of us kids cried much. My parents would tell us, 'When you're already hurt, what's the sense in crying? Crying just makes it worse.' "

The daughter of an Air Force colonel: "On family trips when my brother and I were really young, my father would make us pose for pictures in terrifying situations. He'd make us sit way out on a rock with the river raging right behind and around us. Or out on the edge of a cliff overlooking the Grand Canyon. We would cry and beg not to do it, but that didn't work with him. There could be no crying, no begging. I still have a fear of falling."

The daughter of an Air Force lieutenant colonel: "My dad always had a tough exterior, being a fighter pilot. Nothing ever bothered him; he would never let his emotions show. Even when his mother died, he didn't cry—at least not in front of us. And I believe he was like that with my mom for a long time. He was the same with us kids. When we'd cry, he'd say, 'Oh, stop blubbering like a baby.' It was like he wanted us to be tough."

The daughter of an Army colonel: "We were only allowed to have 'good' emotions, and when it came to pain we were expected to be little soldiers. I remember one summer I stepped on a rusty nail barefoot. I had to be strong and not cry."

It is a lesson that in most cases takes hold. Everyone in the family learns to wear the mask of stoicism, and all pay a price for it.

The first casualties of stoicism are generally family relationships: When the rule is to hold back anything that runs counter to the pristine, untroubled image the family feels compelled to project, there is much that goes unsaid. Family members become walled off from one another. The son of a Marine major said,

> I never had any idea how anybody in the family was feeling, and I wasn't particularly aware that other families didn't operate like that. For example, I never knew you could say to someone, "God, that pissed me off," and they would still love you. The idea that someone might not like what you just did, but would still like *you*, was something I never learned growing up. I'm just beginning to know that now.
>
> I've retained my parents' ways, for better or worse. I don't talk. I have an inability to be angry. I'm nonconfrontational, passive-aggressive. I don't trust people enough to get pissed off at them.

A Navy petty officer's daughter who grew up in a loving but stoic family put it this way: "I stopped showing my pain [over the emotional costs of frequent moving] out of consideration for my parents. I knew they couldn't do anything about it. But that, of course, short-circuited a lot of opportunities for sharing."

That's where the cost comes in. What is unexpressed goes unshared, and the result is a degree of isolation from one another. Family members may ultimately feel, paradoxically, that while they have undergone a lot together—moves, father absence, perhaps war or alcoholism—they have failed to forge strong bonds. Ironically, some warriors may know more about and have stronger feelings for their combat buddies than for their own families, largely because in combat situations stoicism inevitably breaks down. For many warriors it is only in war that they can free their emotional side and open themselves fully to others. The bonding of warriors in war is the kind of communion of the spirit that military families pretend to but rarely achieve.

The other long-term consequence of emotional stoicism is that the children reared in this fashion are often quite out of touch with their own emotions.

The daughter of an admiral described her family as "close" but totally uncomfortable with emotions. The price of displaying emotion, she said, was to be told, "Go to your room." When the children physically hurt themselves, they were ordered not to cry. Nor could they display anger. "My mother told me that when I was young, I threw temper tantrums. You'd never know that from later years, because she and my father certainly took that out of me. Even now, at age forty-eight, it's hard for me to express anger. Sometimes I would like to cry, but I can't. My tears must have gotten really beaten down. We were all very controlled. We couldn't let go to joy, either."

THE MASK OF DENIAL

The last in the trio of masks, and closely related to both secrecy and stoicism, is denial. Military families are masters of the form, as might be expected from the theatrical point of view. After all, denial is a skill that comes naturally to committed performers. If on stage—and of course inside the Fortress one is always on stage—something happens which is not scripted, it is instinctive for the actors either to ignore it or to pretend it was supposed to happen and is perfectly all right. Within the warrior family, it is often second nature to ignore problems, even if they show no sign of going away.

But there is a very good reason why denial is so integral to military life. The possibility of war and death is so real and so close that to constantly feel its imminence would be unbearable. So in order to function, everyone pretends on some level that what they are doing is just a job, an impersonal assignment, unremarkable in every way. The need to deny the implications of this particular line of work is such that even in the face of what one might consider the most undeniable danger, the skein of myth and rationalization holds. Every military family has its law about this: *One must not tear that skein of myth*. For military children, who are often confused by the unnatural strength of this denial, there is a dilemma. Their need to talk out their fears of war and loss competes with their certain knowledge that to do so violates the family code.

The daughter of an Army colonel recalled her own violation of the code, when she was eight years old and her father was in Vietnam on his second tour. "I remember one day walking down the stairs, and seeing my mom sitting in the living room. Right out of the clear blue, I said, 'Mom, what would happen if Dad got shot in Vietnam?'

"I'll never forget the look she gave me. She said, 'Don't—you—ever—say—that!' She was dead serious. So I never asked it, never pursued it after that. I didn't anticipate that kind of reaction from her to a simple question."

This daughter was too young at the time to have fully grasped the forbidden nature of her question. But older military brats almost universally internalize the code of denial and make it their own.

Another Army daughter and her brother, who were both older teenagers when their father was in Vietnam, said that they could not recall ever worrying for a moment about their father's safety. Denial of his danger was in such full swing that even when the mother in this family took her daughter repeatedly to Walter Reed Army Hospital in Washington to comfort gravely wounded soldiers coming in from the war, the daughter never consciously associated her father with the same potential fate.

Other military brats relate similar stories. Denial of potential loss of the father runs strong, although it can take different forms. Some military brats closely followed the course of the war on television and in the papers while their fathers were in Vietnam, making themselves extraordinarily well informed by comparison to their civilian peer group, but they still failed to voice their concerns to anyone else, inside or outside the family.

"I was very afraid my father wouldn't make it back from the war," said the son of an Air Force sergeant who was stationed at Da Nang, refueling bombers on the flight line, during the Tet Offensive in 1968. In that campaign, North Vietnamese troops in conjunction with the Vietcong (South Vietnamese Communist rebel forces) launched simultaneous and highly effective attacks throughout South Vietnam at the height of the celebration of Tet, the Vietnamese New Year, in violation of a truce they had pledged to observe. The Tet Offensive came as a complete surprise to American and South Vietnamese forces, and was such a decisive military setback that it marked a turning point in the war, both militarily and in terms of the willingness of the American public to support it. U.S. media coverage of the destruction wrought by the Tet Offensive was massive, graphic, and ubiquitous.

"I was only nine years old, but I watched the TV news every night," said the sergeant's son. "Whenever I heard 'Da Nang' I'd sit up and listen. There were terrible pictures flashing across the screen. I'd be hoping and praying it wouldn't happen to my father, it *couldn't* happen to my father."

The daughter of a Marine sergeant was thirteen years old when her father was sent to Vietnam in 1968. The family moved into base housing at Camp Pendleton, California, to wait for him.

"That time in my life took on a kind of surreal quality," the daughter recalled.

One of the things we grew up on, of course, was scenes of Vietnam on television. We had a real relationship to this television war, which only in retrospect did I realize was not normal. Our family and other families like us—families of other men serving with my father in Vietnam—would always be home at six o'clock when Walter Cronkite came on the air and reported the war. We always looked very closely at the images on the television to see if we could recognize our father or one of our friends, and that in fact happened on a number of occasions, especially during the Tet Offensive. So here we were, our family and other families in the same boat, having our dinner in front of the TV, looking for Dad. When you think about that, it's really a pretty crazy thing.

So the war was a series of images, and it was like you were connected to your father through these electronic images, distanced from the reality. After a while you see so much fighting and so much carnage that it doesn't make an impression. It was like watching a war movie.

We always spoke of my father coming home. There was never any discussion, any acknowledgment that he might get killed. In my case there was a real fear of that. I knew—especially because of where we lived, in base housing—about the military vehicles that would come through the neighborhoods, and sometimes stop, and there would be a chaplain and an officer and they would go up to the door of a particular house. That was the signal. That was when you were notified that your father had been killed in action. And so of course when you see that green car coming into the neighborhood, you hope it's not going to stop at your house.

But all that was never discussed. There was tremendous denial. In the case of my family, we denied that war experience for years and years.

The children and the spouses of warriors *need* their denial. Anything less would amount to acknowledging the total vulnerability of their way of life, their very identities. It is imperative for the families of warriors to employ denial when the life of a loved one is at stake; confronted with their own helplessness, it is their only weapon.

Warriors themselves, in order to perform their warrior roles, depend completely on denial. Pilots are a case in point: Even in peacetime, their work is full of danger. They fly incredibly complex, state-of-the-art aircraft that are still being developed; a glitch in the machine can cost them their lives. Day after day they get in the cockpit and put their lives on the line. Pilots do not deny the danger—that would be foolhardy—but it is their unassailable conviction that when the moment of danger comes, as they know it must, they will be able to face it down, conquer it, assert their supremacy. Military pilots are accordingly notorious for their enormous egos. According to their lore, as any son or daughter of a pilot can attest, the fault in a fatal accident never lies with the aircraft; it is always a matter of whether the pilot had "the right stuff." And all of them believe they have it. To hold any other point of view would be to admit they do not have absolute control. No warrior wants to face that; and so they don't—as Tom Wolfe illustrated in *The Right Stuff*:

Barely a week had gone by before another member of the Group was coming in for a landing in the same type of aircraft, the A3J, making a ninety-degree turn to his final approach, and something went wrong with the controls, and he ended up with one rear stabilizer wing up and the other one down, and his ship rolled in like a corkscrew from 800 feet up and crashed, and he was burned beyond recognition. And the bridge coats came out and they sang about those in peril in the air and then they put the bridge coats away and after dinner one night they mentioned that the departed had been a good man but was inexperienced, and when the malfunction in the controls put him in that bad corner, he didn't know how to get out of it.

Every wife wanted to cry out: "Well, my God! The *machine* broke! What makes *any* of you think you would have come out of it any better!" Yet intuitively Jane and the rest of them knew it wasn't right even to suggest that. . . . It seemed not only wrong but dangerous to challenge a young pilot's confidence by posing the question. And that, too, was part of the unofficial protocol for the Officer's Wife.[2]

The pilot's mask of denial is as vital to him as any other piece of equipment. It must be seamlessly perfect; any crack could mean the end of his career or of his life. He needs for his family to believe in that mask, too—even though on some level they all know the truth, that even though their father has "the right stuff" there are all sorts of things that can happen to override it: a collision with a flock of geese, an ejection seat that fails, a malfunction in the oxygen mask, a map error that shows the elevation of a mountain to be lower than it is. These possibilities are shut out of the mind and the heart. If the pilot nurtures an irrational belief in his own power, his wife and children do, too.

In January 1986, the families of the astronauts were among the crowd gathered to watch the blastoff of the space shuttle *Challenger*. In the wake of that horrifying explosion, a child of one of the *Challenger*'s military astronauts was heard to cry out, "Daddy, Daddy! You promised you'd never get hurt!"

But to speak of denial in the face of certain danger is to pick only the most dramatic and obvious example of its use in military life. Whether it is because of the hall of mirrors or because denial is the natural survival style of the Fortress, military families are expert at denying the existence of their own problems.

The son of a Navy lieutenant commander gave the example of his parents, whose divorce came as a complete shock to their four children. "My parents had been fighting for five years before they divorced, and we never knew it," he said. "It was just amazing. Apparently they fought all the time, but not in front of us. They always pretended to be happily married." The shock sent the youngest child into a nervous breakdown; she retreated into a fantasy world and was hospitalized for a time.

In another case, the daughter of an Air Force colonel was released from a heroin detox program; when her parents picked her up, they drove her directly to a liquor store, where they bought her a half gallon of vodka. "They somehow thought that alcohol was approved," she said. In general, her parents seemed incapable of accepting the fact of her heroin addiction. "At some point my mother began to give herself medicine by injection," the daughter said. "She's a nurse. She would have a lot of needles lying around the house, and I would steal them and sell them or use them for heroin. It never seemed to occur to her to keep them locked up when I was around. One day when I was in the therapy community, she came to visit. She always has a big black purse with her, and she looked at it, sitting partly open on the floor. She said, 'Oh. I guess I ought to leave my needles in the car.' Can you imagine? With twenty-seven heroin addicts trying to get clean? But her life was based on being the best mother she can. She was in full denial."

The daughter of a Marine sergeant said she became puzzled about how her father dealt with negative emotions apart from anger, since she never saw him in a mood of reflection. "I asked him one time what happens when he is sad or disappointed or feels badly about something that happened in the past, and he said, 'Oh, I don't think about it. I just get drunk.' And that takes care of it."

Denial is certainly not unique to military families, but it is so common that it is one of the characterizing traits. The son of a Navy commander related that when he failed out of the Naval Academy in his last year, his father, whom he knew was crushed, refused to say anything about it. Even in later years, when the son tried to talk to him about it, the father would have none of it. "But avoidance and denial are not temporary mechanisms for my father," said the son, who is now a therapist working primarily with military families. "For a lot of military fathers it is the standard, not the exception."

Just about any military brat can, with some prompting, give examples of secrecy, stoicism, or denial in the way they were reared. But there is one crowning family dysfunction which combines all three in such a perfect melding that it deserves special mention. Not all military families have it, of course, but in its way it is the hallmark dysfunction of military family life. In theatrical terms, it is the most dramatic role there is, a role that supersedes all others and envelops the family in its own tragic script.

It is alcoholism.

ALCOHOL: THE ULTIMATE MASK

If under ordinary circumstances it is usual for members of Fortress families to wear the mask of denial, what happens when alcoholism enters in? The answer is, denial on a grand scale. The alcoholic typically denies the addiction; often the spouse does, too—even as the cycle of emotional and sometimes physical violence spirals upward.

In fact, the horrors of alcohol dependency inside the Fortress involve using all three masks to full effect: The mask of denial cuts off all avenues of help from the outside; the mask of secrecy shrouds the destructive dynamic of the alcoholic household; the mask of stoicism enables the wearer to endure the intolerable past all reason.

In that sense, then, the theatrical company of the Fortress is particularly well equipped to conceal its most intensely destructive personal minidramas behind an immaculate façade of smoothly untroubled conventionality.

The stories of the children, however, give the lie to this picture. In the course of interviewing eighty military brats, I heard a great many accounts of alcoholic families. The following is a small sampling of memories, selected to show the variety of faces of alcoholism inside Fortress families, the way it was seen by the children of warriors.

The daughter of an Air Force general: "Once when my brother and I were teenagers we had a basement we fixed up like a little rathskeller; there was even a parachute hanging from the ceiling. We could kind of escape down there. And one time my brother and I were having a little party, and my father comes down the stairs, drunk as a skunk, and he starts—he's so uncivil—he's going up to the girls, feeling them up.

"And at that time we had this wonderful mannequin, just a head and a torso, no arms or legs, that one of the kids had found somewhere. It was our mascot; we always had this thing at our parties. And my father goes over to the mannequin, talks to it, feels its boobs, finally picks it up and starts dancing and flirting with it, saying, 'You're the most gorgeous girl, you're the only one who doesn't reject me.'

"And that's when I finally went upstairs, sobbing."

The son of a Navy petty officer: "My father would get drunk and break dishes. We had to buy a new set every forty-five to sixty days."

The son of an Army colonel: "My father did have his alcohol. He didn't always *have* to have it, but once he got started he wouldn't drink in moderation. It would go further than it should. His behavior could be described as Jekyll and Hyde: Sometimes he'd be a lot of fun, but it would be very easy for him to snap, and you never knew when that was going to happen. Sometimes it never happened. Sometimes you'd find yourself flat on your back.

"He'd get drunk on a weekly basis, usually in conjunction with a night at the officers' club. He would go to Happy Hour—there were pressures for him to be there—and then he'd come home with a lot of alcohol in him. If it was a school night, I'd avoid talking to him at all. Because if anything came out, he might set you up in front of the family . . . and I mean to the point where you'd be in tears. You never knew what the guy wanted. If you got some idea of what he wanted and it *wasn't* what he wanted, he'd come unglued."

The daughter of a Navy chief petty officer: "My father was not an ugly drinker. He was sweet when he got smashed. But because of his alcoholism he was emotionally unavailable to me. I've been in therapy for years. He never told me he loved me."

The son of a Navy chief petty officer: "My father would get drunk about twice a month. One morning he got up and broke every dish in the house. Another time, when he was drunk and pissed off, he dragged my brother's motorcycle out in the driveway and tried to set it on fire.

"There was always the threat he would smack you in the back of the head with his knuckles or fist. He never beat on people; it was always a single shot when you least expected it."

The daughter of a Marine sergeant: "My father was even thrown into jail a couple of times for drunkenness. But it was always in the context of the Marines, so I don't know that he even thought it was anything really terrible. It was like something you see in a John Wayne movie: a lot of Marines out drunk, punching people out, obnoxious and loud. And it always seemed so innocent and without repercussions when you saw it in the movies. But to live through it was really devastating for the families, because it was embarrassing. It's embarrassing for kids to have their father come home smashed. It's embarrassing when your father is arrested. It's embarrassing and inappropriate when he is slobbering all over you. And it's frightening when he's menacing."

The daughter of a Navy lieutenant commander and pilot: "My father went to detox two or three times, but he still drank. He had cirrhosis of the liver, but he still managed to stay in the service thirty years. He could drive a car home, park it, turn off the ignition, and pass out right there. How he got home—and how he never killed anybody—I don't know. And he would fly, too. He could sober up at will; he had great willpower, and unfortunately, because of it he was allowed to get along with his drinking problem. People knew about it."

The daughter of a Navy captain: "My mother got drunk every day. I'd come home from school and wouldn't be able to find her, and then I'd find her unconscious, wedged between the refrigerator and the kitchen cabinets. Somehow my sisters and I would get her to bed and she'd be ranting and screaming and raving. In the morning we'd ask Dad, 'Do we say something about Mom?' and it was always, 'We pretend it didn't happen.' So we walked on eggshells.

"We were never out with them socially. It may be that Mom was able to keep herself glued together until they got out of the officers' club, and he knew what the signs were and made excuses.

"The times my dad was at sea, my sisters and I survived on glazed doughnuts. I was the one who took care of everybody, who raised my two sisters. I was the mother. I've never been a child."

The son of an Army lieutenant colonel: "Dad abused alcohol most of the time I knew him. From a few beers or a six-pack after work to much more while watching football on weekends, he abused it pretty heavily. To this day I refuse to own a recliner because it reminds me of him getting stoned and passing out with the television on full blare.

"I only remember him being physically abusive [to me] once. But the mental and verbal abuse were worse, and it always accompanied his drinking. The drinking took my father away, although in a real sense, he took himself away. It was a way he used to withdraw from us, his family."

Of the seventy-five military families represented by the voices in this book (there were eighty interviewees, but where I interviewed siblings I counted them as one to avoid skewing the numbers) thirty-nine, or *just over half*, had at least one alcoholic parent.[3] By any reckoning, this is shockingly high[4]—particularly in view of the fact that all of the military brats interviewed were located through word-of-mouth referrals and not by contacting Al-Anon, Adult Children of Alcoholics, Alcoholics Anonymous, or other similar organizations.

It is also quite high considering that studies have shown that denial of parental alcohol problems is very common among children of alcoholics. Claudia Black, a prominent professional in the field who helped identify the common problems of adult children of alcoholics (ACoAs), has said that as many as "forty percent of the people who grow up in alcoholic homes walk out the door not knowing their mother or father was alcoholic."[5]

One is left to speculate, then, whether the high percentage of ACoAs found in this sampling of military brats is attributable to pure coincidence, to exaggeration of a parent's problem by the child, or for some other reason.

While it is possible my findings are the result of mere happenstance—that I somehow stumbled upon clusters of adult children of alcoholics—in my opinion that is not likely to account for very much of the total. For one thing, I received my referrals from a very large and diverse group of sources.

I also rule out exaggeration by the interviewees as the explanation, because I asked detailed questions about the parents' use of alcohol, and interpreted the Alcoholics Anonymous definition of alcoholism conservatively in deciding whether the parent described really qualified as an alcoholic. In my view, a parent qualified as an alcoholic when his or her abuse of alcohol, taking place over a long period of time, became a primary shaper of family dynamics. In other words, the other family members had to have been drawn into the abuser's problem to the extent that they modified their own behavior and attitudes in order to cope, and these roles, all revolving around the parent's abuse of alcohol, came to characterize the family system.

I think the explanation for the high percentage lies elsewhere. First of all, it may well be that alcoholism in the military is in fact widespread—a point that will be discussed later in this chapter. A second reason may be that military brats with alcoholic parents have less of a tendency to deny the problem than other ACoAs. And that might be explained on the basis that use—and abuse—of alcohol has been, until very recently, so open and so accepted in the military that children of warriors grow up sensing less of a stigma attached to alcohol abuse than do their civilian peers. This does not mean that military brats suffer less from the consequences of alcoholism in the family than civilian children, but that they may feel the admission of it does not make them uniquely shamed. In the military, alcohol is ubiquitous, and its abuse tends to fall in the category of "open secret." And while a military brat would never feel free to speak of parental alcoholism while growing up inside the Fortress, once the warrior has retired and the family has left that sphere, the last barrier against talking about it is gone.

Judging by the interviews for this book, it is difficult to imagine a military brat who could not bear witness to the egregious abuse of alcohol inside the Fortress. We've seen it in our own families or the families of our childhood friends, and as an accepted part of the social milieu at the officers' club, the NCO club, and an assortment of military social functions. That, it seems to me, tells us two things.

First, it is imperative for us to find out how this affected us as children and continues to affect us still. Fortunately, a great deal is now known about the effects of growing up in alcoholic families, with the result that information, counseling, and support groups are readily available.

Second—and quite pertinent to our search for roots—it is obvious that we cannot understand the culture we came out of until we understand its relationship to alcohol.

The latter task is best divided into several questions:

How much alcohol abuse is there inside the Fortress? To what extent has the Fortress encouraged it? And if so, why?

The Extent of Alcohol Abuse in the Military

Any examination of alcohol abuse in the military must rely chiefly on studies done over the past few years; there were few large-scale surveys or thorough studies done prior to 1980.

This book examines the effects of growing up inside the Fortress on military brats who are now well into adulthood, rather than those who are currently under the age of eighteen and living in the care of active-duty families. It is therefore important to remember, as a researcher for the Department of Defense pointed out to me, that alcohol abuse was markedly more widespread in the military during the time this group of interviewees was being raised—from about 1940 to the end of the seventies—than it probably is these days, given, among other things, the decline in alcohol consumption in American society as a whole. While alcohol abuse *still* weighs in heavily as a factor influencing family life in the warrior society, we can presume it was even more of a problem for the couple of generations of military brats represented by the voices in this book. This is worth keeping in mind, because statistics describing the extent of the problem in today's military, as alarming as they are, can at best understate the situation that prevailed during the Baby Boom era.

From the perspective of military brats, this is a legitimate sore point. Although the widespread abuse of alcohol in the military was common knowledge during that time, the Department of Defense (DoD) chose to look the other way. Certainly, if rampant alcohol abuse in the armed forces was not a matter of major import to DoD during that period, it comes as no surprise that the possible effects on the children being raised inside the Fortress did not inspire much concern. DoD never authorized a thorough study of the effects of alcoholism on military families—even though, with some foresight and purely out of self-interest, it might have discerned that the effects of parental alcoholism on the large numbers of children born to the military during those postwar Baby Boom years might adversely affect an important pool of future recruits.

In recent years, DoD has begun to show some interest in controlling alcohol abuse, since it remains beyond dispute the number-one substance abuse problem in the armed forces. Its efforts to date, however, have been halfhearted. While penalties have been stiffened for driving under the influence, and nonalcoholic beverages are now also available at social functions, many bases still have Happy Hours with cheap drinks, and all, at this writing, have Class VI stores that sell alcohol tax-free at heavily discounted prices—"a practice that may encourage use or increase the frequency or level of use," according to a team of researchers under contract to DoD.[6] In a comprehensive study published in May 1989 that compared civilian and military consumption of alcohol, the same researchers found that "other things being equal, military personnel are more likely to use and abuse alcohol than the civilian population from which they are drawn."[7]

Just how widespread has alcohol abuse been in the military? Here are a few findings to consider:

- It was reported in 1975 that White House physician Rear Admiral William Lukash had suggested the rate of alcoholism in the military was three times that of the civilian population.[8]
- In the same year, a report found the percentage of "problem drinkers" in the U.S. Navy to be as high as 38 percent.[9]
- A study reported in 1981 found that seven percent of the military personnel surveyed reported suffering from symptoms of alcohol dependence, "and 27 percent suffered some degree of work impairment because of their alcohol use during the previous year. This impairment ranged in seriousness from lowered performance to drunk or high while working. Eleven percent stated that they had worked while they were drunk or high from alcohol."[10]
- The USAREUR (U.S. Army, Europe) Personnel Opinion Survey for 1975–78 reported that "Dividing respondents into five categories on the basis of their answer to the alcohol questions consistently left 30 percent of the soldiers under 21 in the 'problem drinker' or 'alcohol addict' group."[11]
- A study of drinking by military wives in overseas base communities found that nine out of ten military wives drink, that one third of them report drinking more often since coming overseas, and that one in ten

fell into the "heavy drinker" category. ". . . The results . . . indicate that military wives are far more likely to be self-reported drinkers than their civilian counterparts, and that their overall level of consumption of alcohol is higher than other groups of married women." Taking its cues from the fact that one wife in five reported she drinks "to forget her troubles" or "calm her nerves," the report speculated that drinking can be seen as an "occupational risk" of being a military wife, in part occasioned by such factors as absence of the husband, lack of social relationships outside the family, boredom, and separation from relatives and friends.[12]

- The May 1989 study comparing military and civilian drinking patterns found that the percentage of heavy drinkers in the military is nearly twice that of the comparable civilian population.[13] This comparison is considered a meaningful one because the two sets of survey results which were compared were standardized to account for differences between the civilian population and the military population, which is disproportionately young and male—characteristics associated with higher levels of alcohol use. It is worth noting that as of this writing in 1991, there has never been any mass survey of the drinking habits of the *spouses* of military personnel. So the above finding, as alarming as it is, does not begin to present a complete picture of the extent of the problem in the military community.

Encouragement of Alcohol Abuse

As telling as any statistic, however, is the description of alcohol use in the warrior society by the children who witnessed it. These tales of Fortress childhood shed some light on the second key question we are exploring—the extent to which the military and its culture have encouraged the abuse of alcohol.

The son of an Air Force general: "It was *always* there. It was never abused in a very formal setting—that just isn't done—but informally the rule was 'party hearty.' "

The daughter of a Navy lieutenant commander: "My parents were not alcoholic, but they drank heavily. I can remember the pitcher of martinis when my dad came home from work. We kids always thought it was ice water."

The daughter of an Army sergeant: "The socialization in the service is to drink. There was a *lot* of drinking, every weekend drinking until drunk. In Texas, on paydays the men went to Juarez to get drunk."

Drinking is so much a part of warrior culture that it has almost been a requirement. Military wives and mothers interviewed for this book recalled being told by their husbands and by other wives that during social functions they should hold a drink in their hands, even if they never touched it. One officer felt compelled during cocktail parties at his home to prepare his wife a "drink" of diluted coffee on the rocks, in order to keep her teetotaling habits a secret.

Alcohol has in fact been the centerpiece of every social and formal occasion in the military—from formal receptions to battalion "organization days" to ship christenings and Happy Hours. Many children of military pilots tell stories of dreaded Friday nights, when their fathers would come home drunk from Happy Hour at the officers' club with their pilot buddies—a weekly event at which a pilot's presence was de rigueur.

In short, drinking has been "as much a part of the military experience as the duty assignment," according to one team of researchers.[14]

But why? For those military brats who lived with an alcoholic parent—and here I will say that my father, too, was alcoholic—this is no idle question. We grew up understanding that drinking was an integral part of military life and obviously tolerated by the authorities, but we were mystified as to why. Was it merely a natural spinoff of a macho subculture, in which warriors tried to demonstrate control over all things—including the bottle? Was alcohol the anesthetic of choice for men who preferred to forget what they saw in battle, or who were somehow unable to cope with the emotional pain in their lives? Or does the ingestion of alcohol make it easier for warriors—and their wives—to wear the masks their roles require of them day in, day out?

Somehow there has to be an explanation for why heavy drinking was not only tolerated among those responsible for our national defense, but even actively encouraged. For despite the obvious problems generated by alcohol abuse—and those were all too obvious to the children of alcoholics—the Department of Defense continued to make alcohol readily available to members of the service at very low prices, and to reinforce the norm of serving it in abundance at a variety of social functions.

One would think that at some point a hue and cry would have been raised about a situation which to any rational person would seem intolerable. After all, alcohol abuse in the armed forces could legitimately be seen as a national security issue. How secure can our country be, when its defense is entrusted in no small part to a bunch of drunks? It's not even as though one could take any comfort in their remaining relatively sober on the job; alcoholics, until they give up drinking forever, have impaired judgment *all* the time, even between bouts with the bottle. What does "readiness" mean when a huge number of warriors would just as soon hit the bottle as the beach? Or even worse, the bottle *and* the beach? But apparently no one—not tax-paying citizens, nor their elected representatives, nor the brass in the Department of Defense—has chosen to see it that way.

It was not until 1985, in fact, that DoD seemed to show any motivation toward addressing the problem, and to date it has not been nearly as aggressive toward alcohol as toward drug abuse, for which it has a "zero tolerance" policy, even though alcohol abuse involves a far larger segment of the military population. In July 1990, for example—five years after the so-called crackdown on substance abuse by the Department of Defense—a case of canned Budweiser beer cost $15.99 in the town of Ayer, Massachusetts, while in the Class VI store at nearby Fort Devens, an Army post, it could be bought for $12.99, a discount of roughly 20 percent. For bourbon the discount was even greater: At the Class VI a fifth of Jim Beam cost $7.10, 25 percent less than in town.

The double message conveyed by DoD, publicly promoting itself as waging war on substance addiction while quietly continuing to subsidize warriors' drinking habits, would seem to be mystifying. But there is in fact an explanation for why alcohol has been—and to a large extent, continues to be—more than tolerated by the military.

The Partnership of Alcohol and the Military

"Soldiering and alcohol have been almost synonymous since the invention of armies . . ." wrote Lt. Col. Larry H. Ingraham in his ethnographic study of drug and alcohol use among Army enlisted men, *The Boys in the Barracks.* "All armies in all times have faced health and performance deficiencies stemming from the excessive use of alcohol, yet there has remained a singular attraction regarding its use. Alcohol use has been encouraged as a means of promoting camaraderie, cohesion, and group solidarity; on the other hand the high incidence of ensuing fights, property destruction, and inability to function effectively has always been lamented."[15]

Lamented, yes—the verb conjures up images of passive handwringing. But actively, effectively condemned? No. And the reason can only be that from the point of view of the military organization, the payoff of alcohol use, even alcohol abuse, has been greater than the cost.

So what is the payoff?

From detailed observations made by a research team living in the barracks with the men, Ingraham concluded, "Whether the drinking is recreational, affirmational, or ceremonial, one of its primary functions is to provide the participants with a tradition, a history of common experience that gives a sense of depth to their relationships. . . . Drinking also provided one of the few opportunities in the Army to express dependence and nurturance. The classic example was putting a buddy to bed after a drinking bout. . . . Drinking episodes also provided small groups or cliques with a shared history."[16]

In other words, the fact that soldiers are generally strangers to one another presents the military with something of a problem: These men have no common roots, no "shared history," but they may well find themselves fighting and dying for one another on the battlefield. Somehow, in this stiffly formal authoritarian world, they need to bond. In the impersonal theater of the Fortress, some link is needed to connect the wearers of the warrior mask to one another. Historically, traditionally, it has been drinking.

Then, too, there is the other function of alcohol which is useful in Fortress life: It is the anesthetic of choice for those who, for whatever reason, wish to numb their emotional pain. As we have seen, some men arrive in the military carrying a great deal of pain from their early lives. Others can't bear to remember what they have witnessed on the battlefield. Still others need to take the edge off the fear they experience day in and day out as they fly aircraft, handle explosives, or perform other dangerous duty. And some have simply never learned other ways to deal with the considerable stresses of life inside the Fortress. Alcohol serves the anesthetic purpose quite well, and without the social stigma attached to drugs.

The Effects on the Children of the Fortress

Accepting the negative consequences of this arrangement has been something that the military through many generations and until very recently has been fully prepared to do. But if alcohol abuse has compromised national security, damaged relations with the civilian community, and contributed to a negative stereotype of the military, it has perhaps done its worst and most direct damage right inside the Fortress, in the families of warriors.

And if we here describe the problem as not only deeply damaging, but extraordinarily widespread, it is not just this author's opinion. One psychiatrist, on comparing psychiatric records of military and civilian children seen in his practice, wrote, "Military fathers showed an excess of alcoholism, a phenomenon that has been noted by others, suggesting that at least one factor in the background of the military dependents differentiates them from civilians."[17]

In terms of the legacies of having an alcoholic parent, the worst, of course, is the danger of inheriting the problem. According to experts, as many as one in four children of alcoholics become alcoholics themselves, compared to one in ten in the general population.[18] Of the military brats interviewed for this book, eight admitted to being alcoholic themselves; four more admitted to having "an alcohol problem." Nine more, who claimed not to have a drug or alcohol problem themselves, said at least one of their siblings did. Notably, one daughter of two alcoholic parents and an alcoholic stepfather said that she is the only one of nine children to have avoided the family disease. This means that, so far, twenty-one of the seventy-five military families have at least one child with an alcohol problem or an alcohol addiction.[19]

But well before the disease turns up in the children, alcohol has destroyed the fabric of family life. It contributes to violence—70 percent of all family violence is connected to alcohol abuse[20]—and, whether or not there is physical violence, it destroys trust relationships in the family.

Parental alcoholism also leads to a host of other problems the children must face in later life. One doctor wrote that adult children of alcoholics "can best be understood as suffering from a variety of post-traumatic stress disorder (PTSD) in combination with codependency."[21] Although it may be argued that the PTSD designation is coming to be overused in the medical profession, the application here is very interesting—not least because it draws a parallel to the experience of battle-shocked warriors. The doctor cites the relevant symptoms of ACoAs as: a tendency to reexperience the trauma through obsessively dwelling on it; psychic numbing accompanied by a sense of isolation; anxiety that a given situation might progress beyond their ability to control it; survivor guilt and depression; and a tendency to expose themselves to situations that echo the original trauma.[22]

Complicating these symptoms of stress disorder, the doctor notes, is what he calls "codependent dedication to flawed beliefs about willpower and control."

"In essence," he wrote, "the adult children of alcoholics are engaged in a struggle to build their self-esteem based on their ability to exert willpower, a struggle in which their alcoholic parent failed. Unfortunately, failure is guaranteed as long as success is based on the ability to control one's own feelings, to control the actions and feelings of others, or to control the effects of alcohol in themselves or another person."[23]

Control. The heart and soul of the Fortress. The very substance of which the mask of the warrior is made. The first and greatest role model for the military brat. And, for many, our first and most enduring legacy. The tragedy of the mask of the warrior—the controller—is that it is so easily inherited.

That's the bad news. The good news is that the symptoms of the syndrome are considered by therapists to be highly treatable, and ACoAs usually respond very well to treatment. In the 1980s, a national movement arose to identify the ACoA syndrome and help ACoAs cope with it.[24]

The literature distributed at ACoA group meetings often lists various characteristics ACoAs are thought to share. The list is too long to print in full, but some of the characteristics are startling—not only because they frequently apply to military brats who are ACoAs, but because they also apply to many military brats who are *not*. Here are a few of them, from the landmark book *Adult Children of Alcoholics* by Janet Woititz:[25]

- Adult children of alcoholics guess at what normal is.
- Adult children of alcoholics have difficulty following a project through from beginning to end.
- Adult children of alcoholics judge themselves without mercy.
- Adult children of alcoholics have difficulty with intimate relationships.
- Adult children of alcoholics overreact to changes over which they have no control.
- Adult children of alcoholics constantly seek approval and affirmation.
- Adult children of alcoholics are super responsible or super irresponsible.
- Adult children of alcoholics are extremely loyal, even in the face of evidence that the loyalty is undeserved.

These characteristics of ACoAs were echoed by many military brats interviewed for this book. Some had alcoholic parents, some didn't. All had experienced a great deal of mobility, and most had known quite a bit of father absence. Shown the list of ACoA characteristics, some of them—even those from nonalcoholic homes—marveled that they could identify so thoroughly.

When I shared this observation with a social worker who has a clientele of military families—and is also a military son—his words were telling: "A lot of these characteristics are, I suspect, true of adult children of the military as well as adult children of alcoholics," he said, "because the common theme is that bonding and rootedness are interrupted for both. Plus, in both systems the child is somehow secondary to serving parental needs, instead of the parents uniting to nurture the child. I think that's the commonality."

The order of priorities is perhaps the most rigid thing of all about life inside the Fortress: First priority is always, always, the Military Mission. On this there can be no compromise. The second priority is the individual warrior. Third place goes to the spouse, and military brats come in last.

Make no mistake: Warrior families love their children too. This order of priorities is something they don't always find comfortable, though they can't afford to dwell on the point. The fact that children are a fourth-place concern is a truth they are particularly loath to admit, since it flies in the face of conventional American values—and, in accordance with the myth of the Fortress which requires perfection in all things, warrior families tend to see themselves as the epitome of the old-fashioned American way. But the reality is that it is the specific job of military families to adapt to priorities set by the Fortress, not by them. And adapt they do.

That is yet another reason why they become so good at wearing the masks of secrecy, stoicism, and denial. Not only do those masks help families to meet the expectations of the Fortress—to conform, at least outwardly, to the Fortress myth—they help military parents forget about the inflexible ordering of priorities that, where family life is concerned, goes so against their grain. All military brats grow up well aware that their concerns, with rare exceptions, are attended to last— and then only if they have not been overruled by the higher priorities of Fortress life. And while they also know on some level that, as children of warriors, it could not be otherwise, they frequently harbor resentment well into adulthood.

That is not necessarily a permanent state of mind, however. The military brats who are now most reconciled to their childhoods are the ones who view their parents sympathetically, as ordinary, vulnerable people with the usual sets of flaws, who were trying their best to live up to the standards of a particularly rigid way of life. And while it is true that they freely chose to embrace that rigid way of life—and thus are responsible for that choice and its consequences—it is also true that the world of the Fortress is so isolated, and the pressures to conform so great, that it does not take long to lose one's bearings and forget about the notions one once harbored about the best way to live life or run a family. The Fortress consumes its servants totally, forces them to follow its ways, play out the roles it has assigned.

These are roles we look at much more closely as we go deeper beneath the surface of life inside the Fortress to study the family drama.

CHAPTER 3

THE PLAY WITHIN THE PLAY

"Light me another cigarette, darling." As the flame came to her she said, looking into her son's eyes, who quickly dropped his, "Your father has many good points."

"Sure, Mom. They're the knuckles on his left hand."

"Don't try to be so clever, sugah. You and Mary Anne always have to verbally joust with the rest of the world and it's not very becoming to either one of you. And one thing you're not keeping in mind, Ben. One thing that is very important. Your father loves you very much."

"Ha!" Ben laughed. "He's got a fabulous way of showing it." Then a mellowness entered his voice, an exhausted gentleness. "Mama, we've had this talk a million times. It starts out with you leaving him. Then it ends with you telling me all his good points. How much he wants the best for his children. How much he loves us all and sacrifices for us all. Do you know something that I know, Mama? He loves the Marine Corps more than he loves us."

"He's supposed to, son. That's his duty. His job. All men are like that."

"No," Ben said harshly. "It's different. Do you think Dupree Johnson's daddy loved his gas station more than his family? Or Robbie Chambers' daddy loved his doughnut shop more than his wife or kids?"

—Pat Conroy, The Great Santini

About six years ago—I remember it was not long after my father died—I found an old color slide while sifting through a footlocker of family memorabilia. When I held it up to the light and took in the vivid scene from the past, I felt my heart contract.

We were at an airport on a summer day, meeting my father as he came back from a lengthy assignment somewhere. Standing just outside the airport building, behind the rope barrier, are my mother, the very personification of a 1950s housewife in a long-skirted green shirtwaist dress and heels, her hair pulled back in a low bun, and my brother, at fifteen already taller than she, with a crewcut, short-sleeved white shirt and black pants, looking stiff and uncomfortable, his face a mask of dread. I am four years old, in hair ribbons, a frilly party dress, and black patent leather shoes, though the slide does not reveal that detail: It was snapped a moment after I broke free of my mother, ducked under the ropes, and took off. I am a blur caught in space, both feet literally off the ground, a missile of love aimed straight for my daddy, who is striding toward us in his summer khakis, a briefcase at his side.

It is significant, I thought, that the picture does not show the moment of contact. Instead it freezes me in midair, full of yearning, unrequited.

I'd forgotten there was a time when my love for him was so un-clouded, so direct. When feeling was not checked by stoicism. Before fear. Before anger. Before bitterness. The image both restores a lost memory and echoes my sense of emptiness, of incompletion: so much love, seemingly unstoppable, destined to miss its mark.

Another day months later, still grieving over missed connections, over the way things should have been but weren't, I took out the slide again. This time I looked more closely at the cast of characters in this typical scene from the Fortress drama, hoping to uncover clues I had missed before. And indeed, I saw considerably more in that image that day. I saw things that have since come to change the way I view my family and my childhood inside the Fortress.

The first is that, for all the hurt that really did take place in my family, there was also love. Most of it came from my mother, but even where my warrior father was concerned, the connection wasn't totally missed. There were times when love did connect, and in a most satisfying way, as on that summer day in 1955. That those times were few, and that the occasions of cruelty ultimately outweighed the occasions of love from my father, are also undeniable. But that should not lessen the value of the love that did make it through. I began to see that, to do justice to my father and to ease my grief, I would have to learn to value those few times of connection as having a kind of completeness in themselves, an integrity that I should not ignore or violate in my remembering.

Equally important, I came to think as I stared at the slide, is the very real possibility that my mother, brother, and I were not the only ones in our family who wanted more love to make it through than actually did: I forced myself to consider my father's side of it. Perhaps there were occasions when my father was prepared to give love to his family but we were not prepared to receive it. Times when my father even thought he *was* showing love, but we did not understand. After all, we were dealing with a man whose emotional lexicon was doubtless much smaller than his emotional range. I began to realize that, oddly enough, I did not necessarily comprehend what had taken place in my family even though I'd had years of experience as a member of it. I needed to rethink things.

The third realization I had that day was that my parents were not totally in control of what happened inside our family. In a way, I now saw, they were as powerless as my brother and I; things had occurred which they had not necessarily wanted to happen and which they had not known how to prevent. This, too, was a new thought for me, and an overdue one. Now when I looked at the slide I saw that the real determining power in our family resided outside of my mother and father. It was as though I were looking at an invisible member of the family, a secret controller who called the shots yet couldn't be challenged. Someone who orchestrated us, gave us our roles, our script. The one who sent my father away and brought him back, the one who assembled us all at the airport, went with us everywhere, lived inside us even, the one without whom our life would lack meaning. In a sense, I now saw, the old slide could be seen as a portrait of the real paterfamilias, not only of our family but of each and every warrior household.

Oddly, this all-powerful presence usually goes unacknowledged inside the warrior family. But it has a name. It is the Military Mission. It occurred to me that for a very long time, I had been looking at my parents from the wrong angle.

That was the moment I decided to begin this book. Not long after, I began my library research into military families, and did the first interview with a military brat. Over the years since, and by means of the many life stories I have heard from other military brats, still more aspects of that old color slide have come to light. It has helped me not only to grieve for what should have been and wasn't, but to value what was there all along.

This chapter, then, reexamines the two major actors in our family drama, the warrior father and the Fortress mother, noting how they are shaped and guided by the Military Mission.

THE WARRIOR FATHER

When I think of my father, one of the things I remember is his powerful presence. I remember that, even as a very young child, I would know when he had entered the house even though he might be too far away for me to see or hear. And when he quietly looked into a room where I was playing or working with my back to the door, I could feel his personality enter the room and surround me. I couldn't say exactly what it was I picked up on, but I could feel it over my entire back and the back of my skull, and my senses would go on alert. My brother, who experienced the same thing, would say it was instinctual, a foreboding that forewarns. It is true our father had an ominous cast to his nature. Even a good mood could darken in a flash, as we well knew.

But warrior fathers tend to have a strong presence even when it isn't negative. I recall a casual conversation I had with a Navy son a few years ago that addressed that point. This son said he'd always had a good relationship with his father; when he spoke of him it was with admiration, love, and unmistakable yearning. Here was a son who couldn't get enough of his father, who devoured his father when he was home and ached for him when he was away. And his father, like almost all Navy fathers, was away a lot. The son told me that he, too, would know the exact moment his father entered the house, without any obvious cues. He would feel a happy excitement in his stomach, and all his senses would be awakened. But it wasn't limited to when his father was physically near. By way of example, he said, he could remember once coming in from playing outside all day and standing gazing into the refrigerator, as usual, when he suddenly knew that his father had returned. His father had indeed come back, though he was not in the house at the time.

Of such subtle, intuitive responses is the relationship between child and warrior father made. If that seems paradoxical, given the overpowering effect many military fathers have on their children, it is. But the reality of the Fortress family is that the relationship with the warrior is as much divined as it is actually experienced—partly because of the masks of secrecy, stoicism, and denial, which inhibit communication, and partly because the warrior, for one reason or another, is very often not there.

The Warrior as Absentee Father

Looking at the warrior father's absences from the family is at least as revealing as studying his presence. It's like examining the composition of a painting. Art students analyze a painting in terms of positive spaces and negative spaces—the images and the spaces around the images. Negative spaces, they learn, are as critical to the picture as positive ones; the spaces define the shapes, hold them in a certain relation to one another. It would be incorrect to think of negative spaces as mere emptiness; they have a definite construction, a definite meaning. To analyze a picture without taking the negative spaces into account is almost nonsensical; they make the painting what it is. In the warrior family, father absence is the negative space that reveals the images and the structure of the family.

Nearly all warrior fathers are gone from the family for long periods at a stretch, or on frequent short trips. During a twenty-year career in the Army, Air Force, or Marine Corps, a warrior can expect to make four lengthy overseas tours of duty—with or without family—and any number of shorter tours away from home for education, training, field exercises, or special duty.

In the Navy, because of sea duty, father absence is even greater. In general, a Navy father may be away from home fully half the time. These days, during a three-year tour, a sailor typically goes to sea twice, for six months each time. It is common for sailors to miss the births of their children, their first steps, their triumphs and their crises at school. Even now, despite attempts to hold tours to six months, a cruise can be suddenly lengthened if the Mission so requires. And during the two years a sailor is typically "at home" between cruises, frequent two-week cruises take him to sea about half the time. For example, by the time the aircraft carrier Saratoga returned to its home port in Florida in April 1986, its cruise had lasted eight months—and during the preceding twelve months, it was in home port only fifty-six nights.[1]

That's the situation now. When the interviewees for this book were growing up, family separations were even longer. Sea cruises normally lasted ten or eleven months, before adding in surprise extensions.

Such absences obviously represent severe disruptions in family life—but there are even more disruptive patterns, depending on the nature of the command. Ballistic missile submarines, for example, are typically locked into a repeating cycle of three months at sea and three months in port.

This is in peacetime, of course. But any conflict or potential conflict can impose even greater separations. Some of the interviewees for this book have fathers who served two or three tours in Vietnam, for instance. Sometimes those fathers, as we shall hear later, did not come back.

But even under the ordinary circumstances of the peacetime military, absence of the father is a condition of military brat childhood—a condition imposed by that invisible, unchallengeable member of the family, the Military Mission. Warrior fathers are continually leaving, returning, leaving again, or working such long hours that their children can never count on seeing them. Part of the training every military child receives is that one is expected to handle this disturbing fact of life in true stoic warrior style.

"We'd have to drop my father off at the airport in the car," recalled the son of an Air Force colonel, "and he would allow no emotion. We were never allowed to go in and see him off; he thought that was foolishness. I can remember very early feeling that pang when he would leave, this incredible feeling of resisting the urge to cry."

It is actually rather remarkable that this son is able to retrieve the memory of clamping down on his feelings. All of us experienced it, but most of us plowed it under as soon as possible: the mask of stoicism transforming itself into the mask of denial.

In fact, plenty of us deceive ourselves on a grand scale with regard to the effects of our fathers' absences. It is common for military families to imagine themselves as somehow immune to the common psychological stresses of Fortress life, or at least more resilient than civilians who, it is implied, have it easy all their lives. But that is merely the denial mask doing its work. All of us pay a price.

"My father's long absences didn't seem to affect me much at the time," said the daughter of a Marine sergeant,

> but I can tell in retrospect it must have made a tremendous impression on me because of the way I feel now about people coming and going. That's a problem area for me: It's shattering to me when people go. It's only now I'm beginning to get a handle on realizing that when people go away it doesn't mean they're *gone* [forever]. I think I associated his going away with danger, because some of the places he went were dangerous—the Vietnam War. . . .
>
> The sight of suitcases bothers me a lot, even now. I remember my father's green bags, all packed and ready to go. I did and still do love my father very much, and I'm sure it affected me that he was coming and going. Plus the disruption. The transition periods seem to me to have been very difficult, emotional, and painful.

Her reflections speak to effects of father absence that are not generally talked about because they are not quantifiable and therefore not studied. There has been a fair amount of research dating back to World War II showing the effects of father absence on school performance (boys are more affected than girls, and schoolwork frequently suffers), physical health (visits to base clinics by spouses and children for an array of problems go way up during deployments), and emotional well-being (reports of depression and behavioral problems also go up).[2] But there are other effects, too, of the sort that are quite unlikely to turn up in any institutional records, effects that together constitute a different view of childhood, of family, and of events in general than someone from a more stable background is likely to have.

This legacy can be difficult, but the suggestion here is not that such things should be an excuse for self-pity. What is important here, as in the rest of this book, is to see clearly how certain patterns and attitudes were established in the Fortress childhood; only after that has been done is it possible to look squarely at how they continue to influence military brats in adult life. The Marine daughter just quoted, for instance, had recently divorced her husband after a thirteen-year marriage. One of the key issues was her sense of abandonment when he would leave home for long periods to travel or seek work in some other part of the country.

The daughter of a Navy chief petty officer, asked to consider how her father's extended absences affected her, said, "I feel I led two different lives growing up: one when my father was there and one when he wasn't. When he was there, everything had to be neat and tidy, and meals had to be exactly on time. When he was gone it was drive-ins, fast foods, a sloppy house. Two weeks before he came home there was a mad dash to make the house shipshape." But the flip-flops represented more than periodic sea changes in household rules, she said. The family dominated by mother and the family dominated by father were like two very different worlds. She adapted to the changes well enough—outwardly, anyway—but developed no sense of continuity. In adulthood this daughter has alternated between extremes of behavior, including various forms of substance abuse, going from abstinence to reckless indulgence and back. There were other disturbing factors in her childhood besides father absence—for instance, her father was an alcoholic—but she continues to see the "two different lives" of her childhood as emblematic of all the major issues in her life. "When my dad was there and then wasn't there. . . . Everything was polarized, everything was either black or white, nothing was in balance. That's what my struggles today are all about: finding balance."

When the Warrior Is Out of the Picture

How the mother handles the warrior's absences is crucial to what happens with the children, as has been well documented in other research on military families.[3] When she takes the situation in stride, things generally run well enough. The problem with that is the implication that if things do not go well, it is the mother's fault. In my view this is a distinctly unhelpful overstatement. A Fortress mother can do her best, and still the situation crumbles. It is extremely difficult to be a single parent under any circumstances, but it may be impossibly difficult when everyone knows the situation is temporary:

The single parent may not have the opportunity to grow into the role. The kids know it is just make-do until the father comes back, and the mother's authority may accordingly be undermined.

"My mother was an only child," said the daughter of a Navy lieutenant commander. "How could she possibly know how to raise five kids by herself? Sometimes she coped well. Other times it was terrible for her. She'd cry, be depressed. It was just too much.

"We kids took advantage of her when she was feeling depressed and weak, when she'd hear the ship was going to be held over for another month someplace. All that strength she'd built up was suddenly zapped from her. I would stay out past the time allowed, I wouldn't phone in, I'd go where I wasn't supposed to be. It must have been very difficult for her. I feel guilty about it now."

Plenty of military brats take advantage of their mothers when their fathers are away. It tends to look like a typical case of adolescents exploiting opportunities to assert themselves, but seen in larger perspective, the whole family is acting out its resentment toward a situation over which it has no control. Most of the time everyone makes a massive effort to mask this resentment, but one way or another, at that time or much later, it comes out.

For example, there is the bitter story of a Navy son I'll call Brian, whose father, a lieutenant commander, was gone far more than he was home. "I remember he'd be gone six months at a time, home for a month at the most, then out again. He could have turned down some tours that he took; I heard my parents talking about it." This son was twelve years old when his father retired. "I figured when he retired I'd get a dad and we could go camping and do this and that together—but I never got it. He was always away again, back in school, doubling up on his courses just to show everyone he could do it. I was bitter because of that, and I think my mother was too." His parents' marriage declined, to the point that even the mask of stoicism began to break down.

Once I got my mom tipsy and it all came out. She really hurt real bad. She was real jealous of the military. She paid a large price. She didn't work, but she took care of us kids, she took care of everything: bills, raising us, handling all the discipline, just everything.

My dad would come home to a prefab family. It was all taken care of for him. He would go every night to drink with the other men at the officers' club and he could brag about having the perfect family. But it wasn't him that made it. It was my mother. . . . The way she saw it, my dad was married to the Navy, and she was the mistress. Finally, after twenty-two years, she said, "No more."

That was a family that disintegrated: The parents divorced, three of the four children have had problems with drug or alcohol abuse, and the son just quoted has attempted suicide three times.

In some troubled families the warrior's absences are valued more than his presence—or so the family members tell themselves. One Navy son said his mother was "always joyful" when his father, a petty officer first class, went to sea. "It was a real us versus him setup," he said. This son spoke in terms that allowed no middle ground of emotion—but most of the time in such families the feelings about a father's return are mixed. There is anticipation and hope, but it is tied to the cynical realization that the old pattern will probably reassert itself.

"When my father would come home I can remember being happy but also fearful," said an Air Force colonel's daughter, "because I knew we'd go back [to the previous atmosphere of tension and conflict]. It was so pleasant and quiet when he was gone. No nagging or yelling. I knew my brother was in for a hard time when my father came back. My father was very hard on him. Very hard."

Brian, the Navy son from the extremely troubled family, said,

> When I was younger I remember getting excited [whenever my father was coming home]. As we got older, it was more like, "Well, he's coming home again." It was almost better when he wasn't there. Of course, even when he was back, it was like he wasn't there. After work he'd go to the officers' club and drink and come home late. I never really had a father per se. I've talked to people who really haven't had fathers—where the father had died young—and it's weird, there are a lot of similarities. We wished for the same things—a dad to do things with, someone to model myself after a little bit more, someone to go camping with and do things with. That's why I'm not close to him now. He's my father, but I don't know him. [He wants to see me now but] I don't see him because we don't have anything to talk about.
>
> It's kind of like the song, "Cat's in the Cradle." Harry Chapin sings it. The kid says, "I'm gonna be like you, Dad, one day." And his dad's always going away. And finally when the kid grows up, the dad says, "Let's sit down and talk." And the kid says, "I don't have time. I've got to go." That's me and my dad.
>
> I've grown up just like my dad. I'm very unfeeling, unemotional. I don't get close to people. I don't tell people I love them.
>
> Harry Chapin must have been a Navy kid.

The Warrior as Outsider

It would be too simplistic a reading of troubled warrior families to conclude that the whole mess is basically the father's fault, as though he had deliberately set out to inflict pain on his family. It's true he bears some of the responsibility—and more in some cases than others—but what one comes to see after hearing many stories of warrior families is that family dysfunction is a complicated business; one could view it as a system failure caused not by one major break-down but by an unfortunate combination of factors, some of which are within the power of the family to correct and some of which are not. There is no question that where a family is already headed for trouble, father absence exacerbates the situation.

Part of the problem in the military is that father absence is taken so much for granted as part and parcel of military duty that its negative consequences inside the family have typically been taken for granted as well—by family members themselves as much as by the military as a whole. The operating assumption of warrior families, born of those deceptive masks of secrecy, stoicism, and denial, is that everyone should be able to handle the situation perfectly well, and that if problems do turn up it's because the family never had "the right stuff" to begin with.

Social workers in the military have tried, in recent years, to get across the message that no warrior family is immune to the effects of father absence, and that there are steps every family can take to lessen the damage and heal wounds. It may be, however, that the first and best of the recommended actions to lessen the damage is also the one warrior families instinctively find hardest to take: It means taking off the masks, openly acknowledging to one another the problem and the hurt, and figuring out as a family how to handle the situation better than it's been handled up to that point. It amounts to a paradox—a prescription for connecting with one another as the solution to the problem of not connecting with one another. Many warrior families don't have any idea how to find a bridge that will take them from one pattern of behavior to the other. It is hard enough for any family to acquire new skills in communicating, but supremely difficult when that involves adopting new priorities and dropping the habits of secre-cy, stoicism, and denial so essential to the age-old ways of the brother-hood of warriors.

"The gulf that develops between the military man and his children is one of the most hopeless troubles in family therapy," wrote two therapists in a text on problems in warrior families. "Too many times there is little to do about it. The father may be little more than a figure. One discouraging thing we have learned in doing family therapy is the extent to which men reduce the family tension by leaving the family circle. Often such men have no inner life. They have never been intimate with anyone and unfortunately may never achieve closeness with anyone. The military supports that pattern, and in fact endorses

it. It is a very old warrior tradition that says, 'We dare not love too
much for soon we may die.' "[4]

Or perhaps that could be rephrased: *We dare not love too much for
soon we will get orders for another unaccompanied tour.* Since family
separations are inevitable, and families on some level always resent
this, military fathers inevitably learn to protect themselves. Sometimes
it is by physically removing themselves from the home: The father
volunteers for an away assignment and then fakes feelings of distress in
front of the family when the orders come in. Or the father might
remain with the family physically, but distance himself emotionally in
various ways—something that might well come about without him
consciously realizing what he is doing. It is instinctive for him to guard
himself against pain, particularly when he lacks the power or the skills
to do anything constructive about the situation.

"My father had a formal relationship with all of us," said the son of
an Air Force sergeant. "Very, very formal. It would have hurt him too
much to get too close to his kids. And I always knew that, even when I
was very young, so I didn't pressure him. I'd think, 'I can't talk to him,
because he'll hurt.' One time, when I was about nine years old, I wrote
to my father in Vietnam. He was so happy, he sent me a *watch*. But
[the emotional distance between us] was partly his fault, too, because
of the life [he chose]. We had to get used to not being close to my
father, because he always went to these weird places where we couldn't
go: Korea, Vietnam, Alaska."

But again this picture threatens to be too simplistic. Warrior fathers
react to a complicated set of conditions. There is the Military Mission,
of course, against which a warrior father can do little even if he is so
inclined. But there is also the family, which has to deal with its own
anger and hurt in the face of his repeated "abandonment."

For example, the warrior is fortunate if his wife and children have
the communicative skills and resourcefulness to cope with disruption
and loss, and the flexibility to allow him back into their lives despite
what he's missed. But what if they don't? The family may in turn take
steps to protect itself by emotionally shutting him out. And while that
might come as a relief to some warriors, depending on how wedded
they are to the masks of stoicism and denial, most of them in their
unguarded moments probably find it acutely painful. That kind of
rejection may even echo a situation in the father's family of origin that
drove him to join the military in the first place. What is certain is that
in the face of rejection, most fathers will then try even harder to protect
themselves—perhaps by emotionally withdrawing from the family, by
giving vent to anger, or by staying away as much as possible.

One Army major's daughter interviewed for this book described herself as completely alienated from her father, who was away for a great deal of her childhood, including a total of four years in Vietnam, two in Korea, and two in a corner of the United States where his family did not choose to follow. Like the Navy daughter quoted earlier, this military brat described her childhood in terms of two completely different worlds, one mother-centered, the other father-centered. "We actually functioned better as a family without him," she said. "It was a houseful of women. We were very competent, and we did things in a very egalitarian way. Then this guy would come home, and suddenly we were living in a barracks. He gave white-glove inspections and latrine inspections. His language was military, too. There was a lot of conflict when he came back, because he would try to ride herd over people whose lives really went quite smoothly without that need for leadership."

There were other issues festering in that family too, of course, but the father clearly had trouble being heard, or even noticed, apparently, in this house of women determined to form a unit without him. When things finally came to a head for the mother, the family wound up acting out the communication problem that was tearing them apart.

"My mother decided the only thing she could do was stop cooking for him," the daughter said. "One day when my father came home from work, she left the house before dinnertime. When she came home [later that evening], she found my father had disconnected the stove, carried it into the den by himself, and put it in front of the television set so you couldn't see it. But the best part is that my mother and sister pretended the stove wasn't there. They sat there in the den as usual, 'watching television.' "

This, too, was a marriage that ended in divorce—and none of the daughters, all adults now, were in contact with their father at the time of this writing. But this daughter, despite the bitterly comic picture she painted and her avowed resentment toward her father, is not blind to the contribution the rest of the family made to a dysfunctional situation. "I often felt sorry for my father," she said, "because he *tried* to integrate himself into the family, but he didn't have the skills. And we really didn't let him. You know how sometimes you can see a painful situation happening, but it's beyond your skills—or what you want to do—to correct it? But he really did bring it on himself. . . . I haven't seen my father in six years and probably will never, ever see him again. It sounds dramatic, but it's not that big a deal. I think that in many ways, choosing the life that he chose, he separated himself from the family. It was a decision that *he* made."

Stories about father absence are ultimately stories of missed connections, lost opportunities. *He tried to integrate himself into the*

family, but he didn't have the skills. . . . And we wouldn't let him.
Mistakes, regrets on both sides. A moment of opportunity opens up,
passes quickly, is gone.

Lorna is an Air Force brat whose father was a colonel in SAC
(Strategic Air Command), which is known for its long hours of duty.
"It seems to me the times of our family life when Daddy was home
with any regularity, especially any eight-to-five work hours, were very,
very rare," she said. "The norm seemed to be that he was gone most of
the time, often leaving at two or three A.M. and coming home after we
were asleep. I think there was always a longing for him. . . . My love
for him was and is very deep. Even when he was angry with me,
disciplining me, I loved him very much." But his absences made him
an outsider in his own family, and as time went on it was hard, she
said, to find a common language.

"I recall one incident that I *still* feel badly about," Lorna continued.

My brothers and I used to make up plays and stories together, using our
stuffed animals as characters. We had been tape-recording some of this
material, having a wonderful time together for several days.

Suddenly, Daddy was home for a while and Mother told him to go listen
and watch us. He came into the room and asked what we were up to. He
was trying to be friendly and was curious. Unfortunately this was such a
rare event it made us all very shy and afraid; we were afraid he wouldn't
approve of the silly stuff we'd been recording, we felt as if a harsh light had
suddenly been focused on us.

The next instant we all giggled and had a nonverbal agreement to take a
chance and let him listen to the tape—but he had very quickly picked up
on our resistance and he angrily stood and walked away. We knew his
feelings were hurt and we called back to him to come on, it was okay, we'd
let him listen, but he shook his head and kept on walking. We all felt awful
and couldn't undo the situation.

I think that very moment caused a rift between us that never healed.
Somehow we couldn't articulate how much we were pleased that he
wanted to share our game, or how embarrassed we felt that he'd think it
was too silly. We wanted to please him so much, to be close with him. It
really is a sad story, isn't it? But the thing was, our experience was that he
did find our adolescent preoccupations and games to be silly.

If a military brat feels guilty about a moment of missed connection—and who among us doesn't?—then imagine how a warrior
father must feel, particularly after retirement, as his thoughts inevitably turn to what might have been but wasn't, what could have been if
he, if they, had handled things only slightly differently. "Father guilt,"
a social worker once told me, "is a quality of life issue in the Navy."
And the Army, the Air Force, and the Marine Corps. And even if the

warrior successfully manages to force that guilt underground during most of his career, it often comes home to roost in retirement.

The thing is, a man who is out of touch with his feelings to begin with—as so many warriors are—may not even recognize his own guilt feelings for what they are. What he may feel, I speculate, is a combination of extreme discomfort that he doesn't seem to fit into his own family and extreme resentment about that fact, since he doesn't have a clue as to how this disagreeable situation came to be, much less his own role in it. From his point of view—and he may lack experience in acknowledging any other—he's been there for his family all along. When he's shut out, he feels double-crossed. And because his feelings of guilt and regret and longing don't look or sound like what they really are—they may be masked by alcoholism or authoritarianism or stoicism—his family is liable to persist in excluding him.

Coded Father Love

It's easy to see how warrior families find themselves locked into internal dramas of dysfunction and disintegration. So many family problems come down to failures of communication, and communication is all too often not a warrior family's strong suit. Feelings that need to be expressed are frequently kept secret; even if they are not secret they are denied; and even if they are not denied, the natural instinct is to be stoic rather than give them free expression.

Failed communication. Seemingly simple declarations a family longs to hear but that don't make it through: "I missed you"; "I wanted to be here with you, and felt awful that I couldn't be"; "Can we make some time to be together and catch up?"; "I want you to know that when I'm away at sea I think about you a lot"; "I'm home for only a short while and it's very important to me to have this time with you."

And the most important of all: "I love you." Simple words, straightforward, yet very, very hard for warriors to pronounce.

Why is it so hard for them? Partly it's because, as we've noted, warriors tend to be intensely uncomfortable with feelings; many even consider phrases such as "I love you" and "I miss you" to be so unmasculine it makes their skin crawl. It's clearly unrealistic to expect such men to suddenly receive enlightenment and reform their behavior, like a pasture of fierce, snorting bulls turning overnight into flower-sniffing Ferdinands.

"My father never had much affection to share with us," said the son of a Marine Corps sergeant who never used words of affection or allowed his children to touch him. "I don't know that he ever assumed

the father role. He was always a Marine and that superseded everything. To be a father, to him, was to be a DI."

Instead of expecting the impossible, it's worth examining the other
reason warriors avoid those phrases: Many of them actually believe the
words are redundant. Warriors tend to be nonverbal in the first place,
preferring action to words. For them it is natural to assume that by
supporting their families financially and by disciplining their kids as
they discipline their troops, they are showing love. Unfortunately, this
amounts to love delivered in code, which means the message may get
through only occasionally or it may never get through at all.

Military brats are sometimes well into adulthood before they are
able to decipher that code. And by that time the rift may be greater
than the son's or daughter's motivation to repair it.

"I really feel sorry for my father's second wife and stepsons," said the
Army daughter quoted earlier, whose father moved the stove in front of
the TV. "His notion of being a good father is being a good provider. In
this modern world, that doesn't cut it." She had broken the code, and
even come to understand how the family breakup was not just his
fault—but she was seemingly unwilling to take the first step to reclaim
the relationship.

Many warriors, for their part, don't wake up to the damage in their
families until retirement, when the Military Mission is finally out of
the picture. Very often it comes as a surprise to them. What follows,
depending on the family, is either a time of mutual recrimination or
an opportunity for belated bonding.

"I think my father was afraid to love his kids [while he was in the
military]," said an Air Force sergeant's son. "Now that he's retired, he's
starting to tell us things he never told us before. I never knew he loved
me until last year. He's retired now and gets mad when we don't write
him or call him—all this stuff we thought he never cared about." This
son said the first time he ever told his father that he loved him was the
preceding year, when the son was twenty-four years old. "And that was
on the phone," he said. "It felt so funny, I cried. I laughed. And the
first time *he* told me he loved me, I almost passed out. But he couldn't
say the words [out loud]—he wrote them in a letter."

Many warriors don't realize they are in for a really lonely time of it
when they retire. All those words left unsaid leave a painful vacuum
that swallows the warrior whole when the Military Mission is no longer
there to fill his life. The kids, now grown, long ago toughened themselves to his absence: Their letters don't reflect his presence in their
lives. When they call home and he answers, they ask to speak to their
mother.

To be sure, emotional withholding is not the only way warrior fathers waste their opportunities to bond with their children while they're growing up. Some fathers are outright abusive—something we examine in Chapter 7. And some are not exactly abusive, but they harass their children, pick fights, never seem to find anything positive to say, are generally antagonistic toward them. Is this a loving father? Not in the traditional sense. But yes, quite possibly a loving father—or at least one who cannot automatically be branded unloving. This is a point very difficult for civilians to grasp, at least in my experience. But military brats are familiar with the kind of father who lacks the skills to play his macho warrior role any differently—the sort who covers his own low self-esteem with brash and aggressive behavior, who is rigidly authoritarian at work and at home. For such men, harassment is not just a crude form of self-assertion, it is also a form of intimacy.

There is the example of *The Great Santini*. The film made from Pat Conroy's novel has been seen by a wide audience, including almost every military brat interviewed for this book. When I have asked civilians what they think of the father in *Santini*, a Marine Corps lieutenant colonel played to perfection by Robert Duvall (himself the son of a Navy admiral), they tell me that they are horrified by him and consider him abusive and unloving. Military brats, however, see him differently. They recognize Bull Meecham as a very familiar type— just the sort of brash, aggressive warrior mentioned above—and they are convinced that, despite his character flaws, brutal temper, and the undeniable damage he does to his children and his wife, he loves his family.

So at least on some level the coded message does get through, when we choose to acknowledge it. I recall a conversation with an Army brat, the son of a colonel. He described an authoritarian, alcoholic father who frequently set his children up for ridicule. The son said his father never praised him, only snapped at him with questions such as "Why can't you do better?" And yet, when I asked the son, "Do you think your father loved you?" the answer came swiftly.

"I think he loved all of us, yes."

"Would he say so?"

"No."

"Were *you* allowed to say so?"

"Sure. But we never did. He would say it to our mother, and she would say it to us."

Military brats may need to hear it from their fathers—I don't believe any child, from any subculture, is exempt from that need—but they learn not to expect it. There is a clear division of labor in the warrior family: The mother does all the "feeling" stuff, and the father does the rest. But the children don't necessarily conclude the father doesn't love them because of it—they just wish he would be more direct.

"We got different things from my father than from my mother," said the daughter of an Air Force lieutenant colonel. "My father taught respect and responsibility. My mother was the one showing the loving and the caring. He did that, too, but in his own way. He was the authoritarian; he ran the family pretty much like he ran his job. But my father, even though he didn't show any emotion, was telling [us] in his way that he did [love us]—by being the president of our PTA, by coming to our games." Although her words made it sound as though the message of love had gotten through, loud and clear, tears welled up in her eyes and spilled down her cheeks. She went on to say that her father, since retirement from the military, has been trying hard to establish himself emotionally in the lives of his seven children, and they have been encouraging him. "We keep telling our parents that it's never too late," she said.

The daughter of an Air Force colonel spoke of her father in similar terms, and of how she eventually came to understand the code in which he transmitted his love:

> My father was strict in his expectations and held very high moral and performance standards for us in terms of honesty, commitment, our studies—so that even when I resented his demands I also had to respect them. . . . I never feared his punishments as much as I dreaded letting him down. That was a terrible thing to endure, his anger or disappointment, I guess because I always secretly knew he really understood and approved of me. Basically, it seemed he loved us but he saw his main duty toward us to be disciplinary. It was difficult to converse with him unless I brought up questions about his career—the ones he could answer, the nonsecret stuff—or history or math, which were his interests.
>
> The other place we could connect was with my writing. He read what I wrote and praised it, taught me to edit my work and was encouraging of that. That alone made up for a lot of other lacking areas. I still remember in intimate detail the first time he read a story I'd written and realized I was a good writer. I was twelve. He spent several hours with me that night teaching me how to edit my work, going over every damned word in the piece with me. He was really stunned and excited about my skill. I recall feeling so elated, tremulous. I guess it was that I had found a key to gain his approving attention. Maybe that's why I stuck with writing all these years.

The Warrior Who Doesn't Return

Sometimes it happens that the negative spaces in the portrait of the warrior family consume the rest of the picture. This is the father absence that becomes permanent, the loss that hovers on the edge of possibility for every warrior family but becomes quite real for some.

"I can remember when I was in sixth grade, in Germany," said the son of an Air Force sergeant. "The father of one of my classmates flamed out. He was a pilot who stayed in the plane past when he should have, held it so it didn't come down on the village. He died.

"It was heroic, but that didn't help his son. I remember the kid, alone. I felt so sorry for him. Soon after that he disappeared from the class."

The loss of a father, irrevocable and forever, is of course devastating to any child anywhere. But there are some ways in which it may be worse for the military brat: It means the instant loss not only of the father, but of one's identity in the community, and indeed of the entire community and way of life. The family is not permitted to remain inside the Fortress once the warrior is gone. Just at the point where their need for support and consistency is greatest, they are in effect banished from the warrior society.

There is the story of a son we'll call Graham, whose father, a sergeant in the U.S. Army Special Forces, was declared Missing in Action on a secret mission to Laos in April 1961, in the earliest days of American intervention in Southeast Asia.[5] Graham was seven years old, an only child, and living with his mother at Fort Bragg, North Carolina, when the Army chaplain knocked on the door and brought them the news.

"They could have sent a letter through the mail and it would have been just as impersonal as that chaplain's visit," Graham recalled. "I remember he was a very quiet man, very structured in his approach. I sat there and listened to him tell my mother; I really didn't understand. And then my mother took me into another room and explained to me that my father was missing, and that doesn't mean he's dead, but that he's missing from his platoon and they were going to do everything they could to find him, that we'd just have to pray he'd be okay and he'd come home to us soon, but that we had no idea when that would be." That was the beginning of an endless nightmare for Graham and his mother.

First, of course, there was the shock. Because it was a secret mission, his father had not been permitted even to say goodbye when he left that February day, let alone tell his family where he was going or when he would be back. He just put on his uniform and left the house as usual, never, as it turned out, to return. "He didn't have any way of sharing with me where he was going," said Graham, "so I was pretty angry about it [when he left] because I did not know he was going. I had been very shy around that time; I was asthmatic and that made me extremely nervous. My father had helped me overcome my shyness and develop some self-esteem, and all of a sudden he's gone. And then [after the chaplain's visit] the fact was he might never come home to help me grow up into a man. So in one sense I was very bitter, and in another sense I was just a sad child."

Then there was the loss of his friends, neighbors, and the structure of military life when he and his mother were told to move off post and into civilian life.

On top of that, they could not even fully express their grief to those who might have offered comfort. "For a period of two years we couldn't even talk to our family about it," Graham said,

> we were under a lot of scrutiny, a lot of pressure. We had to attend meetings with other wives and family members of men who were missing, and we were constantly drilled [in what we could and could not say]. It was sort of like interrogation, and it was not comfortable. I imagine if you could have measured the stress level, over a period of time it probably would be enough to cause heart problems. I'm sorry I can't give you more details, but to be honest with you, I try to forget about that part of my life. There's nothing but pain, severe loneliness, alienation. I was trying to deal with the fact I might never have a father again. I wasn't sure where he was or why he was there or who was really going to try and get him home.

To make matters worse, Graham's mother, who had been extremely dependent on her husband, fell apart immediately and essentially never recovered. She cried "for weeks and weeks and weeks," he said, and couldn't make any decisions. At the age of seven he was thrust into a role of authority in the family which he could not handle but which, because of his mother's inability to cope, he could not reject. So, on top of the loss of his father, the loss of his community, and the loss of his mother as a functional parent, Graham lost his childhood as well.

A huge amount of loss, none of which he was free to mourn as he needed to: The original commandment not to divulge any information about his father's status, for fear of jeopardizing his chances of return, became thoroughly ingrained. This was enforced Fortress stoicism carried to its extreme, and it exacted its cost, over time, in Graham's detachment from people, his reluctance to share emotions even with his wife and children. "I was always afraid that if you let yourself love someone very dearly, the more chance there is of your total demise if that person were to disappear or die," he said. "So you do not let your guard down to show a lot of affection, and that protects you."

The loss of his father has been as real in Graham's life as any tragedy could be; but because of his father's continued MIA status, that loss has been impossible for him to resolve through grieving. There has never been a funeral, never any goodbye, any closing of that chapter.

Because his father is MIA, Graham remains a prisoner of war, locked in an emotional Vietnam which he can neither win nor abandon. To give up on the issue, Graham has reasoned, would be to give up on the father he loved and who loved him, the father who was the most positive presence in his life, who continues to represent all that is good and worthwhile. So the issue continues to dominate his life, influencing his decisions, casting its shadow over all his relationships. Not one to do anything halfway—"I learned in the military that you do something a hundred and ten percent or you don't do it at all"—Graham has been a high-profile activist in the POW/MIA cause. He has traveled to Southeast Asia in a fruitless search for information. And he has even taken radical action to keep the issue alive in the public mind. He is driven by love for his missing father, by a passionate hatred of politicians, whom he characterizes as fickle and self-serving, and by a need for answers to finally free himself from the painful limbo in which his life has been held.

"I am still torn very deeply by this issue," he said,

> to the point that it rocks the boat a lot. There are constant emotional highs and lows, a roller coaster effect that is hard for me to deal with. I really don't feel I'll be able to stabilize my feelings until the issue has been resolved. . . .
>
> I just wish my father had stayed around. I would be a lot more stable, a lot more of a family man, if my dad had just been there to put his hand on my shoulder and steer me in the right direction. . . . My father was fantastic. He was an authoritarian—that's what military people are all about—and a strict disciplinarian, but he was loving. I liked him. I loved him. I was proud of the way he raised me in the short period of time I was around him.
>
> If I could be like my father, it would be the greatest tribute in my life.

THE FORTRESS MOTHER

It is easy to overlook the role of the military wife and mother in examining the drama of the Fortress family. The Fortress is essentially a society for and about men; the family, too, takes on this character. If the Fortress mother does her job as she is "supposed" to do it in this extremely patriarchal world, she is the family's unseen hand: gentle guide, inspiration, facilitator, nurturer. She mutes the extremes of Fortress life, softens transitions, placates the stern and sometimes frightening father, plays peacemaker, and offers the children their one sure haven of emotional warmth inside the severely stoic world of the Fortress.

But if anything goes wrong with this picture, havoc is unleashed. The mother might abuse alcohol, or drugs, or food. She might lash out at her family, or she might lose her sanity. And if the mother cannot hold the line against the pressures of life inside the Fortress, there is much less chance the children will be able to.

The Navy likes to call the wife's role "the toughest job in the Navy." That's true—for the Navy and for all the other armed services—in that the wife lives with at least as much pressure as the warrior but, as an adjunct presence inside the Fortress, derives less gratification. Although seemingly frank and sympathetic, the comment is made by Navy brass as a pat on the wives' collective back and little more. None of the armed services pass muster when it comes to providing real support to those who hold "the toughest job"; programs and outreach to wives and families still do not begin to meet the need. And at the time the interviewees for this book were growing up, there was practically no support at all.

The kind of woman best adapted to the role of warrior wife, both then and now—for some things about the Fortress never change—is conventional in values, taste, and behavior, and fully willing to play a support role in her husband's career—but she is feisty enough to have a firm sense of self and her own set of interests. She is capable, confident, decisive, flexible. She has a good sense of humor. She likes change and adapts well to it. She's outgoing and comfortable with the constant ebb and flow of people. She enjoys taking challenges in stride.

Unfortunately, the role of Fortress wife and mother doesn't come with a job description, much less a warning label. To be sure, there are women who fit the mold perfectly—or grow to fit it—and are consequently able to do a great deal to ease their children through Fortress life. But there are also women who wake up to find themselves inside the Fortress and wedded to a life that is difficult and demanding beyond their imaginings.

"[Marrying into the military] was a big shock for my mother," said the daughter of an Air Force general.

She came from a very gifted, musical family of California pioneers. They all had great senses of humor and great faith. They studied music and spent their evenings together.

What happened was, my mother was bowled over by my handsome father. His whole world was taking risks. He became a pilot, back when the planes were wood frame. But the hard drinking, the gambling, the smoking, the challenging one another at parties . . . my mother had no idea what this was. My father was unmusical, uncultured, loud. Drinking, flying, balling, drinking . . . that's what [the men] all wanted. They were all handsome. They were all very physical, and did things fast, hard, competitively.

Who knows what appealed to her in all this? She's told me the early years were very hard. But they were dashing, physically irresistible men. There were a lot of Texas debutantes in that generation who were cultured and well educated who were falling for them.

I can understand that, but I can't understand why she stayed. Maybe I never will.

There are wives, too, who adapt so poorly to Fortress life that the marriage, and sometimes the parenting, turn dysfunctional. "The work-oriented, compulsive male married to a dependent, compliant, phobic female" is the description of a common pathological situation in military families, according to two military physicians writing in a professional journal:

He may be a drill instructor, mess sergeant, or brigade commander who has difficulties with heterosexual intimacy and playful regression with children. He uses his work setting and all-male recreations as the only source of gratification. The wife's needs, by default, must be met in the extended military family or with her children, both of which can be adaptive responses or may lead to the following pathology. She is frequently seen in medical clinics, pathetically pleading for relief from a loneliness she cannot articulate. She may become symbiotically involved with her children, forcing them into a premature adulthood to care for her or keeping them in a perpetual childhood so that she can continue to care for them.[6]

This pathology is essentially what happened in Graham's family, according to Graham, although his mother was pushed over the edge into dysfunction only after his father was declared MIA.

And there are wives who are a good match for their husbands and who are generally capable people, but who are gradually worn down by the stress of military life. One daughter of an Air Force colonel brought a small stack of family photographs with her to the interview for this book. First she showed me photographs of her mother from her school years and the early years of her marriage: strikingly lovely, with beautifully arched eyebrows, large brilliant eyes, oval face, small bow mouth. Then I saw pictures as the years went by. In her thirties, still beautiful. But by her forties she was overweight, unkempt, with an indifferent hairstyle and, more noticeable than anything else, an unsmiling face with an expression of defeat. Her daughter said she wears the same expression in countless other pictures.

"I saw the progress of the disease [alcoholism] in my mom," the daughter said. "The bitterness, the hatred. Recently my attitude softened toward her; she was able to talk about her drinking. She said the drinking was about the anger and resentment she felt through trying to be the perfect Air Force wife." Still, through it all the marriage survived, although the family is still struggling with serious problems, primarily in the lives of the children.

But if the Fortress has been a destructive force in the lives of some women, it has also been a strengthening one. Even those women whose families became dysfunctional have often been able to find new strengths and abilities in themselves in the crucible of warrior life— and as far as their children are concerned, as we shall see, those strengths are not wasted, even if the family falls apart. Children observe, internalize, imitate.

What are some of the lessons we learn from our Fortress mothers? Among other things, they show us that even when the situation is bad—problems abound, loneliness prevails, self-esteem plummets—it is still possible to rally, to deepen one's understanding, clarify one's vision, develop new strengths. It is as the Buddhists say: a hidden blessing in every adversity. Raising their children on the move, coping with loneliness, worry, a tight budget, and far away from family and friends, Fortress mothers become practiced at finding the hidden blessing. Many of the stories military brats relate about their mothers reflect such themes: mother overcoming a paralyzing sense of helplessness to discover her own competence; mother finding solace from difficult problems by developing spiritually; mother preserving a sense of accomplishment through countless uprootings by developing portable talents such as artistic or musical skill.

A full portrait of the Fortress mother would include the roles mothers anyplace tend to play: nurturer, teacher, guide, counselor, friend. But there are three roles in particular that Fortress mothers are called upon to perform so often within the family that they come to characterize her part in this play within the play. All three are illustrated in the passage from *The Great Santini* quoted at the start of this chapter.

- The go-between. *One thing you're not keeping in mind, Ben. . . . Your father loves you very much.*
- The spinner of myths. *How much he wants the best for his children. How much he loves us all and sacrifices for us all.*
- The partisan. *It starts out with you leaving him* [Ben says to his mother]. *Then it ends with you telling me all his good points.*

And all of these roles in their own way mirror the number-one function of the Fortress mother: to be the link between the macho male world of the warrior and the opposite, feminine world of home and children. It is a difficult job, requiring endless flexibility, manipulative skill, finely honed intuition, and the sense of balance of a tightrope walker.

Fortress Mother as Go-Between

Quite a few military brats, particularly those from troubled families, speak of being keenly aware of their mothers' powerlessness as they were growing up. It is true, certainly, that consensus management is generally not the style of authoritarian warriors; the wife may be second in command, but she still takes orders. And in truly dysfunctional situations where the father is perhaps alcoholic or abusive, the Fortress mother has scarcely more status than a child.

But she is never truly powerless.

Her power is qualitatively different from her husband's, but for that very reason she can wield it as she wills, without fear of usurpation. Where his power is concrete, hers is abstract, a fluid thing that eludes him completely. The more artful the Fortress mother, the more she can use her power to influence the emotional climate of the family and even orchestrate events or head them off.

The power of the Fortress mother derives in large part from her children. By virtue of their existence she is delivered into a strategic role only she can fill: Her children look to her as liaison to their father; her husband looks to her as liaison to his children. She has the power to change her alliances at will, as the situation demands, acting as advocate one day, adversary the next. She has the power to intervene as keeper of the peace, or to marshal her forces if she wants to wage war. She holds the position of official interpreter for the family, licensed to translate the words and actions of father or child into language the other can understand. And since she is the one and only interpreter, her reports are vested with absolute credibility; she can color them as she pleases, to suit her purpose, subtly altering the way one party sees the other. Many a court vizier would envy such uncontested power. And many a warrior family teems with palace intrigue.

One daughter of an alcoholic and emotionally abusive Army sergeant was able to speak to both the positive and the negative effects of her mother's power. "All my life my mother has run interference and interpreted my father's behavior in a positive way," she said. "Now she still keeps my relationship with him activated, calling to remind me I haven't seen him in a while. If she wasn't around, my father and I probably wouldn't even have the relationship we have." On the other hand, she noted, while her mother's manipulations have been instrumental in keeping the family together, they have also shaped a family architecture that has effectively walled off father and child and kept the mother firmly in the center of power.

"My mother never allowed my father to discipline me, because he had such a violent temper with his mouth," the daughter said. "She always intervened and did the discipline. So of course it got to be that he was the bad guy and my mom and I were aligned against him. And we had to kind of 'take care of Daddy, because you know how he is.'

"My mother is very manipulative with my father," she continued. "She knew exactly how to get around him to get what she needed. It was how she survived and I did too. It was not until I got into early adulthood that I realized it wasn't just him, it was both of them. But [the manipulation] has paid off for her; they're still married, and he's mellowed with age."

Fortress Mother as Spinner of Myths

As interpreters of language and events, Fortress mothers have almost unlimited range to their power. With enough skill they are not only the secret rulers of the present moment and the architects of the family's future, they are also to a large degree the keepers of the family's past, interpreting family history for everyone else and in effect reshaping it as they like.

"There is one thing that messes with my mind more than anything else," said the daughter of an Army major. "I can't tolerate it when people change the past on me. I have lost trust in certain people because of it. My mother will look me in the face and say 'I don't remember that,' when I know damn well she remembers it."

It may be that all mothers have selective memories. But Fortress mothers develop uncanny editorial skill, owing to their need to justify the magnitude of their own sacrifice to the warrior society. Fortress mothers give up a lot for the sake of the Fortress: childhood friends, close relationships with relatives, the possibility of a career of their own. In return, they receive little recognition and sometimes, despite their best efforts, the marriage fails. But even sitting amid the wreckage of a splintered family, no one will cleave to the myth of a happy, unblemished family history like the Fortress mother.

The same Army daughter told a story illustrating her mother's role as revisionist family historian. It seems that during the four years the family was stationed in Europe, they took every opportunity they could to travel and camp, always in the company of another military family with whom the parents were best friends. There are a couple of thick photo albums filled with pictures of those trips, the daughter said, featuring the same group of smiling faces in front of one famous landmark after another.

Later it became known that the whole time they were in Europe, the father of this family and the wife in the other were carrying on an affair. That episode, added to a stack of other festering issues, contributed to an eventual divorce. But many years later, the mother still cherishes those photo albums, still leafs through them to reminisce about the trips as though nothing existed to mar the happy memories. Every picture is still in place. And in every group photo the head of the "other woman" is carefully snipped out.

She is hardly the only Fortress mother to mutilate the facts in order to keep the myth intact. In a way it is reminiscent of the officer who said to a newsman during the Vietnam War, "It became necessary to destroy the town to save it."[7]

Fortress mothers are so good at shaping family myths, in fact, that dismantling those myths becomes a major project for military brats who in adulthood seek to get at the truths of their childhoods.

"One of the things I would rage about when I went into therapy," said the son of a Navy commander, "was that I was raised for a 'Leave It to Beaver' family that never came off. That was the myth and mystique of my family. I can still remember my mother in high-heeled shoes, pushing the vacuum cleaner." According to this son, his family never remotely approximated the model of an intact, cohesive, and overtly loving family that "Leave It to Beaver" epitomized, although his mother did her best to convince everyone that it did.

The same son, embittered by his father's physical and emotional absence from his life, spoke of how he came to believe in a father of mythic stature to fill the painful void. "I had a notion of a superhero male, not macho but courageous, like a Superman or a Batman, that was generated by my mom in his absence, as a way of coping: that he was a good man, that he was doing the best he could, that he missed us all, that he loved us dearly. But you know, I never quite realized that all those messages really came from her *as if they came from him*. She *created* an image of a father for me which had no holes in it whatsoever—until I went to the Naval Academy, and I had to reconcile the fact that he didn't write me at all, and the fact that I can remember doing only one thing alone with my father in my entire life, and that was playing ball with him once when I was fourteen. That was it."

The realization that they've been had, that they've been suckered into trusting a version of reality that was fundamentally false, enrages some military brats when they finally come to it. But later, in calmer moments, they often figure out that for them and for their mothers, these myths were a form of sustenance in a life of emotional hardship. Warrior families frequently have so little in the way of emotional provisions that they need the myths to see them through. It is part of the Fortress mother's job to spin them.

Myth spinning is one of the ways the Fortress mother keeps the family together; unfortunately, it is also one of the ways the mother acts as an enabler of family dysfunction, denying or covering up her husband's alcoholism, child abuse, or wife abuse.

Fortress Mother as Partisan

The role of sole interpreter, negotiator, myth spinner, ambassador, and consultant means the Fortress mother, demure and conventional to all appearances, is in fact a power broker to be reckoned with. But as secretly gratifying as that power might be, it has a very high price. The Fortress mother is not just a dealer; she is also a player. And that means that there are inevitably times when she must choose sides. Because she was never in a removed, neutral position to begin with, and in fact has an enormous amount of investment in both her husband and her children, the middle position can be extremely uncomfortable. And if there is one thing the Fortress mother learns early, it is that neither side will let her off easy. In fact she will be tested to the limit.

"We always thought she was a little bit of a traitor when she took his side," said an Army sergeant's daughter. "Because we knew we had her loyalty. We probably tested her loyalty by provoking situations in which it would have to be clear what side she was on."

Both sides do such testing. And while this happens quite normally in civilian families as well, it may be that in the intensely partisan and frequently polarizing environment in which Fortress families find themselves, it happens to an uncommon degree.

This is most in evidence in troubled families, of course, where loyalty is a particularly loaded issue. The Fortress mother is under heavy pressure to side first one way, then the other. What she is doing is fulfilling her mission as she sees it: to keep the family together at any price. But that mission, so obvious to her, is sometimes lost on the children, who look to her as their only avenue of relief. In warrior families where the father is abusive or threatening, the mother might be relied upon to take up the cause of the children against him—but, as the children find out, there are real limits to her rebellion. For no matter what furious words she hurls in her children's defense, no matter how she tries to shield them, the fact is that every day she remains inside the Fortress is a day she has ultimately chosen to side with her husband. This is one of the biggest question marks military brats from dysfunctional families harbor about their past. *If she was really on our side, what were we doing in that situation? Why did she stay?*

"I'll tell you a really horrible story," said the daughter of an Air Force general.

> A story I've had to talk about a lot with my therapist. When I was about two and a half and my brother was five, my father brought a loaded pistol home. He was drunk. And he said he wanted to show my brother and me how dangerous guns were. My mother said, "You're crazy. Put it away." And he said, "I'm going to shoot this off into the fireplace and show these kids what this is." We're talking about little tiny kids.
>
> My mother started crying and said, "Don't do this." She picked me up, and she tried to get my brother, but she couldn't carry both of us at the same time. She reached out to try and pull him, but she couldn't control that, so she started up the stairs with me. I can still remember: She was crying, and my brother was standing there looking up with his big brown eyes. And then *BANG! KAPOW!* The gun goes off.
>
> Why that woman didn't take her children and go home to her mother, I've never figured out. Why she didn't say, "That's it. It's over, I don't care what you do, I'm not going to have a man coming home and shooting off a gun in the house." I've never figured out what stopped her from taking control right then.

I can't understand why she stayed. It is a question that in stable, functional Fortress families never need be asked. But in the troubled families, the ones that faced alcoholism, child abuse, spouse abuse, it is a question the children harbor all their lives. The answer in some ways is unique to each family; but most of these mothers, if held to account, would probably get around to saying the same thing.

There is of course fear of the unknown, which causes many women, military or civilian, to stay with a bad situation that is familiar rather than venture into poverty and uncertainty with their children in tow.

But there is something else, too, that helped keep them inside the Fortress. Something that military brats still probing their own hurt sometimes overlook.

Despite everything our mothers faced, life inside the Fortress had its compensations for them. It gave them status, a satisfying social life, a fulfilling sense of being part of a larger mission. These things, so much a part of our childhood landscape that we tend to discount them, are not insignificant at all, but integral to our mothers' sense of self. And the very challenges of Fortress life, while cumulatively contributing to major problems, at the same time pushed our mothers to grow in ways they hadn't expected—and they, having come to value this side of themselves, could be expected to harbor a measure of gratitude to the life that brought it out in them.

They stayed in defiance of the bad, in celebration of the good, and in the hope that in the long run all their sacrifice would be proven worthwhile. As with so many other things in Fortress life, their attitude was a mix of courage, stubborn determination, and an enormous amount of denial.

It would be a serious underestimation of a Fortress mother, however, to conclude that her ability to deny the hardships of that life—and their effects on her children—was chiefly attributable to some kind of character weakness. In many cases the decision to stay in the face of stressful conditions and family dysfunction was based on a cold-blooded assessment of her options. What help did civilian society offer women in her predicament? There isn't much help or sympathy *now*; certainly there was far less then. What skills did she have? What means of support for herself and her children? In some cases military wives had been disowned by their families for marrying into the military in the first place. In others, the passage of years had so loosened old community ties that hometown acceptance of a divorcée and her children was not a sure bet.

Military mothers in crumbling marriages have frequently found themselves up against a wall when they tried to resolve this dilemma: On one side is continued emotional hardship in the warrior society, but with guaranteed financial support, social identity, social status, and—provided the father is not abusive—a relatively safe environment for their children. On the other side, in the unfamiliar territory of civilian life, these mothers might be able to find relief from certain kinds of emotional pain—but at the price of financial insecurity, no guaranteed system of moral support, and the burden of wondering if they were doing the right thing by their children.

Complicating the Fortress mother's decision process is the fact that in many cases she does not have even a single confidant to help her think through her situation. For as every wife of a professional warrior knows, it would be recklessly foolhardy even to hint at marital discord inside the Fortress, where it could show up on her husband's efficiency report and quite possibly sideline his career. That, of course, would torpedo any chance of reconciliation, not to mention security.

Surely, under such circumstances, it is no wonder so many military mothers contemplating that decision elected to remain inside the Fortress. Nor is it surprising that, having decided to stay, many of them retreated into full-scale denial to minimize their pain.

That's not all there is to be said on the subject, however.

A great many Fortress mothers in troubled families stayed in that life because of the security they felt it provided them, in recognition of their service. Like their warrior husbands, they believed that in serving their country—and the military had always insisted that is what they were doing—they had earned not only a sense of personal pride but the gratitude of their country as well, in the tangible form of financial security both inside the Fortress and following retirement from it. Where the wives were concerned, however, that proved to be a false illusion.

When marriages finally disintegrated after husbands retired from the military, ex-wives found they were not entitled to any part of their husbands' retired pay as alimony[8]—and since many of the wives, in line with service tradition, had never held paying jobs but had devoted themselves to volunteer work and social activities benefiting the military, they had no income of their own. Women who had helped their husbands through thirty-year careers suddenly found themselves adrift in a strange civilian sea, deprived of status, community, identity, all medical and other benefits, forced to live in strapped circumstances and facing a future of increasing insecurity.

For these women, as their children testify, that fact was every bit as painful as the failed marriage. It was a rejection, a nullification of their service and of them. From their point of view, considering the very different message the military had been careful to give them through their husbands' entire careers, it amounted to a betrayal. The shock of this bitter realization reverberated over the years through thousands of splintered military families.

Eventually, thanks to pressure groups of ex-spouses and the efforts of Representative Patricia Schroeder (D-Colo.), who championed the legislation, as well as of Representatives G. William Whitehurst (R-Va.) and Kent R. Hance (D-Tex.) and Senators Dennis DeConcini (D-Ariz.) and Roger Jepson (R-Iowa), Congress moved to step in and begin rectifying the situation. The Uniformed Services Former Spouses' Protection Act (Public Law 97-252) was passed by Congress in 1982. This law, among other things, permits disposable military retired pay to be considered as property in divorce settlements; payments of the allotment of retired pay may be made directly to the former spouse by the military if the marriage overlapped the period of military service by at least ten years.[9]

But for tens of thousands of military brats, the memory of the way our mothers were demeaned by the warrior society they served remains one of the more disturbing legacies of Fortress life we have to sort out. Probably no other single aspect of our experience has been so directly revealing of the underlying nature of the Fortress. At a time when civilian society is moving toward egalitarian treatment of the sexes, the Fortress remains a bastion of patriarchy, a society which in countless ways affirms men and all things traditionally masculine, and undervalues or ignores women and all things traditionally feminine. And that, despite superficial changes the military undertakes from time to time, is a situation that we can expect to remain essentially the same for the foreseeable future.

This fact of life inside the Fortress, as we shall see, has strong implications for both the daughters and the sons of warriors.

CHAPTER 4

DAUGHTERS OF WARRIORS

"Am I a Meecham, Dad? Can girls be real Meechams? Girls without jump shots. Or am I a simple form of Meecham? Like in biology. Mary Anne, the one-celled Meecham. Or maybe I'm higher that that. Maybe I'm a coelenterate Meecham."

"Yeah, Mary Anne, you're a simple form of Meecham. You're a girl. Now scram. I'm starting to lose my temper. I'm gonna give you a break and just pretend you're not here. I'm not gonna listen to you or answer when you speak," Bull said, hiding himself behind newsprint once more.

Mary Anne began a slow, arduously clumsy dance that began to accelerate as she circumnavigated her father's easy chair. What began as a dramatically delusory ploy to recapture her father's attention turned into a sad tarantella of girlish desperation. She began to sing as she danced around him. "Hello, Dad," she sang, tickling beneath his chin as she circled him. "Hello, Dad, it's me, your invisible daughter. You can't see me, but I'm always here. I'm always here, Daddy-poo. I can't shoot a hook shot. Or a jump shot. I can't drive down the lane or score the winning bucket. But I'm here anyway. Yoo hoo. Dad. It's me. It's the Phantom. Yes, it's Mary Anne the phantom girl . . . always here hovering about, unseen, unheard, and unspoken to. Dad? Dad?"

—The Great Santini

Roxanne, daughter of an Army sergeant, summed it up well. "If you think of *military*," she said, "you think of *male*. The military is about men. Women are just an accessory, a way to keep a man good at his job. *How does a little female child relate to this world?*"

It is the question every military daughter faces every day she spends inside the Fortress, and one she may well ask herself the rest of her life—for it is a question without a ready answer, more in the nature of an impossible task assigned by the wicked king in a fairy tale, or a riddle out of the mouth of a sphinx.

A riddle indeed. For the military daughter must figure out how, in her femaleness, she is valued by her warrior father and the warrior society he represents. A girl-child asking affirmation from the ultimate patriarchy.

Is this different from the task faced by her civilian sisters? In kind, no. In degree, very much so. The basic need for approval from the father may be the same, and so may the challenge posed by a culture dominated by males and male values. But the world of the military daughter, the world of the Fortress, is inherently more intense and exaggerated. It is also more isolated. And that is why the military daughter's search for a positive self-image will be lonely, and long, and of uncertain outcome.

THE WRONG SEX

When the young daughter of a warrior looks about her for clues, what can she learn from the adult women of the Fortress?

They are there in numbers, to be sure: wives, civilian employees, and to an increasing extent, women military personnel. But all are there to support men, who are the "real" warriors, the ones who will see combat and realize the purpose of the community. Even the professional military woman—no matter how sharp—is a second-class citizen in this world of real or potential combat, in which women can never be central players.

So what can the message be for the military daughter, who never asked to be there in the first place? She finds herself born into a society that has little interest in helping her grow and define herself as a woman. This is a man's world, and she is, at best, a son manqué. Much of the work of her childhood will be to shut out the thought that she is somehow trespassing, as though she had been born Off Limits.

To be sure, women are very valuable to the military in their support role. But the message is clear. Women are tolerated inside the Fortress on one all-encompassing condition: In appearance, dress, speech, and behavior a woman must at all times reflect her complete acceptance of the ultimate patriarchy and its implications for women. By that rule any woman inside the Fortress is automatically an accomplice in her own devaluation—whether she is there by choice, as professional or wife, or whether she is there as a daughter, which implies no choice at all.

Within the warrior society, the expectations for a woman are clear enough. She should be beautiful and feminine, thus styling herself as the gratifying object of men's desires, and be dutiful, thus exalting the male system by her servitude. In both cases she is living out male definitions of what it is to be female, and to the extent she accepts these, her growth and individuality are limited.

This sad message of seemingly unavoidable limitation speaks to the military daughter from the heart of her world. Her father commands it. Her mother personifies it. To be female is to be . . . what? Even in the happiest, most closely knit of military families, with the most approving and loving of fathers, the young military daughter daily absorbs a powerful lesson: A female has value only as she is defined by the male. And she will be defined by the male world only in terms of how she can support or reward it. The daughter who wants to know if there is anything beyond this is left staring at her own question marks.

From birth, then, the military daughter faces twin imperatives of Beauty and Duty. And that is her tragic dilemma. To fail at either is to invite the most severe rejection. To succeed at either, however, exacts an equally great sacrifice: It invites alienation from the self, because neither role is of her own choosing, her own making.

What will she do: "succeed" and be alienated, or "fail" and be rejected? As far as the Fortress is concerned, there is no in-between. Shades of gray do not exist here. Once inside the Fortress, one is either right or wrong, for or against, ally or enemy.

From the outset the military daughter is caught in a dilemma with no easy answers—all the more disconcerting because this is a society in which one doesn't ask questions.

NOW YOU SEE HER, NOW YOU DON'T

Put another way, a daughter of the Fortress finds herself with a visibility problem. Born the wrong sex in a man's world, she has trouble coming into focus for the warriors whose recognition she seeks.

If, like Mary Anne in *The Great Santini*, she doesn't measure up in the categories of Beauty and Duty, the penalty is swift and total: She is damned to invisibility.

If, on the other hand, she succeeds at the twin imperatives, about the best she can hope for is an occasional nod of approval that she fits so neatly into a safe, accepted definition of femaleness. If this is visibility, it is the visibility of a person wearing camouflage fatigues under cover of night.

In fact, to be a daughter inside the Fortress is to be a kind of hovering spook: a weightless creature without power, without presence, without context, whose color is camouflage and whose voice is unheard.

Ask any daughter of the military what she learned growing up about what was expected of her as a woman, and the Beauty/Duty indoctrination begins to emerge.

Leigh, now in her forties, is the only daughter of an Air Force general who played a prominent role in World War II for the Army Air Corps. "I always got the feeling my father was genuinely disappointed in me, because I'm small and I was never beautiful. My mother is extremely beautiful, and my father was extremely handsome, and I think they thought any product of their union was just going to dazzle the world. My brother's a very good-looking guy, but I was this squatty thing that came along with buck teeth and one eye that turned in and hair with no body, and I was so tiny that when I was nine years old people thought I was four. I always got the feeling I just wasn't up to snuff. Because if you're going to be a woman you've got to be beautiful and you've gotta have big boobs and painted fingernails."

Michelle's father, an Army colonel, never told her anything about desirable qualities in a woman. "But I got the idea," she says bitterly. "Subservience. My mom was like that always. She gave in to him, always."

Claire, daughter of an Army sergeant, gleaned a similar idea. The role of a woman, she knew, "was to be available for the man, be in the kitchen, and have a son who could carry on the name."

Military fathers tend to be authoritarian. As we saw in Chapter 1, some are drawn to the military because they are authoritarian by nature, while others are heavily influenced by the profession itself. But there are degrees of authoritarianism. Some fathers fit the authoritarian profile in some respects but not others. Some mitigate the effect of their rigid control by mixing in positive attention and fatherly affection. The fathers who are the most extreme authoritarians are those who are sadly alienated from their own feminine side, who have repressed the creative, the feeling, and the spontaneous in themselves to the degree they are rigid, negative, emotionally barren, highly controlling, and even abusive.

If the father-daughter relationship is characterized by control, terrible damage results. To win the approval she needs, the daughter in effect enslaves herself to her father's will; yet no matter how diligently she works to please him, he seems unsatisfied. Somehow she is never able to prove herself.

One variation on the visibility problem is when the authoritarian warrior overlooks his daughter's actual performance and focuses instead on his fantasized fears of what the daughter could do as she grows older and more able to act outside his control. The prospect of her autonomy threatens him, for he believes that whatever she does reflects on him. She may not know her power, but he does, deep in his gut: While his daughter will never be able to add honor to his name—not as a son could—she is fully capable of tarring it with one false step. Or so he imagines. A true authoritarian feels he cannot trust anyone, not even his own superobedient, approval-seeking daughter.

A scene from my own relationship with my father is a case in point. It marked the very last moment of my childhood, when I was eighteen years old and preparing to leave for college.

My mother and I were busy all that morning, packing my things and attending to last-minute details. She was probably feeling anxious, even a little sad, but she covered it over with the genuine excitement she felt for me on that big day. I, however, was subdued and had difficulty rising to the occasion. My father was a particularly ominous presence in the house that morning; I wasn't sure what his mood portended, but I sensed it was not good. For hours he had not stirred from his chair in front of the television set, where he sat slumped, scowling blackly. It was not yet afternoon, but there was no telling how much he'd already had to drink. My mother and I instinctively fell silent each time we passed his chair; in invisibility there is at least a measure of safety.

Finally, sensing the tasks were nearing their end, my father found me in the hallway and said there was something he wanted to tell me before we left. He led me outside the house to the front lawn to say it, which I still find odd. As I followed him, I hadn't a clue as to what it could be, good news or bad, but I remember feeling guardedly hopeful. Was this a change of heart? Was he softening in the face of this momentous occasion? Was it possible I was about to hear the first words of fatherly advice and encouragement I had ever received from him?

He turned to me, gave me a steely look, and said, "You know all those guns I've got in there in the gun cabinet?" I nodded. "You know I keep them loaded?" I nodded. Then he said coldly, slowly, and very succinctly, "If I ever hear of you getting pregnant, or taking LSD, I'll . . . *blow* . . . *your* . . . *head* . . . *off.*" Then he went back into the house.

What I felt at the time was not fear but anger—anger at the affront, anger at its absurdity. I had been the perfectly socialized officer's daughter: obedient, studious, high-achieving, well mannered, conservative in thought and deed, never a moment's trouble to my parents. Clearly all my efforts to live up to what I thought he wanted me to be were for nought; he didn't give me his approval and he didn't give me his trust.

It was years before I related that incident to anyone, but not because

I felt I had to hide it. I simply didn't see anything very remarkable in it; at the time I was ignorant enough to suppose that a great many fathers sent their children off to college in that manner. It was maddening, but surely not that uncommon, I thought. In any case, it was certainly typical of my father. In the context of our family history, it was not an incident that particularly stood out.

Now, many years later, I see it differently. As a parent myself, I find it both astonishing and tragic that anyone could bid goodbye to his child in that manner. As my father's daughter, I deplore the pain he carried within him that he never understood, and that caused him to be so reckless with those he loved. As a journalist interested in psychological legacies, I see alcoholism at work, and rigid authoritarianism, and a value system that, sadly for all concerned, renders females invisible.

What the authoritarian warrior-father dispenses to his daughter is best described as degrees of visibility. For all that I tried, I had never been particularly visible to my father. Probably my impending departure from his house and his control made me briefly more visible to him, and it must have been painful: My father, deep down under his dictatorial manner and his alcohol addiction, was not without sensitivity. It had to have hurt to realize he had botched his opportunity to know his daughter, to express his love and receive it in kind. When he made his threat, it was to cast aside his own pain at having made me invisible. And it was couched in the only terms he knew: to make me even more invisible than I already was—the metaphor, which he may not have meant metaphorically, of blowing my head off.

In the relationship between father and daughter, the father's attention is nearly everything. At its most positive, when he grants her both visibility and approval, the father's attention is his gift and his guide to his beloved daughter. At its worst, when the father is abusive, or in its absence, when he makes her invisible, it can mean her undoing.

Sometimes, especially in a household where the feminine is not valued, an authoritarian warrior uses his power to negate his daughter both through negative attention and through ignoring her.

The following story is of one military daughter caught in that classic trap: All her life she has felt either painfully visible or painfully invisible to the father whose approval she craves.

Georgia's Story: The Disobedient Daughter

Georgia is the oldest child of a Marine colonel. A classic authoritarian who even gave his family surprise inspections, her father was also an alcoholic who came home drunk every Friday night from the officers' club, where he religiously attended Happy Hour with his fellow pilots. Even when drunk, he would rarely lose his temper. An extremely controlled as well as controlling person, it was his way to totally repress his emotions, even to delivering insults in a monotone. During his lengthy assignments away from the family, including tours in Korea and Vietnam, Georgia felt both relieved at his absence and guilty for feeling that way. Her mother was a kind, submissive woman who adored her husband, accepted his behavior, and rarely defended herself or her children against his often brutal verbal put-downs.

From the beginning, Georgia remembers, her father labeled her "disobedient." Always critical of her, he began to harass her about her weight when she was ten years old. It became the central issue of their relationship.

"I was within normal range until I hit puberty," she says. "But even before that my weight was watched very carefully. What I learned to do was stay out of my dad's way, but it was very hard not to be within his reach and notice." He imposed strict regulations on Georgia and supervised her himself, even to approving the contents of her lunch box. Most nights she was not permitted to join the family in dessert. On holidays when candy was given, hers was rationed. There were special exercise programs which he designed and oversaw. And her father weighed her every three days. Georgia nearly always failed the weighing, and was given some kind of punishment, usually a restriction or an extra chore. When she ran out of household chores, her father gave her a broom and sent her outside to sweep the street.

Georgia submitted to her father's rule, but subverted it by eating on the sly.

"My weight got tremendously out of hand," she recounts, "because it was the only control I had, the only way to make my dad really angry."

A watch Georgia's father gave her became a symbol of love withheld. "I was given the watch when I was thirteen, for Christmas. I have it to this day. It's a little skinny thing, gold with a black band. I was so proud. And he said, 'Now, Georgia, I got this watch for you in Japan. You get to keep it for thirty days. And if you have not lost ten pounds in thirty days, I'll take it back.' He took it back. It sat in his drawer for probably ten years, until I finally took it."

During her teen years Georgia was afraid of her father. She couldn't relax, she said, because at any moment he might turn on her. "I didn't want to be in the same room with him. He would walk in and say, 'I can't stand the sight of you. Your arms look like a side of beef. How can I, a physically fit person, be seen with someone who looks like you?' Or he'd pretend I wasn't even in the room." She described a painful incident when she was about forty pounds overweight. "There was a picnic at the Marine base and I didn't want to go, but I had to because it had to be a family thing. But then he said I couldn't go because he was embarrassed to have me with him. Now, when I am an adult, he says to my sister, 'Why doesn't Georgia have confidence?' Why would I?"

Georgia accepted her designated role as Disobedient Daughter, and, at age thirty-nine, still believes in it.

What would have happened if Georgia had not had a weight problem? The story of her sister suggests the answer. Georgia's only sister has always been willowy thin—in her case, the unhealthy result of severe bulimia—and despite being a superachiever, can't seem to do anything right in their father's eyes. Now well into adulthood, this sister, Georgia tells, is plagued by low self-esteem.

Today Georgia is still overweight, though not obese. Her father still derides her during her infrequent visits. Georgia is extremely loyal to a demanding job at which she excels but which allows her very little creativity or self-expression. A pleasant, friendly woman with a dry wit and a love of laughter, she nevertheless has strong defenses against intimacy.

"I have a good time in social situations," she said, "but if someone starts to get too close it's like I put my hand out and hold them off. For years I denied that, but I think it's true. I don't want to be hurt. My family hurt me and I don't want to be hurt like that again."

WINNING THE WARRIOR'S EYE: OCCASIONS OF PRAISE

Like Mary Anne in *The Great Santini*, the military daughter may find herself fighting her own invisibility as she bids for attention from her own father and the warrior culture of the Fortress. She may find through experience that the times she is most likely to get positive attention are when she flatters her father or in some way succeeds at activities traditionally valued by males. In an authoritarian warrior household, the daughter's own female achievements may scarcely draw his notice.

Leigh, daughter of the Air Force general: "I have so few memories of any kind of strokes from my father I can't tell you," she said.

Once when he came back from Japan, he had been promoted in the field. He had two stars on each shoulder. This was the kind of man he was: He decided not to tell anybody. Not my mother, nobody. He just came in. We were all at my grandmother's house, then at my uncle's. I was about seven or eight, and sitting on his lap, looking at his shoulders, I started playing with the stars. And I said, "Dad, how come you have this other star?" And he said, "Well, for God's sake, it's about time somebody noticed!" He went on and on about how bright I was, and went into the room and announced to everyone that little Leigh here is the only goddamn person in the goddamn room that noticed.

I have memories of that sort of thing maybe three or four times in my life: of being thought sharp, perceptive, being right on top of it. That's the only thing I remember being rewarded for. I have very few memories of his encouraging my achievement or rewarding good behavior. I remember once telling him I'd been accepted to the Experiment in International Living. I was so excited. He said, "Of course. Why wouldn't you be?" It was terribly disappointing.

When I was really tiny, about two, I used to get in bed with him in the morning and order him around: "Come on, get up. Go shave." He thought it was the cutest thing, my mother says. I don't recollect it. Then something turned at some point.

My mother tells me he absolutely adored me, I was the apple of his eye. And I just nod. I don't know if I would ever tell her I never felt that love.

Holly's father, an Air Force pilot and lieutenant colonel, was an authoritarian but a loving one. All seven children found him a stern disciplinarian who brooked no opposition, but their unanimous opinion, Holly says, is that he never abused his power. They grew up never doubting his love, although he was not one to say it in so many words.

Still, Holly grew up suspecting he was inclined to do more things with his sons than with his daughters. "We [daughters] knew he was interested in sports, so we played sports in a way to please our father. I don't think I was really that good at sports, but I always tried out and always made the team—so my father would come and watch me."

Just as there are degrees of authoritarianism in military fathers, there are degrees of visibility in military daughters. The more authoritarian the father, the more invisible the daughter is likely to be for him. And the more invisible the daughter—the less she feels affirmed and valued by her father—the more wounded and angry she is likely to feel. Unless this is somehow resolved, when she grows into her own power she may well use it to turn the tables and make her own father "invisible."

Michelle's Story: Rage of the Invisible Daughter

Michelle, one of five daughters of a very authoritarian Army colonel, was thirty years old at the time of the interview and in the midst of struggling with her anger at a father she felt had never been there for her. In this family the father occasionally praised his daughters for their successes, but, Michelle said, "It was almost like it was *his* accomplishment—something for him to brag about." She heard his praise, but never felt validated by it. As she told her story, Michelle was seething with anger over what she considered the latest example of his negation of her: an occasion where she felt strongly she had earned his praise and approval, and yet was denied them.

While growing up, she explained, the sole ambition her father voiced for any of his daughters was for them to finish four years of college. All took this directive to heart, but Michelle harbored many doubts. "I felt so pressured. I was scared to death to get out in the world. I had been so sheltered." She went to college, but quit after two years, which enraged her father. After several more years, she undertook the painstaking process of going back to school, taking a course here and a course there while she worked. Finally at age thirty, with great pride, she graduated from college—but her father did not show up at the ceremony with the rest of the family, later explaining he had a business appointment. The incident touched off feelings in Michelle that erupted in a confrontation with her father two weeks later, on Father's Day.

"I told him he should have been there. He told me he wasn't there for my birth either, or for my sisters'. He even said that during my birth his CO told him he should be with his wife, so he finally went—but it was too late."

She related a dream she had right after the graduation incident. "In the dream he was there but he wasn't there. He didn't say anything; he was like a statue. Just like my childhood."

Having confronted her father with her pain and anger, Michelle is at a loss as to what to do next. "I think, where do I go from here? I've told him how I felt. Now do I just go on?

"He's not the dad I wanted him to be and never will be. I've even thought, He drinks so much and smokes so much and is overweight. . . . If he were to die tomorrow . . . I picture myself at his funeral. All my sisters are crying and carrying on and I picture myself not crying, just standing there, looking at his grave."

Michelle's father called her a couple of weeks after their confrontation, and chatted with her in a light way. At the end of the conversation, Michelle related, he paused and said, "I love you." Michelle said nothing in return. "I was thinking, Do you really love me? Or are you just saying that? Is it sincere?"

MAKING A SON OUT OF A DAUGHTER

Some military fathers are so attuned to the male world that about the only way they can bring a daughter into focus is to treat her as a son.

Many of the daughters I interviewed for this book had received guns as gifts from their fathers. Cynthia's father, an Air Force colonel, gave her a rifle when she was ten years old, and had the stock cut down to fit her arm. "I certainly didn't ask for it," she said. "It was weird."

Claire, daughter of an Army sergeant, said she and her brother received few toys for Christmas, but always, always got guns. "Cap guns, BB guns, a twenty-two. . . . And not just one. The whole set."

This kind of message from the father, particularly when he is also giving signals from time to time that reward conventional femininity, can produce confusion for daughters that takes years to sort out.

My Own Story: Geisha, Get Your Gun

My father gave me a .20-gauge shotgun when I was ten. I remember my mother's dismay. I was shocked too, but simultaneously flattered at his attention. I believe, in retrospect, that it was a very powerful moment of instruction: My father had finally given me a clue as to how I was to mold myself to please him. I was to act like a son. Fine. I became an eager student.

My father taught me to shoot skeet and spoke from time to time of one day taking me hunting. We never went, however, and as I see it now, he was never particularly interested in imparting to me his great pleasure in the hunt. More important to him were the posts' annual turkey shoots, where I would compete against his fellow officers in target shooting and regularly walk off with the turkey. I remember I felt proud, but also confused. At the same time that my father was pushing me to be a sharpshooter and telling me I should join the military, he was sending me to cotillion every Saturday morning to learn ballroom dancing and the fine points of etiquette. During this period he even once remarked, to my utter bafflement, that it was his greatest regret that we were not stationed in Japan, where he could have sent me to a geisha school to learn "real femininity."

Five years after the gift of the shotgun, my father gave me a set of golf clubs—also unsolicited. He paid a pro to give me lessons, and forced me every day of the summer to hit one hundred balls into a field and pick them up. If I'd liked golf it would have been one thing, but I hated the game, never wanted to play it. It was lonely, miserable work hitting those balls in the suffocatingly hot, humid tidewater afternoons and then hunting for them in the tall grass. He would count the balls when I got home.

Only twice did we play golf together. The first time I somehow managed to drive the ball about three hundred yards straight down the fairway onto the green. There was a strong breeze behind me but I still couldn't believe it. My father was astounded and immediately, right on the spot, decided I should play pro golf. I groaned inwardly—I had absolutely no desire to play golf for recreation, let alone professionally, and I had my own ideas about what I wanted to do with my life.

The idea struck me as particularly absurd because I knew all too well I was a lousy player, as I went on to prove in the rest of the game. I could drive but I couldn't putt. In a way that's a metaphor for my whole life at that time. At fifteen I was too aggressive, had no finesse. Boys were terribly confused by me. Outwardly, I was conventionally feminine, and I would obsess over my appearance in the way typical of adolescent girls. But in some ways I was more male than they were: more opinionated, more aggressive, more competitive. As I look back on it I think part of this was normal adolescent confusion—but the other part was because my father, on those rare occasions when he noticed me, was trying to make me into a son.

The confusion persisted for years. By early adulthood, my life reflected what might almost be called a gender gap.

My public persona was that of a relentless bloodhound of an investigative reporter—the kind who divides the world into persecutors and victims, and crusades forth to mercilessly blast the wrongdoers off the face of the planet. I lived for my work, exposing rotten nursing home operators, crooked bureaucrats, hellish prison conditions. In the midst of this my mother once remarked, "How can you be my daughter? You have such a taste for the underside of life!" Perhaps an even more telling remark came, ironically enough, from the newspaper's military reporter. He came by my desk the morning of yet another exposé installment, shook his head, and said, "Mary, I just don't have your taste for the jugular."

My private life, such as it was, couldn't have been more different: I was vulnerable, approval-seeking, yearning for stability and domesticity. The men I knew must have been at a complete loss as to what to make of me.

For a long time I lived a crazy dynamic between those poles, playing Superwoman by day and Earth Mother by night. Finally, as a result of simple aging, some tough experiences, and a lot of hard work at self-understanding, I began to slowly and painfully integrate those parts of myself. The crusading warrior in me was toned down; the feminine side became more balanced, less vulnerable. Almost without my noticing it, the kinds of goals and achievements I valued for myself changed in character; instead of picking goals because they were valued as "male" accomplishments in a "male" world, I found myself rejecting career goals and life paths unless they were consistent with how I experienced myself as a woman.

Some daughters don't have to be coerced into modeling themselves after the son-who-should-have-been. They've already gotten the message loud and clear, and adopted the role as a bid for their father's elusive approval. In some cases this yearning for visibility to the father becomes the central shaping force of a woman's life.

In Catherine's case it almost certainly drew her into the military career her father would have preferred for his son, and that his son rejected. But her story has an added dimension. Once established in the male-dominant world of the military, she never ceased to remind it that it was dealing with a daughter. It is a source of pride to her now that during her career in the warrior world, unlike her childhood, she was a female voice and presence that could not be ignored.

Catherine's Story: Like Father, Like Daughter

Catherine, nearing fifty at the time of the interview, is the oldest daughter of a rear admiral and herself a retired Navy commander. She speaks with love and admiration of her father, but freely admits to the hurt she also carries. At sea fully half the time during her childhood, Catherine's father was also emotionally inaccessible by nature—"so it's as though he might as well not have been there anyway," Catherine says. When he was home, Catherine said, she felt her brother was the favored child. She would try to start conversations with her father, mostly about the Navy. "I think I finally gave up on it. . . . I definitely have that grief, that sadness, that I didn't have a dad like most children do. . . . I attribute it to the fact he was military, but also to his personality."

In many ways, Catherine says, it was a single-parent family—not unlike a great many military families, especially Navy. "My mother had to be both father and mother. In fact, my mother more than balanced out my dad. She was the dominant personality. She always said 'You can do anything you want to do.' " A strong, lively, extremely competent woman, Catherine's mother set the tone of the household and, Catherine notes, "controlled all the emotions—such as there were."

Despite the lack of a strong father presence, home for Catherine was a pleasant and secure place—even though the family moved constantly and she attended five high schools. Very fond of both her parents, Catherine speaks easily of their influence on her life, but says she felt from the outset that she most resembled her father. It has been the task of her whole adult life to understand her emotions and learn to express them more easily.

As a child Catherine liked to play cowboys and Indians and build

model airplanes. She always got the message, she relates, that following boys' pursuits was perfectly all right—until she began to harbor the
ambition of joining the military. "I was frustrated and *annoyed* I
couldn't go to the Naval Academy." At the time the military academies
were not open to women. (Her younger brother later attended the
Naval Academy, although he resigned after a couple of years.) As she
speaks, Catherine's voice warms with the passion of her cause. "Now
that's fixed somewhat," she reflected, "except that the women at the
top of their class at Annapolis still can't go to destroyers and subs. They
can fly planes but not in combat. So they get stuck on tenders and
noncombat ships that are kind of the dregs if you're a top male officer.
It's a very difficult situation."

Her decision to become a WAVE, after graduating from an Ivy
League school where she excelled academically, was not a hit with her
parents: Her father was noncommittal and her mother opposed it,
saying she feared Catherine would "lose her femininity." Her father's
pride in her career was tough to win—but he eventually came around,
particularly after she had chalked up a long series of accomplishments.
"I don't think he was proud of me at first. At least I didn't feel it."

During more than two decades in the Navy, Catherine made a
name for herself not only as a sharp officer, but as a controversial
feminist who argued strongly for women's rights and for nonauthoritarian, consensus-style management. Her efforts sometimes made her all
too visible to her male commanding officers.

"I got a lot of heat," she said. "One of my COs pounded on the
table, saying, 'You've got to be more forceful!' His style was very
authoritarian. He was essentially telling me I had to be like his
destroyer commanders. I told him I wasn't a destroyer commander,
that I do things differently and that what you've got to look for is the
outcome. I was just starting a brand-new command, and it was a
difficult situation. I kept saying my management style was different,
and I was not comfortable with his style. I was just as much of a
warrior; it took that to fight him and run it my way—and I did run it
my way."

Still and all, Catherine is well aware of the paradox of her success. "I
would not have made it as a male Naval officer," she said flatly, "but I
was a very successful female one. I could speak out and get away with
it. The men didn't think I was a threat, in competition with them. And
there was a discounting of women's opinions. I was more emotional—
passionate in terms of causes—and that was acceptable for a woman
but unbecoming for a man. In my fitness reports you can see that they
respected me but also put up with me."

As a professional warrior, Catherine said, she could sometimes feel her father inside her. "I was secure, for instance, and I always felt my father was a secure man. I was always told I am a woman of integrity, and I consider my father to have the highest integrity. And I have courage. Not necessarily physical courage, which he had, but moral and intellectual courage."

Retired from the Navy for six years at the time of the interview, Catherine was still very much a warrior—but this time as a leader of the movement for nuclear disarmament, an area in which she feels military and civilians have a mutual interest. "I was a feminist when it was not popular to be one—in the late sixties and early seventies—and I know I had a lot to do with improving things for women in the Navy. I always called myself the Loyal Opposition—and I still feel that way now, in the peace movement. It fits in with being a new kind of warrior."

MOTHER AS ROLE MODEL

Mother: Our source. Protector. Collaborator. Friend. Competitor. Betrayer. Inspiration. Conscience. First and most powerful teacher. Vision of our future selves.

If the military daughter finds herself on uncertain ground inside the Fortress, there's one thing she can know for sure: She's not up against anything her mother hasn't faced before her.

If the daughter struggles for validation, her mother did too. If the daughter wears the stigma of being the wrong sex in the wrong place, so has her mother. If the daughter in her confusion gropes for her sense of self-worth, her mother has done so also. If the daughter finds herself constantly fighting her invisibility, her mother has too.

The difference is that the mother adapted a long time ago. She had to. And that, in a nutshell, is the most powerful lesson the daughter will learn from her: the example of her adaptation to life inside the Fortress, a world inherently alien to women.

The ways of adaptation are many. Passive dependence. Rigid authoritarian imitation. Sly manipulation. Infidelity. Alcoholism. Spinning of family myths. Almost mystic transcendence. And let us here offer a prayer of gratitude for the fine, strong military mothers who took their knocks but never believed in them, who tried to be there for us, whose nurturance muffled the din of the Fortress, who had the courage and patience to fashion identities beyond those assigned them, whose souls were more than a match for the power of their husbands.

But the fact remains: When the daughter begins her search for a reflection of herself to believe in, her mother is the first place she'll look. And the mirror reflection she sees there may inspire a painful mix of emotions—for along with the strength and resilience for which military wives are justly famous, she is likely to see insecurity, self-doubt, loneliness. And as the daughter watches, the image itself may flicker and fade to invisibility before the unseeing gaze of warriors.

When military daughters describe their mothers, the images they bring forth inevitably reflect the pain of their mothers' invisibility. Here, in their own accounts, are some of the variations on that theme.

Mother as Camouflage Artist

The daughter of an Air Force colonel: "I don't think of my mother as having an ego, or self-esteem. . . . She's friendly and outgoing and can get along with anybody. I get that from her. But when she has problems, she holds them in, lets them eat away at her. I could see it hurting her physically: She has ulcers and other health problems."

Mother as Invisible Servant

The daughter of an Air Force lieutenant colonel: "When I think of my mother, I picture her every morning downstairs, ironing those blue shirts. They all had to be starched, and every crease had to be just right. After fifteen years she finally took them to the cleaners. Secretly. My father never knew."

Mother Who Disappears into Her Own Private World

"My father humiliated her so many times," said the daughter of an Air Force general,

> If he couldn't get anything going with anybody else, he'd turn on her, say something like, "Jesus Christ, why are you so goddamn fat? You're just sitting there, just so fat." She'd look at him and say, "[Steven]?" And about that time I'd say, "May I be excused?"
> . . . I adored my mother while I was young. As an adolescent, with more problems, I began to believe that she was "dumb," as The General stated so many times. She was very dreamy and spent much time by herself in her artistic and musical activities. As I untangle much of this now I realize how good she became at protecting herself from her alcoholic husband. She didn't do me much good in this regard, but I certainly respect her continuing to develop herself as an artist and as a human being. I did not want to be like her when I was a teenager. I would give anything to develop like her in old age.
> I'm glad she's had these years since he died to blossom. . . . Why she's not a bitter, cranky little sick person in a rocking chair somewhere, counting her money, I don't know. I don't have an answer to that. Unless

it's something as simple as a highly developed spiritual life. Her religiosity is so deep and so fine. She has a terrific faith that when she dies she's going to go and be with Jesus. There's nothing goofy about it; it's just rock bottom.

Mother as Accessory

"My mother was the glamorous, vivacious colonel's wife," said the daughter of an Air Force colonel,

She was president of the officers' wives' club several times. She was very charming at parties; my mother had an hourglass figure and wore form-fitting red cocktail dresses. I didn't like the role model of the military wife at all.

Before she married my father she was a WASP [Women's Airforce Service Pilot]. She flew military planes. I was really proud of that and couldn't understand how she could just live a life of leisure and not contribute anything. It bothered me. All this officers' wives' club stuff seemed very frivolous and wasteful and foolish. Of course I know it would have been hard for her as an officer's wife to have a career, because we moved so much—but emotionally I can't respect her. I have more respect for my father because he *did* something.

I recognize that when I am in a new group of people I can turn on the charm, just like she can. The positive aspect of that is that charm is an excellent social lubricant. The negative aspect is that it's phony.

For years my mother tried to make me over in her image, and there was lots of tension between us. It has taken me years of inner work and therapy to realize I was rejecting my mother's stereotype, not her as a person.

Mother Who Was Swallowed Up in Submission

The daughter of an Air Force general and wife of an Army officer: "I very much modeled myself after my mother, as we all do. Mom was a totally submissive person. She was a nurse, but after she had her first baby she never considered going back to it.

"But I have some anger—that I realize I have no right to have—against my mother, for not being aware of other possibilities. I always thought I would be a full-time military wife and mother. I didn't really consider all the possibilities until *late*—largely, I think, because I felt somehow that I *should* be like my mother. Later, in therapy, I realized how much anger I have, and how much I directed inappropriately."

Mother Who Was Visible Only in the Warrior's Absence

The daughter of a Navy commander who was out at sea or stationed away from the family for long periods:

My mother is a strong woman, always has been. Her father died when she was twelve and her mother was sick, so she raised her brothers and sisters. She was a strict mother, but also very generous. She and my sister and I did quite well, really. She never made any problems known to us. We all shared in the work and everything. Then my father came back [after an overseas absence of three years] and expected to move right back into being the head of the household. That's a little tough. . . .

We were transferred right after he returned. I remember being in a nice hotel with two adjoining rooms, after just two days of being back together as a family, and my sister and I were sitting on our bed with our arms around each other because our parents were in the next room fighting and we could hear it. It was so hard. And that was the issue: "You've been gone and you expect to walk right back in here and have things the way you want them. And your kids have grown up and you missed that. . . ." We were terrified she was going to divorce him. You just get your daddy back and you have to worry about losing him again. . . .

During that next year my mother must have put on forty pounds through her unhappiness. Ultimately they worked it out. But he had to recognize her strengths.

We have seen how the stage is set for military daughters to become the ghosts of the Fortress. The authoritarian world of the warrior demands her invisibility, and one way or another—with the powerful example of the mother thrown in—it will get it. If the daughter rebels, she is damned to invisibility. If she conforms, her reward is also invisibility.

But once the daughter leaves the Fortress, what are the psychological legacies she carries with her?

CONSEQUENCES OF HAVING AN AUTHORITARIAN FATHER

When a military daughter becomes invisible, it happens *because* the warrior society requires it: It is the inevitable consequence of being female inside the Fortress. But *where* it happens is on the most intimate level, in the arms of her own family. And her father is the instrument, the voice of authority.

But it would be too simplistic to look at fathers solely in terms of raw authority. They have far more power than that.

The real power of a father is much more subtle, and it's there whether he uses it or not. It resides in what he represents. He is the man who symbolizes all men, the provider who is the bridge to all the world beyond. His approval carries the assent of the entire human race; his condemnation is the quintessential voice of rejection. To be visible or invisible to this man is to be visible or invisible not just to one's father, but to one's self, and to the world.

In her book *The Wounded Woman*, analyst Linda Schierse Leonard writes that a girl's father

> is the first masculine figure in her life and is a prime shaper of the way she relates to the masculine side of herself and ultimately to men. Since he is "other," i.e., different from herself and her mother, he also shapes her differentness, her uniqueness and individuality. The way he relates to her femininity will affect the way she grows into womanhood. One of his roles is to lead the daughter from the protected realm of the mother and the home into the outside world, helping her to cope with the world and its conflicts. . . . Traditionally, the father also projects ideals for his daughter. He provides a model for authority, responsibility, decision-making, objectivity, order, and discipline. When she is old enough, he steps back so she may internalize these ideals and actualize them in herself. [1]

Many of the women I interviewed had suffered at the hands of their fathers. In some cases the fathers were what one might call mildly authoritarian; they weren't cruel or abusive with their daughters, but they were domineering and rigid enough to have been emotionally inaccessible to them, and to rebuff or ignore their daughters' overtures of affection. Then there are the fathers who were classic authoritarians; they were the ones who were not only emotionally inaccessible, but had an extremely strong negative presence.

All of the daughters of these kinds of fathers live with deep, un-requited yearning for the father they needed and didn't have, the father who would have made them solid and visible before the world. And for many of them, the lack of a positive father presence in their lives has made for a set of problems that continues to plague them well into adulthood.

These problems are the negative legacies for military daughters of growing up invisible to their fathers, as ghosts of the Fortress. Every daughter quoted below has sought to be a valued presence in her warrior father's life; every one was thwarted by his inability to "see" her. The results are low self-esteem, crippling perfectionism, difficulty in dealing with male authority figures, extreme fragility, passivity, eating disorders, self-destruction.

Low Self-Esteem

To be sure, not all the daughters interviewed for this book suffered from a low opinion of themselves. But the majority did, and they seemed to fall into three groups of varying visibility.

The most invisible of all, the ones who were negated to the last degree, are those who had been physically, sexually, or emotionally abused. Their story is told in Chapter 7, "Military Brats as Casualties."

Then there are those who seem unable to trust in their own worth and accomplishments, and who are unmercifully critical of themselves for their mistakes; their problems are frequently expressed in a debilitating perfectionism discussed later in this chapter.

Lastly, there is the largest group, composed of those who outwardly seem confident and happy—to all appearances, "successful" military brats—yet who are plagued by a reflexive self-doubt that severely limits them. Cynthia is one of these.

Cynthia's Story: Undermined by Self-Doubt

Cynthia's father, an Air Force colonel, was an authoritarian who was emotionally inaccessible to her and physically and emotionally abusive to her younger brother. Cynthia grew up to reflect one of the classic contradictions to be found among military daughters: She is a high achiever with excellent social skills who is comfortable in any social situation—yet has a poor self-image. When thrown into a new set of circumstances she can pull it off; but left to herself she will rarely seek out a challenge.

Put another way, she is a perfect example of the military daughter who succeeded at the twin imperatives of Beauty and Duty, and who was granted invisibility for her trouble. She was the "perfect" warrior's daughter, yet all her life she has suffered the aching malaise of self-doubt.

"I never got any praise," she said of her father. "I never did anything right [in his eyes], even though I had good grades. When I think back . . . anything that gave me an honor outside the family—National Honor Society, cheerleader—that was almost like a gift to me. I didn't consider I really deserved it; it was just luck. My mom would be very pleased and proud. My dad wouldn't say much of anything. I felt uncomfortable with achievements that made me stand out. I did it, but it was almost like a dream." A complicating factor was that her parents would use her achievements to condemn her brother by comparison.

Cynthia's father was rigid and demanding with his kids, and would stand over them giving orders until their performance either met his standards or until he declared it a failure. "I can remember when I was a little girl of four, trying to learn how to roller skate and not being able to, and my father not letting me off the skates until I could skate without falling down. And I can remember *crying*, pleading, 'Please let me off these skates.' Now I ask you, what was the importance of that? What did it matter if I could or couldn't skate? What purpose did it serve to keep me on them?

"And to this day I will not get into any new situations. I don't want to be caught not doing well. So I set myself up not to do anything new."

Cynthia describes her role in the family as "the Good Girl Who Tried Hard." Her job, she said, was not causing any shame, always doing the right thing. "I can see that in myself even now."

Perfectionism

Many people are proud of what they call their "perfectionism," and with good reason: to them it means a kind of valiant approach to all of life—holding high standards and ever striving to meet them. That's part of it, of course, but there is another side to this trait, a side so dark it can be paralyzing. And it is often found among those who felt, growing up, that they could never win the steady gaze of their father's approving eye.

Perfectionists have internalized their judgmental father voice so well that it comments derisively on every action, every aspect of their lives. It is a bitter way to live, for the internal father voice does not spill over with praise when a thing is done well—but its condemnation is complete and resounding when they miss the mark.

Sarah is an Air Force brat who is now a clinical psychologist in a heavily military part of the country. In an interview she said that perfectionism is one of the biggest problems she sees among her mostly female clientele, many of whom are military brats. "Most of the women I see are superconscientious and responsible," she said. "They have superegos that will not quit. If they make mistakes, they see themselves as 'bad.' The tendency for women perfectionists is to focus on being the 'perfect person.' "[2]

It is a terrible trap—and one of the worst aspects of it is that it is a trap we set for ourselves. We set high standards and compulsively try to meet them as a kind of insurance against the activation of that terrible father voice that damns us to nothingness and invisibility. But since perfection is impossible, the voice comes down anyway: if not about the near perfect performance just executed, then about some other area of life that was neglected in order to accomplish it. And there is no distinction made between the really important things in life and the completely trivial. Tiny things assume inordinate importance, while big ones are allowed to slide.

Georgia, the daughter of the Marine fighter pilot who castigated her for her weight problem, is a compulsive perfectionist. "I can't go to bed if the shoes aren't straight," she said. "Dishes can't sit overnight. Now that's stupid. But growing up, we had to do the dishes even before we ate dinner. My dad couldn't stand to look at the pots.

"I'm a perfectionist, but I don't do things perfectly at all. I'm very rigid, but I don't want to be. And I'm very hard on myself."

The therapeutic thing to do, one might think, would be to throw out all the false standards and start over again, hewing to the middle course to avoid such painful extremes. That is much easier said than done, of course, in part because perfectionism provides a kind of structure that makes it all the more difficult to abandon. And, sad to say, we often choose to live with what is negative but familiar rather than face the void of life without it.

Being a perfectionist is like living on a treadmill that never stops, as one interviewee put it. There is no respite, no satisfaction. Worse, perfectionism may mask an even greater problem: What if the treadmill were to stop? Who would the perfectionist be without an endless succession of tasks to complete? Would she recognize herself? Is perfectionism in part a device to distract one's self from larger issues that are begging to be confronted?

For her part, Sarah believes the military background contributes heavily to the development of perfectionists. "The rigid boundaries of behavior [in the military] are so contradictory to the way life *ought* to be. In the military things are divided into right and wrong, good and evil, life and death; *there is no middle ground*. That's the message: 'This is the way it is.' And that *isn't* the way it is. It's a lie. They live a lie. Kids grow up with this and end up asking, Where is the truth? Who am I? I work a lot with my clients on knowing self. That's the major thrust of my therapy."

Difficulty in Dealing with Male Authority Figures

What happens to the military daughter who is confronted by a man who represents power to her? In interview after interview, military daughters told of being caught in a painful paradox. They are often supremely competent at what they do and, much of the time, models of assertiveness. Yet locked in conflict with a man in power, their shield disintegrates. Just when they are strong and solid and ready to do battle, they feel themselves suddenly dissolve into invisibility. Even more disconcerting, they can't predict when it will happen. One day they carry the confrontation; the next day they crumble.

"Anything can trigger it," said Georgia. "It can be the most innocent thing that comes off somehow as a reprimand. Someone can say something . . . and it just sets me off. I get real upset. I feel like saying, 'Excuse me, I'm just having a flashback.'

"If someone talks to me in a certain tone, I come unglued. It's the same tone my dad used. My boss will do that sometimes. I usually have to walk out and walk around the building, it makes me so angry. It's like being slapped in the face. I can't say that to my boss because he's very sensitive and he wouldn't do that intentionally. But it hurts. Just like my dad."

Michelle has difficulties with all kinds of authority figures. "I get all nervous, don't know what to say. . . . Sometimes I make people out to be authority figures when they're really not. Even bank tellers. Even other teachers at school. . . . I've been a little afraid of them, afraid even to express my opinions."

A military daughter who has grown up being invisible to her father may instinctively react to confrontations by hiding her emotions under perfect camouflage. Grace, asked how she reacts in situations with male authority figures, said, "Until recently, I reacted just as I would had that man been my father. I would withdraw from conflict and acquiesce. Give in. Because I couldn't deal with anger. It isn't that I would have assumed he was more right than I; I just wouldn't have countered with anything." In conflicts with her husband, she tended to dissolve in tears before she had made her points.

Some daughters contrive not to flub confrontations by simply avoiding them altogether, making themselves invisible before someone else can do it for them. Leigh described herself as a "good little soldier," meaning she doesn't make waves, even if avoiding conflict means personal sacrifice or upheaval. "One of the reasons I've taken a leave of absence from my job is that I don't want to deal with a guy in my professional life. He is so much like The General: always pushing, prodding, testing, seeing how far he can push you. I've seen him do really destructive things. He's a real jerk, but he likes me—and I think it's because I go out of my way to make him like me. I don't want him to push me, but I don't want to confront him." When she was a child, she said, her pattern was the same. "My self-defense was staying out of the way, avoiding annihilation. Women are so good at that anyway."

Extreme Fragility

Until I began doing the interviews for this book, my own problem with uncontrollable tears had been one of the enduring mysteries of my life, and a frequent source of embarrassment. Although the problem had lessened considerably by my midthirties, for many years before that it had been very troublesome. When I would feel right-eously indignant and was trying to make my points—and not feeling in the least like crying—suddenly a flood of tears would come and there was nothing I could do to stop it. In no time my bid at assertiveness had literally become a washout, and the battle would be lost. I remember once, confronted by a somewhat loony newspaper editor who had made an unjust accusation, I cried so hard I hyperventi-lated—and then ran out of the building in shame.

But occasional confrontations with authority were hardly the only times I cried. I was liable to burst into tears spontaneously as I was doing some ordinary, mundane task, and not even know why I was crying or what triggered it. I had to avoid sad movies and books and skip over maudlin news stories, because a tale that would bring a tear to the eye of the average reader would send me into mourning for days. I asked many people for advice about my crying problem, but no one had much to offer. It was only after some fifteen years of gradual maturation and a great deal of work at understanding my family and myself that the problem receded to a more or less acceptable degree of sentimentalism. Not, I think, coincidentally, I also met my husband around this time and became truly grounded emotionally for the first time in my life.

For all those years I thought I was the only person afflicted with this mysterious problem. But after doing the first few interviews with military daughters, I came to realize how very wrong that was. Dozens of subsequent interviews only confirmed the impression.

Daughter after daughter poured forth tales of unstoppable tears: One woman said her crying was so unpredictable she would find herself bursting into tears "in front of, say, the orange juice display in the grocery store." Another said she would simply sit down on the couch, not thinking of anything in particular, and her tears would come. Many others told of crying copiously at TV commercials or at other equally absurd moments.

It was the interview with Grace that first brought it home to me. She spoke of the problem as a *need* to cry so overwhelming that she felt compelled to seek out stimuli to help her break through her normally very controlled exterior. "I find I have a need—it's compulsive and almost morbid—to cry at tearjerker television dramas. Last night I watched a show about kids with cystic fibrosis. Even though it was late, I was downstairs crying. And I slept better than I have in a long time.

"When I cry it purges something from me and I can relax. But then it replenishes itself. It seems there is no end to these tears."

As she spoke I thought of a kind of internal lake, filled to the brim with tears, that needed to spill over from time to time. Suddenly it seemed clear that these are tears of grief for a loss so long repressed that it is not consciously accessible—so the emotion seeks any channel it can find to be released. It didn't take long to figure out the probable nature of the loss. Every daughter with a crying problem proved also to be suffering from the lifelong absence of an approving, loving father. The theory resonated within me, and Grace and many other daughters have since told me that they, too, sense it is on target.

The tears are the tears of the invisible daughter, and they will not be suppressed. Nor should they be—for what they are demanding is honest recognition from the daughter who has become invisible even to herself.

Here is how two daughters spoke of their tears:

Holly said that she and all four sisters "cry at the drop of a hat." Although she speaks of always having a good and loving relationship with her father, she noted he was away from the family on unaccompanied tours for a total of four years during her childhood—and when he was home, despite the fact he spent a lot of time with the children, she found his stern exterior forbidding. "That may be why I'm so sentimental now," she said. "First of all, from never communicating with my father as a child, and always being scared of him. I always felt bad when he corrected me. He was so loud, and it was so upsetting. I remember being very timid with him. . . .

"When I look back on it and see who I've become, I know it couldn't have been that bad. I feel I had such a good childhood, and was brought up well. Yet as I look back, too, it seems like I didn't have any relationship with my father growing up. In his own way he showed us attention, but not in such a way that I ever thought, 'Boy, he really cares about me.' "

Anita is the daughter of a Navy chief petty officer, an authoritarian who was at sea half the time, and was emotionally closed to her when he was home. "I cry out of proportion," she said. "I cry at TV commercials, parts of movies. . . . That was the only time it was *acceptable* to cry, too: It was okay to cry at a movie. That I did it *disproportionately* was never looked at. For me it was like 'Go ahead and cry now because you can't cry any other time.' " Asked what she thinks is at the root of her tears, she replied, "Sadness. A sense of loss . . . loss of opportunities . . . something I feel I ought to have had and didn't. Love, probably.

"I'm the only person I know who cries at 'The Donna Reed Show.' " At the time of the interview she had been reflecting a great deal on her relationship with her father. "He's not going to become an Alex Stone [from the television show]—this wise father who's going to talk and share and have a great sense of humor about one's idiosyncrasies or problems. That's not going to happen. So I'm working on acceptance of the fact he's not going to change, and that the only person who can change in the situation is me."

Passivity

Invisible daughters, predictably, have trouble asserting themselves; assertion requires a stronger sense of self than they generally have. They are not necessarily passive all the time; for some, it is the inconsistency within their own personality which is so trying. They know themselves to be one way, but find themselves unaccountably acting in quite another—and are helpless to assert themselves. Paradoxically, an invisible daughter may be the very essence of assertiveness when it comes to arguing someone *else's* cause, but when the moment comes to put herself on the line on her own behalf, she loses her voice and fades from view.

The recurring symptoms of an invisible daughter with passivity problems are these: She has trouble making decisions, large and small. She lacks conviction about her own opinions. Although she may do an impressive job of standing up for someone else's rights, hauling out all the resourcefulness and social skill she acquired as a military brat, she often retreats from her own battles. In group situations she may convey an indifferent "I'll go along with you" kind of detachment that is second nature to her, yet troubling. Often, to the amazement of others who think of her as levelheaded and in control, she fails to make conscious choices about who is going to be allowed to play a role in her life as associate, friend, lover. In general, an invisible daughter fails to take charge of shaping her own life. Reared in an environment where all was decided for her and her opinion counted for nothing, she tends as an adult to sit back and wait for events to sweep her along.

Since passivity is a problem experienced as much by military sons as military daughters, it is treated at greater length in Chapter 11, "Legacies."

Eating Disorders

This book does not purport to be a scientific study, but its journalistic authenticity would suffer if I did not report what seemed a striking incidence of eating disorders among the military daughters I interviewed: About one in four had suffered an eating disorder at some time in her life.

For my purposes here I've defined a person with an eating disorder as one who, for a protracted period, has been seriously out of control in eating habits and has experienced health problems as a result. I have therefore excluded all military brats who spoke of binging around the time of a family move, and other temporary aberrations in eating patterns. The military daughters I considered to be suffering from eating disorders are bulimic, anorectic, seriously obese, or have eating-related digestive disorders. I have included myself in my tally; I was bulimic for seven years during high school and college, although I did not realize the term applied to me until I researched this book. My disorder was not the binge/purge pattern so characteristic of bulimia, but a binge/starve variation. I would binge uncontrollably, then starve myself drastically.

In my view, eating disorders in military daughters are very much tied to the invisibility problem. From their stories it seemed that in each case the disorder could be traced back to at least one of four circumstances, all of which have to do with invisibility:

1. *Sexual abuse.* It is known that sexually abused children some-times develop into obese adults.[3] Simply put, they feel such shame and confusion over their abuse that they wish to "hide" themselves—and do so inside a great deal of excess fat. In a society that holds slimness supreme, it may also be an acting out of their own sense of being social pariahs.

Then, too, for some sexually abused children, food becomes a "drug of choice," and compulsive eating the expression of a desire for self-annihilation. For these children, food may not be the only compul-sion: They are frequently alcoholics and drug abusers as well.

One military daughter had been molested by her step-grandfather at age six. She was about 75 pounds overweight at the time of the interview—but had already lost 170 pounds through group therapy. She was also a recovering drug addict.

Another had been relentlessly abused by her Naval officer stepfather for eight years of her childhood. She told of being obese in her teens, the result of compulsive overeating "as a way of pacifying my miseries."

2. *Stoic families.* In many military families, emotions are re-pressed. In effect the children are taught to "eat" their feelings: swallow them and not show them. Compulsive eating then becomes an acting out of this process.

One daughter of an Army colonel attributed her bulimia to the fact that in her family "we couldn't express emotions." For her it began at a time of great stress soon after she graduated from high school, when she did not know what to do with her life and her parents, although retired, had just decided to move yet again. When a couple of her parents' friends brought over a cake to celebrate the move, she not coincidentally seized upon it when no one was around and "ate" most of it, chewing each mouthful and then spitting it out. It began a bulimic pattern of eating-and-expelling that still plagues her a dozen years later.

3. *Authoritarian families.* Control is what authoritarian families are about, and eating disorders in such families reflect this. Children who act out their problems with excessive control sometimes seize upon food as their medium, "controlling" it (making it do their bidding) almost as an expression of their own helplessness.

The bulimic Army daughter mentioned above told me she tried to "control" food "because in my family we couldn't control anything else. Everything was controlled *for* us. Sometimes I wonder why I didn't become anorectic." The tragedy, of course, is that the notion of "controlling" the food is really an illusion. The food abuser is actually very much out of control.

In some cases the eating disorder might be an imitative pattern, picking up on a parent's addiction. Both eating disorders and alcoholism, after all, are examples of substance abuse masquerading as substance control. One survey of eighty women with eating disorders found that 41 percent had fathers with an alcohol problem.[4] Among the military daughters with eating disorders I tallied for this chapter, the ratio was even higher: Three out of four had alcoholic fathers.

4. *Families where being female is a negative.* This could apply to any one of the above situations or any family where the daughter has a troubled relationship with her father, or witnesses her father's putdowns of her mother. The mother, too, plays a role in this, either by her acquiescence in her own devaluation, or by taking out her frustrations through controlling her daughter. In any case, the perception of femaleness as something inadequate or wrong contributes to the disorder. Compulsive overeating, for instance, becomes a means of giving life to the negative image the father—or the surrounding patriarchy—projects upon the daughter. Georgia, the Marine Corps daughter whose story appeared early in this chapter, is an example.

Eating disorders are dangerous and may be alarmingly common among military daughters. But I see them as symptomatic of a much bigger problem so endemic to the Fortress one might call it a *cultural disorder:* It is the negation of women and women's values, a denial of their inherent worth apart from their usefulness to the warrior patriarchy. This affects all women inside the Fortress, to be sure, but it is particularly manifest in what happens to Fortress daughters, who discover how they are viewed by the warrior culture at the same time they are discovering themselves.

The warrior culture's negative views of women, literally brought home in many cases by the authoritarian warrior father, in effect pit a daughter against her own femaleness. Because she wants badly to win her father's approval, she in effect takes his side and works to negate her own femininity. Eating disorders are an effective means of doing away with the female form. In anorexia the daughter wastes away, losing her feminine curves and often her menses. In obesity she buries her feminine form under obscuring layers of fat. In bulimia she abuses her body, alternately stuffing it and depriving it, treating it as a thing that cannot be trusted, as a vehicle for acting out her self-disgust.

The interview with Maya, daughter of an Army physician, was particularly revealing in this regard. I have assembled the following quotations from four different points in her interview. The parts, when linked, draw the connection between her perception of the invisibility of females inside the Fortress and her eating disorder:

1. I didn't want to be female. I didn't want to be like my mother. It seemed she was part of the baggage that moved along with everything else. I never saw her [accomplish] anything, never saw her be happy. My mother was powerless. What she said didn't matter. Two weeks after having a complete hysterectomy, she moved two kids and a household to Germany. . . . My father was very definitely authoritarian. The message was loud and clear in my family: "It doesn't matter what you think." My father told [my mother, sister and me] directly: "You don't count."

2. I wanted to be like my father so much. So intelligent, so in control.

3. When I was nine and ten years old, I pulled out my eyebrows and all my eyelashes. I don't know why. [This was not a onetime occurrence; the behavior persisted for more than a year.]

4. For five years I was bulimic. I binged and purged all through college. One time I ate a box of raw brownie mix; that was really sick. Then after college I replaced [bulimia] with alcohol and prescription drugs.

Maya knew the score early on: To be female inside the Fortress is to be little more than a burden. She sided with her father and attempted to negate her femininity, first by plucking signs of femininity from her face, then by attacking her body. Later she may have finally come to realize on some level that attacking her femininity was a battle she couldn't win—she was going to remain female no matter what. So she chose to anesthetize herself with alcohol and prescription drugs. Maya is now making a recovery with the help of Alcoholics Anonymous.

In a sense bulimia is an acting out of the battle between terrible "truths" as perceived by young daughters trapped in a negating patriarchy. First there is a "defeat"—the daughter's powerlessness to control eating behavior, which acts out her powerlessness to either change her sex or improve the status of her sex. Immediately following "defeat" there is a "victory"—the daughter's mighty assertion of will, in the form of purging or starvation, to make up for her powerlessness. In the "victory" she is acting out joining the winning side, echoing cultural attitudes that negate women even as she deprives her female body of sustenance. And of course this is followed soon after by yet another "defeat." The cycle continues until she realizes that femaleness is not a correctable condition. At that point she instinctively chooses one of three courses: Like Maya, she can try to block out that truth with any means available; or she can persist in her self-negation in any number of ways; or she can gradually work her way to a more positive view of herself and of women in general.

Eating disorders are one way daughters express confusion or even shame concerning their femaleness, but there are others. And while not as dramatic or dangerous, these too focus on the body.

I have talked with military daughters who fought their femininity almost as an invading enemy, who exercised ferociously to keep their bodies hard and taut as a boy's, who contemptuously rejected feminine decorations of makeup and frilly clothes almost as though in denying gender they could rise above it, be the exception to the rule, win at least a portion of the approval warriors reserve for their sons.

I have also talked with military daughters whose ultrafeminine (and often servile) mothers so exalted femininity, and whose macho authoritarian fathers so devalued it, that they grew up too confused about their femaleness to know what to do. At different times in their lives they have acted out various approaches to it, experimenting with ways of being as though they had to try them on for size until they got the right fit.

"I've had no sense of what it was to be a girl, a woman," said Melody, the daughter of an Air Force colonel. "For a while I was a cocktail waitress, dressed really sleazily. It was a real 'fuck me' look— because that's what I thought it was to be a woman. Other times I've gone to the other extreme of looking really masculine. I was not and am not gay, but people asked me all the time if I was. I didn't care. I'm just beginning to learn what [being a woman] means, and I have a lot to learn." This daughter also suffers from bulimia.

It is possible for daughters of warriors to recover from role confusion and from eating disorders. Counseling is very beneficial. But an important part of recovery is exposure to positive women role models, who demonstrate the strengths inherent in being female, who have a solid sense of self-worth, whose lives demonstrate the possibilities open to women in the far less extreme patriarchy that lies outside the Fortress.

Self-Destruction

It happens sometimes that a military daughter suffers from low self-esteem to such a degree, and with so little in her life to counterbalance it, that she finds herself doing very self-destructive things—courting danger, contemplating suicide, abusing drugs or alcohol or food.

It's almost as if she is crying out to her father, "You want me invisible? Watch me disappear!" Then she begins her very slow dance of death—slow, because she is still hoping he will rescue her from self-annihilation. Here is the story of one such daughter, Melody—the same one just mentioned, who spoke of her confusion about femininity.

Melody's Story: Anger Turned Inward

When we sat down to talk, Melody handed me a picture of herself at age eight. A pretty little girl sat on the edge of the bed staring up into the camera, with eyes that did not match her smile. Unspeakably, unalterably sad, they remained focused on a deep internal grief. There were many other pictures from her Air Force childhood, all the same: a very sad child, smiling on command.

"I don't remember ever feeling good or feeling joy or happiness, before drinking and using heroin," she said. At thirty-two, Melody was a recovering alcoholic and heroin addict. Her parents are both alcoholics, as is her brother.

She described her father as authoritarian and distant. "I remember him being really cold," she said. "I remember him trying real hard to be loving to me. But it didn't fit. Colonels are not soft. They don't make it to colonel if they are." He was tough on her brother, disciplining him frequently, having him make his bed so he could bounce a quarter off it. But he was never violent to anyone in the family. "None of us ever showed any violence. We're all massively controlling—and we need massive amounts of substances to do it. I don't remember any honest emotions. It was always 'keeping up the front.'"

"In my family it was not okay to feel. When I was four or five years old I thought it would kill my parents to know what I felt."

Her earliest memory, she said, is a recurring dream she had for a few years around the time she was five. "I would be sitting in my father's chair at his desk in the Pentagon, when he would walk in and discover me there. Sometimes in the dream he would walk in with a general, other times alone. Always I felt shame and terror. I was definitely where I was not supposed to be."

Melody's early assessment of her relationship with her father was borne out about a dozen years later, when she tried to kill herself by slitting her wrists. She "accidentally" let her mother see—perhaps because she was also desperate for her alcoholic mother's attention, perhaps because it was a lateral way to get to her father. But although her mother did tell her father about the attempt, he never did anything about it, never said anything to Melody.

"I used to think the problem was my family, but I think it's the military too," Melody said.

It's built around what others are going to think of you. I think my parents' problem was that they were very self-obsessed, trying to live up to the role. I took it personally, as though they rejected me. When I had the epiphany—is that the expression? Like a door opening on the truth?—I realized I really didn't have anything to do with it.

Alcoholics Anonymous saved my life. I used to think I was just incredibly self-destructive, out to kill myself. The neat thing is that I keep on learning. Now I see I always take care of myself the best I can. If I could have taken care of myself better, I wouldn't have used drugs. . . .

It seems to me other people have an inner voice to turn to that says "this is okay" or "this is not okay." I don't have one. People tell me that with sobriety I'll start to develop my own values, but it hasn't happened yet. It's not that I didn't have values; it's that I buried them down deep in my need to get approval. I would literally sell anything, say anything, do anything to get that approval.

"Let's face it," Melody said with a short, bitter laugh. "It's not easy for a white middle-class kid to strike out."

Melody's story was dark and foreboding, but it doesn't end there. I first interviewed her in 1986; three years later I wrote to her, and received a reply which read in part:

I can't believe it's been three years. In a lot of ways it seems like another lifetime. I am *not* the same woman you interviewed, and I am really grateful for that. . . .

Things got progressively worse after we met; a lot more struggling with demons and self-hate. I went into another recovery home for eating disorders last December, pretty nonfunctional from mood swings and depressions. But this is where the story gets good—I started taking antidepressants and am working with a very competent therapist. The result is a lot of peace I have wanted for so long. I realize now that part of the problem was biochemical, but you know, Mary, I think I also gave up, too. I seem to have given up trying to meet my expectations, and am a lot happier for it.

I'm back in school, and have only one class left for my B.S. degree. It took a few years to get the self-esteem and faith in myself to go for it, but that's what I'm doing.

And yes, I'm finally finding my own values. I seem to have come to terms with much of who I am, and am not constantly trying to hide it or apologize. I still swear a lot, I laugh much too loud for polite company and only like sex with domineering men. However, I know that I am creative, compassionate and am blessed with a lot of gifts that I no longer want to hide either. . . .

I know I have my work cut out for me [in therapy], but I'm just relaxing more and enjoying the journey instead of waiting to feel good when I reach that elusive "destination."

DAUGHTERS AS WARRIORS:
LIKE FATHER, LIKE DAUGHTER

As we have seen, inside the Fortress there are only two approved roles for a female: dutiful servant or beautiful object of men's desires. Both guarantee a certain kind of camouflage—invisibility. But sometimes a daughter, wishing to avoid these traps, thinks she sees a way out: and that is to become a warrior herself. The kind of warrior Daddy would be proud of. How could a warrior fail to notice a faithful model of himself?

These daughters are like Athena, Greek goddess of wisdom and of war, who sprang full-blown from the head of her father, Zeus, king of the gods. Athena makes herself into a more gratifying "son" than any male could have been: She is intensely loyal to her father, revels in the competition and combat of the world of men, is athletically gifted, courageous, intelligent, wise, cool under pressure, the consummate strategist. In her total devotion to her father and his world, she never marries. And, true to her motherless origins, Athena has little time for the world of women or for any emotion apart from the righteous anger that spurs the warrior into battle.[5]

Catherine, whose story was presented earlier in this chapter, is a classic example of the military daughter who grows into an Athena woman.

Many other military daughters, myself included, exhibit predominantly Athena qualities during some phase of their lives. For me it was the period of about ten years during which I was an investigative reporter. Born as I was to military metaphor, I even imagined myself as a kind of modern-day Joan of Arc. And although my mother couldn't begin to understand what motivated me, my warrior father did. Once, as we reconciled after a two-year period during which we had not spoken to one another, he said he had nevertheless read every story I'd written for the newspaper, and had been proud. No praise has ever meant more.

For several years toward the end of my Athena period I lived in Chicago and devoted myself to working on a history of the Black Muslims,[6] a subject to which I was drawn out of fascination for their evolving ideology, and a desire to study white racism as seen through the eyes of a closed community of militant blacks. It was no accident, of course, that a child of the military should pick another "fortress" community to study. And as alien as one might think that particular community would have seemed to a white, middle-class officer's daughter, the fact was that at times it actually felt comfortably familiar. It was hardly likely I would be thrown off base, for instance, by their male supremacist culture, their nationalism, their paranoia, or by the "battle stories" of their most aggressive period.

Perhaps the best testimony to the warrior bond shared by my father and me was that, to my astonishment, he overcame his own virulent racism to give me his full encouragement on the project. Somehow he reasoned that if his warrior daughter saw merit in the subject, it must be worth doing—and after that his only concern was that I accomplish my mission as perfectly as possible. Specifically, he worried whether I would be able to acquire all the material I needed to do the fullest and *fairest* treatment of the subject. Once in a phone conversation I told him excitedly of the tremendous amount of information I was acquiring from the FBI and CIA under the Freedom of Information Act. He fell silent. "Just remember," he cautioned sternly, "their view is very one-sided!" I think now the greatest gift my father ever gave me was his pride and faith during that time.

For several years the Muslim book seemed the perfect writing project: As an Athena woman, I had a sense of purpose and the joy of using all my abilities to meet the toughest challenge I could find. Although I didn't think of it this way at the time, I was also learning something about how I had been shaped by the warrior society by studying another version of it. But in the end I walked away from the project. Athena to the last, I had a list of perfectly logical reasons why it no longer made sense to pursue it. But in retrospect I think I was also moving out of my Athena phase, and the extremely patriarchal world of militant Muslims was consequently fast losing its appeal. Instinctively I must have felt that if I dwelled there too long, even in my removed observer role, I risked losing my way.

While many military daughters become warriors themselves, as I did, I think many more are less compelled to act it out so obviously. In them the warrior is not so much a life role as a side of their personality which emerges when necessary. This can be something to be really proud of: an assertive, disciplined approach to life that pays off time after time. Growing up in the military, after all, is among other things an intensive course in how to discipline one's self to accomplish an objective.

One such daughter, whose father enlisted in the Army and worked his way up through the ranks to make major, reeled off a list of lessons she had internalized from her father's example. "Always be prepared. Never jump the chain of command. Have high standards of performance. Be disciplined. Understand there's a consequence for actions and also for inaction. Be decisive: Do it, don't regret it."

But the learning of these lessons is a hard road for a daughter of the Fortress. They are not, after all, presented to her as a gift by the warrior society. Frequently she learns them in confrontation with her own father; it is striking to note how commonly in military families it was the daughter, rather than the wife or the son, who would go toe to toe with the warrior. Partly this is because a daughter naturally internalizes the father-model as the masculine side of herself. But part of it, too, may be that the daughter in joining battle with her own warrior father is demanding confirmation of her visibility. If she can win that confirmation, it would help resolve, or at least assuage, the terrible contradiction she senses in their relationship: that her father loves her, but disdains what she is.

Mattie, the daughter of a Navy fighter pilot, spoke to me in our inteview of having had a "close" relationship with her father, saying it was "based on mutual respect"—but in the next breath she said unequivocally, "He hated women."

"He didn't have very positive feelings about women at all," she went on. "He loved me, he adored me, but he didn't trust me. But what he said meant a lot to me."

Mattie said she was the only one in the family who would stand up to her father. "That's why he respected me. Mom and my brother would agree with whatever he said, just to keep the peace, then do whatever they wanted to do and he would never know the difference. But I wanted him to know that I was going to go against him, that I thought he was wrong, and that I had my reasons. We had an awful lot of arguments. But I could *show* him he was wrong, and still it wouldn't have any effect."

Although Mattie wasn't winning the battles, she was at least learning how to fight. There were valuable lessons there about the nature of power: what is and what isn't an appropriate use of power, when to stand up to it, which strategies to use. She also was learning the satisfaction of fighting for principle even if one loses.

When the Athena side emerges, it is unmistakable. The problem for many military daughters, however, is that it is unpredictable. "Athena" comes forward in some situations but not in others. The inconsistency is frequently puzzling to the daughters and to those who know them.

Sometimes the assertive, warrior side of a daughter's personality emerges as a kind of compensation for low self-esteem and passivity. One Navy petty officer's daughter, who has suffered a great deal from low self-esteem and the lack of an approving father, found a counterbalance to her private insecurities by becoming a kind of "public warrior": a leader in several important organizations. The times she feels most solid and capable are when she is giving free rein to the father-warrior within her. "Give me a title, give me a position [read 'Give me troops and a command'], and I'm fabulous," she said. "I can make speeches in front of two thousand people, organize anything. I'm wonderful, outgoing, warm. Call it a party, take away the title, and I'm completely lost. Completely lost." A mainstream political worker and an advocate of social causes, she is a warrior in search of the "good war."

The internalized father-warrior can be far more than a daily guide, as valuable as that is. A woman with a warrior side to her personality can find it a deep source of strength in time of adversity. One of the most interesting things to be heard in the stories of military daughters is how the quintessentially masculine model of the warrior is transformed through their lives to have some clearly feminine aspects: a warrior true to the father, *and to the mother also*. A battle-tested woman warrior who aims not to conquer and rule but to endure and learn; who can defeat the enemy if necessary, but who at the point of victory prefers to abandon the warrior mask for that of healer, teacher, peacemaker.

Olivia's Story: A Warrior in Her Own Life

It was the 1960s in the Deep South. Schools were being forcibly integrated, tensions were running sky high, and Olivia, an Army brat, was one of the black students bused off post to a civilian high school. One day, as Olivia and some friends crossed the schoolyard, two heavyset white boys followed and began to taunt them loudly. When the girls didn't respond, a boy pushed one of them off the sidewalk. That's when fifteen-year-old Olivia did what her daddy surely would have done: She strode out to face the boys, hands on her hips, and stared them right in the eye. "I planted myself in front," she remembered. "I was ready for them."

With the unerring instinct of young predators, the boys gave her a wide berth, pushed someone else off the sidewalk, and the ensuing shouting match inflamed the gathering crowd. Within seconds officials were running to break it up.

It was the first time Olivia had worn her father's mask of the warrior, but it would not be the last.

When I met Olivia, the oldest of six children of a master sergeant in the U.S. Army Special Forces, she was forty years old and doing graduate work in fine arts at one of the nation's best universities. A student of film and video, she was preparing a documentary that would consist of portraits of six "women warriors," she explained, "all of whom have transcended adversity, all of whom have inspired and motivated me."

Olivia herself knows adversity from the inside out, and has reason to be grateful for the solid security she had early on. Her parents, she says, were loving and deeply religious. Her father was stern, but not hard on his kids. Moreover—and this is a crucial difference that separates him from many of his fellow warriors—once he set foot in the house at the end of the day, he ceased to be a sergeant. If there was a problem with Olivia's father, it was that war and other missions took him away from the family much of the time, and when he was home he was not as involved as she would have wished. But on the whole, she says, she came from a home that was rock solid, particularly by comparison to those of some of her civilian relatives and other people she's met along the way: Hers was a family with two dedicated parents, a secure standard of living, and a strong sense of pride in their military identity.

The problems began after she left the nest. She moved to a large city to assume her independence, but soon found herself penniless and with no place to live. Just as she was deciding that joining the Army herself was her best option, she learned she was pregnant. Although Olivia says she "always wanted to marry a military man," she turned down the baby's father, an Army sergeant, on the grounds he "wasn't motivated enough." (Read "less of a warrior than she.") Then began her long struggle to support herself and her baby and secure her own college education. Just when it seemed she had a handle on things, she was involved in a car accident that left one friend dead and sent Olivia to the hospital for months. Over the next couple of years there followed another string of personal losses that kept her reeling. In recent years she's been coping with what she considers her biggest challenge yet: learning how to live with diabetes.

Olivia speaks frankly of the mistakes and misjudgments she's made in her life, but the point is clear: Through it all she raised her son, educated herself, and continues to set new goals. "I can stand on my own two feet," she said. "I've proved that. It was a matter of survival and calling on my resources—and that's a part of the training you receive as a military brat: being able to deal with a situation and not fall completely apart. If one thing doesn't work, you go on to the next thing."

Asked how she "does battle," Olivia replied, "By persevering. And I believe it's *because of* my military background that I'm able to persevere."

Olivia may have learned to wear the mask of the warrior at her daddy's knee, but the perseverance she stresses—at once strategy, method, and goal—is essentially feminine in character. While perseverance also has a place in the masculine warrior's code, it is perseverance for the sake of conquest. Olivia's way, the feminine version, aims at a more passive kind of victory: outlasting adversity to achieve victory as an affirmation of life and will.

THE PARTNERS WE CHOOSE

We have said that from the day a military daughter is born, she has a sphinxlike riddle to solve: In the male supremacist world of the Fortress, of which her father is for her the main representative, she must somehow learn to feel worthy in her femaleness.

It is a lifelong task, of course, and her own confusions, doubts, and insights are inevitably acted out in a thousand ways as she goes. We have already seen the legacies of the invisible daughter and how they work upon her. But nowhere will they be more evident than in the person she selects as a mate. The most important love relationship of her life, by virtue of its intimacy, will mirror every aspect of her struggle for visibility and approval: her securities, her fears, her desires, her dark projections.

The key word here is *choice*. Since, in our society, we choose our own mates rather than have them chosen for us, the mirror is that much more accurate. Put another way, every time we choose a partner, that choice is "perfect." The partner may be far from perfect and the match may be all wrong, but the choice itself is an accurate, authentic reflection of how far down the path we have come, of how much we do and do not understand about ourselves and our family of origin.

Does the choice of partner tell more about a woman than about a man? I think so. To some extent, it is a matter of degree—but that difference is a crucial one.

If a man wants to take the measure of another man, he first looks not to the kind of mate the fellow has chosen, but to what he does and has done in the world. For a man, performance in the world shows "what he is made of."

A woman's performance in the world is also highly relevant information, but it will not tell the whole story. To know her we must know about her relationships. As Jean Baker Miller has pointed out, women develop along a different model than men: A woman's development and indeed her very sense of self are inextricably tied to the emotional context of her relationships with others.[7]

So when it comes to the most important relationship of her adult life, a military daughter's choice will be very revealing. The kind of man she picks, or if she holds herself aloof from men, or if indeed she rejects them altogether and becomes asexual or a lesbian—all these choices in their infinite variations have a great deal to do with how the military daughter has chosen to address some of the most fundamental and persistently nagging questions of her life, from her feelings about her father, to her response to her mother as role model, to the matter of her own visibility to herself and others.

And in the interviews for this book, a military daughter's choice of partner also typically revealed many things that would otherwise have been left unsaid.

The Old Mold

Olivia is a case in point: The revelation is that her warrior toughness is really quite a fragile thing. She has no partner, has had none for twelve years, and has no plans for one—the result of an unshakeable vow of celibacy she took to protect her hard-won independence. Simply put, Olivia is attracted to strong-willed men—but, she explains, her fear is that if she allowed such a man into her life, all her feistiness would inevitably dissolve in a wash of deferrals and self-negation: her mother's pattern. Or as one interviewee termed it, the "Old Mold."

That is not an unreasonable fear, says Sarah, the Air Force daughter who is now a psychologist counseling, among others, many daughters of the military. In fact she sees it as the principal legacy of their military rearing. "It's a weird combination of independence versus dependence," she said. "It really gets out of whack. A lot of [military daughters] have a self-image that's really independent. But when they get into marriage they become dependent, and they can't understand how it happened."

Put another way, it's like the visibility/invisibility problem. Just when the daughter thinks she has successfully, painstakingly constructed a strong self-image to project into the world, it suddenly dissolves into invisibility. And it is no accident that it happens in her most private context, before the one who has supplanted her father as the most significant male in her life. One image has unaccountably faded into another, and this one, while as familiar as her own face, is not one the daughter wants to see. Mother. Suddenly she finds herself back in her mother's pattern.

Hear the words of one puzzled daughter of an authoritarian Marine pilot, talking about a sister who for her was always the very model of assertiveness: "She became very docile for her husband, strangely enough. And she's *never* been docile. But once they were married she went back into the Old Mold. I can't figure it out."

A daughter may not even recognize that it is happening to her. She may think of herself as assertive and independent long after she has begun to change. I recall the interview of an Air Force pilot's daughter who made a point of saying that, in reaction to having an authoritarian father, she and all her sisters chose as mates "mellow men who aren't going to control us." A few minutes later, asked specifically about her own marriage, she said, "What my husband wants, I do. What he says, I do." She never even perceived the contradiction.

Some daughters caught in the Old Mold simply do nothing about it: They live out their marriages in relatively untroubled imitation of their mothers' pattern. Others are plenty troubled by it, and, like Sarah's clients, seek counseling to puzzle it out. Grace, the general's daughter who married back into the military, has used a combination of therapy and a women's group to teach herself a more assertive way to relate to her husband and bring balance to their marriage; we return to her story in the last chapter of this book.

Olivia, from the vantage point of her safely solitary life, fantasized "the perfect solution" to the dilemma. "Marry a military man," she said with a sly glint in her eye, "but make sure he's in the Navy so he'll be gone half the time."

To be sure, the Old Mold is not the only relationship model to be found among daughters of warriors. Here are some others:

Spouse as Antidote

Always intriguing are the military daughters of very authoritarian fathers who have managed, despite problems of low self-esteem and general confusion, to pick the right kind of mate to offset the father's power.

Leigh, for instance, married a man who not only gave her warmth and affection, but was mature and self-possessed enough even when quite young not to be taken in by her father's melodramatic power plays. It was Tom who quickly dubbed his father-in-law "The General," a conversational device that helped Leigh objectify her father and give her room to escape his psychological reach.

In an incident very early in his relationship with his father-in-law, Tom made it clear that he bore him no malice, but he wasn't going to kowtow or be bullied. One afternoon he was driving his father-in-law's expensive car to the airport, Leigh's father beside him and Leigh and her mother in back. On a deserted country lane a dog suddenly ran in front of the car, and Tom braked to avoid it. "The General just blew up," Leigh recounted. "He started screaming about how dangerous that was. 'Goddammit, don't you ever do that again! *Don't you know you've got a general in this car?'* Tom replied that was the most ridiculous thing he'd ever heard. He stopped the car, handed The General the keys, and told him to drive. All of a sudden The General was conciliatory, almost fawning. He couldn't do enough for him. When we got to the airport, he bought us all champagne." The incident set the tone for their relationship ever afterward.

"There is a lot of humor in military life, but it is very dark," Leigh said. "I chose a husband who could see the humor. I can think of a lot of men who wouldn't have put up with it, who would have made me choose [between my family and my marriage] because it was so outrageous. But he's been supportive of me and has seen the humor. In a way it's pretty amazing; the first time my dad met him he was so insulting. . . .

"Tom didn't make issues out of a lot of things. He could have been very competitive and threatening toward my father, but he wasn't. He just wouldn't be baited by him, or threatened, or emasculated."

Déjà Vu

In this group are the daughters who had difficult relationships with their fathers and wind up choosing men who are very much like them. Thus the relationship from the outset is doomed to be a stage on which all sorts of unresolved conflicts are acted out.

Here is the daughter of an authoritarian Army sergeant: "In late adolescence and early adulthood, I'd find the men who were really not appropriate for me. I'd choose men who were similar to my dad, and then find myself thinking at some point, My God, what am I doing here? I didn't like *him*, so what am I doing with *this* guy?" She married a noncom in the Army, and they later divorced.

Cheryl, the daughter of a Navy chief petty officer, told of a sister who twice married—and twice divorced—men very much like their father. "She was better educated than either husband and certainly the breadwinner in both marriages," said Cheryl, "and they made her feel so inadequate. I saw her get the same treatment from her second husband, especially, that we saw our father dish out to our mother."

As for Cheryl, she has been married three times, and her first two husbands mirrored another aspect of her father: emotional distance. "My therapist says, 'Do you see where the men in your life are emotionally unavailable to you?' I was so gullible with my first two husbands. But the man I'm married to now is so emotionally available to me, and I am so distant from him. He's a wonderful man, and yet I treat him so badly. Maybe I don't know how to handle emotional availability."

The Sentry Who Never Sleeps

This is the daughter who finds herself in a positive, committed relationship but unable to trust in it. Even as she is going through the motions of planning with her partner way into the future, some part of her is expecting the relationship to crumble at any moment. In the environment of the relationship she is walking perpetual guard duty, as edgy and paranoid as a Vietnam veteran. In my experience, the military daughters who fit this model were all daughters of alcoholics. It is now well known that adult children of alcoholics often have great difficulty trusting those who are closest to them.[8]

Susan is an Air Force colonel's daughter, and both her parents are alcoholics. "A really big issue for me is that I can't ever relax. I have to hold something back. I have to maintain. Part of me can't lean. It's a real issue in my marriage. My husband is a very secure, well-loved Jewish prince. *His* assumption is that people are there to love and take care of him. *My* assumption is, you never let your guard down."

The Wrong Guy

Some military daughters, time after time, pick such wildly inappropriate men it is a source of wonder and consternation to all who know them. These are the daughters whose emotional needs are so many and so overwhelming that they can't help but choose a partner to fill whatever single need is most painful at the time. The relationship is doomed from the start, because both the initial choice and the relationship which follows are out of balance.

Many of these women are the invisible daughters of very authoritarian fathers, and have problems with low self-esteem. They tend to be attracted to "instinctual" men: men who inhabit the world of feeling, who are spontaneous, dramatic, and capable of great warmth. In other words, the opposite of a rigid authoritarian father who withheld affection. Unfortunately, an instinctual man may have a treacherous dark side: emotions without the balance of maturity or good judgment. At the least, he might make bad decisions that affect her; at worst, he might be dangerous. When I interviewed her, Anita was walking this road.

Anita's Story: No Substitute for Love

When I met Anita, the darkly beautiful, half-Mexican daughter of a Navy chief petty officer, she was twenty-nine years old and every inch a top-of-the-line military brat: poised, collected, articulate, socially graceful, supercompetent at whatever she undertook.

What was not so obvious was that she was also a recovering narcotics addict and compulsive overeater. After almost ten years of counseling and group therapy, she had acquired a great deal of insight and had come a long way toward putting her life in order. Except for her love relationships.

At the time, she was involved with a sixty-four-year-old convicted murderer and former drug addict. And as she recounted a list of past loves, it became clear all of them fit the same mold: instinctual, driven, dangerous. Anita was very unhappy about her habit of going directly to the "wrong guy," but felt powerless to do anything about it.

"I wouldn't know an appropriate man if he walked up and said, 'God sent me,' " she said. "But I know how much I have changed in the last ten years, and I know the change has to come from me; [I have to learn not to] make such crummy choices."

The story of Anita's early life is one of great loneliness, pain, and repressed emotion. She was sexually abused by her step-grandfather at age six, and although she reported it to her parents right away, she has suffered guilt feelings for many years. Her mother was a hardworking woman who held a series of factory jobs and was exhausted most of the time. Anita's father, an authoritarian, was at sea half the year and, when home, would get drunk every payday. "My feeling about men is, they're transitory," she said.

Women stay, but men come and go. Women are to be relied upon and trusted. Men will be here for a little while, but you can't count on them. And they certainly are not going to be around when they're needed.

One of the things I've been dealing with lately, and I can trace it back to my father being gone so much, is a sense of abandonment. It really never occurred to me that my father ever thought about me when he was gone. I got only one letter that I can recall. It was for my sixteenth birthday, and it was such a big deal. He had sent a little one-page letter—I can remember as though it were yesterday—sandwiched between two postcards of the ship he was on. He said the PX didn't have any cards, so he made this one to wish me a happy sixteenth birthday. I still have it.

Anita remembers that when she was little, she was her father's favorite child, and she basked in his approval and affection. Her interpretation is that as she approached adolescence and gained more and more weight, her father became alienated and transferred his affection to another child.

She told of a recent conversation she had with her father—a very rare event. They went out for a meal and talked of ordinary family things. "It was actually very pleasant. Afterwards, he wouldn't come out and give me a hug—that's too much to ask—but he put his hand on my shoulder real quick, so quick you had to pay attention or you would have missed it, and gave me a squeeze. Then he walked on." Later in the day, as she was driving alone to a meeting, she said,

I got all full of tears, and I thought, You can go to bed with a hundred older men, and it's never going to make your father more affectionate than he is. That's the thought that came into my head. I thought, Whoa, where did *that* come from? It's about as Freudian as you can get. But I'm sure there is a connection to my choices of older men.

I always see them initially as strong, solid, someone I can depend on. That never turns out to be the case, but that's how I initially perceive it. What I'm after is the sense that I'm okay, that I'm loved, I'm appreciated—because deep down there's this sense that I am unlovable, I am unworthy, unacceptable.

I have a friend who said I don't give appropriate men a second glance. My response was to think, They wouldn't look at me anyway.

Opting for the World of Women

A few military daughters interviewed either chose or had seriously entertained choosing a life that excluded men as partners. Their reasons—insofar as they had figured them out—were complex. But it was clear from their stories that every one of them felt hurt and angry about aspects of their experience growing up inside the Fortress. At some level they may have reasoned by the law of opposites—that at the other end of the spectrum they might find the self-image that so eluded them in the world of the warrior.

Two daughters, both of whom had been abused as children (one sexually, one physically) were strongly drawn to the convent life. One went so far as to investigate various religious orders as a young adult, seeing it as an answer to her "overwhelming sense of pain, anxiety, sadness." She said, "The only time I felt good at all—which was why I wanted to be a nun—was when I was in church, or teaching children in my faith. That was the only time I didn't feel that wrenching pain." The convent, she said, represented among other things a tight-knit community that would welcome her and perhaps be the antidote to her terrible loneliness. She spoke of her deep-seated fear of men—and the attraction of the convent as a "woman's world." Although she now doubts she will ever take the step of joining, it is an idea that resurfaces from time to time.

The other military daughter actually took her vows and spent seven years as a nun—although she has since left her order and is now married. She explained that she, too, was drawn to the religious life out of terrible loneliness, and because it was a "safe place."

Some military daughters become lesbians. Although the reasons here, too, are complex, it is nevertheless striking that their stories were so full of hurt at their fathers' physical and emotional absence while they were growing up.

One lesbian daughter, after telling of a father who was cold and aloof, said, "I identify with women. And I fought it for thirty years, dated a lot, was engaged, but when all is said and done, I prefer to live with a woman." She never told her father directly of her sexual orientation, but she did finally talk to her mother, who was not surprised. In a splendid touch of irony, that afternoon as she sat in the kitchen talking with her mother, finally "coming out of the closet," her father was in the backyard doing some carpentry work on her bedroom closet door.

This military daughter says she is a lesbian without rancor, who enjoys the company of men and "the male dynamic." Yet her lifestyle revolves around women, and is structured to keep men at an emotional distance.

Another lesbian I interviewed presented a different picture. Although she denied it, her tale was full of the rage of the invisible daughter. She described her father, an Army major, as an authoritarian who showed little caring for his children and humiliated her mother with his endless sexual affairs.

He was also gone much of the time, requesting—and receiving— many tours of duty away from the family. His daughter claims his absence meant nothing to her. "In our family it didn't really register when he was away. We actually functioned better as a family without him." In keeping with the revenge of the invisible daughter, she had made her own father invisible. At the time of the interview, it had been years since she had last seen or spoken to her father, who was divorced from her mother. She was not even sure where he lived. "No one from our family is in contact with him," she said. "We were fatherless for many years anyway. And if I didn't have a father at a time when I would have noticed it, it doesn't feel like there's a hole now!"

Her anger, however, has been displaced onto all men, whom she dismisses as "aliens from another planet." But, she said,

> I do have a weak spot in my heart for what I would call the "modern man": When I see a father in the supermarket wheeling around a baby, a nurturing male, I get a little "Gosh, wouldn't that be nice." When you see nurturing males, it's such a contrast. And I think, My father could have had that. But he couldn't have. Not being the person he was.
>
> I do have a warm spot in my heart for my best friend's father. I've gone fishing with him. He's someone I can do father-daughter things with. I care about him in a soft, mushy way that I think maybe daughters feel about their fathers. The ones that liked their fathers.

These are stories of women to the Fortress born, daughters of warriors, whose life task is to solve this sphinxlike riddle: *How can a girl-child see her own reflection in a room without mirrors?*

For the daughter of a warrior there must always be the hope that if she is resourceful, if she *perseveres*, if she can somehow learn to be a good father-guide to herself, she may find her own unique answer to that riddle. And surely, as she searches for an image she can recognize—an image that will hold, that will not flicker and fade before the gaze of warriors—she can be forgiven her frustration, her rage, and her tears.

But if the young girls of the Fortress face a harsh task, what of their brothers? Is it so lucky to be born male inside the ultimate patriarchy? The sphinx, it turns out, is ready for them, too, with a riddle that may be even more terrible: *How does a boy-child see his own reflection in a room lined with mirrors, all of which show the same image—the father-warrior?*

An image that is much, much larger than life.

CHAPTER 5

SONS OF WARRIORS: MIRRORING THE WARRIOR

Ben was lying on his bed studying the cracked geometry of falling plaster that hung above him. Dreams and imaginary dramas were projected on the ceiling as Ben's brain danced with dazzled portraits of his father and him locked in duels to the death. At these times, alone, Ben consciously extended his frontiers of hatred and longed for a reprieve from his father and the freedom of not being a son.

—The Great Santini

After our father died, my brother David and I conferred by mail on the wording of his obituary for *Assembly*, a West Point alumni publication. My brother made some notations on the copy and sent it back to me with a note, which read in part:

It hasn't been pleasant going over our father's record. I can imagine it is also hard for you. . . . Sometimes I think, well, I never really had a father—but then again, I most certainly did. We never talked. Not once. . . .

I believe that suffering and pain give us a possibility of understanding human dignity and what it means. And we do. Was it worth it? I wouldn't do it again. To live a childhood and adolescence with my father was like being in prison. I hope there is no such thing as reincarnation. As Woody Allen says, if there is reincarnation, it would be awful: One might have to sit through the Ice Capades again. Or one might have to sit through hundreds of meals with the likes of our father.

Some people come to this earth and leave a trail of pain behind them in great and small ways. One usually thinks of criminals in such matters, but there are others who manage with careful attention to detail to accomplish the same, against all odds: quality pain, visionary confusion, a depth of suffering. No shallow accomplishment.

It struck me that my brother's letter was, in its way, also an obituary for our father. A dark and damning obituary, engraved in the shared memory of a painful family history, an obituary that for all its bitterness is as true as the other. For *Assembly* my brother and I had paid respectful homage to our father's warrior persona—the battles, the medals, the commands, the sense of service, the fierce patriotism. It was the part of himself our father valued most; and, giving him his due, so did we. He was not, objectively and subjectively speaking, a good father, but he was a warrior's warrior. He had his faults as a soldier, too, of course; a few years after he retired, he told me, in a moment of self-confession that was never to be repeated, that his worst professional failing was arrogant pride. But, from what my brother and I knew of his career, when it came to duty, honor, country, and to matters of leadership, of dedication to his troops, and of aptitude for war, our father could not be faulted. Two obituaries. Two irreconcilable versions of a man, two ends of the human spectrum. We, his children, standing as witnesses to his soldierly victories, his personal failures. A picture of a man, transformed into the quintessential warrior, who then could not stop going to war. Even in his own home, against his own son.

My brother's note continued. "I remember as a boy of eight or maybe nine wishing with all my might that I was a dog. A common escape, I was later told.

"But," he added, "I never *fully* achieved that wish." A sardonic sense of humor has always been my brother's salvation.

Not long after that, my father's widow—she had been married to him for just the last six years of his life—in a kind gesture sent a fine photographic portrait of him to my brother and me. It is a formal studio pose of my father in a swanky suit and tie—he was fond of fine clothes—taken just a couple of years before he died. His hair is thin and nearly white; age has softened his features and his demeanor. The slight smile and kindly aspect give no hint of the arsenal of verbal condemnation that, in another time, he was ever ready to turn on his family. He no longer looks the formidable warrior my brother once described as "ruthless, unpredictable, always angry, and cunningly, dangerously, intelligent."

Except for the eyes. They are the same clear, cold, gray-green eyes that would register my brother's image on the retina with the assurance of a gunner fixing a target in his sights.

I put the portrait away in a trunk, to be framed at some as yet undetermined time. Later I was surprised to learn that my brother had hung his copy of the picture immediately, in the room where he spends most of his time.

"It's an amazing photograph," my brother commented to me on the phone some months later. "It's as though he's still alive and present. No matter where I stand, no matter what I'm doing, his eyes follow me."

If the problem for military daughters is invisibility, the problem for military sons is surely just the opposite.

From the day he is born inside the Fortress, a son is subject to unending critical scrutiny. Every detail of his appearance and behavior is measured against warrior ideals of manliness, not to mention the even more exacting standards of his own warrior father. While a daughter yearns for some kind of positive attention from the father who can't seem to bring her into focus, a son seeks to shield himself from the glare of the warrior's relentlessly demanding gaze.

To be sure, there are warrior families where the father does not play the heavy, families where the father is caring and affirming, families where the father is even home enough of the time to make that impression stick. I know such warrior families exist; I have met sons who bear witness to the benefits of such a rearing.

And I remember from my childhood a certain Army major, the father of my teenage brother's best friend, Jim Dunning. (Here, as a gesture of tribute, I am using the real names of my brother's friend and his father.)

David would hang around the major's house, talk to him, watch him, instinctively trying to offset the effects of our own fierce father. My brother didn't have very lengthy exposure to Jim's father by civilian standards—military families move far too often for children to have much exposure to any adults apart from their own parents—but by some extraordinary luck the major was assigned to the same places as our father on two successive tours, at Butzbach, West Germany, and at the Pentagon, amounting to a total of about four years of contact. That meant a great deal to my brother then, and it does still, over thirty years later. Major James Dunning presented a different model of manhood from what my brother had seen in our house: the model of a strong warrior with a kind and loving side. "He was a good and decent man," my brother would recollect, "a strong man, with a good sense of humor. And he always had time for his children. The thing that made the difference was that he would *listen*. He wouldn't get angry if you had opinions, and he wouldn't give orders all the time."

I was too young to know the Dunnings well, but the name of

Colonel Dunning—he was later promoted—has nevertheless been invoked as reverentially by me as by my brother over the years. For us he represented a combination of qualities we wanted badly to believe in: courage as a warrior, kindness as a father, steadfastness as a friend. His sons, we thought, must be the luckiest sons in the U.S. Army.

For the sons in a great many military families are not so lucky. Either deliberately or by default, these sons are left to puzzle out a painful contradiction that profoundly affects how they see themselves and later make their way in the world—and like everything else about their young lives inside the Fortress, it is centered on their inescapable visibility.

At the outset, sons say, their visibility is thrilling. On the face of it, every son of a warrior is a kind of crown prince, a child of the correct gender to gain acceptance and affirmation inside the patriarchal world of the Fortress—affirmation that, as we saw in the last chapter, is denied out of hand to his sister. But slowly, inexorably, the visibility of sons is turned against them. By the time they reach adolescence, many sons recount, they have become accustomed to drawing the warrior's eye but not his praise. The warrior father, who for his son represents all warriors, all fathers, does not deliver the overt approval which is vital to his son's self-esteem. The warrior image that seemed so accessible to the sons in their younger years shimmers forever just out of reach; the sons continue to look for affirmation, but with diminishing confidence that they will ever attain it. They are demoralized, confused, self-doubting. From their viewpoint, as young males reared within the walls of a world designed for and about men, it is a problem that should never have been.

Some warriors probably withhold it out of a sincere but misguided conviction that it toughens a son, makes him more of a man. Some, in the manner of authoritarians, are simply not conversant in the language of affection and support, and not particularly sensitive to their children's needs. Saddest of all, perhaps, are the fathers who are both caring and affirming but who, because of the Military Mission that takes priority over all else, are simply not at home often enough or long enough to follow through. Whatever the reason, the result is essentially the same: a son who reaches adulthood harboring doubts about his own worthiness.

It is a common situation. Nearly all the sons who shared their stories for this book said they felt cheated of the father love and male guidance they felt was rightfully theirs. Part of the implication of that testimony is that even in many families where the warrior is basically a decent, civilized, and well-intentioned man, the message of love and affirmation he would have liked to deliver—and perhaps thought he *was* delivering—did not get through. Consequently, the sons, like the daughters, have wrestled in adulthood with problems of self-esteem that are the legacy of the father manqué.

The nonaffirming or physically absent father is only one variation on the story, however. There were also many sons interviewed for this book for whom the principal problem was not an absent father but one who was too much present—the rigidly authoritarian, darkly ominous father in a largely dysfunctional family such as mine, or the one depicted in *The Great Santini*. These sons clearly feel rejected in a more direct and damaging way.

Sometimes the rejection of the son is almost impersonal in nature—the authoritarian father, frustrated at work, needs a scapegoat when he comes home. Practically anyone will do, but the son, in his unavoidable visibility, is the obvious target. He draws his father's anger like a lightning rod. The discipline he receives is harsher, more frequent, more physical than for his sister. Verbal criticism is relentless, approval very rare.

Sometimes the rejection is a few degrees stronger and a few degrees more personal, as when the warrior father seizes upon his son as though on some miniature and inherently unacceptable replica of himself; an unformed, undisciplined, premilitary replica that by its mere existence threatens to tarnish the warrior's image. In such cases it seems to become a secondary mission for the warrior to contain his miniature—as a means, perhaps, of protecting the immaculate military persona the warrior likes to pretend is his true and complete identity. Such a man rarely steps out of his warrior role; he treats his son as an unruly recruit whose very desire for approval is unrealistic and out of line.

And then there are cases of warrior families where the father reserves special and very personal animosity for his male miniature, cases we shall see something of in this chapter and others, where it may be that the father's wrath is a kind of retribution for the supreme offense his little son commits, unwittingly, every time he draws the warrior's eye: the offense of reminding the father of the emotionally needy side of himself he sought to bury in becoming a warrior in the first place. For no matter how the father may have tried to conceal memories of his own painful childhood behind the implacable mask of the warrior, the past has a way of casting its shadow even here, inside the seemingly impenetrable walls of the Fortress, onto the face of his own male child.

Sons in such families are particularly bewildered by their fathers' malevolence. Try as they might to make themselves vanish into the background—and oh, how they come to envy their sisters' invisibility—they remain both exposed and vulnerable. The sons of such warriors—and, judging by the interviews for this book, there are many such warriors—find themselves engaged in a perpetual battle in which they have no weapons, no support, no cover, and which they are permitted neither to win nor to lose. Retreat is not an option. No matter how the sons may wish to capitulate and end the conflict, they find all exit routes blocked.

The most brutal warrior fathers *need* this unending battle—need, perhaps, proof of their continued ability to repress the old emotional hurts they carry—the way tamer men, gentler men, unwounded men, need their sons.

But this is not the way the story begins for the male children of the Fortress.

At the outset, the sons of warriors bask in the glow of their fathers' reflected glory, the cumulative glory of the ages which resides in the person of every warrior, whether or not he has been tested in battle. The soldier-hero is not a storybook abstraction for the sons of warriors: He is an active, powerful, compelling presence, at once challenging and exhilarating, part of a continuum of brave and bold warriors going back to the beginning of history. How wonderful the promise of approval from such a man. How lucky a son feels to bear the mantle of succession.

But while the fact of a son's maleness fires him with visions of his own glorious future, it also delivers him into inescapable, unrelenting scrutiny that is at times oppressive. His tender age makes no difference. Inside the Fortress a male child, no matter how young, is expected to prove his mettle, again and again, beneath the unforgiving gaze of warriors.

IN THE EYE OF THE WARRIOR

We have already seen some of the ways in which childhood inside the Fortress is militarized. Families vary a great deal on that score, of course, but even in families where daughters are let off lightly, there is frequently no slack in the rearing of a warrior's sons. From the beginning a son is expected to work toward merging himself with the warrior image: He is taught to bear pain with courage and self-discipline. By the time he is in nursery school he has learned to append the requisite "sir" or "ma'am" to his replies. While civilian preschoolers are earning gold stars for good habits, a son of the Fortress may be earning demerits and performing punishment duty. And, under the suspicious eye of the warrior father, all vestiges of softness and nurturance will be drummed out.

"My brother and I were taught never to cry, never to show emotion," wrote the son of an Air Force colonel, in a follow-up letter after our interview.

> We were forcibly reminded that men with tears in their eyes were sissies and crybabies. To my father's frustration, this mandate had the opposite effect. Perhaps it was the impossibility of ever living up to such a demand; certainly it was difficult to be a child in the center of a rocky marriage, always uncertain as to what might set off the next ferocious storm, and to be denied any emotional outlet. Living within that contradiction as we did, tears became our first response to family tensions and our father's anger. Even relatively minor disputes with the old man could easily set off a flood of uncontrollable crying.
>
> Of course that would only enrage him further, setting off a flood of invective, and we would be sent to our room, under orders enforced by the threat of violence to remain completely silent. As our frustration grew, our tears got closer to the surface. Our father's anger at our "crybaby behavior" increased, and so did our time on punishment tour.
>
> Perhaps tears were our only weapon against him.

The standard socialization of a young male inside the Fortress takes place in two ways. One is the way just described, in which the intention is to emotionally pummel the son into shape. The other way, more didactic but in a sense equally forceful, is by demonstration. The daughter of an Air Force general provided an example.

"When my brother was little, he had a rag doll," she said. "He carried it around, loved it. My dad found this very objectionable, and he went to great lengths to wean my brother from this doll. He even had a little uniform made for my brother that was just like my dad's uniform. They would dress him up in it and say to him, 'Give us the doll. We're going to take your picture now.' He wouldn't give it to them. There are pictures of my brother in that uniform, clutching the doll. And you can see in his eyes the pain of their wanting to take the doll away so they could take a picture of The Little Soldier."

In such innocuous, ordinary ways begins the indoctrination of a warrior's son. In case his tiny son had not, by the age of three, grasped the implications of his gender for the role of warrior-understudy, the father goes to considerable trouble to dress him for the part. Then a picture is taken of the two of them in uniform, standing side by side, presumably driving home a message of matching images that even a three-year-old could not miss. But the carefully orchestrated attempt at imprinting is not successful, at least not on this occasion; in fact, a different lesson has been taught. The tiny boy now understands that in merging with the warrior image, he will have to surrender an important part of himself.

In a sense it is remarkable that the boy was allowed to have a doll at all. Many of the sons interviewed for this book spoke of how it was strictly forbidden for them to play with dolls—even the popular soldier doll, G.I. Joe—or they risked being derided by their fathers as sissies. Such sex-role stereotyping is hardly unique to the military, but it's fair to say that at any given time the Fortress culture can be expected to promote a more exaggerated version of male stereotyping than that prevailing in civilian culture. Warriors pride themselves on sons who are tougher, more aggressive, more tenacious than their civilian peers; they would be mortified if a civilian kid showed more grit than their own. These, after all, are men who specialize in relentless, single-minded aggression, and they expect no less of their sons. The Fortress is hardly a place where one is likely to find men struggling to deepen their sensitivities; New Age ideas would be blasted out of the air like clay pigeons on a skeet range.

In warrior households, there are any number of barometers of the pressure applied to male children to conform to warrior standards.

Discipline is certainly one of them. "When a son makes an error," noted the son of an Army colonel, "it is rebuked instantly." There are plenty of opportunities for a son to make errors. While a daughter must make her bed in a neat and perfectionistic way, and will often be required to stand inspection the same as her brother, a son will have to go one step further and make the bed so tightly that his father can bounce a quarter off it. A son is typically required to say "sir" even if a daughter isn't. A girl meeting one of her father's friends must merely look pleasant and respectful; a boy must do more, offering a handshake with an acceptable degree of firmness and standing ready to receive further orders. And warrior fathers frequently invent bizarre tasks for sons to perform, presumably to instill an obedience that prevails over any sense of personal discomfort. Military sons tell of direct orders from their fathers to drop whatever they were doing and go scrub the already spotless front steps, or perform a given number of push-ups or laps around the yard.

Sometimes, in the father's zeal to instill toughness, the boundaries between instruction and punishment of sons become blurred. The daughter of an Air Force major, a pilot, told of how, after one of her brothers lost part of his fishing rod during a family expedition, their father forced him to dive over and over again into the deep, murky water until he found it. The same father, in the course of teaching his sons to swim, was not content merely to show them how to spot dangerous whirlpools and avoid them; instead he forced them, in spite of their fear, to repeatedly swim into the whirlpools and get themselves out. "He was a really macho type," the daughter said.

When it came to punishments, he was equally tough: "The boys got boards broken over their rear ends," she said. "But in the classic way, my father didn't touch the girls."

It is a common pattern inside the Fortress: The son of an Air Force lieutenant colonel said, "My brother and I got kicked, bashed around, hit with the belt and sticks. My sister was never touched, although the rules were actually stricter for her."

While sons may typically enjoy a degree of greater personal movement—later curfews, for instance—their visibility is inevitably used against them. It's almost as though their maleness is a license for the authoritarian warrior to violate all boundaries; a son in such a family is typically not granted dominion over anything. For example, he has much less privacy than his sister; even his own bedroom is not a safe redoubt. "I remember laughing at 'Leave It to Beaver' episodes where the father would knock on the door and ask if he could enter the room," said the son of an Air Force master sergeant. "My father would just open the door and walk right in, whenever he wanted. There was no space that was outside his control, safe from his intrusion, and no sense of an area where you could develop yourself."

But if in their unavoidable visibility sons lack dominion over their own privacy, they also lack it over decisions as personal as their appearance, a subject that takes on inordinate importance for authoritarian warriors living in the Fortress hall of mirrors. While a daughter must be neat, clean, and conventional in all respects—the better to be invisible—a son must follow the more stringent standards reserved for warriors, who are always on display. A girl cannot slouch, but a boy must stand ramrod straight. A girl's best shoes must be polished; a boy's must be spit-shined. A girl's hair must be neatly trimmed; a boy's . . . well, the haircut of a warrior's son is a subject in itself. Son after son exploded with resentment at the mention of the word, so symbolic was it of their forced submission of body and will to the iron rule of the father. Typically a son would be hauled off to the base barbershop every two weeks, with the father issuing terse orders to the grim, taciturn barber to make it "high and tight," or "close like a peach, not enough to part." Some of the more unfortunate sons were shorn at home, by the warriors themselves.

"At one point my father bought some clippers and clipped the hair of both us boys," said the son of a Navy petty officer. "He did a terrible, terrible job. A couple of times he did it when he was drunk. I was humiliated. Each time I had to wear a hat for a couple of weeks until it grew out."

The son of an Air Force colonel said, "My father always cut my hair. He butchered it. He used the same clippers on the dog."

Not all the barometers of a son's pressured apprenticeship are as obvious as the haircut, however. In the household of a very authoritarian warrior, another index is the phrasing which has been excised from a son's language. Many sons reported that they—unlike their sisters—were not permitted to use "feeling" words. Phrases such as "I love" and "I feel" were banned outright, confessions of emotion and expressions of affection discouraged. "My father told me never to use the word *love* in my language," said the son of an Army colonel. "I couldn't say 'I'd love to do this, I'd love to do that.' He would tell me, 'Only queers say that.' " The son of an Air Force colonel said, "When you were real young you would say you loved your mom or your dad, but as you got older you *never* talked about your feelings. And my father never asked how we 'felt' about anything."

In some households the authoritarian monitoring of emotions and emotional language in sons extended even to phrases such as "I guess" or "I think"; the authoritarian warrior father would admonish the son, saying, "Either you *know* something, or you don't." In such families there is no tolerance of ambiguity, uncertainty, speculation—all of which, in authoritarian eyes, are weak and effeminate, betraying a less than rigorously rational cast of mind. By the same token, warrior fathers monitor their sons' activities for any hint of slippage from the accepted Fortress norms. Military sons are often forbidden to go on "sleep-overs" at the homes of [civilian] school friends; to even request to do so would bring the accusing question, "What are you, a queer?"

That, of course, is a warrior father's ultimate fear. In some homes that accusing question is repeated with the frequency of a refrain. A son decides not to try out for varsity sports; he hears the refrain. A father returns from a lengthy sea cruise to find his son sporting longer hair; again the refrain. A son loses a fistfight; the refrain.

The homophobia that runs rampant inside the Fortress may be one of the reasons warrior fathers withhold affection from their sons. As we saw in Chapter 3, warriors are not big on expressing affection anyway—but even where they show affection to their daughters, they tend to hold off from their sons. The following is a passage from *The Great Santini*:

> Ben put his nose into the leather sleeve and breathed in rich memories of his own life. He could remember burrowing his head into his father's jacket when he was a child, in the days when he was allowed to hug and caress his father, in the days before his father declared it inappropriate. The sons of Marines all come to a day when their fathers move away from their embrace. The men of the flight jacket. The strong fathers.[1]

"One of the themes in *The Great Santini* that I thought was quite accurate for many fathers," said the social worker son of a Marine colonel, "was the fear of loving their kids too much—especially sons. It's the fear of their love making their sons soft. I was quite touched by that—because with both my brother and me, our dad was much more generous and frank about his affection when we were young adults and he was sure that we had 'made it,' that we were okay, than he had been when we were school age."

Reflecting on the Warrior

If, in the privacy of their own homes, authoritarian warriors tolerate no slack in the training of their son-understudies, there is even less tolerance when the sons are out in the public eye. Just when a young son is trying to bring himself into focus, understand where he stands in his social context, every move he makes is interpreted as a reflection on the warrior who raised him.

Military sons frequently recall with mixed feelings the school team sports in which they participated. On the plus side, many of them note, sports were a quick and effective avenue to friendships, a sense of accomplishment, and a social identity—all the more important when the son may have transferred into a school in the middle of the year and knows he only has a limited time in which to make his mark. But sports can be a real crucible of the spirit if the boy's father is the type of warrior who sees a game less as an opportunity to learn cooperative effort and sportsmanship than as a showcase for the pit bull aggressiveness he has been trying to inculcate in his son since birth. A civilian friend of mine, the father of a ten-year-old girl who plays soccer on a coed team, lives in a heavily military part of the country. All the schools in the area have large numbers of military brats, who are well represented on the teams. My friend says that at most of the matches the military fathers, often still in uniform, shock the civilian parents by "running up and down the sidelines screaming at their little kids, cursing them if they make a mistake."

Such warriors take the mistakes of their children personally, as reflections on their own ability to lead and inspire. The time after the game can be miserable, the sons say, as the fathers analyze what happened in military terms, interpreting flubbed shots or missed passes as failures of nerve or of will—unconscionable acts by troops in battle or, for sons, in peewee league ball games.

It is not hard to infer the kind of backyard coaching the son of such a warrior is likely to receive. "I remember playing catch with my dad one time," said the son of a Marine major. "I must have been eleven or twelve. I had a girlfriend then named Sally. Every time I dropped the ball, my dad called me 'Sally.' I remember him just grinding it in. I can remember how much it hurt, and I remember crying—and not letting it show. God, that was a tough afternoon."

The Warrior Internalized

So far we have seen warrior sons as passive beings upon whom authoritarian warriors work their will—and that, given the disparity in power, indeed seems to be the fundamental nature of the relationship until the sons finally grow up and leave home. But that doesn't mean sons are entirely passive. On the contrary; after a few years inside the Fortress, and especially under the less than subtle tutelage of his warrior father, a son begins to internalize the lessons of machismo and male domination.

A warrior son is typically so saturated with the notion that he must be constantly ready to prove himself that it becomes reflexive to do so. Even if he attempts to reject the programming and wants nothing to do with physical violence, he knows he must be prepared at any time to fake it, because other military sons will almost certainly find ways to test him. His relentless visibility means that his reputation—and self-esteem—live or die by how well he conforms to the mirror image of the warrior reflected all around him.

One testing process nearly all military sons can speak to is fistfights. While fighting is commonplace among boys everywhere, it may be unusually prevalent among warrior sons. Comments from a few of the sons suggested some possible reasons for this.

The son of an Air Force colonel: "There was a lot of fighting. I've often thought about that. I think we fought because there was just a lot of tension and we were just kids and we didn't know what to do with the tension. We were never in one place very long and our homelife was probably shit. Instead of crying and going to bed with it, I'd go to school and beat kids up."

The son of an Air Force lieutenant colonel: "Fistfights? Yes. It was like going into a new dog pack. They all had to sniff you, and one of them always decided he didn't like you. I remember some pretty good fights. I now have a physical revulsion toward fighting. I didn't like it much in school either, but you had no choice. Whenever I could, I'd change it from a fistfight to a wrestling match—you'd get a little less damaged that way."

The son of a sergeant in the U.S. Army Special Forces: "I went through several bloody fistfights just to be accepted. I believe other boys in the military had the same fears I did: Each time you moved in the military you became more isolated. You had frustrations and grief because you had left friends behind and you had to make new ones. Emotionally it was pretty tough. So through aggression you could dissipate some of the emotional stress."

Son of an Air Force master sergeant: "I'm five foot six. For a long time, if someone challenged me, called me 'Shorty,' we were gonna fight, that's all there was to it. I was always in a challenge-oriented mode, from my whole family situation. There was so much violence like that in my life.

"It comes from my father, but it's also from the military. It's a macho environment in which, if you show some kind of weakness, it's shoved down your throat forever."

Another frequent rite of passage in military boyhood is acting on dares. Again, there is an element of this in any boyhood, anywhere— but inside the Fortress dares among boys may be more frequent, more dangerous, and more imperative. A son's personal honor, no small matter in warrior society, must be upheld at all costs. Like fistfights, dares are a natural and unavoidable part of the Fortress culture for young males. As one son of an Air Force sergeant put it, "Dares were a very big thing in our family. It comes from the top down. The father sets the tone—'You're not a man if you don't do this'—and then the kids, the boys, pick up on that and use it to taunt each other."

"Military kids are wild," said another son of an Air Force master sergeant.

They take chances. We always did things we shouldn't. I remember there was this big sawdust pile and we used to dive in it. We could have suffocated. But you were daring because you grew up with this macho-manly thing: All your role models were fighting men, and there were even signs posted around the base about honor, valor, and so on. If someone dared you to do something, *you did it*—or you were a sissy. You'd jump off things, dive in places—and I couldn't swim, and we lost people to drowning—but if they dared you to do it, you'd do it. I don't know if this is different from [civilians], but I think it is; it was part of the society. It was because your father was military. You know how military men are portrayed on TV: They fear nothing.

Another interviewee, the son of an Air Force colonel, said, "Dares and competition were common among the base kids. There would be a group of six or eight of us, and some of the dares we came up with were dangerous. At one base, we'd jump off railroad trestles into the water below, or, even worse, hang by our hands underneath the trestles when the train passed over. That will make you or break you, believe me. But if you did it, you had the authority to dare someone else to do it."

TRANSITION: CATCHING UP TO THE WARRIOR

Nearly every military son I've interviewed who has seen or read *The Great Santini* remembers one particular scene above all others: the scene immediately following the one-on-one father-son basketball match, which the son has won for the first time in his life by a scant but very significant point. The father proceeds to persecute his son for having the temerity to try and redefine the terms of his visibility:

Bull went up to Ben until they were almost nose to nose, as Ben had seen Drill Instructors do to recruits. With his forefinger, he began poking Ben's chin. "You get smart with me, jocko, and I'll kick you upstairs with your mother so you pussies can bawl together. Now guard me. You gotta win by two."

"I'm not gonnna guard you, Dad. I won," Ben said, his voice almost breaking. He could feel himself about to cry.

Bull saw it too. "That's it, mama's boy. Start to cry. I want to see you cry," Bull roared, his voice at full volume, a voice of drill fields, a voice to be heard above the thunder of jet engines, a voice to be heard above the din of battle. Bull took the basketball and threw it into Ben's forehead. Ben turned to walk into the house, but Bull followed him, matching his steps and throwing the basketball against his son's head at intervals of three steps. Bull kept chanting, "Cry, cry, cry," each time the ball ricocheted off his son's skull. Through the kitchen Ben marched, through the dining room, never putting his hands behind his head to protect himself, never trying to dodge the ball. Ben just walked and with all his powers of concentration rising to the surface of consciousness, of being alive, and of being son, Ben tried not to cry. That was all he wanted to derive from the experience, the knowledge that he had not cried. He wanted to show his father something of his courage and dignity. All the way up the stairs, the ball was hurled against his head. The hair short and bristly from the morning haircut, the head this moment vulnerable, helpless, and loathed. Ben knew that once he made it to his room the ordeal would end, and he would have the night to consider all the symbols of this long march: the heads of sons, the pride of fathers, victors, losers, the faces of kicked wives, the fear of families, the Saturdays in the reign of Santini—but now, now, through this hallway and up these final stairs, I must not cry, I must not cry, I must not cry. Until he saw his room. Breaking into a run, he felt Bull release him, free him, his head throbbing, dizzy; and the son of the fighter pilot fell onto his bed face downward, afraid that tears would come if he did not stem their flow in the cool whiteness of his pillow. His father stood in the doorway and Ben heard him say so that the whole family could hear, "You're my favorite daughter, Ben. I swear to God you're my sweetest little girl."

Then turning toward the door, blinded by water and light, Ben spit back, "Yeah, Dad, and this little girl just whipped you good."

The door slammed.[2]

It's a picture of confrontation in a dysfunctional authoritarian family, to be sure—but it's also a picture of a classic milestone in every son's life, when he pulls even with his father, and then, in a moment, passes him. Such a moment, whenever it comes, in no matter what kind of family, military or civilian, authoritarian or not, cannot fail to be telling. Not only does it pinpoint a long-anticipated event of no small Oedipal significance, it inevitably reveals the essential quality of the fathering that has been done over the course of the son's life.

For many sons of the Fortress, childhood proceeds with the pace and drama of a gathering storm. At first bright sunshine with a rising breeze, then far-off rumblings, barely audible; then a bleeding of the sunlight into thick clouds that grow and darken ominously until finally the whole sky looks bruised and swollen, full of repressed fury at the thunder that slams against it. The question is whether those clouds will turn loose their torrential power and drown out the thunder that has so long assaulted and intimidated them, or if the storm will blow over, somehow resolve itself without violence.

For sons who in their inescapable visibility are physically or emotionally abused by their warrior fathers, the question of when and how to put an end to it, physically teaching their fathers that they are now and forever going to be forced to back down, dominates their fantasy life. They long for that moment of transition, for the opportunity to finally turn the tables, back the warrior against the wall, even the score man to man. In the fantasies, the opportunity always comes, the cause is always just, the fight always fair, and the son always wins. In reality, things may not always happen that way.

There were several interviews in which abused sons spoke of the moment of transition, when physical retaliation against the abusive warrior father finally became a possibility.

Joe's Story: Leaving the Father Behind

Joe's father was a Navy chief petty officer from a poverty-stricken background in the rural South. He had been abused, neglected, and finally rejected by his parents, and joined the Navy as soon as he could as a way out of intolerable misery. Joe's father did well for a time, until his drinking got out of hand. Whether his alcoholism sent his career into a slide, or whether a stalled career drove him to drink, the result was the same. Drinking and a corrosive sense of failure went hand in hand. And he turned his anger on his family.

It was that, and the image of his father as a man whose functional
illiteracy enslaved him to a sense of failure, in turn activating his own
personal demons, that hardened Joe's resolve to get a first-class education and leave his father's tortured world far behind, as we shall see in a
later chapter. But first he had to survive.

"In the early years, my father was a standard spanker," Joe said.

> That was nothing unusual in the fifties. But as I got older and his situation
> in the service became desperate, he became a virtual child abuser in the
> frequency, the intensity, and the duration of the violence. From the time I
> was eleven to about fifteen or sixteen, he was very violent. He would just
> beat me—and my brother, but mostly me—with a belt, for a fairly long
> period of time, about five minutes. He would beat me as hard as he could.
>
> The thing for a kid, if you have parents who physically beat you, is
> whether your parents are just punishing you, or whether they're out of
> control. When you see your parents in a physical rage of great irrational
> power, it's extremely frightening. That's more frightening than the beating
> itself, because you don't know if they're going to stop or if they're going to
> kill you or seriously injure you. My father would just lose control. He'd fly
> into rages and beat me unmercifully. He would be screaming. He wouldn't
> say "I'm going to kill you," but he'd say, "You let me down and I'm going
> to teach you a lesson."
>
> By the time I was sixteen it was tailing off, because I was a little larger. A
> big issue for me at the time was physical response. I was about five foot
> eight or five nine. My father was about five ten and very strong, weighed a
> hundred eighty, a hundred ninety. I don't think I would have stood a
> chance. He was an old Navy chief, a brawler type, a barfly, used to
> fighting. The situation was serious enough that a physical response by me
> was something I was always thinking of, planning, fantasizing.
>
> But I never did it. It was unfair in a way, in terms of development, that
> as soon as I finally got big enough to do something about it, he was too
> infirm and old for it to be a fair fight. So you lose your chance.
>
> There's some moment when you're passing each other, when he's still
> vigorous enough and you're finally big enough—and it would have been
> satisfying to physically beat him up. But I never had that.
>
> The people I know who did it just feel horrible. It's not satisfying,
> particularly if you really hurt your father. If you punch him in the mouth
> and knock him down and he sits there, staring at you. . . . You never forget
> that.

For Joe, the moment of transition that mattered the most came very
early, when his own level of education overtook that of his father. By
the time Joe reached parity with his father in physical size and
strength, the question of answering blow for blow had long been
rendered moot. Everything in Joe's life, from his academic excellence
to the company he kept to his highbrow aspirations, was received by
his father as a rebuke. If Joe had managed to fix on that moment of
physical parity as it was passing, when he was strong enough and his

father not yet frail enough to rule out a fair fight, slugging the old seaman from backwoods Alabama might possibly have been unsatisfying, but it certainly would have been redundant.

Many years have gone by, and things have never improved between Joe and his father. They live thousands of miles apart, never see each other, never talk. Joe says that's the way he wants it, and if his father feels differently, he's never said so.

"I never got the sense my father regretted the physical abuse," Joe said.

> Sometimes people apologize to their kids, I'm told. My father always assumed [beating me] was an appropriate thing to do.
>
> There was a time when I thought, He's had a hard life, I should just forgive him. But he continues to injure people and to be a bad person. He's not out of control, he's in charge of his life, and he can see what he's doing to people, particularly to my mother. It would be dishonest to try to pretend that wasn't the case.
>
> So I don't have any hope of any reconciliation with him, and I will actually be very relieved when he dies. I think my mother will be much, much better off; she'll finally be able to begin to enjoy life free of his tyranny.

In Joe's case, his relentless visibility as the son of an abusive warrior father brought him no lack of desire to even the score. It didn't happen in the sense he had imagined, in a physical roundhouse brawl, but it did happen. The score was evened when, in response to the pain of his own visibility, Joe rendered his father invisible. The warrior was made to see that his image cast no reflection.

That's not the cozy ending one might wish for, in which father and son finally meet and reconcile—something that does in fact happen in quite a few broken military families, as we shall see later on—but in Joe's family it is apparently the best that can be managed. There are limits to the reconstruction that is possible in violent dysfunctional families. Disarmament through distance is sometimes the best of the alternatives.

However, distance as a means of defusing family violence is an option that is open to adults, not children. Many a son of the Fortress has longed for the safety of a thousand-mile buffer between him and his abusive warrior father, has even longed for a war to conveniently take the warrior away. But that doesn't often happen. It is the son's task to endure until he is old enough to free himself, and that is what most sons from such families do.

That is what Todd did, too. But, unlike Joe, Todd had his moment
of transition while he was still at home with his father. And unlike Joe,
he took advantage of it.

Todd's Story: Seizing the Moment

Todd's father was an Air Force colonel who by any reckoning would
be described as an extreme authoritarian. He was the father mentioned
in Chapter 1 who forced his children to eat a "square meal" in cadet
fashion, and to stand at attention when he spoke to them. "The role
my father played was the ogre, the man you're scared to hell of," Todd
said. "But we loved him. Especially when we were young children, we
loved him madly. Of course when you're a young child you don't
know any different."

As time when on, the father's iron rule worsened, and the abuse
increased. "Then of course the Vietnam War didn't help things at all,"
Todd said. "The house was completely divided. That's what finally
pushed it. I was beaten up from the time I was nine until I was
nineteen." Family life was a combat zone. "Christ, I remember one
time standing at attention while my father kicked me in the legs. He
was in a rage. He gave me bruises all up and down my legs. I was nine
or ten years old."

There was emotional abuse as well. Todd continued:

> He would criticize us brutally. It was always "You're not good," or "You're
> not good enough." It was a boot camp mentality. And of course when your
> friends came over, his sense of humor was always to put his son down in
> front of his son's friends. *Especially* if you had a girlfriend there. He'd
> make you stand there while he slyly put you down.
>
> My mother, God bless her pointed head, was always trying to get my
> father and me together because she thought it was important that we do
> father-son things. I was always against it, was always saying, "Mom, *please*
> don't ask him to help me with my homework." But she would insist it
> would be good for us, and of course it ended up in disaster. I remember
> one night after my mother prompted him and prompted him and made
> him feel guilty, he came over to help me with my fractions or some
> godawful mathematics I was supposed to do. And I couldn't get it through
> my head; I just couldn't get this notion down. And having my old man
> hanging over my shoulder, and him having no patience at all for teaching
> a kid, made me more and more flustered and unable to deal with it.
> Finally he just exploded. He picked up that math book and started beating
> me across the head with it.

Things went on in that vein for a number of years, with the father
exercising a tyranny of constant denigration and unpredictable, some-

times violent rages, and the son too young and small to do anything but submit—and fantasize about getting back at him.

Then came the moment of transition, and along with it the confrontation Todd had been waiting for.

"The abuse finally ended when I was nineteen years old," Todd recalled.

I was at home, and my father's new wife was there. I had been out all night with some girl, and was sitting having breakfast, with a hangover. My father was in the kitchen being completely obnoxious. I was getting fed up. So I turned around and said, "Would you *please* stop being such an asshole." Well, no one had ever said that to The Colonel before, and I could just see the volcano rising. He turned red, clenched his teeth and started moving toward me with his fists made up, and I suddenly realized sitting there that I wasn't going to take it anymore. I wasn't going to get hit by him. And I also knew I was in great shape and nineteen years old and four inches taller than he was. He was old and hadn't exercised in years.

So as he moved toward me I grabbed him by the wrists and slammed him up against the wall and held him there. Now, when we were younger he used to have this way he'd torture us—he'd take us by the wrists and slap our hands against our faces until it drove us to distraction. And that's what I did to him then. Here was this nineteen-year-old kid making his father slap his own face with his own hands.

His wife was completely freaked out, and my father kept saying, "Let me go, let me go!" and I wouldn't. I said, "I'm not letting you go until you calm down and you decide you're not going to hit me anymore."

That was the last time he tried to touch me.

Twenty years have passed since then. There were times of estrangement, but now, Todd explained, he and his father see each other fairly often. Upon hearing this, I pointed out to him that many another military son with a similar family history has chosen to sever relations with his father completely. I wondered why Todd had not done so.

"What keeps me hanging in there?" Todd said.

I love the old fart. I mean I really *like* the guy. He's a very likable man. In spite of the way we grew up, my father and I genuinely like each other, although it's not in the traditional father-son sense of bonding. It's a superficial male friendship. We talk history, we talk politics, we keep our relationship on a certain level. As we've gotten older we've confided in each other more. I've gotten lots of war stories, but he's never revealed much personal stuff, about his parents, his childhood. That inner core of his is something no one has touched, that I know of.

I can't grab my father and take him down to the bar for a couple of drinks and talk heart to heart. I've never had an honest talk with him. Maybe it has to do with that rigid military environment, and maybe it has to do with the problems he brought into the military with him. Between the two of them, they made this kid from the streets of Bronx into a martinet who didn't mellow out until he was sixty years old.

I think when the old man dies, I'm going to feel hurt again. Not because he's abandoning me, but because there's no way to resolve the things that happened so many years ago. But maybe I shouldn't be asking to resolve them. Maybe I should be content that he and I are now fairly good friends. We like each other, we talk to each other on the phone and in visits, we have lunch together.

Maybe under the circumstances that's the most I can ask for. I'll settle for friendship of a kind. And at the same time I'll have my anger and my hurts, but maybe that's one of those things we have to live with in this world that are never going to be resolved.

Although it would appear from Todd's story that retaliating against the father pays off, it would be dangerous to apply that conclusion to other family situations. Todd himself pointed out that he is lucky his father never kept any guns in the house; another violent father might have followed up that scene in the kitchen by seriously hurting or killing his son. And if, subsequently, the incident did not apparently cast a shadow on Todd's relationship with his father—Todd said that the next day, it was as if nothing had happened—it may be due to what Todd describes as a fortunate confluence of personality traits in the two men. His father, he said, is the sort who moves right ahead, denying or ignoring the crises in his life. And for his own part, Todd says he "can't hold a grudge for more than a couple of hours."

In my own brother's case, fantasies of retaliation figured heavily in his thoughts during his time inside the Fortress. Our father subjected him to constant emotional abuse and physically beat him with regularity during his adolescence. Retaliation never happened, however, and after my brother grew up and left home, he and our father saw almost nothing of one another. My brother's transition from vulnerable son to independent man occurred out of our father's vision, and so went unremarked by him. Until David was thirty-three years old, and came home for a brief visit. I was present, and saw what happened.

It started with something so minor it was clear our father was itching for a confrontation. My brother committed the apparently unpardonable offense of walking into the kitchen barefoot to get himself a snack. Our father, in a predatory state of mind, seized upon this as a personal insult and launched into a string of invectives. Enough years had passed that my brother could keep his cool and respond calmly, trying to defuse the situation. Our father would not be calmed. He worked himself up in the old way, threatened to kill David, and headed for his gun cabinet. "Don't touch those guns," David warned him. "Because I'll have to stop you, and I don't want to hurt you." That David could—and would, if necessary—hurt our father had never before been a possibility in their confrontations. It had been a long, long time since they had faced one another in such close proximity, with the possibility of violence so imminent. My mother and I watched in fear, but there was little we could do; we both shouted at them to stop, but they paid us no heed.

What was clear to all of us was that what David promised—to stop our father with force if need be—was something he could deliver. The transition had come about long before. My brother was taller, leaner, much stronger than our father. In a physical fight there was no question who would win. But our father, a stubborn old warrior blind with rage, went for his guns anyway. And David stopped him, grabbing his arms and forcing him down into a chair. David held him there, his fist cocked back but still talking calmly, refusing to throw the first punch. "Calm down, Dad," he kept saying, over and over. "I'll let you go if you promise not to touch that gun cabinet. I don't want to hurt you. I don't want to hurt you."

It was a crushing moment for the old warrior, our father. I suddenly saw him as a wounded bear, fierce, determined, hurt, in shock. In that moment he was forced to recognize that in this long-running war with his son, his only remaining choices were defeat or withdrawal. Both were for him humiliating; it was obvious that he had lost control of the situation in every way.

He could not control the rage the sight of my brother evoked in him. He could not control his need for alcohol to fuel his anger and dull his pain. He could not control his own aging process. He could not control a physical contest with his son. And, finally, he could not control his son, could not hold him imprisoned in his childhood, subject to his command. It was a battle our father had lost long, long before, but he had not until then faced it. But he was now being forced to face it, held immobile in his own chair, looking fiercely into his son's steady eyes.

Transition: It is always a loaded issue for a son inside the Fortress, even in less violent families. What's interesting is that the manner in which it occurs, sometimes a scene of just a few seconds' duration, tends to match in tone and spirit the essential nature of the father-son relationship from all the years before. I can imagine that in Colonel Dunning's family, his sons' transition was welcomed as a mutual accomplishment to be relished and celebrated. In violent families, as we have seen, the moment of transition is likely to echo the violence or, through equally emphatic declarations of invisibility, the negation.

Of course, in military families where the father is gone much of the

time or is unavailable to his son when he is home, the precise moment
of transition may come and go almost without witnesses. It is discovered later, after the fact, although that moment of realization may
be just as dramatic and is certainly just as revealing.

"I remember when I was sixteen, and my father was coming home
from Vietnam," said George, the son of a Marine Corps major. "It was
supposed to be on a Wednesday, and I was looking forward to it, real
excited. Also nervous and stressed. Then he surprised us by coming
home a day or two early.

"I came home from school, into the hallway which was dark. I
suddenly saw him there, about five or six feet away. And I remember
being surprised, and there was a real foreignness, a strangeness. It had
been thirteen months since I'd seen him. I was a foot taller, twenty-five
pounds heavier, a year older. It was like, 'And who the hell are *you?*' "

For George it was a shocking moment, a moment in which his
resentments crystallized, and which gave the lie to what had been his
happy anticipation. "A lot of anger at military life comes from the fact
my father just wasn't there a lot of the time," he went on. "That year
he was in Vietnam, when I was a sophomore in high school, I was on a
team that won a state championship in swimming. I won three gold
medals. He wasn't there. I got straight A's. He wasn't there. I didn't get
the credit or recognition for a lot of things I did. I'd think, goddamm it,
he's my father, he should have been there for those things. And he
wasn't. I felt I never really had a father. That's not really fair to
him—it's an overstatement—but that's how I felt. I remember spending a lot of time alone, or with my friends, or babysitting my brother.
Not with my parents. Even when my father was 'home,' they'd be gone
every night."

His story in essence is the story of a great many military sons whose
warrior fathers were absentee: The transition itself is like passing one
another in a dark hallway, and experiencing the simultaneous shock of
recognition and nonrecognition. In the space of an instant both of
them sense the enormity of what should have been, and wasn't.

Vietnam and the Draft

For many sons of the Fortress, the issue that foreshadowed their
transition—and brought their relationships with their warrior fathers
into high relief—was the Vietnam War. All of the questions implicit
in a Fortress son's visibility—Does he unquestioningly endorse the
rule of the warrior father? Will he follow in his footsteps?—were
brought to the surface by the war, if the son came of age before or

during the nine years from 1965 to 1973 that our government sent young men in large numbers to fight and die in Vietnam.

Some families were torn apart by dissension over the war. While military households were certainly not the only battlefields for father-son hostilities during the Vietnam War, inside the Fortress it may have been particularly apropos for festering issues inside the family to be expressed metaphorically in the language of war.

Todd, for instance, mentioned that the Vietnam War was a factor in the eventual breakup of his family. The father was on one side, the mother and the children on the other. In that family Vietnam was the perfect metaphor for the combative atmosphere that already prevailed in a family on its way to disintegration. "The war was an incredible issue in my house," he recalled.

The family was split right down the middle. Before my mother left my father, every night at the dinner table there was a fight about the war, and about student demonstrators. My father despised anyone who would march against the country or burn the flag. I remember him sitting there watching the television coverage of student demonstrations, and him clutching the chair, and his teeth clenched and face red and spit flying out of his mouth. It looked like the man was about to explode.

The fight at dinner would just grow until my mother would jump up, go over to a drawer and pull out this FREE HUEY NEWTON button.[3] She'd put it on and march up and down the living room shouting, "Free Huey Newton!" just to drive the old man out of his fucking mind.

By that time Todd's father had retired and his mother was an activist in several antiwar groups. All the children were against the war. Todd participated in the demonstrations at the college campus in his town, although he was still in high school.

For many dysfunctional military families the Vietnam War was an irresistible metaphor for what was going on inside them. Indeed, the war gave them a vehicle for expressing hostility that until then had been for the most part contained, in true stoic warrior style. One might speculate that if Todd's father had not been retired, if he had been sent to Vietnam at the height of the war, the family would have been forced to see things in a different way. But since no one in the family was directly threatened by the war at that time—and since they were no longer living inside the Fortress—they were free to take their identification with the war to theatrical extremes.

There remained, however, the question of what the sons would do when eventually confronted with the draft. Todd's older brother was drafted and served in the Army, although his student deferment kept him from serving until after the U.S. war effort was winding down and troops were no longer being shipped to Vietnam.

Todd did not want any part of the war, either, but felt conscientious objector status was out of the question. As he put it, "I was so goddamn morally straight about everything that I didn't feel I could apply for it, since I wasn't religious. Also, I didn't know if I really *was* a nonviolent person, a pacifist." He had been accepted to a university, and knew he could get a student deferment—but the problem was that he didn't want to be in school. He entered the university, got the deferment, then dropped out after one quarter and spent nearly a year traveling. When he returned, his notice to report for his preinduction physical was waiting for him. He knew that if he passed the physical, he would shortly receive a notice to report for active duty.

As those of us know who lived through that time, young men like Todd who were physically fit, eligible for the draft, and available for duty had several options before them if they wished to stay out of the war. They could go to Canada. They could go to jail. They could do things to make themselves physically ineligible—for instance, starve until they were below the military's minimum weight requirements for their height, or chemically alter their blood pressure. Or, through behavior or attitude, they could present themselves as undesirable from the military's point of view.

The fact there were other options open to Todd makes the method he chose that much more significant. This son from a warrior family that saw the father as symbolic of the authoritarian, patriarchal, military machine, and saw the government at the time as symbolic of all such fathers, refused to sign the Loyalty Oath.

Such an act was, of course, outrageous in the extreme for any American; most young men of the period who fought the draft made it a point to assert that they were against American policy in Vietnam or against the notion of war in general, not against their country per se. For a son of the military itself to refuse to sign an oath of loyalty to his country was practically inconceivable. His act of refusal, of course, subjected Todd and everyone he associated with to months of intensive surveillance. His phone was wiretapped, his mail opened, and he was followed by agents wherever he went. The refusal to sign brought him a great deal of harassment. It also did not work.

The military authorities were not fooled and Todd was drafted, although his student deferment (he had by then reregistered at the university) was, fortunately for him, issued just before his notice to report for active duty and thus took precedence. Like his brother, he escaped the war by remaining in school. By the time Todd graduated, the draft was over. It remained a sore point with his father, however.

"The whole Vietnam era drove a wedge between my father and me," Todd said. "Of course that wedge was probably going to be there anyway, but it was at least ten years before we stopped eyeing each other like a pair of tomcats."

Most of the sons interviewed for this book who were of the right age to have fought in Vietnam did not do so. Some had high numbers and thus were not called up in the draft lottery. Most of the others took measures to stay out of the war, for the most part through student deferments.

But two of the interviewees did serve in Vietnam. One of them, the son of a Navy chief petty officer, was a career Marine Corps officer who said he "loved" the war and looks back on it nostalgically as "one of the best periods of my life." The other, the son of a Marine Corps sergeant, served two tours in Vietnam as an Air Force sergeant. His experience there, related later in this chapter, changed his mind about making the military a career.

Ross, another son interviewed for this book, had a student deferment during the war—but his two older brothers were in the military and served in Vietnam. The oldest had joined the Army thinking to make it a career, although, after Vietnam, he left. The other brother was drafted, served in the Army infantry, and came back a heroin addict. Later he committed suicide by shooting himself in the head.

"His addiction to heroin was because of Vietnam," said Ross, "although if he hadn't gone I'm sure he would have been addicted to something, because we all are. [Ross and his older brother are recovering alcoholics.] But it was heroin, and he wound up killing himself. Now maybe he would have killed himself even without Vietnam, but he definitely had some ghosts from that war."

It would seem, from the way sons speak about their actions during the Vietnam War, that they were either solidly against it or solidly for it (as with the Marine mentioned above, and one other son who had been too young at the time to serve), with no ambiguity of feeling. However, this is anything but true—and the contradictory feelings secretly held by sons who vociferously opposed the war is one thing that differentiates them from their civilian counterparts of the period.

Many sons of the Fortress who opposed the Vietnam War—and did their best to stay out of it—at the same time wrestled with an opposite pull that was the inevitable result of all their conditioning inside the Fortress. Sons of the Fortress are raised to see the warrior path as an inherently noble undertaking, one of the highest expressions of selflessness and duty to society. For them it is an extremely potent idea, an almost irresistible mix of masculine glamour and moral high ground. It is extremely hard for them to reject that notion.

The specific problem that sons of the Fortress were forced to confront revolved around the fact that their exalted notion of the warrior path is an archetype—an image as timeless as it is noble—and which therefore exists out of context. World War II, for many sons and their warrior fathers, typified how the archetype and reality sometimes come together: It was a just war, and to be a warrior on the winning side was to share in one of the most noble, if bloody, enterprises of the century. Vietnam, on the other hand, in its political, military, and moral shoddiness, revealed just how sadly out of sync that noble-warrior archetype can be. Vietnam made clear that to be a warrior, finally, means to transform one's self into an instrument of policy made and controlled by others, with virtually no power to oppose, alter, or escape one's role. It created a dilemma for sons both military and civilian, in which heart and mind were diametrically opposed.

Still, it was not easy, generally speaking, for a military son to throw off his conditioning in the face of Vietnam. To be a son of the Fortress, obvious heir to the warrior mystique, and to oppose that war—any war—was on the face of it as contradictory and painful as for a crown prince to abdicate on the eve of his investiture.

John's Story: The Dilemma of Vietnam

John is the youngest son of an Air Force colonel. Born in 1950, he turned eighteen in May of 1968, not long after the Tet Offensive. At the time, John was involved in antiwar protests. He was also draft age, physically fit, and had decided not to go to college: a prime candidate for Vietnam.

Twenty years later, as he reflected on that time, it was not his imminent danger John recalled, so much as the dilemma he felt as the son of a warrior.

"Even to this day I am really fascinated by the Vietnam War," he said.

> Part of me wanted to go, the whole time I was demonstrating against the war. I was a young male and I felt the pull of "like father, like son." Of course I wouldn't let myself speak out loud about that in those days, not to anybody. But I felt that war [in general] and the military were my father, and the best part of my father.
>
> To see my father standing there in his regalia, when I was a young kid, was the most beautiful thing in the world. He was strong, gallant, dashing. But not only that, he was part of what makes America great. I would hear that in advertisements, see it all around me on the base, and hear it in his voice when I would ask him, "What does the Air Force do? What is it for?"

The slogans all made sense to me: protecting the people, protecting against all aggressors. That meant something to me, and in a lot of ways it still does. The history of America, of the Revolution, the Minutemen—it all blends together. My father was a part of that, and in a sense, vicariously, I was a part of it too because I was his son.

John spoke at length about how the thrill of the military got into his blood, dazzled him, and made it hard eventually for him to take a stand against the war.

"For the Air Force, war is a blip on a screen," he said.

It's very removed from real war because of the nature of their mission. They're a mile up. When I was a kid we were very big on playing Army, with toy guns. That's as close as I got to the real thing, as far as one-on-one combat goes. For me as a kid, war was what I saw in movies or fantasized with my buddies.

But I got to see what war is like to someone in the Air Force. It's a radar screen. You don't see eyeballs, human faces. You see targets, objectives, unidentifieds, incomings, nonresponsives. I saw it at Thule, Greenland, when my father showed me where he worked. It was beautiful, and I was hooked. Thule is a big air transport base; but the Early Warning Site was remote, a white dome on a spit of land.

We went down about twelve stories into the earth. There was a big wraparound screen of the horizon of the whole world at the latitude and longitude of that spot in Greenland. It was very dark, and there are maps drawn out on plastic screens. Everyone has earphones on and screens in front of them, and it was all green light. I'm shaking as I think about it now. It was gorgeous, it was fantastic, it was massive, it was important, and it was something *my dad did*. And of course my father was in uniform and everyone would say, "Good morning, Colonel."

I was fourteen years old, at prime time to be hit by all that. I loved it. I wanted to be part of it. I wanted to join.

That, to me—until Vietnam—was what war was. These guys in front of screens, in green light. They said that in war they would relay information back to the SAC [Strategic Air Command] missile sites.

So I came into my antiwar years with that as background. There was a real dichotomy there. At the same time I was discovering hippies and my own opposition to the war, I felt that ache for "the big organization."

Sons were not the only ones to see that archetype and reality were out of sync in Vietnam. That truth was at least as agonizing for the professional warriors who admitted it as it was for their sons.

Thus it came to be that in some families, like John's, where there had been uneasy silence, or tension, or even conflict between father and son, the Vietnam War, paradoxically enough, brought both a truce and even an alliance that had not previously existed. It was not easy to oppose the war, even very privately, for a professional warrior trained to support any mission assigned to him with heart and soul and blood. John, who in his teen years had rebelled often against a father who seemingly could find no good in him, forged an alliance.

"He didn't want me to go [to Vietnam] either," John said.

> It was one of the few times we saw eye to eye. He said, "This is not a war. This is bad. Too many kids are being killed. It's not like when I was in war. They don't even know who they're shooting at. And kids are coming home maimed and getting spit on." I told him, "If it was World War II, I would go." I meant it and I still mean it. "But I can't go when you're fighting people you can't see and you don't know who the enemy is."
>
> We hugged. And he got me out of the draft. When I was classified 1-A and got my notice for a physical, my father said, "Give me that." He found a shrink and gave him the letter and set up an appointment. I saw him for half an hour. I told him—and I meant it—that if I had to go I would "off" myself. The psychiatrist wrote a letter saying I was suicidal. I took the letter from the doctor to the draft board, and was reclassified 4-F.
>
> I'm proud of it today. A colonel in the Air Force—my father—stood up and told me it was a bullshit war. It made sense. It stuck.

Other sons, too, told of fathers who took on the unlikely role of draft counselors to their sons, ironically trying to save them from the warrior path they had done so much to promote as the boys were growing up. One Air Force colonel pushed his son to go into the Coast Guard, where he at least had less chance of being shot up. Two other officers, a colonel and a lieutenant colonel in the Air Force, tried unsuccessfully to obtain conscientious objector status for their sons.

Other warrior fathers stopped short of giving their sons direct help in avoiding Vietnam and the draft, but took pains to let them know that their sons' opposition to the war would not be an issue between them. Even a hardboiled Marine lieutenant colonel, described by his son as "gung ho," summoned his two sons and said to them, "This is a bad war, and I really wouldn't mind if you stayed out of it."

CROSSROADS

The warrior path is such a powerful magnet for the sons of the Fortress that every one of them must at some point confront the question of whether he will follow it. It is not a question that can be ignored. And while the question can be answered in a surprising variety of ways, the answer will say a great deal about the son, and often much about the father as well.

Those Who Joined

It is common, among sons of the Fortress, to have a father who strongly promotes the warrior path, sometimes to the point of refusing to acknowledge there is any other choice for a self-respecting male. Some sons endorse this view; some sons instinctively rebel, defiantly going their own way. And some wind up joining the military anyway, for a time, as a means of getting out from under their fathers' rule.

Don is the son of an Army colonel. His father, an extreme authoritarian, "encouraged" Don during his elementary and junior high years to follow in his footsteps. "In high school, I was *ordered to,*" Don said. He wanted to get out of the house, away from his father, and ended up enlisting in the Air Force. When his tour was up, he got out and assumed a civilian lifestyle. His father wouldn't speak to him for months, and at this writing still had no contact with Don. "I still think one of the reasons he disowned me," Don said, "was that I didn't follow in his footsteps and become an Army officer."

However, the pressure on a son of the Fortress to become a professional warrior does not come solely from the father or mother. The Fortress at large, in the form of the warrior mystique in which every young boy is steeped, sends a clear message. That alone is frequently enough to persuade a son to choose the military as a career. When a son also has the example of a caring and approving warrior father, it is even more likely that he will go the military route—even if his father, for reasons of his own, tries to persuade him to do otherwise.

Robert is an example. His father, a black Army master sergeant, actively tried to discourage his five sons from going into the military. He didn't succeed; three became career Marine Corps and one career Army.

"He told us that he preferred none of us go into the military," Robert said. "He felt he'd fought enough wars for all of us." Robert's father fought in World War II, Korea, and served three tours in Vietnam. He was an adviser to the Army of the Republic of Vietnam, working with Special Forces, and spoke Vietnamese.

"I was always set on going into the military," said Robert, a Marine captain.

And my father knew it. When my father was in Vietnam, he used to write me letters and in the letters—some people might think this is gruesome, but I have learned a lot from it—he would always send me a picture of the realities of war. One time—I still have it—he sent me a picture of a Vietcong soldier that a South Vietnamese soldier had shot with a grenade launcher right through the chest. It really messed the guy up. In the letter he told me, "There is nothing glorious about war. And I'm sending you this picture so you can see what war is."

To this day I cannot stand to hear officers in the Marine Corps say, "Oh *yeah*—I want to go out and *kill* those guys . . ." I don't think that's a very healthy way of looking at things, since war is not a very glorious sight. We who have never *been* there can sit back and think about all the medals we could possibly win—but once people get there and see how cruel things are, their perspective on things changes. My father taught me that as a kid and I still appreciate it now.

There were a lot of things Robert's father managed to teach him, despite his many tours of duty away from the family:

My father told me as a kid to set a goal, then when I reached it to set another and go for that one. In high school I said I wanted to go to college, graduate and make my parents proud, and then be an officer in the Marines. I attained those goals. Now I'm going after a master's degree.

I look back on my father and think about how he was a *professional soldier*. He wore two pairs of spit-shined boots every day. He wore two starched uniforms every day. When he got one of them sweaty, he'd come home and change.

I guess that's something I picked up as a child. My father would say, "If you try to be something, be the *very best* you can be. If you go out and dig ditches, you be the best ditch digger there is." So I set goals and I try to attain them, and I do my best.

My father is a really, really good image to live up to. I just hope I can impart what my father gave me to my two little girls.

Glenn is another example of a son who, inspired by the example of a father who was a loving parent as well as a fine warrior, found the lure of the Fortress irresistible.

Glenn's Story: Strengthened by the Father

Glenn's father, a West Point graduate and Army officer, applied no pressure on Glenn to choose the military; Glenn said he grew up sensing that his parents wanted him to make his own decisions and would support him in whatever he chose. But his experience growing up in the Army had been so rewarding, and his family life so satisfying, that Glenn early set his sights on an Army career and never wavered. After graduating from a prestigious university on an ROTC scholarship, he entered the Army in the same branch his father had chosen.

"Then and to this day, the Army to me was the *infantry*," Glenn said. "If I was going to be a soldier, I was going to be a *real* soldier and do it right." After graduating with honors from the fourteen-week infantry officer basic course at Fort Benning, Georgia, Glenn went on to graduate from the extremely demanding Ranger training—which entitled him to wear the prestigious Ranger tab on his uniform.[4] He spoke of his next several years in the infantry with evident appreciation.

"It was extremely challenging intellectually," he said. "Unless you've been in the infantry and know how difficult it is to be a leader, to learn infantry tactics and strategy and military history—until you've done that, you don't realize that those people in infantry are pretty damn smart. So it was quite a challenge for me, and I enjoyed that challenge." The challenge remained on an intellectual plane; Glenn is too young to have fought in Vietnam, and there were no other opportunities for combat experience during his tenure in the Army infantry.

It was clear Glenn measured his military performance not only against his own standards of achievement, but against the model his father provided. His father's example is one Glenn aspires to in his private life as well. Glenn described his father as a warrior who was "definitely not authoritarian," who left his problems and military attitudes at work, who is relaxed, playful, funny, a great storyteller, a man who cares deeply about his family and lets them know it.

"It often surprised me that this career military officer with combat ribbons and badges and achievements of all sorts decorating his uniform could be so boyish in his play," Glenn said. "I really enjoyed that, and I thought that showed one *could* be successful in the military without restricting one's behavior to a certain stereotype. And I carried that belief with me into the Army infantry."

Glenn's father had been good at offering love and guidance, but he did his son the additional favor of putting it in writing. "My father sent me excellent letters from Vietnam," Glenn said. He was twelve years old during his father's second tour. "Those letters actually had more impact on me than just about any conversation we've ever had." Glenn told of once writing his father about a youth activity he'd observed in which he saw a lack of integrity which upset him.

"My father wrote back a very memorable reply. He said, 'If you remain an honest person and stay true to your ideals and your integrity, you will be remembered long after what others do crumbles to dust. What you do will have a lasting value.'

"It was an extremely powerful letter. It's difficult not to get emotional just recalling it. I *am* getting emotional. . . . That letter had a strong and lasting impact on me. It has guided me in my life more than anything else my father has done or said, and more than anything anyone else has done or said."

Although Glenn enjoyed the infantry, he left it to go to medical school and is now an Army physician:

I put myself into the future, on my deathbed looking back over my career and thinking, What have I done for society? And I didn't want to answer that I'd spent my life learning how to make war better than anybody else. I certainly respect those in the American Army who can do that well, but that wasn't how I wanted to spend my life's energies. It wasn't the spiritual satisfaction I would expect to have.

Because I've been a dependent as well as having served in the military myself, I have a pretty strong desire to help those who are dependents or who are active duty or retired, as my father is now.

I'm so proud to serve in the Army, after all these years. I'm proud to put on my uniform, although I find myself in hospital scrubs a lot of the time. And when I do put on my uniform, I view it as a symbol of the ideals I believe the Army stands for. Whether the Army fulfills them is not an issue for me. What's important is that it makes the effort to achieve those standards.

Many sons—and daughters—of warriors decide to become career military themselves; what percentage of the armed forces they comprise is not known. At this writing, no one in the Department of Defense had conducted a survey on the subject. Military academies are able to say how many of their cadets or midshipmen are children of alumni—usually it runs about 4 percent—but their data base cannot distinguish between children of career military personnel and children whose fathers may have served only a couple of years as draftees or wartime volunteers.

Although some warrior sons, such as Robert and Glenn, go into the military in large part because they had such positive father role models, others go in because they are still trying to win the father approval they lacked growing up. Perhaps consciously, perhaps unconsciously, they hope that their choice of career will finally bring affirmation from the father, or, failing that, that their craving will be satisfied symbolically through approval by the patriarchal military institution.

Adam, the son of a Marine sergeant, fits somewhere in between these categories.

Adam's Story: The Crossroads of Vietnam

Adam, the son of a Marine sergeant, admired and respected his father. He was awed by his father's ability to survive the horrors of a Japanese prisoner of war camp in World War II. And he believed in the spirit of dedication his father brought to military service throughout his career.

"I was proud of my father," Adam said.

I saw how much power he had as a gunnery sergeant, how much respect he commanded, how he could make people hop to. I was proud of that, and it influenced my own decision to become an [Air Force] NCO. I was always taught that NCOs are the backbone of the military. That's what my father always told me, and that's what I saw. The officers may give the orders, but it's the NCOs who get the job done. And getting the job done was everything as far as I was concerned.

Even though I was only a buck sergeant, I carried myself with that pride of a noncommissioned officer, taking my responsibilities very seriously. That definitely stemmed from my father's attitude.

Adam's father was less successful as a parent, however. Perhaps because of his brutal experience in the POW camp—following which the Marine Corps, according to Adam, never provided his father with the psychotherapy he needed, and on top of that sent him right back to Asia, over his objections, to fight in the Korean War—Adam's father was emotionally cold and frequently abusive to his wife and seven children. "I had a real rocky relationship with my father," Adam said, "but that did not detract from the respect and the love I had for him."

I interviewed Adam barely a month after his father died. Adam spoke of how, in recent years, he'd worked hard to reestablish his relationship with his father. By the time his father died, Adam said, they had done a lot to mend the rift. But twenty-five years earlier had been a time of pain, bewilderment, confusion. Adam had wanted to get away from home at the first opportunity—and what he had experienced in the shadow of the Marine Corps, at the hands of a father who had never regained his mental peace after the tortures of a POW camp, did not deter him from pursuing his ambition of a military career.

"I always enjoyed the military pomp and circumstance," Adam said. "I was enthralled with uniforms and weapons and marching. The spit and polish. Being a military brat always had me in that frame of mind.

"I saw the military as an easy and acceptable way for me to get out of my household and out on my own. I liked being around aircraft and I liked the Air Force uniforms, so in March of 1965 I went down and talked to the Air Force recruiter. They had a slot open for that September. I really didn't think much about Vietnam when I enlisted. In 1965, Vietnam was not a big issue in the news. I figured it was about a fifty-fifty chance I'd get sent there."

Adam still hoped he would be working on an air base in a support capacity. "I didn't realize I was going to be a munitions expert, which means that ninety percent of the time you're going to be stuck in a bomb dump way off in the back forty and nobody sees you. You don't worry about uniforms—you're just fitting five-hundred-pound bombs and shoving twenty-millimeters."

Nonetheless, Adam liked the Air Force well enough. If it hadn't been for Vietnam, he might have stayed.

"I really got a taste of what was going on over there [during my first tour]," he said.

The war had really built up while I was in basic training. And then I spent about six months out of my fifteen-month tour bouncing around from base to base filling in slots, wherever they needed somebody. I volunteered for every project I could find. I rode gunner on chopper search-and-destroy missions; I was in the middle of Operation Rolling Thunder [the massive effort to bomb North Vietnam]; I kicked flares on Puff the Magic Dragon. ["Puff" was the nickname of the modified C-47 transports which were converted into state-of-the-art gunships to support ground troops. During night missions, flares were needed to illuminate the area to prevent gunners from accidentally firing on the "friendlies."]

Vietnam didn't really hit home until my second tour overseas [during and after the Tet Offensive]. My eyes were opened. We were not going to win the war; we were just making the war continue. . . . It was something [the politicians] *couldn't* win politically, and they didn't *want* to win militarily. So Vietnam was a real sore subject, and the military got to be a very negative aspect of my life, where before it had been a positive thing. I had looked at it as a place where I could be somebody and do something with my life, like my father did. Then I saw the military wasn't going to do that for me, because Vietnam took that away.

Adam started on the road to alcoholism in Vietnam: "I began drinking heavily—I was getting bored with what I was doing and I was sick of seeing what I was seeing, of being where I was, with the constant fear of death. If I was not on duty, usually I had a drink in my hand; it didn't matter if it was beer or hard liquor. I was probably drunk five nights out of the week."

And then there was the accident. At a small base in Thailand, Adam and his load team were handling cluster bombs when several bombs accidentally became armed and exploded. Two of the team members closest to the explosions were killed. Several others were severely wounded. Adam was hit by about two dozen pellets (cluster bombs each carry 172 pellets), had part of a toe severed by shrapnel, and lost all hearing for a day and a half. He spent ten days in the hospital, but within a month, despite the horror he had lived through, volunteered to go back on line. For that he was awarded the bronze star.

At the conclusion of his tour, Adam returned home disillusioned with the war and with the military. "Vietnam taught me that war is not the way to solve problems," he said.

A lot of good men died in Vietnam, for nothing. I never really thought the military was the answer to the world's problems, but sometimes you were led to believe that, being a military brat—especially a Marine brat. Until you actually get into combat, you really do not think about war being what it really is: brutal, bloodthirsty survival.

I'm proud I was in Vietnam. I am never going to deny I'm a Vietnam veteran, though I know some guys who do. I did my part, my patriotic duty. We may not have won the war, but *I* won: I survived. That's what I am: a survivor. That's what the military taught me to do, and that's what my father taught me: "No matter what, you will survive."

Those Who Did Not Join

Plenty of sons, of course, choose not to go into the military. Saying no to the warrior path is not always easy, no matter how strongly the son feels about it, because it carries a high price: The son knows he will have to stand firm against the disapproval he will inevitably see in the eyes of every warrior he has ever looked to for affirmation.

The decision about whether or not to go into the military is complicated by a boy's youth at the time he must decide: Just at the time he is ready to take the leap into manhood and the military proffers itself as both the readiest route and the realization of his boyhood dreams, he also feels the powerful need to assert himself as distinct from his parents—in the psychological term, to individuate. The yes and the no do battle within the son, and what eventually happens is sometimes surprising, even to him.

Reed is an Army son first encountered in Chapter 1. His father, a West Point graduate and Army general, was a good father—loving, involved, and not authoritarian. Reed didn't have much cause to rebel, but that has little to do with the need to individuate. When it came to the decision on whether or not to join the military, he was clearly of two minds. Part of him didn't want anything to do with the Army as a career; part of him wasn't so sure. Perhaps hedging his bets, he wound up attending college on an ROTC scholarship. Then he received an appointment to West Point, and he had to take a stand. Although Reed had sought the appointment, he turned it down flat, and in retrospect claims he never intended to accept it. His agitated father wrote from Vietnam to tell his son he was making a mistake— and dispatched a procession of fellow alumni to write and telephone Reed to persuade him to change his mind.

"I'm good under pressure," Reed said. "I knew that was going to happen. I let them tell me I was making a mistake, and I still didn't go. The Army just wasn't what I wanted to be."

Another Army son, Hugh, did things differently. He walked a little farther on the warrior path, which made his decision to turn away from it much more painful—and in his case, dramatic.

Hugh said that although both his parents were emotionally abusive, his father was only mildly authoritarian, and did not specifically tell him what to do with his life. Nevertheless, as an only child, Hugh felt a lot of pressure to continue the military tradition and never really considered doing anything else. In any case, as Hugh saw it at the time, nothing else could compete with the Army. "I fell for the whole line—that the Army was *the* career," he said.

After a year at the Fort Belvoir, Virginia, prep school, he received an appointment to West Point. But right from the beginning—the two-month torment for new cadets known as Beast Barracks—he didn't take to it.

"Some parts of [the West Point experience] were okay, and some weren't," he said. "It was too confusing, too rigid. I don't like taking shit from other people. There, you can't fight back. You have to take whatever they dish out. The whole system grated and grated on me; I had to get out of there."

Hugh could have resigned at any time, but he was still working out his ambivalence. It was not easy to let go of his dream, leave his friends, disappoint his family. But his concerns continued to grow. Finally, after two years at the Academy, he in effect set himself up for the confrontation that would force him to decide.

"The thing that kept bothering me and bothering me the whole time was compulsory chapel," Hugh recalled. "What William O. Douglas had written about the separation of church and state had a big effect on my thinking. I believed in it. But at West Point they had you line up and march to chapel; it was compulsory." At first, to avoid compromising his principles—a point of paramount importance for military brats—he cleverly contrived a way to sidestep the issue. He arranged to be the person to type up the chapel list, and omitted his name so that it would never appear on the chapel roll call. He stayed in his room and slept.

"[The scheme] broke down over spot checks of the barracks," Hugh said.

> A couple of times I was alerted by buddies and escaped, but eventually I got nailed. And that brought a direct confrontation over whether these people had the authority to force us to go to chapel. I saw it as a matter of principle, and I had no idea where it was going to end up.
> They tried to work out a deal: twenty demerits, twenty punishment tours, and go to chapel from now on. I said no. I had these colonels and lieutenant colonels in orbit; they just couldn't believe it. I gave them a constitutional argument.
> Finally I ended up in the Commandant's office. There we were, eyeball to eyeball. He was genuinely trying to resolve this, and I wouldn't let him. I refused to go to chapel. And so I started picking up big-time punishment.

Hugh found himself spending a great deal of time "guarding the clock": walking punishment tours of Central Area for an hour, taking a five-minute break, walking for another hour, taking another five-minute break, then another hour.

Finally a captain on the staff called him in and asked him what he was going to do. That was when Hugh found himself for the first time articulating a desire to leave West Point and turn his life in a completely different direction.

"I told the captain I wanted to go to law school and work for poor people. I had the notion that you could use the law as a vehicle of social change; this was right in the middle of the sixties, the civil rights movement." The conversation was an important one; the act of finally articulating his views felt good, and had the effect of deciding him to leave West Point.

First, however, he had to determine what to do about the matter of principle on which he'd taken such a firm stand. Hugh had been in touch with the American Civil Liberties Union, which had expressed a willingness to take the case to court. Hugh knew that if he pressed suit, the case would undoubtedly go all the way to the Supreme Court. He was initially ready to do that, he said, but in the end backed off: His father was still active duty in the Army, and complained to Hugh that the issue was already affecting his career.

So Hugh resigned, putting an end to the controversy. As he had said he would, he went on to graduate from law school and, as a trial lawyer with an affinity for constitutional issues, has since devoted his career to helping the disadvantaged.

As it happened, Hugh was not the only young man concerned about the chapel issue. A lawsuit brought by midshipmen at Annapolis on First Amendment grounds worked its way through the court system until, in 1972, the U.S. Supreme Court upheld an Appeals Court decision striking down compulsory chapel attendance. Secretary of Defense Melvin Laird issued a directive ordering an end to compulsory attendance at religious services in service academies and elsewhere in the military.

Hugh paid a high price for his intransigence as a cadet on the chapel issue, but through it he found his route to individuation. Reconciliation with his parents was another matter, however. The episode caused a rift that proved very difficult to heal. In fact, the issue continued to fester for seventeen more years, until Hugh's father was dying of cancer.

"My father had been in therapy before that for alcoholism, and had come to some realizations," Hugh related. "He said he had come to see that I had needed to [individuate], and the chapel issue was just how I did it. He told me, 'We have to realize at some time that we can't control other people. Your mother and I tried to do that, and it didn't work. I'm sorry we put you through that.' "

It was a memory that brought Hugh to tears.

"It's made things better, that he said that to me," Hugh said. "It's made it easier for me to look back on the turmoil and pain of those years, especially the years between sixteen and twenty-two, when things that couldn't possibly be my fault were my fault, when I was consistently yelled at, jumped on." Hugh and his mother also reconciled.

I asked Hugh if he were not still, despite having resigned from West Point, a warrior.

"Yes," he said. "I'm very much a warrior. I've been a warrior my whole life."

So it is that some sons of warriors turn away from the Fortress. But even then, a son's refusal to follow the warrior path will not release him from his larger duty, instilled in him from birth: the duty to personify, at all times and in all endeavors, the unvarying definition of manhood dictated by the Fortress.

It is a definition a male warrior child cannot fail to absorb. The world of a son of the Fortress is a room lined with mirrors, all reflecting a single image, much larger than life: the timeless image of the Warrior, macho, stoic, unyielding, ready to sacrifice himself in battle for the sake of a larger cause.

A son can physically leave the Fortress when he comes of age, but it is not so easy to release himself from the compelling power of that image. Every warrior son has had to pay homage to it. Most sons have yearned at one time or another to become one with it.

And most would admit that somewhere deep inside them, the archetypal image of the Warrior is living still, its nobility, its allure, and its challenge still intact.

THE PARADOX

Considering the intense socialization sons receive inside the Fortress, it can come as something of a shock to the warrior father and Fortress mother when a son turns out to be gay.

It happens. Five of the military sons I talked to in the course of researching this book volunteered the information that they were gay. All had "come out" as homosexuals and were living openly gay lifestyles. All had suffered estrangement from their parents, to varying degrees.

One of them, a forty-year-old son I've called Harrison, had a very authoritarian, emotionally and sometimes physically abusive father who was a colonel in the Air Force. "Growing up gay in a family like mine, and in a military environment, was quite difficult, painful, and fearful," Harrison said. "As far back as I can remember, I've been gay—but because of the religious and social prohibitions against it, which I had internalized, I was not able to admit that fully to myself until I was in college. But I was also very aware of it while I was growing up. Harder than anything was accepting the label of 'homosexual.' "

I asked Harrison, who is a psychotherapist, if he thought there might be any connection between homosexuality in military sons and some of the things I had been hearing about in dysfunctional military families—mother-centeredness, for instance, or an absent or rejecting father.

"The party line in the gay community," he answered,

> is that it doesn't matter where homosexuality came from, that even to look at that assumes there is something wrong with it. I think there is some validity to that; no one asks why heterosexuals are heterosexual.
>
> The causes of homosexuality would certainly be multiple, not any one. But I would say . . . the issue has to do with dad, not mom. It's not the overcontrolling mother that seems to be part of the picture necessarily, so much as a gap between the boy and his father—a real desire to receive approval and affection from the father, at the same time there was this gap.
>
> With my dad there was a real sense I wanted his love and approval, and yet with who I was and *how* I was, that would never happen. That was an unresolved area throughout my growing up. There was also an overlay of fear because of his emotional and occasionally physical abuse. And there was anger and outrage at how he treated me and how he treated my mother.

Whether Harrison came to express sexual love and emotional commitment with men instead of women as an unconscious way of compensating for the emotional vacuum he experienced with his rejecting father, is something neither Harrison nor anyone else can ever know. As he points out, in the gay community theoretical notions on the origin of homosexuality are thrust aside as distracting from the central issue: Homosexuality is not something that can be changed in a person, so the important thing for someone who is gay is not to ponder how he may have come to be so, but to work toward self-acceptance and acceptance by others.

It is a tall order, of course, for a gay son of the Fortress to win acceptance from a macho homophobic warrior father. The most cruel and insensitive of warriors, the ones who taunted their sons at every opportunity with the refrain, "What are you, a queer?" must do backflips into some kind of mental hell reserved for human predators when one day the answer comes back *yes.*

I can imagine that in many such families, the moment of revelation marks a final and irreparable breach; the son would be banished and disinherited, left to face the rest of his life as though he had never had a family—unless he could secretly maintain contact with his mother or his siblings. I count it as a nice piece of luck, in fact, that my brother and I turned out to be conventionally heterosexual; otherwise I'm convinced our father would have shot us both on the spot and been done with it.

But I think it may be no accident that of all eighty interviews with military brats done for this book, the two most moving examples of reconciliation between sons and fathers involved sons who are gay. In each of these families, the gap between father and son was nearly unbridgeable by the time the son reached adulthood. In Harrison's case, the father was authoritarian and abusive; in Dan's case the father, a Navy chief, had been physically absent and emotionally withdrawn from his son.

It was extremely difficult for both sets of parents to face the truth when their sons broke it to them, and still harder for them to learn to accept it. But in both cases the fact of the son's gayness acted, over time, like a clarifying agent applied to murky water, precipitating out the impurities. It made unequivocally clear certain issues that in many another family dangle unresolved for decades, until the avenues of communication are finally impassable.

For instance, the revelation of homosexuality made clear that the son was *not* going to follow in the father's footsteps; that in fact his life would take a very different course from his father's, and not just temporarily, but permanently. It made clear that any warming or reconciliation would have to take into account the son's different-ness—that, in effect, the relationship would finally have to be on the son's terms. Not least, it also forced the parents, and maybe particular-ly the fathers, to examine what really counts in their relationship with their sons. Did the value of the relationship reside, as the father had let on over the years, only in the degree to which the son held true to the father model? Or did it lie somewhere else entirely, in something the father could neither control nor even perhaps comprehend, in bonds that are too old, too intimate, too important to reject for any reason?

In each of these families, the son's homosexuality triggered turmoil, sadness, and estrangement. It also triggered a great deal of soul-searching and emotional growth. And in both families, it became an avenue for the warrior father to discover his own ability to give unconditional love.

Dan's Story: Redeeming Love

When Dan was two years old, he and his father were models for a Navy recruitment poster. His father wore sailor whites; little Dan was in a black sailor uniform, perfectly tailored to fit him, trotting joyfully by his side. JOIN THE NAVY! the poster proclaimed.

Their relationship over the next sixteen years was a bit like that poster: both bound by the need to reflect one another, both trying to keep in step, but each in his way the other's opposite, as different as black and white. Dan's father was devoted to sports; Dan excelled at them, but preferred to stay home and play his clarinet. Dan's father was a perfectionist; Dan conformed only as much as he had to, and rebelled at enforced neatness at the first opportunity. Dan's father was unemotional, and did not approve of tears; Dan was at the other end of the spectrum, both emotional and expressive.

While Dan's father was not rigidly authoritarian, he was not overtly loving and was away on sea cruises at least half the time. Dan grew up feeling much closer to his mother, but unable to talk to either parent about most of the things he felt were important, and certainly unable to express his feelings. Dan and both his sisters were "extremely" overweight as children; he attributes this to having to "stuff down" his feelings. "Since I've been able to communicate and express my feelings, I've been fairly slim," he said.

There was no dramatic conflagration when, in young adulthood, Dan revealed his homosexuality to his parents, and no clear rejection followed. On the other hand, it seemed to Dan that he and his parents were keeping a definite distance from one another, and could not speak honestly about his homosexuality or, for that matter, much of anything else. That's where the relationship stayed, on a rather formal, inhibited plateau, and that's where Dan assumed it always would stay—a relationship that was disappointing but at least workable. It was not until Dan hit an overwhelming crisis in his life that he realized how he had underestimated his parents.

His long-time companion, a man I'll call Rob, was dying slowly, horribly, of AIDS. Dan was by his side constantly at the hospital, giving him support and interpreting for him. Rob was deaf, and had taught Dan to sign fluently. It was a time of terrible emotional and physical stress. Dan seldom went home for more than a few hours' sleep, because the hospital had no interpreter to replace him; it didn't take long for Dan to feel physically drained, socially isolated, and totally depressed.

Then, suddenly, his father was there, in the hospital, next to Dan and his dying lover.

"No words needed to be spoken," Dan said. "Just seeing him there was enough." His father's visit that day virtually transformed the relationship. And that was only the beginning of his parents' acceptance and support. His parents would come to visit, driving 180 miles round trip. His mother cooked and delivered meals. They talked with Dan frequently by phone. Most importantly, when Rob died and the world closed in on Dan, his parents were there to share his pain, help him talk it out. In or out of the military, there are too few parents of gays who have stood by their sons as Dan's did.

"I consider myself very, very lucky," Dan said. "I realize now what wonderful parents I have. It was far beyond anything I had imagined anyone doing, and without my ever having to ask. I'll tell you what extraordinary parents they are: They have visited Rob's grave many times, driving all the way from [their city]. Rob's family never goes, and they live just a couple of miles away. I have to keep the grave up, clean it up; his own family won't do it." Even when Dan moved across country for about a year, his parents continued to make the drive north to visit Rob's grave and maintain it.

Rob was the first person among Dan's circle of friends to die of AIDS. In the few short years since Rob's death, Dan has lost eighteen more friends to the disease. His companion now is a carrier of the virus who has developed AIDS-related complex; he's been hospitalized several times already. Dan has tested positive for the virus himself, although so far he has suffered no symptoms. His parents continue to be his emotional mainstay through this nightmare of loss, and in the face of his own potential death of AIDS.

"I just spoke to my mother and father last night about how I am becoming drained," Dan told me one day. "Everyone I know, everyone who's been close to me has either died of AIDS or been diagnosed with it. It's all around me. There's some kind of inner strength that keeps me going; I don't know what it is, but to this day I'm still healthy and doing fine. But I live with this constant threat every day of my life. I know my parents love me, and I love them very much. Without them, I don't think I would have gotten through this time of turmoil. And it is very sad that there are not more families like mine, who support their sons or daughters who are gay or lesbian, who accept them as they are, in their lifestyle. I am very, very lucky."

The very disease that has prompted so many Americans to shun its victims seems to have had the opposite effect on Dan's parents. They understood the message in Rob's death, and in his own parents' abandonment of him. In embracing Dan's loss, they have been embracing their own son, accepting him and loving him while they still have him.

Harrison's Story: Death into Life

Harrison, as we saw earlier, came out of a rigidly authoritarian Air Force family in which his father was emotionally abusive to him and also beat him with some frequency. Harrison was emotionally close to his mother, and very distant from his father. Still, there was a stronger bond with his father than Harrison had ever suspected. It was revealed, as it was in so many warrior households, during the Vietnam War.

Harrison, a teenager and then college student during that era, opposed it fervently on pacifist grounds. His father was a fierce advocate of the war, and could tolerate no dissent from his son. When Harrison drew a low number in the draft lottery and knew he faced a strong possibility of being drafted, he found to his astonishment that his father supported him in seeking conscientious objector status.

"My father wrote a letter of support," he said. "He wrote that although our positions on the war were different, mine was an honestly held position consistent with what he had observed throughout my life. For me this was a *really* important thing, because it was the first time my father clearly supported me in a position different from his own. We had had some nasty fights over the whole Vietnam thing; one night it even turned into a shoving match at dinner." Harrison's petition was nevertheless denied, and he decided to seek 4-F status on grounds he was gay. He received it, but did not explain the grounds to his parents, who did not know of his homosexuality; they apparently assumed he'd obtained the 4-F on "psychological" grounds and never pressed to know more.

That process of revelation began when Harrison's mother found a love letter. "She was horrified and enraged," Harrison related. "Later she took the blame on herself, and finally, after a long time, she saw that I was a pretty good, pretty helpful human being and the same person I'd always been. That was in spite of her fundamentalist Bible study group who told her that I was possessed by the devil." Each of his parents came to accept his sexuality before they died, Harrison said, but their acceptance came about very, very slowly. His father remained essentially in a state of denial about it for some years.

"Then came my mother's death," Harrison went on.

A phone call in the middle of the night. I remember my father and me telling each other on the phone that we loved each other. I don't think we'd ever said that before, or if we had it wasn't in that big, openhearted way.

We went to the hospital. My mother was in a coma. We discussed our beliefs that life should not be extended artificially. Almost as a signal, my mother's vital signs dropped. We had the machines removed. The three of us held hands, and she died. My father looked at her and said how beautiful she was, and how much he loved her. It was like having all his silly veneer removed, and seeing what a good-hearted man he was under all his conditioning. I of course was very emotional, and I cried. And my father told me how much he envied my ability to cry, and that he wished he could cry. I think then he recognized that while I am much more emotional—and from his point of view, more feminine—than he is, he saw there was strength in that. He had never been able to recognize that before. Or not to me.

Over those next eight years I moved ahead with my career and began my practice as a therapist. And my father and I developed quite a fine relationship, considering how different we were. My father at some point made a decision not to get angry at me anymore, and by and large he held to that. He still played games, but by the time he got sick I'd reached the stage where I didn't have any anger at him anymore. I didn't have *any* stuff left over.

It's interesting to note how the issue of mortality broke down the division between my father and me. First there was my mother's death. Then I had a blood test and was found to be carrying the AIDS virus—and I was looking at the possibility of my *own* death coming much sooner than I'd ever thought. And then, three years ago, there was my father's hospitalization. He was hospitalized in September, and died in January.

It was as though, in the face of death, what do our individual differences matter? There was a realization that as much as we had fought in our lives, there was a true and genuine love between us. I remember going to see him in the hospital one day, and sitting on his bed. Some time before, we'd tried to make an investment in life insurance, but it hadn't worked out. First we tried to get a policy on me, but after the blood test I was uninsurable; then we switched it over to my dad, but because of his heart problems *he* was uninsurable. I can remember sitting on his hospital bed and the two of us laughing like idiots at our mutual uninsurability. It was a wonderful moment. It's incredible how much richer life is when we recognize how impermanent it is, how silly a lot of our conditioning is.

Since his death I've found myself fully in his shoes, resolving his business deals, real estate deals, and all that. It's been interesting to see myself in this way. I'd begun to see it in my thirties—that as different as we were, we were also very similar.

The story of warrior sons and warrior fathers frequently begins with one all too visible, one too dimly seen. But time—and an openness of spirit—can bring changes. By the end of the story the mirrors themselves tell the tale.

Two reflections, the same and also different. Undistorted. In focus. Well matched. And both, for all time, warriors.

SONS OF WARRIORS: GHOSTS OF THE FORTRESS

Bull took a long drink and looked at Ben who was reading the sports section of the Charleston Evening Post. *He stared at him as if he were studying the shadows of an aerial photograph. He felt he had failed Ben badly in one critical way: he had failed to drive the natural softness of Lillian Meecham out of him, to root out and expel the gentleness that was his wife's enduring legacy to her children.*

—The Great Santini

It usually doesn't take long, in an interview with a son of the Fortress, to find out where his ghosts lie. They are right there with him, close to the surface, and more than willing to show themselves when summoned by name.

Of course everyone, military brat or not, carries unresolved issues from childhood that figure significantly in how they view themselves and how they deal with the world. But I wonder if many carry ghosts as predictable as those of warrior sons.

For if sons are so much more visible than daughters inside the Fortress, if sons are vastly more susceptible to the power and demands of the warrior image, and if sons enjoy a status and a measure of personal freedom that are alien to daughters, they are also haunted by ghosts that pursue them that much more mercilessly. Worse, they are ghosts of ambiguity: issues that are gray and elusive and emanating from deep within; issues, in other words, with which the black-and-white, surface-oriented world of the Fortress has ill prepared sons to deal.

On top of that, the Fortress trains its sons to suffer in silence, stoically, sharing their ghosts with no one. Sons of warriors can hardly believe it when, in the course of an interview, they are asked questions that in effect name their ghosts. Because they rarely discuss life inside the Fortress with others who grew up there, it is a revelation to them that other warrior sons, too, have these same ghosts.

As I see it, the ghosts, or problem legacies, carried by sons of the Fortress fall into three categories: the unrequited need for father approval, Oedipal issues, and control issues.

THE UNREQUITED NEED FOR FATHER APPROVAL

Craig, the son of an Air Force master sergeant who hit him frequently and belittled him constantly, told a familiar story of increasing estrangement from his father. Like most of the military sons interviewed for this book, he still suffers from hunger for the approving, loving father he needed and, to hear him tell it, never had. And like most of the other father-hungry sons, Craig never stopped hoping that at some point his father would change, and give him the respect and caring he craved.

Sometimes—as we shall see in this chapter and later—that long-suffering hope is justified. The warrior, particularly after retirement, mellows and becomes more receptive to his son's overtures, more willing to reach out himself. That didn't happen, however, in the case of Craig's father, and the hope Craig had for so long nourished transformed itself into a wish bitterly unfulfilled.

"My father was in the hospital, very sick," Craig related.

We got the call he was dying, and got there about midnight. The doctor was just closing his eyes. And I had this intense desire. . . . I wanted my father to explain, say *something*, make me feel better. But of course he was dead.

There are things I wish he'd done differently. Part of it was the alcohol; that was a killer. I've asked my mother about my father's father. Her impression was that my father was treated very brutally. So I share some sympathy for that. And, as I get older and things get harder, I try to recognize that blaming my father doesn't help me. I know that my father is at the root of a lot of things about myself I don't like . . . but blaming doesn't help.

The lack of an affirming father leaves a hole in a son's life that essentially is never filled. The son may do a lot of things to try to fill it—continuing to try and win his own father's approval, or that of a male mentor, or of a large, patriarchal institution such as the military or a corporation—and may well succeed in "fathering" himself in important ways. But there will always be a nagging hunger for the father he wishes he'd had. And plenty of anger.

It may be no accident, for instance, that for years Craig has been a committed Marxist. He attributes that in large part to one of the good things he got from his father and the military—a powerful sense of idealism, and "sympathy for the working man." It is also true, however, that in openly and actively espousing Marxism, Craig has set himself in opposition to the "fathers"—the ruling powers—of the world. (He points out that he is a "progressive Marxist," which means he is also in opposition to most, if not all, of the Marxist leaders of the world.) This in no way cheapens the sincerity of his beliefs; whether Craig came to them because his anger needed an outlet and a focus, or whether he came to them because his own experience with his father sent him in a direction that enabled him to see things differently, the point of origin and the result are the same.

Anger is at the core of every military son whose father was abusive or distant. One could say that of their sisters, as well—and it would be true—but the anger of daughters sometimes disguises itself as grief: the "lake of tears" that from time to time spills over. Sons rarely seem to harbor a lake of tears. For them it is a core of fire—and what spills over into the world is likely to be fiery as well: a quick temper, pugnacity, a choice of career that channels aggression and allows for plenty of confrontation, or, as in Craig's case, an oppositional stance in the world. Perhaps, in contrast to daughters, what spills over in sons could be seen as grief disguising itself as anger.

Fitz, the son of an Air Force lieutenant colonel, was very aware of the connection between his anger and his grief. "Much of my growing up was at the hands of an overbearing, verbally abusive man," he said.

I was also ignored by my father. Dad withdrew when I was very young. Someplace inside of me is a three-year-old who is very angry about that.

Pretty much the only thing my dad and I shared, in fact, was a love of baseball. A movie that spoke to me was *Field of Dreams*. In it, Kevin Costner plays a man who never got along with his father—but he and his father shared a love of baseball. The Kevin character hears a voice that tells him to "build it and he will come." So he builds a baseball stadium in the middle of his cornfield, and sure enough, Shoeless Joe Jackson appears on the field. As the plot develops we learn how Costner left home after arguing that Joe Jackson was a criminal, and how his dad had died several years ago. The climactic scene has the Costner character recognizing his dad on the playing field in his old baseball uniform. It's his dad as a young man, one who doesn't know that Kevin Costner is his son or even that he is going to have a son. Kevin asks his dad to play catch; and so he is reconciled with his dad, but with his dad as a young man who is his peer. They're about the same age, throwing the ball around, and his dad hasn't lost his innocence or his dreams.

Their relationship there on the ball field isn't about fathers and sons. It's about the game, their one area of compatibility, without the rest of the baggage. They can play catch and understand and be with each other.

The Kevin Costner character was driven to find a meeting place where he could reconcile with his father, long after he had died, and he finally found it. I wonder sometimes what it would be like to meet my dad as he was when he was a young guy. I wonder what it would be like to see him not as I knew him—as my angry, withdrawn dad—but as a peer.

Would I understand him? Would that matter? I don't know—but the movie really struck a chord. I think I'd really like to have the chance. There is so much about him that I don't understand. I live an hour and a half away from my father, but it is like the other side of the earth.

How do you begin again? How do you reconcile—or try to? Can you? How do I get over my own anger and resentment? How can I not want to punish him for not being around, or for not even wanting to be around? I don't love him, but he is my father, for God's sake. And I'm thirty years old. I should be over this by now, don't you think so?

Hard questions. And in asking them, Fitz has a lot of company among sons of the Fortress. Fitz remains uncertain about what, if anything, he will do to try and salvage a relationship with his father—but in some ways he's already preparing himself for the effort. He sees the root cause of his anger and confusion. He is realistic about the current state of affairs and wary of pitfalls on the path to reconciliation. He is not overoptimistic about the possibility of change in his father—a hope that could contain the seeds of further disappointment. And it would seem he is not enslaved to a sense of guilt over the estrangement, which could leave him vulnerable to manipulation by his father.

In contrast we have the cautionary example of a military son who was not so clearheaded, nor so self-protecting.

Navy yeoman Michael Lance Walker was a member of the most famous, and most damaging, spy ring of the century in the United States. Michael Walker, his uncle, Arthur Walker, his father's friend, Jerry Whitworth, and his father, John Walker, Jr., a former Navy chief warrant officer and the central figure in the ring, were convicted of espionage in 1985. Michael Walker, who stole documents from the aircraft carrier *Nimitz* at his father's behest, was twenty-two years old when he was convicted, and is now serving a twenty-five year sentence and four concurrent ten-year terms. In much of the coverage of the case, Michael Walker was portrayed as the son of an emotionally neglectful and domineering father who nevertheless so craved his father's approval that he would do anything to please him.

"I was in it because my dad was in it," Michael Walker told journalist Pete Earley. "He was a PI [private investigator], I was a PI.

He was in the Navy, I'm in the Navy. He's a spy, I wanted to be a spy."[1]

But not only does the lack of a positive father presence in a son's life leave him confused, vulnerable, and angry, it also contributes to problems of another kind: It makes it very hard for a son to dissolve the symbiotic bonds with his mother.

OEDIPAL ISSUES

The Fortress, in its very extremes of gender roles, is the perfect stage on which to play out the Oedipal drama. The authoritarian father is the unquestioned ruler of the family and, often, scourge of his son; the mother is her son's refuge and, potentially, the source of his guilt. And the son himself has no lack of rage, of jealousy, of aspiration.

Providing that the Fortress mother is not an alcoholic or dysfunctional in some other way, she can be a wonderful compensating presence in the life of a son suffering under an abusive or neglectful father. She also helps balance out the one-sided macho emphasis of Fortress life.

As one embattled Air Force son put it, "Advice and guidance always came from my mother. It was my mother I talked to about sex and girlfriends. It was my mother who continually reinforced my sense of being a decent human being, and who tried to work something out between our father and us so we'd still have a sense of family in the face of his continual rage."

It is well known that the mother is a profound shaping influence in any son's life. Inside the Fortress, however, where the son feels taunted by the supremely masculine warrior world to which he should be entitled but which remains out of reach, the mother's influence is increased geometrically. In addition, a son of the Fortress spends a great deal more time with his mother than most of his peers in the civilian world, since his father is frequently away from home on sea duty, or temporary duty, or working sixteen-hour days at the SAC base.

Mother-Centeredness

"In father-absent homes," said Dr. Leonard Lexier, a child psychiatrist working primarily with Navy families, "little boys pee sitting down."

There is no way a mother can effectively substitute for the father as a model of masculine behavior, or head off the boy's sense of abandonment. "It's clear that boys have a lot harder time with deployment [and the resulting father absence] than girls," Lexier said. "Much harder.

Mommies and daughters think alike. Women and boys don't think alike. The primary model for a boy in terms of the consolidation of his sense of masculinity, and also in learning about how to get along with females, is his father.

"And let's say you have a sister and dad leaves and then you're stuck at home with mom and your little sister. That's *horrible* for a little boy. And they have a lot harder time in school than their sisters do." Lexier takes the position that father absence is not the same thing as father hunger, and that military mothers can do quite a bit to ease the situation for their little sons, by providing exposure to suitable role models.

Be that as it may, the fact remains that no matter what a mother does, the nature of Fortress life works against a son having the male role models he needs, for the length of time he needs them. When the father is at sea, or stationed away from the family for any reason, the mother is soon overwhelmed with the stress and sheer logistical difficulty of single parenthood; it may be unreasonable to think that she can track down and line up suitable mentors for her son. And in any case, even if a mentor is found, the family—or perhaps the mentor—will likely be transferred out before the relationship can deliver what the son needs.

When the sons of career military men look back on their childhoods, they paint a picture of family life in which the mother is the central figure and the father makes occasional, if dramatic, appearances. Female-centeredness of military families has been measured by looking at which partner usually plays the primary role in handling certain responsibilities, from paying bills and deciding how money is spent to repairing the car. Studies show that in traditional military families where the mother stays at home and the father is the career military person—the situation which applied to nearly every interviewee for this book—the wife, as a direct result of family separations, early on assumes the central role in running the family, and her authority only increases over time. Thus, career military families, in which the father invests at least twenty years in the service, tend to be more female-centered, because female-centeredness increases with the number and length of separations.[2]

Interestingly, the degree of female-centeredness is also greater if the oldest child is male.[3] This means that the oldest son is invited to share in some of the responsibilities and stature that are normally the province of the father. It is a common pattern in the military, but one that cuts two ways. It can build a son's self-esteem and increase his sense of responsibility and independence; a number of sons interviewed acknowledged this as an important part of their character development. But it also adds freight to the already loaded Oedipal issue. When the father returns, ready to take up his former position, the son resents having to yield to him. The father, of course, always prevails—and the son is left feeling impotent, angry, and vaguely guilty.

Female-centeredness of the family, in combination with frequent absences of the father, is one way Oedipal issues are underscored for military sons.

A second way the Oedipal drama is intensified is through the constant mobility of service life. As two physicians writing in a journal of family therapy put it, "[The military child] is used to having his needs met within the family, which makes individuation and Oedipal issues more complicated."[4] What this means is that a boy's need to prove himself gets worked out within the family rather than in the outer community, where his attempts at proving himself are so often interrupted by moving. It also means that the way a boy works out his relationship to women is concentrated unnaturally on the mother— not, normally speaking, in overt sexual ways, but in the day-to-day dynamics that shape his assumptions, his expectations, his attitudes. The problem is considerably worsened in families where an extremely authoritarian father actively deprives the son of opportunities to develop in relationship to girls and women outside the family—by not allowing him to date, for instance, or by openly ridiculing him in front of a date or his sister's friends.

That of course suggests a third way the Oedipal drama is heightened for some military sons: by a father who is negative and rejecting. The pattern is laid down very early. As psychologist Tess Forrest wrote in the journal *Psychoanalytic Review*,

> In the child's early infancy, the father can relate to the child-mother world or he can isolate it. By accepting it, by deriving satisfaction from it, by perceiving it as part of himself, he relates to it and thereby prepares it for penetration. [An important and positive step in the son's development.] By resenting it, by rejecting it, or by indifference to it, he isolates it from the rest of the world and intensifies the twoness. Thus, the intensity and duration of the symbiotic mother-child relationship is from the earliest time influenced by the father. The father can either foster or pierce the symbiosis. I regard it as his primary function to penetrate the symbiotic relationship.[5]

Intensifies the twoness. That, in a phrase, is how military life affects the relationship between the Fortress mother and the Fortress son. It happens in civilian life too, to be sure, but I speculate, having been unable to find any military psychological research on this point, that it happens with much more frequency inside the Fortress. For one thing, military men are separated from their families more often than civilian men, with exceptions, of course. For another, it is part of the macho ethos of the military (something one cannot find in Department of Defense publications, but which nevertheless exists) that in order for the warrior to be optimally "ready" for the Military Mission, which is clearly the warrior's first allegiance, he must cultivate a level of indifference to his family that keeps him from being overly distracted by it. This is one reason the "promise" the son receives by virtue of his maleness—the promise of being personally guided into the warrior path by his own warrior father—is so often broken.

The terrible dilemma for many a son of the Fortress, the dilemma that colors his entire childhood and adolescence and casts its shadow on his adult life, is that he is *supposed* to be bred for the exalted company of warriors, but instead—either by default, because of an absent or indifferent father, or by fiat of an authoritarian, rejecting father—he is abandoned to the world of the mother.

It is not unusual for a son growing up inside the Fortress to recognize on some level that he is being cheated of his birthright, although he is generally confused by this, and assumes it is somehow his fault. Most such sons, it seems, continue to hope the situation will be miraculously reversed.

But there is another wrong inherent in the son's abandonment to the world of the mother that he may never recognize, although he certainly feels the effects. The father's abdication puts him in the psychologically dangerous position of *winning* the Oedipal struggle—not by "killing" the father and "sleeping with" the mother, but by taking over the place in his mother's life the father should by rights occupy. The mother turns to her son for companionship—not sexually, though Freud would say those undertones are always present—but in conversation, sharing of ideas and activities. The son, hungry for some kind of acceptance and acknowledgment of his maturity, not to mention anxious to be seen as interesting and companionable by the woman who represents all women, is usually happy to comply. And thus guilt—the other plague of military sons—enters the picture. Oedipal struggles are not meant to be won.

A Marine Corps mother I interviewed told me that when her husband was in Vietnam, she would frequently make lunch and dinner dates with her adolescent son. "We had an unusual relationship because my husband was gone," she said. "I know I spent much, much more time with him than if my husband had been home. I put so much of my time into [my son] because I didn't have my husband to do it with. It was never to the point that I resented him dating or anything like that. I wasn't possessive of him. It was just an abnormally close relationship." In hindsight, however, it was making her feel uneasy. It had all happened many years before, but at the time of the interview she had recently listened to a radio talk-show guest who warned of the Oedipal implications embedded in such seemingly innocuous patterns of behavior. It was interesting, when I later interviewed the son and asked him about the lunch and dinner dates with his mother, to hear that he had no recollection of them at all, although he said he could remember with great clarity other details of that year without his father.

This same son, later in the interview, noted that although he is over six feet tall and weighs almost two hundred pounds—the same size as his father—"I always think of myself as being smaller than he is. I relate to my mom as being bigger than I am, too." He also said he is "much more intimidated by women than men, because I was raised by a woman." And yet, he said, he goes out of his way to seek out women authority figures; at the time of the interview he had a woman lawyer, a woman banker, a woman accountant.

It is common for military brats to see their parents as larger than life. In addition to Oedipal questions, which are heightened by a domineering, authoritarian father, there is the fact of mobility, which has the effect of reducing the influence of other adults in the lives of transient military children. Part of the task of growing up for military brats of either sex is cutting the parents down to size, and adjusting the mental picture of the relationship to the realities of adult life. Todd, the Air Force son quoted extensively in the last chapter, may have been working on equalizing his relationship with his larger-than-life father by constantly referring to him as "the old man," "The Colonel," "the old fart," and, frequently—although I omitted it from the quotations—by his father's first name. For Todd it may be a harmless way to counteract the effects of having had to address his father as "sir" for the better part of two decades.

Harrison, the Air Force colonel's son quoted at length at the end of the last chapter, described a situation of "twoness" with his mother, which he recollected quite well:

> I was very much my mother's confidant, since she was left alone a great deal by the Air Force life. Therefore I learned rather sophisticated ways to entertain, be a listener, sense feelings, be with someone. I am currently a therapist, and I believe my skills as a therapist have a lot to do with having been brought up in the Air Force.
>
> It was unfortunate that she focused so much of her attention on me. I don't think it gave me enough room to breathe, though that was not my experience of it at the time. I think we both felt we needed each other. Our

world was constantly changing as we moved from one place to another, and my father worked incredibly long hours. So my mother and I were the ones who were around the house, and we were a team. We depended on each other. And in our own way, we did a dance around my father.

The same son made an observation about the Oedipal quality of his fantasy life as a child. The Oedipal drive was represented in symbolic form, of course, but it was obvious enough to him as a therapist, looking back many years later. "A lot of my fantasy material and my interests as a kid were focused on groups of people that were opposed to the U.S. military," Harrison said. "For example, American Indians, especially Apaches. I begged, pleaded, and cajoled my way into seeing every movie about the defeat of Custer that was made during the 1950s. There were a lot of them. They were great. I totally celebrated the defeat of Custer and the cavalry. Boy—Oedipal stuff there!"

Oedipus Unleashed

It was a military brat who shocked sensibilities in 1967 with what is almost certainly the most blatantly Oedipal rock song ever composed. Jim Morrison, son of a U.S. Navy admiral, lead singer of the sixties rock group The Doors, wrote and performed "The End," which takes up more than half of one side of The Doors' first album. Whether or not he had his parents in mind when he wrote it, he didn't mind using it against them. Once, knowing his mother and brother were in the audience of a live show—he had not seen his family in three years and in fact would never see them again in his short life—he made a point of singing it to her, with exaggerated facial expressions. He refused to meet with her after the show.[6] The song includes these verses:

> The killer awoke before dawn,
> He put his boots on,
> He took a face from the ancient gallery,
> And he walked on down the halllll.
>
> He went into the room where his sister lived annnd . . .
> Then he paid a visit to his brother,
> And then he . . . walked on down the hallllll.
>
> And he came to a doooooor,
> And he looked insidddde,
> "Father?"
> "Yes, son?"
> "I want to kill you. Mother . . .
>   I want to FFFUUUUUCKKK YOOOOO!"[7]

Whether Morrison was drawing his sentiments out of his own unconscious, or whether he was just stagily adding fuel to his incendiary image as a particularly iconoclastic bad boy of rock—an image he certainly exploited in other ways that occasionally brought conflict with police and prosecutors—is an open question. He apparently relished his self-styled role as point man in the war against sexual taboos; if in 1967 he was beginning to feel competition from other daring rock performers emerging at the time, he certainly staked his claim to the sexual no-man's-land with "The End." He was often asked in interviews about the content of the song, and consistently gave answers that were singularly unrevealing and essentially manipulative.

Certainly Morrison was a very troubled person; for all we know he may have been born with serious psychological problems. In any case, his self-destructive behavior with drugs and especially alcohol was legendary. When in July 1971 he died in a Paris hotel at the age of twenty-seven, news reports, quoting the French medical examiner, said he'd died of "natural causes." A member of his entourage commented that was like saying "Ernest Hemingway died of extensive brain damage."[8]

It goes without saying that the vast majority of sons, from the Fortress or not, are able to sublimate the rage and guilt generated by the Oedipal conflict. Sometimes, however, the drama is played out to what might be called a worst-case scenario: A son's frustrations and other character weaknesses combine to the point where he can barely restrain himself from fully acting out his rage. It happens infrequently, but it happens—and since the son is consumed by Oedipal guilt, the rage is often turned inward in highly self-destructive acts. Again I quote Tess Forrest, from the journal *Psychoanalytic Review*:

> The boy's crippling bondage to mother and impotent alienation from father cause hatred of mother for her power, demands and enslavement, and hatred of the father for his abandonment, competition, and refusal to provide escape. The murderous impulses are expressed and expiated in guilt. The ingratitude and disloyalty of the destructive impulses toward mother, the only source of satisfaction and security, and toward father, the betrayed progenitor, also provoke self-hatred and guilt. There is, further, hatred of himself, for his pretensions, cowardice, and confusion. He feels guilty as well for his self-betrayal, for his failure to be and live for himself, for his very existence as an extension of mother.[9]

When I first interviewed the Navy son I've called "Brian" in early 1986, he was one of the loneliest people I'd ever met. He was functioning well in his job as a store manager, he told me—he'd always been exceptionally devoted to his work—but his sense of having been emotionally abandoned had plunged him into despair. His marriage was foundering, and he allowed himself few friends. He spoke at length of his deep-seated anger at his father for having been away for so much of his childhood, and for displaying what Brian read as indifference to his family whenever he was home; some of Brian's comments about this are quoted extensively in Chapter 3. He spoke well of his mother in that first interview, characterizing her as "caring, tender, concerned." "I remember her as the person who cared about me," he said. "At the times I needed her, she was there." Nevertheless, as an adult he rarely saw her, despite living in the same city. He had no contact with his father at all.

What struck me most about Brian in that interview and a second one a week later, was that despite a sense of loneliness so painful it was palpable, he refused to take any steps to relieve it and in fact seemed to do quite a bit to isolate himself in his misery.

After several years I caught up with Brian again, and we did a third interview. This time, since long-distance moves had made another face-to-face interview impractical, we spoke by phone and then I sent him a list of questions to answer at his leisure into a cassette tape. A few weeks later, a tape arrived in the mail.

Things had not gone well for Brian in the intervening years, he told me. His marriage, which had been salvaged for a time, had fallen apart again. He was still extremely lonely and insecure. And he told me something he had not revealed in the first interview, that he was a drug abuser and an alcoholic, and had yet to seek help in kicking his addictions. There was one very good thing going for him, however: a reconciliation with his father, who had proved to be both concerned about his son and willing to help him. Brian had approached him first, after hearing his father's health was not good and realizing how much he still longed for him.

The tape continued. Some of the questions had tapped into Brian's sorrow, never far from the surface. "To tell you the truth, I still feel like a child," he said, his voice breaking. "I still don't feel like I've grown up. I feel like a large part of my childhood was taken away . . . I feel robbed. I feel cheated. I feel bitter. It hurts . . . it hurts to think about it."

The last question on the list had to do with personal strengths he felt his military childhood had given him. He ignored that and, after a pause, proceeded to confide an extremely dark and troubling secret:

There's something you didn't ask about. It's hard for me to say this to you . . . but I guess for me in a way it's part of therapy. I have a sexual problem. It deals with domination-type fantasies.

It kind of ties in to your earlier question about decision making. In the military I was always being controlled in the family unit. As a child I was always pushed away, told not to do things. In my adult life it's become a problem in my personal life, and is part of the breakup of my marriage, too. I have this need to be in control.

A year ago the need became very, very strong and to me it was so strong, and the fantasies were so violent that it was driving me crazy. Basically I was a passive personality, but I had this violent side of me underneath. That was about the time I took fifteen Valiums and drank a pint of Jack Daniels—I decided that would be my ticket out of here. Thank God I didn't make it. They took me to a hospital and made me throw up all that stuff.

Anyway, that's the dilemma I'm dealing with now. After a year of therapy we're getting down to the nitty-gritty. I'm seeing how I've programmed myself to create a violent or control situation into a sexual situation. Now we're in the process of reprogramming.

I think it ties in to the military and the insecurities of moving all the time. Because when I moved I didn't have control. I lost all my friends and I didn't have control. And since my dad wasn't there much, I blamed my mother. And that's what my fantasies are about: controlling women. I guess it all kind of ties in.

My wife knows this, and my psychologist, and now you. It's kind of scary telling you this, knowing it might appear in a book somewhere, but if it appears in a book and it helps someone else, then yeah, I guess it's worth it. No matter how scared I am, I guess it's worth it.

Unfortunately, not long after that, Brian terminated his treatment with the psychologist. He was still having rape fantasies, he told me, and still abusing alcohol. We stayed in touch. One evening he called me, drunk, to tell me he'd lost his job. The next day he called back, sober, to apologize for calling while drunk; he couldn't remember anything he'd said. But it was true he'd been fired, he said, and that to him was the last straw, the end of the world.

I had some people from Alcoholics Anonymous in his community call Brian, but he was not interested. I wrote to him and heard nothing back until he phoned a few weeks later "to say goodbye." He was sober, and he told me he was going to kill himself and had already written letters to be given to various people after his death. I was truly alarmed, and talked with him for some time, trying to get him to see how he could draw on the strengths I know he has to take the step of asking for help from AA or the many counselors and agencies that would counteract his sense of isolation and give him hope. He sounded as though he had been persuaded and we ended the conversation—but I wasn't comfortable leaving it at that. I called a suicide prevention hot line in his city and asked them to phone him.

Later I learned that he did the same thing with them he had done with me; he swore he would not harm himself so they'd get off the phone. Then he immediately got in his car and drove to the mountains to slit his wrists. As it happened he didn't follow through that time, as he later told me, but within a couple of days he did make a very serious and nearly successful attempt, using a large quantity of pills and alcohol. He phoned an old girfriend who had since married, and she and her husband came to the rescue.

The last I've heard from Brian was that he had found a job in another state, was still trying to dry out, and still struggling, on his own, to keep from committing rape.

I am not a psychologist, and do not claim to have a handle on what makes Brian tick. But it seems evident to me that his own explanation for his rape fantasies—blaming his mother for his frequent moves and consequent loss of friends—is only part of the story, and not perhaps the most significant part. The way I see it, there is a much larger Oedipal issue at the heart of Brian's problems, an issue of real or perceived abandonment by the father that left Brian a frustrated and enraged young boy imprisoned in the world of the mother. He is still reacting to that real or perceived abandonment, still looking for a way to vent his rage, and still, sadly, unable to see that the first task is to rid himself of the illusion that he can handle it all by himself.

The Masculine-Feminine Split

One of the things characterizing life inside the Fortress is the exaggerated difference between masculine behavior and feminine behavior, masculine values and feminine values. Macho maleness is at one end of the spectrum; passive, receptive femininity at the other.

It's not that a middle ground doesn't exist, at least where women are concerned: In the absence of their husbands, military mothers *must* develop some androgynous qualities, such as decisiveness and self-reliance, if they are to cope well with the stresses of Fortress life. But this middle ground, as necessary as it is, does not fit with the prevailing mind-set; indeed, many wives only inhabit the middle ground temporarily, until their husbands return and they retreat to passive femininity. So the existence of the androgynous middle ground, as crucial as it is to the functioning of the Fortress, is not permitted to alter the notion of what is ideally feminine.

Most parents inside the Fortress came to it from civilian life; they are people well acquainted with other ways of living who freely chose to devote themselves to the exaggerated, theatrical roles required of them in the Fortress company. Their initial grounding as civilians probably helps them balance out in their minds the extremes of Fortress life; somewhere inside them they know that most people don't really model themselves around such gender extremes, and that people inside the Fortress subscribe to this illusion because it somehow reinforces the system. They understand, too, that the system of the Fortress is rigidly patriarchal and conformist, while civilian life allows more latitude.

By contrast, their own children almost never gain any significant exposure to contrasting notions that are strong enough—or can be experienced long enough—to seriously compete with the Fortress polarization and exaggeration of sexual stereotypes. Instead, children of authoritarian warriors grow up in households marked by chronic devaluing of females and the feminine, and they see that attitude supported by the general culture of the Fortress.

Inside every son and daughter of the Fortress this gender split is to some degree mirrored. This has nothing to do with sexuality. Rather, it has to do with strongly contradictory personality traits that can be puzzling to the military brat and to those who know him or her. It has become well accepted in the field of psychology, since the days of Carl Jung, that every human being possesses both masculine and feminine qualities; in a mature and well-balanced individual, these qualities both offset and assist one another. However, the values evident in Fortress life and in the great majority of Fortress families, in which males and the masculine are supremely valued while females and the feminine are essentially negated, contribute to a situation in the Fortress child in which masculine and feminine qualities are driven apart instead of being healthily integrated.

The qualities still exist in each military brat, of course, but they do not assist one another. The person suffering from such a split finds it difficult to bring emotions, thoughts, and actions into harmony; he or she might be attracted to extremes of thought and behavior, might even alternate between them, and has a hard time learning to take a more stabilizing middle course.

This may come about because the original father model and mother model, as well as the masculine values and the feminine values of the Fortress, were not integrated, not in harmony, not equally valued by one another, and not equally valuing of the child.

From a very young age, the warrior son is taught to undervalue the feminine wherever he encounters it, and to mistrust and then deny the feminine aspects of himself. It's a confusing and troubling process, because there is no way to eliminate the feminine aspects of character—for example, the instinct to nurture, or to create. So the son might grow up to experience something on the order of a battle between masculine and feminine aspects of his character that have never been taught how to communicate with one another. Something is seemingly always off balance: The masculine overpowers and represses the feminine. The feminine rages and wars with the masculine. And, in the absence of conscious effort to help restore balance, the military brat frequently harbors clashingly contradictory traits.

A son might grow up to embrace the creative, feminine principle he was forced for so long to deny, but because he is still out of balance, he has trouble figuring out how to combine it with a competitive masculine drive to go out and accomplish things in the world. In other words, he might be a creative or imaginative person who is hobbled by a psychological block that keeps him from producing.

Or he might indulge his creative passion in an explosive, destructive, all-consuming way, paralleling the extremes of Mother Nature, one might say: the son who does not control his creative power but is controlled *by* it—driven perhaps to use his talents to hurt or destroy. Jim Morrison, whether unconsciously or by design, at times appeared to fit this pattern.

Or he might in adulthood choose a traditional masculine course, but experience frustration and a sense of loss at not knowing how to express the "feminine" qualities without compromising the sense of self he has invested solely in the ultramasculine side. In this respect the son might find himself imitating the role of the stereotypical one-sided warrior father, and experiencing the same painful limitations of that role.

At the start of the last chapter we had the image of a three-year-old Air Force son whose father dressed him in a miniature uniform and repeatedly tried to take his beloved doll away. His sister related the image as an example of how her brother was forced into socialization along a model of machismo. That, however, is not all she had to say. Her further comments painted a clear picture of a masculine-feminine split; I quote them because her observations are the kind of material I do not feel one is likely to extract in a first-hand journalistic interview with any son.

"My brother is very artistic," she said. "He loves ballet, even talked about becoming a dancer. Can you imagine? That just made The General quiver." On the other hand, she said, her brother had a very hard time winning his father's approval, even when he threw himself into approved "masculine" pursuits. "My father was ruthless with my brother," she related. "My poor brother. Anything he did was 'bad,' 'stupid,' 'infantile,' 'naive.' That poor kid couldn't do anything right. . . ."

It was the well-socialized macho side that prevailed with him, she said. Her brother badly wanted to be a fighter pilot like his father. "I think he would have been very good at it, and he would have loved it," she said. But his bad eyesight prevented him from passing the physical to become a pilot—a huge disappointment to him. Instead, in what his sister interpreted as a continuing bid for his father's elusive approval, he went to medical school, became a physician, and went into the Air Force as a flight surgeon.

"He's a very conflicted person," the sister said. "He is a wonderful doctor and an extremely compassionate person. And he is also a militaristic, reactionary, fascist person. I can't put the two things together.

"Maybe this is why we'll never be close; I can't fathom it."

The comments of another Air Force son I've called Ross spoke to the unequal valuing of males and females, masculine and feminine, in a typical authoritarian Fortress household. His comments to me suggested how this imbalance is internalized and can produce a split.

Earlier in the interview, Ross had thoroughly established that his father was an extreme and rigid authoritarian who was an alcoholic and emotionally abusive to his wife and all their children. Unlike his father, his mother was a very devout Catholic who wanted Ross to be a priest. For a time he entertained that idea, and even went away to seminary in his sophomore year of high school. He decided against that path, but the path he ultimately chose was no more in line with his father's macho, militaristic notions than the priesthood would have been. Ross became a scholar of Soviet history. He is not a Marxist, he said, although "there is a lot of Marxism in the way I analyze the world," and he considers himself a patriotic American citizen. Still, Ross noted, "I've drifted a long way from what I was raised in, in the military. . . . When I think about being a Soviet historian—it's difficult to get much further away from America. I've moved a long way from grass-roots America, and I don't think that's accidental."[10]

Ross painted a portrait of his family life inside the Fortress in which masculine and feminine, father and mother, were about as divided as it is possible to get. There were always marital problems, Ross said; his mother and father never shared the same bedroom—even though that meant all three boys had to be put in one bedroom, given the size housing usually provided to sergeants in the military. After the boys got bigger, Ross shared his father's bedroom for about ten years, until his father retired. But not only were father and mother, representing masculine and feminine, clearly living in disunion under the same roof, they were both party to the devaluing of the feminine. Here is how Ross speaks of his mother:

"I often don't see the influence of my mother on my life," Ross said. "She was invisible. One of the things I have to work on is to make her more visible; certain of her traits are more positive than my father's."

He pointed to something in the way the household was run, day to day, that for him symbolized his mother's invisibility:

> Something I've observed: In other households, the toilet seats are always *down*. That is their natural position. In our household the toilet seats were always up—and there was never a complaint on my mother's part, never any effort to get us to pay attention to her point of view. She just adjusted to it, and the toilet seats always stood at attention.
>
> But my mother was a role model for me also. Loving, accepting, caring, concern for other people, opposition to racism—all this I got from my mother. I also learned the ineffectiveness of weakness. Her view never counted. She was oppressed by the system.
>
> My method I got from my father: angry, assertive, belligerent. And I got a loving, accepting, caring content from my mother. I don't mean to imply that I didn't love my mother. On the contrary; maybe I loved her all the more for not impressing her personality on us.
>
> I think I'm a feminist. I don't think of myself as a sexist. On the other hand, I don't want to be a woman. When I think of the position of women in our society, I see it as less desirable, for a lot of reasons: the pressures they face socially, the invidious position they're placed in.
>
> I'm happy being a man. I just want to be a different man than the one I am.

Although it is not easy for emotionally wounded military sons to reach out for help in healing themselves, some of them do—and when they do, the masculine-feminine split is one of the core issues to be addressed. There is for example the story of Adam, the Vietnam veteran and son of a Marine sergeant.

His Vietnam experience started Adam on the road to alcoholism— in the last chapter he mentioned that during his second tour he was probably drunk five nights of the week. When he returned to the States and left the Air Force, the drinking subsided for a while. But a few years later, he took up the pattern again.

"It was escapism from problems at work and at home," he related. "And I was feeling a lot of pain from the things I did in Nam; I never *saw* anyone killed from one of my actions, but I know they were. And then the things I did see: the body bags, people getting blown away. Looking at those guys, and knowing *it could be you*. You put that in a secret little place inside you, and it starts to eat you alive."

Adam sought counseling, and tried different therapists until he found one that was a good fit. He's been seeing the same one now for five years; it was this therapist who finally got Adam to face his alcohol problem and go to Alcoholics Anonymous. When Adam spoke to me he'd been sober for eighteen months.

It was also this therapist who addressed Adam's masculine-feminine split. "I didn't really *know* you had a feminine side," Adam said.

I'd heard about it in some of my college psychology classes, but I didn't pay much attention to it until my therapist brought it up a number of times. Then I realized the feminine side of me is what I was running away from: If I did not get in touch with it, I really could not have control of my entire personality.

It was the feminine side of me that was regretting what happened in Vietnam, that felt remorse. It was the side that was hurting, over all the brutality that was committed, and over my having had to be there. The U.S. government turned us into animals. We were just a tool for their politics. The masculine side of you accepts that—you do your job and try to survive—but the feminine side looks at what you're doing and asks, *Is this really me? Is this brutality really a part of me?* And it is ashamed.

I went to Vietnam on my second tour with a completely different attitude about the war. I think all the people around me could sense I was not buying this war. I started questioning what was going on in Vietnam, to the point where it really got hard for me to accept orders from people I thought were incompetent and were giving orders just to be giving orders. I started challenging things and it got me into hot water at times; that's why I never made any higher rank than E-4. But I think it was better for me, because I would have been in a lot worse shape if I had just accepted Vietnam for what it was and not asked any questions. It was the feminine side that was asking—*Is this really me? Is this my fault, or is someone else doing this to me?*—and it was because I was asking questions that I've gotten beyond the pain and suffering I felt all those years.

The emotional aftermath of Vietnam was the immediate impetus for Adam to seek counseling, but the therapy took him back much further than that, to the origin of his masculine-feminine split.

"Growing up in the Marine Corps did affect me, in the way I looked at being male and what it took to get by in the world—the macho image," Adam said.

Some of that's good, some of it's not so good. Not being able to deal with the feminine side was bad for me. But it's not a problem you can't deal with. You have to let go of some of that macho stuff and say, "To be whole, I need to cry, I need to feel, I need the emotion." You can't stuff all that emotion on a daily basis and be healthy.

Now I will cry when it's time to cry and not think anything of it, where before I would hold my tears in, because the sons of Marines don't cry—it's [considered] a sign of weakness. I've had to put that kind of thinking behind me in order to get in touch with my feminine side, and allow myself the luxury of crying, of remorse, of feeling pain, anguish, fear, and then letting *go* of them.

Before, I was an emotional person but the emotions were more like a volcano erupting. I would stuff them to the point there was back pressure and it would just explode. I was very unpredictable. I'm a lot healthier now than I was ten years ago.

CONTROL ISSUES

Children of authoritarian fathers frequently have problems focused on issues of control. For daughters, as we have seen, the problem of control may express itself in an eating disorder. Eating disorders were uncommon among the sons interviewed for this book; control problems for them took four basic forms, although daughters, too, refelected some of these.

Passivity

Sometimes it happens that the daughter in a military family internalizes the father's warrior assertiveness, while the son internalizes the mother's pattern of passivity. For a daughter, this is not such a bad thing; in fact, she can learn to harness warrior assertiveness to overcome the negative legacy of invisibility. For a son, inheriting the mother's passivity is much more problematic. A compliant attitude may help a son survive childhood and adolescence with a combative authoritarian father, but it does not help his self-esteem, or his ability in later life to deal with authority figures who make unjust accusations or unreasonable demands.

"I think I've been as far from being a warrior as I can imagine," said Fitz, the Air Force lieutenant colonel's son quoted earlier.

> I have always been the pacifist, in everything. If somebody is being a jerk, I am the one who tries to find an explanation for it rather than just calling him a jerk. In response to evil or injustice in the world, I am the one calling for mercy and understanding.
>
> Dad was so quick to judge that I have gone completely the other way. Almost consciously, I refuse to judge. Naively, I expect the best from others. I expect fairness and reason. If I don't get it, I tend to ignore them rather than chastise them.
>
> I have never been truly competitive. If I am winning, then I back off a little so that the game is closer. I don't have that killer instinct. I even hate the idea of fishing or hunting; I can't kill these innocent little animals—that would be insensitive to them, don't you think? Even when I was thinking of enlisting in the Army, it would have been as a medic or a radio operator. I would have cringed to shoot at somebody.

Fitz does not feel he has problems with passivity, although from his self-description it is hard not to imagine that he discounts his own feelings when he backs off from confrontation or competition, which would certainly qualify as a form of passivity. Fitz prefers to see himself as having always cultivated a spirit of independence, instead of following in lockstep the aggressive, macho model his father represented. But the flip side of that, which he readily acknowledges, is his difficulty in dealing with authority figures and any kind of hierarchy. By young adulthood, Fitz said, "I had already spent a lifetime hating a world where giving orders seemed to be the main avenue of communication. I mean, I would eventually go on to quit my job at an advertising agency, the epitome of 'hang loose, be creative, and don't conform' thinking, because it was too structured. That's why I'm self-employed. I can work for me."

Those are sentiments echoed among many military sons. Strikingly, more than three quarters of the sons interviewed for this book had either chosen occupations in which they were their own bosses or had deliberately carved out niches with considerable autonomy within larger organizations. There is more on this subject in Chapter 11, "Legacies."

Another son pointed to a different aspect of passivity associated with authoritarian fathers. "We were continually being told by my father that we weren't good enough," he said.

> Whenever we tried to do something he'd always ridicule it, make it seem we couldn't do anything right. Raking the lawn, for instance. . . . he'd be out there in two minutes telling you what a dunce you were because you couldn't rake the lawn correctly. And he'd make you put your hands on top of the rake handle and tell you exactly how to do the sweeps, all the time furious and yelling at you.
>
> I think as I got older it was harder for me to take the initiative. I had no expectations of my own worth or what I could do. My successes came as surprises—delightful surprises, but surprises—as I got older and discovered I wasn't the failure my father continually told us we were.

Perfectionism

As with daughters, perfectionism is a standard-issue legacy for sons of authoritarian warriors. In Chapter 4 I quoted Sarah, an Air Force daughter who is now a clinical psychologist working primarily with wives and daughters of military men. She said that perfectionism is one of the main problems she sees in military daughters, and pointed out the distinction between perfectionism in women and in men. "The tendency for women perfectionists is to focus on being the 'perfect person,'" she said. "Perfectionist men put emphasis more on 'the product': never making mistakes in performance."

I asked a Navy son who is also a therapist if he had observed the same thing. Yes, he said, and he added that he thought he knew the origin of perfectionism in military brats. It comes from the military fathers, he said, because of the fitness reports [known as efficiency reports in the Army and Air Force]. "You won't be promoted in the military if you have anything less than a perfect four-point-oh fitness report," he pointed out. "Anything below four-point-oh is unacceptable. That is a value specifically instilled by the military. Only the people that are four-point-oh make it to the top."[11] In other words, the authoritarian military requires perfection of its members—in part as evidence of total compliance to the demands of authority—and the individual careerist reinforces this programming with personal ambition. The combination makes for extremely powerful conditioning.

Every military brat I interviewed, son or daughter, reported that their fathers—and sometimes mothers—were perfectionists. Most also said they either have the perfectionist compulsion themselves, or that they were equally consumed by a need to react against it. In either case, of course, it is the manifestation of a control problem.

There are variations in degree, of course. In its mildest form, perfectionism is a kind of false illusion that the world, and one's performance in it, can be totally controlled. As one son of a Marine Corps pilot put it, "My brother and I were raised on idealism and perfection. The idealism was that perfection was possible." Until they learn to adjust their expectations, military brats raised on such notions are likely to be dogged by a sense of disappointment in themselves and other people.

The problem is intensified in those military brats whose fathers were not only perfectionist, but authoritarian and condemning. When military sons of this category make mistakes in performance, they do not view them as learning experiences with the potential to strengthen, but as still more "evidence" of their continuing failure to measure up—in other words, failures of will. If that sounds reminiscent of the attitude of an authoritarian warrior father, it is because that's exactly what it is: the internalized negative voice of the authoritarian father, looking for an opportunity to castigate the child.

One son of a Navy commander provided an especially clear example of how perfectionism in performance was passed to him from his father, and how today he can't help using the perfectionism instilled in him against himself:

> My dad was a perfectionist; he couldn't make mistakes. At Christmas Dad wouldn't let us decorate the tree, because it had to be perfect. He laid the tinsel on one at a time; he'd let us put the Christmas balls on the tree, then we'd go to bed and he'd put the tinsel on. I remember once I got up and he'd moved all the balls, because they weren't in the right place. *He changed the tree.*
>
> My dad felt he couldn't make mistakes. The military doesn't let its people make mistakes. And I feel in a lot of ways I can't make mistakes either. I come down harder on myself than anyone else ever can. Yesterday

at work I really lost it because I made a mistake in the schedule. I'd failed to schedule someone to stay late for a slide presentation. I mean I just really got pissed off at myself. I lost my temper, punched a hole in the wall, and got real upset. I just hammered myself for it.

The son of a Navy chief petty officer, asked if his father was a perfectionist, replied, "Dramatically so. The tiniest little imperfection would drive him crazy." It turned out he had given a lot of thought to the matter:

> It's true that in the military the attention to every minute detail of performance and appearance promotes a style of life conducive to the military way. But in the family it's not proper, not reasonable. You have to be able to accept failure in your children and help them deal with it, and not just punish them for it. In the military that's an attitude that just isn't fostered. I don't think my father ever had an inkling of how to accept failure. He was never any comfort when I had a disappointment, just very stoic. I remember wanting badly to do well in baseball, in Little League. But when I first started I was clumsy and struck out a lot. So my father stopped going to the games.
>
> Parents have to find some way of helping their kids deal with failure, and one good way of doing that is showing the child that *you* fail, and you accept it. In military families I think it's rare for parents to allow their children to see their frailty, to see that they don't succeed all the time. That's almost totally absent from *all* hyperperformance families. But in the military it is exacerbated by the way performance is so precisely measured and visible. It's there for all to see. You walk around with how well you've performed written all over you. [12]

Military brats frequently hold themselves to impossibly high standards—higher even than the sometimes unreasonable expectations they have for those around them. "I can*not* fail," said the son of an Army colonel. "Quitting is something I *can't do*. If someone else tells me to quit I can accept it, with reservations. But for *me* to quit? No way."

Breaking the Patterns

When one is raised with only two internal measuring sticks, total perfection and total failure, the need to control can potentially grow so out of bounds that one's ability to judge risks, determining what's reasonable and what isn't, becomes impaired. Brian, for instance, refused for years to get a driver's license—even though, in a city known for inadequate public transportation, he would sometimes have to walk five miles to work. He explained that "a car was a machine you couldn't be in control of totally." His need to control literally stranded him in place, cut him off from possibilities.

A much more insidious problem in the lives of many military sons is drug and alcohol addiction. The control issue works against military sons in two ways.

First and most obviously, the illusion of control leads them right into patterns of substance abuse they find themselves unable to break.

Second, the notions ingrained from growing up inside the Fortress—that any self-respecting child of a warrior should be capable of extricating himself from any predicament unaided—make it that much harder for the son to reach out for help. It's not that daughters are not also vulnerable to the same traps, for they are; but I do believe that where addiction is concerned, sons are at much higher risk and at the same time are handicapped by even stronger conditioning.

The danger for sons is so great, as I see it, that it defies overstatement. Alcoholism research supports this judgment. One study showed that sons of alcoholic fathers are four times more likely to become alcoholic than sons of non-alcoholic fathers.[13] There is reason to suspect the rate may be even higher for sons of the military. For one thing, as we have seen in Chapter 2, alcoholism is considerably more widespread in the military than in the civilian population.

The interviews for this book constitute too small a sample to have much statistical weight, but their revelations are alarming enough to underscore the urgent need for large-scale study: As mentioned in Chapter 2, of the seventy-five military families represented by these interviews (that's less than the total number of interviewees because in a few cases there is more than one interviewee from a single family), thirty-nine had at least one alcoholic parent. (And one additional family had a mother addicted to Valium.) Seventeen of those thirty-nine families have a son who is alcoholic or has an "alcohol problem," by their own testimony or that of a sibling. That's more than three times the rate for daughters; five families have alcoholic daughters.

While these interview results should be viewed as exactly what they are, the results of an unscientifically selected sample, they should also not be summarily discounted. The message is shockingly clear: Military brats in general, and sons in particular, are at extremely high risk for alcohol and drug addiction and should take whatever measures are necessary—including total abstinence and intensive therapy—to counteract that risk. We would be wise to heed the warning our own stories are screaming at us to recognize and heed it without delay. It would make no sense at all to wait and see if these results are confirmed by the kind of large-scale, scientifically controlled research that is warranted; for one thing, I hold out no hope whatever that the Department of Defense will undertake any kind of study to determine what has happened to its children.

Ghosts

I've heard it over and over from the sons of authoritarian, abusive warriors: the waking nightmare that one day they will look in the mirror and see their fathers. All of us from such families are afraid to find we are imprisoned in the family pattern, but it stands to reason that it is a particularly strong fear for sons. The father is their role model. Fortress life itself reinforces that role model in every way. And the physical resemblance to the father is frequently haunting, like a ghost.

"Part of the problem in my own family, with my wife and kids," said the son of an alcoholic, authoritarian Army colonel,

is that I was an awful lot like my father without realizing it. And without wanting to be anything like him, but not really knowing how to be anything else.

I remember one time sitting at the dining room table talking to my family. At the other end of the room was a hutch with a mirror at the back. And I kept catching glimpses of myself gesturing and talking, and it just *scared me to death*—because I saw my father.

It was probably the first time it dawned on me that what my wife had been telling me was really true—I was acting like my father. And she had been around him enough to know what kind of person he was. I would be very short with people. I would preach. Demand. Lecture incessantly. And it did basically one thing: It was causing a barrier between me and my children. They weren't hearing me anymore. They shut me out.

I became terrified, and started listening to my wife a lot more. I really did not want to be like him. My wife has been a tremendous help to me. It's made a big difference, although there are times I revert back, even today. I do tend to have a short fuse. But I try to get my point across and then stop. Part of it is that I've learned how to put words together better than I used to, and I've learned how to be a better listener. Before I was not a good listener. And I've learned to admit when I'm wrong. My father would never admit he was wrong; in the military you almost never saw anyone who could do that.

I want to be a better person than my father. I want to be a good father and a good husband. I'm certainly not as good as I could be, but I'm a lot better than the original product. I give my wife a lot of credit for that.

The worst legacies for any military brat coming out of a dysfunctional, probably alcoholic, family are the destructive patterns that threaten to repeat themselves. The supremely difficult task of the military brat is to recognize those patterns, first in the family and then in himself or herself, and "launch a campaign" to defeat them. It takes every ounce of warrior in us to do that.

But if the Fortress, directly or indirectly, has provided us with enough personal battles to keep us busy the rest of our lives, it has also given us, through no grace of its own, the wherewithal to fight them.

Every one of us has a fighter within. Every one of us has internalized some basics about how battles are fought and won: We know we must study our enemy—in this case, a destructive pattern of behavior—until we know it inside and out. We know we must have a battle plan, with sound strategy and intelligent tactics.

And we know, if we think about it, that an army does not go to war with only one soldier. We cannot—and should not—fight our battles alone.

CHAPTER 7

MILITARY BRATS AS CASUALTIES

"Hush," Lillian hissed at her children. "Not another sound." Her eyes cast a stern, desperate communiqué to her children.

But this time there was no need. Bull's tone had registered. Each child knew the exact danger signals in the meteorology of their father's temperament; they were adroit weathermen who charted the clouds, winds, and high pressure areas of his fiercely wavering moods, with skill created through long experience. His temper was quick fused and uncontrollable and once he passed a certain point, not even Lillian could calm him. He was tired now after driving through half the night. Behind his sunglasses, the veined eyes were thinned with fatigue and a most dangerous ice had formed over them. The threshing winds of his temper buffeted the car and deep, resonant warning signals were sent out among the children. Silence ruled them in an instant. . . .

"Control," Lillian said soothingly. "Control is very important for all of us." She was looking at her husband.

—The Great Santini

In 1986 I spoke with a woman I'll call Victoria, who teaches at one of the elementary schools serving the enlisted housing area of Camp Pendleton, California, one of the largest Marine bases.

"We see a lot of problems with child abuse," she said. "I think the kids I see are basically of two kinds. Either they're overbossed or underbossed. Either the father tells them when to breathe, or he ignores them.

"All of them seem to be lacking affection. You can tell by the way they behave toward their peers. We don't have a lot of caring. So many will pass another child who could be bleeding and they will only stop to look at the blood—not because they cared or wanted to help out in any way. We talk about that *a lot* in class, to encourage caring. We tell them to notice if someone else is hurting emotionally, to see if they can't give them a pat on the shoulder. We have lots of abuse. We're always watching for it; I'd say every year there are three or four abused kids in a class."

At her school, Victoria said, the teachers are very socially aware and motivated to find abused kids and help them. They try to provide a caring environment, and they follow up on the cases they report. "We push to see it's taken care of," she said. But one of the biggest problems the teachers face is the way the Marine Corps initially responds. "When we report suspected molesting and abuse," she said, "an MP [military policeman] comes to talk to the child—*in uniform, with guns, the whole thing*. We've been fighting this and fighting and fighting. We insisted we do not want MPs talking to these children; they look intimidating, and they are not really trained. There are a few social workers, but I guess they are so busy they don't have time for this initial contact. It's a big concern of ours.

"Last year a little boy told his teacher that an uncle was beating him up a lot. So she reported it, and an MP found this kid playing on a football field and says, 'Hey, kid, come over here. I understand your uncle is beating you up.' There were a bunch of kids around, and the kid says, 'No, he's not.' So the MP says, 'Oh, okay. Well, it was reported. We're just checking on him.' And that was it. So it's really a problem; things are just not dealt with in a delicate way."

In early 1989 I again raised this issue with a social worker at Camp Pendleton, who replied that yes, it still sometimes happens that a uniformed member of the military police interviews the abused child. "But frankly I don't see anything wrong with that," the social worker said. "After all, the same thing happens in the civilian community."

The difference, of course, is that in the civilian community it is considerably less likely that the child would have been *abused* by someone wearing a uniform. One of the Camp Pendleton incidents related to me concerned a little girl who was regularly sexually abused by her Marine father and some of his friends on their lunch hour.

The problem is not limited to MPs, however. "The CID [Criminal Investigation Division] guys on the base are just as bad as the MPs," the same teacher continued. "Three years ago I had a little girl who had been molested by a neighbor. The CID guys don't wear guns, but they are just as tactless. They questioned her with *no woman present*. And she was going to court."

In fact on one of the days I did research at the Family Service Center at Camp Pendleton, a Marine was being court-martialed right across the street on charges of sexually abusing a little girl. The girl, who testified against him, was not permitted to have any ally with her in the courtroom—not even her mother or a social worker.

In 1989, there were 759 reported cases of domestic violence at

Camp Pendleton, which has a population of roughly 34,000 active duty personnel plus 45,000 dependents. Of those incidents, 253 involved child abuse. In some respects the way family violence cases are handled at Camp Pendleton is crudely insensitive; in other ways it is exemplary.

If an enlisted Marine at Camp Pendleton batters his wife,[1] for instance, action is taken immediately to stop the violence, protect the wife, and learn what can be done to relieve family stress. The wife is escorted directly from the emergency room of the hospital to the Family Service Center, where she is interviewed by an attorney. The attorney then phones the Marine's battalion commander, who orders him to stay away from his family.[2] The Marine's sergeant major escorts him home to pack a bag. Since Camp Pendleton spans 196 square miles, it is easy to arrange for the Marine to be housed at one of several camps at least a dozen miles away from the family's home, where the wife and children are permitted to stay. The family is put in immediate contact with social workers to begin therapy.

Similarly, when a report on a child abuse incident is made to the command, the social workers make a recommendation as to how it should be handled and what the family has to do. Their power is considerable; their recommendation is fed through the commanding officer (CO) and becomes an order.

Action this swift is almost unheard of in the civilian community. "In the civilian world, if you have a father who's abused a kid, you have to go to the court and get a judge to say, 'You're going to see Dr. So and So every week or you're in contempt of court,' " a local civilian therapist said. "In the military it happens in ten minutes. The CO says, 'You show up or you're in the brig.' You don't have to get a court date or anything. It's marvelous." The effectiveness of the military in ensuring compliance by the abuser stands in contrast to the record in the civilian community. A civilian study has shown that only 13 percent of abusive parents in a voluntary treatment program successfully completed it, and even when treatment was court-ordered the rate of successful completion was only 68 percent.[3]

Of course, when nearly all of the military brats interviewed for this book were growing up, such measures were also unheard of in the military. There were no Family Service Centers, which have only come into being since 1979. Such community centers as there were served primarily social purposes and offered very superficial assistance, such as short-term loans of pots and pans to families whose household goods had yet to catch up with them. There was no outreach, no intervention, no treatment, no preventive education.[4]

Despite the dramatic strides that have been made in recent years, the history of support for families in the U.S. military is on the whole a pathetic one. For many years, as in the civilian sector, problems ranging from alcoholism to wife beating to child molesting were denied, ignored, and protected as dirty little secrets. But while the civilian community began to wake up to its child abuse problem in the early 1960s, with child protection programs in place in nearly all the states by the end of the decade, the military continued to ignore the plight of the youngest members of the Fortress. The old saying "The Army (or Navy/Marines/Air Force) takes care of its own" evidently did not extend to its children.

It can be said with justification that the military delayed addressing crimes against its children until the last possible moment. In 1974 a landmark development in the civilian sector made further delay impossible: It was the passage by Congress of the Child Abuse Prevention and Treatment Act, P.L. 93-247, which among other things created the National Center for Child Abuse and Neglect (NCCAN) under the auspices of what was then called the Department of Health, Education, and Welfare.

With child abuse and neglect now an object of national attention and continuing federal concern, the military reluctantly began to move into line.

CHILD PROTECTION IN THE
WARRIOR SOCIETY

The first military child advocacy program did not come into being until 1975, in the Air Force; similar programs in the rest of the services were not functional until late 1976. Even then, they fell far short of addressing the need. Three years later, the Government Accounting Office, a watchdog arm of the federal government that reports to Congress, issued a report on the military's child advocacy programs, concluding they were "victims of neglect."[5] Among other things, the GAO found that the programs had no direct funding, suffered from a lack of adequate staff, and received no direction at the Department of Defense level. DoD, in an attached letter, agreed with the report's findings and its recommendations.

At this writing, in the summer of 1990, it appears that the military may finally be turning its attention to the problems of its families, although the effort remains on a very small scale. The improvement in the last decade, and most particularly the last five years, has been striking. "The military services are making magnificent strides; they are due appropriate accolades," said noted child abuse expert Dr. Ray E. Helfer, who was among the first to call attention to child maltreatment in the military in the early 1970s. There is enthusiasm, even excitement, among social workers in the military who believe that DoD is finally behind them.

"The phrase that comes to mind is *therapy with a two-by-four*," said an administrator with one of the military family advocacy programs. "That was the title of an article about how difficult it is to get organizations to see they have problems they need to deal with. The military had to be hit over the head to see they had to do something [about child and spouse maltreatment]. But once it became convinced of that, things have moved very fast."

Because of its centralized and authoritarian structure, the military community ought to be able to deal with child abuse and neglect far more effectively than the civilian community. Theoretically, it should be able to institute model preventive programs, treat its abusive parents and abused children, track abusers and families at risk no matter where the mobility of the military takes them, and provide follow-up treatment for as long as needed.

When it comes to dealing with spouse abuse, the military *is* already way ahead of the civilian sector, some say by as much as ten years. It keeps statistics on spouse abuse—something very few states bother to do—provides an array of services, and is undertaking research to develop more solutions.

Where child maltreatment is concerned, the opportunity is there as well for the military to become a beacon to the civilian sector. What has been demonstrated by the military to date—apart from an unconscionable delay in addressing its responsibilities in the first place—is an increasing willingness to tackle the problem. At this point the apparatus of family support services is still being developed, and by any measure is inadequate to the task. In fact, no one knows just how big the problem of child maltreatment in the military is; it is generally assumed that the statistics represent just the tip of the iceberg.

It remains to be seen whether the commitment of DoD—and Congress, as funding agent—is a mere genuflection to public opinion, sufficient only to provide money for a well-meaning but skeletal program, or if it extends to making the military the model of family advocacy it could be. Is DoD's objective to do only enough to get social critics off its back? Or does it aim to frankly acknowledge the considerable stresses of the military life, and offer its families all the support they need and deserve?

What is clear right now is that DoD has made a start on addressing the problem—for which, as Dr. Helfer noted, "appropriate accolades" are due—but it is only a start. The bulk of the job remains to be done: As we shall see, where funding, staffing, and both treatment and prevention programs are concerned, military children still deserve far better than they are getting.

Funding

First, a bit of background. In 1979, the GAO found that there was no direct funding of child advocacy programs in the military. In other words, everyone working in those programs had child advocacy as an additional duty tacked on to their previous job description. By comparison, the funding situation in 1990 is a substantial improvement. In 1982, family advocacy became a line item in the Defense budget for the first time, with an allocation of $5 million to be spread among the four services. By 1990 it had risen to $25.3 million, which funded everything from administration, data gathering, research, and program development, down to the teams of social workers dealing with the problem at the grass-roots level. The program has quintupled in less than ten years.

Still, this should be kept in perspective. With a total 1990 Defense budget of $305.6 *billion*, family advocacy accounts for less than one ten-thousandth of the budget, or, to round it upward, one one-hundredth of 1 percent. As an Army officer not involved in the family advocacy program put it, "Twenty-five million dollars? That's nothin'. We blow up that much in one minute in a firepower demonstration."

A comparison with civilian expenditures is also telling, although differences in the kinds of services provided, as well as out-of-date civilian population data, make direct parallels problematic. It appears, however, that the state of Massachusetts, currently in the midst of a budget fiasco that has left its social programs starved for funds, spends *at least* twice as much per child or spouse on family advocacy as the Department of Defense, without adding in the state's expenditures on preventive education.

The inadequacy of funding is a point everyone associated with the programs agrees on. "There will never be enough funding to staff properly," one DoD employee said. "That's a fact of life." It is a sentiment echoed at every level, from top to bottom.

In early December 1988 I had the following conversation with a DoD employee whose job involved keeping tabs on all the family advocacy programs in the military. She had just finished telling me that *all* the programs in *all* the services were underfunded, and that as a result there were not enough people in the field to treat, train, or educate. I remarked that that was a particularly sad commentary on a community that by its nature is so highly controllable that its programs should be a model for the civilian community to emulate.

"It's a choice of how to spend dollars," the frustrated but realistic employee said. "Do you spend them on the mission, or on treatment programs for child abusers?"

"You *have* to spend it on treatment programs," I persisted, "if for no other reason than many of these military children grow up to join the military themselves, and the problem perpetuates itself."

"Tell that to Carlucci [then Secretary of Defense]," she replied, a cynical edge to her voice. "He's facing budget cuts. Whole weapons systems will have to go. And you want him to spend money on treating child abusers? He'll tell you to get out of here."

The core of the funding problem may be that the highest levels still fail to recognize that there is a real cost in tax dollars *and* in mission effectiveness when family violence and related problems are not caught and treated.

For one thing, personnel under the burden of family stress detract from the mission; that much is well known. For another, DoD research has shown that the number-one reason cited for failure to reenlist is family concerns,[6] which among other things surely encompass the kind of family dysfunctions to which spouse and child abuse bear witness. And every time an experienced member of the armed forces drops out, the Department of Defense loses an investment of hundreds of thousands of dollars in that individual's training and job experience.

By that reckoning, $25.3 million does not go very far either to protect military families or to protect the nation's investment in its fighting force.

Understaffing

In August 1990, all five major Marine bases in the continental United States were understaffed in family advocacy social workers by as many as a dozen positions. In part this was because of a DoD hiring freeze, but it was also because of inadequate funding. As a result, the social workers on the bases were overworked, and some family advocacy functions were carried as collateral duties by other personnel—a situation the GAO deplored in 1979.

In the Air Force, some forty bases at this writing had three-person family advocacy teams based at Air Force hospitals: a therapist, an outreach person to do preventive education, and an administrator. The Air Force recognized the inadequacy of that number, and was conducting a four-year research project to compare the effectiveness of three-person teams with that of the trial seven-person teams located on eight bases.

Although considerable progress has been made—particularly by comparison to the total dearth of family support programs when the interviewees for this book were growing up—family advocacy inside the Fortress remains so uneven and flawed that no military family can be sure the support it needs will be available at the next assignment.

Additional Problems

Anyone trying to get a picture of how well DoD is doing in handling its child maltreatment problem eventually runs into a telling contradiction. The surface looks good, very good. The content could be a lot better.

For example, Family Service Centers, which have served Navy and Marine bases since 1979, are impressive facilities with a broad range of counseling services, educational offerings, and workshops. They have made a valuable contribution to military life, and the Navy likes to boast that its FSCs serve over a million and a half individuals a year—mostly in information and referral services, not counseling. However, the reality is that not all FSCs are alike. An individual FSC may flourish or languish depending on the local base leadership. Funding, which comes partly out of base operating funds, can vary from year to year.[7] Some have more programs, some less. And in some FSCs, many of the programs are run by volunteers rather than trained permanent staff—which means the programs inevitably suffer from uneven quality.

Leadership of the FSCs also varies. The FSC at Camp Pendleton, for instance, as late as 1984 had a director who was not a trained social worker but a tank commander; as late as early 1985, on a base with 34,000 active-duty personnel and 45,000 dependents, the FSC had just one person handling child abuse cases and one handling spouse abuse. But by the end of that year, things had changed substantially: The FSC was revived with the help of a civilian therapist who was given funds to expand staff and initiate educational and prevention programs that should have been in place years earlier. In 1989 there were six licensed therapists working out of the Pendleton Family Service Center, still considered the premier Family Service Center in the Marine Corps; there were plans to have ten more in place by the fall of 1990.

Most FSCs on Marine and Naval bases are not staffed at anywhere near that level. In addition, 80 percent of the FSC directors are military officers and most are not trained in social work, nor have they had much introductory training to prepare them for the job. More than a decade after the creation of Family Service Centers, the Navy provides little more than an annual conference to educate its FSC directors in their duties. And in general, the military approach to social work is a passive one. Outreach, in which the agency works to educate all families in a preventive way, is not common in the military, which is geared to treating individuals who have been referred to the facility after incidents of abuse or neglect have already occurred.[8] There are signs that the military attitude is changing, however; in Hawaii a joint-service program in which visiting nurses brief new mothers on infant care is an example. The Air Force has spent some of its family advocacy money to acquire outreach social workers, and it wants to hire more.

There is another problem with Family Service Centers which the Navy does not mention in its promotional materials: Well over 90 percent of the individuals served by FSCs are enlisted or dependents of enlisted. Officers and their families fear to go near them, and for good reason: There is no guarantee of confidentiality. An officer who is a child abuser cannot risk reaching out for help to an FSC, because it will certainly ruin his or her career. As one FSC director put it, "We tell everyone who comes to us that if there is any spouse abuse, child abuse or substance abuse, it is reportable to the command. There is no confidentiality in those areas. We tell them right away."

This lack of confidentiality affects officers far more than enlisted, for two reasons: First, many of the enlisted who use FSCs may not be career military, and therefore have less to lose. Second, there is a double standard for punishing misconduct in the military, in which the penalties for officers when problems become known are in practice much stiffer, since an officer has a duty to be a model of correct behavior.

For example, if an enlisted man commits incest, he is seen by therapists who then tell the command whether he is treatable. If he is—and if his service record justifies his retention—he is put into a treatment program, and watched carefully. If all goes well, his career can proceed normally. If an officer commits incest, theoretically the same procedure should apply. In practice, however, it often doesn't; much depends upon how his commanding officer views his offense against the background of an officer's obligation to set a moral standard. Opinion among commanding officers is very much divided on this point. There are many COs who would not hesitate to recommend the abuser officer's elimination from the service. This might happen through administrative discharge,[9] or through another provision that permits officers to resign "for the good of the service" rather than face court-martial on criminal charges such as abuse.[10] (If the charge is serious enough, this option is not permitted and the officer must stand trial.)

Even if the officer is retained, he may eventually be forced out in a more subtle way, through being passed over for promotion.[11] What this means is that officers and their families shun Family Service Centers and their counterparts in the other services. "When you know what it takes to be promoted in the military," said a base social worker who was formerly married to a Marine Corps officer, "you know that an officer would have to be *insane* to use a Family Service Center. And that's going to be true until you can offer an officer more guarantees that his career won't be affected."

The same obligation to report holds true for the military medical system. As an Army physician said, "We have an obligation to report the confidences of a patient under certain circumstances—if he confesses to child abuse, for instance." Presumably, most military physicians and medical facilities actually do report incidents of family violence, although even ten years ago, many did not, according to the GAO investigation. The point is that the climate regarding child and spouse abuse has changed sufficiently within the military that an abuser officer can no longer afford to gamble on a military physician's willingness to collude in a cover-up. When officers get help at all, they turn to the civilian community, where their secrets are more likely to be kept.[12] Officers, of course, are also in a better position to afford civilian services than most enlisted personnel.

At the time the interviewees for this book were growing up—long before the climate of child advocacy penetrated the Fortress—abuser officers or the abuser wives of officers rarely needed to go to the expense of having civilians treat their children. They could lie with impunity to military hospital staff and expect their stories to be accepted at face value. The children, of course, would never dare to contradict their parents' story.

The son of a Marine Corps pilot, for instance, related that on numerous occasions as a teenager he was taken to the base clinic or hospital after his father's temper had taken a bloody toll. On one occasion when he was sixteen years old, he recalled, his father had taken exception to his laughter at the absurdity of a family fight. The father, a lieutenant colonel, hurled his water glass at his son's face; it shattered above the boy's left eye. When the son clapped one hand over his eye, blood spurted out between his fingers—and his mother, who witnessed the whole episode, screamed at her husband, "You've blinded him!"

It turned out to be a clean cut across the eyebrow. The son was driven to the base hospital by his mother. During the entire ride, he said, she coached him in the cover-up story he was to give to the doctor: "Now remember," she said, "you were playing a *spirited* game of touch football in the backyard. There was a spigot that stuck up out of the ground, and when you were trying to catch a pass, you stumbled and fell against the spigot."

The son said his mother was very impressive at concocting airtight tales to explain every malevolent wounding of her children by their father. "She always, always had the right sport for the season," he said. "My mother was a brilliant liar—but then, she had to be."

IS CHILD ABUSE HIGHER IN THE MILITARY THAN IN THE CIVILIAN POPULATION?

It is likely that no one who considers the subject of child maltreatment in the military could fail to wonder about the answer to this question. Plenty of people over the past twenty years have made efforts to find out; some have written about it. But the fact remains that it is an extremely difficult question to answer. There are two basic reasons why a comparison is hard to make.

To begin with, there is wide disagreement about the extent of child maltreatment in the *civilian* population.[13] The two most quoted national studies, for instance, vary in their estimates by some 30 percent: According to the National Center for Child Abuse and Neglect, in 1986—the most recent year for which statistics were available at this writing—an estimated 25.2 children per thousand, or a total of more than *1.5 million* children nationwide, were abused or neglected.[14] According to the American Association for Protecting Children, however, 32.8 children per thousand were maltreated in 1986, for a total of *2.1 million*.[15] Other experts on child abuse offer still different figures. And for all the variance in statistics, there is variance in the definitions and methodologies used.

Second, even if there were broader agreement on the amount of child abuse in the general population, the statistics on child maltreatment in the military have been heavily criticized as grossly underreported and therefore untrustworthy.

The Unreliability of Military Statistics on Child Abuse

In 1979, the GAO study complained of "poor reporting" of incidents at the local installation level. "Officials at the field locations we visited said that many child maltreatment cases go unreported. The primary reason is apparently a concern that the information could be used to the detriment of the service member's career."[16] At one Army hospital in California, the report went on to say, a program official said that because information on some cases had resulted in damage to some careers, the hospital had stopped sending reports to the Army registry. Between April 1975 and December 1977, the investigators found, seven Air Force medical facilities did not report any cases of child maltreatment.[17]

In 1980, a research report for the Air Command and Staff College concluded after comparing civilian and military figures that "the military should report approximately 15 times more incidents than it presently does."[18] The author did not infer from lower military figures that there was less child abuse in the military, but that "civilian authorities have generally predicted significantly more actual abuse and reported abuse than the services demonstrate. This difference is a poor reflection on service register performance. . . . The average state child abuse/neglect register collects information on nearly five times more abuse/neglect incidents than the military. This is difficult to explain since the military has a much more structured and controllable population than a civilian community."[19]

The various services have made some important efforts to improve programs in recent years. The way abusers are handled is less punitive and more treatment-oriented, for instance. While the approach to abusers is very much a reflection of the individual base commander, commanders in general are now more educated about the benefits of treatment programs, and the informed recommendations of program therapists have taken considerable pressure off them when it comes to making decisions about whether to keep a reported abuser in the military.

One would think these changes would have resulted in much improved reporting of child abuse incidents at the local level, since the careers of personnel—at least of enlisted personnel—are less threatened, and field workers, spouses, and neighbors would presumably be less hesitant to report them. However, measured against the rate of civilian reporting—which itself is still far from satisfactory—the military incidence of child maltreatment is still seriously underreported.

In 1988 there were 20,715 reports of child maltreatment in the four services.[20] Based on the total number of children of active military members, that works out to a DoD rate of 13.2 reported incidents of maltreatment per thousand children. For the preceding year, 1987—the most recent year for which statistics were available—the National Committee for the Prevention of Child Abuse and Neglect estimated a rate of 34 reports per thousand children, *more than two and a half times higher.* Given the size of that discrepancy, it would seem there is still widespread fear in the military about how reporting of incidents will affect the careers of abusers.

Military statistics on child abuse are unreliable in part because of a registry system that functions poorly, although presumably these glitches will eventually be ironed out.[21] But a far more important reason is the one alluded to earlier in this chapter: Almost all of the child abuse incidents reported in the military pertain to enlisted, not officer families.

In 1988, for instance, 97 percent of the substantiated cases were from enlisted families. As a result, in the military child abuse is commonly referred to as the "sergeants' syndrome." But this is a serious misrepresentation; the only thing those figures show is that reports of abuse in officer families are largely missing. Partly this may be due to failure at the local base level to report incidents involving officers; but an equally important reason may be that abuser officers, as noted earlier, have the wherewithal to make sure they don't get caught.

"Officers are like attorneys and doctors," one military social worker told me. "They can buy silence. They can go out in town and *pay* for psychotherapy, or for medical care for the child they've battered."[22] And if the abused child receives civilian medical care, the incident winds up reported in civilian statistics, not military.[23] There is, however, a reasonable chance that it will not be reported at all; by some accounts, an injured child seen by a private physician is considerably less likely to be reported as abused than if he or she were seen in the emergency room of a public hospital.[24]

Is the Military Population at Higher Risk for Abuse?

Since the statistics gathered by DoD are of little help in determining whether there is more child abuse in the military, and since the extent of abuse in the civilian population is itself in dispute, there is little to keep people from falling back on their own preconceptions and stereotypes suggesting that there *has* to be more child abuse in the military because *warriors are like that*. This, of course, is grossly unfair to thousands of military men and women who are gentle, loving, attentive parents.

At this time it simply cannot be proved one way or the other if the military is more abusive to its children. But certain characteristics of the military are indeed troubling, when seen against a background of sociological studies of child abusers which associate certain conditions with a greater likelihood of child abuse.

1. *Population age.* As of December, 1988, a majority of military personnel—55 percent—were married, and 71 percent were age thirty or under.[25] According to national statistics, this age group is twice as likely to engage in family violence—both child and spouse abuse—as persons who are thirty-one to fifty.[26] In the military the thirty-and-under age group covers enlisted up through the lower-ranking NCO grades, and many low-ranking officers.

2. *Financial stress.* Financial problems have long been known to be a significant stress in families that maltreat children. According to the annual NCCAN study of the general population, in 1986 the rate of abuse was four times higher and the rate of neglect nearly eight times higher for lower income children compared to the higher income group.[27] (Again, this rate of abuse in the civilian population, as in the military, incorporates a bias toward associating abuse with low-income groups because that is where it tends to be "discovered.")

Military pay continues to lag far behind civilian pay. Over the past ten years, the gap has continued to widen—and while no one realistically expects that the gap will ever be closed, the current situation, in which military personnel are not only lagging behind their civilian counterparts but actually *losing* purchasing power, is very grim.[28] Pay for enlisted grades is particularly low, and most of the children in the military are in enlisted families. As of September 30, 1987, 51 percent of enlisted personnel were married, but they accounted for eighty percent of the children.[29]

There are no figures on the number of enlisted personnel who are eligible to receive supplementary income from the government such as food stamps, but it is believed that the number eligible is much larger than the number who actually avail themselves of it. (See Chapter 9.) The 1985 DoD Survey found that in the preceding year, 16,674 enlisted households received food stamps, 41,189 were recipients of the WIC (Women, Infants, and Children) food program, and 12,155 received public assistance checks.[30]

In 1980 in Hawaii—at that time, the only state that noted the suspected abuser's occupation on intake forms, enabling it to statistically describe child abuse in the military—90 percent of the reported child abuse in the military concerned enlisted personnel. The majority of the abusive military caretakers had incomes below the state median income of $21,718 for a family of four, and 17 percent received some form of financial assistance from the state.[31] (This should not be taken to mean that 90 percent of all child maltreatment in the military occurs in the enlisted grades. As noted earlier, abuse in officer households tends not to show up in statistics, for a variety of reasons.)

Where a family lives can also point to higher risk for child abuse—

and many low-ranking enlisted families are obliged to live in depressingly substandard neighborhoods, characterized by overcrowding, lack of privacy, poverty, and a host of social problems. A study of abusive families stationed at Fort Bliss, Texas, found that abusive parents were concentrated in a run-down, low-income section of El Paso.[32]

Interesting to note in connection with the cramped quarters typical of enlisted housing is a 1950 study of the relationship between housing and discipline. The researcher "found a direct relationship between the permissiveness of child-rearing attitudes as a function of the number of rooms in the house: fathers were more likely to endorse the use of power-assertive disciplinary tactics as household space decreased."[33]

3. *The effect of violent occupations.* A 1979 study examined the rates of child abuse in Air Force organizations representing differing levels of occupational violence. It reported that "the lowest rate of child abuse is found in the three least violence-oriented organizations (Air Force Logistics Command, Air Force Systems Command, Air Force Defense Command). All other commands have rates that range from 33 to 111 percent greater incidence of physical child abuse." Further, it found that "the more the command is associated with violence, the greater the prevalence of abusive fathers."

The study concluded, "The more an individual job is related to violence, the greater the rate of child abuse. It is noteworthy that this occurs within the Air Force because even the most violent jobs in the Air Force put one at considerable distance from hand-to-hand combat and the training and mental set required for duty of that type. We therefore think that these are minimal estimates of the effects of being engaged in a violent occupation. The differences might be much greater had this been a study of Army or Marine families."[34]

A 1982 research paper on military child abuse also took note of the association. "The fact that the service member parent is usually the abusive parent compels one to wonder if some of the contributing causes of the problem might well be job related."[35]

It has also been well documented that there is a strong correlation between violent and high-stress jobs in the military and spouse abuse. (See Chapter 1 concerning Peter Neidig's research on spouse abuse by Marine Corps drill instructors.) Child abuse is often found in homes where there is spouse abuse.[36]

In the military, child abusers are more likely to be fathers than mothers.[37] A study of child maltreatment in military families in San Antonio found that male caretakers were responsible for child abuse three times more often than female, although female caretakers were held responsible for cases of neglect.[38] (This, however, is not to let military mothers entirely off the hook. As two noted child abuse researchers have commented, "We believe, as do other investigators, that both parents are involved in abuse no matter which one actually injures the child."[39])

Another related factor of serious concern is that the level of physical injury in substantiated cases of military child abuse tends to be more serious than that found in civilian communities, and the rate of mortality higher.[40] An epidemiologic study of child abuse and neglect at an Army base in Germany over a one-year period showed a very high (9 percent) rate of mortality.[41]

In 1973, a study by a pediatric radiologist of abused children in the Air Force found a mortality rate of 25 percent of Air Force children who were known to have been physically abused, compared to an estimated national mortality rate of 5 percent. Although the percentage is high in part because the reporting of abuse incidents is particularly poor in the military, and therefore the most serious cases represented a larger percentage of the known total, it served to draw attention to the problem. The findings were subsequently confirmed by the Air Force Office of Special Investigations, and resulted in the Chief of Staff of the U.S. Air Force ordering the establishment of policy and procedures to alleviate child abuse in the Air Force.[42]

At the AMA symposium on child abuse in the military in 1974, it was reported that at one Army hospital serving a population of 20,000 military families, "child abuse and neglect was the most common cause of death . . . in children beyond the newborn period and under the age of one year."[43] A study of child abuse in the southeastern United States—including both military and civilian cases—found that over half the child maltreatment incidents in military families resulted in serious injuries, as opposed to 27 percent for the entire sample.[44]

Taken together, the studies just cited suggest the alarming possibility that the violent nature of some military job classifications may present a certain degree of risk to the children of parents conditioned to perform them. At the very least, these findings underscore the critical need for thorough research in the military to answer this question: How much of a link is there between the degree of violence inherent in a specific job and child abuse?

This is the question at the very heart of the family advocacy issue in the Department of Defense, and the question no one in DoD really wants to ask. Up to now, DoD's attitude toward family advocacy could best be described as an increasing willingness to deal with problems of domestic violence that just happen to occur within the military setting. It would be quite another matter to assert, on the basis of comprehensive research findings, that the Department of Defense itself, by virtue of conditioning many of its members to perform violent duties, *shares indirectly* in responsibility for the abuse of military children. If that is found to be true, it would be an exceedingly difficult truth for DoD to face. But if true, it *must* be faced, for there is a moral imperative to face it—and American military families, growing ever more sensitized to these issues and vocal about them, will demand that it be faced. Families need reassurance that the military is doing everything in its power to make sure that warriors conditioned to fight for their nation on a moment's notice do not then turn their aggression on their own children.

If ultimately it is established that the military itself indirectly contributes to child abuse, it would not, I believe, present either military families or DoD with a hopelessly bleak situation. Certainly there are always going to be warriors whose jobs require them to deal in violence, and if present trends continue, most of them will have children. It is also true that the inherently stressful conditions of military life will continue to task these warriors' self-restraint at times of anger or frustration. But in my view this formula does not necessarily have to result in the abuse of thousands upon thousands of military children. Neidig's programs for Marine Corps drill instructors proved that something effective *can* be done to help offset violent conditioning in order to protect the family (and, of course, DoD's monetary investment in the warrior). And if it works for Marine Corps DIs, one would think it could also work for infantrymen, paratroopers, fighter pilots, and many, many others.

4. *Alcoholism.* Alcohol abuse has been tied to child abuse in numerous studies of the general population,[45] and in the military as well. In at least one military treatment program for child abusers, it was found that child abuse by older members of the military is often secondary to alcoholism.[46] This is not to say that alcoholism inevitably leads to child abuse, but that, as many child abuse researchers would concur—although there is controversy on this point—child abuse is strongly linked to alcohol abuse. The same holds true for spouse abuse.

As we have seen in Chapter 2, alcoholism is believed to be significantly higher in the military than in the civilian population.

5. *Social isolation.* One of the prime ingredients in child maltreatment situations is social isolation of the family. Parents whose emotional state is already frayed do not, in such situations, have the option of calling on relatives or close friends to help out. In families beset by problems, the combination of unrelieved pressure and lack of outside support is sometimes enough to tip a parent over the edge into behavior harmful to children.

"I'm not sure that nineteen-year-old parents, one of whom is in the military, are any less prepared for parenthood than the civilian parents of the same age who live across the hall from them," said a social worker at a Navy base. "But I *am* sure that the service couple is likely to have a less intact social support system. The [civilian] folks across the hall are probably in closer proximity to old friends and family, who are the natural helping system not only in times of trouble, but in surviving daily life. The nineteen-year-old military couple is much less likely to have that."

Social isolation is a very common fact of life in the military, made worse by frequent moves. In Hawaii in 1980, military parents who neglected their children said that "social isolation and recent relocation" were the main stresses contributing to the neglect.[47]

Social isolation is a broad term that encompasses not only separation from supportive networks of family and friends, but stress factors such as culture shock in a foreign land. In overseas situations the feeling of isolation is increased by other factors as well, including the financial stress of being surrounded by an unaffordably expensive foreign society, language barriers, and frequent separations from a spouse who is sent away for military exercises or training. Alcoholism among military dependent wives overseas is higher than among stateside military wives.[48] Child maltreatment is also reported to be 33 percent higher on U.S. military bases overseas, compared to bases in urban areas of the continental United States.[49] Roughly one fourth of the active-duty military population is serving overseas at a given moment during peacetime.[50]

All of these factors have to do with high stress, which has been shown to be a major factor in child abuse. In a study that compared abusive and nonabusive parents, two researchers found that the abusers scored much higher on a scale measuring life crisis, which covers such events as pregnancy, change in responsibilities at work, trouble with boss, change in residence, change in schools, and change in number of arguments with spouse.

But stress is not the only factor tipping the parents into abusive behavior, as the researchers pointed out. Their study was of civilian subjects, but their findings have interesting implications for military families.

"From our experience," the researchers wrote, "the abuser is inclined to be isolated, distrusting, impatient, in conflict with his or her spouse, and has a low self-image. Primarily, however, the abuser is in search of a symbiotic relationship—of an attachment with someone who will make decisions for him, assume responsibility for him, take care of him, and in short be a parent to him. Thus, the abuser is likely to subject himself to a state of life crisis as represented by excessive change that requires enormous amounts of constant readjustments."

In civilian life, presumably, such an abuser would make a series of decisions that invite stress and excessive change. The military abuser, however, only has to make one decision—joining the military—after which the military itself takes care of providing the stresses of authoritarianism, constant uprootings, job changes, and, through low pay, financial pressure. The article continues: "The life crisis will put him in a state of exhaustion, with lowered defenses and weakened control over his behavior. The combination of life crisis and symbiosis will predispose him to abuse."[51]

6. *Authoritarian personalities.* A civilian social worker who deals primarily with military families commented on the relationship she sees between authoritarian parenting styles and child abuse. "All families require flexibility," she said. "What we run into is very *rigid* families. When the child goes through developmental stages, the parents want to treat him at age ten like they did when he was three. They don't have the flexibility to grow as the child grows; often the father has a very rigid expectation of 'the way it's supposed to be.'

"I see this with police officers, too—people who are attracted to that masculine sense of power and control. We see chiefs in the Navy who try to run their families like they run their staffs, on a military basis, and it doesn't work. And they get very frustrated and try to control it more and more, and that can lead to physical or emotional abuse.

"I don't think these men purposely want to hurt their families. They have high investments in their families; they don't want to lose them. Insight therapy can be very effective with them."

Rigidity is one of the big problems in abusive families. As one landmark book on the subject noted, "The highest risk of family violence occurs when there is more than one child at home, where there is considerable life stress experienced by one or both of the marital partners, *and where decision-making is concentrated in the hands of one person.*"[52] (Italics added.) The concentration of control in one person is one of the defining characteristics of authoritarian families.

Rigidity and an overcontrolling atmosphere are not the only characteristics of authoritarian families which should inspire concern, however. There is also the matter of low self-esteem. The same social worker went on to make the connection: "Another characteristic of abusive families is low self-esteem," she said. "It's amazing how the military attracts people with low self-esteem—yet to me it seems like in

the military it would be even harder for them to get the buildup they
need." Authoritarian systems by definition are light on praise and
heavy on punishment.

These characteristics of the military population raise troubling questions about the incidence of child maltreatment in military homes—
questions that need to be answered with thorough research. The
definitive comparison of abuse in military and civilian populations has
yet to be done; but in the meantime there is one continuing source of
information that underscores the need for such a study.

As mentioned earlier, Hawaii is one of the few states which, in
compiling information on reported child abusers, takes note of the
suspected abuser's occupation.[53] Thus the state is able to make a
statistical comparison of child maltreatment in the civilian and military communities. In 1979, military personnel comprised 16 percent
of the population but accounted for 27 percent of all reported cases of
child maltreatment.[54] After several bases were closed the following
year, the military portion of the state's population dropped to 11
percent, but it produced 16 percent of the reports of abuse. That ratio
remained consistent every year from 1980 through 1987.[55] As noted
earlier in this chapter, there are significant demographic differences
between the military and civilian populations; the military population
is on the whole a younger one, and youth is a factor associated with
abusive parents. But we also know that reporting of child abuse in the
military is very poor—and *still* the reported incidence in the military
in 1979 was almost 50 percent higher.

What the Hawaii statistics show for certain is that during those years
the military had a major problem in its families which had not been
sufficiently studied, let alone addressed. What the statistics mean in
terms of comparing the military and civilian populations is less clear,
given the demographic differences. In any case, these statistics, coming year after year, should have been sufficiently embarrassing to the
Department of Defense for it to have called for a major, thoroughgoing
top-level investigation, on the order of a blue-ribbon commission, into
the extent of child abuse in the military and the manner in which it is
being handled.

This has yet to be done, although the military has made some
notable improvements in its family support systems in Hawaii, including the addition of some preventive education. In 1988 and 1989 the
percentage of child abuse reports emanating from the military in
Hawaii dropped off sharply; however, even family advocacy program
managers within DoD are hesitant to claim credit for the drop. A
number of factors may be involved, from prevention programs to

demographic changes to data gathering. Again, research is called for. If something is in fact working well in Hawaii to reduce child abuse in the military, it should be pinpointed and then instituted throughout the armed forces. It's not as though the child abuse problems reflected in Hawaii's statistics were unique to families stationed in that state.

Who Speaks for the Children?

Clearly, we still do not have a realistic picture of what is happening to children behind Fortress walls, in the privacy of their warrior families—and our collective ignorance as a society on that score both compromises our ability to help military children and stands as an indictment of our values.

Why don't we know more? Whose responsibility is it to find out? And above all, who can military children count on to protect their interests when their parents fail them?

The military? Historically, the military's track record on protecting its children is abysmal, and although the efforts of the last five years give genuine reason to hope this is being reversed, there is still a very long way to go and much to be proved. In the meantime, given the paltry number of outreach and preventive education programs in the military, and the continued lack of confidentiality that severely inhibits career officers and NCOs and their families from seeking help, the best interests of military children are not being served.

The civilian sector? Hardly. Civilian agencies are already overworked trying to cope with their own communities' child abuse problems, and in any case their jurisdictional authority over military families is mired in confusion. Even if they were ready and able to deal with the problem in warrior families, their efforts would be—as they are now—undercut by the mobility of the families they are trying to help.

Congress? The concern of legislators for the treatment of military children has been sadly inconsistent. The 1979 GAO investigation, triggered by congressional concern, was the best thing ever to happen on behalf of abused military children; it was the impetus for starting DoD funding for family advocacy in 1982. But since then, apart from reactive inquiries in the wake of abuse scandals in military child care centers, and approval of a Defense budget that currently devotes less than one ten-thousandth of its total for military family advocacy, Congress has apparently had little to say on the subject.

Are military children, then, to be the forgotten victims, dismissed with token acknowledgment of their abuse and token programs to address it? Are the children of warriors too mobile, too invisible, too voiceless to draw the attention of those with the power—and moral fortitude—to help them?

It is not clear who represents the interests of military children, if indeed they are represented at all. Even national organizations set up specifically for child advocacy have little idea of how children inside the Fortress are faring. And that is why it is very likely up to us, the older military brats who have grown up and left the Fortress, to raise a hue and cry on behalf of the 1.7 million children now inside the Fortress and the millions more who will be born there, a great many of whom will be abused.

For we, more than anyone else, know the dimensions of the problem, and we, more than anyone else, can speak to its pain.

Of the eighty military brats interviewed for this book, thirty of them—well over a third—had been abused. Twelve had suffered both physical and emotional abuse. Ten had been emotionally abused. Two had been sexually abused—and one of those had been severely abused physically and emotionally as well. Five interviewees fell into a category of emotional abuse and part emotional neglect. I did not tally a category of emotional neglect only; I did not feel I had enough expertise or enough background information on the families to make that classification.

Speaking out for the children—demanding more research, more funding for DoD family advocacy, an end to the ban on confidentiality, and vastly more preventive programs and training—is something we can do for our "kin" inside the Fortress.

CHILD ABUSE AS "DISCIPLINE"

In the Fortress, as elsewhere, there are two kinds of physical abuse. One is the kind that leaves telltale marks: severe bruises and burns, scars, broken bones. This is the kind most likely to be reflected in the statistics quoted above, whether military or civilian, because it's the easiest for outsiders to spot and hardest for the abuser parent to deny, and it falls neatly into a category which can be tabulated.

Then there is the other kind, probably much more common, but greatly underrepresented in the reports agencies receive because it is much harder to catch. In many military homes, this kind of abuse falls under the category of *discipline*.

The following are examples from military brats interviewed for this book:

The daughter of a Navy lieutenant commander: In one Marine Corps family she knew, the father would punch his son hard in the stomach for not saying "sir." In another, where there were no sons, the father did the same with his daughters.

The daughter of an Air Force colonel: She told how her father spanked her little brother when he was two weeks old, for crying. She remembered another severe spanking he received when he was two or three, for not knowing the name of a color. The boy, who developed a learning disability, continued to receive severe physical punishment until he was in high school. "He'd gotten too big by that time for Dad to do that to him," the sister said, "so then it turned into emotional abuse. Before that it was both."

The daughter of an Air Force lieutenant colonel: She recalled how her father would frequently "blow up over nothing." Once when she was ten years old, she related, "he didn't like what I said, so he hit me so hard that I fell down and saw stars." The blow cracked the cast on her father's arm.

The son of a Navy officer: He told of the incidents he recalled among the Navy families living in his cul-de-sac when he was nine years old:

I remember one time a kid had stolen a dart from my friend [Paul's] dart board set. I was with him in the road, trying to get him to give it back to Paul, who was in front of his house with his brother. So the guy says, "Okay, here. *Take* your dart back!" [He threw it] and this little kid walked out from behind Paul and wound up getting hit in the side of the head. Paul turned around and pulled it out; it was a real quick reaction. I remember it so well, because it made a popping sound. I freaked. I thought the kid was dead. But after it was pulled out, [the kid] ran home crying. And then he came outside crying even harder: His dad was beating the tar out of him for crying. And he beat his kid *up*. The kid was all of five years old. Because he cried and the hole wasn't big. That dart had gone *all the way in*. We told his father what had happened, but his father didn't take him to the doctor.

Once when I was at Paul's house he put his feet on the table—and his dad *sat on his legs* to teach him not to put his legs on the table. Paul was about ten.

My next door neighbor, [Ralph], who was also ten years old, was made to bend over and pull his pants down and get beaten in front of everyone. His father would open up the garage door, yank his pants down, make him touch his toes and beat him. I mean right out there in the open.

I remember when my neighbor and I got caught for smoking, when I was nine. I was restricted to my room for two weeks. I consider my dad pretty mellow. But my neighbor got the tar beat out of him, I mean [his dad] just beat the living tar out of him. There were black and blue marks

on his arm from where his dad had held him. I could hear him being hit
from my room.

 This was all in Navy housing. All the fathers were officers. This was our
nice little neighborhood.

And there is the story of Adam, the Vietnam veteran and Marine
sergeant's son who was quoted extensively in the last two chapters. He
told how his father, who had spent much of World War II in a
Japanese POW camp and never later received the proper therapy to
help him deal with that experience, essentially took out his anger on
his wife and children in the guise of "discipline."

"A man who has to deal with three and a half years of constant
torture and being worked to death and starved to death by an enemy in
a foreign country cannot be the same person when he comes back,"
Adam said.

> I think the Marine Corps realized that when he was going through his
> debriefing in Hawaii. From what I can gather . . . they influenced him to
> stay in the Marine Corps because they did not feel he would fit in society.
> He was dangerous. When two sailors tried to rob him in an alley in
> Honolulu after he [collected his back pay and] flashed his money around in
> a few bars, he killed them both. He put his elbow through the rib cage of
> one of them, driving his two ribs through his lungs, and he broke the other
> one's neck.
> He put me and my mother through quite a bit of turmoil and agony
> while I was growing up. My father's answer to any kind of discipline
> problem was to beat you. Some of the beatings were definitely extreme and
> demeaning, to the point where he would lay you across a bed and beat you
> while he was talking to you, and say, "This is for this particular problem,
> and this is for that particular problem." It was something that I felt really
> stemmed from his POW experiences. I felt that he was reliving the type of
> discipline in the prison camp.

For most of the sergeant's military career, he was assigned to a single
Marine base—a most unusual lack of mobility. Whether the Marine
Corps did this to provide him with a therapeutic sense of stability is
unclear, since the Corps also sent him back to Asia, over his objections, Adam says, to fight in Korea. At any rate, for many years the
family lived two hours away from where Adam's father was stationed,
and saw him only on weekends. "All week long my mother would say
'Wait until your father gets home,' and when he did get home on
Friday night, usually all seven kids got a beating, whether we needed it
or not."

Mealtime with his father was particularly tense, Adam said. "My
father, having been starved as a POW, had a fixation about food. You

did *not* waste food in our household. We were physically abused if we did not eat everything on our plates."

None of the above incidents would have shown up in military or civilian statistics, since none were reported. All would fall under the category of "discipline." But, according to a child abuse expert I consulted, all would be properly termed abuse.

EMOTIONAL ABUSE

Some of the above incidents involving systematic berating or humiliation are also examples of emotional abuse—a kind which is rarely reported but which many therapists say is the most insidious of all.

"Physical abuse can be a one-time thing, or infrequent," one social worker told me. "But I don't know how you can have a one-time, isolated instance of emotional abuse." One of the characteristics of emotional abuse is that the psychic wounds, although invisible, remain open and bleeding. Unlike physical abuse, which in many cases is a temporary aberration from the norm in the parent-child relationship, emotional abuse tends to *be* the norm. There is no relief, no opportunity for healing.

The National Center on Child Abuse and Neglect defines emotional abuse as encompassing three distinct forms of maltreatment: *close confinement*, which includes tying or binding a child or confining the child to an enclosed area such as a closet; *verbal or emotional assault*, which constitutes a habitual pattern of belittling, threatening, scapegoating, or other forms of rejecting behavior; and *other or unknown abuse*, which could include attempted physical or sexual assault, withholding of food, shelter, sleep or other necessities, or economic or other exploitation. Of these, by far the most common is verbal or emotional assault.[56]

All abuse produces a difficult legacy for the child in later life: It is that much harder to establish a sense of self-worth and to learn to trust and invest in relationships. With emotional abuse, the patterns of childhood are deeply instilled and very difficult to overcome.

Asked how to spot a child in a classroom who has suffered emotional abuse, one therapist said, "Look for a child who tries to do everything absolutely right, who's afraid to make a mistake, who tries to do everything five minutes before you ask for it."

Ten military brats interviewed for this book had been emotionally abused for years during their childhood and adolescence. Following are two of their stories, one from the officer corps, one from enlisted.

The Officer's Daughter

The daughter of an Air Force general told how her father was gone for fully three years of her childhood. "That was a lot of father absence," she said, "but with him [absence] was sometimes better. He was a general through and through." When she saw the movie *The Great Santini*, she said she sat through it white-knuckled, terrified.

I didn't grow up in a family that was that explicit—my father did not play military games at home—but it was very implicit, and very, very powerful. Our version was a little more genteel, but it was all there nonetheless.

My father was an alcoholic. He could actually be a fairly pleasant kind of guy, until he finished his second drink. Then you were at the mercy of this overwhelming personality, and the harassment. And it seems to me, when I think back, that I can't remember a time when he wasn't finishing his second drink and starting to turn, you know?

He was a big man, he talked loudly, and he wanted everybody's attention all the time. No matter what was going on, he took center stage. And he kidded, he cajoled, he teased, he prodded and he harassed—and as he got drunker, he got nastier. To the point where you'd either get up and go throw up, or have a headache or diarrhea. Finally you'd excuse yourself just to get the hell away from the guy. But he was having a good time. And if you brought someone into the house he could attack, a friend or a date, all the more fun. . . .

He was always testing us, to see how far he could push you before you fell apart. He had different buttons to push with different people. For some reason he just had to do this. He never just came home and sat and read the newspaper. He was always pushing you.

Now, why did any of us put up with that kind of abuse for one minute? Why didn't we three form a coalition and giggle at him? I know why: Because we were scared shitless of this guy.

It also may be intrinsic to the military situation. If the kingpin is in any way undercut, you don't have a military situation; it's something else. Maybe there's a tacit understanding that we behave this way *because we're military.* Maybe from the time we're little tiny kids we figure that out, that he gets to order us around, say anything he wants. We don't get to form political groups inside the family, because *it's just not military.*

The Sergeant's Daughter

The daughter of an alcoholic Army sergeant and his alcoholic wife told of a childhood filled with abuse and fear. She described her father as someone who would drink, gamble, have women on the side, and who took strange pleasure in manipulating his children. As in many abusive families, the abuse was both physical and emotional. But when this daughter tells her story, it is clear that it is the emotional abuse that has left the deepest scars.

"He had two sets of boxing gloves," she recalled,

and he always wanted my brother and me to put them on and box each other. I hated to do that. There were times I was bigger than my brother and could probably get the better of him, but all I can remember is when he was bigger than I was. We're talking eight, nine, ten years old. My brother would hit me in the head, and I would cry, and my father would make us continue boxing. He would be there egging us on like it was a boxing match . . . it was so bizarre. And we would cry. You know, you wanted to *stop* and he wouldn't let you stop. If I let down, then my brother would start whacking me harder. If *he* stopped then I'd just kill him—to win the approval, I guess, of our father. My mother would try to stop my father and eventually she would. I never got physically hurt, but I think my father was sadistic.

He also gave us severe whippings if we did anything he considered wrong, even if it was minor. If he said "don't leave the yard" and we did anyway, we'd get whipped. He would take off his belt, fold it in half, and whip us on the butt and the legs.

One night her parents went out and left the kids, ages seven and nine, at home without a babysitter. They took the opportunity to play with fire, burning up strips of paper in the gas heater. "I guess we left the burnt paper lying around," the daughter said. "Because when they came home my father dragged us out of bed and whipped the shit out of us. Even our mother was crying."

But the worst of it, she said, was the verbal abuse from her father and the terrible fear he inspired. Much of her childhood she has blanked out, she said, and what she does recall of it is almost dream-like. One of her survival tactics was the development of a strange detachment.

"My father would set us up," she said,

and then say "Aha! I told you you were lying to me." And then you realized you were getting trapped, but there was no way out. *No way out.* I was frightened all the time.

But the funny thing about my early military life is that I still look back on it as happy times. Isn't that interesting? It's a tremendous contradiction. I still see us skating in the Motor Pool and all around, playing hide and seek and tag, swimming and bowling, buying hamburgers for a nickel. But it was always outside. Even now I spend as much time as I can outside. For me as a child, inside was danger. So as an adult I'm outside all the time, even though there's no danger here. Outside is freedom. My mind can expand. But when I'm inside, it's like my mind stops. And I think with my father literally your mind stopped—because he could tell what you were thinking.

Maybe he would have told you you can't go upstairs and get your gum, and a little while later you wouldn't remember and start to run upstairs.

And he would say, "Where are you going?" And you'd say, "Outside." And he'd say, "Come in here." And he would *know*. It got to the point where I would be afraid to think at home. It was a form of mind control—but I didn't realize any of this until years later. I really believe that I was afraid to try to have any coherent thoughts, because if my thoughts went in the wrong direction, my father would find out.

How much abuse this daughter and her brother endured even she cannot say, because she has forgotten—or repressed—so much of her childhood. Still, she has a few very telling memories.

"When I was about seven," she said, "we got a pet."

And I'm ashamed to tell this—I didn't even tell my therapist. We had a small house which had a hallway, and the two bedrooms, the kitchen, and the bathroom were all off this hallway. And I remember bringing this dog in there once, a small dog, and I remember shutting all of the doors to the hall so it had no escape, and getting a belt, and *whipping* this dog. Just *whipping*. And delighting in hearing this dog cry. I could cry now to think of it. What a terrible thing. But I remember doing it. *Then* I remember trying to hug the dog, to make the dog realize I really loved it.

And I've never forgiven myself for that. But I also know now that I had to do it, for survival. I had to act it out.

My brother used to be very cruel also. We were both taught how to shoot BB guns and twenty-twos, and were very good shots. When my brother was thirteen or fourteen he used to throw bread out the window to attract the birds, and then kill them. Just like our father used to set us up and trap us.

I consulted a child abuse expert, Dr. Sandra T. Azar of Clark University, about these two examples of children turning their rage on animals. She said, "Such acting out of what happened to them is a common way that children work through trauma. It allows them to gain a sense of mastery over the trauma."

Before she received therapy, this same daughter continued for many years to act out the abuse—against herself:

I've always been *extremely* strict with myself, demanding perfection because my father demanded it. I know that's why. I would always berate myself, call myself all these names, scream at myself. Sometimes I'd even hit myself, bang my head against the wall. Even in high school or college, I'd go crazy when I wouldn't be able to remember something, what the book was about. Later on I'd bang my head, really hurt it. I'd be so angry I wouldn't even sense I was hurt.

Then I'd start provoking myself, which I would *enjoy* doing. Just like you'd have somebody outside yourself provoking you. One part of me would lead the other part of me on, calling me names, grilling and condemning, just like my father would do. I would get madder and provoke myself some more, until in sheer exhaustion I would have to stop, and probably cry.

The turning point for this daughter came after college, when she became involved in a lay religious organization and, for the first time she could remember, began to feel valued for herself. She began building on that, seeking similar associations. At the same time she and her brother, who had a long history of antagonism toward one another, began to heal their relationship and become closer. From time to time over the years she has sought therapy to counter periodic depression, and tells of benefiting greatly from it. She is now happily married to a rooted civilian with a very relaxed personality; they have one child whom she says they are trying to "raise permissively, not rigidly."

No one knows how much emotional abuse there is in the military, or in the civilian community. Experts say it is a very common form of abuse—at least as common as physical abuse—and that it frequently accompanies other kinds.[57]

It is found in all socioeconomic groups both inside and outside the military. But there may be some ground to speculate that emotional abuse is particularly underestimated in the officer corps: It is well known that physical violence often erupts when the verbal skills to manage a situation are lacking. But officers by and large have excellent verbal skills—and, perhaps with the help of alcohol, can easily convert them into an arsenal used against a family member. Verbal attacks are certainly one way to release pent-up aggression—and they don't leave telltale scars that can harm careers.

SEXUAL ABUSE

Although emotional maltreatment is thought by many to be the most damaging kind of child abuse over time, it would be hard to imagine anything more devastating than the abuse of incest, which in a sense wraps all forms of abuse into one. Emotionally, it is one of the most extreme violations of trust; physically it is extreme objectification and degradation of a human being. The child's self-esteem is annihilated, the burden of confusion and guilt immense. And like emotional abuse, it tends to be habitual with the abuser, occurring repeatedly over a long period of time.

According to the National Center on Child Abuse and Neglect, as many as one child in five is sexually abused each day. The known incidence of sexual abuse does not begin to match this—NCCAN found that in 1986 the rate was 2.2 children per thousand—but figures on the extent of sexual abuse are universally considered to be deceptively low because of the highly secretive nature of the act and the rarity with which it comes to light.

In the military, seemingly even less is known: For 1987, the Department of Defense reported a sexual abuse rate of one child per thousand—less than half of what NCCAN found in the general population the previous year. It would be inappropriate to conclude on the basis of those statistics that there is less sexual abuse in the military; it is a great deal more likely that the discrepancy is due to underreporting which, owing to the severe repercussions to career, is even more of a problem than in the civilian community.

A conspiracy of silence reigns in all incestuous families: the members are each reluctant to do anything to destroy the family unit they depend on for their identity, no matter how terrible the situation. And if the ultimate secret is closely kept in civilian families, it may well be locked up even more tightly in military ones.

"This phenomenon [of secrecy]," wrote Commander Patricia W. Crigler of the Navy's Medical Service Corps,

> is particularly true of [incestuous] military families who frequently are relocated and who have often strained or broken their extended family ties. They feel they cannot rely upon neighbors, fellow workers, military physicians, or even schoolmates for fear that the incest information will be turned over to military superiors, resulting in the offender being summarily separated from the service. This action can be a real threat when the service member's skills are oriented toward only military-type jobs, such as gunner's mate, tank driver, combat soldier, or underwater demolition expert. The closed family is kept bonded together, prohibiting anyone from intruding and discovering the "social travesty."

But whether civilian or military, these families have a lot in common. "A further look at the [incestuous] family reveals that there are rigid family rules and role relationships," Crigler continues. "The concept of androgyny is almost unheard of; sex-stereotypical roles and rules are strictly and traditionally assigned and adhered to at all times. The father typically rules the house either with an iron hand or passively with innuendoes, such as implying that if outsiders find out what is going on, he will be sent to jail, thereby splitting up the family. These families do not adapt well to change because their problem-solving skills are few and unreliable. This weakness in the family unit is particularly significant to military families who are destined to move . . . often."[58]

There are several types of incestuous fathers, but the most typical type found in the military, according to Commander Crigler, is probably a "tyrant" type.

He is authoritarian. When he speaks, he appears to be the epitome of a Marine Corps drill instructor or the captain of a ship. He rules, he orders, he demands, and either he receives absolute loyalty and obedience or the consequences will be grave. He brooks no opposition and often uses threats of force or actual physical abuse to have his way inside his family. To his family he is a tyrant, but to his military superiors he may only look like a "good trooper" or a "man with discipline." His family lives in fear of his anger and retribution should they upset him. He is a patriarch and looks at his family as his belongings who must obey him, follow him from one duty station to another, and who are totally subject to his whims. Often, these whims include sex from his daughters. The military macho myth is prevalent in this type. Sex may be the only way such a man has of being close to another human being. He believes that to admit to needs for affection and closeness would be tantamount to admitting weakness. Such an admission would be too damaging to his ego structure, which is built on asserting power and aggression.[59]

The typical incestuous father in the military, on the basis of substantiated cases, is thought to be enlisted with little or no formal education beyond high school.[60] Given the inaccuracy of other military statistics on child abuse, this abuser profile may have little validity; it certainly differs from the civilian profile, which is that of a middle-class male with some college education. In any event, the most harrowing case described to me came from quite a different quarter.

Lisa's Story: A Living Nightmare

Lisa was physically, emotionally, and sexually abused by both her stepfather and her natural mother for eight years, from age three to age eleven. It stopped only when her stepfather's mother caught him in the act. After that the abuse became chiefly emotional, in the form of verbal harassment, threats, and denigration, and she was also relegated to the position of family maid—not an uncommon development in sexually abusive families where the abuser has "finished" with the child in question.

The story of Lisa's abuse is extremely shocking, not least because it violates so many notions of what is usual in sexual abuse cases.

First, incest is a form of abuse that usually stands alone; to find it combined with physical torture and severe emotional harassment and physical neglect is rare.

Second, the perpetrator is usually the male relative alone; the mother may know about it, but she does not participate. In Lisa's case, however, her mother's sexual sadism matched her stepfather's.

Third, at least in the military it is rarely discovered at the status level of Lisa's family. Her stepfather, a graduate of Annapolis, enjoyed a long and successful career in the Navy before retiring as a rear admiral.

Indeed, the abuse of Lisa was never "discovered" by any outside authorities. After the grandmother stumbled upon the scene and confronted her son, he stopped physically and sexually abusing Lisa—but no police, medical personnel, or therapists were ever called in. Neither Lisa, nor her sisters, nor her parents ever received help. Lisa's stepfather turned his attentions to a younger natural daughter and to at least one of her teenage friends. The alcoholism of both her parents also continued unabated, and in her mother's case became incapacitating. Added to the history of severe abuse was horrifying physical neglect of the three children, particularly while the father was gone to sea for months at a time. Lisa remembers surviving with her sisters on jelly doughnuts and soft drinks while her mother drank until she passed out. In only one neighborhood of the many they lived in, both civilian and military, did a neighbor show concern for the obvious neglect of the children; but Lisa, whose stepfather had warned he would kill her if she ever told anyone, tried her best to cover up. When the stepfather was at sea, she became the chief caretaker of her drunken mother as well as her little sisters.

The horror of that family—outwardly so pristinely perfect, with a successful father, a charming mother, and three lovely, obedient little girls—remained a dark secret. Lisa, in a survival response that is common among abuse victims, repressed all memory of the abuse. Severe abuse, particularly sexual abuse, results in what psychiatrists refer to as *overstimulation* of the child: Both the trauma and the child's rage in response to it are too overwhelming for the child to deal with; the recollection is therefore stored in "compartments" of memory and kept walled off and isolated. This allows the child to continue to believe, delusionally, in the inherent goodness of the parent(s)—the most powerful need in childhood—even in the face of the most terrible abuse. Many children lose consciousness or go into a trancelike state during vicious abuse, as a defense against the overstimulation they are powerless to avert or withstand.

Lisa became an almost slavishly devoted daughter to both her parents, continually craving and seeking their approval. She married young, eventually had children, and remained oblivious to what she had suffered—except for a couple of things. She had what she described as a "horrendous fear of men," with the sole exception of her husband, although her sexual frigidity was a problem right from the beginning of their marriage. But where all other men were concerned, it was a matter of raw fear.

"It was just terrible," she remembered. "We'd go to a New Year's Eve party and a neighbor would grab me to give me a kiss and I would fight him clear to the floor. I didn't know why. Everybody thought it was hysterical." And then there was the deep-seated, nagging fear of her stepfather that she didn't understand but because of which she resolved never to leave her children alone with him. Somehow she didn't sense the same fear toward her mother, perhaps because by then her mother was so helplessly drunk so much of the time, and so often institutionalized, that leaving the children in her care was never an issue.

Then in her late twenties, a year after her mother's death, Lisa suffered a nervous breakdown and was bedridden for six weeks. Afterward, a disturbing array of physical symptoms began to surface, ranging from migraine headaches to colitis, pains in her chest, limbs, and joints, and problems swallowing, all of which seemed inexplicable at the time but which were subsequently linked by physicians to the abuse. She began a quest for answers that finally led a therapist to recommend hypnosis, which Lisa undertook with the help of her husband—the only person she trusted enough to put her under.

Several evenings a week, under hypnosis, she poured out the stories of a childhood so horrific it defied imagination. Her husband said she spoke in a slow monotone, with a childlike point of view. Sometimes she would stop and tears would roll down her cheeks. Sometimes she couldn't go on. But then, after a hiatus of a few days, she would go under hypnosis again and the stories would resume. For more than three years the horror poured forth: she had been shut up in closets, suspended by ropes from water pipes in the basement, beaten with sticks and boards, burned with cigarettes, raped by her stepfather while her mother watched, forced to have oral sex, forced to have sex with house servants and many other strangers. The details of these depravities, some of which Lisa shared with me from the hypnosis notes—an act of great personal courage that was very hard on her emotionally—are stupefyingly nightmarish, far too ghastly to repeat on these pages.

After each session Lisa studied her husband's notes and sought to confirm or refute as much as she could of the stories, running up huge telephone bills as she called a procession of family friends, relatives, neighbors, physicians. She was able to confirm a number of details, even learning that she was treated for gonorrhea when she was three. Nothing that came out under hypnosis was ever found to be false. "When it first started coming out, I said to my husband, 'This just can't be true. It must be my imagination.' But then as I checked things out, I could see it was true. Truth isn't the issue anymore. But I live under such tension."

What happened to Lisa was what psychiatrist Leonard Shengold calls *soul murder*. In his book on the subject he writes, "Soul murder is neither a diagnosis nor a condition. It is a dramatic term for circumstances that eventuate in crime—the deliberate attempt to eradicate or compromise the separate identity of another person. The victims of soul murder remain in large part possessed by another, their souls in bondage to someone else. . . . A consummated soul murder is a crime most often committed by psychotic or psychopathic parents who treat the child as an extension of themselves or as an object with which to satisfy their desires."[61]

Unfortunately, by the time Lisa was undergoing hypnosis and finally beginning to realize what had been done to her, both her parents were dead and could not be confronted. She recalled the moment she received the news of her stepfather's death, still years before she realized she'd been abused. "When I got the phone call I went hysterical," Lisa said. "I cried and cried. Now I think back and ask, 'Why was I crying?' But I think the reason I cried at both my mother's and father's funerals is that I never had love. I was crying for what I didn't have, not for them."

Now, at age fifty-three, she continues to see a therapist to help her cope with a variety of continuing problems, including claustrophobia, agoraphobia, panic attacks, and the sexual frigidity that has plagued her throughout her marriage. She feels uncomfortable in any situation she can't totally control, and even has trouble riding in cars. She has had panic attacks while sitting in a dentist's chair and at the hairdresser's, although things have now improved to the point where she can wait in the checkout line at the grocery store. Lisa has never had an alcohol problem—she won't touch it—but is addicted to a tranquilizer.

Even though she now understands what happened to her, and despite the continuing therapy, Lisa still has trouble summoning anger toward her parents. Her husband, who has been supportive throughout, said, "I think [Lisa] feels responsible for some of the things that happened—as though at age three or four or ten she could have stopped it, and because she didn't she's guilty. Obviously, you've got an adult and a three-year-old and you know logically who's responsible, but logic doesn't have anything to do with it."

Shengold has written that rage, overwhelming rage, is the legacy of the soul-murdered. In the case of incestuous soul murder, it is the other, seldom-mentioned side of the Oedipal conflict: patricidal and matricidal wishes of terrifying intensity. These wishes usually reside in the unconscious, because they are too horrifying to conscious thought—and they war with the need to believe in the parents as good and loving. One of the goals of therapy for the soul-murdered, Shengold says, is to "get rid of the invading intrapsychic monster—that is, to undo or at least ameliorate the damaging identification with the soul-destroying parent."[62] If the treatment is successful, the patient gains at least a partial ability to consciously grasp the terrible truth of his or her childhood and hold conflicting feelings of hatred and love in the consciousness at the same time, without splitting them off into compartments. In clarifying the murky horror of an abused childhood, the patient is able—with varying degrees of success—to tolerate the legacy of rage. By naming it, feeling it (at least partially), it is possible to keep from directing it inappropriately. The alternative is to persist in denial, identifying with the soul-murdering parent and quite possibly turning that destructive rage on the self, or on someone else.

Lisa has been trying to come to terms with her rage for years. Typical of soul-murder victims, she will occasionally be able to rise to heights of conscious anger at her parents, feel as though she will finally be able to direct her righteous anger toward them—perhaps, she said, in the form of visiting their graves and yelling at them, or "painting their gravestones black"—only to find herself falling back, unable to sustain the focus of her rage.

"My therapist asked me to fantasize what I would do to my stepfather if I could," Lisa said. "Of course my first reaction was, 'I'd kill him.' Then I said, 'No, I can't kill him.' But you know what I'd do? I'd put him before a whole board of Naval officers, strip off all his medals and his uniform, and tell them everything he did. But then I think, 'The Navy wouldn't believe me anyway.'"

Despite her physical ailments and crippling psychological problems, Lisa comes across as a likable, levelheaded person who's somehow managed to lead a semblance of a normal life. She successfully raised two children—although she faults herself for being "overprotective" as a mother—and now chiefly spends her time in the role of devoted grandmother.

Over the years, her therapists have expressed wonder that she was able to survive her childhood at all, let alone function as well as she has. "My therapist says I should be schizophrenic and psychotic and everything else—because that's what a lot of children will do, have split personalities. I don't know why I'm not, except that perhaps it's because I had a wonderful, loving *amma* [nanny] in my first three years of life."

Shengold writes, "What we do not know about child abuse and soul murder is probably more important than what we do, and in addition there is the mystery of greatly varying inherited gifts and ego strength: these enable some abused children to sustain more abuse and transcend it better than others. . . . Some frequently can or even must function in an 'as if' fashion: they act as if they were psychologically healthy, presenting a façade of normality that covers an essential hollowness of soul."[63]

When I remarked to Lisa that her life is a triumph of survival, she responded, "I'm a survivor, but I don't feel like one. I feel like I'm hanging on by the skin of my teeth. Is that surviving?"

Although Lisa has managed to confirm many key details of the hypnosis material, her life is still haunted by questions—questions that can never be put to rest, that will never lose their edge. How could anyone do such despicable things to a child? How is it that so many relatives, friends, neighbors suspected, but did nothing? What about the doctor who diagnosed gonorrhea when she was three years old? What about the teachers who surely must have wondered why this little girl wore long-sleeved blouses to school every day of the year, even in the hottest weather, to cover her bruises and burns? Not least of her questions, Lisa says, are the ones revolving around the military.

"That's what upsets me more than anything else," Lisa said. "The fact that a man like this could go up the ladder like he did, retire as a rear admiral. He even taught at Annapolis for a while. And of course everybody thought he was the life of the party and he was wonderful. But behind the doors it was a whole different story. How could he get away with all this?"

How indeed? How was it that Lisa's stepfather was able to spend four years at the Naval Academy, which like every military academy prides itself on knowing its midshipmen inside out, without his sadism being discovered? How is it that a dangerous psychotic could have an illustrious thirty-year career in the military, without someone among his peers or superiors suspecting? From what Lisa learned in her exhaustive investigation to assess the truth of the horrors she related under hypnosis, there is reason to believe her stepfather's proclivities could have been deduced as far back as his days as a midshipman. Among the people she tracked down was a widow whose husband— then her boyfriend—had been Lisa's stepfather's roommate at Annapolis for a time. "I told her everything I'd recalled under hypnosis," Lisa said, "and she said, 'I don't deny anything you're saying. That was [Harry].'"

Lisa has clearly suffered many of the consequences of soul murder Shengold refers to in his book: the rage, the inability to experience joy (the victim takes on the guilt that the perpetrator should have experienced but did not), the phobias, psychosomatic pains and illnesses, and "as if" existence. Nevertheless, Lisa transformed my notions of what it is to be courageous. Despite all the vicious means her sadistic parents employed, the soul murder they attempted was not, after all, entirely successful. Lisa, like every other human being, has had choices to make every step of the way in her life—and over and over again, in the darkest moments of her childhood when there was no ally nor any hope of escape, and much later, when the crimes against her were revealed in all their horror, she has chosen to persevere. She has taken the brave road of seeking after truth, at whatever cost. She has endured all manner of abuse, betrayal, and injustice, and years later Lisa is still here, still seeking, still learning, still trying. And she has endured it all not merely to exist, but to give of herself as wife, mother, grandmother. There is no question in my mind, as I later wrote to her, that she is the most courageous woman I have ever met. However, for Lisa, who has a hard time enduring a simple shopping trip, that is a notion difficult to grasp.

Later she wrote to me, "When you said in your letter you think I am 'a woman of extraordinary courage,' it really hit me. I saw the word *woman* written there, and I realized I have never thought of myself as a woman. I have no idea what I think I am. I do know I am a grandma, but other than that I really have no idea who I am. I wonder if I ever thought about it before. I am just this thing on earth with a lot of pain."

Contrary to what many people think, most physically, sexually, or emotionally abused children do not grow up to be child abusers themselves. Recent studies suggest that the rate of repetition of abuse in the next generation is about 30 percent.[64] One study found that a stronger predictor from childhood of future abusive behavior than the fact of having been abused is whether the child felt unloved and unwanted by his or her parents—a perception that can also be found in families where there was no overt abuse. Children appear to suffer the most in later life when the abuse begins at a very young age, lasts a long time, was perpetrated by a close relative, or occurred in a cold emotional atmosphere in the family.[65] Still, researchers are a long way from being able to explain how it is that many abused children grow up to be loving, nurturing parents.

One thing that is now well accepted is that abused children benefit greatly from two things: developing friendships with adults outside the family who are nurturing and supportive, and, even much later in life, undergoing therapy to gain insight into their families of origin and themselves. All three of the abused daughters profiled in this chapter, as well as the abused sons Joe, Adam, and Todd, whose stories were presented in Chapters 5 and 6, have benefited from therapy.

Healing begins, paradoxically, with a very painful step: admitting unequivocally that one was abused as a child. That's a very hard thing for many abuse victims to do; sometimes because they still feel the imperative to keep the family secret, but often because from the outset they accepted the perpetrator's judgment that they "deserved" the neglect or punishment they received. The first task of therapy is to help the abused recognize the injustice done them. If they don't recognize it, the consequences can be high: Denial of having been an abuse victim has been found to be common among those who go on to abuse children themselves.

But therapy goes far beyond the initial admitting of a dark secret. With effort and the passage of time, the abused individual can learn to shed the child's perspective that has kept him or her locked for years in the same psychological dynamic with the abuser. Finally it becomes possible to see with the eyes of an adult, put things in perspective, and adjust the expectations of abuse that are otherwise so often carried into adult relationships.

The pain does not go away, but slowly and steadily it is countered by new strengths that help to balance it. Essentially, the individual is learning resilience.

And resilience is an old friend to military brats.

CHAPTER 8

MILITARY BRATS AS NOMADS

My mother, speaking to one of my military brat cousins: "But you put down roots everywhere you went, didn't you?"

My cousin: "No, Aunt Dorothy, not roots. Vines."

As Lillian wandered about the empty rooms of the house carefully making mental notes about furniture placement and room arrangement, Colonel Meecham herded his children to the front porch for a morale check. . . . With his hands placed behind his back, Bull paced in front of them, clearing his throat, and gathering his thoughts for the traditional moving day speech. . . . Finally, he began to speak.

"At ease, hogs," he began. "I want you to listen, and listen good. We have bivouacked all night and arrived at our destination, one Ravenel, South Carolina, at approximately 0800 hours, twenty minutes before your commanding officer had planned. Now I have listened to you hogs bellyache about moving to a new town ever since I arrived home from the Med cruise. This said bellyaching will end as of 0859 hours and will not affect the morale of this squadron henceforth. Do I make myself clear?"

His children nodded their agreement with expressionless eyes. The swagger stick slapped against Bull's hand in ten-second intervals.

—The Great Santini

For six weeks in October and November of 1978 I was a supremely happy young woman. With the sole exceptions of my wedding and the births of my children, all which occurred long afterward, I still rank that time as the most ecstatic of my life. But virtually no one I knew then understood that.

It was not hard to see why. I was drained from my parents' bitter divorce after thirty-four years of marriage. My own love relationship had recently ended. There had been an exhausting union battle at work. About the only really good thing in my life right then was the newspaper job I dearly loved—and to everyone's shock, I had just quit. There was no new job lined up, and I had very little money. On the face of it, my actions were inexplicable, my attitude surreal.

But I had been seized by a need to move on that was so overwhelming it eclipsed any sensible notions of sticking out the usual cycle of job queries. More than anything else in the world I wanted to get out of Virginia and feel the freedom of the open road. I wasn't worried about jobs; I figured I had enough experience to get me in the door someplace. I also had a head full of freelance ideas and a book I wanted to write.

I packed my yellow Honda Civic with the few things I considered really important: clothes, dictionary, camera, a portable typewriter, a box full of my newspaper clips. Then I hit the road, headed north under clear blue autumn skies, a stack of maps beside me and no particular destination in mind.

Ah, the exhilaration of it! The past was literally behind me, the future literally down the road. I could turn the car—and my life—in any direction I chose. Every road sign signified a new opportunity, a whole new world of choices and decisions, all of which I would make myself. As I drove along, happily pondering whether I should make my new life in Philadelphia, New York, Chicago, L.A., or any point in between, I had no worries. Things would work out—I was convinced of that—and I would become who I wanted to be in the place of my own choice. And if they didn't? Well, I was master of my own fate, I told myself. I'd learn what I could from a bad experience, then pull up stakes and start over someplace else. God knows I knew how to do that. Whatever happened was going to be for the best. Even if I bombed out, I could always write about it. For a writer, I figured, there is no wasted experience.

By the time I reached the Pacific in mid-November, I had fifty bucks to my name. I was worried, but still sure I could pull it off; I had always known I could survive anywhere, make the best of it. That was a truth I'd learned so long ago it was as much a part of me as blood and bone.

Only much later did I realize just how classically military brat that was, and how my odyssey revealed both the best and the worst of rootlessness.

As an Army brat, I was so used to moving, to breaking camp one place, setting up in another, it had become the natural rhythm of my existence. In Virginia I had stayed so long—more than three years in one job—that I chafed and yearned for life on the move. My cross-country adventure was the joyful reclaiming of my identity.

Happy? *Yes*, I was happy—I was going home. And home for me was the comfortable familiarity of constant change and an uncharted future. For me, a modern American Bedouin, life on the open road, destination unknown, was as delicious as a long drink of cool water in the searing desert. It was freedom.

Or was it? For there was another side to it that was not free at all: a fatalistic side in which my wanderings were not so much an exercise in autonomy as an offering up of my life on the altar of fate. It may have looked as though I had taken control of my life, but in effect I had put myself in limbo, awaiting circumstances themselves to make my choices for me—a striking re-creation of my life as a military brat. How long could I keep driving—until I got sick or injured? Until I was sidelined by an accident or breakdown? Until I ran out of money, as I ultimately did? I drove for six weeks, bouncing from city to city in my glorious dance of delusion, about as autonomous and free as the ball in a pinball machine.

The end point turned out to be legendary San Francisco. There I set up camp, ready to pursue my dreams as so many had before me. And things did not work out.

I survived, all right—even made a living from writing. My dream was derailed by something altogether unexpected. Within weeks I found an intense dislike for the city growing within me. A dislike so strong it could not be ignored. A dislike that, ironically enough, centered on rootlessness.

I saw San Francisco as a city cut off from its past, heedless of its future, enveloped almost obscenely in its celebration of the moment. A city where, to borrow the words of someone I met there, "everyone you meet seems to have run away from home." Loudly and self-righteously, I declaimed against it. What I failed to see, of course, was that I had projected my own plight onto an entire city. The mirror image was exact. What I condemned outwardly was the very thing I was loath to face within; inevitably, the image became unbearable. Within seven months I was gone.

This time I chose Chicago—a city I came to love deeply, in no small part because its down-to-earth, see-life-for-what-it-is philosophy helped me finally take a good long look at the legacies of my rootlessness.

And what I found was both good and bad.

There are two questions one can pose that reveal rootlessness as instantly as a litmus test.

The first: *Where are you from?* Military brats do not relish the "where from" question and go through life vainly trying to parry it. Some answer "Nowhere." Others, "Everywhere." There are many versions: citing the last place they've been, or the one they liked most, or launching into a full-blown explanation that reveals far more than the questioner intended. One military son told me, "When people asked me where I was from, it used to be painful, a dilemma. So I had to just sit down and decide something to say and stick to, so people wouldn't think I was lying. Before that, it depended on my mood: *This month I'm from California.*"

The fact is, there is no way to answer the question which is not awkward. The moment it is asked, it sets up a barrier between the military brat and the civilian questioner. A civilian asks the question to get a handle on the person; but no answer the military brat can possibly give will satisfy. The let's-get-acquainted conversation has begun badly, underscoring the gap between our world and theirs.

The second litmus test is a question rarely asked in social situations, but one I posed to every interviewee: *Where do you want to be buried?* A person with roots always knows the answer; he or she probably hasn't given it much thought, but hasn't had to—it's the kind of thing that's answered just by who one is. The response of a person without roots is quite different. "Wherever I am when I finish up," said one military brat. "I have no firm attachment to any geographic location." Another answered, "Buried? Never. I want to be cremated and my ashes scattered. I don't care where."

Cremation can well serve the purposes of a rooted person, of course, since ashes can be interred or memorialized quite easily. In 1987, 15.1 percent of Americans who died were cremated. For military brats, however, it appears to be a much stronger choice. Of those polled for this book who knew how they wanted their bodies disposed of, three quarters wanted cremation—and specifically because it would *not* tie them forever to one place. "Where do you want your ashes scattered?" I asked a Navy petty officer's son, whose answer was typical: "Over the mountains. Or the ocean. Or the desert. Someplace. I don't care." The daughter of an Air Force colonel said, "I think the best thing is to be cremated and scattered to the four winds."

An Air Force general's daughter, told of the strong tendency of military brats to prefer cremation and scattering, remarked, "I understand why. It's so representative of our lives."

The answers of the rest scarcely balanced out the sense of rootlessness. Apart from two who wanted to donate their bodies to science, the responses were equally divided between those who had no idea what they wanted and those who preferred burial—very few of whom had any notion of where they'd like that to be.

Mobility is high among Americans in general; about 18 percent of Americans move annually, although most of these moves are normally within one locality, in proximity to friends and relatives.[1] Even allowing for this tendency in our national character, however, there is a big difference between average civilian mobility and that of the military.[2] Military families not only move much more often than civilians, they move such great distances that it is all but impossible to maintain close bonds with relatives and friends.

One military study noted, "A civilian family that relocates once or twice during the child-rearing period experiences the same initial disruption as a military family. However, when relocation recurs every few years over an extended period of time, a sense of disruption is created. . . . It has been the expressed opinion of many military families that after the initial few moves, additional moves become increasingly disruptive and difficult."[3]

The length of a typical accompanied tour of duty—in which the family goes with the service member to the new assignment—is theoretically three years. In practice, however, military families move far more often. Military personnel are shifted for a variety of reasons— for promotion, to fill a vacancy, acquire new training, or many other reasons, any of which can mean cutting one assignment short in order to begin another.

In conducting interviews for this book, I felt the critical question was not how many times the interviewee moved or how many houses he or she lived in, but how many schools the person attended from kindergarten through high school. Although the number of houses more accurately represents the number of moves—and is usually twice as high as the number of schools attended—the number of schools is the truer reflection of the challenge before the military brat: the number of times he or she had to establish an identity and a network of friends.

The average number of schools for those interviewed was 9.5. I went to twelve. Some of the military brats I talked to went to as many as eighteen. It is not unheard of for military children to go to twenty or more.

From my interviews it appears that Navy children sometimes attend fewer schools than those of the Army, Air Force, and Marines. Navy personnel spend so much time at sea that families sometimes elect to remain in one location as long as possible while the service member goes away on successive assignments. Still, the number of schools attended is higher for Navy children than for most of their civilian counterparts.

We think of ourselves as *nomads*. The term has a nice, definitive sound to it, and suggests, somewhat reassuringly, that our experience fits neatly into a known category. But the term is less a description of us and our lives than an indictment of the language which has yet to reflect the realities of life inside the Fortress.

Nomads in the true sense are groups of people—Inuit, Bedouin, Masai—who move at will in search of hunting grounds, pastureland, water. Like us, they have no permanent home and they move constantly. But true nomads move in entire communities; the social fabric of their lives is kept intact. Nomad children grow up knowing their grandparents, aunts, uncles, cousins. They have lifelong friends. One can speculate that if a nomad were asked "Where are you from?" he would answer, "From my tribe, the such-and-such." And if asked "Where will you be buried?" the answer, too, might be something on the order of "With my tribe." Whatever the answer, it would imply deep rootedness. For while movement is an important ingredient in the lives of true nomads, the most basic reality of all—the sense of identity in community—is as rock solid as it is possible to be.

American military children, by contrast, do not have kinship networks to anchor them. The constant change is not balanced by social stability. For the military brat, each time the family moves, the world dissolves and is swept away.

We are not really nomads. There is no easy label for us.

HELLO-GOODBYE

Resilient is one of the favorite adjectives applied to military children by the Department of Defense in its promotional materials about military family life.

And on this point DoD is indisputably correct. Repeatedly knocked off our feet by frequent moves, military brats develop an extraordinary sense of social balance. By the time we reach adulthood, we've met so many thousands of people, weathered such a diversity of predicaments, that we are unlikely to be fazed by much.

Among the useful traits we acquire: independence, willingness to take risks, flexibility. We know how to read people quickly, initiate new projects, get along with almost anyone, bounce back from disaster.

Most of all, military brats learn to use change as a medium. As children, military brats are not in control of when and how change enters their lives, but typically they teach themselves how to profit from it anyway.

"Moving as often as we did was *extremely* beneficial," said an Army major's daughter, a veteran of twelve schools. "From early childhood I recognized that you can change yourself, and in the next place put into action all the things you learned from the last one. You can be a leader, anything you want, because you are not tied to a community perception of who you are. I picked that up real fast. Some [civilian] people believe they cannot change. A bad boy in a small town is always a bad boy; no one believes he can change. There's too much history, and it's chiseled in stone."

Constant moving is a harsh teacher—but the lessons can be valuable. There are other benefits as well: Military brats who crisscross the country or live overseas acquire sophisticated knowledge that can be an important shaping influence on their lives—improving their self-image, widening their horizons, suggesting their choice of career.

Most military brats grow up with an awareness of the advantages that moving around has given them. But there is another side to the story that is not so well known. It is the story of the pain we carry from so much loss. And it is a story we often do not know ourselves: Early Fortress training in stoicism and detachment from feelings ensures that the first instinct of the military brat is to deny emotional pain.

When adult military brats are interviewed on this subject, it does not take long to see that both the pain of extreme mobility and the denial of that pain are still very much part of their lives.

"How did you like moving around so much?" I would ask in a typical exchange. The answer would come quickly, almost automatically: "I *loved* it." "Would you want your children to move as much as you did?" Again the answer would be quick, and often vehement. "Absolutely not." Not a single interviewee said yes. Clearly there is something missing in that formulation, and it is the pain.

When military brats are drawn out on the subject, the story inevitably expands to include hurt as well as triumph, loss as well as gain. One Army colonel's son, veteran of a dozen schools in five countries, treasures the experiences he had abroad and considers his overseas experience the richest part of his life. He was the sort of survivor kid who thrived wherever he was, making friends easily, doing well in school, winning awards and offices. But that isn't the whole story.

"The older I got, the more difficult it became," he said. With each move he stopped eating, lost weight. In his authoritarian family, the stress of moving with its accompanying losses could not be discussed. Although he clearly profited from his moves, he now says, "If I was to marry and start a family, I wouldn't want to move my kids around that much. I believe it was all the moving around—and because my dad was too busy with his job—that in the end destroyed our family." (His parents divorced in retirement, and he is estranged from his father.)

The first time George, son of a Marine Corps major, came face to face with his pain was when his girlfriend's sister was contemplating marrying into the Corps. He found himself in heated arguments with her as he lobbied against it. "She was in the twilight zone about what it was going to mean to marry into the Marine Corps," he said, still bristling. "She sounded like she'd been talking to a recruiter: 'Oh, we're going to be stationed in Germany, and in Paris . . . ,' and at that time the guy was at Twentynine Palms." (Twentynine Palms is an installation in the southeastern desert of California known for its isolation and considered a hardship post by many Marine families.)

"I mean, there should have been a message in that for her, but she wasn't picking up on it," he continued.

> Then during their engagement he got orders to Okinawa. I remember trying to tell her what it would be like—about the moving, about the times she'd be separated from him for thirteen to fourteen months, that this was probably not the only time he was going to be in Okinawa, about a lot of the shitty places they were going to be stationed. And he was in artillery, so they were going to get the worst assignments of all. And she'd say, "No, no, that's not what it's going to be like."
>
> What I remember about that, though, was how angry I was. So much anger came out at having to move all the time. So I realized that a lot I probably accepted at the time, I still carry around. That was one of the times the anger came out. I was angry at her for not seeing through the bullshit. But of course I was *really* angry at my father, for all the times *I* had to move.

Military children go along with the moves, adapt to the change, survive. But that doesn't mean there is no cost.

One of the costs for children is fear. No matter how many times the family has moved, there is fear about what the next move will bring: How will it change my family? Will I make new friends? Will I ever see my old friends again, and if I do, will they remember me? What will be required of me in the new place? Will my teachers like me? Often the child does not know how to articulate these fears—in authoritarian homes, these skills are not encouraged or developed—and simply lives with the anxiety until the questions resolve themselves.

Barbara, the daughter of a Navy lieutenant commander, had the rare experience of living in one large port city for most of her childhood, while her father left repeatedly on sea duty. The only exception was a two-year stint in Japan, when she was eight and nine. She remembers Japan as a wonderful, enriching experience, but one for which she paid a very high price. It was halfway through third grade when she learned the family would move to Japan in the summer, and the news hit her like a bombshell. "My older brother didn't want to go to Japan either," she said. "We were settled where we were, and Japan was such a foreign country. We didn't understand there would be other American kids to play with. I guess our parents weren't aware we needed to be told." Her performance in school declined so dramatically that she was not promoted to fourth grade.

When the family returned from Japan two years later, it was to the same community, the same neighborhood—a remarkable stroke of luck. But for Barbara it was also traumatic: She went back to her old school, but one year behind—in the same class with the younger brothers and sisters of her friends.

Bouncing around exacts a price, both academically and socially, from every military brat.

The academic costs are sometimes hidden, because military brats so often are high achievers in school. But the high achievement can be deceptive. Frequently it is primarily grounded not in joy of learning or a competitive spirit or superior ability—though all of those might be true—but in something else entirely.

"I think I sought popularity and high grades as compensations for being an outsider," said an Air Force colonel's son who attended eight schools. "I had a very strong sense that in any school setting, certain people would be picked out and pecked to death. Popularity and academic achievement were two of the ways I protected myself. I was pretty neurotic about the grades; I threw tantrums out of fear of not getting things right."

The other thing about high academic achievement is that it was often not true across the board. A striking number of military brats told of getting top grades in everything but math. "I'd go from one school where they were doing new math to another school where they had a different variety," said an Air Force colonel's son who went to thirteen schools, four of them in the same year. "There was always an assumption when you were dumped in a class in the middle of the year that you could catch up. And of course you never really did catch up. Sometimes you were in the dark the whole year because they'd be talking about things you never heard of. I never have been able to deal with math. But I read a lot, so I was always good at English, history, and social studies."

Moving during high school is by far the most difficult. By that time the stakes in social status are much higher, and it takes longer to establish one's self in the new place. One admiral's daughter who went to five high schools found the experience so painful and confusing that she has blocked it out of her memory almost entirely. An Air Force general's daughter who moved only once in high school retains vivid memories. "It was a very traumatic experience," she said.

I was attending a small high school in Illinois, and I knew nearly everyone. I was very active: cheerleader, class officer, head of the French Club and the Pep Club—all of that made me feel very good about myself. Then my parents dropped the bomb that we were leaving all this—in the middle of my junior year—to go to a large metropolitan area where the school would be about three times the size of that one. To try to establish myself in a new school in a year's time. . . . I developed almost a noncaring attitude. I remember thinking, What's the use? Why should I bother? I continued to do well in school—I was always highly motivated to achieve—but the personal investment wasn't there. I feel absolutely no attachment to that high school.

The daughter of a Navy lieutenant commander told of feeling very upset when, in the middle of her sophomore year, her father received orders to go overseas for three years. Her relief was correspondingly enormous when her parents decided the family would not go with him. As much as she loved her father, it was easier to say goodbye to him for three years than to face being uprooted from high school.

COPING WITH MOBILITY

For children, the hardships of moving all revolve around loss: loss of friends, loss of status, loss of security, loss of identity. This kind of loss is part and parcel of military life, and very likely always will be. Even if tours of duty were made twice as long as they were when I was growing up, and families only moved seven or eight times instead of fifteen or twenty, the problems of dislocation and overwhelming loss would still be there. Even if a family knew it would only have to uproot three or four times, it would still be living with the specter of inevitable dislocation, which would inhibit every family member's social invest-ment in the community.

The recurring problem of loss is essentially the same for all military brats. The interesting thing is that some military children obviously handle it better than others. There has been some research to shed light on why.

First of all, it was shown some time ago that families handle any kind of stress much better if they have certain traits, such as stability, affection among the members, a good relationship between husband and wife, good parent-child relations, family council type of decision making, and previous experience with crisis.[4] In other words, the healthiest, most cohesive families are, unsurprisingly, more likely to handle stress better than families that do not meet that description.

Two researchers at Walter Reed Army Hospital compared a group of disturbed military children with a group of normal military children. Mobility was high in both groups, so it was automatically ruled out as the differentiating condition. What the researchers did find out, however, is that certain attitudes held by the parents were markedly different in the two groups. "Mothers of normal children appear significantly more accepting of frequent location, and both mothers and fathers of normal children show a stronger identification with the military community."[5]

What it boils down to is that in most military families, kids take their cues on how to handle the stress of moving from their parents, and most often from their mothers. If the mother handles the move well, chances are the kid will, too. If she doesn't, the child may well have big problems.

This should come as no surprise. Because military children are so transient, they do not have the benefit of extended family or stable community in shaping their sense of self or helping them cope with stress. Even the military child's peer group, though very important, is so fluid that its stabilizing influence is limited compared to that of a rooted child. This means that by far the most powerful influences on the military child are going to be the nuclear family and the military lifestyle in which it is caught up. If there are any major problems in that family—alcoholism, abuse of any kind, marital problems, disruptive mental or physical illnesses—the stabilizing influences are again severely diminished.

The military brats I interviewed who seemed to have handled moves the best came from nonalcoholic families that saw to it the children felt wanted, loved, and respected, and that had two additional characteristics: an unwavering sense of commitment to the Military Mission shared by the entire family, so that the mobility was accepted without question and orders were greeted with excitement; and the full participation of *both* parents in smoothing the transition for everyone.

Holly's family is an example. One of seven children of an Air Force pilot, Holly went to eleven schools in three countries. The logistics of moving such a large family—and all its pets—must have been daunting. "I imagine it was hilarious to see us on a cross-country trip," she said. "Every time we stopped at a gas station every one of us would get out and each one had some kind of animal on a leash, walking it." Holly's mother was there for her children, as so many mothers are. But what was really striking in her story was the role her father played in helping his children adjust to change.

Holly said that whenever new orders were in the offing, her father would come home, gather everyone together, and tell them the list of three or four choices he'd been given so that they could discuss it as a family. "Probably he already knew where he had to go," Holly said, "but he always made us think we helped out in the decision." Once the family was settled in the new place, Holly's father planned outings for the whole family to see the sights of the area; the family has a treasure chest of such memories. In the days before the kids made new friends, he made a special effort to spend time with them, usually playing sports. And one time when his orders called for him to precede the family to an overseas assignment by several months, he regularly sent tapes in which he spoke to his wife and each child individually, describing the new place and answering questions.

Few things could approach the involvement of a loving parent—or especially, *two* loving parents—in helping a child cope with the traumatic losses associated with moving. But even the best parents can't do it all, and not every child has a close family to fall back on.

That's where family pets turn out to be extremely valuable.

The Role of Family Pets

In story after story, military brats told about the critical importance of pets at the time of a move. Dog or cat, bird or turtle, the pet supplied a badly needed sense of continuity—as well as a friend.

"Pets are something you can cling to," said a Navy chief petty officer's son whose family took three poodles with them through every move, even overseas. "They're something that will always be there. You go out for the day and everything and everyone is new and different—then you come home and find your pet. It's safe."

By the same token, military brats say that having to give up their pets because of a move is devastating. Warren, the son of an Army colonel, told of being forced to give up the family dog before every move. "That was probably the single most painful aspect of moving," he said. "By the time I was in high school, we'd had between twelve and fourteen dogs. What happens in the long run is that you develop a certain immunity to getting attached to anything."

Many military brats told stories of how one or both parents wanted to get rid of the family pet at the time of a move. It happened in my family, too. When my brother was thirteen and we were about to leave Germany for the States, our father ordered him to give away his beloved German shepherd. The loss was terrible for him. Some years later, when I was nine, my father received orders to go to France—and told me my pet beagle couldn't come with us. In this case, though, my father also adamantly refused to let me give her away. Over our tearful protests, he ordered my mother to take the healthy, year-old dog to the post vet the next day to be put to sleep. My father never gave me a reason for his position, but I do know that it was an unhappy time in his career. Although my mother and I always feared to cross him, on this occasion we succeeded in giving the dog away behind his back.

Of course, one might expect power confrontations over pets to occur in dysfunctional authoritarian families such as mine. What emerged from the interviews, however, is that even relatively happy, close-knit military families have such stories to tell. One Army colonel's daughter described the emotional climate in her family as on the whole very loving—except for one frightening episode when her parents fought all night, and she felt sure they were going to get a divorce. The issue was that two days before the family was to move, her father had secretly taken the family cat way out into the country and dropped it off at a farm. "It was a blow to my mother and to all of us kids, too," she said.

Moves are severely trying times even in the healthiest families. Fights, power struggles, and other irrational behavior are not unusual, and should not be taken as indexes of a family's overall emotional health. What these stories do reveal, however, is the need for greater sensitivity to the role pets play in helping children handle moves.

Special Adaptations

Military brats go through so many moves, are faced with so many situations in which we must start from scratch to re-create ourselves socially, that it is no wonder we react to the challenge in similar ways. Over and over again, the same adaptations turned up in the military brats I interviewed.

The first adaptation, as noted earlier, is denial of the pain caused by uprooting. The pain of loss is plowed under, and there it sits—not consciously recognized or attended to, but nevertheless informing the way military brats handle situations and relationships, even in later life. Denial of emotional pain is so reflexive to military brats—and others who experience frequent uprootings—that it is the undergirding to most of the other adaptations to change. Following are five of the most common adaptations; nearly every military brat interviewed for this book has experienced at least four of them.

Adaptation No. 1: The Military Brat Antenna

As they weather one move after another growing up, military brats often develop a remarkable intuitive ability that can best be described as an invisible antenna tuned to a special private frequency. With it they are able to detect other military brats at a glance—even though outwardly there are few if any differences from civilian kids. The antenna also enables them to fairly accurately guess the rank of the military brat's father—all without having exchanged a word.

If this seems impossible, consider that nearly every military brat I interviewed, plus quite a few more I asked in informal situations, said they could remember having this ability to detect other military brats, or to guess the rank of a military brat's father, or both. And consider, too, that there were very good reasons for us to have it.

The antenna was activated every time we found ourselves in new surroundings—such as the first day in a new school, or on board ship going to a new destination—and our need for connection with others of our own kind was most acute. Many of us knew we had this ability, and in retrospect many of us know exactly why.

When I asked the son of a Navy commander to speculate on why he had the antenna, the response was instantaneous. "Identification," he said. "Where do I fit in? Who are the folks who are safe, versus the ones who aren't? Who are the military versus the townies and who are the officers' kids versus the enlisted? Because I gotta find a connection with somebody *quick.*"

The only military brats I spoke to who could not remember having the ability to instantly tell another military brat from a civilian were a few Navy brats who went to schools that were almost entirely civilian, and a few brats from other services who went only to military-dependent schools where there were no civilians.

Nearly all, however, could recall knowing instinctively the probable rank of another military brat's father, again before a single word had been exchanged. This ability to tell rank—often so finely honed that one could distinguish between, say, the child of a major and the child of a colonel—is critical for many military brats, because their social world is so thoroughly stratified. Many officer children are strictly forbidden by their parents to play with enlisted children—a subject which will be explored in depth in the next chapter. But since enlisted and officer kids are thrown together in the same schools, both groups need the antenna in order to know from the outset who is who, and avoid uncomfortable social situations.

How the antenna operates is almost impossible for military brats to articulate, perhaps because the ability is so intuitive and nonrational. Although I had a very reliable antenna myself, I am uncertain how it worked. It's true that sometimes visual clues made identity obvious to anyone; for instance, when I was growing up, military sons often sported haircuts that were dead giveaways. But not always.

Another clue was eyeglasses; at the time, the glasses worn by military brats had a certain generic style to them—the frames were either a translucent putty color, or an opaque black. I remember being the hit of my all–military brat fifth grade class after I discovered that when I breathed on the right lens, a small white circle appeared bearing the words *Government Issue.* We thought it was hilarious that it could mean either where the glasses came from or who they were for.

But visual cues do not come close to explaining the antenna, my interviewees agreed. For one thing, they do nothing to explain how the antenna worked in parochial schools, where the children all wore similar uniforms and, presumably, not all the military brats wore GI glasses. It also cannot explain how the antenna still sometimes works in adulthood, when there are no discernible differences between military brats and civilians.

On a number of occasions as an adult my antenna has, unbidden, let me know I was in the presence of a military brat. Once, when I was twenty-seven, I was standing around at a fund-raising party for journalists. It was a large group, and I knew almost no one. Idly I watched a young guy in blue jeans and a plaid shirt, with longish hair, as he walked over to the drinks table. Suddenly I knew, beyond any doubt, that he was an Army brat and the son of an NCO. He turned around, catching my eye, and immediately walked over. "You're an Army brat, too, aren't you?" he said. He also knew I was an officer's daughter. I still don't know what it was our antennas picked up; when it came to dress and demeanor, we appeared to be cut from the same cloth. Another time, in my thirties, I was looking around in a house that our realtor was showing us, when it came to me that he was a Navy brat and his father was a captain. The intuition proved correct. While there have been many times my antenna has failed to tell me that someone was a military brat, when it *has* worked it has never been wrong.

Adaptation No. 2: Ability to Mimic

If the antenna is a shortcut to making social connections, so is the ability to mimic. Most military brats report having at least one of its variations: easy imitation of accents, dialect, and rhythms of speech; an excellent ear for languages; easy comprehension of people who do not speak English well or have speech impairments; an ability to do impressions that are dead-on.

All of these things help military brats cut down the time it takes to win acceptance. And all of them stem from the same basic survival technique. "You have to learn how to watch, and how to listen," said the son of an Air Force sergeant. "Because you don't have much time to fit in."

The ability to mimic serves us well as children, and it continues to serve us well in adulthood: Knowing how to watch and listen is surely one of the greatest gifts bestowed upon us by life inside the Fortress. In some cases it is a tremendous resource professionally, and may even influence the choice of career. A colonel's daughter who is a playwright said she attributes her ear for dialogue to her transient childhood in the Air Force. The son of an Air Force colonel directly linked his transient childhood to the fact that he became a linguist and language instructor. And it may be no accident that quite a few military brats have attained success as actors—Robert Duvall, Faye Dunaway, Swoozie Kurtz, James Woods, Victoria Principal, and Robert Hays among them.

I asked a Navy commander's son, now a social worker, if he had the ability to mimic accents. "Definitely," he said. "Any accent you want. If I can hear it twice, I can do it." He went on to say that he uses the ability daily in his work. "One of the styles of therapy I use is the communication school of therapy. A basic tenet of that style is 'Send your message in their language.' I won't adopt a particular dialect, but I will follow the rhythm and the pattern of however a client is talking, and I will pattern my voice inflections. I'll talk to them using their vocabulary level, rhythm and pattern."

I've certainly done the same thing in my work as a journalist, and have found that even with a hostile subject it helps gain a measure of acceptance for the duration of the interview. We are talking here about something quite effective, yet quite subtle. I doubt if many of the Navy son's clients, or my interviewees, ever knew we were altering our styles in order to be better heard and accepted. What they may well have noted, however, is the intensity with which we listened to their every word.

In fact, the various skills of watching, listening, and imitating come so naturally to military brats that for the most part we don't have to consciously decide to use them; it's all built in, like the military brat antenna.

Occasionally, however, the problem arises of how to shut it *off*. It is very difficult for some military brats in the midst of a conversation to keep someone else's pronounced accent from creeping into their own.

Adaptation No. 3: Forced Extroversion

The teachers I've talked to say that the military brats they've taught tend to be more outgoing than other kids. Some of the other adjectives I've heard are "loud," "assertive," "brazen," and "bold."

These kinds of attributes, in children who are not troublemakers, are often favored by teachers and parents, who tend to interpret them as signs of well-adjusted, thriving, spirited individuals. The point here is not to deny that these are signs of healthy adjustment, but to advance an alternative notion—that, like the military brat antenna and the ability to mimic, these are behaviors acquired for social survival.

For military brats, time is always short. They can't afford to wait around to be noticed or for invitations to drift in. So they often force themselves to take the stage, stand out in the crowd. "You're either going to learn how to be an extrovert," commented the daughter of an Air Force pilot, "or you're going to be a real neurotic person." Or as the son of an Air Force sergeant commented, "The military life either makes or breaks your personality. It *will* force your personality to change. If you're outgoing anyway, you're lucky. But what if you're a homebody type person, and you're forced to move around?"

The lively, bold behavior observed by teachers and others is what I call *forced extroversion:* extroverted behavior whether or not the individual is an extrovert naturally. That would account for the often frenetically outgoing nature of military brats, many of whom are in effect forcing their personalities into an alien style. "My technique was to make jokes all the time," said the daughter of an Air Force colonel. "I was a real contradiction in terms. I was really a shy kid underneath it all, but a comedian on the surface."

And the notion of forced extroversion seems to fit with something else that turned up in interviews: military brats who experience themselves as far less extroverted in adulthood than they were during their military rearing. Extroversion, in other words, is a temporary survival style. If we come by it naturally, it is heavily reinforced—and frequently exaggerated—by the transient lifestyle of the military. If we are not naturally extroverted, we pick it up anyway as a kind of temporary overlay on the personality.

I suspect that forced extroversion is one of the things picked up by the military brat antenna. It may be that, to military brats anyway, there is a detectable difference between a civilian who is naturally outgoing and a military brat who is hell-bent on gaining acceptance. Perhaps military brat extroversion has a more insistent quality to it, a desperation that other military brats pick up on because they identify with it themselves. Where a civilian might see a given military brat as outgoing, socially adroit, and undaunted by new circumstances, another military brat sees the risk-taking social behavior of a kindred soul.

The antenna, though, is capable of great subtlety. Even less outgoing military brats can be picked up by it. In those cases it may be the quickness of a smile, the plea for friendship written in the eyes, or even something else: an air of resignation that seems to say *I've got nothing to lose because I've lost it all before.*

Forced extroversion has its useful side in later life: The behavior becomes so tried and true that even if our extroversion goes underground in adulthood, it can be pulled out when needed. For some military brats it becomes such an important ingredient in their identity that it shapes their lives. The constant role changes, the re-creation of self in new environments. . . . Military brats grow up learning how to put themselves *out there* on the social stage, gambling everything on their skills at attracting attention, winning approval, getting over an image.

Added to the list of actors are a number of successful military brat singers and musicians: Emmylou Harris, Tina Weymouth, Jim Morrison, Kris Kristofferson, John Denver.

In its most positive manifestations during the school years, the forced extroversion of military brats propels them beyond grade-getting into the rarefied company of high achievers in activities requiring public performance. Many tell of going all out for awards, school office, athletic teams, band, drama, and other clubs as a means of integrating into the group in short order. As with high grades, adults interpret this as evidence of superior ability and fine character. They are not necessarily wrong about that, but it might be more in line to view these things as evidence of the skill military brats perfect in answer to a desperate need to gain social footing on new ground.

Military brats learn fairly quickly to exploit the comparatively relaxed environment of most civilian schools. Awards, leadership roles, parts in the play—all are pretty much there for the asking if a kid wants them badly enough and is willing to put in the hard work needed to get them. Other kids by and large fall back in the face of the hard-driving ambition of the military brat. An admiral's daughter told of going to five high schools and, as a gifted clarinetist, playing in all five bands. A number of military brats told of running for—and walking away with —class offices, sometimes within weeks of arriving in a new school. An Army major's daughter, a talented artist, said, "I knew that by using art, wherever I was, I could plug in. We [military brats] were like the traveling Jews: You pick up your violin, and the next place you go, you can join the symphony."

But not all military brats wind up as superachievers. There is another method of social integration that does not invite much approval from authorities but which is a far quicker route to social success: joining the out-group. Out-groups are always looking for new members. If the military brat plays his or her cards right, it's possible to wind up in an out-group almost immediately—or as an honorary member of all the out-groups, for that matter.

Brian, the troubled son of a Navy officer, was a veteran of eleven schools and became very adept at playing the out-groups. "I seemed to pick up friends better among people who weren't in social cliques," he said.

I would be attracted to those who were rejected by the group as a whole. That's the type person I'd make friends with.

In high school, I had friends in every gang. I was into drugs, which was the universal gang. I dealt drugs to all the different groups, so I got along with everyone. When I dealt to the blacks I was real cool and real hip talking—when you dealt with gangs you had to act the way the gang acted, had to conform to 'em. I was playing the role of fitting in with everyone, just to be accepted. If you're in the military, you have to be real easygoing to get into the new group. You're the stranger in town, so you've got to be someone that everyone likes.

Brian, who is white, went to high school in the South at a time of racial strife. He told how one day he was about to be beaten up by a black gang when a powerful black friend intervened to protect him. "That's how I escaped getting into real trouble generally," he explained. "I had friends in all the gangs."

There is another way to describe the effect of forced extroversion in the life of a military brat: looking at the speed with which friendships are made. "How long did it take you?" I'd ask the brat. "About an hour," said one. "Thirty seconds," said another. "Four days at the most," said a third, "and that's in bad times." An Air Force sergeant's son said, "I still do it today: I can make friends with someone while standing in the checkout line at the grocery store."

Sometimes, though, a young military brat's route to new friends was unavoidably rough. A number of military sons said a dreaded part of each move was the certainty that they would have to endure a series of fistfights before things sorted themselves out. Sometimes the fights were with civilian kids, sometimes with other military sons—but, as discussed in Chapter 5, some kind of fight was very frequently the first portal through which a son would have to pass to establish himself with his male peers.

"The worst was going into eighth grade in [a town in New England]," said Craig, an Air Force sergeant's son. "That was the most savage. Those [civilian] kids had been together since kindergarten. It was a working class area, with a lot of toughs just waiting a year so they could quit school legally. Most of my energy the first couple of weeks went to fighting—first one group, then the other. Then they stopped coming to look me up. It was a ritual you had to go through."

The hazards are different for a military daughter, who mainly has to find a way to work herself into a closed group of girls. One technique I heard of repeatedly is something I used myself as a child and which I called, even then, the confessional impulse. The idea is simple: Waste no time in spilling family secrets and personal problems—that sends the clear message *I'm investing in you. Will you invest in me?* If the other girl antes up, as she almost always will, the budding friendship has been cemented by mutual confession. Civilian girls, I noticed over the years, tend to be much more guarded about family secrets; they, of course, have to stick around to live with the consequences if a confessional investment backfires. For military daughters, however, secrets are a cheap commodity, and one of the few resources they can use to manipulate someone else into almost instant friendship. And it certainly qualifies as manipulation. A civilian on the receiving end of a military brat confession typically accords it much more weight and significance than it represents to the military brat. Before she knows it, the civilian finds herself investing heavily in the relationship, unaware that the military daughter, in many cases, can drop it in a flash without a backward glance.

For the military daughter, the problem is that if the new friendship, hasty as it is, turns out to be a mismatch, the military brat has to live with the discomfort of having invested too much in someone who might not respect the confidence. But not for long; mobility will see to that.

Sometimes the confessional impulse persists into adulthood, until the daughter learns to modify it. "When I first taught school," said the daughter of a Navy lieutenant commander, "I lived alone for two years. I got lonely. You get very lonely. One day I said to another young teacher, 'Why don't we go shopping after school?' I told her how much I needed a friend. It was a very vulnerable point for me, and I said too much. I remember after she left I thought to myself, Why did I say all those things? Then it came back in my face that she'd told someone else I was probably a lesbian. She'd misinterpreted entirely; I was just saying I needed someone right then and there to talk to. I got a lot more conservative in my approach after that."

Another friendship adaptation that frequently persists into adulthood—and is as common for sons as for daughters—is for the military brat to play the role of the Needed One, the person others will run to for comfort, advice, or to manage some problem for them. (This is a role which may be exacerbated if the military brat is the child of an alcoholic.) Since military brats are usually quite competent at handling a wide variety of life situations, it's a part that comes naturally. But it does exact a price.

"I have good friends but they're very dependent on me," the Navy lieutenant commander's daughter said. "If somebody's got a problem, it's me they come to. In the last two months, for instance. A friend's wife tried to kill him with a .357 magnum, and he came to me for help. And then there was the case of a teacher who was molesting kids. Another teacher couldn't bring herself to go to the authorities, so she came to me, knowing I would take it on. I did.

"I'm not bragging, because I think it's a detriment. It wrings me out sometimes, and leaves them in the clear. It's terrible. And when you need somebody yourself, it's very hard to turn that around."

Adaptation No. 4: Traveling Light

By the time a military brat with this adaptation reaches adulthood, the lesson has been well learned: Don't invest heavily in relationships. It's painful not to, but the pain isn't as acute as that of investing and losing. Using the mask of denial, which military brats have so readily to hand, it is a relatively simple matter to convince oneself that close friendships aren't necessary anyway.

Grace, the Air Force general's daughter who married into the military herself, sounded bitter as she reflected on this. "Superficiality and lack of intimacy in relationships . . . I really think these are characteristic of the military," she said hotly. "A lot of people thrive on that. It means they don't *have* to get involved emotionally. I see it almost as an avoidance of growing up, a prolongation of adolescence. It is also the nature of the lifestyle, that we don't have the opportunity to develop long-term relationships."

This last point is important. It does not mean that military people are shallow—merely that the lifestyle forces them to limit themselves to shallow interactions. In that world of swirling social currents, where people are washed in and swept away on inexplicable tides, nothing else makes sense. To have a close friendship, after all, is to have a pact of mutual support *over time*; close friends live in the expectation that the investments of yesterday and today will be returned tomorrow. Inside the Fortress, where there is no shared yesterday and no shared tomorrow, close friendships can't take hold.

For military brats, the result is a paradox. We grow up with superb social skills, and are constantly refining ourselves to be more and more likable—but typically we have few friends. Sam, an Air Force general's son who became an Army officer, said, "If I were not married now, and had to count the number of friends I have on my own, I would have next to zero—and that would not be peculiar in the military." He said he feels he has missed something by not having a community of long-term friends, but he's not really sure what. Nearly all military brats share this feeling. We observe a sense of connectedness in others that seems to be deeply satisfying to them—but we do not know firsthand what it feels like, or how to find it. (The search for belonging is further discussed in the last chapter of this book.)

Most of the time this paucity of friends remains a purely private matter. But there are some moments in life when our habit of traveling light in friendships becomes painfully obvious. Judy, a Navy officer's

daughter who married a civilian with deep roots, told of the contrast at
her wedding. Of the two hundred guests, all but a handful were her
husband's friends and relatives.

Some military brats point to thick address books as testimony to the
large number of their friendships; the books are filled with hundreds of
names collected during years of wandering. What this says to me is
that it is very important for these military brats to live with the illusion
of being rich in friendship. And it is an illusion, because most of those
names would fall into the category of enjoyable acquaintances in a
particular pocket of the past, with little likelihood of reconnection in
the future.

It's true that in American English the term *friend* is thrown around
loosely, and civilians also apply it to superficial and sporadic social
contacts. The difference lies in what those "friendships" represent to
the owners of the address books. I suspect that the military brat puts a
lot more stock in the address book, believing the names represent more
than they do. It may be that belief in the illusion of a large network of
friends is a psychological necessity—an antidote to the loneliness that
is the cruelest legacy of the transient life.

Loneliness. For a great many military brats, this is the paradoxical
truth of their childhood in the mobile warrior society: a terrible
aloneness despite the thousands of people who flowed through their
lives. It is also a truth many of them deny well into adulthood, until
introspection or therapy forces it out.

"When I think about my childhood, it is one long, painful wail,"
said Maya, the daughter of an Army physician. "What's surfacing now
[through soul-searching prompted by Alcoholics Anonymous] is the
gut-wrenching loneliness of my childhood. A little-girl-lost type of
loneliness. *Intense* loneliness. I remember crying for one entire summer between my junior and senior years of high school. I would talk to
myself in the mirror to comfort myself."

When I asked this attractive, pleasant, intelligent young woman if,
in adulthood, she finds it easy to dissolve friendships, she said, "I don't
have any friendships I *can* dissolve. I just don't develop friendships; I
don't know how. I mean, I *know* how—you have to call people on the
phone—but I get this feeling of *why bother*. People come, people go.
It's that fear again: fear of loss."

Adaptation No. 5: Ease in Saying Goodbye

If military brats are good at saying hello, we are at least as good at
saying goodbye. Too good, many admit. Call it cutting our losses; call
it scar tissue. Whatever name one uses, it was by far one of the most

common ways we handled loss as children, and it is an adaptation often carried into adulthood. Being the first to say goodbye, or being shockingly cold-blooded about it, is a way we deceive ourselves into thinking we are in control.

This is different from the adaptation of traveling light, which amounts to the withholding of emotional investment. The "goodbye" reflex, by contrast, kicks in whether the relationships to be truncated are superficial or very deep.

A Navy officer's daughter I interviewed has a lively, ebullient personality and is in general the sort of person who moves through life with a phalanx of friends. But, she confided, "I can't identify too many people I couldn't walk away from next week. It sounds cold but it isn't. It's natural to me." The problem, of course, is that civilian friends wind up feeling confused and hurt if they assume there is more of a commitment on the part of the military brat than there turns out to be.

The daughter of a Marine sergeant said, "My task is to learn not to let go too quickly. That's difficult for me. If something looks like it's going to be problematic, it's jettisoned immediately, whether it is a circumstance or a person. Especially people. People, you know, come and go. They can be jettisoned."

One of the things military brats find out quickly growing up is the importance of saying goodbye to the past and all who inhabited it. It's easier to handle the loss—or to trick ourselves into thinking we've handled it—if our first act in the new place is to burn all bridges behind us. Although there were a few exceptions, most of the military brats I interviewed do not keep up friendships once they move on. They don't write letters, don't make phone calls. What's over is over.

One Army sergeant's daughter, asked if she ever wrote letters to old friends as a child, recalled matter-of-factly, "It was my father's world. We were just appendages. We weren't expected or encouraged to keep up with anyone." But it isn't necessary to blame the parents. The tendency to break ties cleanly may be something that just comes naturally to military brats, and for one overriding reason: We need to.

"It's like the Texan who gets rid of his Rolls-Royce when the ashtray is dirty," an Air Force colonel's daughter told me. "I'm excellent at making friends quickly, wherever I am. But I don't write letters. It's a matter of 'out of sight, out of mind.' We develop that as a protective mechanism. If we let ourselves care about all the people we've lost, we'd be crazy."

THE CONSEQUENCES

When I lived in Chicago, I worked in the Loop. Every day I would catch the El downtown and join the great river of urban workers pouring through the streets. The observers of this twice-daily deluge were the street bums and bag ladies huddled immobile in doorways or sprawled along the edge of Grant Park. The curious thing—and I now realize this is a very curious thing, though it seemed quite natural at the time—is that I didn't identify with the thousands of office workers around me. I identified with the street bums.

The thought would come to me as I walked, quietly inserting itself into whatever I had been thinking. *The only difference between me and that bag lady is our position on the pavement.* It was not a dismaying thought or even a striking one—just the registering of an observation I recognized as true in some fundamental way. It never occurred to me to repeat it to anyone else; in the first place, it was just a mental notation, not meant to be voiced. In the second place, the idea would certainly have lacked credibility for anyone who knew me—for in appearance, manner, and lifestyle, I was a long way from a street bum. But there the thought would be, as much a part of my daily life as the packed underground platform at Washington and Randolph.

Occasionally I'd try to figure out how it was I saw truth in it. I never had a clue—until the first interview I did with a military brat, when somehow I happened to mention it. Suddenly I understood. Why shouldn't I identify with street bums? Like me, they're very portable people. They're resourceful. They don't *belong* anywhere. They're physically in the community but emotionally outside of it. And they know that the only thing they really have is inside their skins.

I did not envy them their poverty, their literal homelessness, the emotional barrenness of their lives. There were real differences between them and me. But in some sense, too, there was a kindred spirit.

I remember a rabbi once telling me about the strong emphasis his parents put on education, and why that is so common in Jewish households: "My mother would tell us children, 'They can take everything away from you but the storehouse of your brains.' " Many years later, a Palestinian told me almost the very same thing. He pointed to UN statistics showing that Palestinians have the highest number of advanced degrees per capita of any people in the world. "If we had land, we would work the land," he said. "If we had factories, we would work in the factories. But we don't have land or factories, so we go to school, and more school, and more school."

So it was with a sense of déjà vu that I listened to an Army sergeant's daughter tell me of her mother's words echoing through her childhood: "Get yourself an education. That's the only thing that will always be yours. And if your husband treats you bad, your education will be your escape." There would certainly be no hometown to run to, and very likely no extended family to count on. The message was clear: Prepare yourself, for you have no other refuge you can count on.

The Psychological Diaspora

The first legacy of military childhood transience is what might be called the psychological diaspora. As adults most of us manage to slow or stop the moving—and yet still we find ourselves caught up in a strange migration. It is a migration of the soul, all the more mysterious to us because it has no clear origin and no certain goal.

There is only one antidote to the angst of the diaspora. Belonging. It is not easy for a military brat to learn what that even means, much less to find it. Yet belonging is the single greatest quest of our lives, a quest that lives in many of us as a powerful unnamed yearning.

My feeling is that it is crucial for military brats to put the right name to this yearning, face our unrequited need to belong, and address it as best we can. Because if we do not, the yearning, like anything imprisoned in the unconscious, will play havoc with our lives.

In the last interview I had with Brian, the alcoholic, very troubled Navy son who gravitated to out-groups as a boy, I asked him to describe the first time in his adult life he had felt as though he belonged.

"I still don't belong," he said, his voice breaking. "I still don't fit in anywhere. I feel left out, alienated. That's what's always happened in my life. It hurts."

Those of us born into the psychological diaspora must find our way out of it, or suffer the consequences.

We must find our own answers to the unresolved question of belonging. And we do find belonging, partially—although the nature of belonging, for those not born to it, is that it must be found over and over again.

Another corollary seems to be that for military brats, a prerequisite to belonging is grieving over not belonging and repeated loss. That stands to reason: It is necessary to break down the old immunity to attachment before one can become attached to something new. And belonging, more than anything else, is about attachment.

With concerted effort, it is possible in adulthood for military brats to largely resolve the dilemma of the diaspora. And that holds true for two other difficult legacies of our childhood wanderings as well: delayed maturity, and problems with commitment.

Delayed Maturity

It's no wonder military brats are sometimes perplexing to civilians: We present two conflicting versions of ourselves. The first involves an old-before-our-time, seen-it-all-before composure and savoir faire that leads people to think we are unusually mature for our age. The second, which generally takes civilians much longer to perceive, is an incredible naiveté that leads us to make terrible blunders in our relationships. It's as though in the school of life we skipped a few grades, and in so doing missed the fundamentals.

The fact is, we *did*. Certain lessons about dealing with people, friend as well as foe, cannot be learned on the run. Until we grow up and slow down, we generally do not know how to deal with people long term.

Take, for instance, the problem of how to deal with an enemy. An Air Force sergeant's son put it succinctly: "You make an enemy, you know him at most for two years. By that time either his parents will be transferred out or yours will be." There is no pressure to face things, deal with the matter maturely. But when one day the military brat finds the escape route is no longer open, it can be jarring.

"The worst adjustment for me was in high school, when my father retired," said Mitchell, the son of a Marine lieutenant colonel. "I realized he was never again going to gratify me by coming home and saying, 'Hey, we're going to move!' Always before, if I didn't like a place at least I knew we were going to leave. Part of the painful adjustment in high school was realizing that the kids I pissed off and did not get along with were going to be in the same class with me next year."

The same holds true for friends. The lesson we skipped: how to handle a friend who disappoints you. "That's one thing I didn't get a chance to learn about," said Ellen, an Army colonel's daughter. When her best friend in high school began to change and pulled away from her, Ellen was deeply hurt. But she couldn't bring herself to deal with it, and continued to bleed for the remainder of her time in that school. "I just ignored the situation," she said. "I was really glad when my dad got orders. I was sorry I'd be missing my senior year of high school in that school, but . . . I've always wondered how people who are born and raised in the same town deal with things like that. Because for them it's not something that's going to go away through your moving. Moving was always an easy out."

If through transience military brats fail to learn how to deal mature-ly with enemies and problematic friendships, we also learn little about working through other kinds of problems. An Army lieutenant colonel's son described how his childhood patterns haunt him in adulthood. "I don't have a sense of continuity," he said. "I seem to change jobs and career paths every couple of years. I don't have a strong sense of fighting out problems at work; it's easier to go do something else."

Another lesson we skipped, a lesson critical to developing into a mature adult, is personal accountability. If you don't stick around, you don't have to pay your dues. Eric, an Air Force sergeant's son, told of a brother who styled himself as a troublemaker because it was a very portable identity, and he never had to pay for it. "That was his way of getting attention," Eric said. "My way was to be smart in school. So we each did our own thing. What happens is that you have to decide how you're going to handle this moving all the time; are you going to get in trouble, or what? It was so easy for my brother to get in trouble, because just when things were bad, we got stationed someplace else, or the father of the person he was in trouble with would get transferred. I mean I watched him. He was always saved, like a boxer when the bell rings. There are so many avenues of escape. It's too easy."

After personal relationships and personal accountability, there is a third big area of delayed maturity for military brats: the consistent self.

An essential ingredient of the mature individual is a sense of self solid enough to be one's constant touchstone. It means having a consistent set of values and a way of being in the world that is so natural it is reflexive.

Arriving at a consistent self is very difficult for military brats; it is antithetical to our entire experience. Moving constantly is about changing self constantly. We grow up continually rewriting our personal scripts in order to fit in. We are social chameleons, and we know it. We also know that someday that has to stop, and that learning how to stop is going to be painful: It involves facing the fact that we are who we are, imperfections and all. We can't go on endlessly expecting to be liked by everybody; sooner or later we have to bite the bullet and allow somebody to dislike us, without falling apart.

That may be one reason, aside from lack of geographic roots, that few military brats run for public office despite the idealism and sense of public service that characterize us as a group. Making enemies is a fact of public life.

"If someone doesn't like me, I can't handle it," said Eric. "I think, Why? What did I do? I'm so *used* to fitting in and making friends. There are very few people who, if they don't like me, I can say I don't care. Probably just two percent. It should be a much higher percentage."

Brian is an example of a classic social chameleon. "I used to be . . .

someone who would conform to other people's standards," he said. "If I had five friends, I'd act five different ways. If one friend liked rock 'n' roll and being wild, I would too. If another liked classical music, I'd sit around and be real quiet and make intelligent conversation. And so on. I couldn't handle parties: I had to act too many different ways at once, and I couldn't do it."

I asked Carl, the Navy commander's son and therapist, to comment on military brats as social chameleons. He said that for a long time it was a term he used to describe himself. "The difficulty is finding the real you under the ability to look like anything," he said. "That's the bottom line. Because if you can't do that . . . You see, being a chameleon has advantages, but they are time-limited. Eventually all the people that you're trying to blend in to please leave you. They die. They go away. So basically you're going to be a blank wall—and about that time you better have some Real You down there, or else you're in big time trouble."

Problems with Commitment

If there's one thing military brats know how to do, it's start over. What we don't do nearly as well is *stick things out*. This is strongly related to the problem of delayed maturity, but shows up in so many ways in military brats that it merits expanded treatment.

For an Air Force colonel's daughter I spoke to, the many problems with commitment she'd experienced in her adult life boiled down to one apt metaphor. "I can't commit to kitchen curtains," she said succinctly. Even though she was well into adulthood and had lived in one house for ten years, she just couldn't do it. Kitchen curtains, she explained, are things that you can't take with you; it's a certainty they won't work in the next home you have. And somehow she couldn't shake the notion that there would always be another move.

Military brats do not well understand permanence—whether physical, temporal, or emotional. In fact many of us have trouble thinking more than two years down the line.

Eric, for instance, went to one college for four years and, except for his junior year abroad, lived in the same furnished apartment the whole time—a remarkable exercise in consistency for a young military brat. Except for one thing: He never used the closets or the dresser drawers. "I would fold up my clothes and keep them in a suitcase," he said, "or in cartons I got from Safeway." The idea that he could decamp at any moment had to be a concrete part of his present. Some years later, when I interviewed him for this book, he was agonizing over just having bought his first pieces of furniture; always before he had lived in furnished places. The idea of owning something he would now have to carry around with him was so disturbing he was considering sending it all back.

Temporariness. This is the concept at the heart of our perceptions, our values, our approach to the world. The extent to which this is true—and the terrible danger inherent in that—was made clear by an Air Force colonel's daughter I met early in my research, who spoke matter-of-factly about the way she looks at things. "Everything was temporary when I was growing up," she said. "And that's the way I look at my life now: My job's only temporary. These clothes I'm wearing, this corporate image, is only temporary. My relationships are only going to be temporary."

Eric is another example. He found that emotionally, too, he was forever living out of suitcases. "I always have problems with relationships," he said. "My girlfriends never know it's because I have such a hard time with commitment, but I always do. It's always a fight for me. . . . I remember that until I had one particular girlfriend, I had no understanding of loss. I was more into patterns. I would be with someone for a while, then I would stop it or it would just stop. It was so natural. It didn't affect me; it was really strange. My girlfriends would be hurt and I wouldn't understand why, because I could just stop. It was like it was time to stop. I would be with someone every day for a year, and then I would stop doing it and I didn't know why."

Lorna, daughter of an Air Force colonel, brought up a variation on the problem of commitment in relationships. "I always felt that the men I've been involved with had a problem with commitment," she said. "But I've come to realize I was projecting *my* problem with commitment onto them. I was also choosing men I knew couldn't make a commitment: married, long-distance, seminarian, gay, etc. However, I have always longed for a committed, lifelong partner. At times I've been pretty close to that, but then I got restless." She explained that at the time of the interview, she was in a very gratifying relationship with a man who lived over an hour's drive away from her. Neither one was willing to relocate.

"I do often wonder at myself, that I find it easier to be intimate with those who are geographically distant," she said. "I think there is a connection there to military brat-ism. The fact I choose to be in this relationship and deal with these issues instead of creating a comfortable, secure relationship, says a lot about me."

Of all the military brats I have met, none has exemplified the negative legacies of extreme mobility more than Brian. Although his story represents an extreme, it nevertheless demonstrates the same problem with commitment that plagues other military brats to a lesser degree.

"Moving was something I dreaded," Brian said. "Losing friends . . . it was really painful. Tears were shed. I don't like to be out of control. I had no power over whether we moved or not.

"I don't remember any friends at all in the fourth grade. That's when I was getting paranoid about moving. I was paranoid about getting close to anyone—we would just have to move again. I remember using that against my parents. They'd say, 'You'll make new friends.' I'd say, 'I'll *never* make new friends,' just to show them I didn't like moving. We'd have those kind of battles." The other parts of Brian's life scarcely compensated for the instability. His family was dysfunctional, his father often gone. At school he was constantly in trouble, and his social life revolved, as mentioned earlier, around dealing drugs to gangs. Once, as a young teenager, he even tried to take his life.

When Brian turned eighteen he moved out of his parents' house. He continued to live and work in the same city, but the childhood rhythm of constant moving continued in a bizarre form. As he put it—and his words were chilling—"I tend to dissipate friends after a few years." In short, roughly every two years he moved to another location in the city and cut off all his previous ties. When I met him he was twenty-eight and had been doing this for ten years.

"I've been living in the same city, but I have no friends I've known longer than two or three years," Brian said.

I make a point of moving every two years or so and dropping all my relationships, including two real serious ones. I basically plan their demise. My ex-fiancée—I actually set up a series of things she didn't like to get her to leave. When I move I don't bother to call my friends, tell them I'm still alive. I don't give them a forwarding address. I notify all my creditors and that's it.

I get to the point where I get close to a person and then I start to feel very vulnerable. I tie that directly to moving every two years in the military. I can't become too close to these people because I'll lose them. And if I don't lose 'em on their accord, I'll make *myself* lose 'em. I set myself up to lose relationships in love, and to lose friendships.

I asked Brian more about his friendships. "Lord knows, I've had some really good friends," he said. "If I wrote 'em now, they'd still be my best friends. But I choose not to. It's funny, because I've got a real good friend right here in [the city]. I've been thinking about him lately and wanting to call him. But I know I won't ever pick up the phone and do it."

"How do you feel about that emotionally?" I asked him. "Is it something you feel comfortable with, or does it make you hurt?"

"It makes me hurt," he answered. "But I've accepted it. I will probably be that way the rest of my life. I don't know if it's that I just don't have the energy, or if I just don't want to take the time to change it. It would take a long time. . . . I'd have to dig through my whole past and work into it a lot, and work into my idiosyncrasies in order to change where I am now. Right now I'm not real dissatisfied with the way I am—not enough, at least, to change it."

"It sounds a little contradictory to me," I told him. "You want to talk to your friend, but you don't do it. It hurts you, yet you're not dissatisfied."

"Pretty confusing, isn't it?" Brian said. "But that's my life right now. . . ."

Brian's story remains extreme, but he was hardly the only military brat to describe a pattern of "dissipating friendships," to borrow Brian's phrase, or the conflicting feelings it inspires.

Rebecca, daughter of an Army general, said that after about two years she begins to feel uncomfortable in her friendships, as though they should end. "But I like the friends so much I get determined that I am going to maintain the friendships. Then I find myself undercutting it anyway. The way I start is, I say, 'They don't like me.' My boyfriend thinks I'm nuts. He says, 'Don't you realize they're your really good friends, and you could do anything and they'll still like you?' I know I'm creating these things that aren't true. But I'm working on it. I don't *want* to disengage from my friendships."

Lydia, daughter of an Army colonel, said, "Change has always been part of my life. I'm always prepared to accept change. I expect it. And I think that expectation may work to unconsciously dilute my connections with people, maybe because I'm protecting myself from having to be wrenched out of something. Since I *expect* change, I hasten the demise of relationships, or I withhold becoming as deeply involved as I might otherwise."

John, son of an Air Force colonel, also spoke of the pattern he creates. "I think it has to do with the rhythm of moving when I was a kid, only it happens now over a shorter period of time. Same rhythm, shorter tempo. When I was a kid we got transferred every two to four years. That to me, in my adult years, was typically how long my relationship with a person could last, at the absolute maximum." John has been working on this problem for a while, however, with at least partial success. He's been happily married for ten years.

COMPENSATING FOR INSTABILITY

Although military children frequently manage to deceive themselves and all who know them into thinking they are taking the continual uprooting of military life in stride, on some level they sense they are paying a high price—and they seek ways to offset it.

Childhood Substitutes for Friendship

As noted earlier, family pets can be a very important source of continuity for children, especially because pets return affection at a time when a child's friendships are abruptly truncated. But there are other sources as well. Several of the methods of creating a sense of continuity described to me by military brats involved focusing on something that provided a semblance of interaction, even if it was entirely supplied by the child's imagination.

A number of military brats told of using puppets and stuffed animals as portable friends—and not only to cuddle, but as characters with whom they could have conversations. What is striking is that these were not merely entertaining fantasies, but often relationships of substantial emotional investment for children whose mobile lifestyle and stoic warrior families did not offer many other outlets for feelings to be expressed or returned.

"I developed deep friendships with inanimate objects," recalled the son of an Army lieutenant colonel. "My stuffed animals meant as much or more to me than my breathing friends. They were my support much of the time. I used them as alter egos. I could talk to them and they would 'talk' back and show me sides of myself that I wasn't aware of. I still have puppets, by the way, who are as real to me as if they did breathe—and they still have personalities I recognize as alter egos."

This son was not the first in his family to turn to inanimate objects for continuity from one place to the next. His mother had such difficulty uprooting herself—although in the course of each move she would eventually rise to the occasion and adapt—that she would actually pack up part of the place and take it with her: For instance, when the family had to move from a western state they had all loved, the mother brought along boxes of tumbleweeds, sagebrush, and rocks. The garage is "chest deep" with boxes containing pieces of the places the family lived, the son said.

Falling Back on the Family

Another way military families cope with constant uprooting is for family members to focus on one another to an unusual degree. Parents loom larger than life. The child's sense of dependence and vulnerability is intensified. Because they need to and because it's easier, family members turn to one another instead of to the outside world.

Sometimes parent-child and sibling relationships are asked to do double duty as friendships. Whether the family members profit or suffer from such heavily freighted ties is not easy to say—but there can be little doubt that double-duty family relationships are extraordinary adaptations to extraordinary circumstances.

"I developed a friendship with my [younger] brother," said the daughter of an Air Force colonel.

> We became so similar that we'd wear each other's clothes. He was big for his age and I was small for my age. I loved to wear his shirts.
>
> My brother and I look alike, and when we were kids, we thought alike. We were best friends and confidants. We went exploring together. Our voices sounded identical. When I was in high school and he was in junior high, someone would call one of us on the phone, and we could trade the phone back and forth without the person knowing. Our vocabulary, inflections, everything was identical to the point our friends couldn't tell us apart.
>
> It would even be hard to remember which one of us had done a particular thing because we would come up with the same ideas. Our parents would have trouble figuring it out too, when one of us had done something wrong—so they'd punish both of us. They'd send us to our separate rooms, and that would be the worst thing they could do, because we were so close.

I have read many articles in military publications that claim military families enjoy strong bonds and special closeness as a result of the transient life. As with other aspects of the Fortress myth, however, this is not necessarily wrong but is so one-sided as to be misleading. The tendency of frequently uprooted family members to focus inordinately on one another can also contribute to the intensification of any family pathology that might be present. The sword cuts both ways.

The words of one Air Force colonel's son are an example of how these contradictory notions of family closeness—as boon or pathology—can exist side by side. If taken by itself, his comment would seem to support the notion of military families as stronger, closer, and more loving than many of their civilian counterparts:

"When you compare our military families to civilian ones, I think we have a deeper bond with our families because we were continually thrown back on them," he said. "Your family *is* the fabric of your social life because you are constantly moving around. I went to fourteen different schools before I went to college and moved twenty-one times. When you do that, you're constantly starting over again, looking for some sense of stability. And you get that from your family. Through it all, that was one thing that hung in there: the sense of close-knit family."

However, it is significant that the speaker is Todd, whose story is presented at length in Chapters 5 and 6. His father was an extreme authoritarian who forced his children to stand in military brace when addressing him, who was emotionally abusive to everyone in the family, and who physically abused his sons from the age of nine to about nineteen. After the father retired from the military, the family broke up in divorce. Years went by before Todd and his father repaired their relationship.

Todd's family was dysfunctional, though not alcoholic. In many other military families, the combination of the alcoholic family pathology and continual social disruption is an especially bad combination. Adult children of such families would probably do well to carefully explore not just the legacies of parental alcoholism, but the interaction of that family syndrome with the instability of military life.

Compensating in Later Life

Most military brats in their adult years experience to one degree or another problems that are the legacies of the rootless life. The problems have a function: When they become painful enough, the military brat will instinctively act to correct the pattern, often using skills and strengths that are also by-products of rootlessness. For example, a military brat who can't seem to settle down in a relationship—and who is hurting because of it—might make use of the perceptiveness and intuitive skill gained in the rootless life to benefit from introspection and counseling.

Even if discontinuity prevails in other important areas of a military brat's life, there is often one key island of stability—a primary relationship, an occupation, a gratifying hobby, a home—which the military brat tends with care and protects with zeal. Often, as in John's case, it is reflected in the choice of life partner.

Military brats also have a penchant for building *symbols* of stability into their lives. For them it is not enough to be anchored in a relationship or a career—there must also be concrete evidence of stability, something they can see and touch for reassurance.

"When I was a kid, I always wanted to plant a vegetable garden," said Charlotte, the daughter of an Air Force colonel. "But it was insidious: We *always* moved before I could harvest anything. I was always leaving my garden behind, losing all my friends. Now [in adulthood] I love where I live, I have no plans to move, I have a backyard that is all vegetable garden, and this year I'm turning my whole front yard into a garden, too."

Lorna, another daughter of an Air Force colonel, spoke at length about the disruptive patterns that have persisted in her relationships, jobs, and residences in the twenty years since she became an adult— patterns that she is now trying to overcome. All along, however, she has instinctively created an island of stability for herself in her home. "I've always identified with turtles," she said. "I carry my home on my back. Every place I live, I create a cave place, a very warm atmosphere," she said. "People have said it feels as if I've lived in a place ten years instead of six months. I settle in and create a nurturing, comfy household wherever I go."

It's a common compensation. "If you're a military brat, you go to one of two extremes—either you do nothing to make your space or you do everything for it," said the daughter of a Navy petty officer. "You either make a nest, or you don't worry about it at all." This daughter, who works for a large business, said her cubicle at work "looks like a Victorian parlor," so jammed is it with framed photographs and bits of memorabilia. "I also tend to buy mammoth pieces of furniture," she noted, although for nearly twenty years as a military wife she had to haul the stuff through countless moves. Once when a mover was struggling with a particularly heavy piece, she felt compelled to apologize. "He responded, 'Look at your furniture. It's *all* like that. You're typical military people: It's like you're trying to purchase stability.' "

Creating islands of stability is important, but probably not enough. Such islands stand less as evidence of victory over the old patterns than as instinctive, piecemeal reactions to them—so the results are uneven. Military brats need to bring everything—strengths as well as unconscious patterns of behavior—to the surface, look at all of it squarely, and take stock. Then it should be possible to figure out how to dismantle an old reflexive pattern of disruption and replace it with a new approach. Sometimes it's as simple as realizing, *I'm an adult now. Why am I living my life in this knockabout way, waiting for orders that never come?* Some military brats simply need to recognize they don't have to wait for permission to be decisive in their own lives.

That is the bottom line for all of us who grew up in the rootless life of the warrior society. The negative legacies of rootlessness are many and painful. Overcoming them is difficult. But the same life that bred these liabilities into us also gave us great strengths, and it just so happens they are the very strengths we need to pull us through:

resilience, good social skills, a finely honed intuition, the ability to observe, learn, imitate.

Stable, balanced lives can be ours. We can even come to understand alien concepts such as continuity and permanence. And we do finally grow up. But somewhere inside we will always be children of warriors, marked forever by the transient life we led. To a degree, this means accepting that we must live with contradiction. Part of us will always want to move on; the other part yearns to stay. Our task is to make sure the decisions we make in response to these yearnings emanate from the conscious, not the unconscious self. And we need to learn to appreciate the contradictions that make us who we are.

"I didn't want my own kids to move around as much as I did, and they haven't," said a Marine Corps major's son. "I wanted them to feel a continuity I never felt.

"The flip side is I'm glad I went through that, because moving was an important part of the kind of person I am. I can walk into any situation and adapt. I have a strong sense of survival. I'm more self-reliant emotionally.

"So there's part of me that longs for someplace that's steadfast and eternal, and a part of me that will always be a vagabond."

CHAPTER 9

UPSTAIRS/ DOWNSTAIRS

The upstairs/downstairs thing still affects me in the sense of making me try to peg people by class hierarchy and status. It's something I struggle against all the time because I think it's wrong and I think it's stupid.
— the son of an Air Force officer

Bobbie Sue. I have thought of her hundreds, probably thousands, of times since we were in the fifth grade together. Her hair was light brown and frizzy, her skin fair and freckled like mine. Her eyes haunt me still: They were hazel, bright with intelligence, but full of vulnerability and pain. I was not privy to the secrets of those eyes, but I identified with them totally, felt her pain deep in my heart. Somehow, despite the chasm of "class" difference that separated us, I thought of us as twins.

In a schoolroom of noisy, extroverted military brats, Bobbie Sue was quiet, shy, and to all appearances, lonely. I had friends but I can remember feeling drawn to her—and yet held back. The Taboo. My father was a colonel. Hers was enlisted—I don't know the exact rank, but I knew he was far, far down the totem pole, perhaps the lowest ranking father of any kid in the class. I can remember the mismatched skirts and blouses, the thin pink cardigan sweater, gray along the edges and torn at the shoulder seam. On the rare occasions I heard her speak, Bobbie Sue's soft voice had the twang of the hills somewhere in the Deep South, where her parents were raised.

The only photograph I have of her is one I took on a class field trip. I couldn't ask her to be my friend, but at least I managed to get her in a picture with my friends. The others are smiling, arms around each other, as I snap the picture. Bobbie Sue is standing next to them, staring off someplace to the right, with us but apart.

Bobbie Sue must have laughed and played like the rest of us, but I can't remember that. In my mind she is always unsmiling and alone, though not defeated. There was no belligerence there, no self-pity that I could see. I longed to know her, but she was a mystery to me—and because of the Taboo, she would remain so.

Of all the kids in my class that year, including the girl who was my best friend, it is Bobbie Sue I wish I could see, Bobbie Sue I miss the most. In my fantasies I rewrite the past: walk up to her on the playground, sit with her at lunch, go about the business of weaving a friendship. But I know it could never have happened that way; it was a complete impossibility. The Taboo stood between us, and every time I looked at her it was as if from a great distance.

In my mind, over the gulf of more than a quarter century, I still call to Bobbie Sue:

I am so sorry I could not be your friend, could not reach out to share your pain, to heal your loneliness and mine. We could have been a comfort to one another, dulled the pain of our aloneness. If things had been different, if it hadn't been for the Taboo . . . Bobbie Sue, wherever you are, can you forgive me?

SEGREGATION BY CLASS

The world of the military base is a world divided. Everything about it speaks of hierarchy and the perquisites of power. Its very territory is carved up according to rank, with the presence or absence of privilege apparent at a glance.

The upper echelons of the officer corps live in the most scenic part of the base, on the edge of a lake or the sea, or high on the hills, in spacious, well-appointed old homes with manicured lawns and huge old trees. There is a hushed quality to their neighborhood—the muffling effect of prestige, security, satisfaction. They have their own club, their own pool, their own golf course, as elegant as many a civilian country club.

The housing areas of the enlisted ranks could scarcely be more different: cramped, noisy, dilapidated, with dirt where grass should be, and located at the far end of the base from the officers. The higher-ranking enlisted—noncommissioned officers such as sergeants or petty officers—have a club and pool, of a considerably lesser quality than those of the officers. The lowest enlisted ranks usually have a club as well, though it is little more than a bare-bones recreation hall with a snack bar.

The distance between the "classes" on a military base is geographical as well as social, and that is by design. There is meant to be no intermingling.

Nothing in American civilian life compares to the strict class segregation found in the military. Civilians have their own exclusive neighborhoods and their own ghettos, of course, and even for those in the middle, class status is not irrelevant. But nowhere in America is the dichotomy so omnipresent as on a military base; nowhere do the classes live and work in such close proximity; nowhere is every social interaction so freighted with class significance. And nowhere are the stakes of the game so high.

The thousands of people on a military base live together, have the same employer, dedicate their lives to the same purpose—yet they cannot, must not, socialize outside their class. And this is not merely a matter of custom in a tradition-bound way of life; it is a matter of law. An officer who fraternizes with an enlisted person runs the risk of prosecution under the Uniform Code of Military Justice.[1]

From the military point of view, it can be no other way. In order to function properly, the military must absolutely rely on the expectation that personnel of whatever rank will respect and obey the orders of their superiors. An "improper" relationship between persons of differing rank raises the specter of favoritism, which can lead to a breakdown in discipline, authority, and morale in the command. Few things are so threatening to an authoritarian hierarchy.

So the military goes to great lengths to make as certain as possible that improper relationships never arise in the first place. The 327,648 officers in the active-duty military and the 1,337,556 enlisted under their command all know the social status that accompanies rank, and they know the consequences of overstepping their bounds.[2] Living within the narrow limitations of class and relating to others strictly in accordance with them becomes a matter of reflex, as natural to the organism of the military as breathing.

Exceptions are rare. But it sometimes happens that friends from childhood find themselves serving in the military on opposite sides of the class barrier. If they follow their natural inclinations and attempt to continue their friendship, the outcome is certain to be painful for all concerned. Virginia's parents were both from working-class backgrounds in West Virginia. Her father served in the Army Air Corps in

World War II, then left the service to get a college education, and reentered the Air Force as an officer, eventually rising to the rank of colonel. Arriving at one air base, he was delighted to find that one of his childhood friends was stationed there too, as a master sergeant. They pursued their friendship, the two families socializing together frequently. But the colonel's commanding officer criticized him so severely that his career was threatened; he had to back off from the friendship. "That was very painful for everyone," Virginia recalled, "including us kids in both families."

The result of this strict class segregation is a world with an entirely different dynamic from that of civilian America. The assumption underlying military life is not to affirm and equalize, gradually blurring distinctions and moving toward the goal of one gigantic middle class, but to maintain the most rigid hierarchy possible, built around dominance and subordination and emphasizing class stratification in every way. For the military—any military in any country—this is absolutely critical to the life and purpose of the organization.

And the class differences can be extreme.

In the upstairs world of the officer corps pay scales may increasingly lag behind those of the civilian world,[3] but there has always been an elaborate apportioning of privilege. Not only are the houses often stately and the officers' clubs elegant, there is a whole lifestyle to match: servants, a whirlwind social life complete with fancy balls, and an elaborate etiquette involving calling cards for both husband and wife.[4] There are horseback riding and music lessons for the children, and, later, cotillion classes in which they learn ballroom dancing and the fine points of formal manners.

To be sure, there are gradations of privilege within the officer corps; the status of a lowly lieutenant in no way compares with that of a major general. And even among officers of equally high rank, there is a special insider clubbiness—and what is perhaps an illusion of higher status—for those who wear the rings of the military academies. But then again, even the lowly lieutenant lives a world apart from the enlisted ranks.

In the downstairs world of the enlisted, things are quite different. The NCOs have both power and prestige in the eyes of those beneath them, but very few perks. The housing is often substandard and in poor repair. One Navy NCO's daughter recalled living in a Quonset hut in a housing area with board sidewalks and mud streets. "Whenever it rained," she said, "we had to unplug all the electrical appliances because of the flooding." From 1941 to 1987, when it was finally replaced, the six-hundred-dwelling Sterling Homes housing area of Camp Pendleton was an embarrassment to the Marine Corps. Originally constructed as temporary shelter for workers building the base, it became the primary housing for junior enlisted families for nearly half a century. A 1986 article in the *Los Angeles Times* noted that "the drab, sand-colored structures lack showers, and fewer than one third of the units have telephones. Barbecues and other possessions are chained to the porch posts; clotheslines are the only landscaping."[5]

The pay for enlisted is low—so low that it has been at times a national scandal. In 1969—four years before the All Volunteer Force brought many more dependents of low-ranking enlisted into the picture—a study found that over thirty thousand married Army soldiers "could be defined as poverty cases by the federal government's own standards."[6] In 1978, forty thousand Navy personnel were found to be eligible for food stamps, though only a small number applied for them.[7]

In 1984, national and international attention was drawn to the problem when the thirteen-year-old son of an Army staff sergeant hanged himself following a comment to his mother that "things would be easier if there were one less mouth to feed." The desperate situation in Danny Holley's family was due not just to low pay but to a series of foul-ups by the Army bureaucracy: Upon their arrival at Fort Ord, California, the family was denied military housing, forcing them to find housing off post in an area with a very high cost of living. A transfer of funds from their bank account on a base in West Germany to a credit union at Fort Ord was mishandled and delayed. Their car was mistakenly shipped to New Orleans. The help provided by the relief agencies at Fort Ord was inadequate. On top of everything else, Sgt. Holley's orders were changed so that he would have to serve a year in South Korea before he could join his family at Fort Ord. The family, hungry and penniless, had to fend for itself in his absence.[8] Although the Holley situation was an unusually grim one, even for the beleaguered enlisted ranks, it is difficult to imagine how anything on this order could befall a member of the officer corps.

Indeed, despite the national publicity given to the Holley tragedy, things have improved only marginally for the enlisted ranks since that time. In 1990, six years after Danny Holley's suicide, thousands of members of the armed forces continued to use food stamps to make ends meet,[9] and there is every indication that the number could potentially go far higher—if, for example, the food stamp program were to be made available for the first time to the half-million military members serving overseas. A 1986 Department of Defense study examining the feasibility of extending the program to cover them estimated that thirteen thousand personnel would be eligible based solely on military income. But overseas, as at home, the pride of the enlisted people serving our country often gets in the way; the report goes on to project that of the 13,000 estimated eligible, only 2,550 would be likely to apply.[10]

Upstairs, downstairs. The only equality among officers and enlisted is in dying on the battlefield. And even then, there is no equality in burial. In Arlington National Cemetery, where any current or former career member of the armed forces is entitled to burial, the basic ceremony—called "Modified Honors"—includes a casket team, firing party, bugler, flag over the coffin, and a military chaplain. But the individual must be a warrant officer or higher in order to have "Full Honors": the above plus color guard, escort platoon, caisson with horses, and military band. And only Army and Marine officers holding the rank of colonel or above merit the riderless horse and cannon salute. High-ranking Navy and Air Force officers also get the cannon, but not the horse—since horses were never employed in their services' war efforts.

As we've said, the military has its own authoritarian, hierarchical reasons for making these distinctions, and would probably be dysfunctional without them. But for the sons and daughters of the Fortress, who after all have not volunteered for their particular status, the gradations of rank and their accompanying limitations can be confusing and frequently painful. There is no way to shut out the harsh realities of class difference. To do so, even for a child, would be to walk blindfolded through a social minefield.

And military brats must daily navigate their way through that minefield, because the 1.3 million children of enlisted and the 328,000 children of officers are thrown together in the same schools.[11] Inevitably, military brats become as attuned to the nuances of social class as young mammals learning the deadly hierarchy of the forest. This is one of the origins of the "antenna," discussed in the last chapter, which allows the military brat to intuitively distinguish the rank of another military child's father without ever exchanging a word. The antenna is the military brat's social mine detector.

The Molding of Children's Class Consciousness

Although the military likes to point out that spouses and children have no rank—and therefore shouldn't attempt to wear any—it would be naive to suppose that children grow up unaffected by their parents' social status and attitudes.

Where some young officer kids are concerned, the narrowness of their world and the concentrated classism of their own parents combine to produce a blatant, unselfconscious snobbery.

A child psychologist at a military hospital serving Army and Air Force families said she often sees this in the troubled teenage children of officers. "The kid often has an arrogant, defiant attitude, an attitude of class," she said. "The kids take on the ingrained view of their parents, that they are somehow above the ordinary people in life." She said that she and the other members of the mental health staff find it very difficult to work with such families.

"The officer parents treat us mental health professionals as servants. They say, 'We brought you this child to be fixed. Now *fix* him.' The attitude toward us is so arrogant. And the son or daughter will be sitting there with the same hard-core attitude. It's very difficult for us to make headway with them." I asked her about the NCO families she sees. "The sergeants don't have that attitude toward mental health professionals," she said. "They have it toward their children. The treatment is not sabotaged to the same degree."

Parental attitudes are an important factor in how military children come to perceive themselves relative to others, but hardly the only one. The Fortress itself sees to that.

In *Gardens of Stone*, his moving novel about a military son caught up in the Vietnam War, Nicholas Proffitt, himself a military brat, has his protagonist speak to the pain of class difference. In this passage, Jackie Willow, the teenage son of an Army sergeant, finds himself going to high school on an Army post where there are notably few officers' sons; they've been sent off to military schools or swanky eastern prep schools.

The one problem with such custom, and it was one much discussed at the officers' club, was that it left the girls of Colonels' Row with no alternative but to socialize with the boys of Suds Row.

The colonels' dilemma was Jackie's boon. He dated colonels' daughters almost exclusively, not so much because he liked them better than sergeants' daughters, but because they provided him a passport to the Row itself. The Row was so quiet. There were no Filipino noncom children yapping away in their native Tagalog. No frustrated A. J. Foyts working on superchargers and shattering the golden desert air with the sound of 450 cubic inches. No smells of sour diapers and frying fats. No. Colonels' Row was a dreamy world that whispered, never shouted, and it whispered of power and wealth and *class*. Inside the houses of the girls he took out were exotic items harvested from overseas postings. Not crudely carved lazy susans topped with wooden peasants riding wooden water buffaloes. Not beer mugs from Bavaria that played "Lili Marlene" when you lifted the lid. Not any of the vulgar curios so prevalent in NCO houses that at times it seemed the same cut-rate decorator had done them all. No. The Row had dining tables made of solid oak, not formica. The Row had delicate jade sculptures, not cheap cuckoo clocks that never worked. The Row had hand-knotted Persian carpets on the floor, not yellowing linoleum. The Row had Filipino or Mexican servants in white coats . . . paneled rooms just for books . . . end-tables with damask inlay as complicated as a kaleidoscope . . . Morris chairs of rich leather and padded wet bars adorned with regimental crests. The Row had mothers who were pretty and soft-spoken instead of dowdy and shrill, fathers who gave a boy knowing winks and avuncular pats on the back instead of threats of violence and drunken war stories.

Jackie was never quite sure what the fathers of these girls did in their jobs. "Officer" things, he guessed. They must have been administrators or scientists. There were no Infantry line commands at Huachuca. Jackie always felt vague feelings of inferiority and shame when he entered any of the houses on the Row, and he could only protect his pride and sense of worth by nurturing secret contempt for officers without troop commands. All the boy knew was that the colonels were unfailingly and coolly polite to him. At first meeting they would be friendly and jovial and man-to-man in a burst of inappropriate interest, the way adults often are with adolescents they don't know. Once he told them where he lived and what his father was, they were still polite and still friendly, but polite above all, with everything else suddenly mechanical and forced.[12]

One of the reasons the stratifications of rank have such a powerful effect on military children is that the system itself requires it. Military brats tell of separate scout troops for children of officers and enlisted, separate officer/enlisted seating in post or base movie theaters, and of course separate swimming pools. The very complexity of such arrangements underscores the importance of strict hierarchy to the military: It means, for instance, four Scout troops instead of two: officer/boy, officer/girl, enlisted/boy, enlisted/girl—not to mention officer/Cub, enlisted/Cub, officer/Brownie, enlisted/Brownie. Class difference is not just the external structure of a military child's world; it is an invasive reality.

Nevertheless, military parents do a great deal to reinforce the idea of class boundaries in their children. Not all parents do this, of course— I've been told of some who specifically told their children to ignore such things—but so many do that the message gets across loud and clear, and in a hundred different ways.

Lorna, the daughter of an Air Force colonel, said, "In the base movie theater I was aware that the airmen sat in the back three rows and that we tried to go to movies when they weren't going to be there—they had special times they went. I was afraid of airmen, was given the impression they were subhuman, animals, bad men, that they would hurt a girl."

The son of a Marine lieutenant colonel recalled that his older brother, "a kid of the fifties," was once forbidden by their father to have a crewcut. "We were living on Quantico at the time," he said. "My father didn't allow it because a crewcut would make my brother look like an enlisted man. The standard cut for [officer sons] was none on the sides and just enough on top to part. The part was the privilege of rank."

Sometimes there is even unequal pay for the same work; the daughter of a Navy noncom told of her bitterness at being paid fifty cents an hour to babysit officer kids, while officers' daughters were paid seventy-five.

The Taboo

By far the most important way parents bring class difference to play in the lives of their children is through the Taboo, a force so powerful it twists and inhibits the course of childhood friendship and inevitably affects the child's sense of self.

The Taboo emanates from the officer class, where the injunction against fraternizing with enlisted is such an article of faith that it is frequently and unthinkingly extended to the children. Again, there are exceptions, but the overwhelming majority of the officer children I interviewed all knew of the Taboo and adhered to it.

And yet the Taboo is not something that is discussed directly in officer families. Almost no one I interviewed could recall a specific conversation in which a parent had forbidden them to associate with enlisted children—and yet all knew that this was law. In my own case, the only incident I can remember concerned not an enlisted child but an officer's daughter who was my best friend in third and fourth grades. Her father was a young captain, four grades below my father, a full colonel—and even though her father was an officer, mine felt it was inappropriate for me to be so close with her. So he decided that while she and I could remain "friends," I could never spend the night with her. My brother has one recollection as well: When he was about to turn eleven and the family had so recently moved to the new post that he'd had no time to make friends, he and my mother planned a birthday party in which the guests would be his entire sixth grade class. The class was invited and preparations were well underway when my father learned of the plan and angrily forbade it—on the grounds there were enlisted children in the class.

The fact that such memories are rare is not evidence against the existence of the Taboo, but rather for it. A Navy commander's son, now a social worker, explained:

In families there are two classes of taboo. A Class I Taboo is something you are forbidden specifically to do, out loud. You are told, "You can't do this." The Class II Taboo is a more prevasive and more damaging taboo. It's the thing that is never talked about by anyone under any circumstances. It simply doesn't come up. A Class II Taboo is so dynamite that you know you can't even talk about it; that's more dynamite than something you're forbidden to do out loud. In the case of the Taboo against officer kids making friends with enlisted kids, it was something that wasn't said. It was internalized to the degree that after a point it was literally inconceivable [to violate it]. It's something that operates as an unconscious process.

Indeed, my brother and I were each well aware of the Taboo and were assiduously living by it; the only reason actual incidents occurred was because our father's interpretation of the Taboo was broader than we had imagined.

Sometimes interviewees refer to the Taboo as an "unspoken understanding," which is nevertheless crystal clear to them. An Air Force general's daughter, asked if she had been permitted to date enlisted sons, said, "It was an understanding. . . . My father would have found that totally unacceptable. In fact I think he disapproved of my dating civilians." Dating is a point on which the Taboo revealed itself. In some officer households the children understood they could have "friends" from enlisted families, but under no circumstances could this liberality apply to dating.

But even if officer parents specifically tell their children *not* to pay attention to the Taboo, to make friends with whomever they wish, the children often wind up practicing it anyway, forced into compliance by the Fortress itself. First, of course, there is the calculated geographic separation of the classes, which can be quite effective at dictating who will and who will not become friends. And there are other things. Sam, the son of an Air Force general, insisted that he was allowed to have enlisted friends and that he did have a few. But when I pointed out that an enlisted friend couldn't swim in the same pool as he, he said, "That's right, and that could cause problems. He could come as a guest, but that was frowned upon. I could go to *his* pool, but that also was frowned upon, because that would be invading their turf. That's why your close friends were likely to be officer kids, who could do the same things you did, such as spending a day at the pool and the club, where you could sign a tab for your meals. You needed a friend whose father was also a member of the club."

In fact the swimming pool issue can be traumatic. A Navy daughter, whose father had started out enlisted and worked his way up to become a lieutenant commander, told of a horrifying moment in her childhood when, at the gate of the officers' pool, the young enlisted friend she'd brought along was brusquely turned away.

For the children of enlisted, such incidents burn in the memory. The daughter of an Air Force sergeant recalled her humiliation when she was barred from seeing two of her closest friends, the twin daughters of a major, by their rigidly class-conscious mother. As long as the friendship was confined to the base school in Germany where they were in seventh grade together, things were fine; the officer parents couldn't object to what they didn't know about. Certainly many other military brats have managed to partially subvert the Taboo in this way. But these young girls made a classic mistake. Out of naivete—or possibly rebelliousness—the twin daughters of the major invited the sergeant's daughter to come to their home on a Saturday afternoon. When the sergeant's daughter arrived, she found herself in a very uncomfortable situation.

"It turned out to be their birthday party," she related. "The daughters of the base commander and the wing commander were there; in fact, everyone was an officer's daughter except for me. And because I didn't know it was their birthday, I didn't even have a present." Worst of all, the twins' mother was clearly offended at her presence.

"She was furious," the sergeant's daughter remembered. "It wasn't what she said—she was too sophisticated for that—but how she behaved. I understood it was because my dad wasn't an officer." After that the three girls confined their friendship to school grounds, out of sight of the twins' mother. But when, the following year, she pulled her daughters out of the base school and sent them to a local German school, the only way they could get together was for the sergeant's daughter to meet them once a week at the studio where the twins took ballet lessons. "I'd wait for them until they were finished with the class, and we'd talk until their father's driver came to pick them up," she said. "Then one day when I went to the studio, the ballet teacher wouldn't let me in. She explained to me it was the twins' mother who told her to keep me away. I wasn't allowed to leave a note or anything."

The incident left her feeling shocked and helpless. "I couldn't figure out what to do about it," she said. "She was their mother and she ran their lives. There was nothing I could do. It was tough. Fortunately, my mother and father were very good about it. They said it was one of life's lessons, that there are some people in the world who care more about appearances than anything else. They were extremely supportive, and I'm grateful for that. What if my mother had said something like, 'What do you expect—your father's only a sergeant'?"

This sergeant's daughter, who now lives a civilian lifestyle and has teenage children of her own, realized as she told her story that despite the distance of many years, she has still not left that social trauma behind. "I'm shaking now as I tell you this," she said. "I'm still angry. I guess I haven't finished dealing with it."

It is in order to prevent the pain of humiliation that both officer and enlisted children develop antennas to determine the rank of another military brat's father. There is simply no other way to go about it: Discussing the rank of one's father is yet another taboo. That's one of the paradoxes of military social life. The same parents who force their children to comply with the Taboo also instruct them never to discuss their father's rank. That would be "wearing your father's rank on your sleeve," which, at least in the abstract, is considered grossly inappropriate even by the most rank-conscious parents. The imperative of silence is so strong that even as adults and in totally civilian contexts, the children of officers and high-ranking NCOs report feeling self-conscious when asked their fathers' rank—as though by merely saying it they will be seen as snobs.

So if it is necessary for the military child to know the rank of another's father, yet impossible to ask outright, intuitive skills must come to the rescue.

Military children always figure out what they need to know to survive socially, and then they do what they have to do. As reflected in the above story of thwarted friendship, officer and enlisted kids, determined to defeat the Taboo, think up all sorts of ways to circumvent it. They find places to meet and play outside their housing areas, such as the parade field or the boat harbor or the base theater after the Saturday morning kiddie show. They fraternize in school lunchrooms, clubs, and on sports teams. But such efforts are usually isolated and ultimately doomed to failure; if a friendship cannot be conducted openly, there is no victory at all. And the operative rule is that the officer parents must never ever find out.

The Hostility of Class Difference

Under the circumstances, it is hardly surprising that among military children, resentments develop around class status. Often they reflect the views of the parents, who, although wholly committed to the authoritarian hierarchy of the military, are human enough to chafe under it.

Ask an enlisted child "Is your father an officer?" and chances are you'll get the instant comeback, "No, he works for a living." It's an old military joke, picked up and parroted by the children, and still good for a laugh after untold decades of repetition inside the Fortress because it helps vent the natural tensions of that stratified life. The humor is gentle, but it addresses itself to a raw nerve running through enlisted life: the stereotype of the officer corps as holding cushy, pen-pushing jobs and strutting about with an inflated sense of importance while enlisted guys work their butts off to make them look good—and are paid a pittance for it.

From time to time enlisted fathers bring home stories to their families that seem to bear out the stereotype—and these become seared into the memories of the children. They are almost always stories about the enlisted father triumphing morally over officers who have overstepped the bounds of privilege or who are trying to make themselves look good at an enlisted person's expense.

"When my father went to Hawaii," recalled the daughter of a Navy chief petty officer, "he replaced the chief who was head of the electrical shop. He went in the first day, looked around, and saw toasters, irons, waffle irons, all these domestic electrical appliances. He said, 'What are these doing here?' And one of the fellows said, 'We're supposed to repair them, for free. They belong to officers.' My dad said, 'This is not a repair shop. You send them all out, and tell them we no longer repair home appliances. Our business is with the Navy, not with them.'"

An Air Force son told this story:

At one airbase my father was a first sergeant, and one of the duties of a first sergeant is to sign the morning report in the barracks and certify the status of everyone assigned to that unit. What he found when he took over was that a number of people were still listed under Failure to Repair instead of AWOL [Absent Without Leave], even though they'd been gone for two weeks. Failure to Repair means you're supposed to be on duty at a certain time and you're not there; maybe you overslept. AWOL means you're not in the barracks, you're not on base, you're *gone*. AWOL counts more than Failure to Repair. [13] My father refused to sign the morning report. The colonel ordered him to sign it. My father said, "Give me this order in writing." The colonel wouldn't do that because it's an illegal order. But if my father had signed the morning report, it would be his problem, not the colonel's. Other first sergeants on base had been signing these reports but when they heard about this they stopped, fearing there would be a court-martial or an investigation by the Inspector General. So for three or four days a lot of morning reports weren't signed. Eventually they switched it to AWOL. And two weeks later my father was assigned to another squadron.

There are countless stories like these. Some, like the one about the electrical shop, end on a note of moral triumph: The NCO hero catches the officers red-handed in the exploitation of rank and privilege, and he's bold enough and clever enough to slap their hands, teach them a lesson. A victory for the working guy. Others, like the

one about the falsified morning reports, take the basic story one step
further, revealing a darker truth and, one suspects, the more prevalent
reality: A good, tough NCO can, if he feels like it, seize the opportunity to right a wrong and make an overbearing officer eat crow—but he
may well have to pay dearly for it. Class reality closes in; power
triumphs in the end. The NCO can win the battle, but never the war.

The children of the Fortress are hardly exempt from this reality.
Early on they learn there is no escape from the pain of class division;
their fathers, their families, and the children themselves have already
been frozen into class categories. There is no choice but to live with it,
and with the hostility it breeds.

That hostility gets acted out, of course, often in fistfights or verbal
assaults on the playground. Officer kids are sometimes referred to as
"fags" or "wimps" by enlisted kids, or automatically branded as snobs.

"In every school I went to," an Air Force general's son said,

> I'd always have to fight the school bully, just because I was the general's
> kid. And the school bully was probably an NCO's kid. That was my
> introduction to every school I went to.
>
> The NCO kid would start it, the first day. He'd come up and do
> something to you, dump Coke on you, something. I can remember being
> in mechanical drawing class one day, and the kid walked up and dumped
> ink on my drawing. And I said, "Okay." I knew what was coming. We met
> after school, off school grounds. There must have been five hundred kids
> on his side, and a couple stuck with me, and we had our fight. There was
> no permanent damage done. And then it was okay. It would always be
> okay; I was accepted. It didn't matter if I won or lost; it's whether you stand
> up and fight. All the ones that did this wanted to establish their dominance;
> and the way they would have done that was if I'd said, "No, I'm not going
> to fight you." You really had no choice.
>
> It only happened to me, and to the other generals' kids. I think it was a
> clear distinction. It was because of who my dad was. If my dad had been a
> colonel, it wouldn't have been a problem.

This son's interpretation may not be correct—after all, as we saw in
the last chapter, there are plenty of sons who have to fight their way
into the pecking order of a new school, regardless of their fathers'
ranks—but it hardly matters. His perception of it speaks to one of the
basic truths of military brat childhood: an agonizing class consciousness that runs through every aspect of life.

The effect of this class consciousness on shaping a child's world view
should not be underestimated. The black son of an Air Force NCO
said, "I remember when I was little, I wished I were white, because all
the white people were officers. I know that's a strange way to think, but
I remember that. I equated being white with being an officer. I'd

think, Gee, I wish I could be white. Because you could *see* the difference. We were in enlisted housing. They were in officers' quarters. The quarterback was always the son of the colonel. And the cheerleaders were officers' daughters. They had this by rank."

He seemed to make a distinction between the institutional racism of the military that keeps the officer corps overwhelmingly white, and the largely healthy race relations he experienced on a day-to-day basis with other military brats, both officer and enlisted, in dependent schools. "The military is a caste system," he said, "but it's better than some, because at least you mix with all races, so it's hard to be racist." His point is well taken, as we shall see in the next chapter, for racism is not typically one of the legacies of the military brat. But a powerful class consciousness is.

The same NCO son went on, revealing more of the old bitterness. "You could always tell the son of the CO. He was the football star, he had good grades. They're the kind of people who would blow up Russia without thinking. Because they don't think. They were intelligent, but not creative. They were good at following algorithms or something. You have to be like that to be a West Point person. A lot of officers are so used to giving orders they're not sensitive to the consequences. So that's what enlisted people have to cope with: getting around these guys."

If officer kids bear the brunt of enlisted hostility, being called names and occasionally getting bashed on the playground, enlisted kids, for their part, suffer a crueler fate: They become invisible to the children of higher rank. Officers' children talk past them, avoid them, don't see them. While the arrogance of unearned privilege may play into this, in large part it is a defensive strategy: If there is no eye contact, no verbal contact, there will be no uncomfortable social situation to negotiate. It's no wonder an enlisted kid sometimes wants to haul off and slug an officer kid in the mouth. It's certainly one way to get his attention.

Many of the officer children interviewed for this book admitted they had worked for years in adulthood to tone down the class arrogance with which they'd been raised. What was still evident in a number of them, though, was an attitude that continued to imprison enlisted kids in a stereotype of inferiority. When I asked them to describe their general impressions of enlisted kids, there were phrases such as "not as clean," "a little more hardened, looser," "used more four-letter words," "not as tactful." One said, "Those military kids with drive and intelligence always seemed to be officer kids." A Navy officer's daughter recalled how, at one place they were stationed, the Naval Air Station kids—all or most of whom would have been of the officer class—looked down on the Seabee kids, whose fathers, mostly construction workers, would have been enlisted. "I never understood that," she said. "My father and mother never played into it. But I do believe a lot of the Seabee kids got married right after high school to sailors, and settled down to a military life themselves, as wives. The officers' kids went off to Annapolis."

Class Confusion

The irony of this kind of class perception in officer children is that for the most part, their officer parents were hardly to the manor born. Many of the officer fathers of the interviewees for this book came from small towns, deprived rural areas, or immigrant ghettos of big cities and joined the military during the Depression, when their own families could not afford to feed them. It was, some would argue, the best opportunity going: an honorable profession, a free education, upward mobility, a sense of self-worth. The military at that time drew some of the finest, most able men in the nation. But very likely none of that made it any easier for them to learn to breathe the thin air of the upper echelons of the officer corps.

By the 1940s there was a proliferation of guides and manuals for officers and their wives to give them crash courses in the etiquette befitting their rank. Many of the topics cover the finest points of social behavior, from the number of calling cards one must leave in various situations to who in a group of wives of officers of varying ranks should exit a boat first. But they also covered some extremely basic points. For instance, in *The Army Wife*—a book which, despite its inclusive title, was written solely for wives of the officer corps—the section on table manners advises, among other things:

> The arms should move freely in conveying food to the mouth, but when cutting meat they should stay down near the sides instead of giving a spread-eagle effect. . . .

> Don't encircle your plate with the left arm, clenching your fist while eating with the right hand. Looks as if you are guarding your food! . . .

> Asparagus is definitely not a finger food. It is eaten with a fork.[14]

Officers and their wives who come from working class backgrounds walk a social minefield of their own, with very high stakes. Inside the Fortress, where appearance and performance are everything, a social mistake is more than a faux pas; it is potentially fatal to a career. An Air Force officer's daughter witnessed a painful moment for her mother, a woman of blue-collar origins. "My mother gave a tea," the daughter said. "She was trying so hard to fit in. A senior officer's wife said in a stage whisper, 'What a vulgar display of silver for a junior officer's wife!' That hurt my mother so much. She came from a poor family and already felt uncomfortable."

Many officers' children, exposed to both the earthy backgrounds of their parents and the exacting etiquette of the officer corps, grow up with the savoir faire of upper crust sophisticates—but with an inner sense of class status that is contradictory and unsure. As one Air Force colonel's daughter put it, "There's a way I have two simultaneous views of myself: as a country bumpkin with manure on her shoe, and as someone who can fake her way through any social world, no matter what it is. I think in the military we learn that before we're four years old. My background is confused in the class sense. We're pretty working class on my mother's side. But growing up, all of us had horseback riding lessons, and servants. I sort of think I've lived the whole gamut of classes." Now a professor of sociology, this daughter continued, "I know it made me a sociologist. I had a sensation that this is what I've been doing all my life—I just didn't know there was a name for it: figuring out who's got the power, what are the rules." The benefits of growing up in such an artificially stratified world are few—but this is certainly one of them: a sensitivity to the social subtleties of power, which we can then turn to good use.

An Army daughter told of the lessons she learned from watching her father, a sergeant first class, as he tried unsuccessfully to find the fine line between asserting his own power and bowing to those of superior rank. "I have to believe he never achieved a higher rank because there were times when he had conflicts with officers," she said. "He was so rigid. He's like Archie Bunker; he's always been that way. My mother would try to coach him, tell him what to say and not say, but his attitude always got him in trouble.

"Noncoms are caught right in the middle [between low-ranking enlisted and the officer corps]," she continued. "They don't have *enough* power, but they have enough so that they have the *appearance* of having it. It's a real paradox. The thing is, the military is rigid; that's the way it works. And it takes a rigid individual to do it. But to do it *well* takes flexibility. *Those* are the people who do well in the military—the ones who are very, very adaptable."

The lessons learned from watching the power game at its most blatant can serve a military brat very well in later life. And in its way, the very confusion about social class felt by military brats, both officer and enlisted, is a benefit. It helps us to separate ourselves from it, question it, come to some kind of conscious decision about the role it will play in our adult lives.

LIVING THE LEGACIES OF POWER

Few military brats would dispute that growing up in the hierarchy of
the Fortress has had a powerful effect on the way they felt about
themselves as children. Too often, that early identity is hard to shake.

"It's put limitations on my life," said an Army sergeant's daughter,
who still feels deeply wounded even though she and her husband, a
civilian, live a middle-class life of great intellectual refinement.

> It's made me believe that if someone were smarter, or beautiful, or
> popular, then I could not be in that same category. That was where the
> class angle came in. Not only would I not be there in that category, I
> believed that if I tried, I would be rejected. And the rejection would be too
> great—so I couldn't be vulnerable to trying.
> In my mind it was literally that they were up there, I was down here.
> And I extended this to believe that people I associate with were down here,
> or they wouldn't be associating with me. I'm still very uncomfortable with
> people I put up higher than myself. It's nowhere near what it used to be,
> but I'm still afraid that I don't know how to talk about the right foods,
> or . . . When I was younger, it was dressing right. I saw a picture of myself
> when I was in college; I can't imagine why anyone would have wanted to
> associate with me. I had clothes that looked like I got them from the
> Salvation Army. So that further convinced me that I was of the lower class,
> because I couldn't dress beautifully. Sometimes, with my husband, I think
> he's got a *very* good mind, but the *rest* of him must be lower class—or why
> would he be with me?

There is no question that this military daughter experienced her
place in the class-conscious world of the Fortress as a humiliation.
What is striking, however, is that children from the opposite end of the
spectrum—generals' children—also spoke of feeling embarrassed and
isolated by a status they never asked for and could not understand.

Leigh is an Air Force daughter whose father was one of the high-
ranking generals sent to Japan immediately following World War II to
supervise the occupation. For her the fact of her father's status made
for unbearable isolation, and the story she told evoked a harrowing
image of loneliness. "During the occupation they took over houses of
the wealthy Japanese people and put generals in them," she began.

> I don't know what happened to the people in the houses. We took
> everything—the furniture, everything. We lived in a beautiful modernistic
> Western-style house with a gorgeous Japanese section attached to it. There
> were thirteen servants, including two guys who cut the grass with little
> clippers. They worked on it all the time. My parents went out four or five
> nights a week. It was a huge house. My brother would go up to his room
> and stay there. There was a sign on his door: "No girls, no women, no

sisters. This means you. Keep out." The cooks would bring my dinner out into the dining room. There were beautiful parquet floors and furniture. So I'd sit by myself at the big table and they'd all line up against the cupboard and watch me eat, and giggle. I'd take a bite and sort of smile and they'd giggle. Then they'd take my dishes and go back into the kitchen.

The children of generals and admirals grow up feeling set apart from others, objects of curiosity, envy, or scorn. "I definitely felt the hierarchy," commented Grace, also an Air Force general's daughter. "I have clear memories of being in situations where I felt like a freak. People couldn't wait to see what a general's daughter was like, and there was an immediate reaction. Sometimes I felt pressure to be someone larger than life because of my dad's rank. And there was always a responsibility to maintain appearances." There is also an uncomfortable lack of privacy. "We had an airman aide," Grace continued. "That was odd. Not only did we have a full-time maid, but this man who was always around. It was obtrusive."

Another source of anxiety for children of high-ranking fathers is the class snobbery that seems to go hand-in-hand with their status. Ironically, but perhaps not surprisingly, some of the worst snobbery is found in parents with the humblest origins, to hear their children tell it. Sometimes their children imitate this haughtiness for a time, thinking it is somehow required of them—but then reject it as they see how it contributes to their already keen sense of loneliness. What is harder to shed is the distorted world view that goes with it.

Catherine, daughter of an admiral, said that in her family the prejudice against enlisted was well understood, but very, very subtle. She hadn't realized to what extent she had internalized her parents' mind-set until, as a military officer herself, she was sent to a personnel management school. "It took me a long time to get over my background," she said. "It took a lot of experience, time, and training for me to understand that enlisted are . . . people."

Compensating in Later Life

When they grow up, the children of high-ranking officers sometimes seem to bend over backward to compensate for the classist way they grew up. This doesn't always happen, of course, but the number of people interviewed for this book who fell into this category was striking. Leigh, the daughter of the general in occupied Japan, grew up to become an artist with liberal political views, and a dedicated political activist. Grace, who felt a great deal of pressure as a child to reflect her father's status, became a social worker—as did her sister. The daughter who became a military officer herself became known as a champion of the rights of enlisted and of women. At least three officers' daughters and two officers' sons went to law school specifically to serve society's disadvantaged. A colonel's daughter became a migrant fruit picker for a year and attempted to blend into the underclass—an effort, she reflected, that was her way of "finding out about that scary, threatening world of 'them.' " Several officers' sons interviewed for this book became social workers. In my own case, I became an investigative reporter and attempted to fashion myself into an avenger of the poor and the powerless.

Even where the officer's child did not choose to work out the class dilemma through a profession, there was often compensation at work in terms of political views, and involvement in organizations and religious institutions concerned with human rights. The son of an authoritarian Air Force colonel told me, "I think this upstairs/downstairs setup of the military, which was replicated inside my family with my father treating us children as enlisted men . . . gave me a strong sense of social justice and the importance of egalitarianism. That's probably why both my brother and I are social activists and have been for a long time. My whole life I've rebelled against privilege and authority; I'm sure it came from being raised by an authoritarian military officer in an authoritarian environment." And many officers' children have rejected the class system in the ultimate way—by marrying into the enlisted military or the civilian working class, or by becoming enlisted or blue-collar workers themselves. One Air Force colonel's daughter, now a military officer herself, married an enlisted man, divorced him, then married another—only to divorce him, too. Such a marriage, attempting to bridge the tremendous gulf between the classes within the military itself, would be under tremendous stress; an active-duty woman officer, for instance, could not even take her active-duty enlisted husband to the officers' club for a drink without potentially damaging her career.

Enlisted children, for their part, understand all too well the penalties of low status, and many of them do what they can to change it—even if that means creating an unbridgeable gulf between themselves and their parents.

Joe, the Navy enlisted son who is now a professor at a prestigious university, told of the route to upward mobility he figured out as a child. "You pick up pretty quickly that being an enlisted man's son, you're inferior in social class," he said.

You go to different clubs, to a different pool, you don't play with officers' children.

But I figured out if you were a smart, funny, articulate kid, you could move in any circles you wanted, up to a point. I found that out very early. I went to a very preppy college, and got bids to some of the most exclusive fraternities—just because I was funny and smart.

The fact I was good academically introduces a different class than social class. You don't have to make money, you don't have to achieve materially—you can feel quite superior and quite confident, because you have something the people in that [higher] class want, no matter what else they have. If you do it well and easily, you gain entrée to a social class you wouldn't have if you weren't smart—a special class that preserves you in a way from the humiliation of lower social origin. There's a kind of natural aristocracy among smart people that other people like and associate themselves with. I was actually astonished by it.

In his family, however, there was a price to pay. Joe's family was troubled anyway—as described in Chapter 5, his father had a drinking problem and was abusive to his wife and children—but Joe's academic success unquestionably widened the gulf. By the time Joe was in high school and his father was preparing to retire from the service—a stressful time in every military family—the tension between them was terrific. "Part of it was, in a way, my fault," Joe reflected.

For a long time I thought it was all just his psychosis and I had a tough time forgiving him for it. But as you get older, you realize. . . . I was probably developing into the kind of kid that he would pick up right away would be ashamed of him. There are several thousand ways of letting your parents know that, and all kids go through it. But in my case it was much more dramatic.

My father can't basically write a check, much less write a letter. My mother had to do all that stuff. And by ninth or tenth grade I was winning academic prizes, and my friends who came over were talking a language he couldn't understand. The music I listened to in my room I couldn't talk to him about. I mean, the fact he'd listen to country music or sit around watching wrestling on TV while I was up in my room reading books, must have made him feel funny. He must have felt he had no connection with me at all.

Yet he really did make an effort to go when I was in speech contests, or in Boy Scouts. He would make the effort, but only up to a point. He would be very, very painfully embarrassed if he had to participate in a social function in some way. It was a great stress for him.

I remember when I graduated from high school he had to go out and buy a suit, and it was just agony for him. He didn't know what to buy, and was humiliated that my mother had to come along to give him advice. The suit he wanted to buy—I'll always remember this—was sort of an electric blue. It was real garish, a hillbilly-going-out-to-town kind of thing. I remember him being so humiliated when my mother explained to him that it was atrocious, and he had to buy this gray suit. . . .

It was very difficult for him to participate in the social world of an achieving high school student. He made occasional attempts at it, but it was so obvious that it was very painful for him that I never made a big issue out of it. He didn't come to my college graduation, or my graduate school graduation, or my wedding.

Joe's father suffered from a terrible self-image that got in the way of the father-son relationship. A poorly educated man from backwoods Alabama, and with a horrifying family history of personal rejection, he enlisted in the Navy as a way out. And despite his limited education, he did very well, making it to chief petty officer and retiring, because of a disability, after twenty-three years of service. Clearly he was a smart and able man—though probably he never for a minute believed it.

One of the most common—and hurtful—misconceptions about career enlisted is that they are somehow *lesser* people than officers: less talented, less intelligent, less able. This is simply not so. As a social worker with the military put it, "If they're not with it, they're not going to get past E-6. Now, they may be malicious as hell, screwed up in terms of bonding, have a distorted sense of humor and be flaming alcoholics—but the fact is they aren't going to make chief or master chief or warrant officer if they aren't on top of it. You don't get past E-6 because you outlast everybody; you've also got to pass the exams, and get the fitness reports, same as for officers. Senior enlisted families aren't that much different from officer families. The guys who make it to thirty years are pretty smart cookies."[15]

There's something else NCOs have, too: a special kind of savvy that is directly related to their work. NCOs have a daunting responsibility: They have to make sure morale stays high and the job gets done, whatever it may be, whenever it is ordered, and in spite of any conceivable problems, from supply shortages to bureaucratic snafus to a whole raft of personnel problems. As a result, they become jugglers of circumstance, masters of manipulation, experts at concocting creative solutions on the spur of the moment. The bane of their existence is having to follow the orders of young ensigns or lieutenants whose self-importance is exaggerated and knowledge minimal. While an officer is trained to rigidly follow regulations to the last letter, noncoms learn how to bend them; they aim for an end result that fulfills the order, but get to it by any means they can.

Sometimes this involves minor pilfering of government property, for good purpose. As one Navy hand explained, "In other words, as a chief, you might 'steal' fifteen gallons of ice cream out of the mess, and maybe some cake and peanuts, so your division can have a picnic. What you're doing is misappropriating for unauthorized use. Some-times it's just flat stealing—but more often it's a means of morale building. It's stealing with a wink, because it's going to the right place." In the Navy, there is a word for it: cumshaw, which originally came from the Mandarin Chinese *kan hsieh*, to thank—the expression used by Chinese beggars long ago in gratitude for alms. In latter-day Navy parlance, it has come to mean getting something for nothing.[16]

NCOs in all the services do this kind of thing—circumvent the letter of the law to obey its spirit—and they pride themselves on it. Without it the military would be severely handicapped, if not entirely lost.

NCOs work hard to cultivate this very particular kind of savvy—and NCO kids inherit it. They grow up so steeped in the stories of their fathers and their fathers' buddies that it is second nature to them to know how to read between the lines, sidestep trouble, finesse situations.

Here's Eric, the son of an Air Force master sergeant, talking about honesty:

> For enlisted people, honesty is important—but it's different from officer honesty. I mean, I learned how to *bend* rules. If you hang around sergeants, you learn how to get around those crazy captains—some young green guy who's come out of West Point, and you've been around twenty-five years. Even when I was an ROTC cadet, I got along well with the sergeants. They'd tell stories about what they had to do to keep some young lieutenant in line.
>
> I'm honest, but if there's a way not to tell you something [I'll find it], because that's what enlisted people do a lot. Like staff sergeants, on those forms they have to fill out. You're honest and you don't break the rules and you don't get in trouble, but you learn how to get by. That's one of the strengths you get growing up in the military: My father always told me you have to do this, and this, and this to get around this stupid rule that's not practical.

The son gave an example of how he has applied those lessons in his adult life. When he went to college, he was elected head of the Black Student Union on his campus—and soon found that the organization was headed for crisis. BSU membership had dwindled to the point where the chapter would lose its charter unless a lot of members could be recruited in short order:

> So—and this instinct came directly from my father—I did something that was totally illegal, yet legal at the same time. I gave a party, a dance, because people like to go to dances. Everybody who went had to pay admission and also sign a form that said you were automatically a member of the Black Student Union. So in one day the membership went from ten to about three hundred and fifty. That was totally against the idea that people are supposed to join just because they want to—but it wasn't illegal, because they also signed the forms. It wasn't really dishonest, but it wasn't

totally honest, either. But there we were, the biggest chapter in the state, and people finally did get involved. And that's just the kind of stuff my father would do, under pressure.

I doubt that there's an NCO alive who could read this story without feeling a touch of vicarious pride that this son was such a chip off the old block.

This kind of savvy is something the officer corps is almost wholly without, as are its children. The idea of circumventing the letter to serve the spirit of the law is one of the hardest things for officer children to learn—if they ever learn it at all. Officer kids have book smarts but lack street savvy; enlisted kids frequently have both.

Living in Both Worlds

As we have seen, the social segregation of officer and enlisted is so extraordinarily thorough, the two classes might as well be hermetically sealed.

Only the children mix socially, and then only because even the hierarchical, class-conscious military can't justify the expense of educating its children separately.[17] So it is in the schools, and through the eyes of children, that the two classes get their best views of one another, scanning uneasily while pretending not to see, intuition honed to razor sharpness, warily walking the social minefield like edgy reconnaissance teams behind the lines.

And yet, in this world of social chasm, there are children who have not only observed both worlds but who have lived in them; who have looked at the officer class from below *and* the enlisted class from above; who know what it is to be called both inferior *and* superior, not according to merit but to class.

And no one can better speak to the effects of growing up in hierarchy than they.

These are the children of *mustangs*—men who began as enlisted and, through ability, brains, and sheer grit, worked their way up the ranks to the officer corps. Their children began in the underclass and took that as their identity—then had to recast themselves overnight when their fathers received the crucial promotion. They understand, in a way few others do, how class profoundly affects the way individual children are seen, and how those children come to see themselves.

Beatriz is the oldest daughter of an Army mustang. Both her parents are Hispanic; her father came from a large family in rural Puerto Rico, never finished high school, and enlisted in the military as soon as he could. The Army was his "saving grace," she said, and indeed he served it with the zeal of one redeemed. It was always his policy, she said, to be the best prepared, work the hardest, to not only fulfill the mission but exceed all expectations. He wanted to make it to the officer corps, badly. His daughter had no trouble understanding why.

"In a system with a hierarchy like that," she said, "you're made to feel that officers are a separate breed. That they're better genetic material than enlisted people. That they are better educated. That they're 'white': the elite. So you almost have two systems: a white elite, and a dark underclass. And for a third-world man to make officer is for him to escape the stigma."[18]

The same applies to the children. "As an enlisted kid," Beatriz recalled, "you're made to feel the apple doesn't fall too far from the tree. There is the unspoken question, 'Is your father so stupid that he can't be *more* than an enlisted man?' "

Beatriz said her father would come home from work and make his whole family listen while he practiced making speeches, so they could correct his English. "He was so scared he'd mispronounce something. He always had an accent, and he tried so hard to overcome it, especially as an officer. He enunciated very, very clearly.

"I always felt my father was real smart," Beatriz added. "He just didn't have the education. We [children] caught up to him real quick. We were 'smarter' than he was, and I think that might have been a little frightening for him. He pulled in the reins a little tighter."

Her father was promoted to the officer corps during the Bay of Pigs, in 1961. By the time he retired, some fourteen years later, he had made it to the rank of major. Beatriz was in junior high when he first made officer. She remembers the class transition very well; all sorts of things changed overnight. Suddenly the family found itself in another league. "There were visible differences," Beatriz said,

the housing was better. Your father made a little more money. You had a better car. The uniform looked better. The brass looked better. The hat looked better. It was all upscale. When my father was an enlisted man, we only had beer in the house. As soon as he became an officer, we got a liquor cabinet.

And my mother had to go through a transformation. She had to join the officers' wives' club. Officers' wives have an important role as an extension of their husbands. Enlisted wives are really kind of superfluous. My mother became much more of a power behind the throne as an officer's wife. It's like a corporation. So she had to learn to be a club wife. She always told me, "Beatriz, Americans love to join clubs." She thought that was a really white kind of thing to do. She never quite understood it, but

she did her role because it was important for my father's career. She's a
very charming person, so she pulled it off well—but she always felt it was
like playing a game.

She also had to start doing a lot of volunteer work—at the hospital, or
having bake sales for Traveler's Aid and other things to "help" enlisted
people. It's a kind of noblesse oblige.

I really enjoyed being an officer's kid. It was a real privilege. You're seen
as automatically smarter. Just by association you get brownie points. You
get to go to the officers' club. You get to go to *their* beach. I loved the
privileges. But then more is expected of you, too. I can remember my
father saying, "You're an officer's kid now." Our deportment was supposed
to be different. You had to walk instead of run by the pool.

But I liked it all. It's great to be on the side of people who are winning.
It's every kid's dream to be on the winning team.

But the reality of life inside the Fortress is that not every child can be
on the winning team. A great many are branded losers or less-thans,
not because they deserve it but because they chanced to be born into
that category, and the Fortress itself needs to keep them in that role.

It is a stigma these military brats find difficult to shake. The ironclad class categorizations, coming so early in childhood, may limit
their sense of how far they can go, how much they can achieve.

And it is a stigma that haunts them when, in adulthood, they
emigrate from the stratified, authoritarian world of the Fortress to the
vastly different world of civilian America, a world that places far more
emphasis on achievement than on social origin.

CHAPTER 10

OUTSIDER/ INSIDER

I and my brothers against my cousins;
I and my cousins against the world.
                                    —*Arab saying*

For a child caught up in the transient military life, shaping one's social identity can be as frustrating an exercise as writing on shifting sand. It is to work hard and doggedly at creating something, knowing all the while that the entire effort will be sacrificed to the harsh and inevitable wind of change; not a trace will be left to honor one's industry or mark one's passage.

The reality of life in the military is that it is much too fluid for a child to establish a social identity over time, the way rooted civilians come to understand themselves. And the way in which a military child is always brushing against other people's established communities, ever on the outside looking in, has the effect of reinforcing the sense of apartness.

The rootless children of warriors grow up with confused and incomplete notions of what it is to belong—but they know all too well what it means to be an outsider, and that in fact becomes as much of a social role as they are likely to experience. It is the first and perhaps greatest division between themselves and others.

The interviews for this book showed that quite often, these notions persist well into adulthood. Indeed, many military brats in mid-life were still far from answering the question of where they belong with any degree of satisfaction. They know they are no longer military, in the sense they were as children, but they also feel they are not civilians. These military brats live in the margins of life, observing curiously, and from a distance, the connectedness others seem to have. They may want "insideness"—badly—but they know they may very likely never know what that means.

In his book *The Arab Mind*, Raphael Patai writes about this problem of marginality. He is speaking of Arabs living in countries long subjugated to colonial rule, and which have yet to rediscover their own national identity. But his words could apply equally to military brats:

> "Marginality" denotes the state of belonging to two cultures without being able to identify oneself completely with either.
> An individual becomes "marginal" if, after having been born into a culture and enculturated into it in a more or less normal fashion, he becomes exposed to another culture, is attracted to it, acquires a measure of familiarity with it . . . and strives to become a full-fledged carrier of it—an endeavor which, in most cases, never completely succeeds. The marginal man suffers from his inability to feel completely at ease or "at home" in either culture. . . . Marginal man is marginal, not because he is unable to acquire the intellectual thought processes of the culture to which he wants to assimilate, nor because he is unable to free himself of the thought processes of the culture on which he has turned his back. He is marginal because *emotionally* he is unable to identify with either of the two cultures.[1]

The marginality of military brats is most in evidence among those— the vast majority—who grow up to enter into civilian life instead of going into the military themselves. The son of an Air Force sergeant, reflecting on the path his life has taken, said, "There is a strange way in which [as a military brat] you become alienated from the military . . . but at the same time the military has distanced you from civilian life as well. For example, I see the business community as profit-oriented at the expense of social concern—a perception that I think comes from growing up in the military. And perhaps that led me into academic life, which is neither fish nor fowl. It's not military and it's not business, yet it does have a service component."

OUTSIDER/INSIDER: THE MILITARY

The first world military brats come to know is, of course, the Fortress. But even within the secure confines of the Fortress, a military brat's social identity is couched in terms of *us* vs. *them*.

When I was a small child, I understood that we were something called an "Army family," although I had only a vague idea of what that meant. But I knew one thing for certain: We were most definitely *not* Navy.

Social identity within the Fortress, even for little children, is very much a reflection of the fierce intertribal rivalries that so mark service life. For young military brats struggling to find their footing on the rapidly shifting sand of their social world, tribal identification offers a stabilizing point of reference—even if it is couched as much in terms of who one is *not* as who one *is*.

Inside the Fortress, there is no dearth of cues from which a child may learn the authorized perspective on rival "tribes." The last verse of "The Marines' Hymn," memorized by every self-respecting Marine brat, is an example:

> *Here's health to you and to your Corps*
> *Which we are proud to serve;*
> *In many a strife we've fought for life*
> *And never lost our nerve.*
> *If the Army and the Navy*
> *Ever look on Heaven's scenes,*
> *They will find the streets are guarded*
> *By United States Marines.*

In childhood or later, there is probably no single event that will divide a group of military brats against one another like the annual Army-Navy football game. Air Force brats usually side with Army, and Marine brats tend to go for Navy; it is hardly necessary to point out where the others stand on this all-important loyalty test. When I was growing up, it seemed the autumn proceeded inexorably toward that one monumental event, which more often than not left my father in a scowling black humor.[2]

In the fall of 1965, when I was in the ninth grade, the advancing gloom of November—with its specter of likely humiliation by Navy, which had won five of the six preceding games—was broken by a magnificently electrifying event. A group of cadets from West Point, assisted by some young women enlisted as decoys, managed to sneak onto the grounds of the Naval Academy in Annapolis and steal Navy's mascot, a large billy goat with its massive horns painted Navy blue and gold. They had had to get past a ten-foot-high fence topped with barbed wire and take the goat from a well-lighted pen topped with more barbed wire, just twenty yards from two armed Marine guards.

In military circles, the theft was sensational—particularly since the Naval Academy was off-limits to West Point cadets (just as West Point was off-limits to midshipmen) and the commandants of the two military academies had publicly given their word that the mascots would be safe from such pranks. The uproar was such that the Secretary of the Army intervened; the superintendent of West Point subsequently threatened to confine the entire corps of cadets for the Army-Navy game and Thanksgiving weekend unless the goat was returned. It was, and the ensuing game ended in a 7–7 tie.

As a measure of traditional Army-Navy rivalry, however, nothing about the incident was more telling than what happened when the ringleader of the goat-stealing group appeared before the West Point superintendent to receive his punishment. This part of the story was certainly not revealed to the public at the time, but as related in the 1989 book *The Long Gray Line*, the superintendent in 1965, a two-star general, removed the ringleader cadet's first-class (senior year) privileges for two months—not a particularly stiff punishment—and added, "But I want you to know I'd be proud to have you serve under me in the Army. Well done."[3]

While there is an overlay of humor to all this, there can be little doubt that at least some military people take these rivalries seriously. One Army colonel's daughter told me her father refused to attend her wedding because she was marrying a Navy brat.

Children of the Fortress grow up with epithets about rival services rolling off their tongues as easily as the pro-forma phrasing with which they answer the phone. The lingo of military rivalry is ubiquitous and infectious.

Marines, for instance, are in the habit of referring to sailors as "squids," "swabbies," and "rustpickers," and to Navy ships as "rustbuckets" and "taxicabs for the Marines."

Navy people, for their part, call Marines "seagoing bellhops," "gyrenes," "jarheads," and "weed wigglers," referring to Marine amphibious landing forces making their way onto the beach.

Marines refer to Army infantry soldiers as "doggies," short for "dogfaces." In the Army, Air Force personnel are known as "zoomies," and any active-duty Army soldier caught lounging with hands in pockets is chided for "wearing Air Force gloves," implying that Air Force types are lazy. Both the Army and the Air Force use the terms "squid" and "jarhead," and everyone seems to call Army soldiers "grunts."

Tribal identification is every bit as important to the children as it is to their parents. The transient lifestyle so works against the normal evolution of social identity that a military child might well overidentify with the military tribe, or with the father's rank, or with his job category, as a way of compensating. There has to be some handle for understanding where one stands in relation to the world—and moving frequently essentially rules out certain traditional ways of doing that. It means, for instance, that the child does not have a chance to know his relatives, have long-term friendships, or see his parents function in a fixed constellation of community members over a long period of time. The "tribe" assumes inordinate importance for the military brat, who in turn expects other military brats to hold similarly strong allegiances.

"I remember being in a military-dependent school and always having to represent my branch of the service as though it were a matter of honor," said the son of an Air Force colonel. "I was the only Air Force kid. There were a couple of Navy and Marine kids, and the rest were Army. In a spelling bee, for instance, you wouldn't be competing against other kids, you'd compete against other *services*. I was always the Air Force representative in everything, even out on the playground with bubblegum and who could blow the biggest bubble. It was Army versus Air Force versus Navy. You were always fighting with your friends about which service was the greatest. If you hit a home run, it was for the Army or the Air Force. If you fucked up, people yelled, 'Nyaah, nyaah—*Air Force.*'

"Of course," this son added, "you got this at home, in your family. My father hated and despised the Navy and made no bones about it. He wouldn't even give you a rational reason for it."

Ask military brats, now many years into adulthood, their opinions about the other branches of the service, and it's like uncorking an old bottle: The prejudices of childhood pour forth fresh and vehement and undiminished by time. And although the most vitriolic comments are now often followed by a wry, self-conscious smile at the patent absurdity of the distinctions, it is clear the old tribal textures are still very much a part of their lives.

A Navy admiral's daughter: "We were not good on the Army. Marines were better, but they're jarheads and dumb. Navy was the best."

An Army sergeant's daughter: "I hated the Marine Corps. They were the pits, and they had too much color in their uniforms. Next on the pit list was Navy."

An Air Force sergeant's son, who now lives in a heavily Navy and Marine Corps area: "Air Force was the best, of course. . . . Since I moved here, when I go to a baseball game and they play the Marine Corps hymn, I stand up, because I really respect those guys, but when they play 'Anchors Aweigh' [for the Navy], I don't stand. I also notice that the Navy guys don't stand for the Marine Corps hymn, even though the Marines stand for 'Anchors Aweigh.' It burns me that the Navy guys don't stand up for the Marines."

These strongly felt tribal affiliations are merely the most blatant of the rivalries nursed within the Fortress, and around which children fashion their group identities. But there are many subdivisions of these loyalties, too, based on the rivalries *within* each service.

The Navy has intense rivalries among its three broad categories of aviators, submariners, and surface ship drivers; each considers itself the elite. Naval aviators are known to the others as "Naval radiators," "airdales," or "jet jockeys." Submariners are called "bubble heads." Surface ship drivers have gotten off remarkably easily to date; they're referred to as "black shoes," which does not distinguish them from submariners. (Even though everyone in the Navy now wears black shoes, at one time the aviators wore brown.) Aviators, submariners, and surface ship personnel all dismiss civilian employees of the Navy as "sand crabs."

In the Air Force the principal division is between pilots, dubbed "wing nuts," and "ground grippers," or support personnel.

The Marine Corps uses much the same terminology as the Navy for its aviators, with the addition of "rotor heads" for helicopter pilots, and uses Army lingo for its infantry. Other than that, Marines don't cultivate many names for one another, mainly because, as one officer told me, "We make such a big deal out of just being Marines." However, this mostly applies to Marines in the combat arms, for they have plenty of epithets for noncombat personnel: "pogues," "bean counters" (supply), "data dinks" (computer users), "Remington Raiders" (administrative, referring to typewriters), and "pencil-necked geeks."

The Army is rife with distinctions. Infantry calls itself "the King of Battle," while the other branches refer to infantrymen as "grunts" and "ground pounders." Artillery sees itself as "the Queen of Battle," but its people are known as "redlegs" (after the chosen color of that branch) or "cannon cockers." Armored cavalry personnel (tankers) boast that "If you ain't Cav, you ain't," while the other branches call them "tread heads." Air defense personnel are known as "duck hunters." Helicopter pilots are "fly boys," "taxicab drivers" (if they pilot troop transports), and "chopper whoppers." All noncombat personnel—those who serve in the comparative safety of the finance corps, medical corps, quartermaster corps, or the like—are dismissed as "REMFs," or "rear-echelon mother fuckers."

In all the services, in fact, there is generally more prestige attached to the combat arms branches than to the others. In the Navy, for instance, an F-14 pilot or the captain of a nuclear submarine would carry far more cachet than a "pork chop"—a supply officer, so named because the oak leaves on their uniforms vaguely resemble chops.

Another insider group within each service is composed of officers who graduated from military academies. At their best, academy graduates experience an automatic bonding and camaraderie that is both gratifying to them and well suited to military life, where the ability to make instant connections pays off. Some of them, however—referred to derisively as "ringknockers"—are capable of demonstrating an offensively exclusionary clubbiness. A Navy daughter told of how one November in Hawaii, her father, a lieutenant commander, was barred from entering the lounge of the officers' club to join a group watching the Army-Navy game because he was not a graduate of Annapolis.

I and my brothers against my cousins. . . . Could there be a better phrase to describe the complex tribal rivalries within the warrior society?

But that is only half the saying, and only half the story. For just as the military is capable of endlessly splitting itself into competing factions, it is also capable of closing ranks solidly in the face of outsiders. At those times, all warriors stand as brothers shoulder to shoulder at the gate of the Fortress, staring implacably at the alien world beyond their perimeters.

. . . I and my cousins against the world.

OUTSIDER/INSIDER: THE CIVILIAN WORLD

Most of the military brats interviewed for this book were asked an identical question: "After all these years of living among civilians, do you feel like one of them?" The answer in almost every case was an emphatic *no*. "I have always felt like a military brat," said the son of an Air Force lieutenant colonel. "I will *never* feel like a civilian." The son of an Air Force sergeant said, "No, I don't feel like a civilian, and I don't ever want to."

In perceptions, values, loyalties, habits, military brats well into adulthood still feel distinctly different—even as they live civilian lifestyles, marry into civilian families, raise civilian children.[4]

These feelings of separateness go straight back to childhood. It is next to impossible to grow up in the warrior society without absorbing the notion that civilians are very different and sometimes incomprehensible. By the same token, it would be extremely rare to meet a military brat who did not grow up with an uncomfortable awareness of a converse civilian antipathy toward the military community—something a psychiatrist once described as "a kind of gypsy phenomenon." "Military people are seen by the nearby community as transients and are often targets of mistrust and hostility," he wrote. "Not only does this further isolate the family and cause them to stay within the confines of the base, it presents a difficult situation for the children attending public school. They have to break into peer groups repeatedly as 'the new kid' and are often the school's scapegoats."[5]

Judy, daughter of a Navy lieutenant commander, recalled that learning how civilians often look down on the military came as a rude shock. When she was in high school in a civilian community and her father was stationed overseas for three years, her mother, a teacher in a public school, applied to sponsor a foreign high school exchange student. She was rejected by the board on the grounds she was "a transient"—even though the family had made a decision to remain within the community while the father left on various assignments. Judy was unequivocal in describing her mother's reaction: She took it as a stinging rebuke from a civilian community that did not understand or care to understand military people.

Judy now lives in one of the most exclusive neighborhoods in southern California. She, her civilian husband, and their children are involved and respected members of the community. Yet Judy still feels insecure. "In this neighborhood, when they ask what my father did, I get a funny feeling," she said. "I say he was in the Navy. I don't apologize for it, *ever*, but I always wonder how it's being perceived."

Parker, the son of an Air Force lieutenant colonel, said he grew up conscious of the mixed signals sent by the civilians around him. "I think we were aware there was a certain amount of respect from civilians for the military mission, but there was also an awareness of that old saw, 'He couldn't hack it in civilian life so he went into the military.' We resented that."

Another thing that rankles military families is that civilians often seem to blithely overlook a central truth military people can never afford to forget: that at any moment they may be called upon to give their lives—or lose a loved one—to serve the ends of government. Even if it never comes to that, military people sacrifice a great deal in the course of doing a job that most civilians on some level understand is necessary to the country as a whole.

Often military brats are literally born with an inheritance of civilian contempt; some interviewed for this book told of mothers whose families strongly disapproved of their having married military men, feeling they were "marrying down." In some cases the breach was never completely mended, and the children have grown up unsure of their acceptance in the homes of their own blood relatives.

No matter what the stated objection, the antipathy of many civilians is rooted in a simple fact: Military people are by definition *outsiders*, unknown quantities passing through civilian communities like shadows on a screen, too obvious to ignore, but not real enough to know and understand.

It is unsurprising, then, that military brats, reared with a keen sense of separateness that is reinforced by attitudes within and without the Fortress, find the outsider identity almost impossible to shed in later life.

Culture Shock

The awareness of the civilian community as an alien world comes to children of the Fortress at different times. Many military brats have distinct recollections of when that perception crystallized in their own lives, with the oddly simultaneous sense of being an insider in one community and an outsider in the other.

A Navy lieutenant commander's son said it happened to him at age six, when he started school. "We were on Nantucket Island, living in Navy housing with a hospital across the street. At school I had some friends who weren't military, and I was struck by the difference in their houses and mine. It's weird to think it at that young age, but I remember looking at the houses and realizing I lived in a prefab-type house. The Navy houses were all the same. My friends who weren't in the Navy had real neat houses. I began to look at civilian kids as lucky. They had dads, they had homes, and they had normal lives."

An Army sergeant's daughter: "It seemed we always lived in compounds with barbed wire all around. That was how it was in Japan, and in Germany. It set us apart. I knew we were part of some select group, and others could not freely come and go, although we could. My most poignant memory is when I was about thirteen, and we came back from Germany. For the first time I had to go into a civilian environment. It was a tremendous culture shock, the civilian school. People had fathers at home. People had fathers who helped out. People had fathers who wore ties and suits and casual clothes. It was very difficult."

An Air Force sergeant's son: "The first time I went to a civilian hospital, as a teenager, they were so nice to me I wept."

A Marine sergeant's daughter: "As a child I was always aware that civilians were the 'other.' They were different from us military families, and their lives were different from our lives. They were more settled. They were generally more affluent. They lived in nice neighborhoods instead of these 'projects' we lived in. And their fathers did interesting things. I remember thinking it was really exotic for somebody's father to work at a gas station, or have a music store."

An Air Force sergeant's son: "I had a close friend in high school who was a civilian. It wasn't until I spent a lot of time with his family that I realized not everyone lived like we did. I was truly astonished at this deeply different family pattern. They were calm. They didn't worry about the same things I did. They had a totally different attitude about what was going on. They did things together. They had a regular schedule. If they had neighbors who were alcoholic or abusive, they thought it was scandalous and abnormal—whereas we thought it was the other way around. We really did."

An Air Force general's daughter: "I adored college. It was the first time I'd met men [professors] who were bright, gifted, and nonmilitary. I was so thrilled to meet grownups who weren't generals, who weren't killers, and who wanted to talk about ideas. That turned my life around. I became a very good student, because I immediately grasped the value of teachers. But I had no relationship to the other girls in my dorm. It took me a couple of years to adjust to the civilian mentality; I couldn't understand these people—what they were doing, talking about, or the things they held important."

An Air Force sergeant's son: "You know the strangest thing that ever happened to me? We were at Scott Air Force Base in Illinois and I was in junior high school off base. I became good friends with a kid, because after this he *needed* a friend. He came in after the school year had started, and he was saying 'yes, ma'am' to the teacher. He was polite. And the teacher got upset, and said, 'Don't call me that. I'm not old.' It just happened that his father was still there, standing outside, and he heard that. And his father was an officer. So he walked in and explained to the teacher that at home in the military, this is what you do. He had to explain to her so she wouldn't punish him. I didn't see why she was so offended in the first place.

"But I'll never forget that, because this little kid was so confused. This was *the way he lived*, and it was a good way. To tell him not to say it was traumatic for him, because his father would have killed him, like my father would have killed me, if he hadn't said 'yes, sir' or 'yes, ma'am.' "

Even well into their adult years, military brats who think they have adapted to civilian ways tell of moments when they are brought up short, overwhelmed by the realization that their own perceptions and those of the civilian next to them are impossibly far apart. In the midst of a normal conversation, there is the sense of the floor suddenly opening up, revealing a chasm of differentness. And there is nothing to say.

The same Air Force son who related the story about the boy who called his teacher "ma'am" later ran into a similar situation himself as a graduate student. "I had to force myself to stop saying 'ma'am' and 'sir,' " said the son, who is black. "I said it to my [white] professor one time and he almost *died*. He started talking about slavery and yes'm, no'm—he went off on a whole tangent.

"I concluded he was lacking in social skills, because he might have at least asked before he went way off like that. He just battered me, he was so upset. Once I saluted him, but he took that the wrong way, too. To me that was affection, a very positive thing."

Another Air Force sergeant's son told of taking a trip to South America a few years ago with five civilian friends. "They couldn't believe those countries," he said, "that people could live that way, with military police in the public parks. It seemed perfectly normal to me."

Nearly every military brat can speak of situations where conversation with a civilian stalled on an awkward note. The civilian, upon finding out the other is the child of a warrior, begins asking the usual questions: "How did you like moving around all the time?" or "What was your father's rank?" The questions are natural enough, and hardly offensive, but they have the effect of instantly revealing the lack of common points of reference. The military brat knows that no matter how he or she answers the question, the civilian will not know how to process it.

Military Brats in Civilian Schools

For most military brats, the outsider feeling begins the first time they attend a civilian school. The experience of being "the new kid" is an alienating one for anyone, but for military brats it is complicated by cultural difference: There are sometimes deep differences in values, beliefs, behaviors, interests, worries. If it were not for certain other abilities military brats develop to compensate—such as the chameleonlike ability to conform to the environment discussed in Chapter 8—the situation would be impossibly difficult.

As it is, military brats do not develop these skills equally. And even a military brat who has them can be so traumatized by an ill-timed move that the skills never kick into gear. Henry, the son of an Air Force sergeant, told of the loneliness and isolation he experienced when his father retired and the family returned to the States from Germany. He spent his junior and senior years in civilian high schools where the only other military brats were his brothers. "At one high school I got into a fight because I had a different accent from the other kids. I got kicked out because of the fight, and went to another school. At both schools the kids couldn't accept the fact I'd lived in Europe. I don't know what they were thinking; I don't know if they were jealous or naive.

"I would have felt better graduating from a military [dependent] school than a civilian one. I wouldn't have had to go through so much just to make friends. I can remember a lot of lunchtimes eating alone, or going to the gym and playing basketball alone. I had no stories that related to their past."

No stories that related to their past. In established, stable communities, shared history is nearly everything. Once I had a conversation about belonging with a civilian who was reared in a small town in Wyoming. It's a fine, tight-knit community, he said, but when somebody new moves to town, the people are at a loss as to how to get to know the person. "They've never learned how to ask questions," he said. "When you know everyone else and always have, there is no need for questions; you assume you already know everything there is to know." How different, then, is the military brat—who in effect stands outside the community, the culture, the history of the civilians around him. He is the outsider with no stories that relate to their past, no ready handle for them to relate to him.

As described in Chapter 8, military children entering a new school are extremely sensitive to their status as outsiders, and do everything in their power to break into the social order. They take the fastest route possible, gravitating to the top and bottom echelons but rarely to the middle—because the paths of superachiever and social outcast are the ones most readily open to them. The middle layers usually consist of local civilians who form nearly impenetrable social cliques.

For the military brat whose "outsideness" propels him or her into the superachiever path, there are genuine benefits: a positive social identity, a bettering of chances for higher education and career, a way to get positive parental attention and important validation by the community. High achievement improves self-image and attracts mentors—teachers, coaches, others—who help fill the gap left by an inattentive or absent parent, and the lack of friends. An additional benefit was cited by an Army colonel's son who explained his high-achieving high school record as "displaced aggression"—a way to constructively rechannel the anger he harbored toward his father. But *both* over-achievement and underachievement by military brats can be read as efforts by outsiders to reach out for recognition, inclusion, and the attention of adults and peers.

The child's task of coping with the culture shock of civilian ways is probably far greater than most military parents realize. It is not something that is usually discussed in military families—or indeed with anyone. Many of the military brats interviewed for this book said they were articulating their old feelings of discomfort for the first time. Sometimes their recollections come with emotion as fresh as if it had all happened yesterday.

"I had more difficulty in fifth grade than any other year growing up," said the son of a Marine Corps lieutenant colonel.

> That was the first year we lived in a civilian community. From *my* perspective, these kids were out of their minds. They didn't know how big the country was. They couldn't say Schenectady. They didn't know there was a place called Okinawa. They didn't look at news on TV because they didn't have a stake in it. *I did:* My daddy was over there. My world felt bigger—and to them, it felt false. They said, 'You don't have a father. We've never seen him.' Those were fighting words.
>
> Point of view, and notions about what is right, what feels safe, what is familiar, what's okay, can be very different [for military kids than for civilians]. And all I knew was uniforms, duty, and that security was being in the bosom of the service. That did not feel insecure; it felt *safe*.
>
> It felt *unsafe* to be in a civilian community with a whole bunch of different rules, and to some extent an absence of rules. We had gone from quarters where my father was the senior officer in his building and we knew how we were supposed to behave and other people knew how they were supposed to respond, to living in a suburban neighborhood where there was nobody in charge. My point of view was that this was a very strange way to live, and I was delighted to get back to a Marine Corps community.

Antipathy Returned

Some military brats who felt they were among aliens disguised their discomfort with hostility of their own, sometimes modeled on warrior arrogance. An Air Force colonel's son said he remembered thinking of his civilian peers as "stupid." He said that he and his Air Force brat friends commonly referred to town kids as "tool users."

The son of an Air Force lieutenant colonel said, "I think we looked down a little on the civilian world. After all, we weren't there to make a profit. *Duty, honor, country.* As corny as it sounds, those words still have meaning. Even just as family members we felt we were serving our country. I retain a residual pride in having been part of a military family. There was a common feeling among military families that we were serving a larger need of our society."

Although military brats clearly see many virtues in the civilian community, go to great lengths to integrate into it professionally and personally, and have no qualms about marrying civilians, it seems that their long history as outsiders has left many with a critical view.

Asked to give their general opinions of civilians, adult military brats made almost exclusively negative comments. They characterized civilians as "standoffish," "inefficient," "lazy," "[having] little consideration for punctuality," "sloppy on matters of personal integrity," "disorganized," "wishy-washy on decision-making," and "rule-benders." "They don't go by the book," one complained. "A lot of civilians do just enough to get by," said another, "but in the military you go all out and give it your best."

An Army major's daughter said the gulf is large enough that she has difficulty understanding civilians. "It's always bizarre to me, their sense of place," she said. "The people who have extended families, who grew up in one house. That's very different from my reality. It's real hard to work myself up to empathy when some civilian is fretting and worrying about moving or making a change."

An Air Force colonel's daughter said, "Civilians seemed different. They seemed 'other.' I used to think—and maybe I still do—that civilians don't have as strong a sense of duty as military people. And that they're lazy and undisciplined and narrow-minded. It's like they don't know about the world.

"When I give my word I'll do something, I do it," she continued. "And sometimes I wish I hadn't promised, because then I let myself in for a lot of hassle—but I do it anyway because I said I would. Most civilians I know change their mind and break their word any time they feel like it."

Despite the overwhelmingly negative reviews military brats seem ready to dish out to civilians, these remarks are not exclusively representative of the way military brats think about them. Absent were the many positive qualities military brats were ready in other contexts to credit to civilians—intellectual curiosity, loving families, nurturing fathers, willingness to question authority and speak out. More than likely the question I asked them marked the first time they'd had the opportunity to air complaints they'd been harboring for years but could scarcely share with the civilians in their lives.

Vietnam

Never in the lifetimes of the military brats interviewed for this book has there been an issue that has done more to separate them psychologically from their civilian peers than the war in Vietnam.

It was a wrenching, confusing time for children of warriors, raised never to question the powers that be. For many it coincided with their own coming of age. Some went to Vietnam and died there. Others went and returned, shaken. The rest of us tried to make sense of it, find our voices.

I was a junior in high school in 1968, during the Tet Offensive. The disaster of Tet marked the beginning of the end of American public support for the war, as was apparent even in the small private high school I attended. Although most of my peers were the children of well-heeled, conservative civilians, they were rapidly shedding their willingness to automatically rubber-stamp those values. I, however, was a steadfast Teenage Republican, and gave a speech for Richard Nixon in our school's mock elections that fall. Later the same year I passionately defended the Vietnam War before my speech class, keenly aware that my classmates, most of them apolitical or liberal, could not have seen me as more alien if I'd leaped off a Huey (helicopter gunship) into their midst.

My speech resounded with American responsibilities to the Southeast Asia Treaty Organization, and of course the domino theory, warning that if the United States pulled out, the Communists would seize control of Vietnam, stop all oil tankers passing through the Strait of Malacca, and attack the Western economy through its oil-starved allies. "Japanese industry would grind to a halt," I remember saying fervently. I was very much my father's daughter as I spoke those words, very much a defender of the Fortress.

Within a few months, however, in my job as a summer intern for a daily paper, I was exposed to the world beyond the Fortress for the first time. By the time I arrived at college, I was hungry for different perspectives, thrilled to be out from under my father's authoritarian rule, and filled with the zeal (and newly minted cynicism) of one already bent on a journalism career. The antiwar movement drew me like a magnet.

The raging controversy over the Vietnam War both challenged me to find my own values and offered a convenient medium for the anger I needed to vent. And luckily for me, my father had retired from the military, so any action I chose to take did not run the risk of hurting his career. It was my neck and no one else's; if I could find my moral voice, I was free to exercise it. However, it was not easy to find that voice.

In the fall of 1969, barely a month after I arrived on campus for my freshman year, word spread of a huge peace demonstration planned in Washington, D.C., just a few hours away.[6] The night before the demonstration, one of my civilian friends spotted me on campus and shouted, "Come on! We've got a van going to D.C. and there's just enough room for you! Hurry up!" To my friend's consternation, I refused. "Why *not*?" he asked in disbelief, stopping in his tracks. I had told no one of the conflict that tormented me. Yes I was against the war, but *no* I was not antimilitary. Yes I wanted to protest, but *no* I didn't want to condemn country and military wholesale. What would it mean to lend my presence to a huge, historic demonstration that would be read only one way?

My friend searched my face for an answer. "I can't go," I finally told him, "because armbands only come in black, not in shades of gray." He stared at me blankly, then shook his head and ran off to join the caravan.

At that moment I felt morally right, but still sad and confused. It took me a few days to work it out, but eventually I felt my friend had been right, and I wrong. The important thing at that moment, I came to feel, had been to stand foursquare against the war, in public. Confronted with a moral choice, I had backed off and hidden beind a convenient phrase that in the final analysis meant nothing morally, politically, or philosophically. I realized I had better figure out what it means to exercise free speech in a democracy. It dawned on me that in public protests, positions are stated broadly; the signs do not carry footnotes. Nor are armbands dyed to match one's place in the spectrum of opinion.

After that I went on to protest the war openly and loudly. I had found my voice at last, but there was only limited comfort in that. I was never free of internal conflict, and found myself mentally editing everything I said out loud. "I am against the Vietnam War," I would declare, but add in my thoughts, *This war, not all wars. And I condemn the government leaders promoting this war, not the military doomed to fight it.*

Many other military brats speak to having been torn by similar conflicts. It was particularly hard for those whose parents were still active-duty—whose careers could potentially be harmed by the public protests of a child—and those whose fathers were serving or had served in Vietnam. Many knew, too, how their military parents privately disagreed with the war and felt trapped by it, but were powerless to do or say anything in opposition. Following is a sampling of how some military brats handled the dilemma of Vietnam:

A Navy lieutenant commander's daughter, who kept silent: "Patriotism is an important value in my family. The Vietnam era was very hard for me. I tried to hang on to my loyalty to my country no matter what—to the point of ignoring what was happening in the news.

"I remember in Hawaii my parents talking about it even as convoys rolled by in the background. The buildup was just beginning, and they were both saying it was a mistake.

"I never demonstrated or anything. I would never have done anything to embarrass my father. I just quietly hated that war."

An Air Force colonel's daughter who feared hurting her father's career: "It was hard for me, because I opposed the war and wanted to demonstrate, but I didn't want to get my dad in trouble. So I *did* demonstrate—but I'd hold the sign right in front of my face so no one could tell who I was."

A Navy petty officer's son, who served in Vietnam as a Marine officer: "I went over there knowing why I was going and feeling comfortable with that. I had no problem with Vietnam then, and I have no problem now."[7]

An Army colonel's son who, with his brother, a Vietnam veteran, vigorously protested the war but did not let their father know: "After my father retired from the Army he went to work for the government, in D.C. It was during the Vietnam War, and demonstrations often filled the streets. His friends had to restrain him on several occasions from running into the crowd and grabbing the Vietcong flags some protesters carried. We never talked much about the war with him because we knew it would be a fight." Meanwhile, however, this son helped a group of student radicals storm and take over the ROTC building on their campus—and his brother, who had become very active in Vietnam Veterans Against the War, threw his medals over the White House fence.

Military brats during the Vietnam War covered the whole spectrum of opinion, from those wholly supporting the war, to those wholly condemning it, to those who declined to take a position. What I believe all had in common, however, was a sensitivity to the real human beings serving in the military who were swept into the hell that was Vietnam. The children of warriors did not find it easy to swallow the caricature of the military as a monolithic, inhuman juggernaut thriving on death and destruction. We all knew someone who had served there, someone who had died there. For us the warriors were not faceless and inhuman: They were our fathers, our brothers, our cousins. We could not condemn them. And that point alone was enough to divide us from many of our civilian peers.[8]

Craig, an Air Force sergeant's son who was politically radicalized by the war, told of his personal dilemma. "It was 1966–67. I can remember walking out of the Student Union at noon and seeing the first antiwar protest on campus. There were only six or seven people in a line, carrying signs and committed to saying nothing. I knew them, but I didn't join them. I was walking with a very good friend just out of Marine Corps training and on his way to Vietnam. He needed my help more than anyone else there needed it. This was the contradiction: I understood what the others were *doing*, but I also understood where he was *going*. It's a symbol of where I was caught in the middle of this."

Craig today remains a political radical, but his fundamental point of view is that of a military brat, sympathetic to the men and women of the Fortress. He was drafted but did not serve in Vietnam. As a student he participated in many demonstrations, but often with a strong distaste for what he saw and heard around him. "I could not abide this hatred of soldiers just because they're soldiers," he said. "Emotionally and intellectually I found it repulsive. I was trained to see soldiers as individuals.

"There's a kind of response the Left has to anyone in uniform, thinking of them as fascist," he continued. "And I don't mean a Wehrmacht soldier, either. I mean an SS officer or official in a position of responsibility to engineer the Holocaust. I've spoken in leftist forums of soldiers as working-class people, and I've taken plenty of abuse for it, and it does not endear me to many leftists. At the same time, I despise right-wing types who send other people's children to die. All my life I've grown up with veterans. So I have this distaste for the Right *and* the Left."

The views of this Marxist military brat were echoed in the words of many others self-described as conservative. "I never participated in protests," said Henry, the son of an Air Force sergeant. "I *hated* the protesters, and I still do. I think we shouldn't have been in Vietnam, should never have interfered there all the way back to when Ho Chi Minh was running for president. But I don't think that justifies Americans protesting against the men and women who had no choice about going."

For military brats who opposed the war, no matter what their political point of departure, the question became how to find that fine line where it was possible to protest the war without rejecting one's country, without dishonoring the warrior fathers, without tarnishing the profession we were reared to believe is both noble and necessary. Many of the military brats I spoke to struggled with that dilemma and did not find a way to resolve it. Certainly the way I chose—to join my voice with those of civilian protesters—was not a satisfying one. I was always troubled by the thought that those whose cause I did my part to strengthen were the very people who did not understand the military and never would.

One thing I believe all of us children of the Fortress sensed in our gut: The opposition to the war was too simplistic. It condemned too broadly, too blackly. Where it should have focused clearly on national policy and those who shaped it, the movement blindly condemned those charged to carry out the war, who had little freedom to refuse.

It is true there were individuals in the military who did refuse, and who accepted the consequences. Where these acts were morally driven, it is possible to say those individuals were courageously obeying a higher law. But it was and is unrealistic to imagine an entire armed force laying down its weapons in mutiny against an unpalatable foreign policy. And it is purely fanciful to imagine that soldiers should pick and choose the wars they wish to fight; that's the last thing any country would want, for nation-states depend absolutely on their warriors to do as they are commanded without question or hesitation. Therefore to condemn wholesale hundreds of thousands of soldiers who did not desert or mutiny but went, as ordered, into the nightmare of the Vietnam War, is not only to misplace the blame, but to lack compassion.

On this point military brats of both Right and Left stand united.

OUTSIDER/INSIDER: OVERSEAS

One of the most intense outsider experiences lived out by military brats comes when their families are stationed overseas. Iran, Thailand, Bavaria, South Korea, Ethiopia, France, Japan, Italy, the Philippines, Spain, to mention a few . . . all represent worlds of adventure to families sampling the foreign culture.

Military brats who were in Taiwan tell of typhoons, legions of roaches, rats leaping across the living room floor, and the joys of exploring winding back streets, snacking at the noodle stands. In Paris, where my family was stationed for three years, there were museums and parks, beautiful countryside, and the glories of a culture dedicated to aesthetics.

One Army major's daughter whose mother was from Panama said that when the family was later stationed there, they ventured into the jungle to see the site of her childhood home. "We had to walk a long way, hacking through the jungle with machetes," she said, "then ride in a dugout canoe to the spot. We got back just as the bats came out to suck the blood from cows."

Some families take real advantage of the opportunity—tour quite a lot and learn the language. The children of these families learn the good side of being outsiders. Living overseas becomes an exercise in appreciation, in which soul and mind are expanded. "My feeling is that any experience you encounter becomes *yours*," said an Army daughter. "So what if it's someone else's culture? If you've experienced it, it *is* yours."

An Air Force colonel's son said his family benefited enormously from their stay in Italy, although their decision to move off base into the Italian community drew criticism from those who remained on base. "Military wives would accost my mother in the commissary to say, 'We don't approve of your taking your children away from their own kind.' My sister [who continued to attend the base dependent school for junior high], got the same kind of remarks from kids at school: 'We know your mother's a snob.' "

But the children in that family all learned Italian, had Italian friends, saw a lot of the country, and have a treasure house of memories. "It was illegal to kick a ball in the streets, but we did it anyway," he said, "just like the Italian kids. And then we'd hide the ball from the carabinieri. We went to festivals where there were big floats and people threw confetti in your face and hit you jovially over the head with inflated pig bladders."

Most of the Americans, this son said, refused to take advantage of the opportunity they had to get to know another culture. "A lot of my friends [from the dependent school] left Italy after four years without being able to speak one word of Italian or having eaten anywhere outside of the local pizza joint and the officers' club." By contrast, this son, who remains fluent in Italian, still has friends in Italy and has returned five times to visit them.

Isolation

"My parents were the type who went to Japan as a duty," an Army sergeant's daughter said. "Did we ever visit anyplace? No. They came from lower-class families, and had no sense of reading to their children, or of understanding the Japanese way of life. So we were pretty much isolated. We lived in this compound, and for all we figured, that was the way everybody lived. For . . . years I didn't know other people didn't live this way."

Under such circumstances, often the only foreign nationals military children come to know are the domestics who come to work for their families. Servants have been very common in both enlisted and officer households overseas, because the military from time to time has strongly urged the employment of people in the community as a way of providing scarce jobs and generating goodwill. (Though sometimes very low pay and occasional mistreatment would cause this strategy to backfire.) These foreign servants come to mean a great deal to military children; too often their importance is underestimated by parents.

"In Japan, we had servants," the same sergeant's daughter said,

and I used to get very attached to them. They were so good to me. Eventually they would start to steal things—you have to remember, this was the early fifties, and they were poor and hungry. It would just be a little bit of spaghetti or rice. I remember one time my father called down to the gate and told them to stop one servant. She had a little bit of sugar. That was the end of her; she never came back. That was so cruel. I thought at the time it was cruel. I also thought it was cruel to take this person out of my life that I had learned to love and be attached to and who had some continuity with me.

Once we had this amma, this servant that I must have loved. She must have had great meaning for me. We moved from one place in Japan to another in the summer, and the amma came along with us. And one day I remember my mother and father in the house yelling, yelling, yelling. And I was outside on the swings, crying. I *knew* the amma was being terminated—I have no idea why. We didn't ask questions and we weren't told. All we knew was we had to get outside.

Outsider, insider. In some cases, military children are ordered to forsake even the tiny bit of insideness they manage to winnow from their overseas experience.

It also happens that even living off base is not enough to guarantee the exposure to the foreign culture that some in the family would wish. An Air Force general's daughter whose family lived off base complained of being ordered not to "fraternize" with the Japanese. "And I didn't have the guts to demand it," she recalled bitterly. An Air Force colonel's daughter told of living in a foreign community and having the freedom to associate—but still ending up in painful isolation. The family lived in a tiny French town, in the only chateau. "You can guess how the French kids felt about Americans living in the chateau. There were no American kids around. I was alone most of the time. My sister and brother were around, but they were lonely too. My sister got fat, my brother got rebellious."

But if for many the overseas experience is an exercise in unrelieved outsideness with regard to the foreign culture, it is also an intense dose of *insideness* in the American warrior community. Most American military people live on bases or in housing areas that are walled off from the indigenous population. It is an oddly isolated life, one in which it is possible to delude oneself that one is still on American soil, just relegated to a particularly boring Fortress island out of sight of the mainland. But there are moments, especially in times of crisis, when the larger circumstances cannot be shut out, and the fact of different-ness—different culture, different mission—crackles through the com-munity like an electric charge.

"We went to Germany in 1956, when I was eight," said an Army daughter. "That was the year the Soviets invaded Hungary. My first impression was of long lines of refugees. We lived across the street from the teen club, and there were long lines of people with their possessions in their arms.

"Not long after that it was the Lebanese crisis. *That's* when I thought war would come. We had to have our suitcase packed, complete with water purification pills, and we had to learn to 'duck and cover.' We were going to be evacuated, and the whole base was on alert."

An Army major's daughter told of living on a base in Germany in 1961, during the Bay of Pigs. "Families were issued rations, and we all had to wear dog tags with our name, blood type, and our father's serial number. All the men were told to be combat ready, which meant my father had to keep a bag packed, because at any point he could be called and he would be gone, and you wouldn't know what was going to happen. They were thinking there was going to be an all-out war with Russia."

An Army colonel's son told a bizarre story of finding himself in the middle of a war zone. In the early 1970s, he and his family lived in Thailand and his father went back and forth to Vietnam on missions. Once when his father had leave, he decided to show his wife and children "the most beautiful beaches in the world"—at Cam Ranh Bay, which he called the safest place in Vietnam. "It was July, 1970," the son told, "and we flew into Cam Ranh Bay Air Base during a sapper attack. I remember seeing bodies of Vietcong guerrillas on the airfield, and guns and weapons were firing all around us. The memo-ries of that day are still fresh. It was the first time in my life I was shot at, and the first time I saw dead bodies, some gruesomely dis-membered."

The overseas experiences of most military brats are not nearly so dramatic—but the sense of differentness, of a lonely separateness, is always there.

Standing Apart

Perhaps all pettiness in life is the result of standing outside of someone else's experience, unwilling or unable to bridge the gulf. Military people are not immune to this, and may even be particularly vulnerable. Outsiders—especially those who cannot help that status and do not like it—sometimes feel they have to compensate for their uncomfortable outsideness with a false sense of superiority.

So it is that some military people, children included, come to objectify the foreign nationals they live around, imprisoning them in stereotypes. An Air Force colonel's son told of the unbridled racism toward Iranians he observed among military brats in Tehran:

I remember once going to football practice on the bus. And there was a woman wearing a chador trying to cross the street, which was always a dangerous thing to do in Tehran—you had to very carefully work your way across. The bus was slowly moving past her in the traffic. And this kid brought up a huge gob of spit and waited. I didn't know what he was doing. And then he leaned out of the window and spat in her face. I was so shocked I couldn't believe it. And I turned and looked at the woman and she didn't even show anger. She just patiently wiped it off her face and continued across the street. But the kid was jubilant. I said, "My God, what did you do that for?" And immediately every kid on that bus attacked me. "Nigger lover" is what they called me. That was the kind of racism you'd run into.

And I remember distinctly a teacher in our [dependent] school who was a Persian, and a very sad man. He dressed like an American and wanted to be an American; he wanted it so badly that he would call his own people by the same names that people called him behind his back. Because no matter how well this man dressed and kept up his American accent and mannerisms, for all those little bastards who went to that school he was always a "raghead." That's what they called him, and that's what he called his own people.

An Army colonel's son who spent his early teenage years in France spoke of the French this way:

The lower class are extremely dirty. They're very smelly. They have body odor and are not very desirable to be around. They smoke horrible cigarettes. Occasionally there is the smell of urine. And the bad breath! The French are very nationalistic, proud, stubborn. They think they are the best. They *still* think that French should be the international language. . . . I guess I really thought of the French as a subclass. They were not as educated, didn't dress as well, didn't have the same kitchen facilities or standard of living. So I didn't really see any point in becoming more involved with them.

This particular son attended an American dependent school for three years and had very limited contact with the French. He never returned to France as an adult, and so never corrected his impressions. The stereotypes he cultivated as an outsider have remained intact over the years, frozen in time.

My father was stationed in France from 1961–64. The first year there, when I was ten, I was sent to an American dependent school, and I saw the French only from a distance. It was easy to view them as aliens with habits I couldn't understand and didn't care for. The political situation of the time was tense as well, which exacerbated our sense of being outsiders; it was a liability to be an American. The Algerian revolution was raging, and although President John F. Kennedy and his wife were personally very popular with the French, his early sympathies with Algerian desires for independence rankled terribly. An extreme right-wing terrorist group, the OAS [Organisation de l'Armée Secrète] fanned anti-American sentiment. That first year we lived in a small French town, and the American car we had foolishly brought with us was repeatedly vandalized. "Yankee Go Home" and "OAS" were scratched into the paint, and the antenna and locks were frequently broken.

For most of that first year my views were sadly like those of the son quoted above. Then my parents made a decision for which I will always be grateful: They sent me to a French school for the next two years. It was a difficult outsider experience, one could even say a trial by fire. But after I learned the language and began to make French friends, my perspective inevitably changed. I still felt like an outsider, but now the channels were wide open. I fell in love with the French language, the French culture, the French people. I felt totally challenged and stimulated by that culture, and found myself living on a plane of heightened awareness in which even the smallest, most mundane details of life in the French context seemed exciting. It was immensely rewarding: The more I responded to the culture, the more it seemed to respond to me.

I was nearly thirteen when my father received orders to go back to the States, and the parting from the country I had come to love was almost unbearable. We left from Le Havre, on an ocean liner that pulled away from the docks one June evening at twilight. I remember standing on the deck for a long, long time watching the lights of Le Havre, trying not to blink so I could fill my eyes with as much of France as possible before the horizon would draw the curtain and I would have to turn away, begin my grieving. In France I had found a midway point between outsider and insider which suited me perfectly. I'd learned French and French ways well enough to lose some of my outsideness in that culture, but I also knew I was too American to ever be a true insider there. That didn't matter: I loved the feeling of ambiguity, of standing both inside and outside of two cultures.

In fact I mourned the loss of that delicious ambiguity for years and years, until I was finally old enough to plan my return. And still, after a quarter of a century, I feel a kinship to France, and the sweet sorrow of an old and unrequited yearning.

Coming Home

The irony for a military brat returning to the States after years abroad is that home can seem like another foreign country. The expected satisfaction of feeling enveloped once more in a familiar culture is supplanted by the shock of being almost an alien in one's own land. It's the "time warp" factor—the culture has inevitably changed in the interim—and every school-age military brat reentering American culture has had to deal with it.

An Air Force colonel's son remembered when he first became aware of it; at the time, he and his family were still overseas and knew that in a few months they would be back in the States. "It was 1964," he said. "I was becoming a teenager, and there was this thing we'd been reading about in the U.S. called teenage culture. I remember my parents talking about teenagers in the U.S.: thirteen-year-old girls wearing brassieres and using hair spray. It was shocking news."

Once back home, the period of adjustment takes from several weeks to several months as the military brat becomes updated in music, slang, dance, clothes, movies, TV shows, consumer goods. For those who, like me, attended foreign schools, the shock is greater and the adjustment takes longer. It amounts to reverse culture shock, and for some who have become acclimated to another culture, the initial impressions upon reentry to the United States do not compare favorably.

The Air Force colonel's son who had thoroughly enjoyed Italy spoke to this feeling. "We moved from Livorno, Italy to a lousy, rotten little neighborhood in Arlington," he recalled. "It was boring suburbia: miles and miles of these god-awful garden apartments. We'd come from a city on the Italian Riviera in Tuscany where we were always being stimulated—even walking down the street was exciting. It depressed everyone in the family, and my parents split up for the first time."

The adjustment period is usually not a major handicap—military brats are too practiced at adapting quickly and fitting in to be stymied for long—but it serves as a prolonged reminder that fitting into a social group is not something that comes to us as a natural right, but something that must be learned over and over again.

And even as military brats make the transition, they are profoundly aware of having been changed by their time overseas. They bring a different perspective and a range of knowledge that civilian peers can seldom match. For the sake of acceptance, military brats often find themselves taking steps to deliberately hide their sophistication: feigning ignorance of a foreign language they know fairly well, holding back stories about experiences abroad when the conversation offers a natural outlet for them, pretending to ignorance of international politics.

But the effects of living overseas are very long-term, and continue to be a part of the military brats who have been there. Perhaps there are military brats who have lived in other countries and then put the experience totally behind them, in a sealed compartment of their past, but I have yet to meet one. In some way all appeared to be permanently changed and enriched. Some spoke of a longing for another country such as I feel for France, and they often call it, paradoxically, "homesickness."

Olivia, an Army sergeant's daughter who spent three of her late teenage years overseas, said, "When I came back from Okinawa I was homesick for it. I didn't want to leave, and I cried all the way over. I really enjoyed it there—I was teaching in a missionary school, learning judo, constantly busy. I could have stayed if I'd really wanted to, but I wanted to go to school, and there was no opportunity to go to school there." Olivia returned to the States, attended a university, resumed her "American" life—but her longing for Okinawa and Japanese culture remained with her. Finally she sought out a group of Japanese Buddhists in her community. "I missed the culture so much, and I wanted to be around them—so I joined." At the time of the interview, she had been a practicing Buddhist for twenty years.

OUTSIDER/INSIDER: RACISM

When I was a young reporter, working as a summer intern for a daily, I went to Washington for a day to cover the passage of the Equal Rights Amendment in the House of Representatives. During the debate I sent a page to ask Rep. Shirley Chisholm to come out for a short interview, and to my surprise and delight, the venerable congresswoman complied. She was a strong proponent of the ERA, and said that if it became part of the Constitution it would go far toward eliminating sexism in our country. When I asked her how, she replied, "It's like the civil rights movement and the battle against racism. First you change the laws; then the attitudes will follow."

That, in brief, is what happened in the military. For many years the U.S. military was as segregated and racist an institution as could be found in our country. Prior to 1948, blacks had served in segregated units under the leadership of white officers. Then in 1948, President Harry S. Truman signed an executive order mandating "equality of treatment and opportunity" in the armed forces. Racism did not disappear overnight, but a clear message had been sent that racism in the military, and in federal institutions of any kind, was intolerable. In a hierarchy such as the military, such a message could not be taken lightly. Coming as it did from the very top, the order resonated all the way down the line.

First came the order, the "law"; then a change in attitude followed— slowly in some cases and with some backsliding, particularly in the wake of the demoralizing Vietnam War—but inexorably. Over much of the last forty years, the military has set an example and a standard for civilian society to follow. For example, the dependent schools of the Department of Defense, which compose the largest single school system in the United States, were integrated years, in some cases decades, before civilian school systems in many parts of the United States.

In a sense, it is not hard to see why military attitudes fell into line so quickly. In a rigid hierarchy, rank means far more than race in terms of power and prestige—although often, it is true, power follows racial lines. The point is that every warrior understands that he or she is subordinate to anyone of higher rank, regardless of either person's race. So members of the military already had a powerful alternative way of looking at the world. In addition, behavior between and among individuals in the military is strictly defined and controlled by countless regulations designed to maintain proper respect and harmony. Proper behavior between persons of differing races, therefore, is merely behavior that complies with existing regulations.

Although it still has some distance to go, the military has been remarkably effective at fighting racist attitudes internally, and at changing the mind-set of many racists who join its ranks. Quite a few white military brats tell of parents raised in thoroughly racist surroundings, often in the Deep South, who not only managed to rid themselves of bigotry but impressed upon their children, by word and example, the importance of racial equality. The words must have echoed through thousands of households as military parents instructed their young: "You judge people by what they are, not by the color of their skins."

It is striking how many military brats speak of their parents with great pride on this subject, no matter what problems or sadness their families may have harbored, no matter what issues may yet fester unresolved. Brian, who at the time of our initial interview was not on speaking terms with his father, nevertheless appeared to put all rancor behind him as he proudly told of his father's egalitarian racial views. After his retirement from the Navy, the father moved his family back to the southern community where he'd grown up. It was there his son became acutely conscious of the difference between his father's views and those of the civilians around them. When a black family tried to move into the neighborhood, white neighbors passed around a petition to keep them out. "My dad wouldn't sign it," the son related. "He said, 'They're people, too.' I'm sure he didn't get that from his upbringing. He got it from the military. I think that was something good from the military—it teaches you not to be a racist. My mom, also from the South, agreed with him wholeheartedly. It was one of the times I really respected my dad and liked him."

Other white military brats told similar stories of parents who had been raised in a community where racist views prevailed, but who tried their best to overcome it in the military.

Graham, the son whose Army Special Forces father disappeared in Laos in 1961, said both of his parents were from rural areas of the Deep South, but successfully rooted out their own racism. "My next-door neighbor was black, and he was my best friend," Graham recalled. "I didn't realize he was 'black' until my uncle, who was a member of the KKK, came to visit. He called my friend a 'nigger.' " Graham was vehement at the memory. "That word is not used in my house, and it will *never* be used in my house. I'm not a racist or a bigot. Every man has a right to be judged by his actions and his contribution to society and not by his color."

Ernest, the son of an Air Force colonel, said, "My father came from [the Deep South]. He was prejudiced, but he didn't want me or my sister to grow up prejudiced. He never pushed his views on us. He encouraged us to treat people equally, and didn't show his own prejudices much. My sister and I would go to play at the homes of black friends from Catholic school."

Audrey, the daughter of an Army major, was also aware of how her parents constantly worked to keep their children from picking up their own residual racism. "Once I was dating a boy of mixed racial background," she remembered. "He was half black. My father walked in and saw us holding hands. He drew in his breath quickly but didn't say anything."

Craig's father, an Air Force staff sergeant, had many blacks as peers as well as under his command. "I really think that when I was a kid I had no race consciousness," Craig said.

And I think that's because my mother and father had blacks as company at our house frequently. This was in the early sixties, at the base in Germany, and I remember being very surprised, listening to the news [on Armed Forces Radio], to find out there was racism back in the States.

My father had the best rapport with blacks of any NCO at that base. Black airmen would come to our house to talk to him rather than to their own first sergeants. In some ways I think my father just didn't care about color. You could be black, white, or green—you were still a jerk until you proved yourself otherwise. He just wanted performance, and he was equally hard on everybody.

To some extent, Craig said, his father's private racial views have always been a matter of speculation for him. He said it's possible his father may have harbored some racist ideas, but if so, he never let them show—again, testimony to the reforming effect of the military environment.

Craig learned one of the most moving examples of his father's commitment to human dignity only after his father's death:

One of the things that amazed me when my father died was to see how many people in the town [where he had retired] were genuinely fond of him, and had become fond of him just in the five years since he retired. I was astonished. They knew him as "Sarge." One of them was a black man who lived in that same little town and who'd been in prison three or four times. He'd spent a lot of time there. He said he wasn't bitter, but he was. He was ignorant, and violent as it turned out. He was later killed by a shotgun blast from a man he'd threatened. He worked hard at a meat factory, and he was also a pimp and a gambler. And when my father died, he said to me, "Your father is the only white man who's ever treated me as a man." He offered to dig my father's grave.

Many of the military brats interviewed for this book grew up during the civil rights turmoil of the late fifties and the sixties and remember it well. What stands out in the minds of many white military brats is the contrast between their own racial views and those of white civilians.

A Navy commander's son whose parents were from Little Rock, Arkansas, told of frequently visiting that city as he grew up. "From 1956 on, I carried around the stigma of the Central High School controversy.[9] My mother really raised us with the idea of the value and worth of *all* people, no matter what their social position, or the way they lived, or the culture in which they were raised."

Although it stands to reason that some military brats must have harbored racist attitudes while they were growing up, and even since then, I found no indication of it among the eighty military brats I interviewed. It may be that class arrogance is more easily inherited than racism, since classism is endorsed by the Fortress while racism is not. By the same token, it would be easier for a military brat to develop prejudices—even racial prejudices—against foreign nationals while the family is stationed overseas and trying to cope with feelings of outsideness, than to develop racism against ethnic groups in the military context in which all share some degree of insideness. Also, of course, the military does not put the same effort into eradicating bigoted attitudes toward foreigners as it does to eradicating internal racism that saps morale in the force.

Black Military Brats

Some of the most positive accounts to be found of growing up in the military are the stories of black military brats. Those interviewed for this book spoke of their childhood nostalgically, and described their fathers with obvious love and pride.

"I remember my father as the ultimate in manhood," said an Air Force sergeant's son. "It was so much fun to watch him go to work: Everything was always pressed, he smelled like cologne, his hair was short and neat, he didn't smoke or drink. . . . He was perfect. I used to watch him and try to be like him."

And some black military children grow up acutely conscious of the contrast between their safe, secure life in the military and the tenuous existence of their civilian relatives in small rural towns or big city ghettos. "I never thought I was poor," said Eric, an Air Force sergeant's son. "The things my cousins worried about, I didn't worry about. We didn't have to worry about health insurance, or getting sick. My cousins would talk about whether they could afford to have a baby in the hospital. For us it was all free." And the military fathers were employed, and had rank and prestige and a respected place in an integrated community. Olivia, an Army sergeant's daughter, said that when she grew up and moved away from home to a large city, she sought out the most integrated neighborhood she could find, "so it would seem more like an Army post."

Several black military brats told of experiencing their first encounters with racism in a civilian environment. Olivia related an incident in a German town, when she was nine years old. "One time, my family and a friend of my dad's were walking down the street, and an old German lady came over to us, frowning and saying something. She put her hand on my father's face and tried to wipe his color off. That made a lasting impression on me." She said her father held his temper, stepped back and walked around the woman with quiet dignity and military bearing.

Robert, an Army sergeant's son who was a captain in the Marine Corps at the time of our interview, said,

> I definitely feel that I grew up in a less prejudiced environment in the military. As a kid I never experienced any racism, until one time in 1968. My father was about to go to Vietnam, and we were traveling to Florida, where we would live while waiting for him. We were driving through some little town in Georgia, and the local police officer decided to pull my father over. It was one of those things where he must have decided, "Well, I guess we're going to play the game now." He called a couple of his buddies and they made a few racial slurs here and there, handcuffed my father and took him off to jail. My mother was pleading with them, "He didn't do anything. Please let him go." And they said, "It'll cost you five hundred bucks." All we had was five hundred bucks. So five hundred bucks and two days in jail later, they decided to let him go.
>
> That was the first time I'd ever experienced anything like that. Living in a military environment, you're shielded from that type of thing.

Eric told of repeatedly returning to Alabama when his father was sent overseas to Vietnam or on other assignments. And there he felt like an outsider among both whites and blacks.

"In Alabama I heard little white kids call my father 'boy.' *My father.* And they knew they had the right to do that there. They weren't even afraid." But he ran smack into another kind of prejudice with his own black cousins. "My mother is Creole; she's so light-skinned she has freckles. But I am dark, the darkest person in my family by far, and my cousins didn't like me because I was dark. So when I went there to visit them they would call me 'Little Black Sambo,' and so on. I was shocked. They treated me worse than white people did."

An incident during one particularly long stay in Alabama in 1968 demonstrated to what extent Eric was out of sync with both white and black civilians there. He explained that in that school system, children took seats on the school bus according to race. But instead of having whites sit in the front and blacks sit in the back—after all, this was fourteen years after Rosa Parks refused to move to the back of the city bus in Montgomery—the arrangement was from side to side. And it was not mandated by the school authorities, but by the children themselves.

"It was de facto," Eric said.

> Both sides wanted that, both black and white. They'd decided that front and back wasn't fair, but it was okay to sit on different sides. But I didn't know that. So I sat on the wrong side, next to a white girl, and she started screaming and they tried to say I raped her. They stopped the bus, took me off, and took me to the principal's office. I was only in the fourth grade. I

should have sat next to a boy, but I just didn't know. Where I came from, you sit where you want to sit.

Nothing happened to me, but I got upset about it and after that my brother and I did it on purpose for a month. We sat together, in front, on the wrong side of the bus. And since me and my brother were sitting together, the school realized it couldn't do anything legally to us; they couldn't say I was trying to bother a girl or anything. So they had to call my father in and tell him not to cause trouble. He explained we'd lived all over the country and that's why we were "like that." So then the principal understood. The black kids hassled us too, but I didn't care. I told them they were silly.

Black military brats generally described the racial attitudes of their parents as open-minded and egalitarian, quoting them in almost the same words white military children reported hearing from their parents. Robert said the first time he was ever called "nigger" was in a civilian junior high school in the South. He went home and asked his mother about it. "She just said she didn't care much for the word. My parents never really sat down and said, 'Look, there are going to be white people out there who are going to despise you because you're black.' I can't remember them ever doing that. They more or less taught us that *people are people*. My father always told me, and I still remember it, that 'There are always going to be people who don't like you. The thing to remember is to always be yourself.' "

One result of the racially open-minded upbringing that black children receive in the military is that they arrive in adulthood with a different outlook from that of many of their black peers. The point was perhaps best made by a black civilian woman who described to me her increasing puzzlement as she got to know a young black employee at work who happened to be a military son. "After my first long conversation with him, I asked myself what it was that wasn't quite usual about him," she said. "He was fine in every respect—but, I decided, it was like he had a different *tape* running inside him. All black people have hopes and expectations, but for most of us our hopes are higher than our expectations. It's a matter of being realistic. But with him his expectations were right up there with his hopes. He didn't see any reason why it all couldn't happen for him." Her comment resonated with other black military brats I interviewed subsequently; the lesson they learn growing up in the military is the same one white kids learn: If you are willing and able and work hard, you can move up.

The irony is that sometimes this very laudable attitude reveals a gulf between the son or daughter and the black military parents whose experiences when they were civilians, and sometimes, too, as military people, contradict that expectation. For them, their children say, the best survival tactic is decidedly low profile: *Accept the status quo, even if it limits you.* One of the black military sons quoted above described his father's reaction after he met the son's white girlfriend.

"My father told me, 'There is always a ruling race and a subordinate race, and you shouldn't mix them.' He said it just like that. What he was saying was that *we* should be on the bottom. Now *that's* what holds you back. For my father to say that to his son, who's going to college—that's just terrible. I think hardly any majority person would *dare* say that.

"I understand things differently from my father: that until I take the *mental* chains off, I won't be free. And I don't want to die a slave! I want to die knowing that *I could have done it if I wanted to.*"

Toward Racial Equality

As much as the military promotes the principle of racial equality, and even though military brats testify to their own open-mindedness and the remarkable efforts of their parents to overcome racist mind-sets, it is easy to exaggerate the degree of racial equality to be found in the American armed forces. There are two ways to evaluate it.

Measured against an ideal standard, the military has a ways to go, particularly when one looks closely at the racial makeup of the officer corps. In 1971, while 14 percent of the Army's enlisted troops were black, the officer corps remained 97 percent white.[10] By 1988—forty years after Truman's executive order—the picture was finally looking much better: In the officer corps the percentage of blacks had risen to 10.5 percent, approximating the percentage of blacks in the general population. However, most of those black officers were concentrated in the junior grades, and it remains tougher for a black officer to make colonel or above. According to one black Army colonel quoted in the *New York Times*, the scarcity of blacks in the highest officer grades is partly attributable to the "faint praise" white officers give to their black subordinates on efficiency reports.[11] And the Army was doing considerably less well with Hispanics; only 1.6 percent of its officer corps and 4.2 percent of its enlisted soldiers were Hispanic.

Of all the services, the Navy continued to lag furthest behind, with an officer corps that was only 3.6 percent black and 2 percent Hispanic. (The enlisted Navy was 16 percent black and 5 percent Hispanic.) A 1988 internal inquiry into race relations in the Navy found shortcomings in many areas. "Lack of equal opportunity training for officers is most significant," the report said; in 1987 the Navy spent only $282,000 for advertising designed to recruit potential officers, while the Army spent $9.8 million.[12]

But when the military record in integration is measured not against an ideal standard but against efforts in the civilian sector, it starts to look very good indeed. Charles C. Moskos, a professor at Northwestern University who has written extensively about the sociology of the military, has called the military's integration effort "an American success story."[13] He has written that "blacks occupy more management positions in the military than they do in business, education, journalism, government, or any other significant sector of American society."[14]

The point is that the military keeps on trying, year after year. Eventually it will probably reach its goal of total "equality of treatment and opportunity" for all races, as President Truman articulated in 1948. And the military will certainly reach it long before the civilian sector.

The scene at West Point's commencement in May 1990 was testimony to how far things have changed since my father's day: Gen. Colin L. Powell, Chairman of the Joint Chiefs of Staff, the highest ranking Army general and a black man, stood next to Kristin Baker, daughter of an Army colonel and the first woman ever to be named first captain of the corps of cadets—a coveted honor that goes to the cadet who best exemplifies physical, academic, and leadership skills in the graduating class. It was a telling moment in another, less laudable way, too—for the military has come much further in extending opportunities to black men than to women: Kristin Baker, unlike all previous first captains, did not have the option of selecting infantry, traditionally the choice of first captains, as the branch of the Army in which she would serve; the infantry is barred to women. Instead she chose military intelligence.

Still, West Point's 1990 commencement was a powerful symbol of change in the most tradition-bound of American institutions, and in the military at large. In the class of '90 there were 89 black cadets out of 895, or 9.9 percent. In my father's West Point class of '36, there was a single black cadet: Benjamin O. Davis, Jr., son of the Army's first black general. His life was made as miserable as segregationist policies and other cadets could contrive to make it. In *The Long Gray Line*, Rick Atkinson wrote:

> Davis, a tall, commanding figure, was subjected to "the silence." During his plebe year, he roomed alone, ate by himself at a separate table, and was addressed by other cadets only when official business required communication. Of his classmates in '36, who included two future Army chiefs of staff, Davis later said, "If there were friends, they were silent friends and I mean that literally." He eventually became the Air Force's first black general, rising to three-star rank.[15]

Racism was entrenched at West Point. Even after Truman's executive order, the academy prohibited black cadets from attending dances and dance classes until 1951, and from intercollegiate athletic teams until the early 1950s. Black cadets also could not enter officers' clubs with their classmates during summertime class trips to various Army posts.[16]

Where military brats are concerned, this is important information. The fact that the United States Military Academy endorsed such racist exclusions well into the 1950s, in the face of an executive order by the commander-in-chief, says a good deal about the strength of support for white bigotry that was presumed in the officer corps of which many of us are the progeny.

And that brings the outsider/insider issue, and all its implications, directly home to us. For our white fathers, and many of our white mothers, the exclusion of others on the basis of race—forcing them to be outsiders even as they put their lives on the line for our country against a common enemy—was an important part of their social contract as insiders in the officer corps. This is not merely historical fact; for white military brats in particular, it is historical fact with a challenge attached.

Racism *is* part of the patrimony of many military families, officer and enlisted, and it is a patrimony we the children have by and large refused. We learned we could cut the generational link, stop the advance of racism in our lives and, later, in our own families. And we learned this, I believe, specifically *because* of the Fortress and, sometimes, in spite of it. The refusal to accept the patrimony of racism is one of the most common virtues of military brats, and it makes us, in the best and noblest sense, true children of the Fortress.

In many cases, however, open-mindedness was a virtue that had to be defended early, against one's own parents. Such battles were inevitably lost by the children—although the bitter memories of those defeats are one reason these same military brats have gone on to win the war against racism in their own lives.

The daughter of an Air Force colonel remembered with guilt and shame an incident in which her mother would not allow her to invite a black friend, the daughter of an Air Force NCO, to her sixteenth birthday party. "The friend was a crucial member of my circle of friends at school," she said.

My boyfriend broke up with me for twenty-four hours because I didn't have the guts to tell my mother "no party." I *didn't* have the guts. I was terrified of her and the repercussions.

Not inviting that girl changed her persona *overnight*. Our whole circle fell apart from that day forward, and she seemed to withdraw from us. It was very painful for all of us. I'll never forget the change in her. Sometimes I think maybe up to that day she hadn't had to deal with discrimination, and then her parents had to sit down and explain why she wasn't invited to my party.

I guess I've never forgiven my mother for that one, or myself for not being strong enough to fight it.

The son of an Air Force colonel said, "As early as 1963, when I was fourteen, I felt very strongly about civil rights. I was a ninth grader in Arlington, Virginia, and wanted to go to D.C. for the March on Washington.[17] I was pretty forcibly detained at home. My parents also had very strong reactions against my dating girls of other races."

Another daughter of an Air Force colonel told of a time her parents wouldn't let her accept a ride to the bowling alley with a black friend and her father, even though the father was a major. (In other words, this incident was definitely about race, not about upstairs/downstairs classism.) "My parents found out about the ride at the last minute and wouldn't let me get in the car. I was so embarrassed. It was so racist."

An Army colonel's daughter described her father's anti-Semitism. "I met a couple of young Jewish men, university students, while playing tennis," she said. "A few days later they came to pick me up at my house and my father met them at the door, made a horribly anti-Semitic remark, and slammed the door in their faces."

My own father, as I have stated elsewhere, was a racial bigot (and an anti-Semite), and he felt comfortable enough with other officers to display his bigotry openly—although I have no way of knowing what they may have thought of this behavior. When I was fifteen years old and my brother long grown and gone, a black family bought a house in the small cul-de-sac where my parents had retired. My father immediately put a For Sale sign up in our front yard. My mother and I were deeply ashamed, but, given my father's volatile temper, could not risk taking it down. Instead we made a secret visit to the black family, in which we apologized profusely in an attempt to mitigate the offense. I don't think we succeeded; probably all we did was demonstrate to them how gutless and mealymouthed, as well as outright offensive, some whites can be. And the sign remained in place, branding our house a bastion of bigotry, for months on end.

All of these are stories of battles lost—but in every case, the military brat grew up to become a vociferous defender of human rights.

This is not an unusual situation for military brats. Even where a military parent is blatantly and unselfconsciously racist, the children are likely to grow up much more open-minded. Partly this is because the stated values in our culture of origin, the warrior society, are very clear on this score. And partly it may be due to feeling a kinship with other military brats that is powerful enough to override distinctions of race: We have such an acute sense of outsideness with nonmilitary people, and we experience so much loss growing up—loss of friends, loss of social identity, loss of loved ones in the line of duty—that it is both natural and comforting to identify with other military brats, regardless of race. And for this reason, too, military brats may cultivate a high level of sensitivity to issues of justice and fairness, as will be explored in the next chapter.

THE OUTSIDER SYNDROME

The overall effect of all these experiences is that military brats spend a great deal more of their childhoods on the outside looking in than on the inside looking out. Although military brats have a natural sense of insideness with one another, it is never given a chance to develop because of the highly transient lifestyle of the warrior society. Standing on the sidelines observing other people's in-groups becomes a way of life—and the outsider way of life that was forced by circumstance during childhood is then perpetuated into adulthood by military brats who know no other way to be. Even when they perceive it as a problem, they do not see a way out.

"I always felt I was somehow not quite as good as civilian kids," said the son of a Marine Corps major. "Damn near, but not quite. I can't quite put my finger on it.

"I always relate to myself as an outsider," he said. "I remember thinking, in relation to the in-clique, that I *should* naturally have been a part of it, since I was an A student and a good athlete—but I was for the most part excluded from it. And I would have liked to have been able to say to them, 'Yes, I know you want me, but I don't want anything to do with you.' As it turned out, it was more of a mutual rejection."

This son said he relates as an outsider even now, in his late thirties. "I've never, ever belonged to a group that I felt a part of. Right now I work in an office of fifty people, where there's an 'inside' and an 'outside.' It's real clear I'm an outsider. The other people on the outside are the ones I like the most and enjoy the most, so it all works out real well. But it's the same situation. I'd like to be wanted on the inside so I could say, 'I don't want you anyway,' but that's not the case."

I describe the *outsider syndrome* as an inability to abandon the outsider role, even if it is clearly painful to maintain. It is lonely and unsatisfying to always be on the outside, but for the military brat, outsideness has the familiarity of an old pair of shoes. While it is hard to perpetually live the outsider role, it is harder still to abandon it. The outsider syndrome is the central paradox of a military brat's life. A sense of belonging is our single greatest need and our single greatest quest—yet many military brats perpetuate their own marginality by making choices that are guaranteed to *keep* them on the outside.

This has been at work in my own life in at least two major ways. First, I so longed to return to France that I tried twice to expatriate myself. The first time a family crisis brought me home; the second time, I was defeated by my own refusal to work illegally. I could have stayed and survived as an illegal alien, but I was too much of a by-the-book military brat to reconcile myself to that. Near the end of that second stay, a delightful, elderly museum guard with whom I had struck up a conversation proposed a very French solution to my dilemma: advertise in a newspaper's personals column to marry a French airline pilot. That way, he pointed out, I could have dual citizenship *and* reduced air fare—a brilliant suggestion which I somehow failed to pursue.

The second way I was affected by the outsider syndrome was much more serious. Although from early adulthood I wanted to find the right man and settle down, secure in the stable emotional base I badly needed, I spent a decade dating only foreign men, and only those who were in the United States temporarily. The relationships were not without their rewards, but the long-term unworkability of it was always there, and always more apparent to them than it was to me. None of the foreign men wanted to settle down in the United States. For my part, I was perfectly willing—I thought—to go and live in an alien culture for the rest of my life; it didn't seem all that different from what I'd always done. But the reality was that the best I could have hoped for in a foreign culture was an endless marginality without any hope of gaining true insideness. It works for many people, but permanent marginality happened to be the opposite of what I needed in my own life. I believe now that those many decisions to connect with foreign men rather than Americans—I could not even seem to bring American men into focus during that period—were manifestations of a bad case of the outsider syndrome. What I wanted was *belonging*—yet I went out of my way to make sure it would not become a reality in my life.

Finally, I am happy to say, my own case of the outsider syndrome played itself out. I'm not quite sure how it happened, but the end of my last foreign relationship had a wonderfully clarifying effect on my thinking. It suddenly became obvious that I had been exhausting myself in a long, futile exercise. Not long after that, I met the man who was to become my husband: the son of a close-knit midwestern farm family who, despite living in a big city as a scholar and intellectual, took care to maintain his roots. The first firm step on my own road to belonging was to find a mate who was comfortable with his own roots, and with whom I shared enough cultural commonality for us to communicate easily and well. It has been a happy choice.

The outsider syndrome does not affect all military brats, but quite a few of those interviewed for this book attested to having it.

There is Lorna, for instance, who in Chapter 8 told of projecting her problems with commitment onto the men in her life, choosing as partners only men who could not make a commitment—who were married, gay, in seminary, or who lived far away and refused to move. But the outsider syndrome is not merely a matter of acting out the difficulties with commitment that are often the legacies of mobility. The outsider syndrome is a preferred way of being in the world. Referring to a year in which she immersed herself in the underclass and worked as a migrant fruit picker, Lorna said, "It was another way of stepping outside the culture, as was being a military brat. Maybe it's like a pilot who wishes to go the next step and be an astronaut. Once you've seen the world from the sky, you hunger for more and more distancing. That's what that year was for me."

Todd, too, spoke of continuing his outsider persona, first cultivated as an Air Force brat, in his decision to become a writer: "I don't feel being an outsider stands in my way," he said. "I prefer the perspective. It goes along with my political perspective, which is pretty far to the left. It's my whole approach to the world, the way I walk in the streets."

Eric said that "being black *and* a military brat is like a double dose of outsider." But it is a role he has come to like. He said he spends as much time in Europe as he can, sensing his outsideness. He said when he is there he dates only black American women, so he can experience insideness with his girlfriend at the same time they are both experiencing outsideness in a foreign culture. In the United States, he dates only white foreign women, and for many years secretly planned to find and marry one—"so we'd both be outsiders: we'd be interracial, and she'd be a foreigner. That way we'd have to work through it together and have a bond. I had it all planned." He said a black history course he took in college changed his thinking on that score, but at the time of the interview he still had a white foreign girlfriend.

The outsider syndrome can be a military brat's strong suit, cultivating as it does a spirit of open-mindedness and tolerance as well as a lively sense of curiosity that embraces the world as a marvelously stimulating place. It is also an insidious thing, secretly calling the shots even as we entertain very different ideas about what we want in our lives.

But there is a two-step remedy to the downside of the outsider syndrome: First, to become aware of its functioning in our lives, thus robbing it of its secret power. And second, to counter it consciously, figuring out what it will take to satisfy our need for attachment, and then working to bring that into our lives.

We could rewrite the saying:

> I and my brothers with my cousins;
> I and my cousins with the world.

CHAPTER 11

LEGACIES

It was the first song on all journeys the family took together. Each of the children had heard it first in the arms of their father; its rhythms had come to them through their mother's milk. The song filled each child with a bewitched, unnameable feeling; the same feeling that drove men into battle. The Marine Corps hymn was the family song, the song of a warrior's family, the song of war, the Meecham song.

—The Great Santini

Before I began work on this book I suspected there would be a strong vein of common experience running through the lives of military brats from all the services, but the research bore that out to a degree I had not anticipated. In values, perceptions, life choices, and problems, military brats are strikingly similar to one another. The Fortress put its stamp upon us, and it is a stamp we continue to bear throughout our lives.

One of the most striking pieces of evidence for this was the perception of differentness shared by nearly all the military brats I asked. As mentioned in the last chapter, almost every one answered that he or she still does not feel like a civilian, despite the fact that the vast majority had associated almost exclusively with civilians for the whole of their adult lives. In some undefined way they sensed they were still products of the Fortress, still to a degree outsiders in a civilian culture in which they could function with ease but with which they could not wholly identify.

That overwhelming sentiment was all the more striking because the interviewees had never sat down with other military brats to compare in depth their experiences in the warrior society. These were the responses of military brats who had lived largely in isolation from other military brats, who had no idea that the sense of differentness they continued to experience was shared by others. What I sensed in their response was not only a feeling of innate difference but a realization that there are limits—often self-imposed limits—to their assimilation into civilian America.

"I would like to blend in with people," said an Air Force son, "but my basic nature is different from that of the people around me. The warrior model has been a major part of my life, and my life has felt very much like a warrior path."

Having heard much of this son's life story, I am aware—as he is—that if he had wished, he could have played things differently, with probably less fallout and less anxiety. He has taken some lonely stands at times. But, knowing there was an easier way, he didn't choose to take it. When it required courage to stay the course, he stayed the course. And this son is like many other military brats in that respect. Winning is not so important; putting oneself on the line for principle is. If he had taken a different path, one in which he took fewer stands for what he believed, it would have been completely acceptable in civilian America. But he chose to make his choices—and pay the price—in keeping with the values and perceptions he still carries from the Fortress.

We are the children of warriors. And although it was initially a role not of our own choosing, it is a role perpetuated by many of us with pride. Our minds, our hearts return us time and again to the warrior path. It is an attitude, a way of being. Our souls were hammered out on the forge of discipline and dedication, of mission and service to others, of loss and sacrifice in the name of something larger than ourselves.

Military brats don't really belong in any given place, and most of us chose at some point to leave the Fortress behind. But we most certainly belong to our own lived experience, and we most certainly carry the Fortress within us still.

So far in this book we have looked at a number of the psychological legacies of growing up inside the Fortress, and seen something of how they continue to influence our decision making and our relationships with others.

Like most aspects of the human psyche, each of these legacies has both useful strengths and unsettling implications. But until we understand exactly how these legacies are at work in our lives, we can neither take real advantage of their strengths, nor move to counteract their negatives.

Some of these legacies deserve special examination, partly because they are based so broadly in the military brat experience, and partly because their effects are so strongly seen among us in adulthood. Four legacies in particular are so commonly found in military brats that they come close to describing a profile of us as a group:

- a distorted relationship to time,
- a kind of reflexive passivity that contrasts sharply with outer assertiveness,
- a need for order which is paradoxically coupled with a need to rebel against it,
- and a sense of idealism so powerful that it has an enormous guiding influence on our lives.

THE FIRST LEGACY: A DISTORTED RELATIONSHIP TO TIME

Civilian Time vs. Military Time

Rooted civilians and transient military brats relate to time very differently; the ways of life to which we were born set us up that way. Unfortunately, this does not mean that the two conceptions of time are equally valid. It is the civilian notion of time—seeing it as an uninterrupted flow—that works in American society, and it is indeed the civilian relationship to time that, in the long run, is the healthiest for the individual. It's up to us military brats to understand the difference, and to try as much as possible to recast our relationship to time in the civilian way.

Despite many years of working and living in the civilian world, I don't think I fully realized how my own sense of time was out of sync with reality until I had been married to my very civilian, very rooted husband for a while. One day, listening to him talk with his family, I realized that for them time is a natural continuum: The past flows into the present, which flows into the future. The bedrock assumption of their thinking is that what we did yesterday, and what we do today, determines to a large extent what will happen tomorrow. In a sense this did not, could not, come as a shock to me; some part of me had always known this was one of the basic tenets people have about life, and I probably had always used language in ways that implied I, too, shared this assumption. But the truth I realized that day was that I had never really believed it applied to my own life.

Like many another military brat, by the time I entered college I had

attended twelve schools and lived in twenty different houses. This kind
of mobility seems normal enough as we are undergoing it, but one
consequence is that for us, time hardly unfurls in a smooth continuum. It's true that one year follows upon the heels of another the
same as for a civilian child, and we military brats, too, are able to chart
our growth, record our birthdays and life events in the usual sequential
order. But the reality surrounding these events is so fragmented, so
frequently torn apart and reassembled in different surroundings with
different players, that for us past, present, and future are experienced
as distinct and unrelated. When, as children, we were plucked out of
one environment and abruptly set down in another, our operating
assumption had to be that all our past investments in people outside
the family were lost, and that the new people-investments we were
now rushing to make would in turn be lost when the next inevitable
move came about.

Consider the difference this makes in the way one understands
reality. A rooted civilian—and maybe especially someone like my
husband, who grew up on a farm with his life framed within the cycle
of sowing, tending, and harvesting—knows that in the present, one
can both build on the past and prepare for the future. It is possible—
not only possible, but quite natural—to think long-term. Civilians
thus reared learn to *use time as a medium*. Because they understand
the passage of time, they can conceive of their own lives in terms of it.
They know how to plan and to build and to aim for a far-distant goal.
Equally important, they know the consequences of *not* planning and
not building; and they know that when they make mistakes, other
people are likely to remember them, because the people around them
are long-term witnesses to the same continuum.

Military brats, in contrast, use *change* as a medium. That means
that while, for instance, a civilian child learns early on that every
person in the community has a particular identity and personality
which is merely deepened with time, a military child learns that it is
possible—and indeed necessary—to change as one's context changes,
in order to reap the greatest social benefits in the shortest amount of
time. Our experience teaches us to be chameleons in our relationships. Eventually we also learn that change is a handy way to solve
our problems, essentially by leaving them behind; as a result, we tend
to learn very little about accountability for our actions over time.

The ability to use change as a medium is something that works quite
well during our transient childhood and adolescence, and is a natural
adaptation to a stressful life. The problem is that it doesn't work so well
in the grown-up world. Rewarding adult relationships, whether per-

sonal or professional, are built over time; and try as we might to work it differently, we are bound to find out that there is really no substitute for building bridges from past to present, and present to future.

This is an extremely difficult notion for military brats to grasp. Even words such as *permanent* and *forever*, which roll so easily off the tongues of rooted civilians, are ineffable to us. It is hardly strange that this should be so; our mother tongue, military lingo, is itself incapable of shaping itself around such concepts. Temporary duty (TDY in the Army; TAD in the Navy and Marine Corps) is the term for assignments lasting a matter of months or less, during which the service member is separated from his or her family. By contrast, a permanent change of station (PCS) is a move to a different base in which the service member is accompanied by family. But how permanent is *permanent?* At most, four years—and rarely that long. Even at that, everyone knows that new PCS orders can be issued at any time, so that even the military's notion of permanence is an exaggeration. In the warrior society, time is measured in degrees of temporariness.

The long-term effects of this on children are profound. The child's concept of time is bracketed on one side by the most recent change, and on the other by the expectation of further, perhaps imminent, change. It is an orientation that is very difficult to shed.

"I can *say* the word 'forever,' " an Army major's daughter told me, "but I don't really *believe* the word 'forever.' To me it means 'for right now.' It's present thinking, an extension of the present." The remark is reminiscent of a comment made by an Air Force colonel's daughter, previously quoted in the "Nomads" chapter: "When I was growing up, everything was temporary—and that's the way I look at my life now: My job's only temporary. My relationships are only temporary. These clothes I'm wearing, this corporate image, is only temporary."

Another aspect of this is that a typical military brat, disconnected from the past and keyed in to the present, tends to be almost irrationally optimistic about the future. This attitude is but a transplanting into adulthood of a fervent childhood belief that the next move, the next base, would be better. Never mind that the reality often failed the dream; the need to believe—or should we say, the need to justify our losses—was strong enough to override any evidence to the contrary.

One Army sergeant's daughter, who attended ten schools in three different countries, told of wishing that her family would move even more often than it did. "I would get into ruts, you see," she said. "And I'd think that if only we could move right now I'd have another chance, I could begin again. I had delusions of grandeur. I'd think the next situation would have just what I needed to *become*." A classic example of a military brat using change as a medium: In the face of overwhelming loss, or the inability to gain a footing on new ground, she looked to change for her personal redemption.

That's just the problem. We were always living with one foot in the realm of the temporary, the other in the realm of potential. What was missing was a sense of continuity and permanence, and the idea that what one does today is extremely important because one will have to live with that tomorrow. Military brats understand the concept of potential, but often do not know how to bridge the gulf of time to realize it. It is exceedingly difficult to project what one can become if one does not have a firm handle on what one was—the kind of handle provided by a constant group of peers, for instance. For rooted civilians, the past acts as ballast to hold one steady while preparing for what is to come. Military brats typically do not have this ballast. For us, the past persona keeps disappearing, and the future persona shimmers ahead of us in any number of forms, like a mirage that recedes as we advance.

Because rooted civilians have a more useful understanding of continuity, they are in a better position to visualize their lives over time and set about reaching long-term goals in a coherent way. This isn't to say all rooted civilians do so—just that if they do not, it is almost certainly for some other reason than a flawed perception of time.

Loss of Control

But the temporary mode in which military brats tend to think and act is not the only problematic aspect of our distorted relationship to time. Closely linked is a disturbing sense of lack of control, an outgrowth of our childhood experience of powerlessness in the face of abrupt and massive change. The legacy is a sense of dread that our situation is going to be suddenly altered—by forces with far more power than we—and we will have no warning and no say-so.

An Air Force colonel's daughter told of coming home from school one day when she was about seven to find movers packing up the house; the contents of her bedroom were already boxed up. "What's so odd about it is I know that they told me about the move—later I asked my father and he said he is sure I was told—but somehow I was in such a fog that I didn't realize it." Thirty-five years later, she is still dogged by fear that the scenario will repeat itself.

"For most of my life," she said,

   there has been the sense that my situation could suddenly be taken away
   and a new one imposed on me by 'them' and I would have no choice or say
   about it.

One thing that causes me a lot of trouble is a constant foreboding of being abandoned in my love relationships. I don't trust that anything will last long—which would be okay in itself, except it results in a lot of clinging stuff, fear stuff that gets in the way. I don't know if I'll ever be able to fully separate from that vague feeling that "they" will "rearrange" things: I'll come home and the movers will be there putting my stuff into big cardboard boxes to go to some unknown and unchosen destination. That feeling doesn't seem to go away. In fact, I have always returned from trips braced for big changes and traumas to have occurred while I was absent.

The fear of not having control, of the power really being in the hands of some unknown Other, can lead to two different responses. Some military brats become very controlling, as though in thinking ahead and covering all the angles, or in holding themselves at a carefully gauged distance from complicated involvements, they will be safe. Many adopt lifestyles that marginalize them in some ways, but which allow them to call all the shots: They might insist on living alone, for instance, or being self-employed, or avoiding a whole host of relationships in which they would be subordinates or even equal partners. That way, they might reason, no one can pull any surprises.

The other response, of course, is just the opposite: to resign oneself to powerlessness and simply go along with what life deals out, buffeted about by the winds of change.

Both responses can be found in the same family; the case of two Army sisters poses a useful contrast. The older sister, who grew up to adopt a controlling, independent lifestyle, said that her pattern was set as a child. "I picked up real fast that you can't wait around for something to happen to you," she said. "You have to take charge. You only *have* so much time, and you don't know how much. So you always stay in the present rather than plan for the future." As a kid she was extroverted, a leader. Her sister was quite different: "I always perceived her as shy, quiet, a bookworm. She didn't really interact. Her whole thing was, 'Well, we're going to move soon anyway.' It didn't make any difference to her. My feeling was, 'Quick, let's do this, I might die tomorrow.' "

Many military brats can identify with the attitude of the younger sister, whose survival style was one of least resistance. "I think there was a tendency to feel like, 'We'll be rotating out anyway, so I'll just hang in there until I have to leave,' " said an Air Force general's daughter. "I figured it would all be decided for me, so I didn't have to make a decision. I had a tendency to wait and be overcome by events. And I know I have a pattern of that now." Some military brats with this pattern find themselves giving up control altogether, by surrendering their decision making to others, or delaying important decisions for so long that their options vanish.

Oddly enough, both the controlling response and the resignation response can be found in the same person, and even at the same time. That was certainly true of me when I embarked on the automobile odyssey described in the "Nomads" chapter. I gave the appearance—even to myself—of being in total control, at the wheel, even, but in reality I was surrendering myself to fate: waiting, as the Air Force daughter put it so well, to be overcome by events.

Time and the Crisis Orientation

The expectation that one will be overcome by events may derive not only from the inevitability of the next move, but from the crisis orientation of the warrior society. The byword of the military is "readiness"; what this means in practice is that warriors and their families live a lifestyle of continuous preparation for crisis.

Military brats tell of practice mass evacuations at military bases . . . of being issued dog tags at overseas bases in time of international tension, presumably so their bodies could be quickly identified in the wake of an attack . . . of Strategic Air Command (SAC) bases put on alert, so that movement on and off base is restricted . . . of fathers who slept with red phones by their beds and sometimes disappeared for weeks at a time, unable to stay in touch with their families even by phone. Many have vivid memories of the Cuban missile crisis in 1962; one Air Force colonel's daughter recalled that her father vanished incommunicado for a month, while her mother kept a suitcase packed and waiting by the front door, a map and a loaded .45 sitting on top.

The impression internalized by military brats is that their warrior fathers are essentially instruments of another's will, and that life is about preparing oneself to react to a (possibly imminent) crisis of someone else's making. "My dad was in SAC," said an Air Force colonel's son, "and he always had a red phone in his bedroom. When the alert came, the red phones would ring and all the men would scramble. When I was a kid I spent a lot of time wondering if this was it, if this was really war this time."

For military brats, then, existence takes on a kind of conditional aspect: There is not only the inevitability of change that hangs in the background, but even the suggestion of potential disaster. And through it all, as in a Greek drama, there is the sense of helplessness to change one's fate.

A military brat I once met is an artist whose work consists primarily of realistic pencil drawings. Many of the images are culled from her peripatetic Army life in exotic places. But subtract the exoticism, and the atmosphere they convey is one common to military bases everywhere: mundane surroundings that are nevertheless strangely ominous with danger. Two delicate Japanese geishas sedately sipping tea, a gun and one bullet on the table between them. Three darkly exotic Indian women in saris and Elvis Presley T-shirts, each displaying a small pistol. A group of robed, tiny-footed Asian women seated close together as for a formal portrait, all of them distractedly holding pistols and a rifle, and unaware that behind them, next to a poster of Patty Hearst-as-SLA-guerrilla, a man in a gas mask and kamikaze-style plane are about to turn their sanctuary into an inferno.

Many of the works are subtitled *Moments Before the End*. No matter what the surface subject matter, the images carry the suggestion of a very familiar aspect of the military brat experience: people whose trappings—primarily, their weapons—suggest attempts at exerting control over their lives, but whose body attitudes and facial expressions suggest helpless resignation to their fate. A powerlessness underscored by the climate of imminent danger.

"If there's a noise to accompany my drawings," said the artist, who agreed to discuss her work on condition of anonymity, "it would be a fly buzzing. You know something's going to happen, but you're not sure. My people are like sleepwalkers. There is a feeling that life really blindsides you: You can be as prepared as you like, but what's really going to get you—psychically, emotionally, physically—is buzzing right behind you, and you have no control over that. I think being in the military contributes to that feeling. In the military, there is always some other force that controls where you go or where you've been. Then there is the way that you spend your whole life preparing for a crisis. And when there's a war, you just prepare and prepare and prepare."

Life blindsides you. If that is one's notion of how life works—and for a great many military brats, it is exactly that—it is revealing of our distorted relationship to time. It is a view that discounts both past and future and embraces the present—but with a wariness born of hard experience that the present, despite its seeming innocuousness, could well be "moments before the end."

What kind of impact does this rather fatalistic philosophy have on the military brats who hold it? For many it could lead to either the controlling attitude or the air of resignation described earlier, both of which are forms of self-protection. But that is not all, for there is more than a philosophical attitude at stake here. What we are talking about is the awareness of loss and potential loss on a grand scale. And that means the emotional cost is very high.

The Inevitability of Loss as a Function of Time

Every military brat knows three things about the nature of change: First, it is inevitable. Second, it is beyond our control. And third, while it holds the promise of gain, it *always* means loss: loss of friends, of mentors, of one's contextual identity.

We are all old hands at coping with loss. Some would say that makes us better at handling life's disappointments; in a sense that's true, in that most of us are masters at salvaging what can be salvaged, regrouping, and starting anew. But that has to do with coping techniques more than emotions—and for many military brats, long experience does not make loss any easier to bear emotionally.

Our conviction that major loss is inevitable so colors our approach to life that it leads to what might be termed *trust disorders*. Problems with trust are commonly found among adult children of alcoholics, and, as we know, many military brats fall into this category also; but trust disorders are also found among military brats from nonalcoholic families and, I would like to suggest, are directly linked to the military lifestyle that teaches its children to equate change with loss.

One form of trust disorder is when the military brat develops an inability to trust—for example, an inability to relax in a relationship out of fear it will be suddenly yanked away. An Air Force colonel's daughter earlier spoke of "a constant foreboding of being abandoned in love relationships." And in Chapter 4, a daughter said, "A really big issue for me is that I can't ever relax. I have to hold something back, I have to maintain. Part of me can't lean. It's a real issue in my marriage: My husband is a very secure, well-loved Jewish prince. His assumption is that people are there to love and take care of him. My assumption is, you never let your guard down."

The other common trust disorder is to do the opposite: trust too quickly. Some military brats, myself included, have tended to invest to inappropriate degrees and almost indiscriminately—as though time were so short we could not afford to reject anyone who offered friendship. Our people-investments are therefore sometimes unwise: In effect we give emotional blank checks, and then somehow we are terribly surprised when things turn out badly. Ironically, this pattern, which derives from an excess of loss, leads to even more loss.

These trust disorders are really two faces of the same problem, and represent two ways of adapting. One military brat holds herself aloof from attachment, as a defense against loss. Another attaches all too readily, but lives in constant fear of loss. Either way, the ability to live here and now, to reap the full value and comfort of our human relationships, is undercut. The person who fears intimacy leads a life of painful solitude; the one who invests but lives in constant fear of loss is continually sensing the potential of painful aloneness. Neither one can relax enough to count her blessings.

The fear of loss can be so pervasive that it becomes a motif in the fabric of one's life, and a way of seeing the world. Some of the military brats interviewed for this book have such a hypersensitivity to loss that they must guard themselves from issues of loss in other people's lives as well; they try to avoid sad movies, newspaper articles, or other mirrors in which their own history of loss will be reflected. "I constantly try to prepare myself for loss," a Navy petty officer's daughter said. "Even if somebody at work leaves, it upsets me—because I like my work, and I like the fact that it's predictable who will be where. And if someone leaves, it makes me uneasy temporarily, because I hadn't planned on it or prepared for it. I deal with it by saying to myself, 'Gee, isn't that interesting—there's that issue of loss again. You don't even really care about this person, you just don't want something to change.' "

Other military brats spoke in their interviews of having an extremely strong nesting instinct; their home and possessions carry a significance vital to their psychic stability. "Wherever I go, I settle in and create a nurturing, comfy household," said the daughter of an Air Force colonel.

> People say it feels like I've lived in a place for ten years instead of six months. My familiar trappings around me are part of my root system; I found out how important that is three years ago, when I went through several months of upheaval. None of my normal patterns were in operation and my household was in storage. I went a little crazy, felt out of control, and had a wild, brief, and embarrassing affair. The minute I settled into a new home and unpacked my stuff, I became my old self, called off the affair, and got serious, grounded, and sane again. Until that experience I didn't realize how crucial my familiar nest was to my sense of balance.

On the other hand, some military brats live as though they expect to break camp at dawn tomorrow: They have few possessions and little in their lives to suggest permanence. This is merely the flip side of the same coin: They cope with the inevitability of loss by eternally bracing for it.

In view of our distorted sense of time and the serious implications this has for our lives, it might be wise for us military brats to pose ourselves a question and set ourselves a task.

The question: Is it truly liberating for us to live in the present always, unencumbered by the past and unconcerned about the future? Or are we rendering ourselves prisoners of the moment, like the figures in the artwork described earlier—wary of the danger that may lie just ahead, but somehow helpless to stave it off?

The task: to retrain ourselves in the saner, calmer, civilian mode, gradually learning to live in relation to both past and future, as well as present. The fact is, it takes a great deal of energy to constantly try to live outside the continuity of time; in deepening our understanding of how time works, we can perhaps learn how to use its currents to our advantage. Bringing our patterns to the conscious level is the critically important first step.

THE SECOND LEGACY:
ASSERTIVENESS VS. PASSIVITY

A strength, a weakness. Most aspects of the military brat experience can be seen in this way, including the four legacies examined in this chapter. But few are so oddly contradictory as assertiveness vs. passivity.

The same transient life that teaches military brats to swim like fish in any social setting also teaches a certain kind of passive acceptance. The result is a mix of traits that can be very confusing to those who know us, and to ourselves.

Example: Because we adapt so easily to new settings and frequently go on to be high achievers in them, other people, including parents, teachers, counselors, friends, and co-workers, tend to presume we possess a strong sense of inner direction. There is a terrific irony in this: Even as the military brat acquires a reputation as a strong, capable, assertive person, he or she may secretly suffer the lack of a confident inner voice. The military brat who appears so "assertive" may well be scrambling desperately for external clues as to what he or she should do next.

The key is that the highly transient childhood we credit with teaching us resilience does not really teach how to *assert* ourselves over our new circumstances, merely how to *adapt* to them. A chameleon is not in control of how it changes. And how does it know which of its colors is true? Unless the important decisions we make are dictated from within rather than mere responses to our context, we are not inner-directed.

"I can't imagine a more psychically alienating life than the military," said one Air Force colonel's daughter quoted in the "Masks" chapter. "There is no development of the inner sense of what's right for you. The military doesn't train people to know what they think. You feel feelings and you're not supposed to feel them."

The interviews conducted for this book suggested that this lack of inner direction comes about in the two following ways:

First, it can be bred into children by authoritarian parents, generally fathers, who themselves rely on external rules and direction to give shape to their lives. The dependence on external rules is one of the defining characteristics of authoritarianism. These fathers tend to reproduce the same kind of dynamic within their own families. There are so many rules, and such stiff penalties for transgression of them, that the child has a hard time learning to listen for his or her inner voice and to follow it.

Secondly, lack of inner direction can be a product of constant mobility, which forces children to adapt continually to new situations. When children move a great deal, they focus on conforming to whatever social order they walk into, rather than on asking themselves who they are and what they do and do not wish to be party to.

This was borne out in many personal stories. Children of authoritarian fathers always expressed problems with hearing or following their inner voice. But many children of nonauthoritarian military fathers spoke of the same problems; and some even attributed this to having moved so much and changed so many times that they were not certain who they were.

The lack of a strong inner voice shows itself in several ways:

Indecisiveness: an inability to exercise the power of choice, or to stick with decisions; also, a hesitation to take initiative toward change.

A Marine colonel's daughter: "I'm afraid to make decisions, even about the kind of sofa I want."

The seeking of approval: a quest for affirmation from others which so colors our way of relating that it amounts to a denial of the self.

An Air Force colonel's daughter who attended fifteen schools, and whose father was not authoritarian:

I have always attempted to be such a chameleon, to fit in, that it isn't even a conscious thing. Whatever people are doing, or whatever people want, was fine with me. I suppose I've always been easy to get along with, because I just go with the flow. And that was just fine most of the time, unless one important person in my life was flowing one way and another was flowing a different way and I was stuck in the middle. Then I wouldn't know what to do.

Once I went in for counseling and the therapist asked, "Well, what would *you* like to do?" And I just stared at her and said "I don't know." I had to get in touch with the fact that I didn't know *what* I wanted to do with my life, what my values were, what was important to me. All I wanted was to please other people and be accepted by them. I think that's one of the biggest problems in my life; in a way, it's a kind of cowardice. Very often I won't say things because I don't want to upset people.

I used to think it was because I was a woman and I needed assertiveness, but I think it's a lot deeper than that. It's a sense of not being anchored, of not having roots.

An Air Force daughter whose father, a colonel, was an authoritarian: "A few months ago, somebody told me something that cut me more to the bone than anything else in a long time. She said, 'Sometimes I don't trust you, because I never know what you really believe in. You'll go with whatever the tide is. You'll change to please someone else.' It tore my skin off. But it was true. That's why it hurt so much."

Confusion about one's values: a lack of conviction about one's opinions; failure to stand up for one's rights; a reluctance to take action on one's own behalf.

The daughter of an authoritarian Army sergeant: "I hate myself for being so passive. When I work with someone else I'm not passive, but when I'm on my own I'm so passive I can't stand it. I wish I were more rebellious, more decisive. I wish I would be the type that when someone says something I'd stand up and say, 'Now wait a minute! Clarify yourself! What you're saying isn't right at all'!"

An Air Force major's daughter whose parents were nonauthoritarian but alcoholic: "In the military, everything is seen in terms of black or white. But I have the opposite problem from too much black and white in my life; there's too much *gray*. I have a hard time saying what is right and what is wrong."

A Navy petty officer's daughter, whose parents were neither authoritarian nor alcoholic, but who moved a great deal: "I've been working real hard the past five years or so on cutting the bullshit, on trying to get clear in my mind what it is *I* want. I still don't know. I'm forty-four years old, and I'm still trying to figure out what I'm going to do when I grow up. All these competencies I've developed over my life have been the result of someone asking me to do something. I'm not self-directed; I wait for someone else to point me. I'm a good second banana."

An Air Force sergeant's son whose father was authoritarian:

I've never smoked marijuana or any of that stuff, because I just made up my mind I'm not going to do it. That's just what my father taught me: He always used to say there's danger in breaking rules because then you might find they're so easy to break. The military was a rule-oriented society.

So I have this rule-governed thing. Other people have *values*, but I have *rules*. Like social rules . . . I'm afraid that if I tried marijuana I might like it a lot—and then it would start messing with my system. That's why I don't like alcohol, either. These are rules I set up, and I can never break them because my system depends on rules. That's not good. I have to work it out on other, higher levels. But I'm at the rule stage, like a lot of military people are.

Lack of self-discipline: a tendency to go haywire once the military brat is beyond the reach of controlling authority.

The son of an authoritarian Air Force general, who later chose a career as an Army officer himself: "I had been regimented my entire life. My parents even sent me to a military high school. When I was turned loose at a university, I went ape. I cut about every class possible. I was drifting, and had no self-control or self-discipline— probably because Big Brother had always been watching me as a child at home, and in the military high school."

The umbrella term I use for all of these behaviors is *passivity.* It is important to note that, like the trust disorders mentioned earlier, many of these same aspects of passivity are found in adult children of alcoholics. It may be impossible to untangle whether a passivity problem came about primarily as the result of an alcoholic family, or whether it was occasioned by authoritarianism, child abuse, or constant mobility. It is true that all the military brats interviewed for this book who came from alcoholic families had passivity problems. But military brats who did not come from alcoholic families—whose parents were teetotalers, in fact—complained of these problems as well.

Amy is the daughter of Navy parents who were loving, supportive, nonauthoritarian, and who did not drink. She married another military brat who became a career officer. Although her marriage has been a good one, she spoke frankly of one of the problems they have encountered. "I didn't know I had a passivity problem until fairly recently," she said.

All I knew was I wasn't being perceived the way I wanted to be. It took me years to figure out why. Our family got to a real bad cycle, and we started family counseling.

The problem turned out to be between my husband and me. Neither of us allowed ourselves to ever say anything negative, and I had a neurotic need to please everybody and to placate him. That made it very difficult for us to be close to one another, because we could never say what we were really thinking.

I still see a counselor once a week, although she says that if I had a best

friend I wouldn't need to see her anymore. But it's very difficult for me to
invest in close friendships. I protect myself from getting too invested in
people because they might disappear. Or even more than that, they might
disapprove. Disapproval is an even bigger issue with me than loss.

The way out of a passivity problem is very difficult, but it can be
found. As with the distorted relationship to time, the first step is to
consciously recognize one's patterns. Therapy can be very beneficial,
because it helps the military brat to set up an internal dialogue: One
can learn to interrupt a reflexive pattern, question it, and look for an
alternative.

THE THIRD LEGACY: THE NEED FOR
ORDER VS. THE NEED TO REBEL

Rebellions Big and Small

Having chafed under the rigid rules of the warrior society, many
military brats reach adulthood with a powerful need to rebel. It does
not necessarily mean that the military brat is rejecting out of hand the
values of the warrior society, although it may; it does probably mean
that the need to individuate was so stifled in the authoritarian, rigorously conventional warrior family that when the military brat finally
breaks free of control, he or she may go to extremes of expression or
experimentation—"like a boomerang suddenly being released," as one
Air Force son put it.

Sometimes these rebellions explode in starbursts of great incendiary
power—as with Jim Morrison of the rock group The Doors. Morrison's
deeply resonant voice and defiant language represented the call to
iconoclasm for many of his generation. It was a role he relished; he
once said; in a biographical blurb for Elektra Records, "I'm interested
in anything about revolt, disorder, chaos."[1]

On a much smaller scale, some military brats also found the iconoclasm of the sixties and early seventies both convenient and satisfying;
it was possible to rebel against authority while feeling sustained by an
almost tribal subculture. As with their civilian peers, military brats
found these rebellions were frequently experimental and of fairly short
duration; several military brats spoke of having experimented with
drugs and sex and radical politics, only to later settle down into
conventional lifestyles. One military son told of his intense antiwar
activity while a college student; a dozen years later, having considerably revised his views, he found himself applying for a job with the
CIA.

Actually I heard relatively few accounts of major rebellions among the eighty life stories gathered for this book, if one excludes brief experimental aberrations that were not adopted as long-term lifestyles. I had expected to hear more, and wondered why there was so little material about acting-out behavior in adolescence or full-scale rebellion then or later. A likely explanation returns to two of the roots of so many military brat legacies: authoritarianism and alcoholism in the family.

Children of authoritarian families—and children who were not subjected to authoritarian rule in the family but who are very sensitive to the authoritarian environment of the Fortress—have a particularly strong need to individuate, but they also have internalized particularly strong controls *against* individuating. It's very hard to break out of the pattern.

Where children of alcoholic warrior families are concerned (understanding that many of these families were also authoritarian), a host of worries and of unmet needs will work to mitigate the urge to rebel. The following is an excerpt from an article about children of alcoholics:

> The adolescent child may also have a hard time separating because he or she may still need the nurturing that wasn't provided earlier. Rebellious behavior sometimes makes it easier for an adolescent to separate from home and family. . . . The adolescent child of an alcoholic has a harder time rebelling, however, because the response such behavior will elicit is unpredictable. In fact, the response might not even be directed at the adolescent. One youngster admitted to worrying, "If I stay out too late, will Dad blame Mom as he always does and hit her if he's drunk?"[2]

Most of the military brats I interviewed came of age during the sixties and seventies, and some took advantage of their generation's tribal approach to individuation through dress, music, drug experimentation, and open protest. Some, of course, did not. But the most significant efforts at separation of many, and probably most, military brats have been private and intensely personal. There is for instance the Navy chief's son who married his first wife precisely because his father didn't like her; the Marine colonel's daughter who took up cigarettes and continues to smoke because her father hates it; the Army son who sought and received an appointment to West Point, just so he could have the pleasure of refusing it; the Army son who joined the Air Force to spite his father; the Air Force son who would drive his authoritarian father wild by showing up hours or even days late for every family function.

Not all military families are authoritarian, but in those that are, the children often learn very young the skill of dissimulation, or rebelling *safely:* They become very good at giving the appearance of obedience while secretly harboring feelings of angry defiance.

A Marine colonel's daughter, forced by her father to run laps around the housing area every afternoon, made it her practice to run only in the spaces between buildings that could be observed by her father from their house; she walked every other step of the way. The method worked well until a couple of amused Marine Corps neighbors tipped off her father, who promptly caught and punished her.

A Navy petty officer's daughter whose father held inspections every week would clean and tidy all the surfaces of her room, but stuff her entire wardrobe under the bed, which her father never checked. As a high school student she secretly flirted with radical politics. At school, the extent of her public rebellion was to stand for the national anthem but not sing it. When she was with her family, however, she would both stand for the anthem and sing it, but made it a point to "sway with the music"—an act of disrespect that was totally lost on her civilian peers and probably on her family as well.

A Navy chief petty officer's son said that dissimulation characterized his behavior generally: "When my father was around, I acted as he expected me to act. When he wasn't around, I acted as I pleased."

One military daughter so disliked having to answer "yes, sir" or "no, sir" to her father's questions that she devised a convoluted way of avoiding it. When her father posed an unavoidably direct question, such as "Did you clean your room?," she would respond in oddly stilted complete sentences such as, "My room is clean."

An Army major's daughter said that she nearly always obeyed her father's directives to the letter, but meanwhile cultivated a subversively rebellious attitude: "My father and I had definite power problems," she said. "He tried to be the stern disciplinarian, but I think I had the psychological edge—in that I knew it was his power trip and I didn't have to buy it. So I would do the tasks, but I never really submitted."

The Yearning for Order

To suggest that growing up within a structure as rigid as the military gives one the urge to rebel is to tell only part of the story. That alone does not give an inkling of what it is like to be a military brat—for the thing that makes this legacy so problematic for us is that we not only carry a desire to rebel, but an equally strong desire to surrender ourselves to structure and order. It's a paradox that churns within us at the unconscious level. It can cause great confusion in our lives, and lead to some oddly incongruous behaviors.

There is, for example, the Army sergeant's daughter who attended a large university during the time of political upheaval over the Vietnam War. She became a leftist and was one of the most active members of her campus chapter of Students for a Democratic Society; at one point she even traveled to Canada to meet with a group of North Vietnamese women. During this same period, however, she said it was still very much part of her plans to find and marry a military man and become a military wife. And while she realized that was probably not something she should voice to her SDS peers, she did not herself perceive it as a contradiction.

And there is the Air Force daughter who emerged from the Fortress hating everything to do with hierarchy—yet who chose to teach at a Catholic university known for its rigid hierarchical ways. She still teaches there, but makes it her practice, as she put it, to "undermine the hierarchy in every way I can, in class and out," primarily by voicing her views. "Hierarchy is destructive," she said. "It encourages competition and violence. It also intimidates people, and I don't think students learn best when they're intimidated."

And there were quite a few military sons and daughters interviewed for this book who told of experiencing a powerful attraction to the idea of joining the military themselves. Some, of course, went on to do it and adopt it as their career choice. But many others considered becoming warriors too—even if their lifestyles or aspirations or political views made that idea seem outlandish. Some told of actually visiting recruiters one or more times before finally ruling it out.

I never visited a recruiter, but I have to say that the idea of joining the military has entered my thoughts more than a few times over the years—and this despite the fact that I *knew* it would be a terrible decision for me, that in fact it would be an inexplicable thing to do in light of the person I knew myself to be. But there it was, a magnet in the background that from time to time would exert its pull. I remember that as my thirty-sixth birthday approached—the cutoff age for entering military service—I found myself thinking wistfully, "Only six more weeks left to join up before I lose my chance forever." When I realized what I had been thinking, I was shocked. After all, I was already fully committed to my husband, my small child, my career as a writer—in short, to a life path that took me in a very different direction from the warrior society. I didn't *seriously* want to be in the military—and yet I could clearly see myself donning a uniform and reporting to work in a context I feel I very much understand and in which I believe part of me would be very comfortable.

When I learned that a great many other military brats have experienced the same thing—and been equally puzzled by it—I began to wonder why.

Is this something as simple as nostalgia for a past long gone?

Is is that we yearn for the childhood sense of belonging—however superficial it may have been—that we have been unsuccessful in re-creating in our adult lives?

Or could it be that the powerful urge to go back to the Fortress—or to some other equally structured life—stems from a desire to free ourselves from the choices and challenges of the civilian world? In that case, is the wished-for return to structure a kind of surrender of the self? After all, the society in which we were raised was not at all like the highly individualistic civilian world in which most of us now find ourselves. Do we suffer a kind of *freedom angst*, like émigrés from totalitarian societies, who sometimes speak of feeling as though they are drowning in a sea of choices?

I asked an Army sergeant's daughter who spent a decade as a nun why she chose the convent life. "The spiritual aspect was important," she said, "but on more of an unconscious level. The other thing about it was that you didn't have to make any decisions. You're assigned where to go, what to teach, everything. Later I realized there might be a connection to my military childhood. All the rules and regulations were both comfortable and comforting to me. Even the rules they later changed posed no problems for me."

In the dozen or so years since she left the order, she has married, become an active feminist, and pursued a career. Yet she says,

I've often thought, if I could just go back into uniform myself . . . then I would be safe and secure and I'd be happier. I think that's maybe another reason I went into the order: because there was a uniform. I identify strongly with uniforms. Whether we're all alike or not doesn't matter, because you see we're all dressed alike, and therefore we must all be committed to one thing.

Even just a few years ago I was thinking, Maybe I should be a police officer. I've seriously thought it might be a way out of my unhappiness, of my inability to perform, to do well, to motivate myself to be active and make decisions. It's a crazy thought, I know, because it's just a façade. I know that. But . . . sometimes I even think, maybe I could work at the zoo. They wear uniforms there. And I wonder why I want this. Do I want to be *part* of something? And does that mean that everyone has to dress alike and we all have to show up at eight o'clock for meetings? It would just be a *forced* camaraderie.

But then I think that doesn't matter, because those are my roots. If I could just get back to my roots, that's what I'd do. It would be *home* for me again. And then, even when I went back to visit my parents' hometown, which I hate and despise and detest, it would be all right—because then I could *really* leave and go back to my real home, which would be the uniform.

For those military brats who feel conflict about their own values, as described earlier, the lack of ambiguity suggested by a uniform may hold particular attraction. For others, who have tired of eternally feeling like outsiders, the uniform holds the promise of insideness.

But a military brat does not have to feel confused or set apart to know the longing for a uniform. For many of us the uniform is the essential symbol of all that is good about the military life: It represents order, unity, discipline, purpose. For most of us, uniforms are not intimidating at all; they are reassuring. They stand for something. And to stand inside one seems to many of us to be a privilege and an act of strength: It is a declaration of one's values before the world. If clothing makes a statement about a person, a uniform must certainly be the last word.

That may be why one Air Force colonel's daughter goes to some lengths to create the feeling of a uniform in her life. "My clothing reflects my military background," she said matter-of-factly.

> When I first started teaching I realized I needed some suits, and I had to sew them because I didn't have much money. So I made two suits with skirt and jacket—and I modeled them after my father's uniforms. There was a blue one and a khaki one; I even used some buttons off his old uniforms. So I had a winter uniform and a summer uniform.
>
> My friends still tease me because I like uniform-style clothes. I currently own four khaki skirts, three khaki blouses—two of which are Marine-issue from the base exchange, four khaki jackets, three pairs of khaki slacks, two pairs of khaki shorts, a Marine-issue raincoat, an Army canvas ammo bag which I use as a purse, and a khaki hat which I wear all the time. Yes, I can say the military has influenced my life.

I had to laugh when she told me that, partly because I can identify so well. My own wardrobe is more varied, but only because I fight against my natural impulses. If I didn't, probably everything I wear would be khaki or olive drab, with epaulets and nice, sharp creases.

Finding the Elusive Middle Ground

If military brats with this third legacy have problems reconciling contradictory needs for autonomy and for a sheltering structure, it is no accident: The warrior society itself is a powerful model for this dilemma.

The great paradox of the military is that despite its macho image, its warriors are held in a relationship of extreme dependence on the parent organization. Such macho qualities as independence and decisiveness have no place in the world of modern warriors. As restricted in certain respects as prison inmates, they are permitted to make very few decisions about their own lives: what they wear, how they behave, where they live, what their next assignment will be—all are decided for them. A gigantic organization that requires absolute obedience to authority can function no other way. This is a fact of life to which warriors and their families adapt totally; and inside the Fortress it works well, although this frequently means that retirement from the military and the shock of return to civilian life can be quite traumatic.

The young military child, then, internalizes quite a contradiction: the myth of macho and the reality of dependence, existing inside one another. It is a contradiction that often manifests itself years later, in the military brat's choice of career.

Even those military brats who opt for a great deal of structure in their working lives wind up struggling with the contradiction, often pushing the rules and powers-that-be to the limits. Most of the military brats I interviewed who had become career military as adults recounted having problems as a result of a strong tendency to buck higher authority—even though they had voluntarily placed themselves in a context in which they knew that was not permissible. For example, a daughter who became a career officer said that at Officers' Candidate School she had the highest academic marks, but the lowest military ones. "I had no patience with rules and regulations; I would get furious at OCS. My brother [who went to a military academy] was the same way. I was a devil with my ideas; he was a devil with his behavior."

Other military brats have such problems with authority—from a reflexive fear of authority to the lack of sufficient self-esteem to stand up to it—that the idea of working within a rigid structure is unthinkable. They are strongly inclined toward occupations that represent independence: Some go into business for themselves—as attorneys, small-business owners, brokers, consultants, writers, artists, actors. Some become academics or business managers or field representatives in situations where they have minimal supervision from those above. Some work part-time or strictly freelance to keep themselves at one remove from a structural hierarchy they would otherwise find oppressive. By far the majority of the military brats interviewed for this book had chosen occupations that afforded them a large measure of independence.

"It took me years to realize I was miserable as an *employee*," said one Air Force colonel's daughter who now works as a freelancer. "I think my need to be my own boss, keep irregular hours, eat and sleep when I want, call the shots as much as possible—all this is connected to my rebellion against a rigid code."

This kind of life has its own peculiar form of stress, however: On one side the military brat is successfully evading the specter of oppressive, rigid authority—only to face a life full of uncertainty, financial insecurity, and the equally terrifying specter of the void should the enterprise fail.

It is a gamble many military brats are quite willing to take. But while being one's own boss makes working palatable, in many cases it also limits the possibilities for success. Recognition is hard to come by and there is often no obvious way to move up. Paradoxically, many independent-minded military brats would probably function best—if they only could—in structured environments where their responsibilities are crystal clear and there is a well-defined ladder of promotion. Probably the ideal work situation would be one that offers structure but rewards initiative—and is tolerant of the occasional bullheaded stand that military brats are inclined to take. But then, for this to work, one would have to know more about the politics of small groups than military brats generally do.

One Air Force colonel's son who is now in business for himself told about a job he'd felt compelled to leave. "The agency I worked for was as structured as any structure I'd ever seen," he said. "The difference was that the structure was hidden. The politics were pooh-poohed, but they were there—just less obvious. I left because I didn't like the hierarchy and the politics, and frankly I wasn't very good at it. I did not pretend to support ideas that I didn't like, and I didn't spend time with power people that I didn't like. And that's not sound strategy in an office."

As if finding work situations that offer the right combination of structure and autonomy weren't enough, military brats have another obstacle to overcome. Having grown up as transients, they usually do not know how to function as expected in a long-term community. A rooted civilian seeking to set up a business knows instinctively that it is essential to be actively involved in the life of the larger community; connections and networks are crucial to the enterprise. Military brats, however, frequently have a skewed notion of what community is all about.

For the military family accustomed to a succession of posts and bases, community is a highly fluid situation in which people come and go, linked not by roots but by a like profession. There is a very strong sense of group identity, to be sure, but little of the sense of community-building that is part and parcel of the civilian notion of belonging. Military people do not organize to improve their common lot. They do not cultivate a political voice. They do not seek to change the life of the military community in major ways. They are, with respect to the outside community, consumers of goods and services, not producers. They think short-term, not long-term, and thus hold themselves back from investing in the community outside the Fortress. This is not at all an indictment of the military, merely a description—for, given its essential nature and its high mobility, military life must be this way. But the child exposed only to this definition of community may find the civilian world quite baffling.

Fortunately, military brats are not without the ability to perceive this problem and do something about it. Thanks to the transient life, they tend to have keen powers of observation and imitation—and as a result can potentially make a smoother transition to the civilian world than, for example, their own parents when they retire from the military. But it does not happen automatically. The military brat must consciously use these skills and understand that there is a long learning process involved. It takes both time and effort to finally appreciate that *belonging* is not just a matter of passive assignment to a category, as it was in the military. *Belonging* in the civilian world is a process that is fed continuously, a function of active participation in the spheres of work, education, recreation, religion, culture, politics.

For the military brat, learning this lesson amounts to nothing less than a rebirth into another way of being.

THE FOURTH LEGACY: IDEALISM

The Military Way

The warrior society is one of the most idealistic to be found in American life. The extraordinary devotion to Mission, the self-discipline in service of a cause, the willingness to give one's life at any moment—all are nourished by a pure, unshakable idealism.

This idealism, with its corollary of absolute obedience to principle, is articulated in many ways in warrior society. One example is the Code of Conduct for military men and women (despite its exclusive use of masculine gender), which was established by Executive Order of the President on August 17, 1955 and modified only slightly in 1977:

Article 1. I am an American fighting man. I serve in the forces which guard my country and our way of life. I am prepared to give my life in their defense.

Article 2. I will never surrender of my own free will. If in command I will never surrender my men while they have the means to resist.

Article 3. If I am captured I will continue to resist by all means available. I will make every effort to escape and aid others to escape. I will accept neither parole nor special favors from the enemy.

Article 4. If I become a prisoner of war, I will keep faith with my fellow prisoners. I will give no information nor take part in any action which might be harmful to my comrades. If I am senior, I will take command. If not, I will obey the lawful orders of those appointed over me and will back them up in every way.

Article 5. When questioned, should I become a prisoner of war, I am required to give name, rank, service number, and date of birth. I will evade answering further questions to the utmost of my ability. I will make no oral or written statements disloyal to my country or its allies or harmful to their cause.

Article 6. I will never forget that I am an American fighting man, responsible for my actions, and dedicated to the principles which made my country free. I will trust in my God and the United States of America.[3]

Warrior idealism is pure, strong, and unambiguous. But, seen in a larger context, it also possesses a certain irony: The military exists to protect an almost romanticized version of American life. "We're guarding an ideal," said an Army major, himself a military brat, "and not necessarily the way America actually is." From the perspective of a warrior who knows he may be called upon in the next twenty-four hours to make the ultimate sacrifice, the ideal is a better thing to die for than the flawed reality. This is at the very heart of the military myth discussed in the early chapters of this book. Mission alone is not enough; there must be a strong faith behind it that justifies the stress and sacrifice of military life, and for warriors it is a certain brand of patriotism that glorifies America and—sacrilege to say—exaggerates its goodness.

Of course many a warrior would rightly say that he or she is fighting for the principles of American democracy as embodied in the Constitution, not to preserve life as we know it in Newark, New Jersey. That is correct, of course, but as laudable as it is, it is also not without irony—for the American democracy for which the warrior is committed to die if necessary is actually for *those other Americans*, not for the warrior. There is no such thing as democracy inside the Fortress, or freedom of choice, or even true privacy, since things said or done in private social contexts can legitimately undermine a career.

Nevertheless, the idealism of the military, however out of touch with the sometimes tawdry realities of civilian society, is far from a façade. It is a powerful and sustaining creed, and it resonates throughout the Fortress.

"There is an assumption in the military that absolute values really work," said a Marine lieutenant colonel's son who went to work as a civilian for the military. He ticked off some of them.

"Heroism: the idea of sacrifice, that one risks one's life because something is worthwhile.

"Purity of leadership: the idea that the leader holds our lives in his hands, and won't sleep until the Mission is accomplished.

"Zeal of commitment: dedication even to the point of not questioning whether [the Mission] is worth doing." In fact, one might even say that an attitude which never questions authority is considered a virtue among warriors, and part of their idealistic code. A mind that trusts wholly in authority and desires only to serve, is a mind that can be counted upon to serve without reservation, in purity of spirit.

A side effect of this absolutist approach to idealism is that the distinction between matters of great principle and matters of triviality is sometimes blurred. Thus a quality such as punctuality, surely a comparatively minor attribute in the great pantheon of warrior values, comes to assume inordinate importance—even to the point of being considered a reflection of one's character, of one's intention to fulfill a promise made.

All of these things are strongly internalized in the children of warriors—even the matter of punctuality. I could have set my watch by the exactitude with which military brats turned up for their appointments; and when I drove up to their houses, sometimes they would be already waiting at the door. By the same token, lack of punctuality is one of the most frequently cited military brat complaints against civilians. But if military brats clash with the civilian world over matters as minor as punctuality, it is only symptomatic of a larger divergence of values and ideals.

One of these differences is over the notion of compromise—a decided virtue in the civilian community, but one not stressed among warriors, who are accustomed, after all, to governing their actions in relation to their higher obligation to the Mission, not to yielding ground to another individual for the sake of agreement.

Thus it is that one daughter of a general speaks proudly of the day her father's career was ruined. "My father was a major general at the Pentagon when he was called to testify in a congressional hearing about how money was being spent in the military," she related.

He stood up to [an extremely powerful senator] and called him a liar.
Ironically, he and the senator looked a lot alike. They each had a big jaw and a determined look. He was honest with the senator, and for that he was punished. His CO called him up that night and said, "You're crazy! Your picture is all over the papers. You've just told the most powerful man in Washington to go screw himself. You're out, baby. You're gone!"
So my father left Washington the next day. He was never promoted again, never again given a good tour. And by rights he should have been a

three-star general, should have been commandant of [a military academy].
But I'm very proud of what he did, because he did not betray his sense of
honesty.

So one of the cornerstones of military—and military brat—idealism
is that *one never betrays the cause.* Not even in the short run. Not even
for a moment. Not even when bending a little, or backing off for a
while, might serve the cause better over the long term. In the rule-
governed warrior society, virtue is cleaving to the letter of one's orders
as closely as possible. It is, as the general demonstrated to his misfortune, serving principle without regard for context—a concept alien
to civilian politics, which employs a much more situational ethic.
Fortress morality is a hard-nosed morality, a morality that makes a
point of never giving ground. And if that's something that makes
problems for generals dealing with politicians, it also makes problems
for military brats out in the everyday civilian world, where it is
commonly believed that there is virtue in flexibility, and that rules can
be renegotiated or rejected as the situation decrees.

"The civilian and military worlds work on different principles," said
an Army colonel's son who works for a defense contractor and who,
like many of us, learned that lesson the hard way.

In the military, when you have a rule it's a rule and there is a reason for it;
everyone, if they are working properly, follows the rules. In the civilian
world, they have rules because they *have* to have them, especially if they
are dealing with the government. They abide by the rules only to the
degree it keeps them out of trouble. Otherwise, they have their own sets of
rules, and those seem to be very flexible. If you can bend them and bend
them and they don't break—and you don't get into trouble or get someone
else into trouble—then everything is fine.

But I've gotten in hot water because of that. Once I was following up a
swing shift on a day shift, and I found out the swing shift was doing
something wrong. I reported it to my boss and found out they'd been doing
it for a long time. As far as my boss was concerned, I was to cover up for
them so they could continue doing it. I was absolutely furious.

In civilian life, you bend the rules to your advantage. Maybe you do that
to some degree in the military, too; that's entirely possible. But as far as I
can see, it's *rampant* in civilian life. You do whatever you have to do to
make it work, and if that means bending the rules, then you bend the hell
outta them.

It took me such a long time to learn that, and to learn how to operate in
it, to feel somewhat comfortable in it. It goes against my grain, of course,
but I understand that if I'm going to make it [in the civilian world], I've got
to live with those compromises.

For military brats, the first big drawback of carrying the warrior's
idealistic code into the civilian world is a debilitating naiveté. A

military brat newly emerged from the Fortress commonly expects there
to be a rule governing every situation in the civilian world, and that
civilians will naturally obey those rules and live up to their word. Such
a military brat marches along confidently bearing the banner of warrior
idealism, only to poke himself in the eye.

"I have a lot of the warrior's values without the violence," said an Air
Force colonel's daughter. "I consider myself a crusader, and I get very
judgmental about people who don't live up to what I think people
should be—in other words, to what my father is. The military code of
honor I grew up with seems to me to go all the way back to the knights
in shining armor: They're loyal. They have a sense of duty. They
always keep their word. I think I have inherited a kind of chivalric code
which is part of the warrior mentality. When people would break their
promises to me, I used to go into absolute shock. I could not understand it: 'How can people be so dishonest?' "

An Army sergeant's daughter made a similar observation. "We're all
kind of idealistic and innocent," she said. "We're clean and whole-
some. I mean, at forty years old I shouldn't be so innocent, right? It's a
naiveté that we have, that's preached into us. And we don't see the
harsh side of life growing up, so we tend to see positive images rather
than negative ones. I've always felt other people see things coming
when I don't. But I'm working on it."

It takes a long time to perceive the subtleties and gray areas, and still
longer to learn how to function with the flexibility and compromise
and rule bending that characterize civilian life. Until we grasp this,
military brats are walking contradictions: We project a certain worldli-
ness, an air of having seen it all before, which is regularly betrayed by
our blindness to the most basic operating rules of civilian life.

Military brats are little warriors raised with an Achilles' heel. We
operate on the idea that if we just act honorably, according to noble
principle, it doesn't matter who we are dealing with or what's happening around us. Personal considerations, such as whether we are about
to get totally ripped off, often don't even enter the picture; integrity, we
tend to believe, is not just our guide but our protective shield. So we
play our cards openly, unwittingly setting ourselves up as targets. It
takes a long time, and some tough experiences, to understand the
simple truth that courage without wariness is ultimately self-defeating.
Many a military brat has unhesitatingly gone way out on a limb for the
sake of principle—only to find someone gleefully sawing it off behind
them.

I've done this so many times myself that, in retrospect, parts of my
life take on a cartoonlike quality. For a short time not long after I
graduated from college, I worked for a group of politicians as an

investigator of conditions in maximum security penitentiaries. I went into the prisons, interviewed convicts, guards, and staff, inspected the facilities, and reported my findings to the politicians, who regularly appeared in the media decrying inhumane prison conditions; prisons were the hot social issue of the time. But when some of the findings held grave implications for one of the politicians I worked for—and I doggedly kept pressing the point—I suddenly found myself out on my ear, and my report was squelched. Classic military brat that I am, I was even surprised.

Other military brats have similar stories to tell. There was the Navy chief petty officer's daughter, for instance, who found out that a subgroup of an organization she belonged to was acting in violation of their operating rules: "All these little voices in me were saying 'They're wrong! They're wrong! We've got to do something!' So the warrior in me took it on. And then all my allies faded into the woodwork, and meanwhile the opposition was out there waiting for me, and I got creamed.

"I was able to salvage something from it, and I learned a valuable lesson: Now I won't pick up a battle if I don't have solid support. And that means people who are willing to voice what I'm voicing and support what I'm doing. If there are people with me, I'll do battle even if I lose."

This image of nobly going it alone against all odds, like a soldier braving a storm of bullets to plant the flag on top of a hill, is central to the warrior code. For the military brat, it reflects another side of the outsider/insider dynamic explored in the last chapter: *I and my Mission against the world.*

This bullheaded dedication to principle can cause problems for us, all right. But it is also at the heart of one of the best aspects of military brat character, as we shall see later in this chapter.

Loyalty

In story after story, military brats tell of the culture clash of values they have experienced out in the civilian world. And on no point is this more true than the question of loyalty. Almost every one of the military brats asked said they considered themselves exceptionally loyal—in commitments, relationships, promises, whatever—and significantly more loyal than the civilians they know.

"Loyalty is the pervasive virtue," said a Navy commander's son. "It means you *will* be loyal, *no matter what.* To break a commitment is, to my way of thinking, the worst thing I can do, the cardinal sin."

There is a way in which civilians tend to be more focused on the result, and military brats on the process. Thus for us loyalty becomes an end in itself, no matter what the personal consequences.

The daughter of a Marine colonel: "I try to be loyal at all times. I tend to be loyal no matter what, take that plane right into the ground."

A Navy chief petty officer's daughter: "In relationships with men, I've never cheated—even when they cheat on me. I'm loyal to my friends even when I suspect there's something going on. Recently I got really burned by a woman I'd been friends with for many, many years. I'd been supportive of a lot of things she was going through, but it was one-sided. What happened was that when she was on the upswing, I got dumped. That's not the first time it's happened, just the most recent.

"I tend not to see what's coming," she continued. "Either I don't pick up the cues, or I'm real generous in my interpretation of what's going on."

The daughter of a Marine sergeant: "I am very, very loyal, and I am devoted to my 'duty,' whatever that happens to be. I am devoted to a certain notion of friendship, a certain kind of integrity. In the past I've been much more loyal to friends than I needed to be. Some of those 'friends' turned out to be people who took enormous advantage of my time and energy, and didn't give back when I needed it. Only recently have I begun to discern the kinds of people and circumstances that *deserve* an extended kind of loyalty.

"It's still hard for me to apply this where projects are concerned. I always do much too much work. I have very, very high standards for myself—it's what my father expected of me—so I always do two hundred percent when one hundred percent would do, and most people are doing sixty or forty percent anyway." She gave an example from her job; she is an instructor at a university. She said it has taken her far longer than it should have to return some work to her students, because instead of just grading it and noting a few comments in the margins, she devised an elaborate procedure of taping notes on each paper, writing an extensive report on each, and sending along a checklist of points for each student to keep in mind. "I created an amount of work for myself that was really unreasonable and not necessary given the task at hand. *Above and beyond the call of duty:* That works against me. I recognize that as a problem I have professionally that I will struggle with for the next decade, probably. I hope it won't be for the rest of my life."

These notions of loyalty held true across the board for military brats. With only one exception, all said that they consider themselves more loyal than the civilians they know. One common perception, for instance, was that when a military brat makes an agreement with a civilian and it later breaks down, it is almost always the civilian who has backed out or violated the terms.

It's not that civilians aren't loyal—just that for them, loyalty can at least be questioned. It's a flexible contract, one that can change with circumstances. Not so for the military brat. For us, loyalty is extremely rigid. If our loyalty is triggered, it amounts to a quick freezing of our allegiance—so that we are instantly, by internal fiat, loyal to country, to job, to mate, or to "any damn thing that comes down the pike," as one rather cynical military brat put it.

Once the loyalty gear kicks in, questions cannot be entertained. It can be a wonderfully strong quality—and a precious resource to those on the receiving end—but all too often it can become a decree for the military brat not to think anymore.

What comes of this, of course, is hard knocks: When one is blindly loyal, one tends to bump into reality in sometimes distressing ways. Military brats tend to honor loyalty as a good in itself, an exalted ideal that merits any sacrifice. Of course that's fine when loyalty is well placed, but what if it isn't? Or if the object of our loyalty was originally deserving but later becomes tarnished and unworthy of it? Unfortunately, many military brats find it extremely difficult to turn off their loyalty, even after they've begun to recognize they'd be better off if they could.

The story of one Air Force sergeant's son is a case in point. Like other military brats, he said he considers himself "very loyal" and more loyal than the people around him. "It's had a nasty cost in my life," he said. For a number of years he worked very closely with another person in the same profession. "I stayed [working with him] longer than I wanted to," he related,

> but I had made a commitment. It got harder and harder. Finally he asked me to do something I couldn't do. We were trustees of an account that was not our money, and he spent money he shouldn't have. Technically it was embezzlement, but he wasn't a thief. He was a foreigner and he didn't understand our system. I told him about it but he wouldn't alter it, and I felt responsible.
>
> For me it was a conflict: wanting to protect him and wanting to dissociate myself from this fiduciary misconduct. It became known, and it still is a nasty episode in my career. There is still fallout from it.
>
> I should have quit three or four years sooner than I did, but I kept trying

to make it work as it should have worked. But the signs were all there. I overdid the loyalty thing, and I got punished for it. I think I need to keep saying to myself that I have to be more sophisticated and cut my losses early. But my personality is such that it's not natural.

Semper Fidelis—Ever Faithful—is the motto of the U.S. Marine Corps. It might as well be the personal motto of every military brat ever born. But ironically, part of the military brat problem with loyalty is that, although we grew up steeped in it, we don't really understand much about it. Our notions of it are likely to be too simplistic. A typical military brat grows up secure in the belief that if one is true-hearted and always tries to do things the Right Way—and the Fortress teaches that there is only one Right Way—everything will work out fine.

It takes a few hard lessons in adulthood to understand that, at least in civilian contexts, loyalty is not supposed to be given automatically and unthinkingly. It should be earned. And even then it should be reevaluated from time to time as things change. It comes as a shock to many military brats, but the fact is, it is entirely appropriate to ask oneself questions from time to time: Is my loyalty deserved? What conditions do I attach to it? When is it appropriate for me to withdraw my loyalty?

Such problems are not unheard of among civilians, particularly those who are children of alcoholics or who come from other kinds of dysfunctional families. But that just means that they, too, have something to learn from the prevailing healthier civilian attitudes toward loyalty.

In its largest sense, loyalty is one of the major components of American democracy, and one of the major reasons it works. And this is not merely the basic notion that one does not betray one's country, but something more: Loyalty in its best civilian sense is an organic thing than grows and changes with society. It's about trying to live in accord with one's ideals, but having the strength and courage to question those notions, test them, discuss them, change them.

Patriotism

Alongside the broader concept of loyalty in the pantheon of warrior values is patriotism. For the military brat, indoctrination in patriotic behavior and thinking is early and intense. Consider the daily ritual of Retreat discussed in Chapter 1: On a military base, every military person, every military family member is expected to respectfully stop the car, or stop walking, or dismount from one's bike at exactly 1700 hours when Retreat is blown, and turn in the direction of the flag to stand in silent reverence until the last note of the bugle has sounded. Civilian visitors to the base at that hour may be mystified by the ritual, and might even feel excluded in a sense; the military people by their actions are demonstrating that they are conscious of the flag and daily honor it in a way that civilians do not normally incorporate into their lives.

To draw on an earlier metaphor, in the theatrical world of the warrior society, where costumed actors rehearse their movements and their lines, patriotism is in the atmosphere of every set. It is the unseen element that establishes the tone and is crucial to all the action which follows.

This is so much a part of those of us born inside the Fortress that even military brats who are very jaded on the subject of the military—some of whom have worked politically for such things as the reduction of the Defense budget, or who demonstrated against the Vietnam War—say they cannot watch a parade without feeling a clutch at the heart or having tears spring to their eyes.

Sometimes, it is true, this may have more to do with unresolved issues of childhood than with patriotism itself, for, in a sense, all the legacies of our childhood—positive and negative, resolved and un-resolved—come wrapped up in the flag.

"Even to this day, I can't go to parades," said an Army sergeant's daughter whose childhood inside the Fortress was a dark one, with alcoholic, abusive parents and little in the way of affirmation or support.

> I just cry and cry and cry. It all has to do with the loss we had in the military. The loss my mother had that I never knew [because she died before her daughter could ask her about the difficulties of her life]. It's almost like . . . a wanting to make things better if we could go back to the military again. Maybe we could do it over again, change, and this time make it better.
>
> The contradictions, the sorrow. The men who go off in the war. My father went off to Korea and got shot, though not seriously. My mother cried and cried. My brother cheered when our mother said our father had gotten shot. So we knew, on one level, that he was a very abusive man. And how hard that must have been for my mother. . . . So I'm at a parade, and all those thoughts start coming back. It's very difficult for me.

But there is also a strain of patriotism in military brats that is pure—a native pride in the flag, the military, a way of life. Military brats, no matter what their political views, are often offended by disrespectful treatment of the flag, or even by the cavalier ways other people sometimes display their patriotism—lying on flag-design beach towels, or adorning their clothing and possessions with flag decals, or

hanging the flag outside their homes to advertise their patriotic zeal but
never bothering to take it in at night or in foul weather or to fold it
properly.

"I get upset if I see a flag touching the ground," said an Air Force
sergeant's son. "If I *ever* see *anybody* desecrate the flag, they're in
trouble. And *don't* burn it in front of me, ever—I'm really bad about
that. And being a black male, a lot of people think I'm crazy. They
don't understand that in me. But then they don't understand the good
things about this country, either, because they've never been outside of
it."

That isn't to say that the patriotic feeling carried by military brats is
without nuances. A number of years ago, this same military son spoke
several times with a recruiter and nearly embarked on a career as a
Naval officer. At the last minute he declined, fearing that if war broke
out in South Africa, the United States might intervene on the side of
the apartheid government—and he might find himself in the position
of waging war against blacks with whom he felt kinship and sympathy.
Later he realized that probably was not going to happen, but by then
he had invested himself in another career.

The war in Vietnam, of course, threw into question ideas that had
previously been sacrosanct. Sons and daughters of warriors, and often
their families as well, began to find nuances and clauses in patriotism
that they had never before acknowledged.

"After Vietnam I think my patriotism may have slid to a point where
I questioned the government," said Adam, the Marine sergeant's son
who served two tours in Vietnam with the Air Force, "but I never
questioned my country per se. We are the best country in the world to
live in and I would defend it to the death. I just could never understand why we had to stick our nose into somebody else's business all
the time, try to solve their problems for them. It's okay to question the
government, but you still have to be patriotic about your country."

Gabriela, the oldest child of a Marine sergeant, was still living at
home for most of the Vietnam War. She recalled what a difficult and
bitter dilemma it was for a family steeped in unquestioning patriotism,
particularly during the year her father was in Vietnam. "There was a real
split in my family as to whether the war was right or wrong," she said,

I think we all felt the war was wrong, but we knew we *couldn't* feel the war
was wrong. Making it wrong meant being disloyal to my father. So there
was this terrible schizophrenia, where sometimes we would be discussing
what was happening, and my mother would be against the war, and then
all of a sudden she would say, "My country right or wrong, but my
country." It just didn't make sense to me. I had a very strong sense that the
war was wrong.

When my father came back [he and I] argued it quite a bit, and it caused a great deal of bitterness and division. We spent months not even speaking to each other although we were living in the same house.

But my father came back from Vietnam a changed man in terms of his relationship to the military and to the government. He had known a military world that was much different, a world in which loyalties were very clear and you could tell who were the good guys and who were the bad guys. In Vietnam, all of that broke down. It was a tremendous nightmare for the people who were there.

When my father first came back he couldn't see, or didn't want to see, how untenable our government's position was. So he never hesitated to say what he thought about the protesters we saw on television. He said they were maggots and Communists and if they didn't like this country they should get the hell out. But somewhere along the line, everything he'd seen in Vietnam began to sink in. Now he has very little trust in the government's public rhetoric. For my parents after Vietnam, the world was changed for them. While I would say they are still very loyal to this country, there is also a recognition of people throwing away their lives on useless political charades.

Later on, years later, when there was one of those flare-ups in Central America, there were some rumblings about reinstituting the draft and sending young men there—and my father told my mother that he would move the family to Canada, that he would not allow my brothers to join the military or be drafted in what he considered a stupid and useless cause.

For most of the military brats interviewed for this book, as for many civilians, Vietnam was a formative experience, a prolonged moral dilemma that coincided with their own individuation and forced them to think through patriotism and redefine it for themselves.

For older military brats, Vietnam was a test as well. Many, whether they supported the war or opposed it, found that the experience helped focus their patriotism and in so doing reinforced it; they are clearer about what they do and do not value in American society, and are more willing to speak up about it. That in turn has become the undergirding for a more thoughtful but still affirming patriotism.

Parker, the fifty-year-old son of an Air Force lieutenant colonel, best typified this. Asked if he considers himself patriotic, he responded, "Yes, I'm patriotic. I like what this country stands for as written in the Constitution. But I'm not very proud of the America of Ronald Reagan. It's a selfish and almost swinish America and I don't like it one bit. But it will pass. We always come to our senses in this country."

War and Peace

One of my findings in these interviews was the strong attraction the peace movement has held for many military brats—and not just during the Vietnam War, but in the years since. Twenty military brats said they consider peace their prime social concern and had histories of considerable activism on its behalf.

They spoke of active membership in such organizations as SANE/ Freeze, Beyond War, Mothers Embracing Nuclear Disarmament, World Federalists, and church groups engaged in protests and letter-writing campaigns. Most had worked for nuclear disarmament. Several had actively worked against U.S. military intervention in Central America. Two military brats of my acquaintance—only one of whom was interviewed—have taken the extreme steps of both limiting their income and giving substantial donations to nonpartisan peace groups in order to avoid paying federal taxes they believe support dangerous policies.

Catherine, the retired Naval officer we met in Chapter 4, has been a leader in her city's peace movement and feels she is still fighting for her country. It is a role she does not find inconsistent with her military childhood or with her two decades of military service. "In doing what I am doing now in the peace movement, I'm just as much a warrior, and just as patriotic, as I have ever been," she said.

Leigh, an Air Force general's daughter who witnessed the effects of massive destruction in postwar Japan, said, "That's why I'm in this group," pointing to the Beyond War lapel pin she often wears. "It's too terrifying, too awful. I watched people propping pieces of tin against walls to use as shelter."

Asked if they draw a connection between their childhoods in the warrior society and their involvement with peace, most of the activist military brats answered yes. One of them, the Air Force colonel's daughter I've called Charlotte, is a teacher and author whose longtime activism for peace has led her to write extensively on the subject. She spoke at length about how her military childhood sent her in that direction. Later, I quoted her in conversations with many other military brats, who said they strongly identified with her words.

"You know, living on a military base is living American nationalism at the very extreme," Charlotte said.

> And yet instead of making my brother and me into very narrow, nationalis-
> tic right-wingers, it's made us a lot more tolerant and a lot more global in
> our vision.
>   I think that's the thing that's affected me the most: the sense of being a
> global citizen. Since I don't have one home and instead grew up with
> many different people and cultures, I feel a strong caring for the whole
> planet. Probably I have a stronger sense of empathy with other cultures
> than I would have if I'd lived in the same small town all my life and felt my
> way was the only way.

My parents are right-wingers, and very narrow in their definition of what it means to be patriotic. I consider myself as patriotic as my parents, but in a different way. I feel a sense of love for the beauty of this country and a sense of duty to try and keep us from polluting and destroying it. But I think my sense of patriotism extends beyond the confines of this country alone. I consider myself patriotic in a global sense. I want world peace, and I'm doing certain things to promote it.

It's ironic that, having grown up on many military bases, in a military family, surrounded by weapons displayed very openly, I've come to such an opposite conclusion: What we really *don't* need, I believe, are more weapons and bases. And my brother and my friends and most people I know who've grown up in the military seem to have a perspective which is the antithesis of the narrow, militaristic, nationalistic world view. We seem to see beyond nationalism, even though we grew up in the heart of nationalism. And we have a hope for something beyond military force as a way to resolve conflicts. That's one of the most important things I've learned from being a military brat.

Warrior idealism: a weakness, a strength. The downside for military brats, as we saw in the discussion of loyalty, is the combination of naiveté and rigidity, a kind of recklessly blind innocence that doesn't play well in the civilian world.

But the strength, the great strength, of military brat idealism is its purity of vision. It is a vision of the ideal, fired by the conviction that it is attainable and the certainty that one should try.

"I feel I am more idealistic than others I know *because* I was raised in the military," said Glenn, son of an Army colonel and now an Army officer and physician himself. "I have a strong desire to keep my integrity, and to keep some degree of unselfishness in the conduct of my life.

"Being in the military gives me the opportunity to work toward the achievement of the ideals I feel the Army should be striving for. If I ever were to leave the Army, I would find some sort of cause to serve. Most likely it would not be any sort of political cause, but something I feel would contribute to the betterment of our country or the betterment of mankind."

The Fortress teaches its children well: No matter what path they later follow in life, military brats do not take lightly matters of duty, honor, country. They may interpret those words in a variety of ways, but more often than not they try to echo in their strivings the warrior's code of personal integrity, and of service to a cause greater than themselves. Just like their warrior fathers, the children of the Fortress find that dedication to ideals gives their lives purpose and meaning. It is difficult for a military brat to conceive of life apart from mission, life not informed by and measured against the principles they hold most dear.

Military brats are at once idealists and optimists—and thus offer something to the civilian world that it sometimes sorely needs.

The son of an Air Force sergeant said he decided to become a teacher because he sees teaching as a enterprise that is "noble and ennobling."

"As a teacher I am a warrior on the battlefield of ignorance," he said. "I always wanted to be committed to something I believe in, do battle for something worthwhile. It's the ethos of the military, and it's fundamental to who I am."

CHAPTER 12

MILITARY BRATS
AS SURVIVORS

Mary Anne spoke out brightly, extravagantly. "Let's talk some more about how lucky we are to be military brats."

"I'm so lucky that I get to go to four high schools instead of just one," Ben declared with feigned enthusiasm.

"And I, the lovely Mary Anne Meecham whose beauty is celebrated in song and legend . . . " Mary Anne began.

"Boy is that a laugh," Matt said.

"Quiet, midget, before I feed you to a spider."

"Mom," Matt called.

"We just have a little ways to go, children. So try to get along."

"Or else I'm gonna have to butt a few heads," the colonel growled through his sunglasses.

"Anyway," Mary Anne continued, "I'm lucky enough to be absolutely friendless through an entire school year until the month of May. Then I make lots of new friends. Then I'm lucky enough to have Daddy come home with a new set of orders. Then I'm lucky enough to move in the summer and lucky enough to be absolutely friendless when school starts back in the fall."

"I know you're kidding," Lillian said to Mary Anne. "And I know all of you are upset about leaving Atlanta."

"Tough toenails," Bull growled.

"But there are some wonderful parts about growing up in a Marine family. You learn how to meet people. You learn how to go up to people and make their acquaintance. You know how to act in public. You have excellent manners and it's easy for you to be charming. I've had many compliments about how polite my children are. This is the benefit of growing up in the military and the gift you take with you no matter where you live. You know how to act."

"But the main thing, hogs," Bull said, "you get to hang around me and all my good qualities will rub off on you."

His family groaned in chorus and the colonel threw back his head and bellowed with laughter.

—The Great Santini

Growing up in the military is difficult, even in the most loving and close-knit of families; the frequent moves, the threat or the reality of war, and the requisite masks of secrecy, stoicism, and denial will see to that. In dysfunctional military families—the ones poisoned by alcoholism or abuse or stifled by an authoritarianism so rigid it allows no room to breathe or grow—the difficulty is increased geometrically.

Still, no one ever said growing up is supposed to be trouble free; it avails us nothing to measure our experience inside the Fortress against some frothy fantasy of rooted civilian family life such as "The Donna Reed Show." It is equally clear that, excepting the most horrific cases of abuse, there are worse ways to grow up in America than as a child of the Fortress. And in any case, self-pity is not becoming to the sons and daughters of warriors.

I do not subscribe to any view of military life that paints it as all positive or all negative. Both are obviously wrong from any objective point of view, and speak more to the emotional state of their advo-cates—full-scale denial or unfocused anger—than to anything else.

It is better, I believe, to be as clear-sighted as possible about what we lived and how it affects us: denying nothing, exaggerating nothing, overlooking nothing. That's exceedingly difficult to do, of course. It's so much easier to slip into a version that paints it one way or the other, all black or all white—especially when we have been so thoroughly conditioned by the Fortress to view life in these terms. Our parents, too, were powerful role models in demonstrating the monochromatic point of view; it's part of their art of denial. How many Fortress mothers, like Lillian in the above passage from *The Great Santini*, refused to acknowledge any but the bright side of the military brat experience?

The thing is, our Lillian-mothers were right—as far as they went. We *do* carry some important strengths and useful skills from our experience inside the Fortress, and would do well to appreciate them. However, it's also true that our mothers were transformed by the considerable rigors of their Fortress lives into the most fantastic sort of mental contortionists. Denial is the Fortress mother's specialty; she is capable of excising the most central elements of family history and presenting the tattered cloth for public view as though it were a seamlessly perfect robe of spun gold. So in the effort to understand our experience inside the Fortress, it is necessary to keep the Fortress mother's interpretations in perspective.

The other thing to keep in mind about Fortress mothers—and warrior fathers—is that for the most part they grew up as civilians, and came to the Fortress voluntarily as adults. Somewhere under all their conditioning to warrior ways lie ordinary civilians who were brought up in a vastly different way from the children they later hauled around from base to base and country to country under the rigorously challenging conditions of warrior life. Our parents, in other words, were destined to raise children with whom they could not identify, and therefore could not readily understand.

This seems to be the central problem in communication between military brats and their parents: They have substantially different frames of reference.

That difference in itself is not a barrier to healthy and rewarding relationships. The problem is that the operating assumption in military families tends to be that all *do* share the same frame of reference; so parents often come to perceive the differentness of their children as willful aberrations, and the children, for their part, do not pause to consider that it may be too much to ask of one's civilian-raised parents to see things from the military brat's unique point of view. In story after story related by military brats for this book, relations in the family improved dramatically once one side or the other—and preferably both—lightened up and decided to accept the other's differentness as a central, and valued, part of the relationship.

This kind of misunderstanding is common enough in civilian families too, of course, but it is not necessarily a given. Because military brats and their parents grow up in radically different ways from one another, and because the experience of the Fortress affects them differently as well, major breakdowns in communication are a fairly predictable feature of warrior families.

There are two basic things that Fortress mothers and warrior fathers tend to miss in looking at the experience of their children. One of them is the difference that the lack of roots makes; military brats lack the grounded quality that can be obtained only from growing up in a fixed community of people over time. The internal compass points are bound to look different in a child with no sense of gravity. The second thing military parents miss in their children is, in a word, interiority.

Since warriors and their wives are people who have, by and large, thoroughly adapted to an authoritarian world, they tend to perceive and respond to external realities far more than to internal ones. Every aspect of military brat experience that Lillian Meecham extols in the passage quoted above has to do with how military brats function externally: knowing how to meet people, how to act, how to be charming—in other words, how to skate well on the surface of life.

The problem areas for military brats, however, tend to be matters of an undeveloped interior life, as we have seen throughout this book. Knowing how to get along with people is usually no problem. But learning to find our bearings in the civilian world, listen to our own inner voice, handle emotions appropriately, stick to commitments, correct a distorted sense of time, moderate our missionary zeal and blinding sense of loyalty—these are quite a different matter. We children of the Fortress frequently arrive in adulthood bearing some similarity to the spacious old homes one finds on many a military base: impressive, sturdy, well tended, and with a certain air of déjà vu—but without much in the way of interior furnishings. Typically we put in a request for furniture with the quartermaster—in real life anyone might be tapped to fill this role—and are actually surprised when what's delivered isn't adequate to the task.

I'm not sure how civilians fare in this regard, but it seems to me that we military brats take an astonishingly long time to notice that this lack of interiority is entirely our own responsibility to correct. We are so conditioned in the authoritarian mode that even if we think we have eradicated all authoritarianism from our lives, we still might find ourselves reacting like authoritarians, blaming some person or circumstance for a difficulty that really has at least as much to do with our lack of interiority.

However, what I've seen in eighty adult children of the military suggests that military brats by and large tend to get the message eventually, and then set about the job of correcting their internal balance with the customary purposefulness one might expect of people to the Fortress born. Part of what made the research for this book so interesting was that, over the course of five years, I did repeat interviews with a number of military brats and was able to track their efforts in this regard. Many of them had undergone a striking amount of emotional growth in the interim and gained some extraordinary insight into their families and their lives—which to me signaled that the famous resilience of military brats also applies to the realm of wisdom.

From all I've observed, it seems to me that military brats approach the business of bringing balance and interiority to their lives by breaking it down into four key tasks. I believe this is true for all military brats, whether their families were dysfunctional or not, because what this process is ultimately about is *growing up*. But there is a quantum increase in magnitude and difficulty where there has been severe family dysfunction.

These tasks are: dismantling one's myths, healing the wounds, making peace with one's parents, and addressing the question of belonging.

THE FIRST TASK: DISMANTLING ONE'S MYTHS

One of the characteristics of Fortress society is the unusual degree to which it relies on myth. Everything fundamental to the Fortress, it seems, is tied to myth in one way or another: There is a mythic sense of purpose, a mythic sense of male superiority, a mythic sense of heroism, of danger, of personal sacrifice, and—as in the Vietnam War—of the inherent rightness of one's cause.

I am not using the word *myth* to refer to the powerful tales passed down through the centuries that dramatically illuminate aspects of the human condition. I also do not use *myth* in the sense of a lie or a fiction (although I would certainly take exception to the notion of male superiority, or female superiority for that matter). I use it in the sense of a truth that is greatly exaggerated to serve some emotional purpose.

In some respects such myths perform a vital service. For example, to do its extremely difficult job, warrior society needs to draw strength from powerful myths such as those mentioned above, which are more on the order of highly magnified beliefs that are never questioned. These myths work extremely well, in fact, and are an important part of the heritage of military brats.

But every warrior family, and every member of each family, has another set of myths too: personal myths about the nature of Fortress life, about the overall character of the family, about the roles played by each parent and each child. And as with the myths of the Fortress at large, these myths are usually not fictions at all, but truths exaggerated for a purpose. Like the masks of secrecy, stoicism, and denial, they are extremely useful in defining one's universe and keeping one's bearings within it. But like masks, myths become a problem to the extent one overrelies on them. After a while, one becomes dependent on the myth, and then, quite naturally, protective of it, and then fiercely defensive about it. By that time the damage is done: The myth has come to obscure one's vision, stifle one's reason.

In an earlier chapter we had a dramatic example of a military brat in the process of recognizing how one of her myths of childhood had interfered with her ability to see her childhood clearly. Claire, an Army sergeant's daughter, spoke of her need to believe in the myth of a happy, sunny, carefree childhood even though she had actually suffered terribly from physical and emotional abuse.

She said: "That's always been in my mind, how frightened I was as a child. Isn't it funny, though—even as I talk about being frightened, I have all the windows open in my mind about what a glorious time we had. Isn't that *funny*? . . . There's something about that contradiction. Even in the midst of saying 'I was not safe' my mind is still playing a trick on me—*If you could only return to those glorious days.* Because I see the sun—I literally see the sun, as I'm talking—and I see myself laughing and running and catching and winning. It's so crazy."

In my view the intensity of her pain resulted in an equally intense need for a myth to justify it. Part of her task as an adult has been to try and separate out the myth from the reality so that she can deal appropriately with her pain and grief, and take appropriate strength from the positive aspects of her experience.

Oddly, it is often not so easy to discover what one's myths *are*: They are often the bedrock assumptions of our lives. I was already an adult by the time I stumbled upon one of my bedrock assumptions about my own family, although I did not recognize it as myth when I saw it. I came upon it one day when I sat down to read the great classic novel *Anna Karenina* by Leo Tolstoy. The very first sentence jolted me in a powerful shock of recognition. There was my own personal "truth" about my family confirmed in print:

Happy families are all alike; every unhappy family is unhappy in its own way.

I had always felt my family was unique in its suffering, as though we had been fated to live out our lives in an isolated cell of misery. The line from Tolstoy strengthened me in that belief; I actually imagined I drew comfort from it. If we couldn't alter our miserable fate, at least we had the satisfaction of knowing we were somehow original.

Now, at a remove of some years, during which I was exposed to *The Great Santini*, underwent Jungian analysis, and also researched and wrote this book, I see things quite differently. My own family experience was far from unique. And the first sentence of *Anna Karenina*, at least the way I interpreted it, strikes me now as terribly wrongheaded, and I doubt very much that Tolstoy himself believed it. Indeed, *Anna Karenina*, like Tolstoy's other novels, derives its greatness from the treatment of universal themes of human suffering which we all recognize. In retrospect, I wish I had not vested the one discordant sentence with such authority.

Happy families, for one thing, should not be dismissed as boringly conformist. And more pertinent to my own story, unhappy families are anything but unique in their pain. A troubled family is *never* justified in considering itself uniquely miserable, as though its pain were some form of toxin from which no one else suffers and for which, therefore, there is no known antidote. The very notion adds to the sense of hopelessness and isolation, which is exactly what someone from a troubled family does not need. There is no salvation in apartness; salvation lies in seeing that the pain has a name, and recognized causes, and recognized effects, that it can be talked about with others who have experienced the same thing, that it can even be treated so that it is understood and eased.

Part of that treatment, I believe, is learning to recognize the myths about ourselves and others in our families that we have allowed to grow to disorienting proportions. Bruce Springsteen is no Leo Tolstoy, but about the time I was slowly working my way out of some particularly emprisoning personal myths, I ran across a quotation from him that I felt was much more on the mark.

"Myths don't bind us together," Springsteen was quoted as saying in a *Newsweek* article. "They keep us strangers from each other. Strangers from our communities, from our country, from our friends and our children and our wives. And ultimately from ourselves."[1]

Thank you, Bruce Springsteen, for articulating a notion that has added immeasurably to my understanding of my own life and, incidentally, of *Anna Karenina*.

Some of the military brats I interviewed had discovered this notion long before I did, of course. The son of an Air Force senior master sergeant described how the military brat experience contributes to the invention of a mythical self:

"There's a sense in which you lose your past because you're not in touch with people who can remind you of what you were. And you begin to forge your own past, make it what you want. You operate under all kinds of myths, lies even, about how brave you were, how strong, how successful with women."

Another interviewee, the daughter of a Marine Corps master sergeant, spoke of her own discoveries about the interplay of myth and denial in her family: "In my family we got very good at pretending," she said,

> I recognize it as a defense mechanism when it is incorporated into your daily life. Pretty soon you become good at forgetting, at forgetting whole years. Slowly but surely I am working on issues so that my memory can open up. I've forgotten lots of things: big chunks of my marriage, lots of my childhood. They've disappeared. They're in storage.
>
> I'm finding they're not nearly as painful to deal with as I had imagined. By telling the truth, as I told my mother in a paraphrase of Adrienne Rich, you allow a lot of other truth to happen around you. In military families there is a *lot* of denial on a lot of different levels. So one of the things I'm committed to now is *telling one's truth*.

Yet exposing one's myths and baring one's truths is a daunting enterprise. After interviewing quite a few of us military brats, I still do not know if we are in general particularly bad or particularly good at it. In a sense we should be especially loath to dismantle our myths because so much of our lives is based on them; relentlessly taking them apart would seem to be structurally threatening. On the other hand, military brats are born risk takers.

Classic military brat that I am, I think it's worth it. How is it possible to repair damage in family relationships if one refuses to acknowledge it—or one's own role in it? How can we expect to see clearly until we remove the blinders from our eyes? How is it possible to improve communication with other family members if the price we attach to it is their subscription to our own personal myth about the nature of our family and what happened there? They each have their myths, too. The difficult though not impossible goal, as I see it, is to unilaterally dismantle our myths and work toward truthfulness in relationships, while at the same time remaining kind to our parents and to siblings who have not yet, and may never, dismantle their own myths. Since the sort of myths I'm talking about arise from emotional needs, and therefore mask vulnerabilities, it would be cruel and unrealistic to demand others to forsake what they are not emotionally prepared to forsake.

As difficult as it is to achieve, the clear-sightedness that replaces our overreliance on myth can potentially yield some rewards worth having. From what I've observed among the military brats I know, these are some of the payoffs:

- Ending this overreliance on myth frees us to move forward instead of wasting so much energy on defending an uncompromising myth.

- It is a self-revealing exercise, stripping away layers of fiction to look squarely at one's character, accomplishments, weaknesses, and capabilities.

- It is liberating; abandoning an all-white or all-black view of our families and our experience inside the Fortress, and substituting a full palette that acknowledges subtleties and contradictions, allows us to be critical and appreciative at the same time.

- It helps us take stock of our strengths, the better to make use of them.

Our strengths, in fact, are many—and, judging by the interviews for this book, are frequently underappreciated by us and consequently underused. It is a part of the demythologizing of our past to uncover what we have retained that is genuinely positive, and not merely a compensating delusion in which we indulge ourselves. And, in keeping with the process of bringing balance to our lives, it is also important to understand the darker side of each of those positive traits.

The following is a list of military brat strengths, each one coupled with its potential dark side. All were gleaned from interviews for this book, and some have been treated at greater length in preceding chapters.

- *Responsibleness.* Military brats take the notion of duty very seriously. They routinely give their best effort, and they do everything in their power to keep their word.

  Dark side: As the daughter of an alcoholic Navy chief put it, "I just have to make sure it's not *super*responsibleness." There is a danger of perfectionism, which sets one up for perceived failure, then guilt and self-condemnation. Military brats also tend to take on too much responsibility and then wear themselves out trying to do everything single-handedly.

- *Excellent social skills.* Military brats can get along with almost anybody except authoritarian types, and sometimes even with them. They tend to be very well suited to work involving a great deal of people contact, or where knowing how to quickly fit in socially is an asset.

  Dark side: Military brats protect themselves against loss of friendship, which they tend to consider inevitable, by keeping relationships shallow and short-term. And they assume anyone in authority is an authoritarian, thus creating problems for themselves in the workplace, for instance.

- *Resilience* (or "adaptability," "flexibility," etc.). Military brats seem to be able to cope with almost anything—probably a combination of having moved so many times and of being, in many cases, children of alcoholics.

  Dark side: Military brats are so good at adapting that they can become ambivalent and lose sight of their values. It becomes unclear what they really care about, where they draw the line and take a stand.

- *Loyalty.* It would be hard for anyone to outshine a military brat when it comes to this virtue.

  Dark side: Military brats can be unbelievable suckers.

- *Willingness to take risks.* Military brats rarely balk at anything new or strange, and are generally able to summon whatever it takes to leap into a new and challenging situation. There is an instinctive understanding that the worst that can happen is that the effort will fail, which in itself is a gain educationally. Military brats have taken massive losses so often that they've learned they can survive them and keep on going.

  Dark side: It becomes easier to leap into new situations (or relationships) than to stay with old ones and work through the problems. Military brats might instinctively see to it that they have plenty of change and excitement in life, but they sometimes fall short on actual accomplishment.

- *Discipline.* Those military brats who have internalized a sense of discipline to the point they enjoy controlling and focusing their energies can be extremely productive and efficient.

  Dark side: Too often, military brat discipline is dependent on external authority—which also triggers the will to rebel—rather than being genuine self-discipline. They may give the impression of being very self-disciplined, but in fact are quite inconsistent, and may even go haywire for a time once external authority is removed.

- *Tolerance.* Having had to adapt to many situations and, in some cases, cultures, military brats often learn to appreciate different points of view and the inherent value of diversity.

  Dark side: Military brats can become so tolerant they lose sight of their own values.

- *Idealism.* Military brats can be extremely dedicated to matters of principle and will go to extraordinary lengths to promote or defend them. This can give purpose and a depth of meaning to their lives.

  Dark side: Military brats can be self-righteous, and sometimes make others around them feel guilty and resentful. Also, it's not unheard of for a military brat to sacrifice way too much for the sake of principle— "take that plane right into the ground." Military brats have been known to sacrifice every sort of personal happiness—marriage, family, career, financial security—for the sake of making a point.

- *Handling crisis well.* Military brats often handle emergencies with calm and competence. Others they know sense this and frequently turn to them for help. The daughter of a Marine Corps sergeant, asked to name some of the good things she learned inside the Fortress, said, "I'm very good in a crisis. The more extreme the circumstances, the more calm I get. I'm able to pull everything together at once; I know exactly the kinds of things that should be handled, and in what order. That is something I know I got from my father."

  Dark side: There isn't much of a dark side to this, but it would help if military brats could learn to be better at heading off crisis in the first place. Some military brats, however, seem to thrive on crisis—another trait common to adult children of alcoholics.

Many of the military brats I talked to were making an effort to recognize both positive and negative sides of the same trait. It is part of the search for roots, as well as the search for emotional stability, to take inventory of the legacies of the Fortress.

"A lot of stuff we learned as military brats is powerful and useful," said a Marine sergeant's daughter. "It's just [a matter of] moderating all that behavior so it doesn't become a neurosis. It can become part of a real strong movement forward, a strong and healthy life, a life of self-examination and self-awareness."

THE SECOND TASK: HEALING THE WOUNDS

Not all military brats emerge from their Fortress families carrying painful wounds, but those who do have essentially four choices before them.

They can continue to play out the role of victim, keeping the wounds open and bleeding—not a very comfortable lot in life, although when one is reared inside the theatrical company of the

Fortress it is natural enough to merge one's identity with the assigned role.

They can try to deny that the wounds exist, an enterprise that takes a tremendous amount of energy and which doesn't really work very well; one might end up habitually abusing some substance or other to keep it up.

They can recognize their wounds and give themselves over to anger—an invaluable tool for creating a sense of separation from the hurtful aspects of a dysfunctional family, but which has some serious limitations as an end in itself. It blinds the angry person from seeing any good, and therefore from finding a sense of balance.

Or they can try various ways to heal themselves.

A number of the military brats I spoke to had experienced all of these, often more than once; now in their thirties and forties, they are concentrating on healing their wounds and moving on.

In some ways, healing is the toughest route of all. Inevitably, a great deal of pain is churned up, and the healing itself is a slow process. But there is a qualitative difference between suffering and the constructive suffering that is necessary to healing. I like the way the process was described by Linda Schierse Leonard, a Jungian analyst, in her book *The Wounded Woman: Healing the Father-Daughter Relationship*:

> It occurred to me that my model for healing the wound had been in part a masculine model: the linear notion that progress goes steadily along a straight, hard line to an end point. Whereas my own experience had always been that the path of transformation was more like a circular spiral. Inevitably I came back repeatedly to the central injuries and conflicts, and each time the experience seemed even more painful than the last. The difference was that the period of pain tended to be shorter, that ultimately I had more strength, courage, and an ability to deal with these painful issues. [2]

Most of the military brats I interviewed who were struggling with their wounds seemed to be making progress in healing them. I think this is due in no small part to one of the prime legacies of the Fortress background: the willingness to do battle and to persevere despite setbacks. I could see the warrior at work within them in their courage to face the pain, their determination to see it through to the end. What I saw was a bullheaded fighting spirit, and being the daughter of a warrior myself, I could not help but cheer it on.

Harrison, the son of an authoritarian Air Force colonel and an interviewee quoted at length in the "Sons of Warriors" chapters, was particularly good at articulating this spirit:

"My own philosophy," he said, "is that all of what happens to us in life is fertile ground for our growth toward wholeness—and that includes all of the suffering. So the difficulties of loneliness, of powerlessness . . . have given me a lot to work with as an adult. They are not obstacles so much as sources of growth. In Zen there is a saying, 'The greater the suffering, the greater the enlightenment.' All the dissatisfaction sown by military life makes for a strong drive to resolve that, to find contentment. And there's a very strong sense of perseverance."

Harrison is a therapist, and I am certain he would not want anyone to interpret his comment as meaning that pain is good. Pain is pain, loss is loss, and no one in their right mind wants either. But if that is what we are dealt in large measure, that's what we have to work with—and in their very intensity, pain and loss provide rich material for reflection and strong impetus for growth.

From that standpoint, one could almost conclude that when it comes to totaling up the legacies of growing up inside the Fortress, some of us children of warriors are very rich inheritors indeed.

There are two other observations I have after studying how various sons and daughters of the military are successfully grappling with the more difficult problems they brought with them into adulthood.

It seems to me that a daughter's healing begins when she first says *no* to the patriarchy of the Fortress, and of society in general, that would seek to make her invisible or imprison her in a patriarchal definition of what it is to be a woman.

And it seems to me that a son's healing begins when he first learns to say *yes* to his vulnerable side, accepting the legitimacy of emotions that the Fortress had taught him to repress.

Both of these steps, for which I will give examples below, are the beginning of healing the malady I referred to in Chapter 6 as "the masculine-feminine split." The extremes of Fortress life, I maintain, have the effect of driving apart the masculine and feminine aspects of a military brat's personality—and much of the work of finding balance in adult life is about discovering the sides of personality which had been devalued by the Fortress and learning to develop them.

While a military brat might grow up with a rather lopsided personality—either the masculine or the feminine side underdeveloped in relation to the other—it is more likely that *both* sides are underdeveloped, though one would still be less developed than the other.

Daughters of the Fortress, for instance, tend to grow up with their masculine side, including their internal warrior, denied or grossly undervalued since it is not in keeping with Fortress standards of acceptable femininity; but that does not mean the feminine side has been free to develop naturally. How could it, in a society that places little value on the feminine apart from its usefulness to males? The only feminine traits that are encouraged are those which are quite conventional and in some way serve the Fortress way of life or at least do not threaten it. So a Fortress daughter's task in adulthood is both to discover the masculine, warrior side of herself, and to discover aspects of her feminine side that may have been forced underground.

Sons of the Fortress frequently grow up with their feminine, feeling side undeveloped since it has been depicted as an obstacle to their becoming "true men." This amounts to being cut off from an entire side of the personality and its rich storehouse of strengths that would help them reach out to others, endure emotional hardship, harness emotional power, express nurturance with their children, and free them to pursue interests that bring rich and gratifying diversity to their lives. At the same time, however, the son of a warrior father who was emotionally withdrawn or cruelly authoritarian might suffer the problem discussed in Chapter 6 of being abandoned to the world of the mother, so his masculine side has not been fully realized. As with the Fortress daughter, he must work on developing both sides of his personality.

Fortunately, it seems that one of the first things sons and daughters of the Fortress instinctively seek to do, once they become serious about healing themselves, is bring out the sides of their personalities that have been so long repressed. Again, it is not easy to do, and some military brats—myself included—have enlisted the aid of therapists. Many therapists have the knowledge to help in this regard; in my case I count myself fortunate to have found an analyst who, in the Jungian tradition, was already well schooled in the masculine-feminine split and was very skilled at guiding me in my healing.

A number of military brats come to mind when I think about instinctive efforts to heal the masculine-feminine split.

Among daughters I think of Anita, Maya, Melody, and Gabriela, all of whom have been successful in battling addictions to drugs or alcohol, and who in so doing have come to know and value the warrior and the feminine sides of themselves. I think of Catherine, who as a career military officer herself became a champion of the rights of women in the military, helping them—and, no doubt, herself—find a voice to effectively win their visibility. I think of Lorna, Gabriela, Olivia, Beatriz, and Leigh, who have taken their creativity out into the world to assert their voices artistically. There is Charlotte, who has developed her spiritual life to a high degree—in sharp contrast to her Fortress upbringing—and employs the warrior side of her personality to fight for the cause of peace.

And I always think of Grace, part of whose story is presented in Chapter 4. The daughter of an authoritarian Air Force general and a conventionally submissive mother, she grew up a typically invisible daughter of the Fortress. Grace married into the military and further imitated her mother's pattern, as the efficient but essentially passive helpmate to her officer husband. After a few years, during which there were two children, the marriage began to suffer. As her marriage became more arid and unrewarding, Grace became closer and closer to the priest in their church. It was not just a sexual affair, she said, but something still more powerful—a bond of heart and mind and spirit.

"We 'fell' in love and began spending free time together, laughed and cried—all the lovely things that were no longer taking place in my marriage. It was a glorious time, but one that ended in a lot of pain for five people—my sons also suffered, I think, in the emotional aftermath." The affair ended and the marriage held, though it took a long time for the wounds to heal. Grace sought counseling, among other reasons to better understand why she had entered into the affair in the first place. She came to view it as a form of delayed adolescent rebellion.

"My therapist reminded me that adolescent boys typically turn to vandalism as a form of rebellion, while adolescent girls 'act out' sexually. It occurred to me that my behavior through this relationship [with the priest] may well have been my way of rebelling against my husband's 'fathering' of me. I never rebelled against parental authority at the appropriate time, and needed to pass that barrier to emerge as a fully mature adult." Still, it seems worth noting that when it came to having an affair, Grace did not choose another warrior, but a very different kind of man—a spiritual, emotional man who could bring out the spiritual, emotional side of her that had been locked in or undervalued.

The affair had the effect of awakening a side of Grace's personality—and although she returned to her marriage, that side of her did not want to go underground again. Problems persisted in the marriage until Grace turned to counseling and then, on her therapist's recommendation, to group therapy with other women. It made a tremendous difference in her life. I first interviewed her not long after she had stopped going to group therapy; although she missed seeing the women in her group on a regular basis, she felt the therapy was no longer necessary. She spoke to me about how she had begun to assert herself in her marriage for the first time, and to experience herself as a changed person.

Two years later, during which Grace's husband had retired from the military, I wrote to ask how she was doing and how her marriage was faring, and received a joyous letter of reply.

"I am happier and more comfortable in my marriage now than I have *ever* been," she wrote.

> For the first time in eighteen years I feel that I am able to express *all* aspects of myself—negative as well as positive—and to be understood, accepted, even appreciated in spite of—or sometimes *because of*—them. My unhappiness prior to counseling had to do with feeling boxed in or confined by what I saw as my husband's "definition" of me. This may have had as much to do with *my* definition [of myself]. . . .
>
> Passivity may have been the cornerstone of problems in my marriage [she wrote later in that letter]. For years I "cheerfully" went along with the frequent moves, the social obligations and the expectations that characterize Army life. Since I wasn't confident enough to know that my opinions counted and that my criticism might be valid, I kept them to myself. Eventually, these bottled-up feelings became explosive.
>
> While I [now] recognize my passive tendencies and struggle against them, I can overcome them only by reminding myself how good it feels to be in the driver's seat of my life!

Grace's problems, as I read them, are a classic example of the military daughter who is cut off from her masculine, assertive side, but whose internalized "father voice" had exiled her feminine, spiritual, emotional side as well. The resolution of her split involved not only developing the assertive warrior side of her personality, but encouraging the expression of "feminine" values that had acquired new importance in her life. In the course of our interview and subsequent correspondence, Grace described some of these feminine values, which include connectedness with others, growth and transformation, serving the community, sharing of life stories with other women, spiritual development, creativity—all of them having to do with the "feminine" side. But in all of her activities that reflect these, she pointed out, the degree of gratification corresponds to the degree of assertiveness she brings to them.

When it comes to sons of the Fortress who have instinctively sought to heal the masculine-feminine split in themselves, I tend to think of Ross, John, Harrison, and Adam, who have also been successful in their battle with alcoholism, all of them through the twelve-step process of Alcoholics Anonymous. All spoke of how AA had forced them finally to look at the feeling, vulnerable side of themselves.

I think of several military sons I know who became therapists, helping others to understand and handle their feelings. But the one who stands out most for me is Carl, the son of a Navy commander who was at sea for about half of Carl's childhood and, according to his son, displayed little interest in his children when he was at home.

When I first interviewed Carl four years ago, he was still bitterly angry at his father.

"It wasn't that he was a *bad* father," Carl told me at that time. "It's that he *wasn't* a father. . . . In some ways I think it is harder to try to reconcile a father who simply wasn't there for me but was essentially a good person and still is, and is not a violent man, an abusive man, a chaotic man, but simply a man who had no place in his life for me. I think it would have been easier if he had hated me; at least you know there's a relationship. For you to hate somebody they've got to be important to you. But for my father, taking care of me was right up there somewhere with watering the dog."

Carl went to Annapolis, in part, he said, to win his father's approval. But he was very confused about why he was there, as would be any son who had been abandoned to the world of the mother and then found himself at the very center of warrior culture. "Going to the Naval Academy was a shock," he said. "The thing that struck me so fully was not how painful it was to let go of my mother, but how absolutely disconnected I had been from my father's value system, my father's skills, or any kind of masculine preparation needed to compete in such a wholly and exclusively male world, and a very competitive and caustic system at that."

He racked up a tremendous number of demerits his first year. And then there was the hazing—the practice that is not officially permitted in any military academy but which is a feature of all of them, in which upperclassmen psychologically and often physically harass plebes (cadets or midshipmen in their beginning year at an academy). Hazing can be extremely severe, even sadistic, and from time to time becomes the subject of congressional investigations when it results in injury, death, or other scandal.[3]

"They tried everything they possibly could to get me to give up [and leave the Naval Academy]," Carl recalled, referring to the upperclassmen who had decided to make him a special target. "I didn't break. Something just kind of hemorrhaged inside. I was kind of like a bulldog that just clamps down and holds on. I was as rigid as the system was, but in a different way." He not only held on to become an upperclassman himself, he became one of those who hazed others unmercifully.

"I have personally helped drive a guy crazy," he told me. "We worked him for thirty-eight hours straight, until he cracked. They took him out kicking and screaming, never to be seen again. I unfortunately and regretfully was part of that. Not just as an observer, but an active participant.

"That incident was the incident that let me know that if circumstances were ever changed, I would use all my intuitions about people for positive goals and never again toward negative goals. And I have done that. But that certainly will not help those people I hurt when I was in my second or my first class years."

After he realized what was happening to him, Carl was horrified. "It was anathema to me," he said. "[As a Navy son] I was a product of a system that exalted loyalty, justice, honor. I was deeply offended by what I saw in the very incubator of the upholders of that tradition, on the most hallowed and sacred ground. I saw social injustices and acts of barbarity in the hazing system that ruined my taste for the whole thing." And of course there was his complicity in some of those acts, which has been a source of guilt for him ever since.

Over the course of his last two years at the Academy, Carl's grades gradually deteriorated. When, in his last semester, his grade point average dropped below the acceptable limit of 2.0, he was dismissed and then offered the opportunity to "turn back," repeating his senior year. Carl chose to leave the Academy instead. He graduated from a civilian university and then went on to obtain a graduate degree in social work. He also underwent therapy himself over a period of five years—with a therapist who, on the last day of Carl's therapy, revealed he was a graduate of Annapolis.

For some years now Carl has been a clinical social worker, counseling primarily military families. "Now the irony of this whole thing— and it doesn't take a great mental jump to see it—is that basically I took that entire negative experience [at the Academy] and formulated it as my life task: to help people individuate, to gain nurturance they haven't had in their own lives, and to make peace with my own world in the process. The thing a lot of people don't realize about therapists is that they gain as much as they give."

Carl told me he knows what he wants to be his epitaph: "I'd like it to read, 'He gave at least as much as he took away.' If I can do that, my life has been a contribution."

During that first interview it seemed to me that Carl had already accomplished an impressive amount of emotional growth since his days at the Academy. He had lacked a father growing up, and on his own had figured out a way to "father" himself: As Carl himself pointed out, his role as a therapist was in a sense his chance to play the positive father figure to his clients, who perhaps represented wounded parts of himself. In his case it worked, and it had the additional advantage of helping him repay a debt he felt he owed through his participation in some especially brutal hazing at the Naval Academy.

Yet one critical area remained: his unrelieved bitterness toward his father.

Two years after our initial interview, I wrote to Carl with some follow-up questions. He replied at length, and told me of a major change in that last critical area.

It turned out that a few months after I interviewed Carl the first time, his father sent a letter to each of his children essentially ordering them to shape up and act like a family. The letter infuriated Carl, who fired off a long and angry letter to his father. The fight continued by mail for a few months, but they got a lot off their chests and then found themselves sharing their feelings about other things. Finally they were standing on common ground. Carl then visited his father several times, and they discovered a mutual interest in computers that has added another avenue of sharing. What Carl had to say in assessing his new relationship with his father was indicative, I think, of a man who had healed his masculine-feminine split. He sounded like a son who had come to understand his feeling side and who was free enough to make use of it in taking action in his life.

"We've both decided to let bygones be bygones," Carl said.

There has come a point where punishing him for what he is not, and his punishing me for what I am not, simply doesn't make sense anymore. I've tried to establish a positive relationship with him, and he with me, and I think we're doing okay with that. We struggle with every letter to try to share some of the intimacies of our lives, and we try to find some thread of experience to unite us other than our common history.

I do not choose to go into the second half of my life hating my father, or bearing grudges, or crying over things that might have been.

I do not see my father as a warrior anymore. I do not see him as a hero whose standards I cannot live up to. I now see him as just a man, like myself, trying to get by the best way he knows how, having done some things well and having made some mistakes. We are negotiating with each other delicately.

I feel in some ways that the weather outside today is like my relationship with my father. It is a bit crisp, but it is clear, and there is the possibility of warming. I am happier than I have ever been in my entire life. I'm at peace with my past, I have a loving family, and my father and I have forgiven each other. It's good to be alive . . . [there was a pause] . . . and I'm proud to be his son.

And that brings me to the third task I have now seen many military brats undertake in their search for emotional balance and maturity: making peace with one's parents.

I have heard many stories of military brats who, like Carl, have been successful at this. Many of them give primary credit to their fathers for changing in ways that at last permitted the relationship to flourish. That is true to a degree—many military men soften in retirement, and as they age—but I don't believe improvement in the relationship is best explained by that. For one thing, the scenario of waiting upon the father to change puts the military brat once more in a position of static powerlessness reminiscent of childhood.

The thing that is often overlooked in the stories of reconciliation with formerly unapproachable warrior fathers is that the military brats had first worked very hard toward healing their own wounds—which means they no longer saw themselves as powerless children, but as adults responsible for their own lives. In the stories I heard, "transformations" in the warrior fathers almost always followed hard-won self-acceptance in the children.

THE THIRD TASK: MAKING PEACE WITH ONE'S PARENTS

During the course of my own Jungian analysis, in which it is customary to pay close attention to dream material, I had a dream that was extremely striking and which I have thought about many times since. It was an unusual dream not only for its power but for its brevity and its obviousness. This was not a dream that had to be unpacked and interpreted in the context of dozens of others. This was a dream in which my unconscious hit me over the head with a sledgehammer.

It took place in the backyard of our quarters on some Army post of my childhood. I had the impression it was either our backyard at Fort Bragg or the one at Fort Myer, but I could not glean many details from just my peripheral vision; my gaze was focused entirely on my father's face, and he was standing so close I could feel the warmth of his breath. My mother was standing there too, equally close, so that the three of us formed a kind of tight triangle. I was an adult, the age I was when I had the dream.

My father was looking intently at me. But instead of the usual hard, cold glare, his eyes were vulnerable and pleading. He opened his mouth and after a moment's hesitation spoke a single sentence, with great feeling. It was obviously an enormous effort for him to keep his voice from breaking. Still searching my eyes, unblinking, he said, "Tell me what it takes to be a good father."

Even in the dream, the question stunned me. It was something I had never imagined I would ever hear my father say, so incompatible was it with everything I had observed in this fierce and unrepentant man. In a flash all sorts of other questions were raised in my mind.

What had happened to change him so? Why was he asking me now, after my brother and I were adults? Was this an admission of accountability for so much of our pain? Was it an apology?

He was still staring at me, pleading with his eyes. I realized in the most profound depths of my being that I must not hesitate longer. I must answer, and my answer must respect his pain, his dignity, and the seriousness of his question. Above all, my answer must offer him a chance.

"First of all," I said slowly, as our eyes held, "thank you for asking me." I paused. "The most important thing for a good father is to *keep the lines of communication open.*"

His eyes, still vulnerable, registered gratitude. I had said the right thing. In that instant, still holding one another's gaze, I felt a connecting of our hearts, and I knew our relationship had redefined itself.

That was the entire dream. In Jungian terms, it could be seen as a conversation between myself and my own animus, as Jungians refer to the masculine element in a woman's personality; a woman's father is usually the prototype for her animus. As such, the dream marked a turning point in the analysis: It was clear that my animus and I were finally on speaking terms, and it would now be possible to forge cooperation.

But the dream for me was more than evidence of progress in analysis. It was so startling that it had the effect of getting me to take a fresh look at my relationship with my real, living father; perhaps there was something about him, or our relationship, that I had overlooked.

Indeed there was. Cued by my dream, I began—slowly—to consider that I had better get to work on dismantling a whole package of myths about my father's villainy, and perhaps about my own self-proclaimed innocence. It took a while—and indeed my work on this book has been part of the process—but I eventually came to see how I had imprisoned my father in the role of a ruthlessly cruel and all-powerful ruler, an evil king who was beyond the possibility of change.

It had been a formidable fortress, this myth of mine. I had taken it as an unshakable article of faith that my father had the two-dimensional character of a fairy-tale despot, and like a fairy-tale despot he could not alter or escape the part. I remember once, as a young adult, telling my brother that if there was one thing in life I knew with *absolute certainty*, it was that our father would never change.

As the author of my own fairy tale, I suppose I was exercising my editorial prerogative. Having cast my father in the role of intransigent bad guy, I proved to be equally intransigent about editing my story. But this was serious business, I came to see. In denying that my father was capable of change, I was denying his very humanity. By fiat I had chosen not to see his vulnerability, or his need—the very generative heart of change. And in our infrequent dealings over the better part of a decade, I had treated him very much like a two-dimensional mythic figure who would chimerically appear from time to time to torment me, and who had to be either escaped or beaten off with any psychological weapon I had to hand.

In retrospect, I think I was extraordinarily lucky that my father lived long enough for me to sort out some of this. Our relationship had already begun to change by the time I had the dream—otherwise I am sure I would not have had it—but I suppose I was still so blinded by my own myth I had refused to trust in those changes or build on them.

The background to all this was that after my parents' divorce, which became final about five years before I had the dream, my father cut off relations with my brother and me. At the time, neither of us considered that a major loss. From what I've been able to piece together since, my father lived for the next couple of years in a small apartment and kept almost entirely to himself. The loneliness must have been excruciating; he could no longer even dull his pain with whiskey because the medication he took daily precluded the use of alcohol. He'd had to quit drinking cold turkey following a heart attack, and after that he managed to stay dry by sheer force of will. Unfortunately, my father's victory over the bottle was not accompanied by any corresponding triumph of personal growth. He was too much a victim of his own hubris to turn to Alcoholics Anonymous or other such groups, and thus cut himself off from that source of support and friendship.

It was revealing in a way that when he finally reached out, it was to a bank teller at a drive-in window; he had to choose among the impersonal human contacts to which his life had been reduced. For all that, his choice of the bank teller was felicitous. He began by trading pleasantries with her, then making jokes, then, when he was on a roll, sending roses to her up the pneumatic tube. She turned out to be a very nice woman—affectionate, kind, motherly, appreciative of his little jokes, and exceedingly patient. And of course she had the advantage of knowing my father only as he was then, a chastened warrior who had mellowed with age, and not as he had been.

In that relationship my father finally found the redemption to be experienced in another human being's faith in one's humanity, the ability to love and give and grow. They married, and for the last six years of his life my father, who was exceedingly grateful for the chance to begin again, enjoyed a measure of happiness and the opportunity to grow into his best self—bounties he had certainly denied himself through his destructive conduct in the long marriage to my mother, when he was blinded by arrogance, egotism, and driving ambition.

It was no coincidence that around the time my father met his sweetheart–bank teller, he began, tentatively, to reach out to me. I was slower than she to realize this was a new phase of his life, with new possibilities—but that was to be expected, given our history, and my slow response was I think for the best. My father and I needed time to learn to trust one another, to feel out what kind of relationship we could manage.

My father's first step was something I have already referred to: He phoned me in Chicago and showed friendly, supportive interest in my research on the Black Muslims. It was a big surprise to me, and a welcome one—but I did not trust him yet. He phoned several more times, and the conversations were not always successful. They would begin fairly well, but the safe topics would be exhausted in about two minutes and he would slip into some intolerable tirade. However, we were establishing one thing that was very important—that we wanted to be in touch, and were willing to keep trying. What remained was how to manage the relationship.

That part fell to me. In what amounted to a kind of role reversal, I set down some explicit ground rules for our phone conversations: I would be happy to talk to him anytime, I said, as long as he did not bad-mouth me, my mother, or my brother. If he tried, I would give him a warning—and also gently try to change the subject. If he persisted in his diatribe, I would tell him I could not tolerate that and would have to hang up, but hoped he would call again soon to talk about something different.

Initially I was forced to hang up on so many occasions that I wondered why either of us was persisting in this exercise. I still had so much anger toward him that it would have neither surprised nor disappointed me greatly if the whole thing had fallen through. But my father eventually learned to talk within the rules, and we came to have some enjoyable conversations.

Most remarkable of all, he was able to tell me he loved me, for the first time since I was a little girl—or perhaps it was the first time in many years I had not been deaf to it. He even left "I love you" messages on my answering machine. And since by this time I knew that I was wholly committed to salvaging whatever I could from this relationship, I made it my secret rule to tell him I loved him three times for every time he told me.

Now, to keep things in perspective, my father did not metamorphose into Alex Stone of "The Donna Reed Show"; this is not another fairy tale. He was still quite recognizable as the testy and belligerent old warrior, narrow-minded, egotistical, paranoid, capable of great and sudden cruelty, and, so far as I could tell, completely disinclined to self-reflection, let alone remorse. We never had any soul-searching conversations. We did not "resolve" any old issues. We did not speak of the past at all.

This was most definitely a relationship that could only function within strict limitations: We had to keep to safe topics such as gardening or the weather or politics, which was safe only because I kept quiet except for feeding a question to him every now and then to draw out his views, which in their extreme difference from my own were quite interesting. He was reluctant to speak of his own family background, or his military career, or war experience. We had almost no cultural touchstones: He read very little, rarely saw a movie, had no interest in theater or museums. He probably would have liked to talk about golf, but I had put that out of my life years before and found it difficult to muster interest. His other area of competence was television, which he watched almost continuously, as far as I could tell, but which I barely watched at all.

It was fortunate we lived over a thousand miles apart; things were much more manageable over the phone than they were in person. Although I always benefited from my visits to his house, they had to be so carefully managed I would feel perpetually exhausted. I always had to be on my guard; long experience had taught me my father was a master of the sneak attack. Even so, with all sensors activated, I sometimes had to learn the hard way where the weak spots in my relationship-management system lay.

For instance, I found out after one disastrous visit that when I flew to see my father I had to rent a car, even when my budget could ill afford such a luxury, so that I would not be put in the childlike position of asking permission to use his, and so that it was absolutely clear I could—and would if necessary—leave his house instantly rather than tolerate the intolerable. It was an important part of reformulating our relationship for me to prove I could no longer be trapped. In fact, the presence of my rental car in the parking lot despite his protestations that it wasn't necessary had a significant calming and equalizing effect on our relationship.

From time to time my father would casually mention that he was thinking about coming to visit me in Chicago. I am grateful he never forced the issue, because it was clear to me that our visits could work only on his turf, not mine. It was a safe bet he would not have approved of my neighborhood, which was ethnically very mixed, or the books I read, or much of anything about my life, including my friends, many of whom were Jewish or black or Hispanic.

A limited relationship, yes—and I realize it sounds like slim pickings to people who have benefited from much closer and richer father-child relationships—but for us it was the very best we could do, and so much more than we'd ever expected. Like those other, much richer relationships I have observed from a distance, it was founded on mutual respect and an agreement that our need to love one another outweighed our differences.

We had to stretch ourselves to make it. My father clearly had to learn some basic rules of civil behavior. I had to learn to see him differently, and constantly renew my willingness to give him a chance. In the course of this frequently difficult business I found I was learning a great deal about the nature of forgiveness.

Frankly, I had always considered the matter of forgiveness, at least where my father was concerned, to be a mystical notion that was beyond my ken, not to mention my application. As a child of a dysfunctional family of the Fortress, I was perhaps more attuned to Old Testament wrath.

But I came to see that "forgiving" my father did not have to involve a godlike absolution of him for his sins. Indeed, his responsibility for decades of abuse of my mother, my brother, and me is beyond question: It is a fact, a part of family history I cannot change and that I choose not to deny or forget. The notion of accountability for one's acts is a cornerstone of my value system.

But forgiveness as I came to understand it has a lot to do with being just plain realistic. The fact was that there was no way my father could make restitution for the abuse; the damage was done and it was not the sort of damage that can be undone or for which there can be compensation. It would have helped quite a lot if he had apologized, but he was unlikely to do that and in fact never did.

But if my father's guilt was an immutable truth, there was another as well: He was still my father, and I his daughter, and we still needed one another. Forgiveness came to mean recognition of that fact above all others, and a determination that whatever transpired next in our relationship would be firmly based on it.

There was no absolution for the sins of the past—neither my father's abuse of his family, nor my imprisonment of him in myths that did not respect his humanity. But there was a kind of healing grace in our willingness to move forward together, with a new attitude of mutual respect, and with gratitude for little things—a shared joke, a word of approval, a long and satisfying hug.

The past was not forgotten, but we robbed it of its power to stop us from building something new and better.

A number of the military brats I talked to were involved in the same process of reconciliation with a parent, almost always the father. Here is some of what they had to say:

Holly, the daughter of an Air Force lieutenant colonel who was not abusive to his children and who was loving to them but in a rather formal, even coded way that left Holly, for one, hungry for much more: "The only reason I feel lucky now is that my parents are still young enough that we can make it up. In the past five years our relationship has improved enormously. It is not what it should be, but we're getting there. Father is mellowing; last year we gave him a surprise party and actually saw him cry. He's finally finding out it's okay to show feelings and it even feels good."

Roxanne, daughter of an alcoholic Army sergeant who was frequently emotionally abusive:

I love my mother to death and I'm real close to her, but at this time I choose not to be around my father that much. I can spend short periods with him, but then it gets into that old feeling again. He just . . . he can be a miserable human being.

I'll still have him over for birthdays and dinners, but every time he'll try [to provoke me]. And what I've learned to do is simply tell myself "It's not important. It's simply a power struggle. Let it go." Because if he doesn't get feedback, he can't continue with it. And he doesn't. For instance, he'll say, "Good God. What have you done to your hair?" And I'll say, "Oh, I don't know. It looks a mess, doesn't it?" And he'll go about his business.

So I see that in order to accept him, I just have to remember that there's nothing he can say or do to me that's really worth fighting about. I love him. I know I do. And I know he loves me. . . . We're never going to see eye to eye on things, but why should we? Nobody ever said we had to be exactly alike, think the same way.

John, the son of an Air Force colonel who was emotionally abusive to him but who, as described in Chapter 5, came to offer his son moral support during the Vietnam War:

My father died eight months ago. It still seems odd to say he's dead, he was such a big part of our lives for so long. I miss him.

When I was growing up he would withhold affection or be condemning—say things like "You're no son of mine." "Nothing you do is any good." "You'll never make anything of yourself." He'd put me on restriction for a month at a time for not mowing the lawn on time. For years I strived for his approval, lived for his approval. It was meted out rarely, like nectar from a honeysuckle—sweet but teeny. Never enough.

At some point much later, he gave up trying to mold my life, and at about the same time I gave up trying to be his "boy." I was an adult then, and I told him what I was going to do, and if he didn't like it that was fine, I was prepared to accept the consequences. At that point it had been many years of battling, and he'd seen where it got him—either I would self-abuse with drugs or alcohol, or I wouldn't call home for months at a time and even then wouldn't talk to him. The only tool I had was to withhold affection—exactly the same thing he did.

What happened was that he got very sick, and I came to him. He said, "John, whatever you do, if it's going to make you happy, it makes me happy." He was finally giving me approval. I think it was because his mortality was staring him in the face.

Over the next five years, we pretty much cleared up what we wanted to clear up, thank God. I feel good about that. I told him things I thought I had to tell him. I forgave him for a lot, let it all go. It helped. It worked.

It's so ironic: Just prior to his death we got closer than we ever had been in my life.

Gabriela, daughter of a Marine Corps sergeant who was alcoholic and emotionally abusive:

Right now my relationship with my parents is very positive. We've all grown up—my mother, my father, and myself. It's been a struggle at times but I think we've gotten to a very nice point where we can talk to each other as friends.

A lot of this has happened in the last eight years, since my father had his heart attack. He was in the process of changing even before then, but that brush with death really made him think about what his life was like and what kind of relationship he wanted with his children and grandchildren. He's changed dramatically. As a matter of fact, I told my mother I really don't believe the man who lives with her is my father. My personal feeling is that he's a clone who was left behind by Martians who took my real father someplace else, where he's probably torturing them and causing a great deal of aggravation.

He's done a one-eighty. He's become a very thoughtful and nurturing individual. He and I collaborate closely on all my art exhibitions; he does all my framing for me and he helps install the show. As a result of our association, he's been able to move off into his own creative areas. He's a very accomplished woodworker, and he's been doing a kind of naive folk painting that's really quite wonderful. I'm encouraging him to do more of that. He has a very interesting style.

I don't think it was until after I was married that my father finally began to change. And that may have been due to something my husband noticed first—that my father was very isolated. Whenever any of us visited the house, we always went to see my mother first and left my father alone in the den with his drink, watching television. And I guess I realized that he was lonely. I began to make an attempt to speak to him when I went over to visit, and that began to open things up. That, coupled with his heart attack, really changed things.

Here, as throughout this book, much space has been given to the relationship between child and father. This is not just a reflection of my own life experience; the interviews for this book showed that for almost all of the military brats I interviewed, the most painful problems within their families had to do with fathers.

In fact I think that with the important exceptions of military mothers who were dysfunctional themselves—substance-addicted, abusive, or mentally disturbed—the issues to be resolved with mothers are of a different kind altogether. By far the majority of mothers of military brats interviewed for this book were gentle, nurturing, loving women who were invaluable emotional anchors for their children. The bonds between child and mother had always been strong and remained strong in adulthood. So in adulthood the primary issue between military brats and their mothers is usually not one of reconciliation, but one of understanding how to interpret the mother as role model in the most constructive way: It takes some effort to bring the mother into sharp enough focus so that her positive traits can be fully appreciated and her less laudable attitudes and ways of coping can be understood and avoided.

What I heard in the stories many military brats told of their mothers was that there was a lack of unity between the mother's inner self, the one she protected or denied altogether, and her outer self, the one she showed to the Fortress. Even though the mother was carrying out her role inside the Fortress by her own choice, in the full belief that it was a life of sufficient meaning and reward, there were ways in which she was not fully realized as a person. This is something children are sometimes better able to perceive than the mothers themselves, because the mothers are accustomed by disposition and long experience inside the Fortress to discount the sides of themselves they were not free to develop.

This gap between the inner and outer self is very common in military wives, I believe—something I would attribute in large part to the patriarchal order of the Fortress which has historically devalued the feminine, and to a life of such extreme mobility that the military wife is cut off from growth that would otherwise be encouraged by rootedness in a community where her own women friends were learning to develop themselves.

It is also true that some of these military wives, particularly those of my own mother's generation, were raised to expect nothing more than what they received inside the Fortress. Perhaps they would accuse me of unfairly applying the standards of my generation to theirs, and there may be truth in that as well. Nevertheless, this phenomenon I am calling the gap between the inner and outer self is a very real issue for military brats when we come to think about our mothers as role models; in that sense it is our perception of them, not their perception of themselves, that matters. And that is why I think many military brats are trying to sort out what they know about their mothers into what amounts to two distinct categories: what their mothers had to do to survive inside the Fortress, and what their mothers really were in themselves, regardless of the Fortress.

It makes a big difference in how we apply the lessons of our mothers' lives. In a sense it becomes our responsibility to learn to make distinctions our mothers for one reason or another did not make—to be the peacemaker without being passive, to be supportive of a spouse's professional persona without allowing ourselves to be subsumed by it, and to keep the elements of constancy and tolerance in our love without slipping into the role of enabling a spouse's destructive or self-destructive behavior.

Military brats are indeed fortunate when their parents live long enough for the relationship to enter a new phase of clarity and closeness. Certainly I count myself as one of the lucky ones, where both my father and my mother are concerned. But I also believe very firmly that our relationships with our parents can continue to evolve and improve even if our parents are no longer living or no longer in communication with us. Enough of our parents reside in our memories and in ourselves that we can continue the dialogue.

I have said that one of the most interesting aspects of research for this book was seeing how some interviewees changed over a period of a couple of years, growing in maturity and wisdom. One of the most striking examples of change in attitude, however, occurred in the course of just a few days.

As was my practice with interviewees who lived too far away for me to interview in person, I sent a long list of questions to Ross, the son of an alcoholic, emotionally abusive Air Force senior master sergeant. The project of reexamining his childhood inside the Fortress hit him at just the right time; a recovering alcoholic, he was in his sixth month of sobriety with Alcoholics Anonymous, and at a point in the twelve-step process in which it was necessary to review his life. The story poured out of him, enough to fill six ninety-minute tapes. He made the tapes in segments, over the course of perhaps a month. And there was a striking contrast between his attitude toward his parents at the start of the tapes, and at the end.

Both of Ross's parents had been dead for a number of years by the time he sat down to tell his story for this book—a fact that certainly complicates the major task of coming to terms with them. And there was the additional factor that Ross had not made peace with his father before his father died. (The relationship with his mother had not been in jeopardy.) At the beginning of the tapes he painted an angry picture of his father as an emotionally abusive alcoholic and depicted his mother as manipulative, an enabler of his father's alcoholism, and— his word—"invisible."

"I've had a lot of anger in my life, a lot of *rage*," Ross said in a more reflective tone. "I think I've looked at the unfairness of life and concentrated on that, and it's colored my whole vision of things. I would look for something wrong to justify my wrathful approach to life. I got in a lot of fights." His tone in the tapes was still very angry, but somewhere around the middle of the interview it began to change.

"One of my relatives told me my father's mother used to take him outside in the front yard and give him a whipping, just for no reason. They were poor sharecroppers, and his father was an alcoholic. My father grew up in a sick environment. I have to remember all this. He grew up in a much sicker environment than I grew up in, and I have him to thank for that."

Later in his narrative—it must have been many days later, during which he had attended many AA meetings—Ross picked up that thread again, and his voice was softer, his tone no longer strident:

I've worked very hard recently. I try to "image" my parents in positive modes. I try to "image" myself being very physically close with my father, hugging him, kissing him. The same thing with [Lou], my brother who killed himself. And with my mother I just try to imagine her in all the positive ways.

I don't want to make my mother a saint and my father a demon. But I don't want to look at them with glaring, realistic glasses either. I want to see them in the loving modes they could have been in if they'd been able to get help the way I've been able to get help. I don't see them as bad, I see them as sick.

I'm grateful to my parents for the fact they raised me, they fed me, clothed me. They kept a roof over our heads. We never went hungry. There are plenty of alcoholics who go off the deep end, go on welfare.

I'm grateful for who I am physically; I'm very strong. I'm grateful for my intelligence, my sense of humor, my work ethic, my commitment to education. My parents imparted values to me. That sense of values is the thing I'm most grateful to them for.

[Even though my parents are dead], I'm trying to forge for us the relationship we *could* have had, given another scenario, another environment. And to make amends to them, too, by the way. Because it's not just a one-way street. I've told lies about the way my father treated me, making it worse than it was so I would seem more noble than I was. I've rejected some of my mother's values because I couldn't accept the burden of some other parts of her legacy. I did not involve myself with her relatives the way

she felt I ought to. So there are a lot of things I need to take care of on *my*
side of the street. It's not just changing the image of my parents, getting
them to be the way *they* "should" have been. It's a dynamic, organic,
integrative transformation of my whole family scenario.

And then I want to bring that out of myself, take it to my students. I can
almost physically feel the opening of my heart . . . prying that thing open,
letting out the light and the joy and the gifts my parents gave me, using
them for everyone around me.

Whether one has already "resolved" things with living parents, or
whether one has had to work on it in their absence, I believe the
internal dialogue of resolution continues for all of us, for several
reasons.

First of all, it would be presumptuous at any point to imagine we
had understood all we need to of our parents' lives and concerns.
Secondly, as we age and change ourselves, the relationship with our
parents needs to be constantly reformulated. And since we're only
human, we also backslide now and then into old attitudes of resentment which must then be brought round again.

At the conclusion of Chapter 6 I presented the story of Harrison, the
gay son of an Air Force colonel who was able to make peace with both
his parents before their deaths. He wrote me a letter in response to
some follow-up questions which was so revealing of the continuing
need to work on parental relationships, and so helpful in showing how
he is dealing with this himself, that I will quote from it at length:

> You mention the issue of parents. Today I realize, because of my experi-
> ence and training in psychotherapy, that the view I had of my parents was
> tremendously one-sided. Certainly I'm not advocating denial. What I've
> remembered about my childhood difficulties and pain certainly helps
> explain my conditioning, patterns, and limitations. Those insights, howev-
> er, have *not* necessarily led to change. In fact when I identify with them
> too much, they become a good "story" for why I am the way I am.
>
> More importantly, these memories of "what my parents did to me" are
> only one part of the picture. They seem to be founded on some ideal
> notion of perfect parents, and frequently too on some childlike belief that
> parents are "Parents" rather than people with limitations, struggling against
> their own conditioning and with the sometimes overwhelming task of
> raising children "without the directions."
>
> In retrospect I feel quite fortunate that I was able to reach a basic
> understanding with my parents before they died. Still, since they died I've
> begun to appreciate their contributions to me as never before. . . .
>
> In the last year I've been working with a tool called Naikkan, one part
> of a psychotherapy/way of life called Constructive Living. Its method is
> to reflect upon the past and allow neglected parts to surface. Reflecting on
> one's parent, for instance, during a particular period of time, and asking
> one's self three questions: 1) What did this person do for me? 2) What did I

do for this person? and 3) What trouble or bother was I to this person? Note that the question that is left out is "What trouble or bother were they to me?" That information has usually been *carefully* encoded in memory!

The answers are to be specific. Not "She fed me every day," but "One day in sixth grade when we were living at Pease Air Force Base in New Hampshire and there was snow outside, my mother gave me a steaming bowl of Campbell's vegetable soup and a peanut butter and jelly sandwich." As these memories surface, they can be written down or shared with someone trained in the practice. One then continues through segments of time, usually in three-year blocks.

As a result of my first experiences with this practice, I was asked to write a letter to each of my parents telling them two kinds of things: specific things I wanted to thank them for, and specific things for which I was sorry. As asked, I took this letter to their graves and read it.

My own experience of this has been quite profound. I realize now how *much* I was loved and cared for by my parents, and it baffles me how I held together a construct of only my parents' flaws for forty years. I don't mean to deny any abuse or difficulty, but what has emerged is the sense of a foundation of love, care, and generosity in daily, concrete form. I also realize how truly difficult I was for my parents in an already very difficult, pressured, and constantly changing life.

I also recognize now that my parents did not reject me, I rejected them in so many particular points in my life. And their support continued. For me, Naikkan caused a total paradigm shift. My personal history no longer looks like it once did.

So, humbled, I recognize my parents' incredible efforts—and they're gone. What to do? I feel fine talking with my parents since their deaths. I don't know if I'm talking only to my own inner psychological father and mother, or to more. I do know it works. At times, I must admit, I have yelled at them. I also try to honor the best of their values in the things I do, in the people and concerns I help. From time to time I extend myself to their families, even when I feel no need to, as a way of returning their care for my needs. Or I attend one of their friends' funerals, or have my father's flag flown at the cemetery on patriotic holidays. My grandmother used to say, "If somebody gives you something, don't try to give it back to them; turn around and give it on. That makes the world go 'round." Enough said.

An "attitude of gratitude," as I've heard it is called in Alcoholics Anonymous. Like the process of Naikkan that Harrison described, it is about recalling with as much specificity as possible the positive acts of our parents, and according the appreciation that is long overdue.

I must say that despite what my father and I accomplished in reestablishing a positive relationship before he died, I had a rough time after his death. All of the ugliness in our family was churned up again, and it seemed as though every waking moment I was assaulted by powerfully intense and contrasting emotions, all jumbled together. I would miss him terribly, find it unbelievably unfair that I couldn't just dial his number and hear him speak to me again. Then I would be seized with fury at the recollection of some rotten thing he'd done or said to me or my mother or brother; then I would think of a dozen more rotten things. Then there would be a flood of guilt at what I should have done or said and never did, followed by a flood of compassion at what I think he must have suffered in his own childhood, at the hands of an alcoholic father who withheld affection. And the cycle would begin again, interrupted only by long bouts of crying for the father I needed him to be and that he never was.

I was hard on him, very hard. I remember thinking that I seemed to have lost all the ground I'd gained through so much labor at reconciliation in the last years of his life; I was back to looking at him all out of balance again, not putting events in perspective, not seeing my own role in them, not giving him proper credit for the good he'd done, and totally indulging my bitterness. I didn't *want* to be in that frame of mind, but there it was. At one point I decided to sit down and earnestly make out a list of things for which I was grateful to my father, in an attempt to force myself back into a more stable and clear-sighted emotional state. It quickly became obvious I wasn't ready for that; all I could come up with for my "gratitude list" were three short items: 1) his role in my conception; 2) his genetic contribution; and 3) the fact that he never sexually abused me.

That was the whole list. According to me at that moment, my father might have done just as well by me if all he'd done was visit a sperm bank. The odd thing was that I *knew* there must have been more to list, but I couldn't remember any of it. My anger flooded out everything else, except the sharp pain of my missing him.

Now I see that period as a necessary part of my grieving process, in which I in effect released some emotional toxins. After a while my vision began to clear. I still felt the rage, but for shorter duration, and it would be followed by some positive memory—the time we went fishing when I was five, when he praised me for a good report card, one of the satisfying hugs we had toward the end of his life, a gesture of kindness he made to a neighborhood child. My list grew, my perspective widened.

My father was a difficult and often destructive human being, yes. But that wasn't all there was to him. He gave me some things for which I am deeply grateful, despite being emotionally wounded himself.

And by far the most important thing of all was that over and above his good traits, and in spite of his bad ones, I loved my father. Really loved him. And I miss him still.

Because reconciliation with one's parents is so terribly important, most of us, as I've said, need to continue this process whether in dealings with our still-living parents or in internal dialogue with our absent ones. But having heard a few truly horrific life stories, I must also say that in a very few cases, the model of reconciliation with one's parents may not be appropriate.

Lisa, for instance, whose story was presented in Chapter 7, is the most badly scarred person I interviewed; in view of what she suffered, Lisa's very existence, not to mention her ability to function and even to have rewarding human relationships, is truly astonishing. The crimes committed against her by her sadistic parents put them, as I see it, in a category apart. To urge Lisa to reconcile with such soul murderers would be to commit yet another crime against her dignity and spirit. Indeed, as Lisa's therapists have suggested to her, she could benefit from harnessing her anger and learning to focus it precisely on the memories of her deceased parents.

What victims of soul murder can do in addition to understanding their anger is look to persons other than their parents as role models and mentors with whom they can share kindness, affection, and trust. In so doing they fill in some of the void, and learn to parent themselves.

I believe very strongly, however, that cases where reconciliation with parents is to be avoided are rare, and the fact some cases exist should not be used as an excuse not to pursue it.

Most of us, including those of us who suffered abuse to a lesser degree than Lisa, need to come to terms with our parents, empathize with their problems and appreciate what care they did give us. Just because one was abused or neglected, as bad as that is, does not mean one was soul murdered; there is an important distinction there. A soul-murdering parent employs abuse to deliberately bring about the annihilation of the child as a separate identity capable of feeling love and happiness. Very few abusing parents would fit the psychopathological profile of this extreme category.

For the child who was abused but not soul murdered, I think the stories presented in this chapter of John, Gabriela, Ross, and Harrison may hold special benefit. All were abused, primarily emotionally, and all have worked hard to understand their anger and move beyond it to find genuine love and appreciation for their parents.

THE FOURTH TASK: ADDRESSING THE QUESTION OF BELONGING

In the course of some background reading for this book, I ran across an essay by a civilian social services administrator who had worked extensively with military families. At one point he observed, "If military life poses so many problems, why do people remain in it? The answer is that it also offers many distinct advantages aside from the more obvious fringe benefits. One of them is a strong sense of belonging to a community."[4]

I wouldn't dispute it. But the sense of belonging he refers to is one that applies far more to the parents than to the children.

Children inside the Fortress grow up with the feeling of being tolerated, not celebrated, by the military establishment; this indeed is the most likely origin of the term *military brats*. One of the notions the military tries to put across to its members is that it constitutes one enormous "family." And to our parents, it probably seemed so. Men who are training for war, not to mention men who actually go to war, form extremely tight bonds. Over the course of a military career, warriors and their wives frequently meet up with their friends at various duty stations and military schools, and renew those bonds. But the notion of the military-as-family is largely fraudulent from the child's point of view, and it's another way in which the frame of reference of military parents differs from that of their children.

Our mothers and fathers may have viewed new orders with, among other things, an expectation that it would likely bring an opportunity to renew old friendships. But children, after a time, grow calloused to such possibilities. The collective brat-wisdom on the subject was that even if you did run into someone you knew on another base, chances are it wouldn't be your best friend but someone you knew only as the one who always claimed the coveted backseat on the school bus, or who smashed a popcorn box on your head during the contained anarchy known as the Saturday morning kiddie show. And even if it was someone you knew and liked reasonably well, there would likely be some other wrench thrown into the works: Perhaps this time around the kid would be sent to parochial school, or his family would choose to live far away from the base, or the father would have been promoted over yours so that playing with the child would now be complicated by all sorts of inhibiting protocol, or you would only have two months with the kid anyway before his family—or yours—would be rotated out.

Another implication of the military-as-family concept is the familiarity of military life. It is true that military bases are so similar in appearance, layout, and routine that their predictability is comforting, particularly by contrast to the intimidatingly alien world of civilians. In that respect they may echo, to a slight degree, the feeling rooted civilians have about their hometowns. But this is only an illusion, and military people mine it for all it's worth because it is all they have.

What military base retains any memory of the people who have served there? It cannot—not in the way a real town can—because there is absolutely no permanent community of inhabitants, no collective memory. Warrior families pass through them and leave not a trace of their passage.

Our parents—most of whom experienced the privilege of having been raised in a definite place with a unique character—were able to find a sense of belonging in the warrior way of life they freely chose to join. It was a life that rewarded them with an identity, status, and a gratifying sense of purpose—what more could one ask of any hometown? But inside the Fortress, unlike a real hometown, these are things in which the children do not share, unless it is in the upstairs/downstairs class system that twists the natural course of friendship with their peers.

Some of the military brats I interviewed spoke of the nostalgic feeling they have whenever they visit military bases. I know this feeling; I have it myself. But I believe it is not nostalgia for a sense of belonging we once felt; it is nostalgia for the sense of belonging *our parents* felt there, and that we yearned for but never really had.

Indeed, what the research for this book clearly showed was that military brats have no idea of what it is to belong. I asked almost every military brat to define what *belonging* means—and in almost every case, the answer came back "I don't know."

Even more striking were the responses of those who purported to know. When I asked the daughter of a Navy petty officer who was also a military wife for many years, she said, "Belonging is a comfort level. When you feel comfortable, you belong. When you don't feel comfortable, you don't belong."

I said, "But belonging by that definition is very transitory. You can belong at one moment and not belong the next."

"That's right," she replied, and considered the case closed. I couldn't help thinking about what my husband's midwestern farm family would say if they could listen in on our conversation. I suspect they would have been shaking their heads in disbelief.

When I've asked civilians about their sense of belonging, I've found that their definitions have everything to do with time: connections, identities, experiences forged over a long span. Military brat definitions, such as they are, have almost nothing to do with the passage of time: They describe belonging almost as a collage of brief experiences that may have nothing whatever to do with one another. Their definitions, in other words, are definitions that reflect the distored perception of time described in the last chapter.

"Belonging?" said the son of an Air Force colonel. "I suppose it means to feel comfortable with a set of people or a geographical location. In my adult life I can't ever remember *not* belonging, maybe because I am a very independent person. Maybe that's an important part of belonging: feeling you belong to yourself."

I interpret that definition as classically military brat: an adaptation of the concept of belonging to reality as we have always known it—a function of self and moment. Everything outside the self is undependable; our instinct is to draw our perimeters as closely as possible, attach ourselves outside of the perimeter only to the extent we can still break camp quickly if need be. Obviously this has major repercussions in the way we live our lives.

"It does not come naturally to me to know how to belong, or even to *want* to know how," said the son of an Air Force sergeant.

Or as an Army son put it, "We develop a certain immunity to attachment."

That's the crux of the matter. Military brats do not know what belonging is about. Military brats even cultivate a sense of apartness, partly because it comes naturally anyway, and partly because it is protection against loss. But I do not for one second believe that military brats are immune to the desire to belong. We may not know what it is, we may even fear what it may cost us, but we seek it without end.

"I don't know how to define belonging," said the daughter of an Air Force colonel. "I seem to want to be part of some group, identify with that group—and that's something I am able to do, and have done, *temporarily*. Right now, my church is my community. It's where people greet me and make me feel welcome and feel a part of them. That's probably why I'm so committed to that church: There is a spirit of belonging and caring. It's something I've wanted all my life."

Other Americans may see themselves in light of the pursuit of happiness. I wonder if we military brats aren't most accurately seen in light of the pursuit of belonging.

Must it always be so elusive?

In a sense it seems so: I have now met a great many military brats who have pursued belonging in a dazzling number of ways, yet who say they still do not feel their search is over. One Army son talked to me for over an hour in rapturous tones about the deep sense of joy he felt in attending, for the first time, a reunion of military brats who had attended Verdun (France) American High School—and then immediately afterward, in response to my query, proceeded to tell me he had no idea what "belonging" meant.

I met two military daughters, one Navy, one Army, who had converted to Judaism—partly to see if it could bring them a sense of belonging, and partly to guarantee their children a sense of connection they had never had themselves. They did not really feel like Jews, they said, but they received enough out of the experience, spiritually and to some extent culturally, to make it a worthwhile investment.

One of the most common ways military brats seek roots is to marry them. Nearly every military brat I interviewed who was married or had a long-term partner had chosen someone who to them represented rootedness. The rootedness doesn't rub off on us, but the close proximity to it seems to add a valuable dimension to our lives. Sam, the son of Air Force parents who had moved fifty-two times in a thirty-two-year military career, married a woman who grew up in one house. The great majority of the military brats I interviewed, in fact, had partners who had grown up in only one or two houses. Perhaps, in the great statistical scheme of things, this is not unusual. But the fact remains that we've all known plenty of other military brats as well as civilians nearly as mobile as ourselves, and for the most part we don't choose to settle down with them.

Religion is another avenue down which military brats search for belonging, instinctively looking for ways to participate in community, and to find or nurture a spiritual sense of roots. Some of the military brats I met, such as the two daughters who converted to Judaism, demonstrated a preference for very old religious traditions. "When I went through the ceremony to become a lay Buddhist teacher," said an Air Force son, "one of the things I was given was lineage papers which trace the line, teacher to teacher, back to a big circle, and the red line comes back around to me. I feel roots in that religion."

I've met military brats who have devoted themselves to investigating their family genealogy, and others who have delved deeply into their ethnic roots.

And there are those who roam the country or the world until they find a place that suits them, and set about weaving their lives into it. They do not exercise the same claim that the civilians around them have by birthright, but it would be hard to surpass them in their degree of community involvement, or in the strength of their almost mystical attachment.

In my case I've done some of all of these: I sought out unknown American cousins, went to Wales and tracked down my Welsh relatives, became an active church member, married a rooted civilian, bought a 240-year-old house in New England, had two children. And for all that I still don't have a sense of belonging in the way I've imagined belonging to be—but I feel I've added some important elements of it to my life in each of these ventures.

When I began this book, it was partly another facet of my continuing search for belonging. And I've learned much in the course of listening to the stories of so many other military brats, including several things about the nature of my own quest that surprised me.

The first is that the search for belonging is not just my own obsession, but one of the driving forces in the lives of all military brats. It is the impetus behind many of the most important decisions we make in our lives.

The second is that we probably cannot ever put that longing to rest. The yearning to belong has been part of us for so long that it is one of our defining characteristics, for we are by nature outsiders. We will always envy the sense of belonging in others, we will always hunt for it ourselves, always find parts of it, always believe there is something more to be found, always convince ourselves that we will find it in "the new place."

The third is that this endless seeking is one of our best traits. It keeps us stretching, learning, experiencing. The odyssey itself is the reward: The search for belonging, in the many creative ways we undertake it, leads us to learn a great many things we need to know but could not learn inside the Fortress. Through it we learn about commitment over time, about contributing actively to the life of a community, about working through disappointment, about adjusting our idealistic expectations, about making our *own* choices and living with their consequences. It is perhaps paradoxical, but the search for belonging which can never be completed is the very vehicle through which we seem to complete ourselves.

And there's something else, equally paradoxical. I used to believe that the perpetual state of *not belonging* was a liability—until a very insightful and articulate military brat, a Marine Corps daughter to whom I will always be grateful, taught me otherwise. She made me see that the quality of not belonging is in fact the birthright of the unrooted, and an asset of immense value if we learn how to use it. Through her I began to see that while as children of the Fortress we have the ability to learn and incorporate some of the facets of belonging that truly rooted people enjoy, we also have something most of them lack and can never acquire: an ability to exploit the value of not belonging.

I quote Gabriela:

> I do not feel I belong to any one particular group or place. That used to cause me a great deal of anguish, until I came to terms with it. I realized that because I didn't belong anywhere in particular, I could belong *everywhere*, and to any group. And that's been a great source of comfort to me, and a source of strength as well.

I certainly do at core feel my military background is my foundation. And because I grew up in the military I was able to develop the kinds of skills that will be very positive in the next twenty years. The world is changing so rapidly, and those who don't change with it are going to be left behind, or left with models that are anachronistic. I'm able to move around, into new circumstances, adjusting quickly and feeling relatively confident.

In graduate school it was made clear to me I wasn't Hispanic enough to be an Hispanic artist, nor Anglo enough to be an Anglo artist. So basically I've been rejected by both groups. That caused me a lot of pain until I realized it offered me a tremendous amount of freedom. It allowed me to act as a bridge or a facilitator between those two groups, and between other groups, too. The whole thing for me in the future is to be able to *connect* ideas, people, art media—people who wouldn't normally speak to each other, things you wouldn't normally associate with one another. I feel I have an ability to bring them together, because I don't have an investment in any particular group—which is not to say that I don't *care* about those groups, but I am not so tied to them and to the dogma associated with them that I can't make connections.

So what is it like to belong? In the traditional sense, I don't know. I do have a desire many times to go home. Sometimes I feel it very strongly—right now of course because I'm going through a divorce—and I want to go back to the way things were because I knew what it was like to be married, what that person was like and what the circumstances were like, even though they were not satisfying. At least it was something recognizable, that I could hold on to. For me to go into the future now means that I must go into uncharted territory, without any recognizable boundaries. It's a double whammy. It's frightening. It's like falling out of a plane in a controlled free fall.

The only thing one can do at that point is set aside the fear long enough to go forward, so you can get used to the new territory, get settled in, and realize it's not frightening. And then use that as a new launching pad to go on again into new uncharted territory.

In the old traditional sense of belonging, I guess I don't belong to anything concrete. I belong more to an idea, a process of becoming. I'm committed to that process of becoming, which means that my self is constantly under construction; certain parts of it die off or are discarded, and other parts come up and are nurtured. *That's* where I belong, in that process, and with other people who are in that process.

From here on out, my life, by my own choice, is going to be carved out of territory that has no boundaries. No personal boundaries. No ethnic boundaries. That's scary; it makes me want to retreat. It's a good thing I don't have anything to retreat to.

At times of stress, one does want to go home. *But there is no home,* except the one that one makes in the spirit and the mind.

The home that one makes in the spirit and the mind. That is the home I was looking for when I began this book.

And that is the home I have found, the home I share with other military brats. Our home is not a place, but the shared experience of the Fortress and its many legacies. Our home is hardship and what we learned from it. Our home is a rich fund of values and ideals. Our home is a special quality of freedom that one can obtain only, ironically enough, inside the ironclad Fortress.

"Home" for a rooted civilian is a place to return to so that love and values and memories and a sense of continuity can be replenished. What I found is that we military brats have a home like that too, a home that we all share, that lives in each of us, that we can visit in one another.

I could not have found it without the help of the many military brats who shared their stories with me. The sharing of stories, I learned, is what roots are all about. Subtract the sharing, and what do you have? Only a bit of dry knowledge fit to be filed in a dusty folder somewhere. Real roots are about *connection*—the bonding with others who share a similar lived experience—and the recognition that who we are individually is due in large part to that lived experience.

After devoting almost five years to intensive study of military brat stories, I have come to two definite conclusions.

First, beyond any doubt, our lived experience inside the Fortress shapes and influences us to such a degree that we bear a distinct identity as military brats and always will.

Second, I like who we are. Military brats are brave, capable, idealistic. We are seasoned by tribulation, honed by our sense of commitment.

I am proud to be a military brat, and despite the high price exacted by the Fortress, I would have it no other way.

NOTES

CHAPTER 1. "TROUPERS"

1. Navy and Marine bases tend to carry the names of the places in which they are located. Army posts in the continental United States are sometimes named for places and sometimes named for Army heroes, so Army brats, too, are occasionally given the names of the posts where they were born.

2. Since I was a child, an interesting new hymn has been added to the standard armed forces hymnal: "Bless Thou the Astronauts Who Face." The first verse reads, "Bless Thou the astronauts who face / The vast immensities of space; / And may they know, in air, on land, / Thou holdest them within thy hand. / O may the small step each doth take / Aid others giant leaps to make." *Book of Worship for United States Forces* (Washington, D.C.: U.S. Government Printing Office, 1974), p. 194.

3. Lt. Col. Kenneth W. Estes, *The Marine Officer's Guide*, 5th ed. (Annapolis: Naval Institute Press, 1985), p. 125.

4. There is a memorable scene about this in the novel *The Great Santini*.

5. Devil Pups, Inc. is a private, nonprofit, charitable California corporation based in Los Angeles. It was founded in 1954 by a group of Marines in the wake of an incident at Beverly Hills High School in which teenage boys burned the U.S. flag. The name Devil Pups appears to derive from the Marine Corps mascot, the bulldog.

6. Doubtless this military wife had experienced white-glove inspections many times herself. For many years, and certainly at the time she would have been involved in military life, it was usual for the military police at a given base to perform a white-glove inspection before a service member preparing to leave could be officially checked out of his quarters. At that time it was the service member's—or more likely, his wife's— responsibility to make sure the quarters passed the inspection. Any spots that were dusty or dirty were tidied instantly, in front of the police. White-glove inspections are no longer the norm, although they may still be performed on some bases if the base commander so decrees. The more usual practice is for the inspection to be performed by a civilian employee of the base housing office, who does not normally hold the occupant to the standards of the white glove. After a number of years in which some aspects of final clean-up were typically handled by a government cleaning crew, however, the full responsibility for leaving the quarters in immaculate condition has returned to the service member.

7. In some enlisted families, this may be a cultural carryover from the parents' background. In the South, for instance, it is customary to say "sir" and "ma'am" to adults as an expression of politeness. However, many of the enlisted families that required this form in their children were not of southern origin. See note 8 for additional information.

8. Although noncommissioned officers are never addressed as "sir," recruits in boot camp are not yet members of the military—they don't gain that status until they have

successfully completed their basic training course—so the standard rules of interaction do not apply to them. They are taught to address their sergeants as "sir" in order to impress on them the necessity of respect for one's superiors. This may be one reason why children of enlisted are often made to say "sir" and "ma'am" to their parents.

9.   In 1985, at the time of my visit to MCRD, there was a waiting list; a team of Army generals had just paid a visit to MCRD to gain insight into the Marine Corps's recruitment techniques. However, the Corps's history is checkered on this point. During the Vietnam War, 85 percent of Marine recruits were draftees who had opted for the Corps instead of another service. Immediately following the institution of the All Volunteer Force in 1973, the Marine Corps experienced a steep drop in recruitment and had to lower its standards in order to fill quotas. Eventually it improved its recruitment methods and raised its standards, only to have to drop them again in 1989, along with all the other services, in order to meet quotas. In 1990, however, the Marine Corps was back to more selective standards; over 95 percent of its recruits had high school diplomas or had passed equivalency tests.

10.   Air Force Regulation 35-10 states in part, "Headgear will not be worn . . . while indoors except by armed security police in the performance of their duties."

11.   From the *New York Times*, March 26, 1986, pp. A1, A18.

12.   See, for example, *Dimensions of Authoritarianism: A Review of Research and Theory*, by John P. Kirscht and Ronald C. Dillehay (Lexington: University of Kentucky Press, 1967), p. 72.

13.   Ibid., pp. 72, 132–34.

14.   The study was headed by Dr. Peter H. Neidig, Ph.D., of Behavioral Science Associates, Beaufort, S.C. The results quoted here are from the publication *Military Family*, which carried a three-part series on his findings entitled "Domestic Violence in the Military," beginning with the May-June 1985 issue, Vol. 5, No. 3.

15.   NCO is short for noncommissioned officer, an enlisted member of the military who bears a rank of E-4 to E-9. There are four grades of warrant officers, who hold superior rank to the enlisted noncommisioned officers. Distinct from these and superior to them in rank are commissioned officers, with ranks graded from O-1 (ensign in the Navy, second lieutenant in the Army, Marines, and Air Force) to O-10 (four-star admiral in the Navy, four-star general in the Army, Marines, and Air Force), with special ranks of five stars reserved for Fleet Admiral of the Navy, General of the Army, and General of the Air Force. Since the Marine Corps is part of the Navy, it has a commandant but not a five-star general.

16.   Peter H. Neidig, "Domestic Violence in the Military, Part II: The Impact of High Levels of Work-Related Stress on Family Functioning," *Military Family*, Vol. 5, No. 4, July-August 1985, p. 4.

17.   Neidig makes a distinction between verbal threats and physical threats. A physical threat is counted as marital violence, although it falls short of actual physical abuse.

18.   Neidig found that certain violent behaviors *are* gender specific; women tend to be more verbally abusive and men tend to make more physical threats—but the husbands and wives he studied tended to be equally abusive physically. He stresses, however, that in a physical battle the wife was much more likely to be seriously injured than the husband. From the evidence of the wife's heavy involvement in physical abuse, he infers that "interventions must be directed to the relationship rather than just one half of the relationship."

19.   Neidig, op. cit. p. 4.

20. Don M. LaGrone, M.D., "The Military Family Syndrome," *American Journal of Psychiatry*, Vol. 135, No. 9, September 1978, p. 1042.

21. Ibid.

22. A moving account of another such nonauthoritarian military father and his tight-knit family is to be found in the book *My Father, My Son*, by Adm. Elmo Zumwalt, Jr., and his son, Lt. Elmo Zumwalt III, with John Pekkanen (New York: Dell Publishing Co., 1987).

23. Allen Frances, M.D., and Leonard Gale, M.D., "Family Structure and Treatment in the Military," *Family Process*, Vol. 12, 1973, p. 173.

24. Nancy Shea, *The Army Wife: What She Ought to Know About the Customs of the Service and the Management of an Army Household* (New York: Harper and Brothers, 1954).

25. See "Air Force Rethinks Socal Demands Made for Years on Officers' Wives," by Adam Nossiter, *The Atlanta Journal and Constitution*, Nov. 2, 1988. Chapter 3 of this book includes additional treatment of this subject.

26. Clella Reeves Collins, *Army Woman's Handbook* (New York: McGraw-Hill, 1942), p. 181. Although this text dates from 1942, this point is considered to hold largely true even today.

27. Ibid., pp. 181–82.

28. John K. Miller, M.D., "Perspectives on Child Maltreatment in the Military," in *Child Abuse and Neglect*, ed. by Ray E. Helfer et al. (Cambridge, Mass: Ballinger Publishing Co., 1976), p. 272.

CHAPTER 2. "MASKS"

1. This was in 1962. In 1965 the U.S. military left France at the demand of President Charles De Gaulle. Since then the USAREUR headquarters has been in Heidelberg.

2. Tom Wolfe, *The Right Stuff* (New York: Bantam, 1980), p. 9.

3. In 23 families, the father was the alcoholic. In 5, the mother was alcoholic but the father was not. In 11, both parents were alcoholic.

4. Naturally, one wants to know how this compares to the civilian sector. There are several reasons why that is not easy to answer. First of all, my sampling is not a scientifically controlled survey and should not be considered as such. Second, since the alcoholic parents referred to here spanned quite a long time period, there is no way to compare these findings to national alcoholism statistics for any given year; this is important, because national patterns of alcohol consumption go up and down over the years. Third, a true comparison would have to statistically adjust the figures to correct for demographic differences, since the military is not a comparably representative population. In addition, possible differences in operating definitions of alcoholism and alcohol abuse might preclude direct comparisons of civilian and military surveys.

However, if one is merely curious about national figures on alcoholism—keeping in mind the above, as well as the fact that national figures cover *both* the civilian and military sectors—the National Institute on Alcohol Abuse and Alcoholism (NIAAA) estimates in its 1990 report that there are 10,980,363 alcoholics age 18 or over in the U.S. population. This is based on a national survey done in 1979, but is statistically altered to project the estimate for 1990. Since the estimated population of adults 18 and over on July 1, 1989—the most recent information available from the U.S. Census Bureau at this writing—was 184,679,000, this means that, according to the NIAAA, alcoholics comprise approximately 5.9 percent of the adult U.S. population.

If the 7,306,319 "alcohol abusers"—as distinct from alcoholics—are thrown in as well, the percentage of adults who abuse or are addicted to alcohol rises to 9.9 percent.

5.   "Children of Alcoholics Battle Trauma as Adults," *Los Angeles Times*, Sept. 24, 1985.

6.   Robert M. Bray, Mary Ellen Marsden, and Michael R. Peterson, "Standardized Comparisons of the Use of Alcohol, Drugs, and Cigarettes Among Military Personnel and Civilians," paper presented at the annual meeting of the American Public Health Association, October 23, 1989, Chicago, p. 15. This paper was based on the study cited in note 7.

7.   Robert M. Bray, Mary Ellen Marsden, and Sara C. Wheeless, "Military/ Civilian Comparisons of Alcohol, Drug, and Tobacco Use," Research Triangle Institute, May 1989, p. 31. Their study, prepared for the Department of Defense, was based on data concerning military alcohol use drawn from the 1985 Worldwide Survey of Alcohol and Nonmedical Drug Use Among Military Personnel, and on data of civilian use drawn from the 1985 National Household Survey on Drug Abuse. Civilian data were standardized to reflect sociodemographic distributions of age, sex, race/ethnicity, and education in the military.

8.   Marianne Lester, "The Alcoholic Wife," *The Times Magazine*, Oct. 8, 1975, p. 16.

9.   D. Cahalan and I. H. Cisin, "Final report on a service-wide survey of attitudes and behaviors of Naval personnel concerning alcohol and problem drinking," Navy Dept., Bureau of Navy Personnel, Washington, D.C., 1975.

10.   William C. Louisell, Jr., Deputy Assistant Secretary of Defense, Drug and Alcohol Abuse Prevention, "The Military Problem with Drink and Drugs," *Defense 81*, October 1981, pp. 20–23.

11.   Larry H. Ingraham, *The Boys in the Barracks* (Philadelphia: Institute for the Study of Human Issues, 1984), p. 213.

12.   Gerald R. Garrett, Betty Parker, Suzan Day, Jacquelyn J. Van Meter, and Wayne Cosby, "Drinking and the Military Wife: A Study of Married Women in Overseas Base Communities," in Edna J. Hunter and D. Stephen Nice, eds., *Military Families: Adaptation to Change* (New York: Praeger Publishers, 1978), pp. 222–37.

13.   Bray, Marsden, and Wheeless, op. cit., pp. 22–26.

14.   Garrett et al., op. cit., p. 236.

15.   Ingraham, op. cit., p. 91.

16.   Ibid., pp. 124–25.

17.   James Morrison, M.D., "Rethinking the Military Family Syndrome," *American Journal of Psychiatry*, Vol. 138, No. 3, March 1981, p. 356.

18.   "Alcohol and the Family," *Newsweek*, January 18, 1988, p. 39.

19.   If drug problems are added in, the number rises to 23 (there were actually 9 families with drug-addicted children, but 6 have been previously accounted for because of their children's simultaneous alcohol addictions). If eating disorders are added in as well, the number of families with substance-abusing children rises to 32 out of 75.

20.   The words of Dr. Jerry Flanzer, director of the Mid-America Institute on Violence in Families at the University of Arkansas, as quoted in "Domestic Violence: The Alcohol Relationship," by Lt. Serge R. Doucette, Jr., MSC, USNR, and Cdr. Robert D. McCullah, MSC, USN, *U. S. Navy Medicine*, Vol. 71, March 1980, p. 5.

21. Timmen L. Cermak, M.D., "Children of Alcoholics and the Case for a New Diagnostic Category of Codependency," *Alcohol Health and Research World*, Summer 1984.

22. Cermak, op cit. I have paraphrased his list of symptoms.

23. Ibid.

24. See books such as *Adult Children of Alcoholics*, by Janet Geringer Woititz, and *It Will Never Happen to Me!*, by Claudia Black.

25. Janet Geringer Woititz, *Adult Children of Alcoholics* (Deerfield Beach, Fla.: Health Communications, Inc., 1983), pp. 104–105.

CHAPTER 3. "THE PLAY WITHIN THE PLAY"

1. "Separation of Families Hurts Navy Retention," by James Gerstenzang, *Los Angeles Times*, San Diego County edition, May 19, 1986.

2. There are scores of studies on the effects of father absence. See, for example, the following. On poor personal and social adjustment: Barbara B. Dahl and Hamilton I. McCubbin, "Children of Returned Prisoners of War: The Effects of Long-Term Father Absence," U.S. Navy, Naval Health Research Center, Center for POW Studies, San Diego; Thomas L. Trunnell, "A Review of the Psychosocial Significance of the Absent Father," paper presented at the Western American Psychiatric Association meeting, August 1968, Seattle. On behavior problems: Gentry W. Yeatman, "Paternal Separation and the Military Dependent Child," *Military Medicine*, Vol. 146, No. 5, pp. 320–22; Frank Pedersen, "Relationship Between Father Absence and Emotional Disturbance in Male Military Dependents," *Merrill-Palmer Quarterly*, Vol. 12, 1966, pp. 321–31; C. Seplin, "A Study of the Influence of Fathers' Absence for Military Service," *Smith College Studies in Social Work*, Vol. 22, pp. 123–24. On the effects on IQ, quantitative ability, and behavior: Elizabeth D. Hillenbrand, "Father Absence in Military Families," *The Family Coordinator*, George Washington University, October 1976, pp. 451–58; L. Stolz, "Father Relations of War-Born Children: The Effects of Postwar Adjustment of Fathers on the Behavior and Personality of First Children Born While Fathers Were at War" (Palo Alto: Stanford University Press, 1954). On development: Gael E. Pierce, "The Absent Parent and the Rorschach 'T' Response," Ch. 4, *Children of Military Families: A Part and Yet Apart*, ed. by Edna J. Hunter and D. Stephen Nice, #008-040-00181-4, U.S. Govt. Printing Office, Washington, D.C. On increase in psychosomatic complaints at military clinics during deployments: A. I. Snyder, "The Effects of Husband's At-Sea Time upon the Role-Playing Behavior of the Submariner's Wife," Technical Report No. 3, Arlington, Virginia: Office of Naval Research (Code 452), Organizational Effectiveness Research Program, 1978.

3. See, for example: A. J. Marsella, R. A. Dubanoski, and K. Mohs, "The Effects of Father Presence and Absence upon Maternal Attitudes," *Journal of Genetic Psychology*, Vol. 125, 1974, pp. 257–63; L. Stolz, "The Effect of Mobilization and War on Children," *Social Casework*, Vol. 32, 1952, pp. 143–49.

4. David W. Keith and Carl A. Whitaker, "C'est la Guerre: Military Families and Family Therapy," in *The Military Family*, ed. by Florence W. Kaslow and Richard I. Ridenour (New York: Guilford Press, 1984), p. 151.

5. Despite the early date, Graham's father was not the first American soldier to die or be declared MIA in what was to become the American war in Vietnam. The first Americans to die were a major and a sergeant who were killed by guerrillas near Bienhoa, South Vietnam, in July 1959. But it was still years before the United States made a major military commitment to fight in Southeast Asia. American military

advisors were not sent in large numbers until early 1962, a year after Graham's father disappeared. Congress did not pass the Tonkin Gulf resolution, which in effect gave President Lyndon Johnson the power to wage war in Vietnam, until August 7, 1964. American planes bombed North Vietnam for the first time later that month. U.S. Marines did not land on the shores of South Vietnam until the spring of 1965.

6.   Allen Frances, M.D., and Leonard Gale, M.D., "Family Structure and Treatment in the Military," *Family Process*, Vol. 12, 1973, p. 176.

7.   The comment was made by a U.S. Army major to television news correspondent Peter Arnett after the town of Ben Tre had been reduced to rubble by American firepower. See *A Bright Shining Lie: John Paul Vann and America in Vietnam*, by Neil Sheehan (New York: Random House, 1988), p. 719. It was a phrase that, as Sheehan points out, came to epitomize the "mad logic" of the American war in Vietnam.

8.   Over many years, court decisions had supported this interpretation of the law. In 1981, the U.S. Supreme Court finally had a chance to rule on the subject in *McCarty v. McCarty*, and found that under existing federal law, the former spouse of a military service member was not entitled to any part of that member's military retired pay as part of a property settlement in divorce. However, the Court invited Congress to correct this situation, as Congress had previously done with regard to federal civil service and foreign service annuities.

9.   P.L. 97-252 does not apply to divorce settlements that became final prior to the *McCarty* decision on June 26, 1981. However, in some states it may be possible to retroactively reopen a case in order to obtain a portion of the former spouse's military retired pay. At this writing, Rep. Schroeder has introduced another bill, the Uniformed Services Former Spouses Equity Act, in response to the U.S. Supreme Court's May 1989 decision in *Mansell v. Mansell*, which supported a retired military husband's right to convert a portion of his retired pay into disability benefits, thereby making it untouchable as divisible property.

CHAPTER 4. "DAUGHTERS OF WARRIORS"

1.   Linda Schierse Leonard, *The Wounded Woman: Healing the Father-Daughter Relationship* (Boston: Shambhala, 1983), p. 11. This book is an excellent resource for those wishing to explore the complications of the father-daughter relationship or to understand the implications of being female in a patriarchal society. Leonard, too, addresses the approved roles of beauty and duty mentioned earlier in this chapter, but from a slightly different angle and at much greater depth.

2.   Sarah was contrasting that to the way perfectionism manifests itself in men, which is, in her words, "to put emphasis more on 'the product': never making mistakes in performance." See a discussion of this in Chapter 6.

3.   Patricia Crigler, "Incest in the Military Family," in *The Military Family*, ed. by Florence Kaslow and Richard I. Ridenour (New York: Guilford Press, 1984), p. 121.

4.   The survey was conducted by the Renfrew Center, a residential facility for the treatment of anorexia and bulimia in Philadelphia. It was cited in *Shape*, October 1987, p. 78.

5.   For much more on Athena and other archetypes in women, see Jean Shinoda Bolen, M.D., *Goddesses in Everywoman: A New Psychology of Women* (New York: Harper and Row, 1984).

6.   I have used the term *Black Muslim* here because it is the name by which most people know this black separatist community, which began in the 1930s but attained public notoriety in the late 1950s with the rise of their famous spokesman, Malcolm X. However, the use of this term necessitates an apology to members of the community

itself, for the name was not one they chose or ever used for themselves; it was coined by the press during the 1950s. Members of the movement, the mainstream portion of which is no longer racist or separatist, have always preferred to use the simple term *Muslim.*

7. Jean Baker Miller, *Toward a New Psychology of Women* (Boston: Beacon Press, 1986). See especially Chapter 8, "Ties to Others."

8. Janet Geringer Woititz, *Adult Children of Alcoholics* (Deerfield Beach, Fla.: Health Communications, Inc., 1983), p. 39.

CHAPTER 5. "SONS OF WARRIORS: MIRRORING THE WARRIOR"

1. Pat Conroy, *The Great Santini* (New York: Avon Books, 1976), p. 216.

2. Ibid., pp. 141–42.

3. For those too young to remember, Huey Newton was one of the cofounders and, later, principal leader of the Black Panther party in the 1960s. He was militant, charismatic, photogenic, articulate, and thus was anointed one of the heroes of grass-roots opposition that swept the country like a brushfire during that period.

4. The 12-week Ranger course is a grueling indoctrination in survival and guerrilla warfare. Some Rangers are subsequently assigned to a Ranger battalion, but for the most part graduates of the course are scattered throughout the Army infantry and other branches of the service. The training is for both officers and enlisted.

CHAPTER 6. "SONS OF WARRIORS: GHOSTS OF THE FORTRESS"

1. Pete Earley, *Family of Spies: Inside the John Walker Spy Ring* (New York: Bantam, 1988), p. 263. See also the interview with Dan Morain, "Walker Son Says He Became Spy 'to Please My Father,' " *Los Angeles Times*, May 20, 1986.

2. Janice G. Rienerth, "Separation and Female Centeredness in the Military Family," in *Military Families: Adaptation to Change*, ed. by Edna J. Hunter and D. Stephen Nice (New York: Praeger, 1978), pp. 169–84.

3. Ibid., p. 182.

4. Allen Frances, M.D., and Leonard Gale, M.D., "Family Structure and Treatment in the Military," *Family Process*, Vol. 12, 1973, pp. 171–78.

5. Tess Forrest, "The Paternal Roots of Male Character Development," *Psychoanalytic Review*, Vol. 54, No. 1, 1967, pp. 51–67.

6. Jerry Hopkins and Danny Sugerman, *No One Here Gets Out Alive* (New York: Warner Books, 1980), pp. 134–38.

7. Ibid., p. 96.

8. Bernard Wolfe, "The Real-Life Death of Jim Morrison," *Esquire*, June 1973, p. 106.

9. Forrest, op. cit., p. 66.

10. I believe that my own attraction to the Black Muslims as subject matter for a book was for much the same reason. I did not want to become a Muslim or a member of their community, but studying them and their formerly antiwhite viewpoint—as I now see in hindsight—was one way of bringing my own father's bigotry into focus even as I distanced myself from it. The irony for both Ross and me, of course, is that Black Muslim racism was a mirror reflection of white bigotry just as pre-glasnost Soviet

history was a mirror reflection of the repressive, militaristic aspects of the American Fortress establishment Ross instinctively opposed.

11.   The rating system on efficiency or fitness reports changes from time to time. At this writing in the Marine Corps, for example, the point scale is no longer used on fitness reports for ranks E-5 and above. Instead, across the top of the sheet are columns labeled, from left to right, Not Observed, Unsatisfactory, Below Average, Average, Above Average, Excellent, and Outstanding. However, the same rigid standard of perfection obtains: A perfect rating is no longer "four-point-oh," but "all to the right," meaning outstanding in every category. Ironically, a fitness report that marks a Marine "excellent" in every category might well signify the end of his or her career, since it almost certainly means that Marine will be passed over for promotion in favor of someone whose record is "outstanding."

12.   That is, as evident in the rank displayed on one's uniform, and also in one's age relative to that rank.

13.   D. W. Goodwin, "The Genetics of Alcoholism: A State of the Art Review," *Alcohol Health and Research World*, Vol. 2, No. 3, 1978, pp. 2–12.

CHAPTER 7. "MILITARY BRATS AS CASUALTIES"

1.   A consideration of how spouse abuse cases are handled is not irrelevant in this context; a seven-month study of child maltreatment cases in military families in the San Antonio area in 1976–77 revealed that in 20 percent of the homes, spouse abuse also occurred. Sandra M. Schnall, "Characteristics and Management of Child Abuse and Neglect Among Military Families," in *Children of Military Families: A Part and Yet Apart*, ed. by Edna J. Hunter, D. Stephen Nice, U.S. Govt. Printing Office, Washington, D.C. 20402, p. 150. Another study of 87 male spouse abusers and 95 nonabusers, all of them active-duty military personnel, screened them for child abuse; 36 percent of the spouse abusers had elevated child abuse scores, as opposed to 9 percent of the nonabusers. Joel S. Miner and Ruth G. Gold, "Screening Spouse Abusers for Child Abuse Potential," *Journal of Clinical Psychology*, Vol. 42, No. 1, January 1986, pp. 169–72.

2.   This order amounts to the revocation of the Marine's privilege to go home at the end of the day to be with his family. The Marine Corps considers a Marine to be the property of the Marine Corps twenty-four hours each day; the time he associates with his family is a privilege, not a right. When that privilege is revoked, the Marine still has freedom of movement around and even off the base, but he may not associate with his family.

3.   David A. Wolfe et al., "The Importance of Adjudication in the Treatment of Child Abusers: Some Preliminary Findings," *Child Abuse and Neglect*, Vol. 4, 1980, p. 131.

4.   In the Army, the term is Army Community Service Centers. They have existed since 1965, but until recently had a primarily social function. Problems such as spouse abuse and child maltreatment were not addressed at these centers until 1978. The Air Force established five prototype Family Support Centers in 1981; since then FSCs have been established on all major bases. However, FSCs do not handle family advocacy. Unlike the other services, the Air Force bases its family advocacy teams in base hospitals and clinics. The Navy Family Support Program was established in 1979; there are now 75 FSCs serving Navy and Marine families.

5.   "Military Child Advocacy Programs—Victims of Neglect," U.S. Government Accounting Office, Washington, D.C., Distribution Section, Report No. HRD-79-75, May 23, 1979.

6. As an article in the *New York Times* put it, "Longer range, the ability of the military to retain experienced noncommissioned officers often turns on how well families are looked after. 'The Navy enlists sailors,' says a naval officer, 'but we reenlist families.' " "Women, Blacks, Spouses Transforming the Military," by Richard Halloran, *New York Times*, August 25, 1986.

7. As previously noted, funding for family advocacy comes directly from the DoD budget. The bulk of the work of Family Service Centers is not family advocacy, however, but other kinds of support services.

8. The civilian sector has been just as remiss in instituting preventive programs. For a damning indictment of the treatment-over-prevention approach, see Gertrude J. Rubin Williams, "Child Abuse Reconsidered: The Urgency of Authentic Prevention," *Journal of Clinical Child Psychology*, Vol. 12, No. 3, 1983, pp. 312–19.

9. See Army Regulation 635-100, para. 5–12, regarding elimination of officers for misconduct or moral or professional dereliction: "Failure to respond to rehabilitation efforts regarding repeated acts of child/spouse maltreatment or abuse and/or other acts of family violence in a reasonable length of time." See also Army Regulation 635-200, para. 14-12c, regarding discharge of enlisted soldiers for commission of serious offenses.

10. See Army Regulation 635-120, ch. 5. In fact, courts-martial are exceedingly rare on charges of child abuse not involving sexual abuse. In the Army, "only one out of every 183 soldiers whose nonsexual abuse of his child has been substantiated . . . is tried by a court-martial, but one out of every six soldiers is tried by court-martial when child sexual abuse is substantiated. . . ." See Alfred F. Arquilla, "Crime in the Home," *The Army Lawyer*, April 1988, pp. 6–7.

11. See Army Regulation 635-120, ch. 11, regarding the elimination of certain officers not selected for promotion.

12. This behavior has been known for some time. See Donald E. Cowing, "Psychiatry and the Air Force: An Uneasy Alliance," *American Journal of Orthopsychiatry*, Vol. 44, 1974, pp. 274–75.

13. It should be noted that statistics for the U.S. population are for the population *as a whole*—so military as well as civilian incidents are included in the total. Any comparison between military and civilian statistics—even if the methodology of the studies were exactly the same—would therefore be a comparison between the military population and the civilian-plus-military population.

14. *Study Findings: Study of National Incidence and Prevalence of Child Abuse and Neglect, 1988*, U.S. Department of Health and Human Services, Office of Human Development Services, Administration for Children, Youth and Families, Children's Bureau, National Center on Child Abuse and Neglect, p. 44.

15. *Highlights of Official Child Neglect and Abuse Reporting, 1986* (Denver: American Humane Association, 1988), p. xiii.

16. GAO report, op. cit., p. 29.

17. GAO report, op. cit., p. 30.

18. Maj. James R. Silliman, USAF, Air Command and Staff College, Air University, Maxwell AFB, Alabama, "A Joint Service Child Abuse and Neglect Register," April 1980, p. 2.

19. Ibid., p. 27.

20. Department of Defense Child and Spouse Abuse Statistical Report, Fiscal Year 1988, p. 1. Of these reports, 9,378, or 45 percent, were substantiated.

21. Administrators at the three service registries, which maintain computer records of domestic violence in the military, like to talk about how much the reporting of abuse incidents has improved in recent years. Nevertheless, serious problems remain in the way the system functions. In the summer of 1990, for instance, the Navy registry, which covers the Marine Corps as well, showed that one Marine command had not a single incident of child or spouse abuse in all of 1989—a virtual impossibility. A Marine who questioned that picture found out there were eighty incidents of spouse abuse alone in that command. The command had reported its statistics, but through a computer coding error at a Navy hospital which was not caught at the registry level, none of these reported incidents appeared in the Marine Corps profile.

22. The same argument could well apply to the senior enlisted grades of E–6 through E–9. Senior noncommissioned officers, because they are in leadership positions and have invested heavily in their careers, also have a great deal to lose if they become known as child abusers. Most of the reported child abuse comes from families in pay grades E1–E6. The reports drop off sharply for the senior enlisted pay grades of E7–E9, although the rate of 2.6 substantiated cases of child abuse per thousand children is still five times higher than that of the senior officer pay grades of O–4 through O–10.

23. To its credit, DoD has been encourgaing states to pass legislation so that information on military abusers gathered by civilian agencies is passed back to the military; the coverup route of officers and senior noncoms would then be closed, and the military would be able to take appropriate action with respect to abusers and victims. In most states this is theoretically possible, but what actually happens varies according to individual state and county restrictions, and the degree of motivation of the local military base to work out an understanding with the civilian sector. Privacy issues are a sticking point—such constitutional issues will always be an area of contention between the authoritarian, nondemocratic military and the civilian sector—but it may also be that some civilian communities are waiting for the military to further improve its services to families before they will feel comfortable in cooperating.

24. Murray A. Straus, Richard Gelles, and Suzanne K. Steinmetz, *Behind Closed Doors: Violence in the American Family* (New York: Doubleday/Anchor, 1980), p. 145.

25. Statistics computed from *Defense 89 Almanac*, U.S. Government Printing Office, Washington, D.C., tables on pp. 28, 31.

26. L. A. West, W. M. Turner, and E. Dunwoody, "Wife Abuse in the Armed Forces," Center for Women Policy Studies, Washington, D.C., 1981, as quoted in *The Military Family*, ed. by Florence W. Kaslow and Richard I. Ridenour (New York: Guilford Press, 1984), p. 129.

27. *Study of National Incidence and Prevalence of Child Abuse and Neglect: 1988*, National Center on Child Abuse and Neglect, pp. 5–26. In this study, the cutoff level dividing low-income and higher-income families was $15,000 a year. The study found that among lower-income children, physical abuse was 3.5 times more frequent, sexual abuse 5 times more frequent, and emotional abuse 4.5 times more frequent.

28. Grant Willis, "Civilian-Military Pay Gap Will Keep Widening in 1990," *Army Times*, October 2, 1989. Based on a DoD analysis.

29. Computed from *Defense 89 Almanac*, tables p. 31.

30. Internal Analysis Memorandum D85–001, 1985 DoD Surveys of Officer and Enlisted Personnel and Military Spouses, "Households of Enlisted Personnel Receiving Food Stamps," February 1986, p. 2.

31. State of Hawaii, Department of Social Services and Housing, Public Welfare

Division, *A Statistical Report on Child Abuse and Neglect in Hawaii, 1980*, pp. 56, 71. The forms of state aid received included Aid to Families with Dependent Children (AFDC), food stamps, and housing assistance.

32. D. B. Sattin and J. K. Miller, "The Ecology of Child Abuse within a Military Community," *American Journal of Orthopsychiatry*, Vol. 41, No. 4, July 1971, pp. 675–78.

33. The study by K. Roy, originally published in *Journal of Home Economics*, Vol. 42, 1950, was cited by Ross D. Parke and Candace Whitmer Collmer of the Fels Research Institute in "Child Abuse: An Interdisciplinary Analysis," *Review of Child Development Research*, Vol. 5, ed. by E. M. Hetherington (Chicago: University of Chicago Press, 1975), p. 527.

34. Capt. John A. Schwed, USAF, and Murray A. Straus, Univ. of New Hampshire, "The Military Environment and Child Abuse," July 19, 1979, pp. 9, 13, 15.

35. David C. Larson, "A Comparative Study of Child Maltreatment in Military Families," National Law Center, George Washington University, Fall 1982, p. 14.

36. See Milner and Gold, op. cit.

37. See, for example, Schwed, op. cit., p. 9; also "Child Abuse in the Southeast: Analysis of 1172 Reported Cases," Clara L. Johnson, Regional Institute of Social Welfare Research, Univ. of Georgia, Athens, 1974.

38. See Sandra M. Schnall, op. cit., p. 150.

39. Blair Justice and David F. Duncan, "Life Crisis as a Precursor to Child Abuse," *Public Health Reports*, Vol. 91, No. 2, March–April 1976, p. 111.

40. See, for example, David C. Larson, op. cit., p. 14: "[T]he younger age of the abused child coupled with the higher reported incidence of physical abuse . . . creates potential for a more injurious degree of child abuse in the military community."

41. Casimir R. Wichlacz et al., "The Characteristics and Management of Child Abuse in the U.S. Army—Europe," *Clinical Pediatrics*, Vol. 14, No. 6, June 1975, p. 546.

42. See Silliman, op. cit., p. 1.

43. Ray E. Helfer, M.D., "A Report of a Symposium on Child Abuse and Neglect in the Military," American Medical Association Conference, 1974.

44. Clara L. Johnson, op. cit.

45. According to the Public Health Service, 80 percent of child abuse cases show some connection with alcohol abuse. Cited in Robert D. McCullah, "Effects of Family Dysfunction on Military Operations: Mental Health Needs," in *The Military Family and the Military Organization*, ed. by Edna J. Hunter and Thomas C. Shaylor, The Adjutant General Center, Washington, D.C., 1978, p. 35.

46. J. K. Miller, "An Interdisciplinary Approach to Child Protective Services in the Military Community," American Humane Association, Second National Symposium on Child Abuse, Denver, 1973, pp. 24–30.

47. *A Statistical Report on Child Abuse and Neglect in Hawaii, 1980*, p. 75.

48. Gerald R. Garrett et al., "Drinking and the Military Wife: A Study of Married Women in Overseas Base Communities," in *Military Families: Adaptation to Change*, ed. by Edna J. Hunter and D. Stephen Nice (New York: Praeger Publishers, 1978), pp. 222–37.

49. Schwed, op. cit., p. 11. Schwed also notes that child abuse is 25 percent greater among personnel stationed at rural military bases, where isolation is greater and resources are fewer, than in urban military areas.

50. Based on statistics in *Defense 89 Almanac*, p. 26.

51. Justice and Duncan, op. cit., p. 114.

52. Straus, Gelles, and Steinmetz, op. cit., p. 197.

53. Virginia's intake form for reported child abusers has a blank for the individual's occupation, but at this writing most field workers do not complete it, so the state is not in a position to say what percentage of reported abusers are military.

54. U.S. Senate Committee on Appropriations, Department of Defense Appropriations Bill, 1980, 96th Congress, 1st sess., 1979, Senate Report 96-393, p. 76.

55. State of Hawaii, Department of Human Services, Family and Adult Services Division, A *Statistical Report on Child Abuse and Neglect in Hawaii, 1980–1987,* p. 56.

56. Study Findings: Study of National Incidence and Prevalence of Child Abuse and Neglect: 1988, National Center on Child Abuse and Neglect, pp. 4-8, 4-9. In 1986, 1.9 children per thousand, or 120,800 children nationwide, were found to have been verbally or emotionally assaulted. This number is widely believed to be grossly underestimated.

57. James Garbarino and Anne C. Garbarino, "Emotional Maltreatment of Children," pamphlet published by the National Committee for the Prevention of Child Abuse, 1986, p. 6.

58. Patricia W. Crigler, Commander, U.S. Navy, "Incest in the Military Family," in *The Military Family*, ed. by Florence W. Kaslow and Richard I. Ridenour (New York: Guilford Press, 1984), pp. 101, 102.

59. Ibid., p. 106.

60. Ibid., p. 101.

61. Leonard Shengold, *Soul Murder: The Effects of Childhood Abuse and Deprivation* (New Haven: Yale University Press, 1989), pp. 2–3.

62. Shengold, op. cit., p. 67.

63. Shengold, op. cit., p. 6.

64. This was found in a survey of intergenerational studies done by psychologists Joan Kaufman and Edward Zigler of Yale University, and reported in the *New York Times*, "Sad Legacy of Abuse: The Search for Remedies," January 24, 1989.

65. Ibid.

CHAPTER 8. "MILITARY BRATS AS NOMADS"

1. Statistic cited in D. Ley, A *Social Geography of the City* (New York: Harper and Row, 1983), p. 239.

2. Certain parts of the civilian population, such as the ministry, the State Department, and the corporate world, experience mobility approaching that of the military. Corporate kids sometimes refer to themselves as "IBM": I Been Moved. From conversations I have had with such children now in adulthood, it seems likely that any child who has moved frequently, whether military or not, will identify with most of the benefits and liabilities of rootlessness detailed in this chapter.

3. Diane D. Broadhurst et al., "Child Protection in Military Communities," U.S.

Department of Health and Human Services, Publication No. (OHDS) 80-30260, p. 9.

4. Reuben Hill, "Generic Features of Families Under Stress," *Social Casework*, Vol. 39, Nos. 2 and 3, February–March 1958, pp. 139–50.

5. Frank A. Pedersen and Eugene J. Sullivan, "Relationships Among Geographical Mobility, Parental Attitudes and Emotional Disturbances in Children," *American Journal of Orthopsychiatry*, 1964, pp. 575–80.

CHAPTER 9. "UPSTAIRS/DOWNSTAIRS"

1. Uniform Code of Military Justice, Article 134, Paragraph 83. As the article states, not all association between officers and enlisted persons constitutes an offense; it must be shown that the association resulted in "the prejudice of good order and discipline in the armed forces." The penalties for violation of this article are high: the maximum punishment for fraternization is dismissal, forfeiture of all pay and allowances, and confinement for two years. The individual services also have regulations covering fraternization; violation of these regulations can result in an unfavorable efficiency or fitness report (which works against future promotion), relief of command, or other measures. (See for example Army Regulation 600-20, paras. 4-14, 4-15 and 4-16.)

2. September 30, 1988 figures from the Department of Defense, as published in *Defense* 89, September 1989 almanac issue, p. 31.

3. This has been true of the military as a whole, and it is still true. In fact, the gap continues to grow. In 1989, after nine years of Republican stewardship, the gap was wider than it had been under President Jimmy Carter. Grant Willis, "Civilian-Military Pay Gap Will Keep Widening in 1990," *Army Times*, October 2, 1989.

4. Calling cards are still very much a part of military protocol for officers. The 1985 edition of *The Marine Officer's Guide* devotes three pages to their proper use. A commonly used reference for officers published by the Navy, *Service Etiquette* by Oretha D. Swartz (Annapolis: U.S. Naval Institute, 1977), devotes a 17-page chapter to official visits and calling cards. The entire hefty tome (582 pages) covers everything from the proper size and appearance of place cards at official dinners, to how to eat an artichoke, to how much to tip the crew of a charter boat.

5. "Looking for More Good Families," by Jenifer Warren, *Los Angeles Times*, San Diego County Edition, April 5, 1986.

6. D. Saunders, "Poverty in the Army," *Social Service Review*, December 1969, pp. 675–78.

7. R. D. McCullah, "Effects of Family Dysfunction on Military Operations: Mental Health Needs," in E. J. Hunter and T. C. Shaylor (eds.), *The Military Family and the Military Organization*, proceedings of a symposium held at the 1978 American Psychological Association convention, Toronto, September 1, 1978, pp. 32–41.

8. The specifics of the Holleys' predicament came from an article in the *San Diego Tribune*, "Mother Wants Son Buried in Ireland," August 30, 1984, p. A-9. The problems of the Holley family did not end there. In 1986, during another tour in West Germany, Sgt. Johnnie Holley, after 13 years of service, was ordered out of the Army. His commander refused to cite his reasons for the reenlistment ban. ("Soldier Whose Son Killed Himself Is Ordered Out of Army," *Los Angeles Times*, November 14, 1986, p. I-37.)

9. The Department of Defense seems to have great difficulty determining the exact number of military members who use food stamps. The most extensive information available at the time this book was researched was from a 1985 DoD survey, in which

16,764 enlisted, representing 1.1 percent of the enlisted military, had reported using food stamps during the calendar year 1984. The figure is not considered particularly reliable, because the survey was not given to any enlisted personnel with less than four months' service, nor were surveys forwarded to members who had served more than four months but had left the service before the survey was distributed.

10. "Feasibility of Having the Department of Defense Issue Food Stamp Coupons to Overseas Households of Members Stationed Outside the United States," A Report to Congress Pursuant to the Conference Committee Report on the FY 1986 DoD Authorization Act, prepared by the Office of the Assistant Secretary of Defense, Force Management and Personnel, Feburary 28, 1986, pp. 7, 8. The report goes on to recommend against extending the food stamp program overseas until more cost-effective methods of addressing the problem had been explored. In other words, the relatively small number of persons expected to actually apply for the food stamps would not justify the start-up costs of the program.

11. The figures, rounded off, are for September 30, 1988, as reported in *Defense 89*, p. 31.

12. Nicholas Proffitt, *Gardens of Stone* (New York: Carroll and Graf, 1983), pp. 173–74.

13. The difference in severity is actually extreme. Failure to Repair is a minor violation of regulations; an individual who is Absent Without Leave is subject to court-martial and can be sent to prison.

14. Nancy Shea, *The Army Wife: What She Ought to Know About the Customs of the Service and the Management of an Army Household*, 3d rev. ed. (New York: Harper and Brothers, 1954), pp. 177–79.

15. There are nine enlisted grades: E–1 through E–9. In the Navy, an E–6 is a petty officer first class; in the Marines, a staff sergeant; in the Army, a staff sergeant or specialist 6; in the Air Force, a technical sergeant.

16. See *American Heritage Dictionary*; also *Sea Legs, A Handbook for the Navy Family*, Navy Military Personnel Command, Family Support Program Division (Washington, D.C. 20370).

17. The military tries, however. On bases that are sufficiently large to have a great many children, the military builds separate schools to serve the enlisted and officer housing areas, which are always widely separated geographically.

18. Although the military has led the civilian sector in many ways concerning opportunities for minorities, it has a long way to go, even by its own admission. In the Navy, for instance, although the number of black officers doubled between 1978 and 1988, blacks still represented only 3.5 percent of the officer corps. There are even fewer Hispanics. The chief of naval operations ordered an inquiry in the summer of 1988 after it was revealed that the Navy lagged behind the other three services in recruitment and promotion of minorities. ("Navy Probes Lag in Minority Promotions," New York Times News Service, Worcester [Mass.] *Sunday Telegram*, July 24, 1988, p. 15A.)

CHAPTER 10. "OUTSIDER/INSIDER"

1. Raphael Patai, *The Arab Mind* (New York: Charles Scribner's Sons, 1976), pp. 188–90.

2. Between 1950 and 1987, a total of 38 games, Army won only 12 times, or less than one game in three. On three occasions, in 1956, 1965, and 1981, there were tie games. The biggest Navy blitz in that period was in 1973, with a score of 51–0. Army's most decisive win in that time was in 1969, when it defeated Navy 27–0.

3. The story of the theft and its aftermath are from *The Long Gray Line: The American Journey of West Point's Class of 1966*, by Rick Atkinson (Boston: Houghton Mifflin, 1989), pp. 129–33.

4. This question was not posed to military brats who were active-duty members of the military.

5. Don M. LaGrone, "The Military Family Syndrome," *American Journal of Psychiatry*, Vol. 135, No. 9, September 1978, p. 1042.

6. The first giant "Moratorium" on the war drew a quarter of a million demonstrators in Washington, D.C., on October 15, 1969.

7. Another veteran's point of view is that of Adam, the Marine brat who served with the Air Force during two tours in Vietnam. His story is presented in Chapters 5 and 6.

8. Obviously, not all civilian protesters took so facile a position with regard to the military—but so many did, and persisted in it for so long, that it has left a bitter legacy for military people, especially Vietnam veterans.

9. The controversy over desegregation in public schools in Arkansas grew rapidly and culminated in President Eisenhower's issuing an executive order in September 1957 for federal troops to assist in enforcing federal law in Little Rock as integration proceeded. More than a thousand paratroopers from the 101st Airborne Division at Fort Bragg were sent; they surrounded Central High School, fought back white mobs, and, inside the school, acted as bodyguards for the black students.

10. Atkinson, op. cit., p. 367.

11. Richard Halloran, "Blacks and Women Find Roads for Advancement Through Life in Military," *New York Times*, August 26, 1986, p. 9.

12. Richard Halloran, "Wide Bias Against Minorities Found in Navy," *New York Times*, December 20, 1988.

13. Richard Halloran, "Women, Blacks, Spouses Transforming the Military," *New York Times*, August 25, 1986.

14. See note 11.

15. Atkinson, op. cit., p. 62. This passage is incorrect on one point: Davis was not forced to eat alone, although many cadets openly tried to avoid assignment at his table. For years after his graduation from West Point, Davis and his wife Agatha were subjected by other officers to various humiliations. However, they stayed the course and went on to make a major contribution to the improvement of race relations in the U.S. military. See the autobiography *Benjamin O. Davis, Jr., American* (Washington: Smithsonian Institution Press, 1991).

16. Atkinson, op. cit., pp. 62–63.

17. The March on Washington drew 250,000 people on August 28, 1963. At the time it was the largest demonstration for civil rights in the history of the country. In the TV series "Call to Glory," about an Air Force family, the oldest boy, Wesley, is 14 years old and living just outside Washington in 1963 when the March on Washington takes place. A strong proponent of civil rights (he'd already been roughed up for his beliefs by small-town toughs in a previous episode), he makes a placard and joins the march. At that point, however, the story loses all credibility: The father, *in uniform*, finds his son and marches beside him. As any military person knows, that would certainly have marked the end of his career. Military personnel are not permitted to join demonstrations, let alone wear their uniforms to them.

CHAPTER 11. "LEGACIES"

1. Jerry Hopkins and Danny Sugerman, *No One Here Gets Out Alive* (New York: Warner Books, 1980), p. 155.

2. Ellen R. Morehouse, "Working with Alcohol-Abusing Children of Alcoholics," *Alcohol Health and Research World*, Summer 1984.

3. As published in *The Naval Officer's Guide*, 9th ed., by Vice Admiral William P. Mack, U.S.N. (Ret.), with Captain Thomas D. Paulsen, U.S.N. (Annapolis: Naval Institute Press, 1983), pp. 515–16.

CHAPTER 12. "MILITARY BRATS AS SURVIVORS"

1. "Myths Keep Us Strangers," *Newsweek*, International Edition, November 2, 1987, p. 53.

2. Leonard, op. cit., p. 167.

3. An incident in December, 1989 focused attention on the United States Naval Academy at Annapolis. A 19-year-old female midshipman was handcuffed to a pipe near a urinal by a group of older male midshipmen, one of whom photographed the incident. Two men were given campus restriction for one month as well as demerits on their academy records, and six others received letters of reprimand. The woman, citing disillusionment with the handling of the incident, resigned from the Academy. An Alabama congressman called for a congressional investigation, and the Chief of Naval Operations asked a subcommittee of the Academy's governing board to investigate how the incident was handled. See "Harassment Case Shakes Annapolis," by Felicity Barringer, *New York Times*, May 20, 1990. In all, there were five separate investigations of the incident resulting in reports. The Academy's internal report, released in October 1990, blamed negative attitudes toward women in the Academy's brigade, and reported that two-thirds of the female midshipmen complained of sexual harassment. See "Four Reports Cite Naval Academy for Rife Sexism," by Felicity Barringer, *New York Times*, October 10, 1990, p. A 12. (The fifth report, by the General Accounting Office, had not yet been released.)

4. John K. Miller, "Perspectives on Child Maltreatment in the Military," in *Child Abuse and Neglect: The Family and the Community*, ed. by Ray E. Helfer and C. Henry Kempe (Cambridge: Ballinger, 1976), p. 274.

INDEX

About the Author

MARY EDWARDS WERTSCH was raised in a military family and lived in several different countries and twenty different houses by the time she was eighteen. She is a seasoned investigative reporter who has extensively covered prisons and consumer rights. Wertsch earned a B.A. in philosophy at the College of William and Mary. She currently lives in New England with her husband and two sons.

In the wake of reading the hardcover edition of this book in the summer of 1991, an Air Force daughter named Pamela James founded an organization for U.S. military brats around the world, the motto of which is "Clarity, Compassion, Connection." Originally called Adult Children of Military Personnel, Inc., the name has since been changed to Military Brats, Inc. For further information, write or call:

Military Brats, Inc.
P.O. Box 82262
Lincoln, Nebraska 68501-2262
800-767-7709